WE GOTTA HAVE IT

TWENTY YEARS OF SEEING BLACK AT THE MOVIES, 1986–2006

ESTHER IVEREM

Thunder's Mouth Press
New York

For Phyl Garland and Fred Ho.
And for Mazi, my most faithful movie companion.

WE GOTTA HAVE IT
Twenty Years of Seeing Black at the Movies, 1986–2006

Published by
Thunder's Mouth Press
An imprint of Avalon Publishing Group, Inc.
245 West 17th Street, 11th Floor
New York, NY 10011
www.thundersmouth.com

First printing April 2007

Library of Congress Cataloging-in-Publication Data is available.

ISBN-10: 1-56025-916-7
ISBN-13: 978-1-56025-916-9

9 8 7 6 5 4 3 2 1

Interior design by Bettina Wilhelm
Printed in the United States of America
Distributed by Publishers Group West

CONTENTS

Acknowledgments xxv

Introduction: Covering the "New Wave" of Black Film xxvii

Chapter 1: Seeing Black 1

Chapter 2: The New, Black, Hot . . . 13

She's Gotta Have It—*August 8, 1986* 13
Black Star—Whoopi Goldberg in Jumpin' Jack Flash—*October 10, 1986* 14
Hollywood Shuffle—*March 20, 1987* 15
Black Star—Whoopi Goldberg in Burglar—*March 20, 1987* 16
Black Star—Whoopi Goldberg in Fatal Beauty—*October 30, 1987* 16
Black Star—Denzel Washington in Cry Freedom—*November 6, 1987* 16
Eddie Murphy Raw—*December 18, 1987* 17
School Daze—*February 12, 1988* 18
Action Jackson—*February 12, 1988* 19
Coming to America—*June 29, 1988* 19
Black Star—Whoopi Goldberg in Clara's Heart—*October 7, 1988* 20
I'm Gonna Git You Sucka—*December 14, 1988* 21
The Mighty Quinn—*February 16, 1989* 22
Do the Right Thing—*June 30, 1989* 22
Sidewalk Stories—*November 3, 1989* 23
Harlem Nights—*November 17, 1989* 23
Black Star—Whoopi Goldberg in Homer and Eddie—*December 1, 1989* 24
Glory—*December 15, 1989* 24
House Party—*March 9, 1990* 25
Black Star—Whoopi Goldberg in Ghost—*July 13, 1990* 26

Chapter 3: Mo' Betta? 29

Mo' Better Blues—*August 3, 1990* 29

To Sleep with Anger—*October 12, 1990* 30
Et Cetera—The Price of a Date with Starring Power —*December 5, 1990* 30
Black Star—*Whoopi Goldberg in* The Long Walk Home —*December 21, 1990* 32
Black Star—Laurence Fishburne in Cadence—*January 18, 1991* 32
New Jack City—*March 8, 1991* 32
The Five Heartbeats—*March 29, 1991* 33
A Rage in Harlem—*May 3, 1991* 34
Straight Out of Brooklyn—*May 22, 1991* 34
Jungle Fever—*June 7, 1991* 34
Boyz n the Hood—*July 12, 1991* 36
Livin' Large!—*September 20, 1991* 37
Black Star—Denzel Washington in Ricochet—*October 4, 1991* 37
Strictly Business—*November 8, 1991* 37
Daughters of the Dust—*December 27, 1991* 38
Juice—*January 17, 1992* 38
Mississippi Masala—*February 5, 1992* 39
White Men Can't Jump—*March 27, 1992* 39

Chapter 4: Isn't He Lovely 41
Et Cetera—In TV, It's A Different World *Indeed—March 24, 1993* 41
Deep Cover—*April 15, 1992* 44
One False Move—*May 8, 1992* 45
Black Star—Whoopi Goldberg in Sister Act—*May 29, 1992* 46
Sarafina!—*September 18, 1992* 46
Boomerang—*September 24, 1992* 47
Black Star—Wesley Snipes in Passenger 57—*November 6, 1992* 48
Malcolm X—*November 18, 1992* 48
Black Star—Whitney Houston in The Bodyguard—*November 25, 1992* 49
Queen—*February 14, 1993* 49
CB4—*March 12, 1993* 50
Interview—Martin Lawrence—April 29, 1993 51
Posse—*May 14, 1993* 55

Menace II Society—*May 26, 1993* 56
Sankofa—*May 28, 1993* 57
Black Star—Whoopi Goldberg in Made in America—*May 28, 1993* 58
What's Love Got to Do with It?—*June 9, 1993* 58
Poetic Justice—*July 23, 1993* 59
Black Star—Wesley Snipes in Rising Sun—*July 30, 1993* 60
Interview—Robert Townsend—August 9, 1993 60
Bopha!—*September 24, 1993* 62
Black Star—Wesley Snipes in Demolition Man—*October 8, 1993* 62

Chapter 5: Black Like Me 63
Black Like Who?—*October 23, 1993* 63
Black Star—Will Smith in Six Degrees of Separation —*December 8, 1993* 72
Black Star—Denzel Washington in The Pelican Brief —*December 17, 1993* 72
Black Star—Denzel Washington in Philadelphia—*December 23, 1993* 72
Sugar Hill—*February 25, 1994* 73
Black Star—Ice-T in Surviving the Game—*April 15, 1994* 73
The Inkwell—*April 22, 1994* 73
You So Crazy—*April 27, 1994* 74
Crooklyn—*May 13, 1994* 74
Fear of a Black Hat—*June 3, 1994* 75
Betcha By Golly, Wow: Black Culture Looks Back—Crooklyn, The Inkwell, *and* The Jacksons: An American Dream —*June 19, 1994* 75
Black Stars—James Earl Jones and Whoopi Goldberg (Voices) in The Lion King—*June 24, 1994* 79

Chapter 6: A Place of Our Own 81
Projecting Hope in Harlem—Harlem's Victoria 5—August 9, 1994 81
Black Star—Laurence Fishburne in Searching for Bobby Fischer—*August 11, 1994* 86
Black Star—Whoopi Goldberg in Corrina, Corrina—*August 12, 1994* 86

Fresh—*August 24, 1994* 86
Black Star—Samuel L. Jackson in Pulp Fiction—*September 23, 1994* 86
Jason's Lyric—*September 24, 1994* 87
Drop Squad—*October 28, 1994* 87
Drop Zone—*December 9, 1994* 88
Higher Learning—*January 11, 1995* 89
Tales from the Crypt Presents Demon Knight—*January 13, 1995* 89
Black Star—Laurence Fishburne in Bad Company—*January 20, 1995* 90
Black Star—Laurence Fishburne in Just Cause—*February 17, 1995* 90
Black Star—Halle Berry in Losing Isaiah—*March 17, 1995* 90
Bad Boys—*April 7, 1995* 90
New Jersey Drive—*April 19, 1995* 91
Friday—*April 26, 1995* 91
Panther—*May 3, 1995* 91
Black Star—Samuel L. Jackson in Die Hard: With a Vengeance —*May 19, 1995* 91

Chapter 7: Am I Black Enough for You? 93
Searched at the Cinema—July 11, 1995 93
Black Star—Denzel Washington in Virtuosity—*August 4, 1995* 96
The Tuskegee Airmen—*August 26, 1995* 96
Black Star—Wesley Snipes in To Wong Foo Thanks for Everything, Julie Newmar—*September 8, 1995* 96
Clockers—*September 13, 1995* 96
Devil in a Blue Dress—*September 29, 1995* 97
Dead Presidents—*October 4, 1995* 98
Black Star—Wesley Snipes in Money Train—*November 22, 1995* 98
Black Star—Laurence Fishburne in Othello—*December 15, 1995* 98
Waiting to Exhale—*December 22, 1995* 98
Once Upon a Time . . . When We Were Colored—*January 12, 1996* 99
Don't Be a Menace (to South Central While Drinking Your Juice in the Hood)—*January 14, 1996* 99
Interview—Theresa Randle Has Hollywood's Number Girl 6—March 17, 1996 100

A Thin Line Between Love and Hate—*April 3, 1996* 103
Et Cetera: The Real Villains of Jonny Quest—*May 29, 1996* 103
The Nutty Professor—*June 28, 1996* 107
Black Star—Will Smith in Independence Day—*July 3, 1996* 107
Black Star—Denzel Washington in Courage Under Fire —*July 12, 1996* 107
Black Star—Shaquille O'Neal in Kazaam—*July 17, 1996* 107
Black Star—Laurence Fishburne in Fled—*July 19, 1996* 109
Black Star—Samuel L. Jackson in A Time to Kill—*July 24, 1996* 109
Black Star—Wesley Snipes in The Fan—*August 16, 1996* 109

Chapter 8: Our Story, Their Story, Whose Story? 111
Get on the Bus—*October 16, 1996* 111
Set It Off—*November 6, 1996* 112
The Preacher's Wife—*December 13, 1996* 114
Ghosts of Mississippi—*December 20, 1996* 115
Gridlock'd—*January 29, 1997* 115
Rosewood—*February 21, 1997* 116
Miss Evers' Boys—*February 22, 1997* 116
Rhyme & Reason—*March 7, 1997* 118
The Sixth Man—*March 28, 1997* 119
B.A.P.S.—*March 29, 1997* 119
Black Star—Wesley Snipes in Murder at 1600—*April 18, 1997* 120
Interview—LisaGay Hamilton—May 13, 1997 120
What About Black Romance?—Love Jones, Waiting to Exhale, Jason's Lyric, Naked Acts *and* Sprung—*May 25, 1997* 124
Black Star—Will Smith in Men in Black—*July 2, 1997* 131
Black Star—Samuel L. Jackson in 187—*July 30, 1997* 131
Black Star—Laurence Fishburne in Event Horizon—*August 15, 1997* 131
Hoodlum—*August 27, 1997* 132
Black Star—Wesley Snipes in One Night Stand—*August 31, 1997* 132
Interview—Ice-T—September 14, 1997 132
Soul Food—*September 26, 1997* 137
Gang Related—*October 8, 1997* 137

Chapter 9: History and Mystery 139

Et Cetera—Late-Night Wannabes—October 9, 1997 139

Black Star—Keenen Ivory Wayans in Most Wanted*—October 10, 1997* 145

Jackie Brown*—December 25, 1997* 145

Black Star—Denzel Washington in Fallen*—January 16, 1998* 145

Ruby Bridges*—January 17, 1998* 145

Porgy and Bess: An American Voice*—February 4, 1998* 147

Black Star—Samuel L. Jackson in Sphere*—February 13, 1998* 149

The Wedding*—February 22, 1998* 149

Black Star—Wesley Snipes in U.S. Marshalls*—March 6, 1998* 149

Always Outnumbered*—March 21, 1998* 150

The Player's Club*—April 8, 1998* 150

He Got Game*—May 1, 1998* 150

Woo*—May 8, 1998* 150

Black Star—Halle Berry in Bulworth*—May 15, 1998* 150

Black Star—Samuel L. Jackson in The Negotiator*—July 29, 1998* 151

How Stella Got Her Groove Back*—August 14, 1998* 151

Black Star—Wesley Snipes in Blade*—August 21, 1998* 151

Why Do Fools Fall in Love?*—August 28, 1998* 151

Chapter 10: Fight the Power 153

OPM—Family Name*—September 15, 1998* 153

Beloved*—October 16, 1998* 155

Belly*—November 4, 1998* 155

Black Star—Denzel Washington in The Siege*—November 6, 1998* 155

Black Star—Will Smith in Enemy of the State*—November 20, 1998* 156

Down in the Delta*—December 25, 1998* 156

Black Star—Laurence Fishburne in The Matrix*—March 31, 1999* 156

Foolish*—April 9, 1999* 157

Life*—April 16, 1999* 157

OPM—Star Wars: Episode I—The Phantom Menace*—May 19, 1999* 157

Black Star—Will Smith in Wild Wild West*—June 30, 1999* 157

The Wood*—July 16, 1999* 158

Black Stars—LL Cool J and Samuel L. Jackson in Deep Blue Sea *—July 28, 1999* 158
Introducing Dorothy Dandridge—*August 21, 1999* 159
Urban Menace—*September 7, 1999* 159
Blue Streak—*September 17, 1999* 159
The Best Man—*October 22, 1999* 159
Black Star—Denzel Washington in The Bone Collector *—November 5, 1999* 159
Adwa—*November 20, 1999* 160

Chapter 11: Let the Good Times Roll 161

The "New Wave" at the Millennium—Feburary 7, 2000 161
Interview—Vin Diesel—February 18, 2000 172
Black Star—Vin Diesel in Pitch Black*—February 18, 2000* 174
Freedom Song—*February 27, 2000* 175
3 Strikes—*March 1, 2000* 177
Ghost Dog: The Way of the Samurai—*March 17, 2000* 178
*Black at the Oscars—*The Hurricane, The Green Mile, The Cider House Rules, *and* The Matrix—*March 20, 2000* 179
Romeo Must Die—*March 22, 2000* 182
Erasure at the Oscars—March 27, 2000 184
Black and White—*April 5, 2000* 186
Third World Cop—*April 14, 2000* 187
Finding Buck McHenry—*April 16, 2000* 188
The Corner—*April 16, 2000* 189
Love and Basketball—*April 21, 2000* 191
Black Star—Djimon Hounsou in Gladiator—*May 5, 2000* 192
From Mammy to Mama—Mother's Day 2000 193
Held Up—*May 12, 2000* 195
Dinosaur—*May 19, 2000* 196
Black Stars—Thandie Newton and Ving Rhames in Mission: Impossible 2—*May 24, 2000* 197
Big Momma's House—*June 2, 2000* 198

OPM—Me, Myself & Irene—*June 15, 2000* 199
Shaft—*June 16, 2000* 200

Chapter 12: Acapulco 2000 and Summer Madness 203
Acapulco Black Film Festival—Dancing in September —*Acapulco, Mexico*—*June 5–10, 2000* 203
Acapulco Black Film Festival 2000—Simeon 204
Acapulco Black Film Festival 2000—For Da Love of Money 205
Acapulco Black Film Festival 2000—Nothin 2 Lose 206
Acapulco Black Film Festival 2000—Love the Way 206
Acapulco Black Film Festival 2000—Under Suspicion 207
Acapulco Black Film Festival 2000—Same Difference 207
Acapulco Black Film Festival 2000—Box Marley 208
Acapulco Black Film Festival 2000—Field Guide to White People 208
Acapulco Black Film Festival 2000—*HBO Short Film Competition* 208
Acapulco Black Film Festival 2000—Something to Sing About 209
Acapulco Black Film Festival 2000—Bellyfull 209
Scary Movie—*July 7, 2000* 209
Black Star—*Halle Berry in* X-Men—*July 14, 2000* 210
The Nutty Professor II: The Klumps—*July 28, 2000* 211
A House Divided—*July 30, 2000* 212

Chapter 13: Urbanworld 2000 and Black Women on the Verge of a Film Breakdown 213
Urbanworld Film Festival—*New York, New York*—*August 2–6, 2000* 213
Urbanworld Film Festival 2000—The Visit 214
Urbanworld Film Festival 2000—Voice of the Voiceless 215
Urbanworld Film Festival 2000—30 Years to Life 216
Divided We Stand—*August 8, 2000* 217
The Original Kings of Comedy—*August 18, 2000* 218
Catfish in Black Bean Sauce—*August 24, 2000* 219
Black Star—*Wesley Snipes in* Art of War—*August 25, 2000* 220
Orfeu—*August 25, 2000* 222

American Pimp—*August 31, 2000* 222
Turn It Up—*September 6, 2000* 223
OPM—Nurse Betty—*September 8, 2000* 224
Backstage—*September 8, 2000* 224
Black Women on the Verge of a Film Breakdown—Big Momma's House, Black and White, *and* X-Men—*September 9, 2000* 226

Chapter 14: We're *Bamboozled* and Black Stars Rule 229
Bait—*September 15, 2000* 229
Uninvited Guest, Asunder, *and* Shafted—*September 22, 2000* 230
Remember the Titans—*September 29, 2000* 233
The Ladies Man—*October 13, 2000* 235
Love Beat the Hell Outta Me—*October 19, 2000* 236
Bamboozled—*October 20, 2000* 236
Interview—Spike Lee—October 20, 2000 238
Cora Unashamed—*October 25, 2000* 241
Loving Jezebel—*October 27, 2000* 242
Black Star—Will Smith in The Legend of Bagger Vance—*November 3, 2000* 244
The Invisible Soldiers: Unheard Voices—*November 9, 2000* 245
Men of Honor—*November 10, 2000* 246
What's Cooking?—*November 17, 2000* 248
Boesman & Lena—*November 17, 2000* 249
Half Past Autumn—*November 30, 2000* 250
Love Song—*December 1, 2000* 252
Interview—Julie Dash—December 1, 2000 253
Snatch—*December 6, 2000* 257

Chapter 15: Pimps, Hos, Brothers, and Sisters 259
Disappearing Acts—*December 9, 2000* 259
OPM—What Women Want—*December 15, 2000* 260
Finding Forrester—*December 19, 2000* 261
Pimps Up, Hos Down—The Director's Cut—*January 15, 2001* 262

OPM—Traffic—*January 5, 2001* 263
Jazz—*January 8, 2001* 264
Bojangles—*February 4, 2001* 265
Double Take—*January 12, 2001* 267
OPM—Save the Last Dance—*January 12, 2001* 268
The Queens of Comedy—*January 27, 2001* 269
Black Films at 2001 Film Festivals—*February 12, 2001* 270
Down to Earth—*February 16, 2001* 273
The Caveman's Valentine—*March 2, 2001* 274
Blacks at the Oscars 2001—*March 20, 2001* 275
The Brothers—*March 23, 2001* 277

Chapter 16: Challenging the American Culture Machine—And Not 279

Et Cetera—*Blackbuster: Haile Gerima's D.C. Store Rents a Different Kind of Black Film*—*April 9, 2001* 279
Kingdom Come—*April 11, 2001* 282
Filmfest DC—Lumumba—*Washington, D.C.*—*April 17–29, 2001* 283
Filmfest DC 2001—Samia 284
Filmfest DC 2001—Cuba Feliz 285
Filmfest DC 2001—Brother 286
Filmfest DC 2001—Bob Marley Live in Concert 288
Filmfest DC 2001—Andanggaman 289
Filmfest DC 2001—Faat Kiné 290
Two Souls at the Acapulco Black Film Festival—*Acapulco, Mexico*—*June 4–9, 2001* 291
Acapulco Black Film Festival 2001—Love Come Down 292
Acapulco Black Film Festival 2001—Blue Hill Avenue 294
Acapulco Black Film Festival 2001—One Week 295
Acapulco Black Film Festival 2001—Van Van: Let's Party 296
Acapulco Black Film Festival 2001—Lift 296
Acapulco Black Film Festival 2001— A Huey P. Newton Story 298
Black Star—*Halle Berry in* Swordfish—*June 8, 2001* 299
Baby Boy—*June 29, 2001* 299
Pootie Tang—*June 29, 2001* 300

Scary Movie 2—*July 4, 2001* 301
OPM—The Score, Made, *and* Sexy Beast—*July 13, 2001* 302
OPM—Planet of the Apes—*July 27, 2001* 302
Movies for Black Children—July 1, 2001 303
Black Star—Chris Tucker in Rush Hour 2—*August 3, 2001* 304

Chapter 17: Epic Lives and Fantasy 307
Urbanworld Celebrates Five Years of Building Black Film—New York, New York—August 1–5, 2001 307
Urbanworld Film Festival 2001—Beyond Tara: The Extraordinary Life of Hattie McDaniel 308
Black Star—Mekhi Phifer in O—*August 31, 2001* 309
Two Can Play That Game—*September 7, 2001* 311
Glitter—*September 21, 2001* 312
Life and Debt—*September 27, 2001* 313
Africa—*September 27, 2001* 314
Training Day—*October 5, 2001* 315
Bones—*October 24, 2001* 316
The Wash—*November 14, 2001* 317
OPM—Harry Potter and the Sorcerer's Stone—*November 14, 2001* 318
Black Knight—*November 21, 2001* 319
Et Cetera—Talk Show Mammies?—December 11, 2001 320
Ali—*December 12, 2001* 323
OPM—Piñero—*December 13, 2001* 324
Black Star—Danny Glover in The Royal Tenenbaums—*December 14, 2001* 325
OPM—The Lord of the Rings: The Fellowship of the Ring—*December 19, 2001* 326
Sins of the Father—*January 2, 2002* 327

Chapter 18: Battling Words, Beats, and Story 329
OPM—Black Hawk Down—*January 18, 2002* 329
Middle Passage—*February 7, 2002* 330
Monster's Ball—*February 8, 2002* 331

Black Star—Denzel Washington in John Q*—February 15, 2002* 333
Queen of the Damned*—February 22, 2002* 334
Interview—Alice Walker—February 28, 2002 335
Joe and Max*—March 3, 2002* 338
All About the Benjamins*—March 8, 2002* 339
Black Star—Eddie Murphy in Showtime*—March 15, 2002* 340
Black Star—Wesley Snipes in Blade II*—March 22, 2002* 341
Not All of Us Are Oscar Happy—March 28, 2002 342
Black Star—Morgan Freeman in High Crimes*—April 5, 2002* 345
Black Star—Samuel L. Jackson in Changing Lanes*—April 12, 2002* 346
Filmfest DC 2002—La Tropical*—Washington, D.C. —April 17–28, 2002* 347
Filmfest DC 2002—Karmen Geï 348
Filmfest DC 2002—Ali Zaoua 349
OPM—Star Wars: Episode II—Attack of the Clones *—May 16, 2002* 350
Black Star—Morgan Freeman in The Sum of All Fears *—May 31, 2002* 351

Chapter 19: Big Laughs and the Unkindest Cut 353
Undercover Brother*—May 31, 2002* 353
Mama Africa*—June 7, 2002* 354
Black Star—Chris Rock in Bad Company*—June 7, 2002* 355
OPM—Sunshine State*—June 21, 2002* 356
American Black Film Festival—Fun, Films, and Fans in the Sun —Miami, Florida—June 26–30, 2002 357
American Black Film Festival 2002—The Riff 359
American Black Film Festival 2002—Crazy as Hell 360
Men in Black II*—July 3, 2002* 360
Like Mike*—July 3, 2002* 362
Black Star—Vin Diesel in XXX*—August 9, 2002* 362
The Adventures of Pluto Nash*—August 16, 2002* 364
Undisputed*—August 23, 2002* 365

Barbershop*'s Unkindest Cut—September 13, 2002* 366
Snipes—*September 20, 2002* 367
OPM—The Four Feathers—*September 20, 2002* 368
LaLee's Kin: The Legacy of Cotton—*September 26, 2002* 369
The Rise and Fall of Jim Crow—*October 1, 2002* 370

Chapter 20: Sanaa Rules, Drumline Beats, Denzel Directs 373
Brown Sugar—*October 11, 2002* 373
Knockaround Guys—*October 11, 2002* 374
Paid in Full—*October 20, 2002* 374
I Spy—*November 1, 2002* 375
8 Mile—*November 8, 2002* 376
Standing in the Shadows of Motown—*November 15, 2002* 377
Friday After Next—*Who You Callin' a Ho?—November 16, 2002* 378
Rabbit-Proof Fence—*November 29, 2002* 379
Black Star—Taye Diggs in Equilibrium—*December 6, 2002* 381
Leguizamo's Latino Empire—*December 6, 2002* 381
Drumline—*December 13, 2002* 383
Antwone Fisher—*December 19, 2002* 383
OPM—Gangs of New York——*December 20, 2002* 384

Chapter 21: Who's Zoomin' Who? 387
Interview—Spike Lee to Black Audiences: "Grow Up!"—January 10, 2003 387
Black Star—Busta Rhymes in Narc—*January 10, 2003* 391
City of God—*January 17, 2003* 392
The Murder of Emmett Till—*January 20, 2003* 393
Brother Outsider: The Life of Bayard Rustin—*January 20, 2003* 394
Biker Boyz—*January 31, 2003* 395
Unchained Memories: Readings from the Slave Narratives—*February 5, 2003* 395
Deacons for Defense—*February 5, 2003* 395
Good Fences—*February 5, 2003* 397

Deliver Us from Eva—*February 7, 2003* 398
Interview—Dan Haskett, Master Animator—February 7, 2003 398
Lockdown—*February 14, 2003* 402
Amandla!: A Revolution in Four-Part Harmony —*February 19, 2003* 404
OPM—Dark Blue—*February 21, 2003* 405
Bringing Down the House—*March 7, 2003* 406
Tears of the Sun—*March 7, 2003* 407
Black Star—Morgan Freeman in Dreamcatcher—*March 21, 2003* 408

Chapter 22: Truth Be Told 411
Head of State—*March 28, 2003* 411
Black Star—Delroy Lindo in The Core—*March 28, 2003* 413
A Man Apart—*April 4, 2003* 413
Dysfunktional Family—*April 4, 2003* 414
Race: The Power of an Illusion—*April 24, 2003* 414
Black Star—Morris Chestnut in Confidence—*April 25, 2003* 416
Black Star—Halle Berry in X2—*May 2, 2003* 417
Daddy Daycare—*May 9, 2003* 417
Only the Strong Survive—*May 9, 2003* 418
The Matrix Reloaded—*May 15, 2003* 419
Black Star—Don Cheadle in Manic—*May 23, 2003* 420
Black Star—Morgan Freeman in Bruce Almighty—*May 23, 2003* 420
2 Fast, 2 Furious—*June 6, 2003* 421
Wattstax—The Special Edition—*June 13, 2003* 422
This Far by Faith: African-American Spiritual Journeys—*June 19, 2003* 423
Black Star—Bernie Mac in Charlie's Angels: Full Throttle—*June 27, 2003* 424

Chapter 23: Film Can Be Fierce 425
Unprecedented—*July 1, 2003* 425
Black Star—Naomie Harris in 28 Days Later—*June 27, 2003* 426
Whale Rider—*July 4, 2003* 427

Bad Boys II—*July 18, 2003* 428
Dirty Pretty Things—*July 18, 2003* 429
OPM—Lara Croft Tomb Raider: The Cradle of Life—*July 21, 2003* 430
Black Star—Samuel L. Jackson in S.W.A.T.—*August 8, 2003* 431
Civil Brand—*August 29, 2003* 431
The Fighting Temptations—*September 19, 2003* 432
Matters of Race—*September 23, 2003* 432
The Blues—*September 28, 2003* 433
Out of Time—*October 2, 2003* 435
OPM—Kill Bill—*October 10, 2003* 435
OPM—Pieces of April—*October 17, 2003* 435
Scary Movie 3—*October 24, 2003* 436
OPM—The Human Stain—*October 31, 2003* 436
The Matrix Revolutions—*November 5, 2003* 438

Chapter 24: A Troublesome Property 441
Tupac: Resurrection—*November 14, 2003* 441
Black Star—Djimon Hounsou in In America—*November 26, 2003* 442
Honey—*December 5, 2003* 443
Love Don't Cost a Thing—*December 12, 2003* 444
Cinderella, the Bond Girl, and the Big Girl—Maid in Manhattan, Die Another Day, *and* Real Women Have Curves—*December 23, 2003* 445
OPM—Cold Mountain—*December 25, 2003* 448
The Battle of Algiers—*January 9, 2004* 449
Appreciation—Ron O'Neal—January 17, 2004 451
Citizen King—*January 19, 2004* 452
You Got Served—*January 30, 2004* 453
America Beyond the Color Line with Henry Louis Gates Jr.—*February 3, 2004* 453
Barbershop 2: Back in Business—*February 6, 2004* 456
Sisters in Cinema—*February 8, 2004* 456
Mighty Times: The Legacy of Rosa Parks—*February 8, 2004* 457
Nat Turner: A Troublesome Property—*February 10, 2004* 457
A Place of Our Own—*February 17, 2004* 457

Lost Boys of the Sudan—*February 18, 2004* 458
Against the Ropes—*February 20, 2004* 459
Beah: A Black Woman Speaks—*February 25, 2004* 460

Chapter 25: Those Bad Mother (Shut-Yo-Mouth!) 463
OPM—James' Journey to Jerusalem—*March 5, 2004* 463
Interview—Danny Glover—March 15, 2004 464
Black Star—Ving Rhames in Dawn of the Dead—*March 19, 2004* 467
New African Films Festival—The Silence of the Forest—*March 24, 2004* 468
Black Star—Don Cheadle in The United States of Leland
—*April 2, 2004* 469
Johnson Family Vacation—*April 7, 2004* 470
Filmfest DC—Nina Simone: Love Sorceress—*Washington, D.C.*
—*April 21–May 2, 2004* 470
Filmfest DC 2004—Soldiers of the Rock *and*
Asshak: Tales from the Sahara 471
Man on Fire—*April 23, 2004* 472
The Agronomist—*April 23, 2004* 473
Carandiru—*May 14, 2004* 474
Control Room—*May 21, 2004* 475
Baadasssss!—*May 28, 2004* 476
Soul Plane—*May 28, 2004* 477
Something the Lord Made—*May 30, 2004* 478
The Chronicles of Riddick—*June 11, 2004* 478
Black Star—Ossie Davis in Bubba Ho-tep—*June 14, 2004* 479

Chapter 26: Unbought and Unbossed 481
OPM—Fahrenheit 9/11—*June 25, 2004* 481
Everyday People—*June 26, 2004* 482
OPM—King Arthur—*July 7, 2004* 483
Black Star—Will Smith in I, Robot—*July 16, 2004* 483
Black Star—Halle Berry in Catwoman—*July 24, 2004* 484

The Twentieth Anniversary of Purple Rain*—Purple Rain Pimpology —The Missing Link Between* The Mack *and the Many Macks of Hip-Hop?—July 27, 2004* 485
Black Star—Denzel Washington in The Manchurian Candidate *—July 30, 2004* 487
She Hate Me*—July 30, 2004* 488
Urbanworld's Tricky Pop Culture Terrain—August 4–8, 2004 488
Black Star—Jamie Foxx in Collateral*—August 6, 2004* 490
The Cookout*—September 3, 2004* 491
Black Star—Bernie Mac in Mr. 3000*—September 17, 2004* 491
Chisholm '72: Unbought and Unbossed*—September 24, 2004* 492
Woman Thou Art Loosed*—October 1, 2004* 492
Black Star—Will Smith (Voice) in Shark Tale*—October 1, 2004* 493
Black Star—Queen Latifah in Taxi*—October 8, 2004* 494
Black Star—Derek Luke in Friday Night Lights*—October 8, 2004* 495
Moolaadé*—October 13, 2004* 495

Chapter 27: Big-Boned Cinema 497
Ray*—October 29, 2004* 497
Black Star—Nia Long in Alfie*—November 4, 2004* 498
Fade to Black*—November 5, 2004* 498
Black Star—Samuel L. Jackson (Voice) in The Incredibles *—November 5, 2004* 499
Black Star—Wesley Snipes in Blade: Trinity*—December 8, 2004* 499
*OPM—*Million Dollar Baby*—December 15, 2004* 499
Hotel Rwanda*—December 22, 2004* 500
Coach Carter*—January 14, 2005* 502
Unforgivable Blackness: The Rise and Fall of Jack Johnson *—January 17, 2005* 503
Black Star—Laurence Fishburne in Assault on Precinct 13 *—January 19, 2005* 504
Are We There Yet?*—January 21, 2005* 505

Slavery and the Making of America—*February 9, 2005* 505
Black Star—Will Smith in Hitch—*February 11, 2005* 506
Sucker Free City—*February 12, 2005* 507

Chapter 28: State of the Union 509
Lackawanna Blues—February 12, 2005 509
Unstoppable—*in Ossie's Own Words—February 13, 2005* 510
Diary of a Mad Black Woman—*February 25, 2005* 512
Interview—Ruben Santiago-Hudson—March 4, 2005 513
Their Eyes Were Watching God—*March 6, 2005* 518
Can the Michael Ealy Era Begin?—March 6, 2005 519
Sometimes in April—*March 19, 2005* 521
Guess Who—*March 25, 2005* 523
Beauty Shop—*March 30, 2005* 524
Filmfest DC—We Don't Die, We Multiply—*Washington, D.C. —April 13–24, 2005* 524
Black Star—Erykah Badu in House of D—*April 15, 2005* 525
King's Ransom—*April 22, 2005* 526
OPM—The Interpreter—*April 22, 2005* 526
Death of a Dynasty—*April 29, 2005* 527
Black Star—Ice Cube in XXX: State of the Union—*April 29, 2005* 528
Black Star—Mos Def in The Hitchhiker's Guide to the Galaxy *—April 29, 2005* 528

Chapter 29: The Changing Same 529
OPM—Crash—*May 6, 2005* 529
Shake Hands with the Devil—*June 3, 2005* 530
The Honeymooners—*June 10, 2005* 530
Silverdocs Documentary Festival—Sweet Honey in the Rock: Raise Your Voice—*Silver Spring, Maryland—June 14–19, 2005* 531
Rize—*June 24, 2005* 532
Hustle & Flow—*July 22, 2005* 532
Black Star—Jamie Foxx in Stealth—*July 29, 2005* 533

Four Brothers—*August 12, 2005* 534
Ralph Ellison: An American Journey—*August 24, 2005* 535
OPM—The Constant Gardener—*August 31, 2005* 536
G—*September 16, 2005* 538
Proud—*September 23, 2005* 538
The Gospel—*October 7, 2005* 539
The Untold Story of Emmett Louis Till—*October 14, 2005* 539

Chapter 30: Get Rich or Make a Real Movie 541
Congo: White King, Red Rubber, Black Death—*October 21, 2005* 541
OPM—Wal-Mart: The High Cost of Low Price—*November 4, 2005* 541
Get Rich or Die Tryin'—*November 9, 2005* 542
Black Star—Jeffrey Wright in Syriana—*December 9, 2005* 543
Appreciation—Richard Pryor, Giant of Comedy—December 12, 2005 544
OPM—King Kong—*December 14, 2005* 546
Glory Road—*January 13, 2006* 547
Last Holiday—*January 13, 2006* 548
On the Outs—*January 20, 2006* 549
The Boys of Baraka—*January 20, 2006* 549
Black Star—Tyrese Gibson in Annapolis—*January 27, 2006* 551

Chapter 31: African-American Lives 553
Something New—*January 29, 2006* 553
Black History Month—February 2006 554
Tsotsi—*February 24, 2006* 558
Black Star—Cuba Gooding Jr. in Dirty—*February 24, 2006* 559
Dave Chappelle's Block Party—*March 3, 2006* 559
Big Pimping at the Oscars—March 7, 2006 560
Inside Man—*March 24, 2006* 561
OPM—Manderlay—*April 7, 2006* 562
ATL—*Boyz in Another Hood—April 7, 2006* 563
C.S.A.: The Confederate States of America—*April 9, 2006* 563
Preaching to the Choir—*April 14, 2006* 565

Akeelah and the Bee—*April 28, 2006* 565
Black Stars—Laurence Fishburne and Ving Rhames in Mission: Impossible III—*May 5, 2006* 566

Chapter 32: Baller, Shot Caller 567
Tyler Perry's Feminist Appeal—May 17, 2006 567
Heart of the Game—*June 9, 2006* 569
Silverdocs Documentary Festival—His Big White Self *and* Beyond Freedom: The South African Journey—*Silver Spring, Maryland —June 13–18, 2006* 570
Waist Deep—*June 23, 2006* 571
Little Man—*July 14, 2006* 572
Shadowboxer—*July 21, 2006* 572
Black Star—Jamie Foxx in Miami Vice—*July 28, 2006* 573
From Florida to Coahuila—*August 9, 2006* 573
Black Star—Shareeka Epps in Half Nelson—*August 18, 2006* 575
When the Levees Broke: A Requiem in Four Acts —*August 22, 2006* 575
Idlewild—*August 25, 2006* 577
Crossover—*September 1, 2006* 578
Black Star—The Rock in Gridiron Gang—*September 15, 2006* 578
The Last King of Scotland—*October 6, 2006* 578
Catch a Fire—*October 27, 2006* 579

Chapter 33: Dreams and Dreams Deferred 583
American Blackout—*November 5, 2006* 583
OPM—Bobby—*November 22, 2006* 584
Black Star—Denzel Washington in Déjà Vu—*November 22, 2006* 586
OPM—Three Needles—*December 1, 2006* 587
Ithuteng—(Never Stop Learning)—*December 3, 2006* 588
OPM—Apocalypto—*December 8, 2006* 589
Blood Diamond—*December 8, 2006* 591
The Pursuit of Happyness—*December 22, 2006* 592

OPM—Children of Men—*December 25, 2006* 594
Dreamgirls—*December 25, 2006* 594

Epilogue: The Lists 597

Permissions 603

Index 607

ACKNOWLEDGMENTS

I have been encouraged by editors like Sylviane Gold of *New York Newsday*, mentors such as the late, great Phyl Garland of Columbia University and my high school English teacher Carolyn Pritchett (who always encouraged me to think and write about the theme of literature). I have been influenced by the writings of thinkers such as Amiri Baraka, Larry Neal, Edward Said, and Homi K. Bhabha, to be confident in my ability to make a critical analysis that makes sense in my world. Beginning my arts career in New York brought me into contact with the more liberated wing of the press and writings by Thulani Davis, Gene Seymour, Jill Nelson, Nelson George, Greg Tate, and Lisa Jones. It also brought me into contact with others in the arts community making their way and establishing the rules of engagement as they went along.

In recent years, as I have left my life of large newspapers, I have been encouraged and supported by many writers who also work, in large part, outside corporate media, including Robin D. G. Kelley, Mark Anthony Neal, Karen Juanita Carrillo, and my good friend Makani Themba-Nixon. I thank Retha Hill, vice president for content at www.bet.com, for hiring me to be the site's first contributing film critic and for supporting my independent vision for the development of www.seeingblack.com. (And thanks to all the contributors and users of www.seeingblack.com.) Thanks to James Hill, at www.bet.com until recently, for our many conversations, debates, and plots about the definition and coverage of our movie universe. I thank my editor of this book, Anita Diggs, for her insights and her valuing of Black voice.

Introduction

Covering the "New Wave" of Black Film

We Gotta Have It represents twenty years of seeing a new generation of Black movies. Before this journey began in 1986, with Spike Lee's *She's Gotta Have It,* a Black movie meant one of the increasingly mindless productions starring comedians Richard Pryor or Eddie Murphy. Black voice and context in these movies was whatever wisecrack each comedian could insert into the script or be scripted by writers who were often not Black.

Twenty years later—ending roughly with another Spike Lee joint, *When the Levees Broke: A Requiem in Four Acts,* Hollywood's ability to script and validate its own Black reality still exists and this era of film has created an explosion in the number of people recognized as Black movie stars. At the same time, there has also been a relative explosion of Black film *auteurs*—director-producer-writers who, though toiling increasingly in the obscurity of the film festival circuit, have created and brought to the screen a fuller panorama of Black life.

What has happened between these two points in time is an amazing film journey referred to as the "new wave" of Black film. This film movement, for me, involves a new generation, my post–civil rights generation, asserting its voice, telling its stories, and—most importantly—unabashedly addressing the Black community in tone and content. The key disciples of this film movement, our Matthew, Mark, Luke, and John if you will—Spike Lee, Robert Townsend, Keenen Ivory Wayans, and the Hudlin brothers—first proved that a Black audience exists for new films written by and about us.

It's not just about Black being "in style" or relevant; decisions to include us or speak to us are also financial decisions. African-Americans make up at least 25 percent of the moviegoing audience, spending $2 billion annually, not to mention what we shell out for renting movies, pay-per-view services, and legal cable and satellite television connections.

Once it was established that this audience could be a profitable one, it did not take long for Hollywood to piggyback, first with its own entrenched star system. For several years in the late 1980s, there was an odd juxtaposition of this "new, Black, hot," represented by often-controversial films by Spike Lee (*Do the Right Thing, Jungle Fever,* etc.) and some movie starring Whoopi Goldberg like *Jumpin' Jack Flash* or *Ghost* that had little or nothing to to do with the Black community or a Black voice. It wasn't just that Goldberg, a talented comedian, was presented to the Black community by Hollywood as our new star, her films were obviously not made with us in mind. The learning pace of the studios quickened, however, and new Black stars, with grassroots credentials in the new wave movement, were tapped for standard Hollywood action, drama, and comedic fare that we gladly claimed as our own. Going to a "Black" film meant going to a Spike Lee film but it also meant going to see Denzel, Samuel L. Jackson, Laurence Fishburne, or Wesley Snipes. Standard Hollywood fare outside the new framework of Black voice usually meant (and still means) that these big Black stars—all men except for Halle Berry—are often steered into stories obviously not made with us in mind. (*To Wong Foo Thanks for Everything, Julie Newmar*—What the f#@*?) Of course a disproportionate number of their roles were/are as cops, soldiers, or some other type of law enforcement. So breakthrough, fight-the-power roles, such as Morpheus in *The Matrix* or the bad-ass vampire Blade, were revolutionary and welcome.

The learning pace has also quickened with productions allegedly about the Black community but written by those outside of it, such as *Monster's Ball, Hustle and Flow,* and a myriad of lesser-known efforts that take some seeds of Black history and culture, plant them in foreign soil, and reap some very strange fruit. Compiling this book has reminded me of this strange fruit, how our voices become diffused, mutated, or lost when tumbled around within Hollywood's system for green-lighting work and creating movie stars. As a screenwriter explained recently at the Reel Sisters of the Diaspora Film Festival in Brooklyn, "They tell me to bring them a script that Halle Berry can star in—otherwise they're not interested."

I am also painfully aware of how much the last twenty years have also revealed other shortcomings of the "new wave." It has been far too much a Black *male* new wave of film. Most of the directors, screenwriters, leading actors, and decision-makers have been men—and most of the stories have been about men. The result has been an erasure of the lives, voices, and contributions of Black women, outside of some ways, some truly wack ways, that we are framed and rendered by others. (Some consider this male state of affairs as continuing payback for that era in the early 1980s when Black women writers turned out a series of novels that many felt bashed Black men, culminating, of course, in Alice Walker's novel *The Color Purple*, which became a popular, though controversial, film in 1985.) Even as technology has made filmmaking cheaper and more accessible, creating a movie still takes money that many in our community still do not have or are not willing to risk on an artist's dream. Spike Lee would not have gotten his early films off the ground if it had not been for his grandmother writing big checks. I believe that this disparity is one reason that I find myself frequently reviewing important films, especially documentaries like *Race: The Power of an Illusion,* that are produced by Whites about the Black experience. (All the while come asinine studio productions with Black casts such as *Soul Plane* or *Big Momma's House*.)

With such cash money in mind, it is the commerce side of the entrepreneur, not the artistic side of the auteur, which is driving many of our more recent independent productions. Many of our movies, like many movies in general, are viewed as monetary investments that, with the right variables and luck, might turn a few million into more than $20 million in a matter of months. That's a return that not many hustlers can pass up. Much of the new wave has simply turned into a new way to get that paper—not to tell our important stories, pose new ideas, questions, or controversies.

Included here are reviews (many excerpted), interviews, and essays about movies that we sort of claimed as ours. Whether "we" made them or not, they had something to say either to us or about us, so at the very least, we went to see what was being said behind our backs. They are a mixture of films—"Black" films that were decidedly Black in content and tone, movies featuring Black Stars, other people's movies (OPM) that were of some significance to us, and, to the extent that space allowed and my ego could exert its will, my coverage of happenings outside the Black movie universe (Et Cetera) that are relevant to our movie experiences.

When I started watching these movies, I was in my twenties. Now I am in my forties. I have watched these movies as a journalist and film critic but also as a friend, girlfriend, wife, mother, single mother, aunt, sister, daughter, and movie lover. In every instance, I have watched them first as a Black woman. Movies bring words and images to us but we also bring who we are to the movies—to laugh, to cry, to tremble with fear, to gaze in awe, to grow angry, to contemplate, and, hopefully, sometimes to learn and grow.

We do keep bringing ourselves to the movies—in droves.

It seems we gotta have it.

1

Seeing Black

Chocolate City, D.C.—The post–civil rights generation of African-Americans comes wrapped in the armor of our art and culture. A colorful, intricate armor, it is shaped by Stevie Wonder and the Jackson Five, Marvin Gaye and Aretha Franklin, James Cleveland and James Brown. It is textured by the 1970s—funk from bands such as Parliament-Funkadelic and War, potent screen images from that decade, and dance moves we perfected in humble living rooms before they went worldwide. It is polished by the 1980s—beats of "The Message" by Grandmaster Flash and the Furious Five, the explosion of hip-hop, post-soul grooves like new jack swing and, beginning in 1986, with Spike Lee's *She's Gotta Have It,* a "new wave" of Black film created from our voices and speaking directly to us.

We have grown up witnessing the assertion of our own voices, the postmodern affirmation of ourselves as auteurs and of our own signifying perspectives and personalities. That voice professes our varied humanity, rather than our status as animal-other-lesser. Because of this assertion, we are acutely conscious of the issue of voice. We are especially conscious of whether we are speaking for ourselves or being spoken for, gazed at, analyzed, explained, and framed by others. And as post-civil rights adults, we find it disturbing to witness the disjunction between the plethora of that art and culture we create—and the centrality of that culture to our lives—and the scarcity of our voices given authority to speak on it in the mass media.

Like being put on intellectual lockdown, we are limited in our ability to make our own analysis of what we create in music, film, theater, visual arts, and dance. With the partial exception of some of our own publications and some alternative press—and even these are often lacking in Black critical voices—we do not often tell our own story. What Black artists produce is selected, framed, and filtered outside the Black community in a manner that marginalizes both the artists and the community. This marginalization has increased as media have become more corporate, concentrated, and homogenous. The political climate post–September 11 has also made it increasingly risky for both artists and critics who stray too far from flag waving—a narrow definition of patriotism or support of the status quo.

This collection offers one critical voice and one particular journey. I'm not claiming to speak for all of us, but I am claiming status as one of us. I am claiming "first voice" as an African-American to write about African-American culture. That "first voice" is a voice that comes from our culture. What we feel, experience, and think about our culture comes first. All other voices, though possibly important, must come second. As a former colleague, Jon Jeter, used to say, I'm flashing my "Black card," with knowledge and faith that our universe has its own history, references, and traditions. With these words, I am honoring that history and tradition and offering faith in a future not framed with nihilism, pathology, simple mindedness, or ridicule.

It never occurred to me, when I was eight years old and sent from my Black working-class-neighborhood school in North Philadelphia to a school downtown, that I was supposed to feel inferior to the White students who formed half of the new student body. To this day, I think it was because I brought my cultural armor. I really believed there was a soul power. I really believed when Don Cornelius ended *Soul Train* with the immortal words, "love peace, and *soul!*" that there was energy in his words just for us.

My armor was welded together with an eight-year-old's sense of moral authority and the Black pride of the times: We *are* beautiful. Our cause is right. I have the same rights as anybody else. Can't you see how beautiful I am? If anything, I probably felt sorry for White people. They didn't have what I had. By my sense of reason, our music, dance, and images were just as powerful a force transforming the measure of our humanity as marchers or rioters in the streets. With the explosion of soul, funk, disco, post-soul grooves, and hip-hop—which was just one segment of the third Black arts renaissance of the last century—we have become accustomed to being center stage, or at least holding our own among an assortment of competing stages.

Most of us have come through the idea of integration still quite segregated, especially when it comes to culture. We travel in our own parallel and overlapping African-American universe with BET on television, Tom Joyner on radio, and lively clubs for regional music like go-go in D.C., bass in Miami, and bounce in New

Orleans. The UniverSoul Circus tours the country, as do hot gospel acts, as do authors ranging from Toni Morrison to Walter Mosley to Terry McMillan. New literary talents are hailed at poetry slams, seasoned artists are honored at exhibit openings, bawdy theater productions like *Beauty Shop* draw a faithful crowd. We fill our churches with stained-glass images of Black gods and saints and have gathered by the thousands to worship more earthly icons at sold-out summer music festivals. With athletes treated like pop heroes, we have elevated the humble sneaker into the realm of sculpture and male fetish. Our childhood symbols of Americana that used to never be Black—like Miss America and superheroes—have definitely been made Black.

Nurtured on blaxploitation flicks, we are not afraid to laugh at ourselves, as long as we know the director is laughing *with* us and not *at* us. The Wayans family has built a career creating a Black laugh track. Bertice Berry's book *Sckraight From the Ghetto* makes us acknowledge and giggle at our roots. We can poke fun at the hackneyed traditions of Black History Month. Our generation's version of the bad niggas Shine and Staggerlee has moved beyond the realm of bar, barbershop, or basement jokes to the national stage of music videos and sitcoms.

Raising Our Voices

Though our representation among the ranks of critics has increased slightly above what it was in the early '90s, when one national poll of minority journalists revealed that fewer than ten were critics, our numbers remain few. Because of this scarcity, our voices are often not heard in the cacophony of daily discourse in newspapers, news magazines, television news programs, what Tavis Smiley calls "the conservative citadel" of talk radio, or in proliferating sites on the Internet.

This scarcity happens for a number of reasons: First of all, as soon as you start talking about art and culture, you enter a realm treated as rarified and elite. The sense is that you must possess particular knowledge, taste, and authority in order to be a critic. And, to be fair, this assessment is true to some extent. The tricky part, however, is this: Who decides what knowledge that is and what sense of taste that is? And who grants that authority? I believe that there are lots of elitist and, as an extension, racist decisions being made every day by editors—representing this country's powerful mainstream news organizations. Often, they simply cannot acknowledge that an African-American or any person not White and middle class is educated enough, urbane enough, or sophisticated enough to offer valid criticism. Often there is a disjunction in what is known and valued. We walk in different circles. We speak in different languages.

Often there is no field of vision between the Black and White universes. A White editor reads a story by a Black writer about the rise of Southern influences in Black culture and it does not register for him because the impact of these changes has not registered in his world. But, in the other world, the Black writer has seen rap influenced by the Southern twangs of Outkast, acts hailing from New Orleans and Houston, or the transplanted Southern sound of California-based artists like Snoop Doggy Dogg. We've heard Steve Harvey, Tom Joyner, and J. Anthony Brown on the radio and television. We've seen the increased use of the South for sets in movies like *Jason's Lyric, Down in the Delta*, and *Eve's Bayou*. The Black writer cannot graft the Black story's content onto a White framework. The fields of vision do not converge.

The commonplace nature of our exclusion was reinforced for me in Miami Beach at a reunion of fellows of the National Arts Journalism Program. A Black music critic at a Midwestern newspaper related that, when he wanted to write about the gifted and emerging jazz vocalist Kevin Mahogany, his editors responded that they wanted, as a prerequisite, to know what *Time* magazine or the *New York Times* thought of the singer. Such disrespect of this writer's voice is outrageous. His editors were stating clearly that they placed a higher value on the thoughts, taste, and authority of the White critics at these other publications than of their own writer. This sort of thing happens all the time, if not as blatantly, when yet another White-boy is plunked from among the ranks of general assignment reporters and made a music or film critic. The same White boy and his voice is suddenly ordained with a certain legitimacy, simply because he is chosen by other White men to have it.

This old-boy network, in most cases, cannot be distinguished from racism, sexism, and elitism. As the French art historian Pierre Bourdieu has written, "The upper class propriety treats taste as one of the surest signs of true nobility and cannot conceive of referring taste to anything other than self."

And to be fair, we also deny ourselves opportunity. I believe we have so internalized the idea that we don't have the knowledge, ability, or taste that we don't fight for our voice. We accept that someone else has more right to a voice. We silence ourselves. We are so accustomed to being framed and represented by others that we acquiesce and accept their gaze or their dismissal.

The hip-hop world, in particular, acquiesces and is complicit in shortchanging itself when it accepts that the only value at stake in the world of culture is commercial success and fame. As a result, any unfavorable assessment of a film or musical performance is considered to be simply "hating"—an expression of jealousy by the critic of wealth and fame. Under this model, it is very difficult for some of us to accept a critical assessment of Black female talk-show hosts in relationship to the historical role of the Black mammy. It is difficult to see through the ethnic burlesque of Jennifer Lopez or through what I have come to call the "Berry-ization" of Hollywood. (Not all Black actresses should have to do nude or sex scenes with White men in order to "make it.")

At the same time, acutely aware of the power of images, we rebel when certain lines are crossed. Witness the outrage and protests in 1998 over the television show *The Secret Diary of Desmond Pfeiffer,* a sitcom set during slavery, which really turned out to be more stupid than racist. Witness that, even with the power of the Academy of Motion Picture Arts and Sciences over all things cinema, Black people still spoke knowingly when Denzel Washington could not win an Oscar for his performance in *Malcolm X* or *The Hurricane,* but could win one for playing a rogue cop in *Training Day.* Witness the shame felt by so many of us at the humiliation of young Black women on the popular minstrel freak show *The Flava of Love,* starring Flava Flav, on the Vh1 cable channel.

Being Defined from the Outside

Of course, one of the reasons the dominant culture feels privileged to make a representation of us is because we have been stripped naked, literally and figuratively, in this society. Literally on auction blocks, under whips, and during brutal rape. Figuratively, over and over, in narratives we did not write, such as *The Birth of a Nation* or *Monster's Ball,* which assault us with the cinematic power of turning lies into truth. Whites feel they "know" us and our simple little lives, partly because they have always had such a role in shaping the narrative about us. And as the popularity of our art explodes, we as a people become a commodity along with it, to be picked apart and framed within a context acceptable to the dominant culture.

With questionable "images" of us ever present, plastered and billboarded—and often created by us—there is a sense of exposure, a glaring light shown on often the least attractive, the most criminal, the most seedy part of us, that is then made large to become representative of us all. Our lives become one nonstop rap music video, porno flick, lowbrow comedy, or straight-up horror movie.

The critic who takes a post-colonial view of culture—meaning in part that they are conscious of all the borders of race, ethnicity, gender, sexual orientation, class, and history connected with their subject—is aware that images are powerful. You can't help think that when a New York police officer stops a car driven by an elderly Black woman and then proceeds to abuse her as a suspected drug dealer that his atttitude has at least something to do with images of us all as animal-other-lesser.

Or why does a police officer feel he can get away with sodomizing us with a broomstick; shooting us, as we stand unarmed, forty or fifty times; or beating us bloody on a crowded New Orleans street?

The Black artist's exclusion can be seen as an extension of the Black community's exclusion. When Anna Deavere Smith thought about the scarcity of Black female voices in the theater, she told me, "We're missing a lot. We're missing another kind of humanity, which comes from a Black woman's experience, which is being on the outside not just in terms of race but in terms of gender. It makes me very sad to think about this erasure really, this way that we are not seen."

Or, if we are seen, perhaps we are not seen in a way that values who we are. Consider, for example, the attack by Arlene Croce, a White critic, on Bill T. Jones's 1995 production, *Still/Here,* which dealt with the ravages of AIDS. In a vitriolic essay in the *New Yorker,* Croce dismissed the production as "victim art," meaning not really art at all. "In quite another category of undiscussability are those dancers I'm forced to feel sorry for because of the way they present themselves: as dissed Blacks, abused women or disenfranchised homosexuals—as performers, in short, who make out of victimhood victim art," she wrote. "I can live with the flabby, the feeble, the scoliotic. But with the righteous I cannot function at all." Well, when the Croces of the world "cannot function," and cannot recognize Black voices of pain or protest as art, we are the ones labeled dysfunctional. It is this kind of racism and "victim art" labeling that does not occur when assessing work by Whites in response to the September 11 attacks or the ongoing so-called "war on terror."

All a writer has and, as an extension, all we as a people have—is our voice. Voice is especially critical in this time we live in of heated rhetoric and competition between texts, narratives, newspapers, magazines, little magazines, and proliferating Web sites on the Internet—where the number of sites including hate-filled material calling for our destruction are outnumbered only by those selling pornography or UFO conspiracies. A very important point about voice was made several years ago to me by the critic Ellen Willis: "Journalists' understanding of what they are doing has often not caught up with what they are in fact doing," she said at a gathering of the National Arts Journalism Program. "I think of criticism as a way of interpreting society."

By raising our own voices, we can "interpret society" and speak to each other rather than simply be spoken to by others or through a hostile mask or filter. It becomes the job of our critics, especially those conscious of the post-colonial, imperialism-ruled state of our existence, to analyze not only the fashioning of our images but the impact of those images as well.

For example, it might be argued that Black artists offering images of African-Americans as hookers, hos, pimps, players, and drug dealers are representing themselves (and us?) through their art. But pop artists more often present a producer's vision, a record executive's vision, a vision considered marketable. The line between art and commerce gets so fuzzy that it ceases to exist. And when the added element of race representation is added—and let's not fool ourselves, it is always added—we'd better be careful about what vision is accepted.

In this world we live in, we have to distinguish between what we are creating and what is being sold back to us. Just like the economic model of imperialism—when poor countries ship off raw goods and materials from the earth (or labor) at incredibly cheap prices and are sold back prohibitively expensive manufactured goods—there is an insidious and slick cultural imperialism at work in our lives as well. How do we ship off the Jackson Five and get back a 1980s Michael Jackson with a pale, hacked face? How was Oprah Winfrey created? How was Mike Tyson created? How was Michael Jordan created as a role model? How high of a price do we pay for such creations, good or bad?

When we understand what is being sold back to us, and to everyone, we will understand how images—exported worldwide—come home to roost. We can understand why a new immigrant just off the boat might barely speak English but already know how to properly enunciate the word *nigger,* or understand that Black women are to be disrespected. We can understand how domination and control of the means of cultural production supports the larger social domination.

When film producer Warrington Hudlin thought about the spate of ghettocentric dramas sprouting up in the 1990s purporting to show "authentic" Black urban life, he put it this way: "The reason why 'hood' movies are gratifying to White critics is that when you show the inner city as the jungle, you're doing two things: you're providing the White audience and the White critic a voyeuristic view of this hyper reality in which violence, sex is all raw right there on the surface. And second, you're saying something very important to him. You're [allowing him to say,] 'No matter how bad my life is, it could be worse. I could be a nigger.' It just makes us two different classes of human beings."

Or how about how the culture comes to roost in our own psyches? We are the first generation to be fed a steady dose of Black images not only in film and on television, but integrated into all manner of advertising as well. If we aren't going to be simply passive consumers of culture, then we must question what we are seeing. Take, for example, how for so long we were not shown as lovers. I mean the kind of lovers portrayed in countless Hollywood films as well-rounded, beautiful, passionate people. Sure, in recent years, we've made some progress, particularly with Sanaa Lathan's portrayals in *Love and Basketball* and *Brown Sugar,* and with *Love Jones* and *Sprung.* But the fact is that in the thousands of films and television shows that Hollywood has produced, only a handful have depicted any substantial relationship between a Black man and a Black woman.

When I spoke to Ruby Dee about this, she spoke poignantly. "I guess that exclusion is something I've known about all my life," said Dee, who appeared in her first film in 1949 and played in her own real-life love story with her husband of more than fifty years, Ossie Davis. But she told me she has never starred opposite a Black man in a full-scale love story. "It's one of the things stuck in your subconscious and it eats at you in little ways," she said. "You've received a certain type of propaganda about yourselves, about your relationships, about White people. Something creeps in of the enemy's propaganda."

As I was screening and researching dozens of films, I felt deeply the damage that has been done to any Black person who has learned "through an aesthetic of White faces, aquiline features and flowing hair" what love, and as an extension, humanity, is. All those images of Black women as either trashy hookers or asexualized mammies had created more than a parade of pathetic stereotypes—which are damaging enough in the larger society. There is internal damage done as well. Doug McHenry, director of *Jason's Lyric,* agreed: "We swim in a sea of culture," he said. "And that sea alters our expectations and how we treat each other."

The critic aware of our post-colonial existence is aware of more than the textual and social underpinnings of our images and what images are being sold back to us. It is also becoming increasingly important to acknowledge that some of our best artists and the most important cultural stories may not be the ones that are swept up into the cultural-industrial complex, that they may not be considered a good investment risk or receive the hype that others do.

If the bottom line is used constantly to measure the newsworthiness of an artist, then we miss out on the deep undercurrents of Black culture that have always been and continue to be there. If only the hype model is followed, then it is possible to ignore our roots and many veterans who where holding up the sky for us well before we were born—people like Elizabeth Catlett, or an old subway blues singer named Carolina Slim—or an unhyped filmmaker at your local Black film festival. It becomes possible to let hype rather than our own judgment and taste rule us.

It is also possible, in a world where more rap albums are purchased by Whites than Blacks, to forget that there is often a big difference between our art as it intersects with the dominant culture and as it connects with us.

Making Our Own Definitions

When we look at art and culture as it connects with *us* in the last twenty years, we have to recognize that we have experienced a third Black arts renaissance, following Harlem in the 1920s and the Black Arts Movement of the 1960s. This current blooming—which one Washington, D.C., group of artists calls the Golden Age of Black Art—consists for me of four major streams: the explosion and dominance of Black popular music and its impact on video, fashion, street culture; the building of Black media such as BET; the maturing of the "new wave" of Black film, and the presence and continued influence of veteran artists and institutions that got their start more than three decades ago during the Black Arts Movement, such as Amiri Baraka and the Third World Press of Chicago, headed by writer Haki Madhubuti. Related to the last group is a corps of academicians and "public intellectuals" who have kept alive serious debate about Black culture.

Also, for me, is the issue of to whom I am speaking. Mass media implies a mass audience, and for Black critics employed by mass media, the day-to-day job entails speaking to the majority (still Euro-American at this point in time). As I have attempted to frame my thoughts for this book, I wrote a note to myself that asked, "Am I a voyeur?" I asked myself this because of how, when employed by large, corporate media, I was pulled and pushed to represent our art in a way that conforms to how Whites see us/experience us/frame us. That mission, if I chose to accept it, involved walking outside my body/experience/parallel universe and then looking back at my world, and seeing how it looks from the other side. Needless to say, I have consciously not chosen this mission and fought attempts to force me into such a role, which is really just another way of silencing our voices and perspectives.

To speak *to* us through most corporate media usually involves convincing some editor, who lives outside of our universe, that our conversations within the Black universe are newsworthy, that how we experience and relate to our own culture is just as valuable as how he or his children experience it, even if for a whole different set of reasons. It means convincing the editor that our conversations are newsworthy even if they involve interweaving issues of race, sex, and class that many still pretend have nothing to do with the creation, dissemination, or criticism of art. If race, sex, and class have nothing to do with it, then why are the lists of top TV shows among Blacks and Whites almost mutually exclusive?

How did *Antwone Fisher* fail to make most top-ten lists, yet Blacks recognized it as a masterpiece?

Let's look at another example. The story of David Driskell, a curator, art historian, and painter, is of tremendous importance to African-American art history and to American art history in general. But because his story does not fly high on the radar of important White art, his story might not be told, unless we tell it, unless we assert our authority to say that this man is important and this is why—even if he is not on the White radar right now, along with the traveling Van Gogh exhibit, the debate over Britney Spears's breasts, the gross excesses of Marilyn Manson, or the latest interpretations of long-dead composers by the local symphony orchestra. The critic looking at our art should be aware of how it is making history now.

After the question of *who* or *what* gets covered, there is the question of what is said. Did Tupac possibly "get what he deserved" (as one White writer wrote) when he was murdered? What does the McDonald's Gospelfest tell us about the state of Black sacred music? As much as *The Cosby Show* depicted wholesome Black life, did it leave something out? What *was* R. Kelley thinking about when he wrote those immortal words to a woman: "You remind me of my jeep"? What did happen to '70s soul? Did Phyllis Hyman's death really say more about Black women's lives? Let's debate it: Maybe we might see the peculiar tradition of Black actors performing in a wig and high heels—Flip Wilson, Dennis Rodman, Wesley Snipes, Ving Rhames, RuPaul, and Nickelodeon's Kenan and Kel—as less amusing and more troubling than do Whites. Can art be the catalyst to revitalize and liberate our communities? These are some of the questions that will be examined, poked at, or blasted by the critic who is speaking specifically to us.

We can expand the universe of Black cultural stories beyond the tabloid variety that the dominant culture uses to either make us a pathology/freak show or a burlesque comedy—a response that I like to call the "Ooh-chile-look-at-dem-niggers!" syndrome. Frantz Fanon described the effect more simply and elegantly when he told of an encounter on a street with a young French child who turned to his mother and said, "Look! A Negro [or Nigger or Black]!"

Often, it is not a matter of such blatant depictions of us as the Other. Sometimes we are defined by how we are marginalized and framed within the art world. Not only will some subjects simply not be covered, some are covered but are offered little space, or are positioned "below the fold" or at "the bottom of the page" or are not allowed into print at all.

One of the most important things the post-colonial critic can do is return the gaze. Rather than looking solely at the art of African-Americans, it is important to look at the work coming from the dominant culture that portrays us, even when it is not portraying us, and offer a critique based on our reading of history, culture, and taste. So when *Porgy and Bess* shows up again sixty years after its Broadway debut in a PBS documentary and a stage production at the Kennedy Center, it's time to gaze back at the production written by a White Southern aristocrat and scored by a New York Jewish composer. When a young White filmmaker interrogates slavery by poking a microphone in the faces of Black people and asking, "My family could have owned yours. How does that make you feel?" it's healthy to be able to critique the work and explain why such an approach might interest Whites but could thoroughly offend Blacks. When the critical kudos and awards begin to rain down on Steven Spielberg's *Saving Private Ryan*, it's healthy for the course of American dialogue for someone to point out the impact of excluding Blacks from such a powerful film about World War II. Sure, World War II was segregated; Blacks and Whites did not fight alongside each other. But our fathers and grandfathers were "over there." Our grandfathers and fathers died "over there." The film, as tightly directed as it was, excluded us entirely from the picture of a generation now being lauded as this century's most heroic and "best." Just as we are not shown as lovers, we are rarely shown as heroes, except in the rare gem like *Glory.*

By speaking as I do, I know I will invite some people to accuse me of "advocacy journalism," of not adhering to some sort of standard of objectivity and fairness. Well, I reject this notion. I know that the very nature of criticism and journalism in general is highly subjective. I know that decisions about what is covered and how it is covered are made based on a set of experiences, assumptions, and ideas that are very individual and limited by human foibles. What I am claiming is my authority to assert the value of the experiences, ideas, traditions, and knowledge that I bring to the table. I reject the assumption that I must be White, usually male, and of middle-class or elite origin to have this authority.

I also reject that I must be an academic, ensconced in the halls of ivy to make an impact. In fact, an assistant director of the National Art Journalism Program said that academic criticism is becoming more and more marginalized and that academics feel that mainstream arts journalists and critics are "stealing their thunder."

I have also felt apart from many arts and entertainment journalists who seemingly become a part of the story as near-promoters through an endless supply of fluff in their content, or by continuing to write about artists or groups of artists whom they have befriended or joined in some sort of creative movement. It's not as if I don't believe this sort of writing is valuable. I just know that it makes a difference in my level of fairness if I sit down to write about a friend or someone with whom I have established a personal or professional relationship.

It's been tricky to maintain my consciousness and my own insider status through knowledge and experience, yet try to employ the tools of journalism that I trust. It has been difficult as someone who has also established a career as a poet to somehow try to maintain my own work as an artist within this renaissance while at the same time also writing about the renaissance.

Sometimes it has been difficult to be a woman, not only inside the newsroom but out in the field, where many popular artists in particular assume that all women, including journalists, are approaching them in response to their wealth and status. It has been very disappointing to learn that the actions of some female journalists have given them reason to doubt our collective professionalism.

As I compiled these articles, I realized my own growth and how voice is an evolving process, affected just as much by issues of race, gender, and class as what we write about.

I will always remember one day, way back at the start of this journey, when I was covering art and artists in the "outer" boroughs of New York City, having a conversation with Kellie Jones, who was then curating the exhibit space at the Jamaica Arts Center in Queens. Though I was new at the arts game, the rules presented themselves clearly to me. I felt that my voice was being marginalized at my newspaper. While I had a tremendous freedom to roam, I still had to find a way to comment on the arts closest to my own life, which included music, dance, film, and video. Those granted access and authority to write about these things were all White boys, White boys who in turn hired other White boys, who walked in off the street and were given a greater voice than I was. I don't remember the precise art being discussed but I remember Kellie facing me squarely and saying, "Well, you have just as much right to write about it as they do. After all, it's *your own culture*. What you have to say about it is more important than what they have to say."

2

The New, Black, Hot . . .

She's Gotta Have It

August 8, 1986

I am introduced to this new era of Black film in a small movie theater on the Upper West Side of Manhattan. Outside this dark space, I live in a media image–saturated environment, filled with heated and subtle racist speak from President Reagan on down to local talk radio. Within that saturation, there is buzz among my friends about this new film, *She's Gotta Have It*, and there are small advertisements for it in the newspaper I work for, featuring a photograph of a quartet of young Blacks—one woman and three men.

The house lights dim and a montage of black-and-white images appear on the screen that look to be of everyday Black folks in Brooklyn. Then come the characters, starting with Nola Darling, who address the camera and make it clear that this film will be about Nola's sex life. I am sure that I have never seen anything like this on the big screen before—first, a Black woman of my twentysomething generation playing the part of an everyday Black woman (as opposed to some larger-than-life Pam Grier superbabe or trashy hooker). Finally, that Black woman is dealing with a subject near and dear to my heart—men and dating. Another montage comes, this one hilarious, with a series of Nola-described sorry brothers with even sorrier come-on lines, such as: "You're so fine, I'd drink a tub of your bathwater." Even in their sorriness, I know these men are talking to me, that these jokes are meant for me and that, under no scenario, am I the object of another culture's joke that I don't understand.

When Nola and her main man, Jamie, are nude in bed and the screen coddles her bare, dark breasts and their lovemaking, I know I have never seen anything like this. The White man sitting in the row in front of me begins to breathe very heavily.

Beyond the novelty of a young, brown-skinned Black woman starring in and featured as a beauty in a film—and the film's artistic and comedic touches—I am fascinated by the premise of the story: that a woman, Nola (Tracy Camilla Johns), is the one openly juggling three men (and her reputation), as opposed to the normal scenario these days of a man doing or trying to do the same. The writer, director, and producer, Spike Lee, a recent graduate of New York University's graduate school of film, obviously doesn't feel any reluctance about feeding derogatory stereotypes about the supposedly sex-crazed Black woman (in fact, he seems to delight in thumbing his nose at such racist ideas).

For much of film, anyway, he subverts the macho pecking order in the Black community and gives Nola control over her relationship and sexual choices with three distinctly different men—Jamie (Tommy Redmond Hicks), Mars (Spike Lee), and Greer (John Canada Terrell). That control continues until one brutal scene between Nola and Jamie flips the script and a macho brutality seems to prevail.

Through Lee's character, Mars, *She's Gotta Have It* offers hints, primarily through sports references, of the common nationalism and race speak that still occur among young Blacks in the I-gotta-git-mine 1980s—such as a rejection of the Boston Celtics and their media-adored Larry Byrd. Nola creates a painting and collage on the wall of her loft apartment and pastes up headlines about police brutality, including one about the case of Eleanor Bumpers, an elderly Black Bronx woman killed by police in this city two years ago. This film is also fascinating for how it features an artist lifestyle, as opposed to a lifestyle based on the 9-to-5 rat race. It offers an alternative vision to being a baller, an entertainer, a suit-and-tie guy (or gal), or some type of cop (as in one from Beverly Hills).

For all the sex going on, I don't see any condoms, not that there are none there. When it comes to Nola Darling, I am fascinated, infuriated, jealous, disdainful, and curious. But I know I have seen something new, including the parts of her that are me, on the screen.

Black Star–Whoopi Goldberg in *Jumpin' Jack Flash*

October 10, 1986

As things are brewing in the "new" independent wing of Black cinema, Hollywood has found a new star in comedian Whoopi Goldberg, the comedian and stage artist who showed her film-acting ability in last year's *The Color Purple*, directed by Steven Spielberg. In this first so-so comedic role, she plays Terri Dolittle, a bank employee who, through her work on the computer, gets caught up in an espionage plot and with a mysterious stranger named Jack. None of this story has anything to do with another Black person, issue, or place. Throughout, I'm not sure what is so funny.

Hollywood Shuffle

March 20, 1987

With its hilarious satire, witty sketches, and over-the-top depiction of the life of Black actors, *Hollywood Shuffle* is a sure classic that entertains while making searing commentary about 1980s Black movie images, art, life—and Hollywood.

Produced by a newcomer, the director-actor-comedian Robert Townsend, who has made a name for himself with his story of financing his film on a shoestring with credit cards, *Hollywood Shuffle* follows a few days in the life of a young Black actor, Bobby Taylor. When we first meet him, he is standing in front of his bathroom mirror rehearsing a ridiculous scene in which he is to play a street thug named Jimmy, who "jive talks" and "cool walks" in some sort of way that makes him seem like a different species of human. "I ain't be got no weapon!" is my most favorite Jimmy line.

While Bobby is going through his audition process, he has a series of flashbacks, always with a comedic twist, to the kinds of movie images we've come to know: runaway slaves or slow-talking butlers who don't understand why everyone wants to leave the house of massa, who's been "good to us." Then there is a cut to another scene with the same actor (Townsend) doing an advertisement for the Black Acting School, where Whites teach Blacks to play "TV pimps," "movie muggers," and "street punks" in courses including Jive Talk 101, Shuffling 200, and Epic Slaves 400. A successful graduate brags about how he is currently playing the role of a prison inmate trying to rape his cellmate.

It is also a send-up of Hollywood in general—two brothers "sneaking in the movies" act as film critics offering their opinions on satires of *Dirty Harry, Indiana Jones*, and *Amadeus*. There is the conceited Black actor with the crappy job starring as a giant bat in a sitcom called *Batty Boy*. There is a villain named Jheri Curl, whom you can find by following the empty activator (hair-care liquid) bottles and who can be tortured into confession by depriving him of his prized hair juice.

Written in conjunction with Keenen Ivory Wayans, this is humor that can tickle you and make you cry. It is really the first comedy that I feel was written with any acknowledgment of my generation's humor or our angst over "making it." To a score by Patrice Rushen, *Hollywood Shuffle* makes me laugh about one of the ridiculous aspects of my existence as a Black person in America, a very important aspect that has implications for me here at home and for how people see me and the larger African-American community all around the world—where Hollywood images are exported.

Just as writer George C. Wolfe is exploding Black theater conventions in his off-Broadway hit, *The Colored Museum,* Townsend rips the horrible business as usual in the film industry. Here, the industry is represented by a trio of White casting agents–directors–producers who listen to a series of Black actors—mainly buppies and trained artists—try to transform their real selves into some caricature of cinematic Blackness: a slave, butler, or street hood. The White trio gets to decide what is "Black" and genuine.

Veteran actress Helen Martin plays Bobby's grandmother, who represents his better conscience and dreams. When Bobby dreams, he sees himself playing the first Black Superman. He doesn't dream of continuing to jive talk and shuffle in Hollywood.

Black Star–Whoopi Goldberg in *Burglar*

March 20, 1987

Goldberg is still trying to find the right Hollywood fit. This piteous little flick, where she plays a burglar and bookstore owner, ain't it.

Black Star–Whoopi Goldberg in *Fatal Beauty*

October 30, 1987

In this film, Goldberg plays an L.A. narcotics detective with lots of goofy disguises. Reportedly a love scene between her and her buddy Mike (Sam Elliott) was cut at the end. Perhaps this is the first hint that Goldberg, the most visible Black actress in Hollywood, is viewed by Hollywood as an asexual being.

Black Star–Denzel Washington in *Cry Freedom*

November 6, 1987

As people of conscience the world over focus on the struggle against apartheid in South Africa, *Cry Freedom* would seem the natural vehicle for an exploration of the subject on the big screen. Unfortunately, because this story is based on a book by the journalist Donald Woods, the filmmakers have opted to make it mainly about him, played by actor Kevin Kline. I am not putting down the book or story by

Woods—he has a right to his narrative—and it could be that White people can best relate to the horrors of apartheid if told by a White person. But the focus on Woods in this film feels lopsided and ill-conceived. The bigger drama, the genocide faced by South Africa's twenty million Black inhabitants, is only hinted at through minimal appearances by Denzel Washington in the role of Steven Biko and brief flashes to important people's victories in that country.

Eddie Murphy Raw

December 18, 1987

As a movie star freed of the confines of *Saturday Night Live,* Eddie Murphy has developed a stand-up routine that is, indeed, "raw," filled with all of the profanity, bathroom humor, blue social commentary, and misogyny that he can muster. Some of his favorite routines include ridiculing homosexuals and celebrities—this time Bill Cosby, Brooke Shields ("the Whitest White woman"), and Mr. T.

Much of the comedy being created by the rising male stars of today centers on the so-called battle of the sexes and the sudden access that their fame and money has given them to hordes of gold-digging females—especially if these nouveau celebrities weren't always thought of as so attractive. Murphy even goes the extra mile to claim that, in order to avoid the habit of American wives getting half in a divorce, he will go to Africa and get a "bush bitch" who is too ignorant to know her rights or the law.

There are some funny jokes—like the one about the homemade hamburger—but, in general, *Raw* is a bit much for anyone with even an ounce of feminist sensibility. Murphy's bitterness—who knows where it comes from—outweighs the heart that even salty old Richard Pryor could show when talking about matters of romance. Let's just say that, for my money, Eddie Murphy can never be a convincing high priest of relationships. Finally, I wonder if all the parents who brought young teenagers to this New York City concert knew what the content would be for Murphy's stand-up routine, compared to the content of Murphy's action films that they have loved and that have made them Murphy fans.

Though this film is directed by Robert Townsend and produced by Keenen Ivory Wayans, Murphy seems too much a part of Hollywood—its star system, and the comedy routine as usual—to be part of a new sensibility in Black film.

School Daze

February 12, 1988

If we've somehow forgotten, Spike Lee reminds us that *School Daze* weren't always the best days. In his sophomore feature effort, set at the historically Black, fictional Mission College, conflicts about light- versus dark-skin complexion, "good" versus "bad" hair, career aspirations versus social activism, and a host of class and moral issues are tackled in a lighthearted and eclectic format that includes musical performances and satires about Black Greek life.

The result feels a bit disjointed, offbeat, and dissonant, like a Thelonious Monk solo, but isn't also African-American life? There are two main adversaries. One is Dap (Laurence Fishburne), who is trying to lead a campus campaign to have the college divest from South Africa. The other is Julian (Giancarlo Esposito), head of the campus chapter of Gamma Phi Gamma fraternity, which is bringing in a new line of pledges with a series of demeaning tasks and tests—many in public view of the larger student body.

It is obvious that Lee reserves the most disdain for Julian, the frat guys, and their female support group, the Gamma Rays. It seems that he not only finds their lifestyle superficial, silly, and morally bankrupt, he also takes special aim at the hierarchy in many Greek organizations that, even in the 1980s, practice intrarace discrimination. The Gammas and the Gamma Rays obviously prefer members and associates with light skin, long hair—whether real or artificial—and keen facial features that are closer to the features of Whites.

Most of the drama about looks is played out among women, who are vying for attention on campus and compete for various titles of Queen this-or-that. The longest musical number is a face-off between the wannabes (as in wannabe White or "wannabe better than me") and the jigaboos (a derogatory name that is similar to "spook" or "sambo" in meaning). It is also obvious that the school administration is supportive of the beauty standards and general status quo represented by the Gammas and the Gamma Rays. In contrast, they do not appreciate Dap, his band of student activists, or their goals.

While Lee touches on the issue of intracolor discrimination, he does not explore it beyond female cattiness or link it to any history or class schism in the Black community. Casting for the women who face off is also very uneven, with up-and-coming actresses such as Tisha Campbell and Jasmine Guy cast against Kyme, Joie Lee, and other dark-complexioned actresses who aren't styled to exude glamour appeal. Perhaps such points seem nitpicky, but in the treacherous war of race beauty standards, all sides must be equally armed.

This is obviously far from a textbook perfect film, but it illustrates how Lee is willing to sacrifice convention for social relevance. You cannot look at this movie and come away with no sense of this era's issues in the Black community.

Action Jackson

February 12, 1988

Though starring Carl Weathers and featuring Vanity and Bill Duke, *Action Jackson* is solidly in the mold of standard Hollywood action movies, filled with lots of vapid chase, crash, and burn scenes, a dose of T&A, and amusing musical sound effects. Most tellingly, it has nothing to do with the Black community and has nothing to say to us, except perhaps to try and convince us, as did *Shaft* and *The Mack,* that we have an actual stake in the macho aspirations and exploits of one Black man. At some point, Vanity's character teases the star about his nickname: "Action?! Fine-looking woman like me and you don't even touch me all night? You either gotta be queer or a cop." Vanity is the junkie-mistress of the evil White villain who is engaging in antiunion violence (a bit of relevance) and who is married to the good White woman (Sharon Stone). Both women help Action Jackson achieve ultimate macho supremacy. I am forever changed by what I have seen that is new and fresh in Black film, which speaks to me—and this ain't it.

Coming to America

June 29, 1988

After Eddie Murphy's routine in last year's *Raw,* during which he referred to an African woman as a "bush bitch" and belittled African culture, he would seem the least recommended actor or producer to create a film having anything to do with "the motherland." But, with his industry clout, he has teamed up with his buddy, talk-show host Arsenio Hall, in this new romantic comedy.

It does have its funny and romantic moments. In America, there are definitely jokes, like what is now the running gag among Black filmmakers about jheri curls or other types of juicy hair-care processes. But before we get to America, most of the jokes are set in Africa and all I can say is, listen with an open mind—if you can.

Murphy plays Prince Akeem of the mythical kingdom of Zamunda, where he exists in a comical pampered state with rose petals always strewn on his walking path, with his butt wiped after taking a crap, and with naked women bathing him in a pool-sized tub. We meet him on his twenty-first birthday when, according to his country's custom, he is to meet and marry the wife chosen for him by his parents.

But, hold on—the young prince questions this custom, and, after a disappointing meeting with the beautiful chosen wife (Vanessa Bell), he decides he wants a wife who is an independent thinker and who challenges him mentally. He decides that he can best find this woman in America, in New York City, and, where else but in Queens? With his servant Semmi (Arsenio Hall) at his side, he decides that he wants to live in the most common surroundings as possible because he wants the woman of his dreams to love him for who he is, not for what he has.

After a series of disastrous encounters with women in bars, he decides to attend a "Black Awareness" rally, where he sees Lisa McDowell, daughter of a fast-food businessman, and decides that she is the one he wants to be his queen. The rest of the story involves his effort to woo and win her.

The direction by John Landis (*Animal House, The Blues Brothers*) keeps the comic tempo upbeat and, while some of the scenes "set" in Africa look cheesy, the overall production values are befitting a reasonably budgeted film. The script by David Sheffield, presumably peppered with inserts by Murphy's own humor, makes the most fun of the ridiculous excesses of royalty and the materialism of Americans. That's all good, but what ain't good is how Murphy is able to make these jokes at the expense of the women who are supposed to be his servants, concubines, and wannabe wives. Most of the women put in these pitiable positions are dark-complexioned, while his choice of a queen, Lisa, is light-complexioned. This is powerful and obvious commentary that is not lost on Black viewers. And while this observation is by no means meant to cast aspersion on Shari Headley's fine performance, it is meant to point out the continued subtle and not-so-subtle messages of Murphy's movies.

Black Star–Whoopi Goldberg in *Clara's Heart*

October 7, 1988

Goldberg has finally wrestled free from some mediocre comedy scripts, but she has wound up as—you guessed it—a maid! Here she plays Clara Mayfield, the newly hired housekeeper for a wealthy couple whose marriage is falling apart. The couple's son, David (Neil Patrick Harris), is drawn to Clara as the only person to give him attention and care. He winds up spending his weekends in her Jamaican neighborhood. No better proof is needed than this film that Hollywood has very few options for Black women, and mammy is one of them. The menial trappings make it hard to like what might be good about the movie, such as the rapport between Clara and David. The plot also takes a weird twist when Clara reveals that she has a secret past. At least mammy gets to cross her arms and say, damn, I got my own problems.

I'm Gonna Git You Sucka

December 14, 1988

Keenen Ivory Wayans is obviously tickled by the world around him. His penchant for social satire was first seen in a big way in last year's *Hollywood Shuffle,* which he wrote in conjunction with director Robert Townsend. With a series of unsparing jokes on the big screen about jheri curl chemical hair treatments (which have been picked up by other comedians and scriptwriters, or, who knows, maybe Wayans heard them first from someone else?), he may be singularly responsible for the welcome decline of the chemical curl business.

In *I'm Gonna Git You Sucka,* he finds other trends and excesses of Black popular culture to skewer, including the fad for numerous gold chains, pimp grandeur, and, most especially, the peculiarities of '70s blaxploitation flicks. Even when it tickles the funny bone, his comedy is very sophomoric and very male—including jokes about a seemingly attractive woman who, it turns out, has very few parts of her that are real; the middle-aged mother who can fight better than her army son; and how a woman's menstrual cycle makes her turn into that devil-possessed girl from *The Exorcist.*

The story follows a young man, Jack Spade, who comes home from military service because of the death of his brother. Once home, he realizes that the local gangster, Mr. Big, is trying to extort $5,000 from his family to pay off the debt supposedly owed by his brother. To fight Mr. Big, he enlists the aid of aging heroes—stars of the '70s action flicks that we know and loved (or hated). So into the picture come Jim Brown, Bernie Casey, Fred Williamson, Isaac Hayes, Antonio Fargas, and a martial arts fighter, Steve James, who sort of takes the place of Jim Kelly for this genre. United, they all plan to bring down the notoriously evil Mr. Big, who, of course, is White.

It's all in good fun, enjoyed best in the company of young men. Wayan's comedy is on top of the latest trends and fads. It is not clear if the jokes will be as appreciated years from now when there are new fads and trends that are equally ridiculous, and when younger film viewers do not understand references to the blaxploitation era. Like *Hollywood Shuffle,* this film is loved for its wit, for not taking itself too seriously, and for Wayan's conversation with us.

Postscript: In 1990, Wayans created the weekly television comedy show In Living Color, *which aired for four years and launched the careers of many of his family members, including Damon Wayans, Shawn Wayans, Marlon Wayans, and Kim Wayans. The show also catapulted the careers of Jim Carrey, Jennifer Lopez (as a dancer), and Jamie Foxx.*

The Mighty Quinn

February 16, 1989

Denzel Washington is the big draw and best asset here as a police officer in Jamaica who is trying to solve the case of his friend Maubee, who has been implicated in a murder. Though the story is not inspiring and Denzel's Caribbean accent needs work, the island setting beckons.

Do the Right Thing

June 30, 1989

Do the Right Thing is best understood in the context of our tumultuous 1980s, with its extremes ever more exacerbated in New York City—the widening gap between the rich and poor, the disappearance of many urban jobs that had sustained the working and middle class, and high-profile cases of police brutality and racial violence or killings.

Working as a journalist at a New York daily newspaper, I cannot help but place it also in the context of media and voice, which the Black community lacks. In this "new wave" of Black film, this is the first drama to move beyond the much-appreciated better portrayals of our interpersonal lives to address larger social conditions in the African-American community.

The setting is a block in the Bedford-Stuyvesant section of Brooklyn on the hottest day of the summer. This is Spike's best job at writing so far and the neighborhood includes all the usual and unusual suspects—the neighborhood pizzeria, Sal's Pizza, run by Sal (Danny Aiello) and his two sons Pino (John Turturro) and Vito (Richard Edson); their deliveryman Mookie (Spike Lee); the neighborhood old man Da Mayor (Ossie Davis); the neighborhood old lady (Ruby Dee); Mookie's girlfriend (Rosie Perez), sister (Joie Lee), and a friend named Buggin Out (Giancarlo Esposito).

There are also the neighborhood choruses or crews who occupy stoops and corners—a trio of three men, anchored by the comedian Robin Harris, hold forth on the sidewalk under a beach umbrella; a group of rowdy teenagers, anchored by the comedian Martin Lawrence, fritter away their days and nights. There is also a circle of Latino men, a family of Korean grocers, and, of course, police. There is a radio deejay (Samuel L. Jackson) who broadcasts from a neighborhood storefront and, in a category all himself, Radio Raheem, a football-player–sized young man (Bill Nunn) who carries a massive boom box that always plays "Fight the Power" by the rap group Public Enemy.

The story, which is really about a neighborhood rather than any one person, unfolds in conversations within and between these various camps. It's Saturday. The only people we see working are the Italians, Koreans, and Mookie. The heat acts like a burner beneath a pot, driving forward aggravation and frustrations. The tenuous state of peace that exists in the pot only needs the heat, or one spark, to begin to boil. In addition to the heat as aggravator, Buggin Out, who represents the unschooled nationalist—a more hotheaded version of Mars Blackmon from *She's Gotta Have It*—moves around the block trying to get everyone to support a boycott of Sal's Pizza until Sal adds photographs of Blacks to the walls of the pizzeria, where pictures of Italian-Americans like Frank Sinatra and Sylvester Stallone currently hang. All the various dramas on the block, including the heat, fade away when this one issue of images and representation boils to a head, resulting in a street riot and death.

As much as *Do the Right Thing* serves as an anatomy of social unrest, it does not give us the kind of insight we need into some of the characters—Mookie, in particular—to help us know more about their motivations to riot. It is less an avocation of violence than it is a meditation on it—all kinds of violence, the kind seen and unseen.

Sidewalk Stories

November 3, 1989

This very touching silent black-and-white movie by Charles Lane follows a homeless artist as he tries to find the mother of a baby whose father has been murdered. The photography, performances, and direction are all very good and contribute to the feel of a modern-day fable about what it means to be rich and poor.

Harlem Nights

November 17, 1989

The word about this movie, executive-produced by and starring Eddie Murphy, is that it was made because Murphy always wanted to act in a period piece. It is supposed to be set in Harlem circa 1918, but the acting and dialogue, particularly from Murphy and Richard Pryor, sounds like the setting could be the '60s, '70s, or '80s. *Harlem Nights* makes me believe that I'm in the Harlem Renaissance as much as I believe that I am America's sweetheart Meg Ryan. It's all substandard fare. Quick (Murphy) and Sugar Ray (Pryor) run an illegal after-hours spot with gambling, liquor, and prostitution. They develop a scheme to overcome pressure from the White mob and a crooked cop (Danny Aiello). Veteran comedian Redd Foxx delivers a few good lines, but, all in all, *Harlem Nights* feels like someone playing at making a movie that has no good jokes, flavor, or atmosphere, and, unfortunately, is of no consequence.

Black Star—Whoopi Goldberg in *Homer and Eddie*

December 1, 1989

In this flick, Eddie (Goldberg) is half nuts, and she's trying to a help a mentally challenged guy find the father who abandoned him. Not only is Goldberg asexualized, here her name is even Eddie! (Eddie Cervi, what kind of name is that for a Black woman?) It feels like these Whoopi roles are obviously written for Whites and she gets shoehorned into them.

Glory

December 15, 1989

The slave rendered as a modern around-the-way brother, full of swagger, heart, and venom, is but one of the reasons to recommend *Glory,* the heart-rending historical film about the 54th Massachusetts Volunteer Infantry Regiment that fought in the American Civil War. Denzel Washington, known to most from his roles in *Cry Freedom, The Mighty Quinn*, and as the handsome Dr. Philip Chandler on *St. Elsewhere,* is the irascible Private Trip, who obliterates the image of the servile darkie and instead imbues a runaway slave with what he had to have: spirit, tenacity, and daring.

This is, for my money, one of the best war movies ever made, with an incredible ensemble of Black actors including Washington, Morgan Freeman, and a young Andre Braugher making his film debut. Too bad that once again, stories that honor our history are given short shrift by so many White critics and buzzmakers. I guess it is too much for them to see Black men not in the roles of street thugs or in the less-threatening role played by Freeman this year, as an elderly White woman's chauffeur in *Driving Miss Daisy.*

Directed by Edward Zwick and drawn from the collected writings of the regiment's young White leader, Colonel Robert Gould Shaw (Matthew Broderick), this is another one of our stories told from the perspective of a White person. But, unlike other films, it also offers tremendous insight into Blacks, who should be at the heart of the story. In *Glory,* we learn about discrimination faced by the Black soldiers and regiment inside the Union Army and the particular journey and camaraderie of the Blacks. Most poignant for me was the campfire service on the night before the soldiers went into their historic and courageous battle at Fort Wagner in South Carolina. "I stand here this evening, heavenly father, to ask your blessings on all of us," says Morgan Freeman in the role of Sgt. Major John Rawlins. "So that if tomorrow is our great getting up morning, if tomorrow we have to face the judgment day, heavenly father we ask that you let our folks know that we went down facing the enemy, that we went down standing up amongst those who fight against our oppression. We want them to know, heavenly father, that we went down fighting for our freedom."

Washington obviously made the role of Trip his own by contributing his own particular flava to the dialogue and scenes with the other Black soldiers. His addressing his colleagues, variously, as "buck," "field hand," and "house nigga" is dead-on. At some point, when Andre Braugher's character, Thomas—a free Black who has known Colonel Shaw since childhood in Massachusetts—is reprimanded by White superiors, Trip takes the opportunity to tease him. "You thought you were different, didn't you?" he says, raising Thomas's hat from his face. "What you think now? You just thought you were so smart, didn't you, nigga? Well, you in the real school now."

So many of the pivotal scenes involving the soldiers—the fact that they were not given regulation shoes, uniforms, or pay—show Trip standing up or making moves for it to happen. A critical and powerful scene, when he is about to be whipped, shows his back already scarred. Trip represents the spirit of Black rebellion in a regimented White man's army.

This is an amazing performance in a movie the likes of which I have never seen before.

Postscript: For this year, Driving Miss Daisy *won the Oscar for Best Picture and Denzel Washington won his first Oscar for the role of Private Trip in* Glory.

House Party

March 9, 1990

The high school movie of comedy and coming-of-age calamity is given a hip-hop twist in *House Party,* a film by two brothers, Warrington Hudlin and Reginald Hudlin.

Hip-hop comes in the form of the rap duo Kid 'n Play, who are the stars of the film. Play (Christopher Martin) is the chocolate part of the duo, with the low curly fade haircut. He is also the one giving the house party in question while his parents are out of town. Kid (Christopher Reid) is the tall, slender, light-skinned half of the team, with the very high high-top fade that makes him look like a pencil with an unused eraser on his head. Most of the story unfolds as Kid tries to attend Play's party, even though he is grounded.

It is through Kid that we travel through *House Party*'s way stations of comedy with their decided references to those of us who grew up Black and urban. His widowed father, called only Pops, is played by the hilarious comedian Robin Harris, who delivers one-liners with his signature grumbling and big eyes. Pops wonders aloud why his son's hairstyle resembles a broom and why he ever got involved with Kid's White mother. Harris represents the old-school, no-nonsense parent in the Black community. Kid's school buddies include Play and Bilal, played by another rising comedian, Martin Lawrence (*Do the Right Thing*). His nemesis is a muscular jheri-curl clad trio (members of the musical group Full Force) that looks as if it was just released from prison.

As Kid tries to reach the party, he is accosted by the Full Force brothers several times on the dark streets. Pops is also looking for him, and there is a possible romantic entanglement with either Sharane (A. J. Johnson) or Sidney (Tisha Campbell), the finest girls in the school. The remainder of the gags include Sharane's family living in the projects, various boasting, schemes and efforts to engage in teen sex, and the fact that Bilal has very bad breath.

It is all in bawdy good fun, which is only odd in the sense that *House Party* is a bit too mature, with too much sex, sexual references, and profanity, for what would seem to be its natural audience: the PG-13 crowd. On the other hand, mature adults, while enjoying the action, might feel we are too grown for a flick about high school. Of course most of the actors, while certainly youthful in appearance, are also not really high school age. Kid 'n Play are in their mid- to late twenties.

All these semi-oldheads on-screen make *House Party* a very mature but funny take on high school.

Black Star—Whoopi Goldberg in *Ghost*

July 13, 1990

With newly realized psychic powers, Oda Mae Brown (Goldberg) helps the ghost of a husband communicate with his wife and try to protect her from the same forces that killed him. This movie really isn't about Oda Mae at all. Goldberg, who can't get any love at all in Hollywood, gives a big assist to a tale of eternal love. How cruel.

Postscript: Goldberg won an Oscar for Best Supporting Actress for Ghost.

3

Mo' Betta?

Mo' Better Blues

August 3, 1990

For much of its 130 minutes, *Mo' Better Blues* feels like the film equivalent of rappers bragging about their assorted sexual conquests. Romantically sophomoric and bordering on misogynistic, the film nonetheless takes what is probably a realistic view of the love landscape traveled by Spike Lee and other Black male members of the "Black Pack," the new Black glitterati of the music, film, and sports worlds.

The film features the dashing Denzel Washington, known to most from his Oscar-winning role in last year's *Glory,* as Bleek Gilliam, a rising jazz trumpeter. Gilliam is juggling two women: Clarke (Cynda Williams), an aspiring singer, and Indigo (Joie Lee), a schoolteacher.

Bleek's relationships with the two women, who know about each other and try to nudge Bleek in their direction, allows Lee to explore the dating terrain among our era's male jet set, wannabes, and buppies in general. It is a very male world (perhaps represented best in spirit by those 1986 Oran "Juice" Jones lyrics: "This is my world, you just a squirrel tryin' to get a nut").

Subtly, Lee presents the same issues of color stratification in the Black community, wannabes versus jigaboos, that he presented in *School Daze,* in casting Clarke as a light-complexioned women with straight hair and casting Indigo as a brown-skinned woman who wears her short hair in a crinkly natural style. (And in this subtle battle of aesthetics, Joie Lee's stylists and the cinematographer surely let her down, as the doe-eyed beauty appears in scene after scene with her hair and skin looking less than its best.)

Other than these superficial differences, there are not obvious deeper social, political, or intellectual differences highlighted between the two women, except that Clarke seems to take more of an active interest in Bleek's career and work than does Indigo. Though we might initially think otherwise, this is not a choice necessarily between an earth mother and a jet-setter, or the deep versus superficial. Williams actually infuses a lot more life and bubbly into her character, which outshines the somewhat cool and brooding role played by Joie Lee.

Outside the realm of Bleek's bedroom, this film is notable for its ensemble of male actors around Washington, including Wesley Snipes as a saxophonist, Giancarlo Esposito as a pianist, Bill Nunn as a bassist, Samuel L. Jackson as a henchman, the real-life drummer Jeff "Tain" Watts as the drummer in Bleek's band, and the comedian Robin Harris doing bits of his hilarious stand-up routine.

The good news on the love front in this film, which was initially titled *A Love Supreme,* is that its randy, male-centered narrative gives way to a more balanced and mature view of romance, love, and—(gasp!)—even marriage. But perhaps it also sends the message that such maturity is only possible for men when they reach a dead end in their life, and that they will take the female dream of love only after their own male dream of conquering the world has faded.

To Sleep with Anger

October 12, 1990

Charles Burnett's acclaimed film about a man named Harry (Danny Glover) and his impact on one family is eccentric and surprising, from beginning to end.

Et Cetera—The Price of a Date with Starring Power

December 5, 1990

What do you get when you mix models, actresses, and date-hungry women with filmmakers, rappers, and other assorted male luminaries? Well, you get more glitterati than literati, more hair weaves, blond dye, and sequins than dreadlocks and kente cloth.

This was the mix at Monday night's First Annual Black Models Ball, which included a Go to the Movies with a Movie Star auction to benefit the Black Filmmaker Foundation, the twelve-year-old organization nourishing rising young Black filmmakers like the Hudlin brothers and Charles Lane.

With a dozen offerings on the block, the auction attracted hundreds to the cavernous, chilly nightclub The Building, on West Twenty-sixth Street in

Manhattan. High bidders won a movie date and popcorn with the star of their choice.

The night felt like a highfalutin but friendly meat market. Maybe the meaty feeling started with the auctioneer, Kim Coles, the comedian best known for her TV commercials selling Burger King hamburgers. Maybe it was the crowd of shrieking women in scanty dresses who bid as expertly as mechanics looking over used cars. Maybe it was the shenanigans of one of the members of the rap trio Full Force (B-Fine, Bow-Legged Lou, and Paul Anthony), who swiveled his tongue out lasciviously. Or maybe it was just Sam Silvera, the Chippendale's dancer who stripped to the waist, flexed his copper-colored pectorals, and promised to bring his G-string along on the date.

"I don't want them to feel like beefcakes," Coles said of the auction lots at the start of the night. But then she couldn't resist pointing out each man's more promising attributes. "Look, ladies," she said as Channel 2 news anchor Reggie Harris stood "on the block" beside her. "He's got big hands."

Sometimes the guys went into a sales pitch as well: "A movie with Heavy D. just ain't no movie," said the overweight rapper, dapper in a tan sportcoat.

"If you buy me," said Silvera, "I'll pay such close attention to you."

"I'm shocked. I don't believe it," said one woman in an elaborate black-and-gold gown, after someone bid $430 for a date with Reginald Hudlin, the writer and director of *House Party.*

The woman who won the date with Hudlin, Karen Alpert, of Bedford, New York, thought the price "was cheap." And she wasn't the only one to bid more than the price of a car payment for a date. This was a crowd of climbers, and the bidding seemed to have less to do with the looks and physique of the men than their rank in the "What Can You Do For Me?" department.

Some bids topped Manhatten rents. Nelson George, *Village Voice* columnist, and Ed Eckstine, a director for Polygram Records, drew the night's largest bid of $1,450, split between two women.

Heavy D., however, generated the most excitement in the house. When he drew a bid of $360 in the early going, it seemed impressive. But the top price for an individual date went for Warrington Hudlin, producer of *House Party,* paid by twenty-three-year-old Gisele Marcus of the Upper East Side.

"He's had a lot of accomplishments," said Marcus, a Manhattan management consultant.

Tai Mak, a karate master known for his appearance in *The Last Dragon,* kept stabbing at the air with a high kick of his left foot, but only garnered a top bid of $95. Despite his promise of attention, Silvera drew $150; G. Keith Alexander, a TV reporter, drew $400 after promising the winner an appearance on *The McCreary Report.* Even after promising free passes to *Saturday Night Live,* cast member Chris Rock couldn't do better than $150.

In one case, it seemed the winner might get more than she bid for—or less. Despite the tease about Reggie Harris's hands, it turns out he's been happily married for twelve years. Jameliah Green, of Stuyvesant Heights, Brooklyn, tried to mask her disappointment after placing the winning bid of $450.

"I've always respected him," Green said. "I respect that he is married."

As Harris's wife, Diane, waved from across the room, Harris said, "My wife agreed to it [the auction]; it's for a good cause. She will probably go to the movies with us."

Black Star—Whoopi Goldberg in *The Long Walk Home*

December 21, 1990

Whoopi is a maid again, but this time in the context of working for an upper-crust White family in Montgomery, Alabama, when the historic bus boycott occurred there in 1955. She plays opposite Sissy Spacek, and both women turn in powerful and nuanced performances.

Black Star—Laurence Fishburne in *Cadence*

January 18, 1991

Currently known as Larry, Fishburne adds some flava to a movie featuring Charlie Sheen as a rebellious inmate in an army stockade.

New Jack City

March 8, 1991

The dominance and devastation of crack cocaine in the 1980s Black community provides *New Jack City* the perfect opportunity to create this film era's first Black *Scarface* or New Jack *Superfly.*

The gangster is Nino Brown, played by Wesley Snipes, an ebony man with chiseled features and a steady gaze (*Mo' Better Blues*). The setting is Harlem in particular and Reagan-era America in general, where a drug-saturated nation is treated to a "just say no" antidrug slogan from the First Lady, where the rich get richer, the poor get poorer, and, as Nino tells us, "you gotta rob to get rich."

With cinema's favorite organized crime icons as models, *New Jack City* sets up the typical double consciousness in viewers, where we want to root both for and against the bad guy. After all, on some level, the Nino Browns of our world are getting over in a system we think is designed for their and our failure. Even if it is in a twisted way, and even if our community pays the ultimate price, we are lured into admiring the outlaw, knowing full well that there are just as many moral outlaws on the supposed right side of the law—shysty investment bankers, prostitutes, high-end drug pushers and users—that are not being prosecuted. *New Jack City* also appeals to a Black nationalist streak as Nino combats the traditional and powerful Italian Mafia, which has always controlled a portion of his past criminal activities.

We are seduced by the outlaw's big houses, fancy cars, stylish clothes, the richness and new jackness of it all. The outlaw, it seems, always lives the high life and, in this era, it means that Nino and his Cash Money Brothers crime syndicate party at fictional fancy clubs in Harlem, where they are feted by popular entertainers such as Flava Flav, Keith Sweat, and Teddy Riley, inventor of the new jack swing style of music that gives this film and era its rhythm and attitude.

Rapper Ice-T also brings a gangster hip-hop aesthetic to the movie in the role of an undercover police officer who is Nino's chief adversary and counterbalance in the plot. Director Mario Van Peebles, producers Doug McHenry and George Jackson, and writers Thomas Lee Wright and Barry Michael Cooper—almost all newcomers to feature-length films—have succeeded in creating a believable environment and story where we watch Nino Brown and his crew take over a large Harlem building and set up a production and distribution center for crack cocaine.

This film does not present us with new ideas, just perhaps new jack ways of framing and speaking them. Women, of course, do not fare very well, but Vanessa Williams does hang with the boys as a steely and no-nonsense assassin named Keisha. Some compare the story line to that of *The Untouchables,* involving the prohibition-era gangster Al Capone. When the story line gets predictable toward the end, it must rely on very good performances, particularly by Snipes, Ice-T, and Chris Rock, to carry it off.

The Five Heartbeats

March 29, 1991

Even though since *Hollywood Shuffle* Robert Townsend has directed *Eddie Murphy Raw* and his own *Partners in Crime* television show, this feels like his sophomore feature film. Also written in conjunction with Keenen Ivory Wayans, it tells the story of a 1960s singing group that goes pro and encounters problems both professionally and privately. The performances, especially by Townsend and Leon, are memorable.

A Rage in Harlem

May 3, 1991

Imabelle (Robin Givens), beautiful paramour to a gangster, is on the run with gold from a shootout, unaware that the bad guys are hot on her trail. Help comes in an unlikely form. Lots of shoot-'em-up. Little context or meaning.

Straight Out of Brooklyn

May 22, 1991

This film's director, Matty Rich, is receiving a lot of buzz in film circles as "the next young Black hot . . ." Reportedly only nineteen years of age at the time he made the film last year, Rich gained even more buzz when he won special jury recognition for *Straight Out of Brooklyn* earlier this year at the Sundance Film Festival. The film itself, which tells the story of four young people growing up in a Brooklyn housing project (Rich himself grew up in that borough's Red Hook Houses) is very raw and mostly difficult to watch.

As he tells the story of one beaten-down family, the Browns, he treads familiar turf—the bitter and brutal father (George T. Odom), the long-suffering wife (Ann D. Saunders), and the teenage son, Dennis (Lawrence Guilliard Jr.), who thinks he has found a sure but illegal way to get his family "straight out of Brooklyn." Most of the scenes, characters, and dialogue are constructed in a slapdash sort of way. Though the effect gives the film a near documentary style, it also gives the viewer the sense that this movie—and the larger stories of our community—are not important enough for more time and care.

Jungle Fever

June 7, 1991

Jungle Fever is, undoubtedly, the first film to take on so boldly the American taboo of interracial dating. To explore the subject, Spike Lee picks at the same sensitive spot that he did in *Do the Right Thing*—the thorny relationship between Italian-Americans and African-Americans living in New York City.

Such a jumping-off point, of course, allows Lee to poke at racism in general, as well as at the intra-racial neuroses of both Blacks and Whites. One half of the interracial couple is a successful architect named Flipper Purify (Wesley Snipes). Purify is a very dark-complexioned Black man married to a very light-complexioned Black woman named Drew (Lonette McKee), who is a buyer at Bloomingdale's. They live on Striver's Row in Harlem. The color subtext of the Purify family (as in purify the race?) is interrogated a bit, as well as the color baggage carried by each of Flipper's parents, and by the Black community in general. We are also privy to a startling "war council" of Black women castigating Black men who only date White or very light Black women, and White women who are always throwing sex at Black men.

The other half of the interracial pair is Angela Tucci (Anabella Sciorra), a temp assigned to work for Flipper at the architectural firm where he is employed. Angie comes from the Italian working-class community of Bensonhurst in Brooklyn, where in real life two years ago, a Black teenager was killed while there to answer an advertisement for a used car. Angie is coming from a very traditional family, where she is expected to cook for her father and two brothers. Her mother is deceased, as is the mother of her boyfriend, Paulie (John Turturro), who lives with his father. We learn through their conversations that Angie's family, friends, and neighbors, though some of them are darker and have kinkier hair than some "Black people," hold bigoted views of African-Americans and reject any notion of Italians dating "niggers."

These emotionally laden scenes make for fascinating cinema that confronts rather than escapes the social conditions of each community. They are presented as a result of a late-night office tryst turned romance between Flipper and Angie. The actual affair, the onset of the "jungle fever" as it were, comes quickly and is not as visceral as the reaction to it. If Lee, as the writer and director, wants us to believe that the pair simply acted out of curiosity, then the affair, on-screen scenes, and dialogue between them still needs some spark of lusty curiosity. The pairing would also be more believable if Flipper and Angie had anything in common aside from their workplace.

Much of the film's passion is directed, instead, to a powerful drama of crack addiction unfolding in Harlem and in Flipper's family. His big brother, Gator (Samuel L. Jackson), is a crack addict who is constantly leaning on Flipper and on his mother, Lucinda (Ruby Dee), for money. His father, the Good Reverend Dr. Purify (Ossie Davis), has disowned Gator and, as a Black son of the American South, takes a hard line against Flipper's association with a White "whoremonger."

It is the crack fever that gets more passion from Spike Lee. Perhaps in his choices, he debunks the myth of the importance, or even existence, of jungle fever.

Boyz n the Hood

July 12, 1991

Five years into the new wave of Black film, we are entering the "hood."

On the heels of this year's popular *New Jack City,* about a Harlem drug pin and empire, comes a flick that switches coasts and tells a tale of youth and coming of age.

Written and directed by John Singleton, a newcomer who trained at the USC School of Cinema, *Boyz n the Hood* is an unflinching and close-up story of four young boys growing up in South-Central Los Angeles. This story and setting allows Singleton, with a better-than-average script, to explore the issues of absentee fathers, teen pregnancy, lack of education, police brutality, and violence that plague so many of our communities—not just South-Central.

It is also a tremendous coming-out party for the actor Cuba Gooding Jr. who, along with rapper Ice Cube, turns in a performance that never lets us doubt the story's truth. Gooding plays Tre, a young boy sent to live with his father, who lives across from a single mother named Brenda (Tyra Ferrell). Brenda's two sons, Darin, known as Doughboy (Cube), and Ricky (Morris Chestnut), do not have their fathers in their lives. Though Tre, Doughboy, and Ricky live on the same street, attend the same schools, and play together, the boys—beginning at a young age—are on two different paths. Tre not only has his father and mother in his life, his parents are educated and are conscious of the pitfalls and dangers for young Black men.

These class and education differences are shown in the film, but they are not prominent given the fact that Tre's father, Furious (Laurence Fishburne), lives right across the street and his crib is not much different in appearance than Brenda's house. What winds up being the focus is gender, with Brenda and a crack-addicted mother on the same street seen as wholly incompetent parents. In contrast, Furious is seen, as Doughboy says in one scene, as the equivalent of "Malcolm Farrakhan." Gender differences are also highlighted because of the disrespectful manner in which Ice Cube's character and many of the young men refer to women as bitches, hos, and hoochies. Though women in the neighborhood seem to be denigrated for their sexuality, the one girl in the neighborhood, Tre's girlfriend Brandi (Nia Long), who holds onto her virginity is hounded, especially by Tre, to relinquish it.

Singleton is ultimately just as critical of the wanton and stupid attraction that men have to guns and violence. While he does blame much of this wrong path of young Black men on absentee fathers, there is also some consideration given to the act of violence and its heartrending consequences. According to statistics stated in the film, one in every twenty-one African-American men will be murdered, with most of these deaths at the hands of another Black man.

If there is any hope in ending both the war on the streets and between the sexes in this film, perhaps it lies with Tre and Brandi, who seem to understand that united we stand, divided we fall.

Livin' Large!

September 20, 1991

Michael Schultz's comedy takes a deft look at the process of being upwardly mobile as a young Black news reporter (T. C. Carson) loses his identity and soul.

Black Star–Denzel Washington in *Ricochet*

October 4, 1991

Washington plays a Los Angeles assistant district attorney, Nick Styles, who is in a literal fight to the death with an ex-con determined to destroy the man who sent him to prison. Often riveting, it is similar in tone, to me, to *Fatal Attraction,* because a family and children are threatened and because the arch villain, Earl Talbott Blake (John Lithgow), commits a series of violent acts with a maniacal drive. The script does not link Blake's obsession to race. It is difficult for us to imagine that there isn't a connection.

Strictly Business

November 8, 1991

This is a likeable and lightweight romantic comedy that pokes fun at male and female buppies, white-identified Negroes, and the pretensions of street savvy among young Black men. Waymon Tinsdale III (Joseph C. Phillips) is the straight-laced executive who is dying to meet a gorgeous waitress (Halle Berry), but feels he lacks the Black mack-daddy vibe needed to pull it off. He turns to a hip mail-room employee, Bobby Johnson (Tommy Davidson), to hook him up in exchange for getting Bobby into a trainee program at the company. This is Berry's coming out as the new Black sex symbol and beauty ideal, and the beginning of the craze among many Black women to copy her signature short, spunky hairdo.

Daughters of the Dust

December 27, 1991

Julie Dash's meditative tale about the Black island people from off the coasts of Georgia and South Carolina. Referred to by many as the Gullah or Geechee people, they have retained more of the African ways and sensibilities than African-Americans who live on the mainland. This film, set in 1902, actually chronicles the decision of some members of a family, the Peazants, to leave their rather desolate island home and "cross over" to the mainland for more opportunities. Though most do leave, many stay with the elderly family matriarch, Nana Peazant, who movingly urges her family, wherever they may be, not to forget their cultural heritage. This film captures the magic of this landscape, as well as the beauty and sensibility of Black women in a way that I have never seen before in a movie. It won the award for cinematography at this year's Sundance Film Festival.

Juice

January 17, 1992

The primary merit of *Juice* is as a warning about hanging around with crazy people—and making a movie about crazy people. Rapper Tupac Shakur plays the part of Bishop, an over-the-edge Harlem teenager who hangs with three other boys—Q (Omar Epps), Raheem (Khalil Kain), and Steel (Jermaine Hopkins).

The film follows these three truants in a dead-end ghetto travelogue from their houses, to the video arcade, to stealing from a record store, to getting cigarettes, to running from the cops, to planning a petty crime. It is all of minimal interest, intellect, or action. And then Bishop takes petty crime to a whole other level.

Part of what is infuriating about the movie is its insistence that we elevate the decisions of these four wayward young men, most especially Bishop, to be important enough to meditate on for two hours. It is all nihilism, pathology, and senseless murder writ stylishly on the big screen by Ernest Dickerson, best known as Spike's cinematographer.

By making Bishop the vehicle through which we understand the lives of young Black men, it creates the misguided sense that they are all animals with a moral compass that is different from other human beings. Perhaps *New Jack City* and *Boyz n the Hood* changed the course of this new Black film renaissance toward pathology, nihilism, and death. If so, I hope that *Juice* represents the most senseless—and depressing—that it will get.

I don't believe these films are reflecting the reality for the majority of people in our community, who are hardworking adults and young people hoping to break free of the madness, not contribute to it. I believe these films, as well as music videos and some so-called hip-hop journalism, are creating a reality, a perceived reality, that is not us.

Mississippi Masala

February 5, 1992

Denzel Washington stars in this close-up look at a romance between an African-American man and an Indian woman in the Deep South. Directed by Mira Nair, it is one of the first films to take a frank look at the racist attitudes of new immigrants toward African-Americans.

White Men Can't Jump

March 27, 1992

This movie is a likeable comedy mainly because its two stars, Wesley Snipes and Woody Harrelson, are likeable, and despite the fact that it stretches a one-note joke, about White men not being able to get air on the basketball court, into a full-length movie. The pair, Sidney Deane and Billy Hoyle respectively, work as basketball hustlers, taking money from young Black ballers who assume that Billy is a pooty butt. They are also in the crosshairs. Billy owes money and some thugs are on their trail. Rosie Perez (*Do the Right Thing*) makes an appearance as Billy's girlfriend.

4

Isn't He Lovely

Et Cetera—In TV, It's *A Different World* Indeed

March 24, 1993

"After six years of marriage, we're looking old and tired [to the network]," said Susan Fales, the thirty-year-old executive producer and head writer for *A Different World,* which has been on hiatus since January 28. "It's time to go to Victoria's Secret and get some lingerie to pique their interest." The series is expected to return later this spring, and its fate will be decided May 17, when NBC announces its fall schedule.

Buffeted at the start of this season by its head-to-head competition Thursday nights with *The Simpsons* and then "kicked in the pants" by Fox's *Martin* during its last three months, *A Different World* and its fans are facing the fallout from the first head-to-head competition between two popular shows aiming for the same young, predominantly Black, audience.

"The thing selling *Martin* is that it's a 'couple show,'" Fales recalled network bigwigs telling *A Different World*'s producers. "You've got to get more Dwayne and Whitley stuff," referring to two key *World* characters played by Kadeem Hardison and Jasmine Guy.

"It kicked us in the pants," Fales said of *Martin.* "They were neck and neck with us. They beat us."

Frequently pausing with a joyful, light cackle, Fales offered a behind-the-scenes glimpse of televisionland during an informal talk and interview this week at the Museum of the Moving Image in Astoria, New York. Some hot topics among the Black Hollywood set:

1. Will the success of the recent miniseries *Queen* spawn a new crop of Civil War–era, "rag on the head" dramas?
2. There are so many light-skinned Black actresses and so little skin-tone variety at auditions that they are sometimes sarcastically called the "mulatto follies."
3. Other Black comedians, including Sinbad and David Chapelle, may be getting their own shows, reflecting an industry trend to build series around comedians.

"What I do find depressing is that the networks are thinking, 'Hey, he'll be *big funny,*'" Fales said. "There are so many gifted actors and actresses who are being passed over."

Fales, who grew up on the Upper West Side the daughter of actress Josephine Premice and stockbroker Timothy Fales, began her career fresh out of Harvard as a junior writer on *The Cosby Show.* She said that the specific effect of this emphasis on comedians could mean less focus on social issues that *A Different World* attempted to address in recent seasons, and even less chance that serious Black dramas will be developed.

Most Blacks in television "are like the fools in Shakespeare," she said. "I think they are going to try to bring on some Black dramas because there was so much flack over the fact that all the new [Black] shows are comedies."

When it comes to a show like *In Living Color,* Fales questions the tastefulness of some of the spoofing, but—citing Robert Townsend's landmark *Hollywood Shuffle* or George C. Wolfe's *The Colored Museum*—said she is not uncomfortable with the idea of Black satire.

"Why can't we have our Charlie Chaplins? Our bozos," she said. "We have our clowns, but people get concerned when that is all they see."

The pressure on producers to be "big funny" rather than substantial is greater than ever, Fales said, because of efforts by a small group of religious fundamentalists who continue to target prime-time shows that address issues such as teen sexuality, AIDS, or racial tensions.

As an example, Fales screened a 1991 episode of *A Different World* in which a semiregular character announced that she had contracted AIDS. On the same show, Whitley was deciding whether to lose her virginity.

"I got a call from [NBC Entertainment President] Warren Littlefield saying, 'Please don't do this. The sponsors are all going to drop out,'" Fales said. "But we were insistent."

In the end, the episode lost some sponsors. But it was one of the highest-rated episodes of the season.

"And networks are profit driven, not ideologically driven," Fales said. "It's not about depicting Blacks in one way or another. If they thought it would make money, it would be, for God's sake, bring CANCER! LEPROSY! THE DISEASE OF THE WEEK!"

To drive home the point, Fales emphasized that the network wanted Whitley to lose her virginity if it could be during the "sweeps" period when a show's viewership is measured.

That the series developed a reputation for being issue-oriented—it has addressed the Los Angeles riots and date rape—is ironic. When it debuted in 1987 as a *Cosby* spin-off, it was remarkable in its lack of controversial issues for a show set at a college campus. Fales said that, even though it was a Black college, the writers couldn't deal with racial issues or explain the presence of regular character who was a White student.

"Debbie Allen [the show's director] is the one who turned it around," Fales said. "Debbie started the ball rolling by saying that the show has to be of our time. It can't exist in this bubble."

As a reality check or bubble check, Fales and other show staffers annually visit Atlanta to interview students at Morehouse and Spelman. And Fales's eight-member writing team, which includes four women and four men, half of them Black—rare even as Blacks make progress in Hollywood—debates everything from plots to dialogue.

As a recent example, Fales said, the youngest member of the team, an intern, was angry that a show was being produced on Black memorabilia, highlighting the servile "mammy" image.

"She said, 'A mammy was just somebody who flipped pancakes and didn't stand up for herself. I'm ashamed of her.'"

As a result, the intern's feelings were transformed into dialogue—almost verbatim—and included in the episode. Such debates reveal the continued need for more Black writers and producers, Fales added. She then laughed, referring to another show, where the frequent use of "Girrrrl" as a sentence opener was written to "make the dialogue authentically Black." She tells a funny story of a White producer for the show *Rhythm and Blues* confronted with this pattern, who replied, "I read [Terry McMillan's] *Waiting to Exhale* and that is how they talk."

"It's not about being Black to write Black but it's about finding people who have sensitivity to and respect for the culture," she said. The challenge for such shows as *A Different World* is to stay topical, Fales said. "Sometimes I think the [network] attitude is, 'C'mon ladies, let's just get out there and be entertaining,'" Fales said. "C'mon. You should be happy you're on the air."

Deep Cover

April 15, 1992

The era of Black film is giving the industry's few Black directors, who had been primarily relegated to television episodes and perhaps commercials, their first opportunity to direct a feature-length film. Bill Duke, a big, imposing man best known to most of us as an actor, is one such directing talent. Last year, he directed the standard fare *A Rage in Harlem,* and in his new project, *Deep Cover,* he again deals in the realm of the underworld of crime and the police.

Deep Cover is the first crime drama that I have seen starring a Black man that feels as much like a psychological thriller as it does a crime thriller. Russell, also known as John (Laurence Fishburne), is an undercover cop who is assigned to bring down the Mexican cartel that controls cocaine distribution in the western half of the United States. Through his assignment, he works his way up the ladder of those in the operation, including Eddie (Roger Guenveur Smith), a fast-talking dealer who seems too eccentric for the street trade, and David (Jeff Goldblum), a crooked attorney who is padding his income considerably with laundered drug money. He also meets Betty (Victoria Dillard), a stylish art dealer who uses her gallery as a front to launder money for David.

As Russell finds success on the case, he is increasingly in conflict with both his boss, a little man with a Napoleon complex, and his own sense of morality. He wonders if, while acting undercover as a drug dealer, he is not contributing to the drug problem in the Black community as opposed to solving it. As his internal and work conflicts increase, he becomes, as the movie tagline tells us, "a dealer, snitch, junkie, and hustler." As in so many of these stories, the aim is to be the player, not the person getting played. We root for Russell not to be played; he's the underdog with a heart and conscience in a world without either.

His character grapples with the work conflicts of members of the post–civil rights generation of African-Americans, who often find themselves in work environments that challenge or directly conflict with their sense of responsibility to the Black community. As Russell finds a way to resolve his personal conflicts, his decisions represent some group resolution as well.

Throughout the film we are drawn into his mind through his voice as the narrator and through scenes that stress intense conversations and tense relationships between characters. *Deep Cover* is gaining a cult following perhaps partly because of its often raw, race-conscious, and funny dialogue. At some point, as John considers how he has been double-crossed, he confesses that he'd "been turned out like a two-dollar ho."

Postscript: One scene of John, cleaned up in a designer suit and long, dark coat, foreshadows Fishburne's appearance as the kick-ass leader Morpheus in the mega sci-fi hit The Matrix.

One False Move

May 8, 1992

With a Black director, Carl Franklin, and Cynda Williams (*Mo' Bettter Blues*) and Michael Beach in the cast, *One False Move* is getting buzz among my buddies as a Black movie to see, even though, it seems, the primary characters are White.

I was unprepared for the visceral impact that this movie—particularly the opening scenes—would have on me, probably precisely because it is set outside of what has become the setting-as-usual for drug violence and mayhem.

In the story, we meet Ray (Billy Bob Thornton) and Pluto (Michael Beach), hardened criminals who decide to rob a known Los Angeles drug dealer with Ray's woman, Fantasia (Cynda Williams). In the process, they commit a grisly murder among some partying middle-class Black folks and find themselves on the run and hunted into Texas and Arkansas. A small-town Arkansas sheriff (Bill Paxton) has learned of the trio of outlaws and that they might be headed to his town, where both Ray and Fantasia have roots. For much of the movie, the L.A. police and the Arkansas sheriff try to set a trap, and the trio of increasingly desperate outlaws try to cash in on their crime.

The combination of Franklin's moody direction and Thornton's screenplay turn what could easily have been a corny movie into a gripping and haunting classic of the crime genre. The interracial romance between Ray and Fantasia adds a layer of intrigue to both the story and the outlaws, who are cool killers. Maybe the fascination is that we are looking at a close-up portrait of sociopaths. The interracial romance takes another twist when the trio arrives in Arkansas.

Perhaps it is unfair to characterize every story like this one, involving a story line about a mulatto, as a "tragic mulatto" tale. While it is true that no one is to blame for their heritage, it is also equally true that film and literature never seem to tire of the subject and theme. In each new generation, new narratives that blend both mulattos and tragedy are rolled out for us in all their bitter poignancy (this time, by a White man, Thornton, the writer on this project, who was in real life married to Cynda Williams from 1990 to 1992, during the time I assume this film was being made).

I, admittedly rather reluctantly, put the character of Fantasia, who is also known as Lila, into this tragic mulatto category. Not only do we learn that she has a White daddy who she never knew, we also learn that perhaps this lost-daddy tragedy has contributed to her choice in and quality of relationships, adding more tragedy to her already tragic existence. Perhaps unrelated, Lila is seen, by Ray and Pluto anyway, as somewhat unstable, and therefore the erratic element in what could have been a more perfect crime.

Despite my misgivings, I still find *One False Move* to be an engaging and fascinating film that has held my attention time and time again.

Black Star–Whoopi Goldberg in *Sister Act*

May 29, 1992

Sister Act is kind of corny and obviously made more for Whites who will get a kick out of seeing nuns sing pop tunes and cut a rug. But it is likeable in spots, despite its formulaic plot and tired faux-urban set. Goldberg plays a lounge singer who witnesses a murder ordered by her mob boyfriend. She is placed in the witness protection program at a convent, where she begins to teach the nuns to liven up themselves and hopes that the mob doesn't find her.

Postscript: A sequel, Sister Act 2: Back in the Habit, *is released in 1993.*

Sarafina!

September 18, 1992

Film version of the hit Broadway musical about life for young Black South African antiapartheid activists. Leleti Khumalo, the radiant lead actress, has always presented the duality of her beauty versus the ugliness of her country's system of government.

Boomerang

September 24, 1992

For this ardent fan of romantic comedies, also often known as chick flicks, *Boomerang* gets my money for one of the best and funniest contributions to the genre.

It gets some mileage by flipping the script on the age-old saga of the ladies' man/modern-day dog among the buppie set in New York City. To make this story line work, director Reginald Hudlin (*House Party*) makes use of the services of Eddie Murphy, Hollywood's Mr. Black Everything for at least a decade. The misogyny that Murphy freely exhibited in *Raw* and, to a lesser degree, in *Coming to America* makes him the perfect leading man to play the part of the conceited and doggish Marcus Graham, a successful marketing executive at a Black-owned cosmetics company.

When we first meet Marcus, he is asking his secretary to send seven different women a single red rose with "the usual card" that says "thinking only of you." We see and learn of his history of wooing and discarding women. We hear him and his boys Gerard (David Alan Grier) and Tyler (Martin Lawrence) speak endlessly about women, relationships, and their word for sex, starting with the letter "p." Things seem to be going swimmingly with Marcus's fly crib, fly wardrobe, and revolving-door interactions with women until his company is acquired by another one and his world turns upside down.

The merger brings him into contact with the new company's namesake (Eartha Kitt); Jacqueline (Robin Givens), the new head of marketing; and Angela (Halle Berry), an artistic director. Murphy and Barry Blaustein, who also did the script for *Coming to America,* have lots of fun, at the expense of Marcus, men, and career women by giving Jacqueline many of the attributes typically associated with insensitive men in relationships (forgetting to call, wanting to watch "the game," and asking their partners to fetch them a beer). But, more importantly, they have a ball turning Marcus into a whining girl, full of the complaints typically attributed to women in relationships (asking why you didn't call, waiting by the phone, getting all whipped in bed). There are enough gags in this vein, plus contributions from Martin Lawrence and Chris Rock, to keep the story and jokes rolling. When Marcus thinks that perhaps love is through beating him down, fate has yet to deal him one more hand.

This is one of the best roles I have ever seen Murphy play and it is probably because this script allows him to show a vulnerable side that we haven't seen before. The direction, production values, and script are also great.

Even so, I am conscious, however, of how, ultimately, the classic dog is able to still choose which woman has a relationship. He gets to have a happy ending, while all kinds of women—the crazy model played by Grace Jones; the career-minded woman played by Robin Givens; the aging vamp played by Eartha Kitt; the crazy, jilted ex-lover played by Tisha Campbell—are all left ass-out.

Black Star–Wesley Snipes in *Passenger 57*

November 6, 1992

Launching into the action-hero niche, this time Snipes plays an ex-cop, John Cutter, who is aboard a plane when terrorists take over. His memorable line to the villain: "Always bet on Black!"

Malcolm X

November 18, 1992

Race and race history exists at the heart of the African-American experience and our everyday lives. Ask any racially ambiguous friend who floats between cultures, like maybe a White Puerto Rican, about the difference between White and Black parties and they'll tell you that at Black parties, any group conversation sooner or later gets around to racism and the state of the race. This hardly ever happens at White parties.

This seemingly simple observation occurred to me as I was absorbed by this powerful biography of the Black nationalist leader who was gunned down in 1965. Yes, at well over three hours, it is longer than the flicks we're accustomed to seeing, but it is well worth the sit. Best to sit and learn something—or remember. This is our conversation that we never hear on the evening news, in the right-wing rhetoric about "pulling ourselves up by our bootstraps" and certainly never in feature-length movies. Whether we realize it or not, the result of this absence must be similar to looking into a mirror that shows only part of our reflection.

In telling the story and journey of the man born Malcolm Little in 1925, *Malcolm X* also provides a sweep of history for that generation who grew up witnessing racial terror in this country and were then the mature foot soldiers for racial justice in the 1960s. The first hour of the film, which covers the time when Malcolm X was still a street hustler and prison inmate in Massachusetts, includes several flashbacks to his childhood filled with terror in the Midwest, where his parents were followers of Marcus Garvey. His father is believed to have been murdered by White supremacists in Michigan; his mother was institutionalized and her children, including Malcolm, were taken from her and put into foster care. At the home and school where Malcolm was sent, where he was the only Black child, he was called "nigger" so much that he thought that slur was his name.

Of course we hear and see all of Malcolm's history and story through the amazing actor Denzel Washington, who holds us spellbound in the belief that he *is* Malcolm X. From a petty thief and numbers-runner with his hair conked, to a prison inmate first learning about the Nation of Islam, to an international advocate for human justice, Washington turns in a flawless and remarkable performance that will make this film stand the test of time. Spike Lee also makes an appearance, which feels odd, as Malcolm's young hustling buddy, and Angela Bassett is superb in the role Malcolm X's wife, Betty Shabazz.

Though based on *The Autobiography of Malcolm X* by Alex Haley, the movie does not include some aspects of Malcolm's family life, such as the rift between him and his brother, also a Muslim, or mention of his sister, whom he first lived with in Boston. It does support the belief that he was murdered by members of the Nation of Islam, perhaps with knowledge of or assistance by government agents. This film sizzles, from its fiery prologue to its heartrending then uplifting end.

Black Star–Whitney Houston in *The Bodyguard*

November 25, 1992

Kevin Costner portrays a thoughtful former Secret Service agent named Frank Farmer, opposite a selfish, unthinking diva, Rachel Marron (singer Whitney Houston). Houston's poor acting, her diva pose and sleepy eyes that render her unlikeable, generate little sympathy, and even sour our voyeuristic interest in the taboo interracial romance between her and Costner. Unlike films featuring our other Black female star, Whoopi Goldberg, this film does hint that Houston "gets some," but, of course, it is only hinted at.

Queen

February 14, 1993

Alex Haley's story about his father's side of the family is depicted in this TV miniseries starring Halle Berry. It tells the touching story about the horrible life faced by the mulatto daughter of a slaveholder's son and a slave but, overall, it is too long and too unrelentingly painful. It is also challenged by such poor makeup and hair styling for Berry that she could easily walk to another set, switch costumes, and play the crack addict in *Jungle Fever* all over again.

CB4

March 12, 1993

Told in the form of a fake documentary, *CB4* is a funny and insightful comedy for all of us who are tired of the trend in the music industry toward so-called "gangsta rap" and who can laugh at the ridiculous aspects of popular culture, like three rappers named M. C. Gusto, Stab Master Arson, and Dead Mike.

This is a deft satire about appearances versus reality in the entertainment industry. On stage, Gusto (Chris Rock), the leader of the group, wears a long jheri curl and shades, Arson (Deezer D) drinks a forty of malt liquor, and Dead Mike (Allen Payne) is obviously not afraid to pay the ultimate price for his gangsta-ness. Chalk outlines, like those from a crime scene, are taped on their stage floor. The group is named after a prison's cell block four.

Off stage, the three are really middle-class kids who had to learn to curse, dance, and assume a street pose. This perpetration of gangsta roots is what has catapulted them into stardom. In a brief history of the group told by Gusto, we learn about the different gimmicks they tried in order to make it, including a stint where they all wore plastic shower caps on their heads and another where they stuffed their clothes to imitate the Fat Boys. In this film's story line, we watch as their fake game goes too far when Gusto takes the name and identity of a local real gangster who wants his identity back.

Other funny scenes include interviews with celebrities such as Halle Berry, Ice Cube, Ice-T, and Flava Flav about CB4, and one scene when the group is about to get a record contract. "Do you cuss on you records?" asks the record company executive before he signs the group. "Do you defile women with our lyrics? Do you fondle your genitalia on stage?"

There is also enough time to ridicule music videos, political opportunists who blame rap for all evils of the world (like kids wearing baseball caps backward), sex scenes in hood films, Afrocentrists, crack addicts, and hair weaves. Some of the group's biggest hits are titled "Sweat of My Balls" and "Straight Outta Locash."

The film's writers, Chris Rock and the former music journalist Nelson George, together have enough comedic edge and knowledge of the music industry to keep *CB4* fresh. (Look out for the hip-hop retirement home.)

Interview—Martin Lawrence

April 29, 1993

"HIP HOP Hooraaaay!! Ho!! Heyyy!! Ho!!"

The Naughty by Nature recording booms at the sold-out BAM's Majestic Theater in Brooklyn, where the crowd, sitting stadium-style on risers, erupts in "Heyyy," "Ho," and stomping feet. Then as a lone, slight man walks stage front, a young coiffed woman, then two, then several more, jump up from their seats, cheering. The "Hey" and "Ho" explode into theater bedlam.

"Oh, I'm fine, now," says Martin Lawrence to the shrieking females as he steps center stage and cuts a few dance steps under the spotlight in a loose-fitting, green leather suit. His baggy pant legs are stuffed into black combat boots.

"I'm not going to let you make me think I'm fine. I'm still the big-eared #$% I always was."

He stages an imaginary sex scene with one of the many women who now throw themselves at him.

"Martin, there's just something about you," he says, affecting a female voice.

"Could it be the $100,000 in my pocket?" he answers, back in his usual tones.

Best known as the star of *Martin,* Fox's Thursday-night comedy in which he plays Detroit DJ Insane Martin Paine, Lawrence is the latest comic to make the leap from stand-up to sitcom success, a route traveled by the likes of Roseanne Arnold, Tim Allen, and Jerry Seinfeld. The TV exposure has also jump-started his stand-up act, which features material that's definitely not for prime time.

Lawrence now routinely sells out venues across the country, including three SRO shows around New Year's Eve at Radio City Music Hall. And because of his success in both worlds, Lawrence's fans range from grade-schoolers who have installed Martin Paine's expressions—"Whazzup?!" and "You go, girl"—into their vocabulary to adults, who crack up at his blue stand-up routine.

No doubt about it, the man is hot. A veteran of several small film roles (*Do the Right Thing,* both *House Party* flicks, and *Boomerang*), Lawrence will soon star in his own movie: Last week's sold-out performances in Brooklyn were filmed for his first concert movie, following the path of Eddie Murphy and Richard Pryor.

"Martin is dumb large," said music/TV/comedy impresario Russell Simmons. (Lawrence hosts the Simmons-produced *Def Comedy Jam* on HBO.) "He is so large. He's like the first in a new wave of comics behind Robin Harris. He's part of a whole new generation that is a little freer. The energy is different. It's not shock humor. The language is so natural. It was a shock thirty years ago, but not today."

Lawrence's appeal is easy to understand: His fans sense that they know him, that he is one of the trash-talking, posturing, but good-hearted around-the-way guys they grew up with. This "brother from the corner" persona puts Lawrence closer stylistically to his idol, Pryor, or his mentor, the late Robin Harris, than it does to Murphy (it's tough to envision Murphy playing basketball, for one).

"I'm that kid in the neighborhood, I haven't changed," Lawrence says in a penthouse suite at an Upper East Side hotel. "I'm that little beady-haired, snotty-nosed kid that ran around, but I'm also that kid that believed in something, who always believed that I could be something.

"When the fans say, 'We feel like we know him,' feel like I'm that brother next door, it's because I am," he says, lounging in loose-fitting clothes, sneakers, and a baseball cap that reads, "You So Crazy," the name of his stand-up tour.

"When I act the way I act, I'm just doing what I know," he says. "It's where I'm from."

Unwarned, those who know him primarily through his TV show might find themselves blushing or wincing at his live act, which contains references to masturbation and oral sex.

Sometimes, though, he veers into territory—prison rape, intimate bodily functions, and hygiene—that makes his audiences squirm, even as they're laughing. No one is spared—Blacks, Whites, gays, the incarcerated, crack addicts. Not even Magic Johnson, who, according to Lawrence, "should just sit down and take his medication" rather than try to counsel Black youth angry at the Rodney King beating.

And at the same time, it is clear that this twenty-eight-year-old—struggling to stay focused in a sea of cash, easy women, and temptation—sees himself as a teacher. He finds humorous ways to make points about topics as varied as racism, using condoms, or his favorite: male-female relationships.

His focus on how men and women relate to each other offers parallels between Martin Paine the television character who has a girlfriend, and Martin Lawrence, the stand-up comic, who is single. Much of the action on the sitcom that he helped develop revolves around the relationship between Insane Martin Paine and his girlfriend, Gina (played by Tisha Campbell). In the story line of three highly rated episodes, Martin and Gina fought, broke up, and reunited. Before the final episode, viewers were invited to call a 900 number (the proceeds were donated to charity) and vote on who should apologize. Their verdict: Martin should get on his knees.

On stage, he is a sort of Dr. Ruth for his contemporaries. He gives advice not only about sex but about the intricacies of relationships—communication, doing the "little things," and leaving a person who is, in terms he repeats throughout his act, "crazy" or "deranged." In fact, he says, it is because of this subject that he is making his movie. It is of this part of his act that he is most proud, and it is on this subject that he is most sincere. Lawrence knows that many of his fans will not attend marriage counseling, but will find a kernel of truth in what he says.

"If he's crazy, deranged, leave him," he says. "And it's not just putting men down because I give you both sides. There are jealous women and possessive women out there, too."

Lawrence's focus on relationships stems from his own childhood. He was born in Germany where his father, John Lawrence, was stationed in the military. When the family moved back to the states, they lived in a variety of places including Queens. His parents' marriage dissolved. As a result, Lawrence jokes that one moment he was running around a house with a private backyard and the next he was "ducking cars in the projects."

If you ask him, he'll tell you that he loves his father, that they get together periodically for drinks. But you walk away knowing that he still feels bitter because he and his five brothers and sisters grew up with little or no support from his father. His mother, Chlora Lawrence, struggled with a series of cashier jobs in Landover, Maryland, where the family eventually settled.

"Even if the relationship does not work, if you have kids, both of you have the responsibility to spend time with the kids," he says.

On stage, he's more blunt: "I can understand parents breaking up, but take care of your &%$# kids.

Lawrence was a bad, hyperactive little boy, so bad that his mother tried to leave him with his father. But when he was in the third grade, he joined the family in Landover, where he is remembered as the boy who stood against the wall cracking on everybody who walked by. The teenager who was such a class clown that some of his teachers gave him time to tell jokes at the end of class if, in turn, he would not disrupt while they taught. The boy who fought and was a Golden Gloves boxer at fifteen years and ninety pounds. The boy who secretly stayed up until 2:00 A.M. to see Pryor's R-rated act on cable TV.

After high school, Lawrence tried the local comedy scene and even came to New York for a short while, working outdoors in Washington Square Park, passing his jacket for donations. Returning home, his first break came when he was a contestant on *Star Search.* He won once and then lost, returning to Landover, where he worked on a maintenance crew buffing floors, trying in vain to impress his friends with his small success.

But in 1987, executives at Columbia Pictures saw his *Star Search* tape, which landed him a role in *What's Happening Now!* a syndicated update of the '70s sitcom. That lasted for a season, then Lawrence found himself looking for work. Meanwhile, his savings dwindled.

In 1989, he landed a supporting role in Spike Lee's *Do the Right Thing.* Though it was a small part—he was one of a group of neighborhood boys who hung out and harassed the neighborhood drunk—he made an impact on the screen and behind the scenes. In a pivotal moment in the film, one neighborhood resident is angered that the local Italian-run pizzeria has no pictures of Blacks on its walls and tries to organize a spontaneous boycott. He approaches Lawrence and his friends.

"Man, you must be crazy," Martin's character, Cee, responds. "Good as them &%$# pizzas is." With that memorable line, delivered with such dead-centered authenticity, he stole part of the movie for himself and imprinted himself in the minds of African-Americans always searching for portrayals of authentic Black characters, in this case the comically sad brother who won't even let a minirevolution get in the way of his appetite.

Behind the scenes, according to the *Do the Right Thing* companion book, Lawrence kept the cast laughing. "It was a jovial set," said actor John Turturro. "Martin kept us laughing throughout. Danny [Aiello] made him do his impersonations about 150 times. The poor guy was burnt out. . . . 'Martin, Martin,' Danny would say. 'One more time. Do Sugar Ray Leonard.'"

Martin, the TV show, was one of the few new series to succeed during a dismal TV season. Even if, by Lawrence's own admission, the writing was often weak.

"We've gotta get stronger writing," Lawrence says. "That's very important to the show. This year, we had a lot of shows where the story line wasn't really a strong story line. But through the grace of God, my craziness, I was able to make something out of nothing."

Martin was also one of several sitcoms aimed at Black viewers that premiered last fall. Even if the writing was occasionally weak, most TV critics considered it a notch above the others, especially *Rhythm and Blues* (now off the air) and *Out All Night* (which *Entertainment Weekly* said was notable for its "leering stupidity"). The critics were on target: *Martin* won an NAACP Image Award this January.

However, in a well-publicized speech last fall, Bill Cosby made little distinction between the new sitcoms, labeling them "stereotypical and vulgar."

Lawrence shrugs off Cosby's criticism.

"Everybody can't do what Cosby did," he says, his disappointment apparent despite his protestations. "I saw Cosby on *Arsenio* and he was saying there are Blacks that have graduated from Harvard or whatever schools he was talking about. Yes, there are. And he can come on TV and do the family-man show and the Harvard school and all that. But what about the Black people in the ghettos, in the neighborhoods—that can't afford college? You know what I'm saying?—that want to laugh at what they experience every day and need to laugh at it to help them get through it?

"But me and Cosby are cool," he adds. "It's not a beef. I'm not sitting around, you know, saying 'Forget Cosby!!!'"

Lawrence credits such African-American directors as Spike Lee and Reginald Hudlin for allowing him to express and develop his true comic potential. He is most comfortable on stage, but, in the steps of his mentors, he has his sights on film and increasing the number of Blacks working behind the scenes in TV and movies.

"But one thing about Martin Lawrence, I can always go home," he says. "I know where I come from. So if you edit me on TV you can't edit me live. You can't stop the people who come to see me in my personal appearances.

"And there's home in the sense of family," he continues. "I can go to kick back at my mom's. Mom'll make a sweet potato pie and I'm chillin . . . and gettin' fat."

Postscript: The film version of Martin Lawrence's Brooklyn concert was released as his first film, You So Crazy, *in April 1994. Because the MPAA gave it the harsh rating of NC-17, equivalent to the old X-rating, the original distributor, Miramax, sold it to another company, Samuel Goldwyn, which released it unrated.*

Posse

May 14, 1993

A cast of hip celebrities, including Tone Loc, Big Daddy Kane, and Mario Van Peebles, make for a good-looking movie poster, but a crazy, rambling script does not allow *Posse* to deliver on its unspoken promise of a take-no-prisoners Western. How could we lose in a Western with a man named Big Daddy on our side? I imagine that several years from now my infant son might appreciate all the gunfights, explosions, and Black cowboys, but I expect more of today's Black filmmakers than business as usual in blackface.

Posse has an interesting prologue about the history of Blacks in the western United States, mentioning the cowboys Nat Love and Cherokee Bill, and how almost one-third of the original cowboys were Black, as were half of the original settlers of Los Angeles. "But we never hear their stories," says the old-timer telling us the tale. Then he tells us the story of Jesse Lee and his posse, which started in the Spanish-American War. By this tale, it looks like a Black infantry was doing all the fighting, while the White soldiers relaxed, played cards, and had their war portraits painted. The heartless commander sends Jesse and his men on a suicidal mission to steal supplies behind enemy lines. Jesse and his men succeed at the impossible mission and then must turn on the commander when they are double-crossed.

Hiding out in coffins, Jesse's men get to New Orleans where, inexplicably, street performers that sound like Take 6 are singing on the corner and one member of their group, Weezie (Charles Lane), has a Staten Island accent. The commander catches up with the posse, which heads out West. They wind up in a town lorded over by a foul-tempered sheriff and infested by the Ku Klux Klan, where Jesse was once arrested and forced into the army as a sentence. Jesse proceeds to mow down various White people with a vengeance.

Finally, here, the movie settles down into a familiar Deep South–styled struggle for Black justice and begins to make some sense. We actually care about the fate of Jesse and the town, though the film is not consistently a comedy or drama, lighthearted or poignant. With all this confusion, it even manages to slip in a sex scene.

Posse does feel like more of a period piece than *Harlem Nights,* but not enough to convince us that Black cowboys freely peppered their dialogue with mf-bombs. This is a big production with what looks like a fairly big budget. Too bad it does not have enough meat to go with all those potatoes.

Menace II Society

May 26, 1993

Just as *Juice* forever stamped in our minds the young Black sociopath in New York City, *Menace II Society* does the same for Los Angeles. In New York, his name was Bishop, in Los Angeles, his name is O-Dog, played not-so-convincingly by the cherub-faced Larenz Tate. Like many of the movies of its genre, it asks us to watch two hours of pathology and nihilism—petty crime and easy murder—all in the claim that "this is the truth . . . this is what's real." Directed by two young twin brothers, Albert Hughes and Allen Hughes, who aren't from the ghetto, *Menace II Society* has blaxploitation II written all over it. Its main redeeming quality comes in the character of Ronnie (Jada Pinkett), a young mother who insists on raising her child with values not set by the streets. She thinks of bettering herself for her son's sake.

Sankofa

May 28, 1993

Haile Gerima's evocative meditation on American slavery and African-American identity is gaining respect as an independent production flying in the face of the well-oiled film distribution system. "Footwalked" or "four-walled" across the country, often showing in a single theater in each city, the film nonetheless is gaining a following among those interested in continuing to support films that touch on the African-American experience, such as last year's *Malcolm X.* Gerima's film explores the meaning of "Sankofa," an Akan word that means, "We must go back and reclaim our past so we can move forward; so we understand why and how we came to be who we are today."

It is visually stunning as it follows an African-American fashion model, Mona (Oyafunmike Ogunlano), from a slave castle in Ghana—the kind of place that was a holding pen and departure point for millions of enslaved Africans being transported to the Americas—to a slave plantation in the U.S. The scenes in Africa and the castle are moody and haunting—accompanied by dialogue from Sankofa, an old griot who chides tourists, including Mona, for violating sacred ground, as well as a rich musical score credited to David J. White.

When Mona dismisses the old man and ventures into the lower levels of the castle, she is suddenly transported back in time and becomes one of dozens trapped in the room waiting to be whisked away. These scenes are the best in the film, combining the production's overall theme, symbology of the Sankofa bird, music, and mood. In contrast, when Mona arrives in the United States, much of the movie has the feel that we have come to expect in slavery dramas. Some of it is frustrating. For example, several scenes of Mona being brutally raped are shown close up, while, in contrast, when she is able to shoot her attacker we are not shown a close up of him meeting his fate. The effect has left many of my generation of filmgoers, though respectful of the Ethiopian-born Gerima, feeling disappointed that a film about reclaiming our past hammers away our mental and physical slavery but does not fully show the effect of our determination to fight back.

Black Star—Whoopi Goldberg in *Made in America*

May 28, 1993

Race and racial identity get the comedic treatment when a young Black woman (Nia Long) finds out that her father was a White sperm donor (Ted Danson). Her mother is played by Whoopi Goldberg and her boyfriend is played by Will Smith.

What's Love Got to Do with It?

June 9, 1993

Tina Turner's 1984 multiple-platinum solo album, *Private Dancer,* again made her an international star. Her biography, *I, Tina,* is the basis for this tour de force biopic.

Laurence Fishburne and Angela Bassett turn in searing performances as Ike and Tina Turner, the rhythm-and-blues duo responsible for hits including "A Fool in Love," "River Deep—Mountain High," and "Proud Mary" during the '50s, '60s, and '70s. The story begins in 1939 when Tina Turner was born Anna Mae Bullock in Nutbush, Tennnessee, before going to live with her mother in St. Louis as a young woman. There, she met the dashing guitarist and bandleader Ike Turner, who loved her voice, recruited her to join his band, and then became a driven, domineering, and frequently abusive husband.

The intensity and brutality of the film, rendered equally by the story, acting, and production, is difficult to watch. For much of the story Tina exists in a claustrophobic bubble with unexpected moments of torture and agony. The visible signs are the frequent beatings, her bleeding and swollen face, Ike's sniffing of cocaine. Then the merciful relief comes in the form of a divorce.

The human drama that we see unfold happens without melodrama or moments to regret. Bassett is so amazing that we never doubt for a moment that she is Tina Turner. She obviously worked out for the role, transforming her body into a thicker, more muscular frame similar to Turner's. She pours herself into every stage performance, with perfect execution of Turner's signature energy, gait, and vocal style. Fishburne is equally magnificent as a monster—a brutal, controlling man who projects his frustrations on the one person who vowed to never leave him.

This is an important story about women, African-Americans, domestic violence, and families, and I am very interested in knowing how this film and its artists will be treated by those who hand out awards. This is one of the most gripping stories I have ever seen on the big screen. I will never look at Tina Turner or any other musical artists with assumptions again.

Postscript: Both Angela Bassett and Laurence Fishburne were nominated for Oscars for their roles in this film, in the Best Actress and Best Actor categories, but did not win.

Poetic Justice

July 23, 1993

It is so refreshing, in our nonstop stream of movie testosterone, to have a movie starring a woman and told from her perspective. (What a concept.) Written and directed by John Singleton, *Poetic Justice* is far from a feminist tale, but at least it does begin to explore the world and voice of one woman.

Justice (Janet Jackson) is a Los Angeles hair stylist and aspiring poet who works in a salon owned by a businesswoman named Jessie (Tyra Ferrell). The shop is frequented by her gregarious friend Iesha (Regina King) and the neighborhood mailman, Lucky (Tupac Shakur). When Justice needs to attend a hair show in Oakland, she winds up sharing a ride with Iesha, Lucky, and Iesha's boyfriend, Chicago (Joe Torry), in a U.S. Postal Service truck. What starts out as another tale in the hood turns into a road-trip movie, filled with various stops that allow the travelers to meditate on relationships, family, community, and tragedy in their lives.

While the story does belong to Justice, Singleton renders her and most of the women in the film as a troubled lot, plagued by depression, cynicism, alcoholism, drug addiction, and any number of other maladies. Collectively, they would seem to earn the harsh moniker of "bitch" and "ho" from Lucky, Chicago, and the other men around them. Jackson reportedly gained weight to play the part and she does a serviceable job in the role of a somewhat sheltered around-the-way girl who is afraid to love again. The show is stolen, however, by King, who with every gesture, expression, and tart remark plays to a tee a modern-day urban princess, with perfect hair and nails and a selection of men to keep her supplied with cash and alcohol. When Justice goes into a snit and gets out of the truck in the middle of some desolate California hills, Iesha is the one who talks her back into the truck and delivers one of the movie's best lines: "Girl, I *know* you ain't gonna let no nigga make you walk all the way to Oakland."

I do think that, just as Singleton and other new filmmakers are working with today's musicians to provide original and evocative music for their movies, he could have also used the work of Black poets of his generation for Justice's voice.

Compared to his past film roles and real-life exploits , the very photogenic Shakur turns on his charm in the role of a young Black man holding down a legitimate job and caring for his young daughter. We watch him rescue the tyke from the home of her mother, who is using crack and perhaps engaging in prostitution to support her habit. There are layers and nuance in both the script and Shakur's performance that allow Lucky to break out of the usual depictions of young Black men that have no sense of responsibility, decency, or respect.

Black Star–Wesley Snipes in *Rising Sun*

July 30, 1993

Snipes plays police detective Web Smith in this whodunit with a Japanese flair adapted from the Michael Crichton novel. He plays opposite Sean Connery, an expert in Japanese affairs, called in to help solve the murder of a hooker inside a prestigious corporate office. Snipes and Connery make a good team, with Snipes assuming the role of the unseasoned junior officer.

Interview–Robert Townsend

August 9, 1993

If you saw *Hollywood Shuffle,* you might have suspected director Robert Townsend would one day return to the screen wearing a bodysuit and cape.

The aspiring actor whom Townsend played in his 1987 debut film dreamed of flying in Superman's blue and red colors. As he sped to save the day, the scene elicited cheers of recognition from Black baby boomers in theater audiences—finally on the big screen there was an African-American superhero, a character who they grew up realizing was never Black, just as at one time Miss America was never Black.

Now, six years later, Townsend has expanded his hero dream with *The Meteor Man,* a new comedy he wrote, directed, and starred in about a Washington, D.C., schoolteacher who acquires special powers when a meteor hits him. In conjunction with the release, Marvel Comics has also released the first *Meteor Man* comic book.

"I've always wanted to play a superhero," Townsend said, visiting New York City last week for the premiere. "I've always seen myself doing, you know, STOP THIEF!!" he says in his best mock every-superhero voice.

"I've always seen myself doing that," he said. "Meteor Man will be the first true superhero, who happens to be Black, that a lot of these little Black children will see. That all children will see. You know what I'm sayin'?"

Townsend has taken on stereotypes before: *Hollywood Shuffle* skewered Black movie myths. His second film, *The Five Heartbeats,* a sentimental family film about a singing group, fell flat at the box office. The thirty-five-year-old director is now back on surer footing, using comedy to communicate his message.

"I think that with all the crime that is happening in the country, I felt like I had to make a statement that people can work together and make a difference," he said. "And rather than do a public service announcement, I'd rather make a movie that is entertaining. When people look at it on a deeper level, they'll say, 'There's a message here.' I think that is the best way to get a point across, for me as an artist at least."

Townsend said he wanted to make his hero someone with whom the audience could identify. An everyday guy with human flaws and a pair of quirky, amusing parents. So Jefferson Reed, the unassuming schoolteacher who dreams of a music career, is cowardly. He has learned to survive by avoiding trouble. Even as a superhero, he retains his frailties, such as his fear of heights.

"All the superheroes that I watched and studied while I was writing the script, they were kind of not accessible. And I think that everyone who sees Meteor Man, they can identify with him. He's the cat who crosses the street. He's the cat who doesn't want to get involved. You know, he's not happy with his gig. He wants to get another gig. And that's what I really wanted the most, the human side of a superhero."

Townsend chose to work with a meteor because he wanted something to come from outer space. "So when the concept came to me, I said, 'Bet. Meteor Man.'

"And there was never a comic book called Meteor Man. There's been a Comet Boy. There's been a Meteor Boy and Meteorite. I called the place where they clear titles and they said, 'It's all yours, Mr. Townsend.' So I was like, 'I AM METEOR MAN,'" again, using a superhero voice.

If you wonder, while watching the film, how Townsend tries out his shtick, forget scientific test audiences. Picture him alone at his desk laughing to himself.

"I trust myself," he said. "I know exactly what I want to do. When I write it, it makes me laugh. And I go, 'Oh, that's silly. Ooohhhhhhhh, it's funny.' Then I shoot it."

And don't tell Robert Townsend that movie heroes don't matter.

One Friday, during his high school years on the West Side of Chicago, Townsend and his friends went to see the movie *Superfly,* and by that Monday, some of the crew had "fried their hair," or were imagining themselves with cool coke spoons, or worse, as drug dealers.

"I just remember thinking how powerful movies were—even at a young age. It was like I'm gonna get me a coke spoon and I'm going to sell drugs."

With this film, Townsend feels he's made it cool again to be a good guy.

"Kids—white, black, brown, red, yellow—come up to me and say, 'I want to be Meteor Man' because they've seen the film," he said.

"And that's how it should be—Spider-Man, Batman, Superman, Meteor Man—it shouldn't be any other way."

Bopha!

September 24, 1993

Bopha is an emotionally complex tale set during South Africa's mass movement to end apartheid and told from the perspective of the country's Black majority. It was directed by Morgan Freeman and stars Danny Glover, who plays a South African cop caught between drawing his salary as a pawn of the government and joining the rising tide for change.

Black Star–Wesley Snipes in *Demolition Man*

October 8, 1993

Rambo versus Nino Brown. Snipes is the crazed futuristic criminal Simon Phoenix, who had been cryogenically frozen and is "thawed out" on parole. He goes on a new spree of killing and mayhem. Society's only hope is to also thaw out John Spartan (Sylvester Stallone), the police officer who originally brought Phoenix to justice.

5

Black Like Me

Black Like Who?

October 23, 1993

Spike Lee tells a college audience that Hollywood only wants to make Black films about urban violence and drugs.

Bill Cosby calls Russell Simmons's *Def Comedy Jam* a "minstrel show."

The Rev. Calvin Butts thunders from his Harlem pulpit about Black musical artists who refer to all women as "bitches" and "whores."

Is this blaxploitation II?

Perhaps not since the 1970s has the subject of how Blacks are represented in the popular media provoked such debate among artists, critics, and the consuming public. But back in the 1970s, Blacks, as a general rule, were in front of the cameras, not behind them, when films such as *Superfly* and *The Mack* cast Blacks as pimps, prostitutes, and drug dealers. Now, Hollywood includes Blacks at many levels of the filmmaking process. Similarly, Blacks in music and television have made greater strides in controlling what they produce.

However, profit, not ideas, drives these industries. And if images glorifying a small criminal element within the Black community can make a buck, the money machine will quickly shift away from films like *Malcolm X,* which fed a flowering interest among young people to educate and enlighten themselves.

"There is a lot of pathology in these images," says filmmaker Warrington Hudlin, who, along with his brother Reggie, produced the hits *Boomerang* and *House Party.*

"Every film shouldn't have to be about some urban, hip-hop drug thing," Lee told 5,000 people at Siena College, just north of Albany, New York, last month.

"This is not the only African-American experience. It's getting ridiculous." Filmmaker and television producer Robert Townsend agrees, but thinks that Black artists who make the films are equally to blame.

"What's happening now I call the Black-on-Black film crime, the Black-on-Black television crime, because a lot of people creating this stuff happen to be African-American," Townsend says. "Nobody wants to blow the whistle because they say, 'Hey, that's a brother trying to make some money. He's getting paid.'"

Women in the entertainment industry are concerned about how young female fans will build self-esteem and self-confidence in the face of misogynist lyrics characterizing women as sex-for-sale gold diggers—lyrics embraced by many young male artists who find that their newfound money and fame attract groupies who would otherwise shun them. In a recent interview, rapper Dr. Dre described his Los Angeles–area home as a place where he hangs out with friends "and about twenty to thirty women."

Another element that distinguishes the new blaxploitation from that of twenty years ago is the degree to which much of the art by Blacks is also consumed by Whites. Artists such as Ice-T, Ice Cube, and LL Cool J generate more sales in America's suburban malls than in city shopping districts. *Def Comedy Jam* has an audience that is 60 percent White.

Music

"I can see it now," said Speech, leader of the group Arrested Development, in a *Billboard* magazine essay earlier this year. "Some 'chef' wanting to get rich so he adds a tablespoon of - - -to his lyrics, two cups of blunts and spliffs, an album cover with at least three guns showing, and a sister with her stretch-marked booty hanging out. There you have it. . . . A supposedly 'real Black' song with majority White listeners."

Even vociferous critics of today's culture are quick to make two points: First, that racy subject matter is not new. When Bessie Smith sang, "Need a little sugar in my bowl, need a little hot dog in my roll," in 1931, she spoke plainly of sex. Second, they don't want their criticism misinterpreted as a belief that youthful Black culture, seen by many as a voice for the disenfranchised, is any more vulgar, violent, or gangsterish than a larger culture that includes the likes of Howard Stern and Guns N' Roses. They simply fear this focus on violence, nihilism, and misogyny has a particularly pernicious effect on a community already battling a host of social problems.

"Black people have been faced with such negativity from day one that we really can't afford to perpetuate the stereotypes foisted upon us," says Kate Ferguson, editor of two fan magazines, *Word Up* and *The Best of Rap and R&B.*

To pinpoint the beginning of the current cultural wave is difficult, but by 1989, there was already criticism of artists in the male-dominated world of rap such as Slick Rick, Too Short, and the group N.W.A. for their sexist lyrics.

Slick Rick, for example, included on his 1989 album *The Great Adventures of Slick Rick* the cut "Treat Her Like a Prostitute." The group N.W.A. was one of the first groups to refer to all women as "bitches" and "hos" in its seminal *Straight Outta Compton.* Even after N.W.A. disbanded, solo acts spawned by the group, including Dr. Dre, continued the tradition. And as the first popular gangster rappers, N.W.A. also launched a barrage of violent images across the country: "When I'm called off / I gotta sawed off / Squeeze the trigger / And bodies are hauled off;" the group also rapped in "Straight Outta Compton."

"I think the gangster image is excellent," says rapper KRS-One. "I think any image that makes America afraid of us is good. Any. They have their images to make us scared of them, so this is our image—we'll blow your [expletive] brains out."

But most of the violence in Black video (and film) depicts Black-on-Black crime. And rather than being afraid, young White America embraced gangster rap. During the late '80s, as hip-hop's popularity grew, many White pop- and dance-music stations played controversial rap groups banned on Black radio stations—and lured young Black listeners. Though White pop stations traditionally target youth, Black radio stations such as New York's WBLS have historically served a wide variety of musical tastes. Even as some Black stations have loosened their restrictions to woo back listeners, it's not uncommon for Onyx, Ice-T, and 2Pac to receive their first airplay on White pop stations.

This change, combined with the rise of the music-video industry and alternative marketing strategies by independent record labels, which target college stations and dance clubs, has diminished Black radio's historical role in the community as an important arbiter of taste, and its power to make or break musical careers.

As difficult as it may be to believe, groups such as N.W.A and 2 Live Crew sold hundreds of thousands of albums with virtually no radio play. 2 Live Crew leader Luther Campbell produced "clean" and "dirty" sides of the group's first single, "Throw the D," a dance highlighting male genitalia. Initially an underground hit, the record was available at mom-and-pop neighborhood stores, flea markets, and at college parties. Radio wouldn't touch the group—though they later gained airplay, which spurred sales of their four albums. 2 Live Crew gained national notoriety in 1990, when *As Nasty As They Wanna Be* was the first record in the history of the country to be found obscene by a federal ruling.

In New York recently to promote his new pornographic album, *In the Nude*, Campbell said he made a calculated business decision to sell sex raps, because no other artist had.

"If I was a White man, I'd be a genius," said Campbell, a thirty-three-year-old millionaire. "It would be like, wow, he took *Playboy* out of the magazine and put it on vinyl, and what did he do next? After he made those nasty rap records, he's got all this rhythm and blues stuff rolling now."

By rhythm and blues, Campbell was referring to groups,, such as H-Town, on his label, Luke Records. With the hits "Knockin' Da Boots" and "Lick U Up," H-Town has continued the recent pattern of leaving violence and misogyny to rappers, while rhythm and blues acts push sexuality as far as they can.

"Hey, Hugh Hefner's a genius," Campbell says. "What is the difference between him and me?"

Video and Performance

Nothing has had a greater impact on the overall music industry in the past decade than music videos. Though record companies were slower to provide video budgets for Black artists and MTV was slow to give videos by Blacks airplay, videos are now an integral part of the marketing strategy for most artists. Today, *MTV Jams,* which highlights Black music, is one of the most popular programs on the cable channel. Like radio, MTV competes successfully against Black-owned BET for young Black listeners, even though BET plays a wider variety of Black artists.

Because popular images of Blacks have always been an emotional issue in the Black community, music videos were subjected to scrutiny from the start. Until recently, for example, the biggest complaint was the predominance of light-skinned, long-haired women, to the exclusion of darker women reflective of the larger Black population.

Now, however, the complaints are more likely to be about the preponderance of images that are violent, insulting to women, or glamorizing a criminal lifestyle. This year, Onyx flashes semiautomatic weapons on "Throw Ya Gunz in The Air"; the first female gangster rapper, Boss, does a drive-by shooting of young Black men on

"Progress of Elimination"; dozens of scantily clad women dance provocatively on Wreckx-N-Effect's "Rump Shaker."

Butts, pastor of Harlem's Abyssinian Baptist Church and a leader in the Black community's response to offensive messages, says that coming across three videos—one by Luther Campbell, Apache's "Gangsta Bitch," and "Ain't Too Proud to Beg" by TLC—in part spurred him to get involved.

"I was appalled at what I saw and heard," says Butts, sitting at his desk at the church's office. "It was so vulgar. I had seen some things in music before that didn't quite jibe with my sensibilities, but I knew that these things were doing important commentary. However, what I saw that particular night had no socially redemptive value at all."

The cable channel that Butts came across, Video Jukebox Network, commonly known as the Box, plays videos that viewers have paid to see, often ones that MTV and BET won't play. In its major markets—the New York area is its number-one market, with 1.75 million households receiving it—the station is dominated by videos by Black artists. Many racier or violent videos show up on the Box first, such as Madonna's steamy "Justify My Love," in 1990.

"The perception that we don't turn down anything isn't true," John Robson, the Box's director of programming, said from the station's Miami offices. "We do get complaints. . . . We have the ability to remove videos from a particular market."

There are signs, according to record executives, that the Box is trying to clean up its act, pressing companies to eliminate violence, sex, and illustrations of marijuana use. But unlike MTV, which operates on advertisers' dollars, the Box draws a large portion of its income from viewers. The Box is trying to generate more ad revenue, which, observers say, could make it more vulnerable to the whims of record companies. For example, recently Russell Simmons, who heads Def Jam Records and promotes artists on the Box, let a reporter listen as he pressured a Box executive to air a new video depicting drug use.

According to Ralph McDaniels, who has produced videos for artists including Stevie Wonder, Whitney Houston, and Boyz II Men, new artists are at the mercy of the record company, which will shape the artists' identity in videos. Established artists have more leverage.

"A problem we have as video-makers is trying to put certain positive images into videos," McDaniels said at WNYC's studios in Lower Manhattan, where he produces and hosts the local *Video Music Box* program. "If I have a Black male in a positive light—let's say he is a lawyer—a lot of people in record companies will feel like, 'Well, can't we have someone else in that role?'"

Also, live performances compete with videos. Big Daddy Kane, an artist whose image is built around his rumored sexual prowess, has appeared on stage in see-through pants and barely-there briefs. At a recent performance at the Apollo, H-Town brought up women from the audience, sat them on chairs, and faked a sexual act.

What do parents think? "I don't think it's appropriate for children to hear and see some of the things out here," says Leslie Green, a thirty-five-year-old mother living in the Bedford-Stuyvesant section of Brooklyn. "I do tell them, 'I do not care for a certain song.'" But like other parents interviewed, she feels unable to monitor what her children watch and listen to while she's at work.

Film

Taken as a whole, the new wave of Black filmmakers is producing diverse films such as Mario Van Peebles's *Posse,* Spike Lee's *Malcolm X,* and Charles Lane's *Sidewalk Stories.* But there is no doubt that Hollywood sees green in what some directors call "hood" films, centering on criminal elements of the Black community—starting with *New Jack City,* and *Boyz n the Hood* in 1991 and followed by films such as *Juice, South-Central, Trespass, A Rage in Harlem,* and, this year, *Menace II Society.* Some have starred rap artists.

"It becomes a self-fulfilling prophecy," says Helena Echegoyen, director of development for New Line Cinema, which released *Menace II Society.* "We have to look at the movies being made, at what is making money, and you make movies like those."

Some directors and Hollywood executives say that they are being told, in essence, to make hood movies or nothing. But fearing a studio backlash, they prefer to remain unidentified. Townsend, however, speaks on the record: "I just hope it gets to the point where they respond to more in African-Americans than just the savage side. Because, right now, when the savage side comes out, everybody is at home. When the buffoon side comes out, everybody is at home. When the middle ground, real life, comes out, then all of a sudden it's, 'I'm uncomfortable. . . .'"

In addition to coping with Hollywood's formulaic machine, artists and executives say Black films get comparatively low budgets. And, they say, the finished product is marketed by White executives who fail to see its nuances and promote every Black film as just that, a Black film, a widget, while White films are sold as romances, Westerns, children's movies, and so on.

And once their films are in the market, Black filmmakers contend with a virtually all-White corps of arts writers and critics, many of whom, directors say, feel more comfortable with ghetto stereotypes and violence than with other depictions of Black life.

For example, when Kenneth Turan panned *Boomerang* last year in the *Los Angeles Times,* he cited his feeling that the movie's star, Eddie Murphy, had been better in his previous hustler roles, and his sense that an all-Black cast playing successful professionals was "silly and arbitrary." The review provoked a rare written outcry from Murphy, director Hudlin, and members of the public.

"If this were a movie about gun-totin' drug dealers, it would be praised for its gritty authenticity while the complaints would be about encouraging violent behavior in the wake of national riots," Hudlin wrote in a letter to the *Times.*

"The reason why hood movies are gratifying to White critics," Hudlin says, "is that when you show the inner city as jungle, you're doing two things: you're providing the White audience and the White critic a voyeuristic view of this hyperreality in which violence, sex is all raw right there on the surface. And second, you're saying something very important to him. You're saying, 'No matter how bad my life is, it could be worse.' . . . It just makes us two different classes of human beings."

But producers of some of the violence- and drug-centered films say they are not bending to the will of White Hollywood. Both John Singleton, director of *Boyz n the Hood* and *Poetic Justice,* and the Hughes brothers, directors of *Menace,* say their films, all set in Black Los Angeles, describe an important reality of urban life, a reality their generation identifies with even if it is not their own personal experience.

"That kind of stuff happens for real," says Albert Hughes, who was raised in the suburban community of Pomona. "We did research," adds his brother, Allen. "So we said, let's show America the way it really is. No sugarcoating. No escape," Albert says.

Hudlin says that the difference in approach between some of the directors is generational. The Hughes brothers, twenty-one, and Singleton, twenty-five, are younger than pioneers in the recent film wave.

"I think that in the late 1960s and 1970s, the African-American artist was shaped by politics," Hudlin says. "If you were a playwright, screenwriter, or whatever, you had to take a position in this political dialogue that was going on. In the absence of the dialogue, I think there is a criminal subculture that right now is shaping art. I think that gangster rap comes out of that criminal subculture. And if you're only twenty or twenty-five years old, then you missed the debate, then you missed being shaped by that. The echoes of the political debate have faded for this generation. And that is why the movies are so different."

Comedy

At thirty-six years of age, Russell Simmons is certainly old enough to have been shaped by the race debates of the 1960s and 1970s. But, in his role as head of Rush Communications, which includes the record label Def Jam and *Def Comedy Jam,* he finds himself championing artists and trends of what writer Nelson George calls the post-soul culture of Black America. And Simmons is not concerned that many of his artists as well as *Def Comedy Jam* serve a largely White audience. Reflecting a general comedy explosion in this country, several Black comedy shows have cropped up in the past two years, including *The Uptown Comedy Club, The Apollo Comedy Hour,* and *Comic View.* But none of these draws the audience or controversy of HBO's *Def Comedy Jam.* A recent show, for example, peppered with what is the standard profanity, included several comedians graphically illustrating oral sex.

Responding to criticism leveled by Bill Cosby, Simmons says of his program, "I don't feel it's a minstrel show. If he's offended by their language or whatever they do, hey, those are real people. And they are mostly moral and very straightforward people."

Stan Lathan, director and executive producer of *Def Comedy Jam,* says the show fairly represents the kinds of material being presented in Black comedy clubs across the country. "The problem is that people zero in on the raunchy material," Lathan says.

Some comedians say that the success of *Def Comedy Jam* has encouraged upcoming comics trying for a crack at celebrity to be raunchy. "I'm sure it probably could," Lathan says. "But, again, I don't think the material is anything different from what the comedians were doing."

Sandy Wernick, another executive producer of the show and president of Brillstein-Grey Entertainment, which manages several *Saturday Night Live* artists, including Dana Carvey and Adam Sandler, says the show appeals to Whites in part because Blacks have become secure enough to laugh at themselves.

Wernick, who is White, says he was intrigued by Simmons's idea because of its crossover appeal, and thought Simmons, who sold rap music to White America, was the right man to make the concept successful.

Wernick concedes that the show's White viewers would probably never venture to hear the same comics in a Black comedy club, traditionally intimate places where Black comedians know, when they tell racially sensitive jokes, that the audience laughs with them, not at them.

Similarly, he says, the show's White viewers are laughing with the comedians, not at them.

How does he know that?

"I do know. You know by the testing," he says. "You cannot sustain for two-and-a-half years on people being voyeuristic."

What's Next

If those concerned about Black messages and images in pop culture are searching for relief, they might find it in the fact that the entertainment machine has to get new parts when the current ones wear down. What is coming could be a backlash against current artists who have reduced the panorama of Black life to a single grim snapshot.

Artists who followed Public Enemy in the last wave of "conscious rap," such as X-Clan, A Tribe Called Qwest, Chubb Rock, Heavy D, Queen Latifah, De La Soul, and Poor Righteous Teachers, are being joined by newer artists rejecting images of death and nihilism, such as Arrested Development, Nefertitti, Das EFX, and Get Set V.O.P.

"People are tired of hearing about people shooting somebody with their nine," said the rapper Heavy D. "Now it's getting monotonous. In the beginning, it was creative because it was somebody telling the rest of the world about a certain place they are from. Now you have a million and one people making those records who aren't even from the ghettos."

Coming from Hollywood next year is *Sugar Hill,* starring Wesley Snipes and centered on a Harlem drug kingpin trying to go straight. But there is also *Crooklyn,* Spike Lee's sensitive drama about a Black Brooklyn family.

And, artists say, Black consumers must show that they are willing to support films other than action-packed ghetto-dramas. For example, after years of hearing complaints about there being no films for Black children, Townsend released *Meteor Man* this year—which received positive reviews in all three New York City tabloids—but poor box office response. When Black directors hear about gears changing, they don't want the change to be: Black films out, some other films in.

"I think things will change," said *Billboard* magazine rap editor Havelock Nelson, who at twenty-nine has been living with hip-hop since his adolescence. "I can see the change in myself. I loved N.W.A. When their first album came out, I played it every day. But I didn't question anything. But I think that as you get more of this, it's going to be a tipping point when it becomes tired and we're going to go for a new flavor."

Black Star–Will Smith in *Six Degrees of Separation*

December 8, 1993

The stage play *Six Degrees of Separation* is adapted for film by the playwright John Guare. Mocking of rich White Manhattanites and sounding a warning about Blacks, it tells the story of a Black, gay hustler, Paul (Will Smith), who convinces a Manhattan couple to give him food and shelter in their swanky home.

Black Star–Denzel Washington in *The Pelican Brief*

December 17, 1993

In the role of an investigative reporter, Gray Grantham, Washington stars opposite Julia Roberts in a gripping film adaptation of the John Grisham novel about the assassination of two Supreme Court justices. Grisham's novels read as though they were written to be adapted for film and they make for fast-paced thrillers. Through this role as a college graduate and professional, Washington offers a cinematic counterbalance to the current parade of Black thugs in films and music videos.

Black Star–Denzel Washington in *Philadelphia*

December 23, 1993

Washington plays a small-time Philadelphia lawyer, Joe Miller, who is small-minded about homosexuality but bighearted toward victims of discrimination. When a man (Tom Hanks) is fired from a fancy law firm after contracting AIDS, only Miller will represent him. The resulting poignant scenes allow this film, directed by Jonathan Demme, to marry the newer issue of AIDS discrimination to America's imbedded issue of racism.

"We're standing here in Philadelphia, the city of brotherly love, the birthplace of freedom, where the founding fathers authored the Declaration of Independence," says Miller. "And I don't recall that glorious document saying anything about all straight men are created equal. I believe it says all men are created equal."

Miller also puts one of the law firm's Black employees, a young woman with large earrings, on the stand to explain how the inhospitable environment may have also had racial overtones.

Joe Miller: Have you ever felt discriminated against at Wyatt Wheeler?

Anthea Burton: Well, yes.

Joe Miller: In what way?

Anthea Burton: Well, Mr. Wheeler's secretary, Lydia, said that Mr. Wheeler had a problem with my earrings.

Joe Miller: Really?

Anthea Burton: Apparently Mr. Wheeler felt that they were too . . . "Ethnic" is the word she used. And she told me that he said that he would like it if I wore something a little less garish, a little smaller, and more "American."

Joe Miller: What'd you say?

Anthea Burton: I said my earrings are American. They're African-American.

Postscript: Tom Hanks won the Oscar for Best Actor for this film, which also won several other film and human rights awards.

Sugar Hill

February 25, 1994

The repeated theme of leaving the game is explored in *Sugar Hill,* which functions as sort of a reprise and coda for Snipes and *New Jack City* (Barry Michael Cooper, writer on *New Jack City,* writes the screenplay this time). Here, Snipes plays Roemello Skuggs, a drug dealer who wants to walk away from the streets and live with his girlfriend, Melissa (Theresa Randle). Of course, walking away is never easy, if not impossible.

Black Star–Ice-T in *Surviving the Game*

April 15, 1994

Crazy film about a group of rich White men who decide to transport a homeless Black man (Ice-T) to the wilderness to use as hunting prey.

The Inkwell

April 22, 1994

Director Matty Rich and writer Trey Ellis tell an unremarkable story about a troubled adolescent boy and his family's summer vacation in the Black middle-class section of Martha's Vineyard during the 1970s. The exploration of class rifts in the Black community is welcome though formulaic. Some of the story lines, like one about a May-December romance, are not developed enough to be believable. The cheesy afro wigs also lend the production an unintentional faux quality.

You So Crazy

April 27, 1994

Martin Lawrence is an endearing comic. When we listen to him hold forth on stage, for this movie of a Brooklyn show I attended last year, it's like we're watching our brother or play cousin joke it up on the front porch. Martin can make you laugh so hard you pee on yourself. That's all good, but we just don't want to hear our play cousin's blow-by-blow (or lick-by-lick) breakdown of his sex life or experiences with poor feminine hygiene. Ill . . .

Crooklyn

May 13, 1994

Just as Spike Lee's movies, so far, have explored the adult world of the post–civil rights generation, *Crooklyn* explores with just as much vigor its coming of age. The setting is in Brooklyn in the 1970s and the prologue here, vital to understanding his films so far, is filled with nostalgic looks at childhood games like double-dutch rope, spinning tops, and Rock'em, Sock'em Robots.

This is also Lee's second film, after a long bout of testosterone, to focus so much on the experience of a female, in this case, a young girl growing up with four brothers. Written in conjunction with his sister Joie Lee and brother Cinqué Lee, *Crooklyn* seems to be the most autobiographical of Spike Lee's productions.

In it, the Carmichael family, headed by Carolyn (Alfre Woodard), and Woody (Delroy Lindo), struggle on Carolyn's salary as a schoolteacher and his sometime income as a musician. There are lots of dinners with black-eyed peas, some experience with food stamps, as well as a time when the electricity is cut off. Still, compared to many of their friends and neighbors, the Carmichaels have a rich life—both parents in the household, parents with education and careers, they seem to own their home—no matter how humble it is—and existence on welfare isn't a given.

Troy (Zelda Harris) is the little girl here who we watch grow up over the course of a summer. A ten-year-old is a bundle of purpose and we see how she chooses to direct that purpose—in games, teasing, defiance, dishonesty, and generosity.

Like so many of Lee's movies, this narrative doesn't follow a typical plot that lets us know fairly soon what the primary conflict will be. Instead, life itself is the conflict and action that we watch unfold in scenes that are sometimes funny, sometimes poignant, but always ringing emotionally true about the life of a child. Because the action is relatively benign, without much danger or big action, this film may feel slow to some but it can be just as engaging to those of us who feel a connection to the characters. I will say that the family does experience a major crisis and change and that change propels Troy to mature even more.

The movie does a service by describing how not every urban childhood, though perhaps touched by the possibility of danger, is bad or even regretful. Spike Lee makes his cameo appearance as the neighborhood glue sniffer. Isaiah Washington is the Vietnam War veteran who is not running on all cylinders. Like the documentary *Wattstax,* it recalls the images and sounds of the decade that either birthed or raised many of us.

Fear of a Black Hat

June 3, 1994

While last year's *CB4* took a more satirical approach to ridiculing the hip-hop music industry, the humor in *Fear of a Black Hat* is more subtle but no less searing. Written and directed by Rusty Cundieff, it is also in the form of a fake documentary, this time by a Black filmmaker (Kasi Lemmons) who feels the group represents a sense of consciousness but also possesses the typical "disdain for women" common in the genre.

This time, the group is N.W.H. or Niggas With Hats. A member of the group, Ice Cold (Cundieff), explains the significance of the name to the filmmaker by recalling the days of American slavery when slaves worked in the hot sun without anything on their heads. Ice Cold explains that the group's name is a declaration of attainment because, in contrast to slavery days, they do be rockin' some hats. (Their rival rap group, the Jam Boys, release a single titled, "Hats Ain't Shit.")

Fear of a Black Hat is punctuated by several "music videos" for the group's hits, including, "My Peanuts," "Guerrillas in the Midst," "I'm Just A Human," "Booty Juice," "I'm Gonna Kick Yo Black Ass," and "Buried and Bald (Wear Yo Hat!)."

Betcha By Golly, Wow: Black Culture Looks Back—*Crooklyn, The Inkwell,* and *The Jacksons: An American Dream*

June 19, 1994

"It was the baddest of times, it was the worst of times. It was the time of Walt Frazier, it was the time of Richard Nixon. It was stickball players on Saturday morning, it was Krazy Glue–sniffers on Saturday night. It was the Jackson Five, the Partridge Family, Afro-Sheen, Don Cornelius, Peace, Love and Sooooulll . . ."

So goes a promotional spiel for Spike Lee's new film, *Crooklyn.* But, with its hard push on the nostalgia buttons of the post–civil rights generation of Blacks, it also could describe the era of Matty Rich's recent film, *The Inkwell,* or the '70s spirit of new Nike commercials featuring NBA players in a fictional barbershop in the hood.

The era also is re-created in Snoop Doggy Dogg's popular music video "It's a Doggy Dogg World," in which Snoop plays a pimp named Silky Slim, surrounded by aging actors of the blaxploitation movies of the '70s, including Fred Williamson, Antonio Fargas, and even a Pam Grier look-alike. Thumping throughout these productions is the steady backbeat of classic 1970s rhythm, blues, and funk: popular cuts such as Curtis Mayfield's "Superfly" or more urban, esoteric offerings, like Manu DiBango's "Soul Makossa."

Are the soul '70s back? You bet your afro puffs they are.

Interest in the '70s isn't new. But the embrace of the decade by young Blacks may extend beyond the trendy revivals of platform shoes and *The Brady Bunch* to include precious memories of a time when Black pride flourished, and a time—pre-AIDS, pre-crack, pre–Ronald Reagan and his economic "restructuring"—when Black neighborhoods had more cohesion.

Both *Crooklyn* and *The Inkwell,* says cultural critic and author Michael Dyson, "are trying to reconstitute a space where it is safe for Black cultural expression and Black social expression to run their course."

As depicted in these films, commercials, and videos, the '70s represent "the urban terrain before urban terror was at such a peak that people couldn't have safe domestic relations or a sense of community," says Dyson, whose book *Reflecting Black* was published by the University of Minnesota last year.

In *The Inkwell,* which focuses on a shy and awkward sixteen-year-old boy, we relive teenage parties when daring girls wore hot pants and "sizzlers" (very short skirts or dresses with matching bloomers) and boys wore platform shoes and loudly colored polyester jumpsuits with matching jackets. On a recent night these getups drew hoots of laughter from the Black audience at the Sunrise Multiplex Theater in Valley Stream, Long Island.

Memories of childhood, of music, dances, fashions, and hairstyles of the past, become the route back into a more innocent time.

In *Crooklyn,* which focuses on the Carmichael family and their neighborhood in Brooklyn, children play outdoors, racing down sidewalks, jumping double-dutch rope or playing hand-slapping games, Rock'em, Sock'em Robots, stickball, skeelies, and hot peas and butter.

"I look back, and I see a time when kids could have a lot more fun than they have today," says Lee, thirty-seven, who grew up in a family and neighborhood in Brooklyn similar to the one in the film. "I never had to worry about getting shot in school or in front of my house. The worst thing that could happen was that somebody might take your lunch money. Maybe you'd get a fat lip or black eye. But it was fists. Nobody was pulling an Uzi and spraying bullets."

Rich, who is in his twenties, says what attracted him to *The Inkwell* project "was the sense of family values championed in the screenplay. One of the strong elements in the movie is the caring and hope that exists within the family."

That both films are about nuclear families, with both mother and father present, is telling. Since the 1970s, the percentage of Black families headed by both parents has declined steadily. Now 46 percent of Black families are headed by single women.

But writer Michelle Wallace sees more than nostalgia for traditional families in these films, noting that both *Crooklyn* and *The Inkwell* contain plenty of family conflict. For example, in *The Inkwell,* the father has difficulty communicating with his shy and quirky son, and the father in *Crooklyn* is trying to reconcile his fledgling musical career with the need to support his family.

"*Crooklyn,*" Wallace says, "raises issues about current dissonance in the Black family. In general, Spike Lee engages in a critique of masculinity. I don't see it as nostalgic at all. Maybe some people feel that he idealizes the Black family, but I don't think so."

Even if there's a mixed message about Black families coming through in these movies about the '70s, the message on the soundtracks is unequivocal: In that decade of shifting social and racial ground, music and dance were pivotal to the development of a sense of personal and group pride for Black youth.

Lee uses no fewer than twenty-two vintage songs, including "People Make the World Go Around" by the Stylistics (who also crooned that classic, "Betcha By Golly, Wow") and "Ooh Child" by the Five Stairsteps. And in the new Nike commercials, repeated often during the NBA playoffs, music—including "Express Yourself" by Charles Wright and the Watts 103rd Street Rhythm Band, Mayfield's "Superfly," various James Brown riffs, and even "Strawberry Letter 23," by the Brothers Johnson—immediately set a soulful mood.

A pseudo-'70s nightclub is the setting for the video of "It's a Doggy Dogg World," which also features a *Soul Train* line. And vintage footage from that show appears twice in *Crooklyn,* once when the Carmichael children imitate trendy dances like the robot and the rubberband, and at the end, as the credits roll. These dancers with bobbing afros and limb-stretching moves drew laughs of recognition recently from Blacks at the Plaza Twin Cinemas in Brooklyn. ("Look at her!" said one woman, rocking an infant carrier. "She looks like Diana Ross!")

There also is nostalgia for the house party, a social element of Black culture that has diminished as urban fear has increased. It appears in *The Inkwell,* where adults do the bump—that then-scandalous dance—the dog, and other moves inviting below-the-belt contact between men and women.

But during the '70s, it was pointless to get to the basement party with your hot pants and knowing the latest songs and dances if your 'fro wasn't together. Although images of the afro are in heavy rotation in the current revival, the afro is used primarily for its evocative value. There's just a single reference within these various productions to the controversy this hairdo stirred in the Black community, splitting children from their parents—particularly girls from their mothers—as the natural look was embraced as either a political or fashion statement.

Activist Angela Davis, whose image from that time, with a full-size afro, often is recycled (the March issue of *VIBE* magazine, for example, ran a fashion spread featuring actress Cynda Williams in various poses as Davis), says the meaning of the afro as a political statement is being lost today.

"It is both humiliating and humbling to discover that a generation following the events which constructed me as a public personality, I am remembered as a hairdo," says Davis in an essay that will be published this fall in *Picturing Us,* a book from The New Press about African-American identity.

"It is humiliating, because it reduces the politics of liberation to the politics of fashion; it is humbling because such encounters with the younger generation demonstrate the fragility and mutability of historical images, particularly those associated with African-American history."

As with the representation of the afro without its social scenery, Dyson, who is thirty-five, warns about the popular media embracing the "politics of nostalgia without offering a critique." He worries that this generation seeks, like all generations, to make their age the golden one, and that the current crop of feel-good images don't convey the fact that "the seeds of what we've reaped in the 1990s"—unemployment, the gutting of neighborhoods—"were sown in the 1970s."

In a speech in April at Princeton University, Manning Marable, director of the Institute for Research in African-American Studies at Columbia University, said, "In the generation since the civil rights movement, there have been many real examples of African-American upward mobility. . . . More than one in seven Black families currently earn above $50,000 annually.

"By contrast, since the late 1970s," Marable said, "the general conditions for most of the African-American community have become worse . . . Economically, by 1990, about twelve percent of all Black families were earning less than $5,000 annually."

Dyson points out that "Black folk have always harkened back to a period of achievement when they were better off," citing even interviews and research in 1914 by the scholar W. E. B. DuBois. Even a few decades after emancipation, people were telling him that the community had been stronger before.

"In one way, that is positive. You always have an endless pool of resources or moral regeneration," Dyson says.

AFRO DOS AND DON'TS: WILL THE REAL AFRO PLEASE STAND UP?

Advertisements promoting *Crooklyn* feature tall, slender women walking on Brooklyn streets sporting "blown out," moon-size afros and sunglasses. This crowning glory also makes its appearance in *The Inkwell.* But the difference in approach to the hairdo by the films' directors is striking.

Spike Lee, who appears in *Crooklyn* wearing an afro, insisted the cast let their hair grow out naturally. Matty Rich, on the other hand, relied on wigs—the worst Hollywood hair since *The Jacksons: An American Dream,* which at least had the excuse of being a made-for-TV movie.

Of the current crop of afros in popular media, our vote for most authentic goes to George Gervin, the 1970s basketball star included in new Nike commercials. One ad shows Gervin in full 1970s regalia—well-rounded afro and shirt with a large, pointy "butterfly" collar.

Right on, brother!

Black Stars—James Earl Jones and Whoopi Goldberg (Voices) in *The Lion King*

June 24, 1994

With its striking cinematography, lush African setting, and the voice of James Earl Jones as a regal elder, *The Lion King* is easily embraced as the closest that Disney has gotten to depicting anything African or Black in a positive manner. But just as Jones is the voice of what is regal, Goldberg is the voice of a group of sleazy hyenas who sound and act like caricatures of ignorant Black folks. Despite this obvious annoyance, *The Lion King* is an instant classic.

6

A Place of Our Own

Projecting Hope in Harlem—Harlem's Victoria 5

August 9, 1994

Even on Sunday along this prime stretch of 125th Street, vendors with displays of colorful kitsch set up folding metal tables end-to-end along the sidewalk, almost obscuring the entrance to the Harlem Victoria 5, one of only three movie theaters operating in New York City's Black neighborhoods, and one of a handful of theaters owned by Blacks across the country.

The black, white, and red marquee in front of the theater reads: *Alma's Rainbow, The Lunatic,* and *The Women*—Live. But this morning, if you go through the theater's swinging doors and up the wide stairway to Theater 4, you find evangelist Michael Patterson baptizing a new member of his church in a cow trough.

"I bought it upstate," Patterson says of the black plastic tub sitting on the theater's unfinished wood stage. "They're also used for goldfish and outdoor ponds. But we use them to baptize people."You see, this is no ordinary movie theater.

With five theaters on two floors, the Harlem Victoria 5 could be described as aiding a different kind of homeless: movies produced by Black independent filmmakers that have no place to go, live theater productions lacking cash or connections, lecturers looking for a mass audience, and even the Central Harlem sector of the New York City Church of Christ, which believes that its members' hard-earned offerings are better spent on salaries than on a building mortgage.

But the shining hope among those who operate the Victoria is that the process of gathering these "homeless" itself creates a sense of community—as well as a place in an African-American community to spend entertainment dollars.

"I feel badly that I have to go downtown to a restaurant," admits Warren Blake, the retired New York City police detective who holds a twenty-five-year lease on the Victoria, which is owned by the Harlem Urban Development Corp. "When you go down to Eighty-fourth Street, there are hundreds of places to sit down and eat, and then you can go to a movie. That's a night out for most people.

"I feel badly because a neighborhood should be complete," says the seventy-year-old Blake, who has lived in Harlem for nearly fifty years. "It should fulfill your entertainment, religious, clothing—all your needs. You know, there is not a proper sit-down restaurant on 125th Street." He gestures with disgust eastward down the street from his second-floor office near St. Nicholas Avenue. "There's nothing here! Nothing!"

But Blake is obviously trying to create something new in Harlem, especially with his recent efforts to make the Victoria a center for Black independent film. Despite his moments of despair, his eyes light up when he twirls this idea in his mind. Visitors who come to talk about the theater quickly realize that for this childless man, who has jars of spice drops, chocolate-covered raisins, and gummy bears in his office, the Victoria is his baby now.

Weekday afternoons are quiet at the theater. Past the foyer, you come into a vast two-story mint-green lobby, with a mixture of old detail and modern renovation, including a shiny stainless-steel concession stand that is oddly out of place. Straight ahead is Theater 1, where in the darkness three people are watching *Alma's Rainbow.*

More than five years in the making, this coming-of-age tale by New York–based director and producer Ayoka Chenzira follows the twists and turns of a girl growing up in a West Indian middle-class community in Brooklyn.

Staying through the credits, the three Black women in the audience obviously have more than a passing interest in the film. The last to leave is Karen Perry, a native of Harlem who now lives in the Bronx and works as a costume designer. (She worked on the recent film *Above the Rim,* which included a scene shot at the Victoria.)

"I grew up in this theater. My God, I saw *Sweet Sweetback's Badass Song* here!" says Perry, scanning the ceiling, which retains original ornate details.

"It's so important to have this theater back," she says. "We have to go into White communities and sit in little rooms to see our films. . . . I was looking in the *Village Voice* last week thinking that I had missed this film. Their listings only go to Ninety-sixth Street." For Chenzira, the Victoria was a logical stop after a series of film distributors declined to pick up *Alma's Rainbow,* her first feature film since she graduated from New York University in 1975.

Chenzira's dilemma is not unique. Today's generation of Black filmmakers has learned to overcome roadblocks to making a film. But once it is made, there is often no place to show it.

Some of the filmmakers argue that the same mindset that has locked most Black Hollywood movies into predictable ghetto, gangster, drug, and comedy themes blocks any effort at the distribution level when a different kind of independent movie is made.

The fact that Black communities, not only in New York but around the country, have so few movie theaters only compounds the situation, they say, because there are hardly any theaters whose audience base has a natural interest in the subject matter.

They add that traditional art houses, such as the Film Forum, are not the answer, because they often don't show enough interest in the films and don't have promotional outreach to the Black community.

"The Victoria is the home for Black independent film not only in this country but internationally," says Chenzira, pointing out that Blacks from around the world are planning to show films there. "It's marvelous to be at the entry level of it all," she says. "Slowly, the space and the productions are coming together."

Since it started the trend last January with *Neria* by Godwin Mawuru, the Victoria has shown about a dozen independent films, including *Daughters of the Dust* by Julie Dash, the 1960s classic *Nothing but a Man, Sankofa* by Haile Gerima, *Murder Magic* by Windell Williams, *The Lunatic* (filmed in Jamaica by Lolcreme), and *Alma's Rainbow.* So the fact that the Victoria could be deemed the "home" of Black independent film indicates both the desperation and the promise of the theater and its filmmakers. In many ways, theirs is a match made in heaven; in order for either to thrive, they both must thrive.

The financial results have been mixed. By far, the most successful independent film to be shown at the Victoria has been Gerima's *Sankofa,* which mounted an aggressive grassroots promotional campaign. (WLIB Radio host Gary Byrd essentially told his listeners that if they didn't see *Sankofa,* they weren't good race people.) The film is currently playing at the Village East Cinema on Second Avenue at Twelfth Street. But lacking the promotion that most people have come to expect for movies, many of the films play to near-empty theaters. *The Lunatic,* for example, did not gross more than $500 in six weeks. And Blake pays a full-time projectionist about $212 a day.

"I have a lot of money in the street," says Blake, referring to artists who have used his space and owe him money. "And it's not helping me at all."

In addition to working with filmmakers to improve promotion of the films, the theater needs to adopt stricter business practices. Some productions, such as *Camp Logan,* the recently staged play by Celeste Bedford Walker, have left the theater owing them money.

But Blake is learning. With upcoming films such as *Let's Get Bizzee,* starring Doug E. Fresh and directed by Carl Clay, the theater stands to benefit more if the films do well.

"I take my hat off to him," says Clay of Blake. "No one is doing what he's doing, and there just aren't many people like him out there at this stage of the game."

The Victoria turned to independent film after operating from September 1992 to March 1993 as a first-run theater with films such as *Posse, Just Another Girl on the I.R.T., Malcolm X,* and *Candyman.* But the fees charged to receive such films, the percentages taken by the studios, and the inability of the theater to fill its seats made that venture a financial failure. (The Victoria did receive a burst of publicity, however, when Gramercy Pictures initially refused Blake's request to screen *Posse* because it didn't want the film to be shown in Harlem. Indignant Blacks kept calling Gramercy Pictures until the film was released to the theater.)

One continuing problem, Blake and general manager Harold Sharp believe, is that, even though it has changed hands, the theater has not shaken the bad reputation for violence that it gained during the late 1980s, when Cine 42 Inc., which had run four theaters on Forty-second Street, had control of it.

Built in 1917 as a vaudeville house, the Victoria was designed by the theater architect Thomas Lamb. Remnants of its neoclassical design are still apparent underneath decades of change. Gradually, movies took over such halls, of which there were many. Sharp, who is forty-five and grew up in Harlem, remembers, on 125th Street alone, the West End, the Sunset, the Apollo, the Loews Victoria, and the Harlem Opera House, as well as an RKO theater just north on Seventh Avenue.

But as the housing stock deteriorated and people began to move out, these theaters lost their patrons. "It almost seems like I woke up one day and all the theaters were gone," he says.

In 1978, the Loews Victoria was the last of the once-grand movie houses to close in Harlem. Only one other theater, the Nova, which at 148th and Broadway some consider to be a part of Latino Washington Heights, remains in the community.

"In the '60s and '70s, there was too much going on on the street," recalls Karen Perry, sitting in the Victoria's lobby. "People got uncomfortable with sending their children out to the movies alone. Then they discovered they could go to Eighty-sixth and Third Avenue. There was a time you couldn't pay Harlem people to go to the Village. We thought only freaks lived down there.

"You know," adds Perry, whose daughter is studying film at New York University, "I watched 125th Street burn down and be rebuilt."

The "downtown factor" is something that all Harlem arts and entertainment groups must face. In essence, they are confronting ingrained images of the community as dangerous, dirty, and filled with rowdy youth. And when people go out, they want to go out to a space that is clean, safe, and offers a variety of entertainment options.

Blake has invested in renovations that include new projection and sound systems in each theater and new lavatories. But operators of the Victoria know that they must do more. Among other things, the vast space lacks the decorative touches to compete aesthetically with first-run theaters a short trip downtown.

Already, though, visitors here feel like they are seeing something special. About three hours after members of the New York City Church of Christ filter out from their Sunday-morning service, the audience in the same space, Theater 4, watches *The Women,* a song revue put on by Irene Datcher, Ebony Jo-ann, and Gina Breedlove, who entertain the dozen gathered with songs such as Bill Wither's "Grandma's Hands," Chaka Khan's "Through the Fire," and the traditional gospel "Jesus Is Real to Me," as well as reminiscing about dances such as the "Camel Walk" and the "Hank Ballard."

"I wish we had more of this in our neighborhoods," Harriet Chittick, an "over-fifty" resident of the South Bronx, says after the show is over. "We don't have anything like this where I live."

On the next night, colorful orange kente cloth is draped from the same stage for the Monday-night lecture series that costs $5. City Councilman Adam Clayton Powell IV, a candidate for Congress, tells the audience that he wants to "engage in a debate about what your common concerns might be."

More poignant comments come from a man in the audience named Jerome who rises to his feet during the question-and-answer period: "It's hard on me to come to these seminars. I struggle to pay my rent," he says, wearing a cap and jogging suit. "But I take pride in coming to this theater. I would love to see our people buying in our own stores.

"People with money won't open up a vegetable stand," Jerome says. "And those without money are always talking about what they're going to do. But they can't because they don't have anything to do anything with."

Out on the street, after 8:00 P.M., when in other parts of the city the nightlife is just getting started, most of the stores have closed and metal gates are pulled down on the storefronts. Up and down this block, between Seventh and Eighth Avenues, the vendors are also gone and the vacant sidewalks are heavily strewn with garbage.

Tony, a vendor who's packing up, is asked about the filth on the street and replies, "Oh, they'll be by to clean it up. It will be swept up by tomorrow."

Postscript: While the Harlem Victoria 5 has not survived as a movie theater—at our deadline, its fate was still being decided—a new multiplex, Magic Johnson Theaters, was built by former NBA star Earvin "Magic" Johnson in 2000, less than a block away.

Black Star–Laurence Fishburne in *Searching for Bobby Fischer*

August 11, 1994

Fishburne brings his trademark intensity to the role of Vinnie, a speed chess wiz who shows the ropes to a young chess prodigy.

Black Star–Whoopi Goldberg in *Corrina, Corrina*

August 12, 1994

Whoopi plays a maid again but this time she's sassy and smart. She stars opposite Ray Liotta, a widower who needs help with his daughter Molly.

Fresh

August 24, 1994

Samuel L. Jackson stars in this formulaic film about a twelve-year-old drug dealer living in a foster home.

Black Star–Samuel L. Jackson in *Pulp Fiction*

September 23, 1994

As the Bible scripture–quoting, jheri-curled hit man Jules Winnfield, Jackson is a pivotal figure in Quentin Tarantino's bloody and unsparing montage of life among outlaws. Tarantino intertwines four separate stories and, in the process, takes stylish violence and 1990s cynicism to a whole new brutal level. He connects with today's Black ghetto gangstas, as rendered in our own films, by positioning them as killable, irreverent fodder in the bigger gangsta world that includes White men (and, of course,

Black men with White wives). Accordingly, the terms "nigger" and "dead nigger" roll easily off the tongues of White characters and Tarantino saves the ultimate indignity for virile, macho Ving Rhames, who is supposed to be the baddest Black mother (shut-yo-mouth) of them all. The macho White action hero, Bruce Willis, is Ving's savior.

*Postscript: Tarantino won an Academy Award for Best Screenplay (written directly for the screen) and many actors, including Jackson, John Travolta, and Uma Thurman received Oscar nominations as well. This film redefined the acting career of Travolta, who had been languishing in a post–*Saturday Night Fever *purgatory. After his role as a hit man in* Pulp Fiction, *he would go on to play more leading and hardened characters, as would Jackson.*

Jason's Lyric

September 24, 1994

This variation on boys in some hood has more heart than most films of the genre and a more expansive take on the issues of family, the streets, and romance. Allen Payne (*New Jack City*) stars as Jason Alexander, a young TV salesman living in Houston who is battling bad childhood memories, a troubled younger brother's predilection for the streets, and his own fear of love. Like *Juice* and *Menace to Society, Jason's Lyric* creates the out-of-control monster. When Jason meets a young woman named Lyric (Jada Pinkett), he turns his attention toward wooing her.

Their developing romance provides some very steamy love scenes, which were so hot that the Motion Picture Association of America, which rates films, gave this film an NC-17 initially—equivalent to the old X-rating—until some footage was cut. Director Doug McHenry cried foul, saying that there is a double standard to how sex acts by Blacks versus Whites are viewed by the MPAA and the organization responded, defending its decision and claiming that McHenry was only seeking publicity for his film.

Drop Squad

October 28, 1994

Any of us who have spent time meditating on the state of the race have, in some conversation or another, come to the conversation about, in essence, vigilantism within our own ranks. Such is the intriguing premise of *Drop Squad,* a drama about a team of men and women who abduct race traitors, transport them to secret locations, and try to deprogram them from their destructive ideas and actions.

The story line interrogates the ideas of nationalism, community, and responsibility to the race versus responsibility to self. It challenges the "I gotta git mine, I gotta get paid" mentality that seems to justify getting money by any means necessary, regardless of the resulting larger impact.

While we see various abductee cases—including a drug dealer, a young man who refers to women as "bitch" and "ho," and a corrupt city councilman—the primary abductee the story follows is Black advertising executive Bruford Jamison Jr., also known by his family as Boo-boo (Eriq La Salle). Bruford spends his days and nights developing ads directed toward the Black community for products such as malt liquor and fried chicken. Though he is happy to have his campaigns accepted by Whites, he draws criticism from Blacks for the ads' stereotypes and other demeaning content—a near-naked Black woman straddling a large bottle of malt liquor between her legs, or a gospel choir of obese women cackling over chicken. One member of the drop squad, Garvey (Ving Rhames), tells him, "Niggers like you laugh at nigger jokes with your White friends."

Bruford has been recommended by his sister for deprogramming but, from his perspective, he sees much of his family as a lot of embarrassing underachievers. He is so sure that closer proximity to his family will ruin his fragile web of acceptance among Whites that he fails to offer an easy recommendation for a cousin who badly needs a job.

This film is directed and cowritten by newcomer David C. Johnson with another newcomer, David Taylor. While the overall film has the feel of an expanded short subject, the script does offer depth to Bruford's character and the production values and direction are good. What enriches the plot is that Bruford isn't depicted as all bad and that the faults of his family, like laziness and ignorance, are shown, too. There are also internal issues within the drop squad—about its methods, including the degree of talking versus physical coercion used. "The problem today is that people today ain't trying to hear nothing," says Garvey. "You got to get their attention first." Most of this conflict is set up between younger members of the squad and the founder, Rocky (Vondie Curtis-Hall). The film does make us wonder, in such a community of vigilantism, who will monitor the vigilantes.

Drop Zone

December 9, 1994

Wesley Snipes, now a bona fide action hero, is a sky-diving crime fighter in this thriller.

Higher Learning

January 11, 1995

John Singleton's take on college life, which will undoubtedly be compared to Spike Lee's *School Daze,* also explores the college campus as a microcosm of the ills of society. But rather than the historically Black school dissected by Lee (who attended Morehouse College in Atlanta), Singleton (who attended the University of Southern California), looks at school life at a predominantly White university attended by a diverse student body.

The assortment of characters at his fictional Columbus University include Malik Williams (Omar Epps), depicted as a young Black man who expects something from Whites; Remy (Michael Rapaport), a White student who adopts White supremacist ideology; and Maurice Phipps (Laurence Fishburne), a professor who challenges Malik's expectation of a pass for mediocrity. "So, Mr. Williams thinks I am an Uncle Tom, hmmm?" Phipps says to Malik. "Well, well, well. What does that have to do with your ability to place a comma in its proper place or put a period at the end of a sentence, hmmm?"

I am just as interested in Singleton's attempt at addressing social issues involving Whites as I am in his singular dissection of Black pathologies in *Boyz n the Hood.* Few movies in this era look frankly at American racism and fewer still take a look from the perspective of a young Black man or woman, so I do not find his story lines or characters to be unrealistic. Singleton still struggles with his Black female characters. Either they have major issues or are, like here, largely missing in action.

His effort to pack so many issues into two hours leads to situations and characters that are not very nuanced but this flaw does not outweigh, for me, the bold tackling of racism that remains at the center of African-American life.

Tales from the Crypt Presents Demon Knight

January 13, 1995

Tales is not, by any stretch of the imagination, a Black movie. It only gets mention because Ernest Dickerson is the director, because there are those of us who were fans of the *Tales from the Crypt* television series (that always featured the talking skeleton), because it includes Jada Pinkett and CCH Pounder, and finally, probably because of the latter two reasons, it received advertising rotation in media targeting African-American filmgoers. It stars Billy Zane (*Posse*) as a demon known as The Collector, who is seeking the final key that will allow him to bring chaos upon the universe. It probably fits the bill for horror film lovers—with gore and mayhem—and probably includes too much of it for those like me who do not think a vomit bag should be a date accessory.

Black Star–Laurence Fishburne in *Bad Company*

January 20, 1995

Fishburne narrates and stars in this crime drama about a CIA agent who owes "the company" a large amount of gold. He appears opposite Ellen Barkin and has a hot sex scene with her.

Black Star–Laurence Fishburne in *Just Cause*

February 17, 1995

One thing positive that I can say about this murder mystery is that it keeps you guessing until the end. It also brings together Fishburne, Sean Connery, and Blair Underwood. Underwood is in the role of Bobby Earl, who is facing execution for the murder of a young girl in a small Florida town. He calls in Paul Armstrong (Connery) to help him prove his innocence. There are lots of twists and turns in the plot as we try to figure out if the cherub-faced Bobby could possibly be a killer. As a matter of fact, there are probably too many twists and turns, as the plot seems to spin out of control and give me a headache. Fishburne plays the town's steady sheriff who is sure the right man is behind bars.

Black Star–Halle Berry in *Losing Isaiah*

March 17, 1995

Berry stars as a crack-addicted mother, Khaila Richards, who abandons her son in the trash then tries to get him back from the White social worker (Jessica Lange) who had adopted him when no one claimed him. Samuel L. Jackson also stars as Khaila's attorney and Cuba Gooding Jr. is her boyfriend. While the story seems to have the most sympathy for the social worker, it is still a decent effort at considering the complex issues of drug addiction and child abandonment in the United States.

Bad Boys

April 7, 1995

An early summer action flick, *Bad Boys* pairs Will Smith and Martin Lawrence as detectives in a likeable, action-packed crime drama.

New Jersey Drive

April 19, 1995

The world of a group of Newark, New Jersey, carjackers, perhaps best appreciated by other teenage males, is the subject here. Jason Petty (Sharron Corley) and Midget (Gabriel Casseus) live for stealing cars and joyriding, but their days may be numbered when one stolen car is a police vehicle.

Friday

April 26, 1995

Despite its simplistic plot of one (funny) day in the hood, *Friday* has become an instant classic for gen-exers who enjoy watching two seemingly unemployed friends, Craig and Smokey (Ice Cube and Chris Tucker), sit on the front porch and get blunted. The pair tries to pay back a debt to the local gangster, Worm, before he hurts or kills them. In the process, they contend with a host of neighborhood characters, including Craig's parents and Deebo, known as the area's meanest thug.

Panther

May 3, 1995

Set in Oakland in the mid-1960s, this is a decent effort by director Mario Van Peebles to tell the story of the beginnings of the Black Panther Party for Self Defense. The script is just so-so and production quality is not great—for the most part it looks like a made-for-TV movie—but important scenes about police brutality, the goals of the party, and the role of the local police and FBI in destroying the party make it informative and worthwhile.

Black Star—Samuel L. Jackson in *Die Hard: With a Vengeance*

May 19, 1995

Pair Bruce Willis with Samuel L. Jackson, add lots of American racial tension, and you have what is almost an anti-buddy flick. *Die Hard: With a Vengeance* makes *Lethal Weapon* (Mel Gibson and Danny Glover) look like two guys playing patty cake. In this third version of the *Die Hard* franchise, John McClane (Bruce Willis) is separated from his wife and working clear across the country for the NYPD. He pairs up with a Harlem electrician, Zeus Carver (Samuel L. Jackson), to foil the plot of a master bomber, who has threatened to blow up several sites in the city. While they go through those motions, race features prominently in the plot as Carver isn't the kind of Negro who just loves himself some White people. Though we understand that Carver's skepticism of Whites is well founded and not the same as so-called "Black racism," the script sometimes says otherwise. In one scene, he instructs his two sons that they shouldn't take help from White people; in another, his conversation with McClane goes something like this:

McClane: "I'll tell you what your problem is, you don't like me because you're a racist!"

Zeus: "What?"

McClane: "You're a racist! You don't like me because I'm White!"

Zeus: "I don't like you because you're going to get me killed!"

The most memorable "race" scene, of course, is when Bruce Willis, as a ploy, nearly incites a riot while walking in Harlem wearing a large placard that says, I Hate Niggers.

Die Hard: With a Vengeance makes fast and superficial and entertaining comments about Zeus's personal prejudices and allows those to be referred to as racism, while saying nothing really about the real racism faced by Black people in Harlem or in New York City in general. Still, it is entertaining and gives Jackson a reputation as an outspoken, blue-collar race man on film.

7

Am I Black Enough for You?

Searched at the Cinema

July 11, 1995

It's girls' night out in southeast Queens. Time to head to the movies and gaze at Denzel in *Crimson Tide.*

Only it's not so simple. As I park the car, my neighbor Kim, who always carries food with her because she is diabetic, starts worrying about whether her pop-open can of sliced peaches will be allowed into the theater.

"They'll say it's a weapon," she mumbles as she closes the car door. "I'm going to see what they say. The last time, I had a little bottle of orange juice, and they said I couldn't bring it in because the bottle could be a weapon."

Welcome to the movies—America's favorite entertainment—Black-community style. Here at the Sunrise Multiplex Theater just over the Nassau border in Valley Stream, not only are glass bottles suspect, but everyone passes through a metal detector, and all bags are searched. "It makes me think of going to a prison," says Kim, a thirty-seven-year-old mother of two who works as a word processor. After shedding his belt, jewelry, and keys, one patron recently had to remove his metal-tipped cowboy boots and walk through the detectors in his stocking feet. Carl, a lifetime resident of Queens, stood nearby, watching the man repeatedly go through the detector: "I thought to myself, damn, good thing he didn't have a metal plate in his head."

Stricter security measures were put into place after a series of violent incidents at the theater, the last and most serious of which was a shooting that killed one and injured three on Christmas Day 1990 at a screening of *Godfather III.*

But the safety measures don't soothe everyone. Some people consider the theater still too dangerous to visit. Others are so turned off by the detectors that they refuse to go. But whatever their sentiments, most people I know out here have a strong reaction to Sunrise.

"I would prefer not to go there," says Kevin, a thirty-five-year-old father and businessman living in the Hollis section of Queens. "I would prefer not to go anywhere where I am subject to a search. It's a police-state mentality.

"It does further damage to how we think about ourselves and our communities. Going through metal detectors, going to stores where they pass your food through a hole in the bulletproof shield—it creates the idea that where you live is not a good place."

Kevin says such security measures reminded him of a supermarket that opened in East Orange, New Jersey, where he lived before coming to Queens. Not only were shoppers greeted by a large stop sign asking them to check their bags, the store also erected poles around the entrance that prevented patrons from rolling grocery-laden shopping carts to their cars, a convenience taken for granted in suburbia.

"I could drive ten minutes away to Montclair and not have to put up with any of that crap," Kevin says.

I have mixed feelings. Southeast Queens is the nation's largest Black middle-class community; yet, like most Black communities around the country, it does not have a single movie theater. So the Sunrise is a potent symbol of both the economic disinvestment in my community and of how crime creates a prison culture in Black communities. I hate the infuriating toy police attitude of some of the guards, who treat many of us who pass through as suspects.

On the other hand, despite past violence, Sunrise is serving my community, a community no one else chooses to serve. I'm sure the theater's owners are not motivated by altruism. They have obviously identified Black films as an important part of their market. Every new Black film is shown there, while the neighboring Green Acres Cinema seems to religiously avoid such offerings.

Similarly, in Fresh Meadows, the closest White neighborhood to the north, one of the two first-run theaters rarely if ever screens films that appeal to African-Americans. Though I occasionally go to movies there, and to Green Acres, I am torn when I do: Why should I support theaters that don't support me?

Longtime residents of Queens remember when a series of community theaters served southeast Queens, including at least three on Jamaica Avenue and others in

Cambria Heights, St. Albans, and, more recently, Rochdale Village. But most were old-fashioned, single-screen theaters that did not show first-run features. Like such community theaters all over the country, they eventually lost patrons and closed during the 1960s and 1970s.

I sometimes dream about a shiny new multiplex opening right in my own community. I would support it enthusiastically, just as I choose to support a Black community by living where I do.

Then I ask myself: If such a theater opened, would I feel safe if there weren't metal detectors? The theater would serve everybody in the community, including people who might be carrying weapons—and who I still choose to live around rather than around people who don't want me in their neighborhood. And who will cheer the Black hero along with me in darkened theaters.

Maybe Kevin is right. Maybe by becoming conditioned to routine heavy security, African-Americans are conditioned to see themselves and particularly young Black men as criminal.

But a friend who is not Black says that the Oklahoma City bombing and the subsequent revelations about just how armed and increasingly violent this nation is made her realize that the security measures taken in Black communities may become the norm in many places. I don't know if I agree with her. I can't imagine residents of Forest Hills being required to check their bags at the grocery store, even if one day they are required to pass them through metal detectors. There is a difference between a security culture and a criminal culture.

I definitely don't want to raise my two-year-old son in the latter. He was oblivious to the metal detectors at Sunrise when we went to see *The Lion King,* his first movie-theater experience, last Christmas. But at some point he will notice that at one movie theater, where he sees lots of people who look like him, he steps through metal detectors and a man searches Mommy's purse. But if we go about three blocks to Green Acres Cinema, where there are fewer of us, we just walk right in. Later still, he will be looked on as a possible suspect wherever he is.

Kim makes it past the guard with her peaches. This guard is actually a nice guy, who banters about the high price of movies and how he cannot afford movie theaters any longer. "I wait for the videotape," he says.

Kim, who has lived in Queens all her adult life, says that she still prefers to go to a movie theater where she can "walk right in."

Not too much to ask, she says, just for a night out to sit in the dark and gaze at Denzel.

Black Star–Denzel Washington in *Virtuosity*

August 4, 1995

In a plot that stretches the definition of plausible, Washington stars as a police lieutenant hunting a virtual-reality killer who escapes into the real world.

The Tuskegee Airmen

August 26, 1995

A great ensemble cast headed by Laurence Fishburne tells the story of the Tuskegee Airmen, African-Americans who overcame racism within and outside of the military, to become the first Black fighter pilots to go into combat during World War II. The cast also includes Allen Payne, Malcolm-Jamal Warner, Courtney B. Vance, and Andre Braugher.

Black Star–Wesley Snipes in *To Wong Foo Thanks for Everything, Julie Newmar*

September 8, 1995

Of course none of us are ready for Wesley Snipes in a dress. Our brave action hero is only the latest Black man to heed the urgent call of a blond wig and a pair of pumps (Dennis Rodman? RuPaul? Flip Wilson?). America loves it. He plays one of three cross-dressers, along with Patrick Swayze and John Leguizamo, who are traveling cross-country when their car breaks down in a small town. The best thing is his name—Noxeema Jackson. (C'mon, you know you laughed.)

Clockers

September 13, 1995

Bombarded by Black popular culture images glamorizing drug dealers, shiny guns, and various elements of "thug life," Spike Lee finally offers his take on the subject in his eighth theatrical release, *Clockers,* an unsparing and claustrophobic film that refuses to offer easy answers or easy outs.

While in *Jungle Fever* he explored the residual destruction in Black families wrought by the crack cocaine epidemic, *Clockers* takes its name and focus from the hordes of young Black men who are seemingly on the corners twenty-four/seven in open-air drug markets selling their wares. Added to the mix, through conversation, is the growing scourge of AIDS in the Black community; racist NYPD officers; the defeat of the city's first Black mayor, David Dinkins, to Rudy Giuliani; and the debate over "gangsta rap." On these subjects and their intersection with the clockers, Lee is obviously both sympathetic and literally nauseated.

His main character, Strike (Mekhi Phifer), who sells rock from the benches at the Nelson Mandela public housing project in Brooklyn, is a complex character who is suffering from an ailing stomach that causes him to wince, vomit, and bleed internally. On the one hand, Strike has the decidedly non-thug hobby of model trains and, on the other, he wants to please his kingpin boss, Rodney (Delroy Lindo). He must keep his drug-dealing troops in line, win the friendship of a neighborhood boy whom he is recruiting into the criminal business, and stay steps ahead of the police officers who periodically raid his business site—even to the point of strip-searching him in public.

The story revolves around the murder of another of Rodney's lieutenants, and for much of the film we are wondering if Strike committed the murder or if it was committed by his older, straight-laced brother, Victor (Isaiah Washington). We are maneuvered through the case by a dogged Det. Rocco Klein (Harvey Keitel), who senses something strange in Victor's confession to the crime. Ultimately, we figure out that the success of the business-as-usual drug trade relies on the existence of cops who are not like Klein—who are supposed to be immune to the mounting body count of young Black men like Strike.

The story, written by and based on a book by Richard Prince, explains Rocco's dogged pursuit with his insistence on controlling his streets. "You don't play me," he tells Strike. "I play you."

We get far less insight into Victor to understand how he could possibly get involved in a murder. In the plot, he is sort of set up like a straw man whose actions don't make sense and, therefore, make a big part of the story feel emotionally untrue, especially when compared to the impact of the movie's many corpses.

In *Clockers,* Lee's signature preamble is a montage of "crime" scenes, almost all assorted young Black men with gruesome gun-shot wounds. Some lay in pools of their own blood. There is the yellow crime scene tape surrounding the victims, and sometimes there is the crowd standing outside the yellow tape, watching the scene and passing time.

Devil in a Blue Dress

September 29, 1995

Denzel Washington stars in this moody and sexy murder mystery based on Walter Mosley's novel and series about the Black detective Easy Rawlins.

Dead Presidents

October 4, 1995

The Hughes brothers again concern themselves with the illegal hustle for cash or "dead presidents" as it is known. The production is above average and the action keeps moving, but Larenz Tate is still not believable to me as a grown man, even less so as the Vietnam Veteran/bank robber that he is supposed to be here.

Black Star–Wesley Snipes in *Money Train*

November 22, 1995

Wesley Snipes and Woody Harrelson reprise their buddy act, with both playing New York City transit cops and Harrelson again playing the ne'er-do-well. This time, his name is Charlie and he hatches a scheme to steal the "money train," which carries weekly revenue from the New York City transit system. His foster brother, John (Snipes), has always bailed him out of his problems but may not be able to this time. They both have the hots for an undercover officer (Jennifer Lopez) who is helping them catch a sicko who's setting fire to token-booth clerks.

Black Star–Laurence Fishburne in *Othello*

December 15, 1995

Shakespeare's *Othello* has always struck me as extremely demeaning to Black men and totally out of step with the ideal of a brother with savvy and street smarts. This film, the first to have an African-American man in the role of the Moorish King Othello, is beautifully shot in such a way that highlights even further the sex scenes between Fishburne and Irene Jacobs, who plays Desdemona.

Waiting to Exhale

December 22, 1995

This Black chick flick event of the decade succeeds in spite of its self-consciousness. Based on Terry McMillan's best-selling novel of the same name, the film follows four women, played by Whitney Houston, Angela Bassett, Lela Rochon, and Loretta Divine, "waiting to exhale" as they navigate the bumpy road to relationship rightness. Bassett, whose husband (Michael Beach) leaves her for a White woman, has, literally, the hottest scenes in the flick, while Devine, the movie's big girl, has the happiest ever-after. The diva makeup and styling, which make Bassett and Houston look ridiculously perfect when they wake up in the morning, gives these characters and the film a certain artifice.

Once Upon a Time . . . When We Were Colored

January 12, 1996

The heart of this release is in the right place. Through the eyes of a young boy, it tells the story of a Southern Black community during the days of segregation, from the years 1946 to 1962, a period when the relative prosperity in America was paralleled by continued racial segregation and oppression in the South. The performance by young Charles Earl "Spud" Taylor Jr. is heartwarming, and the film's pivotal controversy, about an effort by area Whites to force the Black ice man (Richard Roundtree) out of business, illustrates the tie between so-called civil rights and economic justice. That all being said, I find the movie to be emotionally simplistic and a bit of a snooze. It doesn't expand the narrative of what we have already seen—whether in literature, film, or on television.

Don't Be a Menace (to South Central While Drinking Your Juice in the Hood)

January 14, 1996

Enough gun-drug-pathology films and clichéd South-Central L.A. rap videos now exist to provide ample material for the Wayans family to do what it does best: poke fun at other people, this time in the hood with *Don't Be a Menace.* The trick is to make the already ridiculous completely outrageous. Sometimes the family succeeds, like in Keenen Ivory Wayans's 1988 spoof of '70s films, *I'm Gonna Git You Sucka.* Sometimes they fail, like in the waning days of the Fox television series *In Living Color.* In this movie, they succeed, for the most part.

The film, partly written by Shawn and Marlon Wayans, relies on its audience's knowledge of current Black popular culture. To understand most of its references, you should know, for example, John Singleton's *Boyz n the Hood* and *Poetic Justice,* the Hughes brothers' *Menace II Society,* Spike Lee's *Do the Right Thing* and *Jungle Fever,* and at least one music video by Dr. Dre or Snoop Doggy Dogg.

Don't Be a Menace—complete title, *Don't Be a Menace to South Central While Drinking Your Juice in the Hood*—follows two young men, Ashtray (Shawn) and Loc Dog (Marlon), in an effort to explain "how it really is" living in South-Central, the premier "ghetto" in film and videos today.

The result is more a pastiche of parody than a story. Loc Dog asks Ashtray for fashion advice. Should he carry the Tech-9 or the Uzi? Which expensive leather sneakers? He finally settles on pink bunny rabbit slippers that he wears out in the streets.

Outrageous is the key word here. In many successful scenes, the Wayanses deftly play on our assumptions and clichés. They catch the viewer sleeping and deliver deadly punches: a gray-haired grandmother who is not sweet and, instead, uses the trendiest hood profanity, smokes blunts of marijuana, and out-dances Rosie Perez. A mother comes home, catching her teenage daughter having sex and, rather than the usual boy-escapes-out-the-window scene, Mom dons her dominatrix outfit and wants to join in the fun. We think Loc Dog is making crack, but he's not. Ashtray's big love scene, rather than tender and romantic, becomes the funniest moment in the movie. Let's just say that it involves Kool-Aid, hot dogs, and hot sauce.

At other times the filmmakers miss by a mile, overusing clichés like malt liquor (in one case given to a baby in a bottle), or when an elderly woman is held up for her walker and in the beginning scene when two men are quickly shot dead in the street.

The viewer may pause, aware that what is being parodied is film reality, a hyper-reality that may not be true to life, that may not, in fact, be real. When you laugh, what are you laughing at? The parody? The memory of the original film? What are the filmmakers laughing at?

Don't Be a Menace constantly draws attention to the fact that it is a movie. It makes no effort to pull us into a fictional world or to draw our sympathy. At the beginning of the film, as Ashtray's mother takes him to live with his father, she tells him she won't see him again because "you know there aren't any positive females in these movies." Later, Ashtray tells a little boy that both of them are part of an endangered species. "Why, because we're Black males?" the boy asks him. "No," Ashtray replies, "because rappers are taking all the good acting jobs."

We remain on the outside looking in and, in some cases, laughing.

Interview—Theresa Randle Has Hollywood's Number

Girl 6

March 17, 1996

Her role in Spike Lee's new joint, *Girl 6,* is the first starring film role for Theresa Randle. So she wants to put the right spin on her career.

"I don't want that stuff attached to me—you know, the new, Black, hot . . . the 'new sister on the block' kind of thing," she said, looking pensive and direct during a recent visit here.

She's about twenty-nine, but doesn't want to give her age. (You can't blame her. Hollywood treats actresses over forty like they're ready for Jurassic Park.)

She doesn't want to be boxed in, Blackballed, or Blacked in.

Blacked in? Well, that's what you might call Hollywood's recent trend of casting Blacks in roles "originally intended for Whites," or something like that. When a film part "goes Black," as they say, it does create an opportunity for someone. But when such a change is publicized as racial progress, is the message that the actor got the role because of talent or because of race?

"I would never want to be in something because they decided to 'go Black,'" she says. "I would love to be in it because you said, 'This is a brilliant role. I saw Theresa Randle in that movie. I'd love to have her in it.'"

Well, we'll see, Theresa. We'll see.

Hollywood hasn't served up many high-quality starring roles for Black actresses. Even in the new wave of Black film, women have primarily played supporting roles to men. A challenge to that pattern is likely to be the legacy of *Waiting to Exhale.*

In her new movie, which opens Friday, Randle plays a struggling young actress in New York who aspires to try her luck in Hollywood. To pay her bills, she takes a job with a phone sex company, where she is identified only as Girl 6. She tells herself that her job is acting. She is really good at what she does. Then she lets it get out of control.

Despite its promotion as "The Outrageous New Comedy From Spike Lee," this movie is not a thigh-smacker. As a matter of fact, those who fear that the sex industry makes women vulnerable to danger might find that this movie makes them very uneasy and, at times, very scared.

"It should be a dramatic comedy," Randle says. "I was surprised when I saw them marketing it solely as a comedy because I knew what I had done—unless they cut the film in some way that I didn't know about."

To prepare for the role, Randle wanted to go undercover at a phone sex company but didn't. She decided instead to be upfront and say she was "doing research." But the companies—three outfits, each grossing millions of dollars a year—weren't having that. So she worked with a few consultants, people with experience in the phone sex industry who filled her in on the inner workings and sent her copies of letters from clients to help her construct a character identity.

"I never crossed the line and actually listened to them speaking to their clients, but there are phone lines where you can actually hear a two-party conversation, if in fact you choose to—anyone in the public can do that," she says.

"But specifically, I had things I wanted to ask them, like, 'Did you ever have a client that you fancied and wanted to meet?' One of the women said, 'Yeah, but when I met my guy, it didn't work out. We met a couple of times and realized that we had nothing in common.' So all those things helped," she says. "Because I knew that I had to focus on falling in love with a voice and envisioning what this voice will look like.

Randle credits writer Suzan-Lori Parks for "doing her homework" in developing a realistic plot that includes the burnout she says so many phone sex workers experience, as well as the idiosyncrasies of an industry that relies on the fact that its customers don't know whom they're speaking to.

"Unless [the clients] request 'other than,' the assumption is that you are a white woman," Randle says. "Think about the commercials you see on cable late night. They usually have images of blondes, brunettes, redheads—whatever—but they are all White women. Unless you turn to the soul channel and you see a bunch of sisters in bathing suits, or turn to the Asian hotline. Usually you know what hotline you're calling. At our company [in the movie] we specialize in White housewife types.

"There is one caller who [gets excited by hearing] the Puerto Rican woman going through her grocery list. He loves to hear her accent."

Girl 6 fits into the crazy mix just fine. We know she's desperate for money, desperate to be an actress. So desperate that we have seen her, though traumatized, obey the command of a film director to bare her breasts during an audition. That scene also gave Randle pause.

"I just wasn't going to do it," she says. "I hadn't done it [in any roles] up to this point because there just wasn't a reason, and now there was a reason but I still wasn't going to do it. But then I said to myself: 'Girl 6 would do it. Theresa, stop it.' Girl 6 is at that point at the start of the film. She's hungry. She's clueless as to what it's all about, so she'd do it."

The rawness of that scene along with the sexual subject matter has made this role an expansion for Randle, who had been thought of as a "good girl" type after playing Wesley Snipes's doe-eyed girlfriend in *Sugar Hill*. This was in the prime of Snipes's days as a big heartthrob, and Randle's character not only did not have sex with Snipes, but she put down his drug-dealing self for most of the movie. She's also had a featured role in *Beverly Hills Cop III* and had bit parts in Lee's *Malcolm X* and *Jungle Fever* and Robert Townsend's *The Five Heartbeats*.

Randle thinks Hollywood too easily typecasts actresses, not allowing them to stretch beyond the last role they did well.

"We as actors have to find vehicles where we can show what we're capable of," Randle says. "Otherwise they don't know, and in conversation they will say things like, 'Oh, she does this well' without really knowing what you do. Once you do something well in one film, God forbid if you're labeled as that and you don't get to do anything else. A lot of people don't understand what acting is. An actor should be a chameleon. You should be able to do anything."

Parts and films that really upset her are ones that depict her native South-Central Los Angeles—and all inner-city neighborhoods—as places primarily of pathology, instead of homes to working and striving families. Her mother, Admonia Johnson, who cared for children and the elderly in their home, raised Theresa, as well as her sister and brother, to be the performer she had always wanted to be but couldn't because of her strict Jehovah's Witnesses upbringing.

Randle remembers a childhood spent rehearsing and touring with a community arts group. She tested well and attended better-appointed public schools in West Los Angeles while continuing private acting lessons.

Like Girl 6, Randle has found the politicking for jobs in Hollywood a bit too much. She spends a lot of time in her Los Angeles apartment. The other day, she was watching *What Ever Happened to Baby Jane?* She marvels at the longevity of the careers of divas like Bette Davis and at the quality of the stories their characters told. But can Hollywood, with its increasing number of Black directors, create roles with depth for Black actors, roles that will let Randle live out her Bette Davis dream?

Well, we'll see, Theresa. We'll see.

A Thin Line Between Love and Hate

April 3, 1996

This is a sophomoric version of *Fatal Attraction* starring comedian Martin Lawrence. A wealthy woman (Lynn Whitfield) makes an abrupt about-face from being dismissive of a small-time deejay to being obsessed by him. The story line serves as an extention of hip-hop's recurrent theme of dizzy and gold-digging women. This time the woman is beyond dizzy, and a "playa" meets his match.

Et Cetera—The Real Villains of *Jonny Quest*

May 29, 1996

It's a signature trailer shot for classic *Jonny Quest* episodes: Africans, in skins and feather head wear, gesture with crude instruments and murmur unintelligibly, something like "wooga-booga-ayaa-agaa." Their hurled spears clink futilely against the door of the sleek jet spiriting away eleven-year-old Jonny; his scientist father, Dr. Benton Quest; bodyguard Roger "Race" Bannon; young Hadji; and miniature bulldog, Bandit.

The scene flashes on the television screen for only a matter of seconds, but that is ample time for the cartoon images, in classic *Quest* fashion, to paint the dark natives as both evil enemies and foolish savages. It is also enough time for post–civil rights parents, who are not having any of that, to grab and click the remote, especially if there is a young child in the house.

But what if, instead, we crank up the volume? What if we treasure our nostalgia? After all, 200,000 videotapes of classic *Jonny Quest* shows have been snapped up since their rerelease nine weeks ago, according to Dan Capone, director of marketing for Turner Home Entertainment.

Judo student Jonny tosses "lizard men" three times his size. Hadji, adopted by Dr. Quest from the streets of Calcutta, performs magic with the evocation "Sim sim sala bim!" Dr. Quest triumphs over villains with his high-tech inventions. For many of us, *Jonny Quest* was the first modern science-fiction adventure, a prequel to *Indiana Jones.* And it had a slammin' musical score.

This is our heritage, these are our memories. Some of us wouldn't dream of clicking the remote. We say, of course it's racist. Of course, of course. The series was launched in 1964 (and aired on and off until 1980), before it was incorrect to be so blatantly imperialist. It was during the Cold War, so Russian accents are thick among the few White villains. After all, it's not as if our peers in Hollywood's new wave of Black filmmakers have provided many alternatives for our or their children, other than Robert Townsend's brilliant, underrated 1993 effort, *Meteor Man.*

Most important, we don't watch vintage television shows the way we used to. By watching a show like *Jonny Quest,* we can also wrestle it to the ground. We can have a big laugh at television benighted enough to present the world in such a screwed-up fashion. We can choose to take from shows what we want, while struggling over the issue of how old but powerful images will be presented to our children.

It seems like a lot of backflipping over just a cartoon. But Black folks have been backflipping for a long time, adjusting sensibilities to the dynamics of American popular culture. Earlier generations of African-Americans were initiated into popular culture by shows such as *Amos 'n' Andy, Tarzan, Our Gang,* Shirley Temple movies, or Looney Tunes. Similarly, *Jonny Quest* required then and now an unconscious but sophisticated and computer-quick series of calculations. We want to tune in and enjoy the hero-and-adventure fantasy but survive the racial assault and insult. That survival, the victory, is one of those earth-moving, quiet miracles not picked up by the radar of racial progress.

It is a miracle that we can survive sour images and still claim them. Lots of artists have, for example, claimed Aunt Jemima. They've painted, acted, and danced her in a different role, using the spatula in her hand to liberate her from her passive pose on the pancake box. New York composer Fred Ho has taken the inscrutable Charlie Chan and made him into a revolutionary.

And an important reason we can survive them is all the work done by the generation before us that demanded the media take responsibility for cleaning up the international image of Blacks as subhuman. The last three decades have offered images of Black people that weren't all negative—beginning, roughly, with the 1968 series *Julia,* going through *The Cosby Show,* hero movies like *Glory,* and the obligatory appearance of everyday Blacks in commercials. With some positive representation out there, each television or film image does not have to carry the weight of being "positive." We can accept Black villains and bad guys—and even the occasional feathered headdress.

The creators of *Jonny Quest* are not unaware of these issues. Preparing for a new *Jonny Quest* series that will start in the fall, the Turner Entertainment Group in Atlanta had cablecast a *Jonny Quest* Farewell Weekend at the end of April, showing the classic episodes on the Cartoon Network and then taking them off the air for good, according to Capone. From now on, they'll be available only on videotape.

Capone said that he gauged consumer interest in the Quest classics by noting requests to the network, putting feelers out on the Internet, and researching what had been written about the series. *Quest* fans told the Cartoon Network that they like the cartoon's action and think that: Jonny is spirited, brave, and has adventures in foreign lands; "Race" is strong, sturdy, and "a perfect figure of protection"; Hadji is mysterious and has special powers; Dr. Quest is intelligent and able to use his intellect instead of violence. Bandit is adorable. And they looove to hate Dr. Zin, an evil Asian scientist.

Those offering such descriptions clearly separate the good guys from the bad guys, and most of the bad guys are dark-skinned. Dr. Zin is always hatching some evil scheme. An East Indian man attempts to murder Dr. Quest. Hadji is brown; he's not a villain, but he is made into a compliant exotic. Except for him, the people of color wind up shot, exploded, electrocuted, buried under an avalanche, snatched by a giant crab. . . . The list goes on.

Female characters are nearly nonexistent. Jonny's mother is dead. The only regularly appearing female is Jade. She is equipped with a gun and has some adventure-hero credentials, but she is conniving and a vamp.

In 1993, producers Hanna-Barbera eliminated most such racial and sexual stereotypes in the feature-length *Jonny Quest vs. the Cyber Insects.* Hadji is more assertive. Dr. Zin doesn't look brown and evil as much as ugly and evil. And a young girl, Jesse, is an important part of the Quest Team. In addition, the Quest Team in the movie works for a military-intelligence outfit that has a Black man in charge and a well-integrated staff. Capone says that in the new series, *The Real Adventures of Jonny Quest,* care was also taken with such matters.

The old stereotypes, Capone said, "are part of the reason why it's been updated. *Jonny Quest* is great. But it includes some things that you just can't do now, things that you could do thirty years ago. We definitely want a series that makes improvements upon that."

Sometimes it seems that the war over "political correctness" has a sound-bite quality and rhetorical content that misses an important consideration—the children. Why should any child, anyone, have to be denigrated by a cartoon? Or ignored?

"I want to see Dr. Zin in 'Master of Evil,'" a three-year-old tells his mother.

She pops in the tape. One of two episodes on that tape is a favorite of hers, with a Zin-made spy robot that looks like a giant spider. Later she asks her son who is the bad guy and he says, "Dr. Zin." She tells him that, yeah, Dr. Zin is bad but not everyone who looks like Dr. Zin is a bad person. "You know, Julie from [the PBS show] *The Puzzle Place* looks like Dr. Zin and Julie is cool." Yeah, he says, he likes Julie.

She asks him why Zin is bad. The boy says, "Because he has a giant bad spider and some giant ants."

The mother feels a slight sense of relief. But she wonders what her son would do if, today, at this very moment, he were given one of those tests with Caucasian dolls and Asian dolls and asked to pick the good guys and bad guys.

She hopes he would say, "I don't know," and ask, "Who has the giant bad spider and some giant ants?"

And what is his favorite thing about the cartoon, she asks. No. It's not Jonny, or Race, or Hadji, or Dr. Quest, or any human, he answers.

"The pterodactyl, that's what I like," he says, referring to the prehistoric flying creature on the show's intro sequence.

She is relieved again, thinking that at least for now, in his dinosaur-fever stage, he is not overly concerned with how people are painted, or with heroes who never look like him.

The Nutty Professor

June 28, 1996

In this remake of the 1963 film starring Jerry Lewis, Eddie Murphy does double-, triple-, and quadruple duty in the role of Professor Sherman Klump, a grossly obese man who has created a serum to make him—poof!—into a slim man. Klump's slim alter ego is an obnoxious egomaniac named Buddy Love who, unlike the professor, seems to have no sensitivity or scruples. The makeup and special effects in the film, transforming Murphy into Klump as well as assorted members of the Klump family, are amazing, but Murphy's zany overdrive in the part of Buddy Love recalls his more annoying performances. And although it is obviously part of the gag, you know there is *no way* any woman who looks like Jada Pinkett, nerd or not, is going to try and get with someone who looks like Sherman Klump. C'mon now.

Black Star–Will Smith in *Independence Day*

July 3, 1996

This is a film that we like and laugh at because we get to see a Black man kick some alien butt with the advantage of all the special effects that Hollywood can muster. Will Smith is Captain Steven Hiller, part of a team assigned to fight aliens that have already destroyed major cities around the world. His girlfriend (Vivica A. Fox) is a stripper. They had to go *there.*

Black Star–Denzel Washington in *Courage Under Fire*

July 12, 1996

Lt. Colonel Nathaniel Serling (Washington) investigates whether Captain Karen Walden (Meg Ryan), killed during Operation Desert Storm, deserves the Medal of Honor. *Courage Under Fire* works as a taut detective tale that, as they often do, spins out of control at the end.

Black Star–Shaquille O'Neal in *Kazaam*

July 17, 1996

In the modern fairy tale *Kazaam,* Shaquille O'Neal, the seven-foot-one, three-hundred-pound center for the Orlando Magic, plays a genie who has just been awakened.

Alas, the movie's producers could use a genie of their own.

Surely, if granted three wishes, they could have produced a better film. And since they were banking on O'Neal's appeal to kids, they could have made better use of his budding musical ability.

In the film, twelve-year-old Max Conner (Francis Capra) lives with his single mother, Alice (Ally Walker), in a struggling community in downtown Los Angeles. Their apartment is replete with the faux-seedy decor Hollywood uses to evoke the inner city. The effect is to say: This place is really depressing, and these people are real losers. Max is White, but he is tormented by a predominantly Chicano group of boys who chase and beat him.

As Max nonetheless attempts to curry favor with his persecutors, the setting and tension are ripe for a good, old-fashioned celluloid lesson in values and maturity. But this ain't it. The main problem is that, though the movie is built around Max and Alice, the script, direction, and acting fail to give these characters the necessary depth. We gradually learn that Max's father hasn't been around since Max was two. But parental absence is not reason enough to empathize with Max, who is a chronic whiner around the apartment. We also learn very little about his mother—like what kind of work she does, what happened to break up the marriage, or what she cares about other than her fireman fiancé. She flits in and out of scenes—nervous, clueless, and ineffective—always reacting, never in control.

The effect of such thinly painted characters, of course, is to make the movie implausible to start with. And that makes it all the more difficult to suspend disbelief and accept the supernatural genie Kazaam—a hip-hop-tinged apparition with rhyming pearls of wisdom, boombox, tasseled turban, and Persian slippers.

The other reason *Kazaam* fails is because it fights with itself. It was obviously created as a vehicle for O'Neal, who is also a professional rapper. But director and producer Paul M. Glaser (who played Starsky in the television cop series *Starsky and Hutch* and directed the feature films *The Air Up There, Band of the Hand, Running Man,* and *Cutting Edge*) does not build on the hip-hop performances, which are among the more entertaining scenes in the film. Young children may like some of the special effects. Those who are in the gross-me-out stage might laugh at the hamburgers, tacos, and other junk food that goes splat on the floor in one scene. But there's not much for anybody else.

Shaq's performance is also mixed. In his 1994 feature-film debut, *Blue Chips,* he was on familiar turf—playing a college basketball player. But in *Kazaam,* he doesn't seem sure what kind of genie he wants to be. One moment he's being a big brother to Max, the next he's a rapper, and then he's taking all kinds of abuse from Max, being called Godzilla or told that he smells like "hippopotamus butt." But he continues to follow Max around like the big slow kid on the block, a huge '90s version of Bill "Bojangles" Robinson serving little Shirley Temple.

Black Star–Laurence Fishburne in *Fled*

July 19, 1996

A pedestrian remake of *The Defiant Ones* starring Laurence Fishburne and Stephen Baldwin as two chained-together escapees—one Black and one White—from a prison work gang.

Black Star–Samuel L. Jackson in *A Time to Kill*

July 24, 1996

Though *A Time to Kill* is considered by many to be John Grisham's best work of literature, it is the least-satisfying film adaptation. It lacks a sense of gravity for the crime involved—the brutal rape of a ten-year-old Black girl by two White racists. It is also overly theatrical at inappropriate moments; a scene about dueling demonstrations by the Ku Klux Klan and the NAACP looks like bad staging for a film musical. It also sets up these groups as equals among extremists. Jackson, firmly now in his niche as a working-class Black hero, turns in a passionate performance as Carl Lee Hailey, father of the molested girl, who takes justice into his own hands by killing her attackers. The bulk of the film centers on his trial and his representation by a young local lawyer (Matthew McConaughey) who is assisted by a law student (Sandra Bullock). Though the subject matter should be compelling, the film is not and does not know what it wants to be.

Black Star–Wesley Snipes in *The Fan*

August 16, 1996

Snipes is a star baseball player who becomes the object of obsession for a fan played by Robert DeNiro. (Oh hell. You do not want DeNiro on your ass.)

8

Our Story, Their Story, Whose Story?

Get on the Bus

October 16, 1996

In *Get on the Bus,* the new Spike Lee film about a group of Black men traveling to last year's Million Man March, there is a riveting scene. One passenger on this journey from Los Angeles to Washington tells a secret: In a former life as a gang member, he killed so many people—primarily other young African-American men—that he needs two hands to count them all.

The confession by Jamal (Gabriel Casseus)—who is now a Muslim and works to end gang violence—is not a pivotal moment, but it is defining. It illustrates the way this energetic, poignant, and funny film succeeds, and the way it does not.

Jamal's scene, in which he pulls up his sleeve to reveal a Crips gang tattoo, is confession and revelation—what we filmgoers demand from drama. Here, Lee serves it up without a lot of flash or tricks. There is just a lone man with a humble demeanor who's perched on a bus seat. His story could easily be dismissed as another from a criminal class of Black men given media exposure well beyond their percentages in the Black population. He might represent a social nightmare. But with his new faith, Jamal has turned his life around. If he represents a nightmare, he also represents hope.

Jamal's story is contrasted to that of a police officer on the bus named Gary (Roger Guenveur Smith). The cop's father was killed in street violence. Gary confronts Jamal, saying he's the kind of person responsible for such carnage; he dismisses poverty as justification for murder. While Jamal might represent the power of personal atonement, Gary represents atonement to the larger society.

As in the real-life march one year ago today, this convergence of diverse Black manhood is what is compelling about the film. The bus serves as Lee's metaphor for Black America. On it, the issues of unemployment, single-parent families, and a crippling nihilism among youth travel along with the men. When stories like Jamal's are delivered, the movie is at its best. In other story lines, a Black gay couple and homophobia are treated as more than just the butt of jokes. The jagged rift between sons and absentee fathers is handled in a way that is moving and comical.

As he has in the past, Lee gets a big assist from Ossie Davis, who plays Jeremiah, the elder statesman of the group. Andre Braugher, known for his role in *Glory* and his current work on *Homicide: Life on the Street,* provides much of the glue for the journey. He plays Flip, a glib and obnoxious actor who fancies himself the alpha male of the group.

With so many stories to tell and so much ground to cover, however, the film sometimes has the sense of being constructed by committee. A simpler vision would have allowed a closer look at fewer lives. When life stories like Jamal's require a little more than just a telling from a bus seat, they suffer. There is not much of a preamble to the trip. We don't see the men in their ordinary lives before they board the bus. Most of the movie has the feel of a handheld-camera documentary. There are no flashbacks. We travel only in the present.

Despite its meandering, the movie ably bounces along until the end, when it fizzles. It's as if Lee can't figure out how to wrap up the film in a meaningful way. Instead, he simply kills off a character on the bus, for little apparent reason. It's sad—not just the death of the character, but Lee's maddeningly predictable habit of flawing each of his movies.

But the bulk of the movie is refreshing, even if it lacks much of a plot. It shows Black men talking compellingly about their lives in ways rarely glimpsed in Hollywood shoot-'em-ups-in-the-hood.

Set It Off

November 6, 1996

Just in time, now that all the election doublespeak is over, F. Gary Gray's new film, *Set It Off,* hits hard at a central theme in American life today: scoring big money by means respectable or not. *Set It Off* could also serve as a bellwether for race relations in this country. To the extent that Americans of all tribes understand the rage of its four women whirling through young adulthood in South-Central Los Angeles, we might all be saved.

In two hours, and with a big assist from gripping performances by Queen Latifah, Jada Pinkett, and Vivica A. Fox, Gray turns upside down popular, racist images of lazy Black "welfare queens." He shows, instead, four women more representative of not only poor Blacks but poor Americans in general. They work nights for a janitorial service. They earn so little that they have no hope of escaping the claws of a crime-ridden environment and a lack of education.

So they decide to rob banks.

Maybe there will be other movies about crazed postal workers, graduate students, or professionals mangled in the white-collar maw who decide to take up the gun. But this is a story of women—literally cleaning the dirt of corporate America for a living—who redefine what is legitimate. They decide to break the rules when they realize the game is set up for them to lose.

Frankie, the character played by Fox, turns criminal after being fired from a bank for knowing one of the young men who robbed her branch. They grew up in the same housing project. Her suit splattered with the blood of someone killed during the holdup, she pleads, "I can't help who I know!" This emotionally charged opening sequence of the robbery and her firing has to rank alongside scenes in *Norma Rae, Matewan,* and *Silkwood* as one of the best about the American workplace.

When the foursome, wearing wigs and sunglasses, begins robbing banks, the urban drama turns into an action flick. This story line may divide audiences the way *Thelma & Louise* did in 1991. The divisions may be along racial, gender, or class lines. Law-and-order types and those who have been victims of a crime may be turned off. But the scenes work, just as surely as those from *Butch Cassidy and the Sundance Kid.* We root for the four women as underdogs and models of the 1990s antihero. Tisean, played by Kimberly Elise, for example, needs money to retrieve her son from the clutches of a social services agency. He was taken from her after she couldn't afford a babysitter and took him to her job, where he was injured.

Set It Off grants bank robbers more than cinema chic. It bestows them moral authority.

Most of this legitimacy is created through performances by the actresses. Pinkett, as she has in the past, plays the tough pretty girl. But here she is more than a girlfriend. She is beginning to lose that sleepy-eyed look of a young seductress. Like her character, Stony, she is beginning to open her eyes.

Queen Latifah steals the show, investing a lot of fire, spit, and vinegar into the character of Cleo. By taking the role of a lesbian, Latifah thumbs her nose at those who have labeled her and other female rappers as gay. In perhaps stereotypical fashion, Cleo acts as the tough of the group. She mows down her foes, handling a Beretta submachine gun with one hand. She gives the movie its hip-hop flavor, articulating, with every scowl, crooked smile, or expression of dead-serious intent, the attitudes of twentysomethings who have hit society's wall.

Latifah's performance goes a long way toward giving the film its power. Gray could have done more with the office-work scenes, which are rendered sterile in comparison with the nasty work cleaning crews often do. The actresses work hard to give spark to some of the predictable scenes and dialogue in the screenplay by Kate Lanier and Takashi Bufford. Their fine work eclipses the fact that the film gives us very little information about most of them. Latifah's character's past, for example, is almost a complete mystery. But we accept her swagger and anger because something shown this convincingly must be real.

The Preacher's Wife

December 13, 1996

In *The Preacher's Wife,* an angel in the form of Denzel Washington comes to Earth to give strength and support to an embattled church pastor. Maybe the film could have used some heavenly intervention as well.

It's not a bad movie. In fact, in this remake of the 1947 *The Bishop's Wife,* director Penny Marshall manages to paint one of the more realistic recent portraits of African-American working-class communities. She avoids the hyper-reality of nihilistic thugs that so many directors use as a sort of ready-made kit for constructing scenes of Black life. It was shot in Northeastern cities like Buffalo, New York, and Jersey City and Paterson, New Jersey, with big, old, turn-of-the-century houses and churches. One century later, though, the buildings—a bit too conspicuously marked by graffiti in the film—are deteriorating. The scenery, what cinema types call the mise en scene, contributes mightily to this story of a community striving amid the ruins, people fighting an overwhelming tide to maintain what they have.

As Christmas approaches, things are breaking down in the community where the Rev. Henry Biggs (Courtney Vance), his wife, Julia (Whitney Houston), and son, Jeremiah (Justin Pierre Edmund), live. In Biggs's church, there are cracks in the walls and the boiler is about to blow. Young men in the neighborhood are being carted off to jail and foster homes.

With this milieu established so well, the story still founders. It's not that it tries to tell too many stories at once but that the stories seem predictable and disjointed.

The script and directing fail to draw us close enough to the main characters so that they appear more than cutouts. Even the immensely talented Washington has to pour on a little extra charm in the role of Dudley to be more than just a bright-faced Ken doll.

The other problem is Houston. Though obviously selected for her drawing power and singing talent, she has so far proven herself unable to carry a starring role in any film that requires us to sympathize with her. Her unemotional diva mask, stiffness, and dated look (especially tired wigs) make her an odd romantic heroine. She is like a walking stop sign in the course of the plot.

Vance somehow transcends the script and is a likeable preacher. And, by far, the best scenes in the movie are those with children. Jenifer Lewis, who actually looks better than Houston in the film, steals most of her scenes as Julia's sage and sassy mother, a widow of a minister who now puffs on the occasional cigarette.

There are many good reasons for going to see *The Preacher's Wife.* Just don't go looking for a blessing.

Ghosts of Mississippi

December 20, 1996

This is a heart-wrenching and inspiring account of the effort to bring the murderers of civil rights activist Medgar Evers to justice twenty years after his death. Whoopi Goldberg is excellent in the role of Myrlie Evers, the widow of Evers. Alec Baldwin is the persistent assistant district attorney, Bobby DeLaughter, who is pursuing the case, despite the personal and professional repercussions. While we learn very little about how the family of the slain leader fared after his death, we are given too much information about DeLaughter's failing marriage and the Southern world that protects Byron De La Beckwith, long believed to be the killer.

Gridlock'd

January 29, 1997

Gridlock'd is an often exasperating junkie travelogue starring Tupac Shakur, Tim Roth, and Thandie Newton. Not a comedy (as in funny) and not quite a drama (as in you can take it seriously), it follows a day in the life of two drug addicts (Shakur and Roth) who try to kick their habit after their friend (Newton) overdoses and is hospitalized. Trudging with this intrepid duo through public assistance offices or as they dodge henchman does not make for fresh or engaging cinema. The film does try to tap into the growing interest in poetry and spoken-word performance, but even this artistic foray can't relieve the gridlock of frustration.

Rosewood

February 21, 1997

This is definitely John Singleton's finest film to date. In a riveting fashion, it tells the story of how in 1923 a Black town in Florida was burned to the ground by a White mob. Superb performances by Ving Rhames, Don Cheadle, Akosua Busia, and Esther Rolle.

Miss Evers' Boys

February 22, 1997

Early in the new HBO film *Miss Evers' Boys,* Eunice Evers—an African-American nurse played by Alfre Woodard—approaches groups of rural Southern Blacks, explaining that the federal government wants to provide them with free, high-quality medical care.

This is the height of the Depression. And the poor sharecroppers she is facing have seen the federal government turn a blind eye to decades of lynching and social inequality. So naturally, they greet Evers's offer with suspicion. "Why the government helping us all of a sudden?" responds one voice in the crowd.

These moments turn out to be among the few that ring true in the two-hour drama. As most viewers will know, the story the movie tells is based on fact. The "free medical care" turned out to be a heinous government experiment in which hundreds of Black men with syphilis went untreated for forty years. While the government lied to the men and pretended to heal them, they suffered blindness, deafness, deterioration of bones and the central nervous system, insanity, heart disease—and, ultimately, death.

But don't expect this film to hammer home the magnitude of this tragedy, which is a touchstone for African-Americans and has provided ammunition for government-conspiracy theorists. Based on the play by David Feldshuh, it is neither a big-picture exploration of what is known as "the Tuskegee experiment" nor a penetrating study of the key players involved. Rather, producers Kip and Kern Konwiser have created a film that steers down the middle, providing few sparks in the process.

The story is told through the eyes of Evers, a fictionalized character based on an actual African-American nurse who signed on to the project. She thought the study would improve the health of the men of Tuskegee, Alabama, which at the time had the highest syphilis rate in the nation. Within a short time she knew better but continued merely to look after the untreated men, not attempting to change the situation.

As a starting point, the focus on Evers appears promising. Too many films, including *Mississippi Burning* and *Cry Freedom,* have told stories of Black tragedy, drama, or heroism by focusing on Whites—often a singular brave White man.

But looking at the story through the eyes of Evers puts too large a focus on her. There is nothing wrong with a portrait of Black complicity, just as there would be nothing wrong with a film that focused on Africans who sold their brothers into slavery or Jews who collaborated with the Nazis. The film tells us that the common-sense talk of nurse Evers was pivotal in persuading many men to participate. But it makes her role more significant than a single nurse's could have been, and fails to focus its camera on the government officials who made the evil decisions.

Of course, it's possible that the filmmakers were trying to make a taut, personal drama exploring the inner turmoil of Evers and the lives of the men participating in the study. But this doesn't happen, either. We know from the start that Evers took her Florence Nightingale oath seriously, "to devote myself to the welfare of those patients committed to my care." But the film does not adequately explain the forces that prevented her from fulfilling that oath—by going public about the study once she realized its intent, or by secretly injecting the men with lifesaving penicillin, which by 1942 was recognized as an effective treatment for syphilis.

It's hard to know what to think of Miss Evers, an aging spinster who lives with her father (Ossie Davis). Is she blindly obedient to authority? Is she a Southern belle trained to take orders? Is she just long-suffering and naive? Is she afraid she can't meet the mortgage? She even turns down a chance at romantic happiness with Caleb Humphries (Laurence Fishburne), a man crazy about her, out of a supposed "duty" to the people in her care—a duty best described as deceiving them while she comforts them.

Some scenes are downright chilling, among them the "treatment" sessions, spanning decades, in which the men think they are rubbing one another's backs with a healing mercury solution but in fact are applying a useless oil. All the while, Evers urges them to keep on massaging.

The motives of Dr. Brodus (Joe Morton), a fictional Black physician in charge at Tuskegee Institute, are clearer. He is ambitious and has been fooled into believing the ridiculous notion that the study will uplift both the university's medical program and the race by proving there is no biological difference between Blacks and Whites. "We have a chance to make history here!" he tells Evers, sounding like someone unaware he is marching into hell.

With scenes like this, it is difficult to feel sympathy for Evers or Brodus. Still worse, the lives of the victims and the pain they suffered are compressed into a few low-wattage scenes. At the end, text is flashed on the screen explaining how these human guinea pigs and their survivors were eventually given a monetary settlement by the government. This information is interesting, but it makes you wonder where all those wives, daughters, and sons were during the course of the story.

Rhyme & Reason

March 7, 1997

Rhyme & Reason, a documentary released this week by Miramax Films, bills itself as "the ultimate backstage pass." Perhaps such hyperbole can be justified in a film about hip-hop, which as an art form relies on braggadocio and swagger. But when you boast, you have to be able to back up what you say. And truth be told, *Rhyme & Reason* cannot claim ultimate status.

It is a fast-paced, fuzzy, feel-good ride. It presents another face of hip-hop: the big family atmosphere at Heavy D's annual picnic in New York; Salt-N-Pepa reminiscing about hearing their music on the radio for the first time; members of Pharcyde exhibiting some of the comical aspects of improvisational freestyling. This film is so smooth, it makes even old gangsta rapper Ice-T seem likeable.

It colorfully recounts the birth of the music form, beginning in the Bronx in the 1970s, when rapping, DJing, dancing, fashion, and graffiti were all vital elements of the culture. It shows how, over the years, the other elements have taken a backseat to rapping and the music industry.

While the film includes interviews with dozens of artists, *Rhyme & Reason* sounds like something a hip-hop fan has heard before. It's sort of like *VIBE* magazine on video. For much of the film, you could just as well be watching a series of Bill Bellamy interviews on MTV or "Box Talk" features on the Box cable channel—just add plenty of cussing. It's short, sweet, and light. It's not too deep or critical. It does not advance the discourse. Its freshness springs from the concentration and arrangement of voices for consumption in one sitting. The most fun will be had by those who consider the celebrity talking head as a sort of eye candy.

But at a time when the hip-hop community is still reeling from the murder of rapper Tupac Shakur, the documentary skims the surface of issues such as lyrics with strong violent, sexual, and misogynist content. It covers the issue of women in hip-hop with mainly a smiling and happy shot of Salt-N-Pepa sitting on a couch. The pair talk about being dissed as newcomers, and how happy they were to be referred to as the female equivalent of male pioneers Run D.M.C.

Some shortcomings of the film stem from its form. Director Peter Spirer relies almost exclusively on spoken word on camera, quickly cutting from one scene to the next, from one face to the next. While this technique gives the film a grittiness and authenticity that would seem required of a film on hip-hop, the form seems to limit opportunity for depth or for the injection of facts or statistics—even as text on the screen—that could place some of what is being said in a larger context. Because Spirer relies so much on interviews to create the film's narrative, omission of some key players in hip-hop, such as Russell Simmons, Grand Master Flash, and Snoop Doggy Dogg, seems to create gaping holes in the story. Given how often such artists and executives do not or cannot grant interviews, there must be ways to do a comprehensive film without them. But Spirer hasn't shown that way.

The Sixth Man

March 28, 1997

Marlon Wayans and Kadeem Hardison star in a lukewarm comedy about a basketball player assisted by a ghost.

B.A.P.S.

March 29, 1997

Robert Townsend's comedic genius is deft and furious. It mines—without explanation or apology—the psyche, foibles, and possibilities of African-Americans. Beginning with his landmark *Hollywood Shuffle,* in his underrated *The Meteor Man,* and now with *B.A.P.S.,* he has provided viewers with some very funny film scenes.

As he remains true to his artistic vision, he slips beneath the radar of most film critics and the film industry, which has yet to prove that it knows how to market his work. It's as if Hollywood is not comfortable with the idea of African-American comedy unless it is in the often tasteless, one-note variety produced by the Wayans family—those stars of Fox's unmourned *In Living Color.* (How fitting that *B.A.P.S.* opened on the same day as the foolish but more heavily promoted *The Sixth Man,* starring Marlon Wayans.) They root for the lunacy of Whoopi Goldberg or Bette Midler or Danny DeVito, but they just can't get with Townsend.

Despite its idiotic promotional trailers, *B.A.P.S.* is a very funny movie. In it, Townsend and writer Troy Beyer use the Bama—the term African-Americans give to unsophisticated Southern Blacks—to tell a modern fairy tale with a decidedly off-color tone. Nisi, played by Halle Berry, and Mickey, played by Natalie Desselle, are two homegirls from Savannah. That's homegirl as in down home. They have so many gold teeth that they set off metal detectors. Their hair is Patti LaBelle to the tenth power. It is so done, so big, that it blocks the movie screen on an airplane. Nisi is so tired of her boyfriend's perm that she refers to him as her "broken-down Superfly."

But, as in any good fairy tale, Nisi and Mickey have a dream—to open the world's first combined restaurant and hair salon: a place where you can buy both eggs and hair extensions. Nisi has a plan to earn money for their dream by flying to Los Angeles and winning a video dance contest sponsored by rapper Heavy D. She fails miserably but the pair accept another offer to help a rich, elderly man, Mr. Blakemore (Martin Landau), to be happy in his final weeks of life. Little do they know that they are being set up by Blakemore's evil, scheming nephew. The only other thing to say about the plot is this: Pity the fool who tries to set up two homegirls from Savannah.

Townsend has fun with the idea of clashing cultures—Black waitresses from Savannah and a filthy-rich household in Los Angeles—without letting the film descend into predictability. He uses a different twist to explore the tired fairy tale of the poor and pure of heart somehow working restorative powers on the rich and barren. In the process, he even makes a comment about the term *B.A.P.*, which stands for Black American princess—usually an affluent, spoiled girl. Nisi and Mickey aren't rich, but they—and this film—have a lot of heart.

Black Star—Wesley Snipes in *Murder at 1600*

April 18, 1997

In a boiler-plate but entertaining whodunit, Snipes, a D.C. cop, and a Secret Service agent (Diane Lane) team up to get to the bottom of a possible murder cover-up at the White House.

Interview—LisaGay Hamilton

May 13, 1997

On stage at the Kennedy Center in Athol Fugard's *Valley Song,* LisaGay Hamilton pours so much pubescent life into her role that it is impossible to take her for anything but a lanky, sweet-faced South African teenager. She has a lilting accent and trills her Rs, calls her grandfather (played by Fugard) "Oupa," and has that universal pout of adolescence down to a T.

In reality, Hamilton is a native of Long Island, thirty-three years old, and, unlike her character, Veronica, has moved past merely dreaming to become accomplished in a field that offers few prospects for Blacks.

"She's one of the most crafted actresses I've ever worked with," says the sixty-five-year-old Fugard, who has written nearly two dozen plays and has worked with Hamilton on this one over the past two years. When the Washington engagement is over, they will part ways.

"When I auditioned her I had an enormous sense of her intellectual maturity," he adds. "She has a stunning good head on her shoulders, and that is matched by an equally fine mastery of her craft. Audiences who have had a chance to see her have seen a great American actress at the threshold of her career."

In a profession more comfortable with actresses who are easily classifiable commodities—the bod, the blonde, the bad girl, the girl next door—Hamilton brings contradictions and issues to the table, as well as her talent. With bright eyes and high cheekbones framed by a rounded face, she looks young enough to play characters half her age—which has hurt her in auditions for more mature roles (Spike Lee once told her she looked about twelve). She did, however, recently land the role of a legal secretary in the ABC television series *The Practice* and will appear in the upcoming film version of Toni Morrison's *Beloved.*

She says she has always been fiercely conscious that Blacks are generally typecast on stage and screen. And by avoiding musical theater, she has cut herself off from a lot of the opportunities that are available for Black actors. By insisting on serious roles, in Shakespeare and other classic works, she has usually found herself appearing before audiences that are predominantly White.

"*Beloved* is one example where it's about craft and art, and challenging each other," Hamilton said on a recent day off, wearing jeans and a sweater at her hotel apartment near the theater. A film like *Booty Call,* she added, "is okay. But there's so much more we can do. We're just beginning to tap into that."

You could say that Hamilton's career is an indicator for the depressed state of Black theater in this country. She grew up influenced by the work of the Negro Ensemble Company and by playwrights like Ed Bullins and Ron Milner, but today the NEC—which nurtured Denzel Washington and Samuel L. Jackson, among many others—is all but dormant. She made her Broadway debut in August Wilson's *The Piano Lesson.* But when there's rent to pay, waiting for the next play by August Wilson must feel a little like waiting for the next album by Stevie Wonder. This graduate of the drama programs at New York University and Juilliard, who won an Obie Award for *Valley Song,* often finds there are few places to take her talents.

"It's frustrating to do this performance before a sea of White people," she says. "The play is not just for one person or one race. Athol and I just knew that the play would attract a diverse audience here in D.C. But then, on the first night, we looked out there and it was like, oh Jesus God!"

It happens that a soap-opera-ish all-Black gospel musical, *A Fool and His Money,* recently drew mostly Black audiences across town at the Warner Theatre. Hamilton looks at such shows—referred to collectively as "the chitlin circuit"—and admits that she's concerned about their possible impact on more serious Black theater. But she acknowledges the marketing skill of producers like *Fool*'s David E. Talbert, who saturate popular Black radio stations and churches with news about their productions.

In contrast, marketing for *Valley Song* did not include the area's most popular Black stations because of what Kennedy Center officials say is a comparatively limited advertising budget. Newspaper advertisements for the show feature a picture of Fugard, who plays both a White man and Veronica's "colored" (the South African term for mixed-race) grandfather, hugging Hamilton. Hamilton contends that the campaign does not make clear to Blacks that the play, which deals with the painful legacy of apartheid, is for them. "I can just imagine someone seeing that [ad] in the paper," she says. "They'd say, 'What is this? Who is this White man playing a Black man? Isn't apartheid over? I ain't seeing that [expletive].'"

While the chitlin circuit rolls on, grossing millions around the country, Hamilton is looking for roles that are a little meatier.

Like Veronica, for example. The character walks her tiny South African village with rope-thick braids hanging over her shoulders and wearing shorts and a T-shirt, a well-worn sweater tied carelessly around her waist. She has big dreams. Unlike generations of coloreds in her town, this teenager is not gearing up for a lifetime of scrubbing white people's floors. No, in her country's post-apartheid world, she wants to be a singer—a performer with big hair, a shimmering gown, and gloves up to her elbows.

Studying for her role in the play, which is based on events in Fugard's life, Hamilton traveled to South Africa, interviewed people, and took in the scenery in the country's Karoo region, where the play is set. She purposely did not see the South African production, preferring to develop her own version of the character. She studied with dialect and singing coaches. In interviewing the real Veronica's family, she learned that the girl liked to wear shorts. So she had her costume changed from the skirt Veronica wore in the South African show. Her face brightens at the thought that some theatergoers were convinced she is South African.

"I had to ask myself what about my own life was useful for this part," she says. "What about my life do I relate to this play? I don't think I can tell you what it is to be a Black South African woman, but I can tell you what it is to be a Black American woman, what it's like to live in a sexist society, what it's like to live in a racist society, what it's like to be loved by my parents, what it's like to leave home. There's probably more of my two-year-old niece in this character than any material I've gathered through anthropological research."

On *The Practice,* Hamilton also made her creative presence known. She knew that the young receptionist and legal secretary she plays would dress to impress in the office. Instead she was issued cheesy outfits that she believed were more appropriate for a streetwalker. So she appealed to producer David E. Kelley and got some adjustments in the wardrobe.

"When she read for us, there was such breathtaking honesty that we immediately signed her up," says Jeffrey Kramer, coexecutive producer of the show, whose creators are hoping it will be renewed for the fall. "For somebody like LisaGay, who has fully invested herself in her character, you have to trust that she knows what her character would feel and look like. You can't put an actress of that caliber into clothes that don't make her comfortable."

To hear Hamilton's older sister, Connecticut-based attorney Heidi Hamilton, tell it, LisaGay was born to be an actress. As a child in Stony Brook, New York, she entertained her family by lip-syncing to the cast album of *Purlie* and acting out parts from Broadway productions that her mother and sister took her to see.

Perhaps she was influenced by the soap operas that her grandmother, who lived with the family and babysat for LisaGay as a toddler, watched religiously. Her mother, Tina, worked then, and still does, as an administrator for the Girl Scouts. Her father, Ira, was an entrepreneur in real estate and construction. Her parents divorced while she was in middle school, and the Hamilton household suddenly became a house full of women. They lived in a predominantly White neighborhood, so LisaGay learned in school play auditions to fight for roles that weren't intended for Blacks.

Hamilton is outspoken on the issue of nontraditional casting. She wrote an article for the *Village Voice* about being rejected from a White production because of race. Then, during the recent debate on the subject between August Wilson and critic Robert Brustein, she reevaluated her position.

"I have come to a place in my own career where I'm beginning to rethink what I really want," she said in an interview this year. "I have spent all of my life, literally . . . fighting to get into White plays, arguing that I have every right to be there. And I've come to that place where I think that's pretty stupid."

Says Heidi Hamilton: "I think she's feeling like she's not making a contribution because she's not communicating to her people." In *Valley Song,* "it's really a communication thing you're doing—you're bringing life to the dreams and aspirations of a young African girl."

But rather than just bemoan the lack of quality parts and the sad state of Black theater, Hamilton now thinks about doing some writing herself and seeking out the work of Black writers of her generation. A turning point for her came four years ago when the veteran theater actress Mary Alice (*Having Our Say, Fences*) told her that she no longer wanted to do Shakespeare. "I was devastated when she told me that," Hamilton admits. "I was doing so much Shakespeare. But I understand that now. Because as an artist, you do want to tell your story, your own story."

What About Black Romance?—*Love Jones, Waiting to Exhale, Jason's Lyric, Naked Acts* and *Sprung*

May 25, 1997

> *This is for the lover in you . . .*
> —sung by Howard Hewitt and Shalimar

Sitting in the sunny restaurant at the Park Hyatt Hotel in Washington, D.C., Theodore Witcher is asked to name a Hollywood Black romance. Pausing a moment, he leaps back decades and offers a dusty *Mahogany,* the inauspicious 1975 directorial debut of Motown music mogul Berry Gordy. It featured a painfully thin Diana Ross with a broad smile and bouncy hair playing opposite heartthrob-of-the-decade Billy Dee Williams.

Any others?

"I can't say that I recall," Witcher says. "In the last generation of films, you pretty much arrive back at Diana Ross and Billy Dee."

Witcher is the twenty-seven-year-old director of *Love Jones*—which has made a name for itself as a new Black romance. Opening last week was director Rusty Cundieff's *Sprung,* which is quirky but offers more of a traditional, head-over-heels love story. What makes both films remarkable, first and foremost, is that they are actually Black romances. The fact that Witcher, culturally savvy like the poetry café regulars in his film, cannot name a few recent Black love stories, says a lot about Hollywood's avoidance of Black love and sexuality on the screen. In the thousands of films and television shows that Hollywood has released, only a handful have depicted any substantial relationship between a Black man and a Black woman. As recently as the 1980s, *The Cosby Show* was unique on television in that it was often the only place to see a Black man kiss a Black woman.

"I guess that exclusion is something I've known about all my life," says veteran actress Ruby Dee. She appeared in her first film in 1949 and has played in her own real-life love story with her husband of nearly fifty years, Ossie Davis. But she has never starred opposite a Black man in a love story. "It's one of the things stuck into your subconscious and it eats at you in little ways. You've received a certain type of propaganda about yourselves, about your relationships, about White people. Something creeps in of the enemy's propaganda."

Two years ago, *Ebony* magazine published the results of a survey of film historians, filmmakers, and actors, who were asked to name the most romantic Black movies. A forty-year-old musical, *Carmen Jones,* topped the list. Rounding out the top ten were: *Nothing But a Man* (1964); *For Love of Ivy* (1968); *Sounder* (1972); *Claudine* (1974); *Coming to America* (1988); *Jason's Lyric* (1994); *Lady Sings the Blues* (1972); *Mahogany* (1975); *Paris Blues* (1961); and *A Warm December* (1973).

Only two movies from the last two decades made the list. And a strong argument can be made that some of the movies aren't romances so much as dramas and comedies containing a thread of romance.

There is no comparison between these films and real love stories from Hollywood. Consider just the hits of the past film season. In *Jerry Maguire,* Tom Cruise finally realizes the wispy blonde he married is his true love. In *The English Patient,* dashing, wealthy Brits—smug benefactors of a colonized world—live risk-taking, interesting, and passionate lives.

Through an aesthetic of White faces, aquiline features, and flowing hair, we have been given a vision of what love and, as an extension, humanity, is. We've seen them all: average, well-meaning White people (*Sleepless in Seattle*); mob love (*Bugsy*); funky musicians (*A Star Is Born*); hooker as Cinderella (*Pretty Woman*); communists (*Reds*); military love (*An Officer and a Gentleman*); dying White people (*Love Story*); White people speaking in foreign languages (a favorite: *Wings of Desire*); elderly White people (*On Golden Pond*); even unattractive people (*Inventing the Abbotts*).

"There's something about the simplicity of a love story," says actress Theresa

Randle, who has played the girlfriend/wife opposite Wesley Snipes and Michael Jordan, and is the star of Spike Lee's *Girl 6*. "That's why I love Lauren Bacall and all those people because they were in real movies. You sit there and you cry and you wait for who comes in the door."

For a substantive Black film romance, go back to 1963, to *Nothing but a Man* with Ivan Dixon and Abbey Lincoln. Go to a foreign film, *Black Orpheus.* In literature, turn to works like James Baldwin's *If Beale Street Could Talk,* Zora Neale Hurston's *Their Eyes Were Watching God,* or last year's novel *Tumbling* by Diane McKinney-Whetstone. (But even romance in literature may not make the transition to the screen. The hot affair between Easy Rawlins and Daphne in Walter Mosley's *Devil in a Blue Dress* was reduced on the screen to a single steamy scene.)

Or turn to the imagination. No doubt there was an African willingly captured by slavers just to follow an abducted loved one; recently emancipated Blacks who walked the length of the country to find a lost spouse. There were fashionable lovers of the Harlem Renaissance; militant lovers of the 1960s.

"I miss seeing those images," says rapper and actress Queen Latifah of the scarcity of Black lovers on-screen. "I would like to see every aspect of Black human life in the world on the screen. But that is only going to happen if people write it and market it.

"I think that *Waiting to Exhale* did a lot in that it sold," she adds.

A Question of Economics

Talk to directors, actors, and film executives about the reasons for this love drought and, as always, when the subject of Black film comes up, you will be presented with catch-22s. The spiel starts something like this: Yes, Queen Latifah and everybody else, scripts with Black romance are being written. But few if any Blacks in Hollywood are in a position to green-light a film, and Hollywood will only invest in Black films that White executives believe are sure moneymakers.

In recent years, the biggest Black films have either been urban (ghetto) dramas or urban (ghetto) comedies. Director John Singleton's first film, *Boyz n the Hood,* grossed $57.8 million domestically and was nominated for an Academy Award. His next effort, *Poetic Justice,* was—though thematically scattered—sort of a love story, starring Janet Jackson and Tupac Shakur. But it grossed $27.5 million and was picked at by critics.

"The question becomes, 'Am I going to risk something on an unproven quantity?'" says Doug McHenry, director of the love story *Jason's Lyric* and producer of such films as *New Jack City* and *A Thin Line.* "These are the type of calculations that filmmakers go through because we are being pressured."

"Because we are not entrenched in decision-making positions at the corporate level, we have to work even harder and be rejected even more," says actor Roger Guenveur Smith, who had his first and only film love interest in Spike Lee's *Get on the Bus.*

"And a lot of that has to do with the cyclical nature of the business," Smith adds. "A Western or a silly comedy will do well, and then every studio has to do a Western or a silly comedy. For a while, there were five or six Black Panther projects floating around, but because *Panther* did not do well, all of those projects were squashed."

But the issue of Black romance in film gets even more complex. If anyone is going to take a risk on a film, they are less likely to take such risks on Black films, which are considered appealing to a niche market. McHenry estimates that there is perhaps a core audience of six to seven million people—primarily age fourteen to twenty-five—for such films. In contrast, there is an estimated audience of between forty to fifty million for each "general audience" film. While African-Americans support general audience films—comprising up to 25 percent of moviegoers—White people generally do not support Black films in the theater.

Smith thinks that expanding the currently limited marketing strategies for Black films could improve the chances of success for Black romances. He points to the success of independent films of the past season such as *Fargo,* which earned a respectable box office draw and was allowed to slowly build a following. The movie that ushered in the new wave of Black film, Spike Lee's independently produced *She's Gotta Have It,* utilized an alternative release strategy with some success. The film, which followed a young Black woman, Nola Darling, and her love affairs with three men, was arguably the first American film to treat lovemaking between Black actors and the naked Black body in an artistic fashion.

"*She's Gotta Have It* didn't necessarily depend on the big opening weekend," Smith says. "And as it stands now, if films don't do big business on the first weekend, then they disappear."

On-Screen Sexuality

Yet the lack of Black romances cannot be dismissed as merely an understandable corporate prerogative. To accept that reasoning would require ignoring Hollywood's extreme avoidance of Black sexuality and its continual promotion of European standards of beauty as the romantic film ideal.

Half of the equation for a film romance, for example, requires a beautiful heroine. In the Hollywood version, the role is filled by White women—Meg Ryan, or Julia Roberts. They offer accepted models of sincerity and vulnerability. When Ryan gets that wide-eyed, glassy look in her eyes, she's the all-American daughter or sister wrestling with emotions and mating.

But no such sympathies or romantic sensibilities are developed for most Black women on the screen. Up into the 1960s, the most common role for a Black woman was that of a maid devoted to the care of Whites. In the 1950s, the first television show to star a Black woman, *Beulah,* featured a large, bandanna-wearing actress, Louise Beavers. She declared herself in one episode to be so busy as a domestic that she wasn't "in the marketplace for a husband." The film image of the asexual Black woman has carried down to the present day in the person of Hollywood's highest paid Black actress—Whoopi Goldberg—who has played mammy roles (*Clara's Heart, Corinna, Corinna, The Long Walk Home*) or played one of the guys. The one semi-romance Goldberg is most easily remembered for, *Made in America,* was opposite a White man, Ted Danson. Similarly, when Primestar, the satellite television service, polled Americans last year, singer Whitney Houston—who appeared opposite White actor Kevin Costner in the blockbuster hit *The Bodyguard*—was the only Black actress cited as a favorite romantic heroine.

During the last three decades of film, the most consistent image of Black sexuality shown on television and film has been that of a Black prostitute. In '70s blaxploitation flicks such as *The Mack* or in seemingly innocuous television shows like *Starksy and Hutch,* the Black hooker was marked by, along with her hot pants, high heels, and rabbit-fur jacket, all of America's sick mythology about the loose sexuality—and availability to White men—of Black women. Today's hooker images are sometimes more subtle. Even in the love relationship between actors Will Smith and Vivica A. Fox in *Independence Day,* the Black woman worked as a stripper.

"Black women and White women have totally different sexualized histories in America—two totally different paths," says Bridgett M. Davis, director of an independently produced film, *Naked Acts,* that focuses on a young Black woman's quest to love her body. "What is the effect on Black women whose sense of their bodies has been based on them being placed on an auction block, stripped down to their waist, being raped, and then being told that they asked for it? That's a heavy history, and how do you climb out of that?"

Singer Toni Braxton, who is creating a stir with her nearly nude pose on the cover of *VIBE* magazine, told the publication there is a double standard for exposure and idealization of Black vs. White bodies. "If an artist like Madonna is wearing her booty hanging out, she's considered a genius. But if a Black person does it, we're considered skank whores or sluts," she said.

On the male side, the historical racial stereotype of the Black buck seems to translate easily. Black actors like Wesley Snipes and Laurence Fishburne have been able to slip into lead roles in action dramas such as the current *Murder at 1600 Pennsylvania* (starring Snipes). While twenty years ago Hollywood wasn't ready to accept Billy Dee Williams as sort of a Black Cary Grant, Fishburne has played very sexual roles opposite Ellen Barkin in *Bad Company* and opposite Irene Jacob in *Othello.* In contrast, the sex in *The Bodyguard,* between Houston and Costner, was only hinted at with the hokey symbolism of his erect sword cutting her sheer scarf. When Vanessa Williams played opposite Arnold Schwarzenegger in *Eraser,* no hint of any sexual attraction was allowed between them.

Even the best of the vintage Black romances, *Nothing but a Man, A Warm December,* and *Claudine,* avoid sex scenes, as if the lovers might burn a hole in the celluloid. The notable exception to this, of course, is *Jason's Lyric,* starring Jada Pinkett and Allen Payne. In fact, the film was considered so hot that the movie ratings system initially threatened to slap it with a NC-17 rating. Director McHenry protested, saying that the ratings board was unaccustomed to seeing Black lovers on the screen, and that acts that were no more risqué than what had appeared in other films were considered "pornographic" because the bodies involved were Black. He eventually shaved some footage to get an R-rating, yet some critics still described the film's sex scenes as "raw" and "graphic."

"If you have two Black people making love, somehow that's steamier than other people," McHenry said at the time. Motion Picture Association of America President Jack Valenti denied his group was racist and accused McHenry of milking the press to promote his film. McHenry countered that the MPAA was picking on his film as a way of proving that it was doing its job.

Plastic America

Movies such as *Jason's Lyric* are often the efforts of emerging Black directors. For many of these filmmakers, it has been a mission to portray on film the romantic and intimate relationships they have witnessed or experienced in real life.

"*Love Jones* was something that, if we pulled it off, would be something we hadn't seen before," says Witcher of the film's depiction of romance among young, urban creative Blacks. In Cundieff's *Sprung,* there is a startling moment that offers a self-reflexive comment on both the rarity of this type of film and the state of Hollywood's Black films in general. Two lovers are in the park. He tells her his dream, to one day make a movie with friends and lovers who sit around and talk.

"Is it a Black film?" she asks.

"It's Black."

"There are no gangsters? No drugs? Nobody getting shot?"

"None of that."

"Humph. You ain't gonna make no money."

He differs.

"It's a love story," he says. "And everyone loves a love story."

The new wave of Black directors has not always been successful in its attempts to depict romance. Independent film critic Jacquie Jones, for example, has been critical of how Black women have been portrayed in the new crop of films. Despite its marketing strategy, *Love Jones* is less a love story than a story about the difficulties of connecting in the '90s. *Sprung* sets up a disquieting comparison between the more genuine love of its light-skinned stars (Tisha Campbell and Cundieff) and the tawdry attraction between its dark-skinned supporting actors (Joe Torry and Paula Jai Parker).

A major roadblock for Black romances is that such films typically must be star driven. Of the two leading star contenders, Denzel Washington has expressed no interest in sexual scenes, and Whitney Houston—who comes off as stiff and artificial as a Black Barbie on-screen—has not yet developed the acting muscle to be a romantic heroine who elicits our sympathies. The two of them, starring in *The Preacher's Wife,* were supposed to produce a romantic blockbuster. Instead, the chemistry between them was flat.

But in the hands of new directors and producers, Hollywood may creep closer to depicting actual Black love on the screen. Think of all the baby steps. For example, in *Waiting to Exhale,* a full-figured Black woman walked away with the happiest ending of all. Though just a subplot in *Jerry Maguire,* Cuba Gooding Jr. and Regina King gave one of the more realistic portrayals of a young Black couple in recent film history. And in *Sprung,* Campbell actually gets to play a pretty ingenue with normal drives for life, love, and sex.

"It was a mandate and agenda to include tenderness between Black men and women in my film because it's so rarely seen," says *Naked Acts* director Davis. "I think that it speaks to the whole of my creative effort, which is to reveal Black folks' humanity in whatever guise."

Directors who have such an agenda believe that these images have a powerful impact.

"We swim in a sea of culture," says McHenry. "And that sea alters our expectations and how we treat each other."

"In all of this, we have not yet gotten to the point where we can celebrate our sexuality and beauty," says Davis. "I don't think that most White women know that even to be [angry] about objectification is itself a certain luxury. It suggests a certain history. I feel like, 'Objectify me. Make me the objective standard of beauty.'

"We all want to see our lives reflected on the screen," she adds. "The heart of our lives really is our sexuality. It cuts to the core of who we are as human beings."

Black Star–Will Smith in *Men in Black*

July 2, 1997

As part of the *Men in Black* duo, who routinely search New York City for aliens, Agent J (Will Smith) tries to thwart a bigger alien plan to destroy planet Earth. Big fun and funny summer action flick with amazing special effects.

Black Star–Samuel L. Jackson in *187*

July 30, 1997

In this very Hollywood rendering of the inner city, Jackson stars as Trevor Garfield, a high school teacher who, after being brutally beaten by a student in New York City, relocates to Los Angeles. There, he steps into another violent scene, this time with members of a street gang.

Black Star–Laurence Fishburne in *Event Horizon*

August 15, 1997

In the year 2047, Fishburne is captain of a rescue crew sent to salvage a spaceship, the *Event Horizon*, which has recently reappeared after disappearing into a Black hole seven years before.

Hoodlum
August 27, 1997

The story of the lucrative numbers racket in 1930s Harlem is rendered as a nationalist struggle when gangster Bumpy Johnson is played by Laurence Fishburne and the chief Black numbers runner, Stephanie St. Clair, is played by the venerable Cicely Tyson. Together they face the notorious Dutch Schultz (Tim Roth), who wants profits from the street lottery all to himself.

Black Star–Wesley Snipes in *One Night Stand*
August 31, 1997

Snipes in a ho-hum interracial love tryst.

Interview–Ice-T
September 14, 1997

Ice-T is such a hustler.

At this moment, he is in the Burbank, California, studio where his new NBC drama, *Players,* is being shot. Wearing a magenta shirt, with leopard-print vest and shoes, he looks like an MTV pimp. His trademark fedora, with an upturned brim, is pulled down to within an inch of his thick brows and hazel eyes. Hustler is his clothes, which just happen to be his on-camera wardrobe. Hustler is his sly expression and hair slicked back into a ponytail. Hustler is his nonstop-motion body language. To be honest, this rapper-rocker-actor-author-peep-show-host is more of a hustler than anything else. Right?

"For life. Full blown. When I got up from the rap game, I had three pagers," he says in a low whisper, as the taping goes on in the next room. "I was in the streets. I was making money. I would hook up with these rappers and they were like, 'We're going into the studio, we're going to get blunted and kick back.' And I was like, 'I don't get high.'

"'Let's go get drunk.'

"'I don't drink.'

"I said: 'Let's go get this MONEY, man.'

"And I always counted my money, who had my money," he says. "I always checked my people. Double-checked. Made five phone calls about a hundred dollars:

"'Wheremyhundreddollarsat?'

"A lot of rappers got caught out there—oh, he's making the money. He's cool—but people are ripping them off hundreds of thousands of dollars. Now they're broke. My thing is, I got my [expletive] on so many different levels, you can't count my money. You can't comprehend it—he made a rap record, then he made a rock record, he made a couple of movies, then he got a TV show, he's got [stuff] he's doing in Brazil, he's got a book. . . . I'm not here because I particularly love acting.

"It's a hustle."

It may indeed be a hustle but it's not the illegal type—robberies, break-ins, credit card schemes, and prostitution—that Ice and his homeys back in South-Central Los Angeles would scheme.

He means he's getting paid.

He's getting action.

He's also getting a role—that of Isaac "Ice" Gregory—that fits him just fine, fits him to a T. The TV Ice is one in a trio of prison felons, along with Alphonse Royo (Costas Mandylor) and Charlie O'Bannon (Frank John Hughes), who have been paroled in the service of crime fighting. In the pilot episode, Ice wears his goateed I-don't-play-that face. He takes the menacing fringe types he's played in films like *New Jack City* and *Trespass,* loses some bleakness, and adds a little felon humor. ("You don't miss watching *Soul Train* with two hundred inmates?" he asks one of his partners.) This is Ice-T Lite.

The lightening of Ice's usual heavy brooding is not what he envisioned when he developed the idea. In his original version, which he thought would be a perfect HBO movie, the trio of felons were not connected to the police at all. They took the law into their own hands, stalking down and sometimes offing fiends selling children, selling drugs.

"They would take them out by any means necessary," Ice says in his trailer on the set. "They kept money [they confiscated] to operate on. They themselves were being chased by the cops and they had a parole officer that kept them one step ahead of the police.

"Too hard for television," he sighs.

But the stars of *Players* are still felons. Though they do good, they come from the other side of the law. The heroes aren't straight-up cops.

After all, this is a world envisioned by a rapper-rocker who turned the establishment upside down a few years ago with the track *Cop Killer,* which encouraged the killing of brutal police.

His sentiment against bad cops hasn't changed much since that episode of his career, during which he drew the wrath of police forces and the likes of Dan

Quayle and Charlton Heston. As he wrote in his book *The Ice Opinion,* published last year: “Cops don’t walk up to people in the ghetto, especially members of the Los Angeles Police Department, and say, ‘Hi, how are you doing?’”

So it only figures that Ice-T has developed his own ideas about law enforcement, the enforcement of justice, and the definition of justice.

“I had this idea for *Players* for a few years,” he says. “I had it ever since *New Jack City* because they told me then that the only way you can fight bad guys is to be a cop. And I’m, like, what if a criminal wanted to stop something bad? He’d probably be better at it than a cop. And that’s when my brain started working.

“I’m not a cop and I don’t necessarily feel you have to be a policeman to right wrong,” he says. “I think there are a lot of human beings out there in the world who have problems with crime and would like to stop it.

“I just like playing bad guys,” he says. “I think with playing good guys, the tendency is to be corny. I haven’t really met any straight-square people that I found extremely interesting.”

But really, now. Playing a straight-up cop—not like the edgy cop he played in *New Jack City*—really wouldn’t fit him. Wouldn’t fit his hustle of being an authentic thug-gone-Hollywood. Would it?

Adhering to the street credo, Those who say don’t know, and those who know don’t say, he doesn’t get too specific about his criminal past. “Let’s put it this way,” he says. “I did the whole scope of crimes, from armed robbery to kidnapping for ransom. Hard-core [expletive].” But he says he never killed anyone. He says he doesn’t want to sound as though he’s glorifying criminal behavior or waving it like a flag of true ghettoness. But his past, including some gang connections, is stamped on him. Just as a good breast job is the branding mark of the latest would-be starlet, his street allure is a brand that markets him in this industry searching for what translates as real on the screen.

“He’s extremely charismatic on screen,” says Dick Wolf, executive producer of *Players* and the creator and executive producer behind the hit shows *Law & Order* and *New York Undercover.* “It’s charisma. It’s something that is larger than life and instantly accessible.”

This certain something is what Ice’s friends recognized when they told him to take a chance at a legit hustle. “Go with it, man,” Ice says they told him. “White people like you.”

This was back in the early ’80s, when Ice got the chance to appear in the film *Breakin’*. Ten years later, he was one of the first rap stars—after Will Smith, the

"Fresh Prince"—to parlay his name recognition and aura of street authenticity to the screen. Since then, artists like Ice Cube and Queen Latifah have made the same leap. They've proved that, while it is next to impossible for established screen personalities—Eddie Murphy, Bruce Willis, John Tesh—to be taken seriously as musicians, African-American rappers and singers like Whitney Houston or Janet Jackson have been able to move in the opposite direction to the big screen. This is partly due to how cheesily Black films and TV shows are treated, marketed to an audience assumed to be more concerned with big names than big art. And maybe it's because each big-name rapper is accepted first of all as a distinct charismatic personality, a symbol, made up of a particular face, voice, and aura. And that persona, as long as it keeps its charisma, can translate through film, TV, popular books, fashion runways—all the way stations of modern celebrity.

It was actually through guest appearances as a hardened criminal on *New York Undercover* that Ice first caught Wolf's eye. After viewing dailies from the first day of shooting, Wolf was so taken with Ice's screen presence that he decided Ice's character would not be killed off as soon as planned. So months later, when Ice wanted to pitch his idea, Wolf, who is a big honcho out here, actually took a meeting with him.

Like rap lyrics, the images that African-Americans sell can prove controversial. Ice-T caught flak from a largely White pro-police faction for *Cop Killer,* which included the chorus "Die pigs, die." But he has also incurred the wrath of Blacks objecting to his misogynist depiction of Black women, his glorification of a small criminal class, and his claim to be an angry spokesman of the people. The contrarian pundit Stanley Crouch has compared Ice-T and other gangsta rappers to Zip Coon, a crazy, razor-toting urban character in old minstrels.

Maybe old Zippy was a hustler in his own way, too—sticking up old ladies and threatening White people. Hustlers are about the money. On the one hand they present an appealing picture of success. Ice lives in an expansive house in the Hollywood Hills with his girlfriend of several years, Darlene Ortiz, and their son, Ice Jr. He says they live a married life but that he doesn't believe in the contractual institution of marriage. (But probably not many married men would parade their wives near-naked on an album cover as he has.)

As a naked rags-to-riches tale, Ice-T's story works. There is an up-and-coming rap group called the Comrades who say:

I'm out to make unsurmountable amounts of cheese [money].
I won't stop 'til I get a house next to Ice-T's.

"Once I drove a Benz, I never wanted no low-rider anymore," Ice says. "White people come over my crib and say this is nice, like I'm not supposed to know how to even decorate my [expletive]. They're like, 'Why you do live here?' I say, 'Do you think Black people want to live in the ghetto?' I mean, the ghetto is not a Black neighborhood, it's a poor neighborhood. If I lived in the hood and I had some money, niggas would rob me and they would move out of the hood."

Money rules the hustler and the hustler will cross a lot of lines to get it.

Take, for example, *Ice-T's Extreme Babes,* a national cable show he hosts featuring naked women. As photos and videos of the women are shown, he comments. "This is Tasha, she's from Chicago." Men phone in and vote for the most extreme babe. Winners move on to the finals.

"It's cool," he explains. "It's kind of like a—um—beauty contest. You call from your house. It's a free call, though. It's something to do. Luke [Luther Campbell of 2 Live Crew infamy] does *Luke's Peep Show.* My thing is classier. It's cool. It's something to do. It's pay-per-view and I make money."

Hustlers stay on top of their game and they can change quick as lightning. Ice enjoys watching the grips on the set, how quickly they change lights, move a desk, whatever. They are the real hustlers here, he thinks. After Ice-T peaked as a rapper (his album released last year, *VI: Return of the Real,* sold only 84,000, according to SoundScan), he moved into rock with his group, Body Count. It was a bit much for his remaining rap fans. He would be at shows rapping with his black stocking cap on, then whip it off for the rock segment and start swinging his straight hair around like Axl Rose.

"I've been doing rap for fourteen years and this is my sixth album," he says. "So when people compare me to, say, Biggie Smalls, I say, yo, that's Biggie's second record. Twelve years from now, I don't know if you'll want to hear it. I feel like John McEnroe, who's won Wimbledon. I've been on the cover of every rap magazine ten times. I've done tours around the world so I can step off and let Nas and the new guys come in. I gracefully exit. I'm not mentally bent on still being the best rapper. But I always make rap records because I enjoy it.

"And who knows?" he adds wistfully. "I could put out a hit record next year. And it could blow up. Music could go through a cycle like, 'We're ready to hear some new Ice [expletive].'

"Blam. I could be the [expletive]. You never can tell."

Hustlers also know the rules of the hustle. He may not be able to do the part he'd originally conceived in *Players.* But that's okay. The number-one rule out here is that if someone else is paying for it, you do what they say. Just as he is starting his own rap label, he wants to maybe do an independent film that he will control.

He is playing the game. Every year, he tries to tighten his hustle—return all phone calls, get up early, make the moves, run. He gives his age as thirty-eight. He never thought he'd be on the Universal Studios tour. Trams filled with gawking tourists slow down near his trailer. He hears the guide say something like: "In this trailer is Ice-T shooting the new drama. . . ." He's hustling what he has: Charisma? Charm? Talent? Flava?

"You know what it is?" he says. "I don't think it's even the flavor. It just made money. Don't even reach for art. This is not an artistic game. It's money. If I walked on there [on the set], they might ask, 'What did he do?' You and I might call it flavor. But they're like, 'Damn, people like it. Let's get more of it.'"

Soul Food

September 26, 1997

The ensemble, which includes Vanessa L. Williams, Vivica A. Fox, Nia Long, and Mekhi Phifer, delivers part of the richness promised by any production that takes *Soul Food* for a name. In the story, Big Mama's children are challenged to keep family unity after she is hospitalized due to diabetes. Much of the story is told through her grandson Ahmad, played by the adorable Brandon Hammond. Some of the action feels stilted and unreal and the script takes special aim at the daughter who is a lawyer, Teri (Williams), stereotypically casting her as a bitch.

Gang Related

October 8, 1997

Released more than a year after Tupac Shakur's murder, *Gang Related* is a middle-tier rogue cop drama starring James Belushi with Shakur as his young partner. It seems more of a vehicle for Belushi to try and create a film presence for himself and another attempt to exploit the tired buddy cop mold for a younger audience. It might be notable for a rare romance between a White man (Belushi) and Black woman (Lela Rochon), but any possibility that the relationship could be treated with quality is overshadowed by the fake-gritty drama and the casting of Rochon as a stripper.

9

History and Mystery

Et Cetera—Late-Night Wannabes

October 9, 1997

It has never been easy being Black in Hollywood.

Since the *Keenen Ivory Wayans Show* and *Vibe* debuted August 4, and with a show hosted by Earvin "Magic" Johnson expected next year, there's been a growing struggle. The stakes and the prize: the younger, hipper, and certainly Blacker late-night audience left homeless when Arsenio Hall's show went off the air in 1994.

Producers guard their guest lists. The tape of Johnson's pilot show is under lock and key. Hip-hop artists such as the Lost Boyz and Puff Daddy bounce like ping-pong balls between *Keenen* and *Vibe,* the latter hosted by Chris Spencer. The wisdom here is that all three shows won't survive.

National ratings for *Vibe* and *Keenen* aren't great (both have dipped well below 2.0, roughly equivalent to two million households). But they are faring much better in urban areas with a high percentage of African-Americans.

On the other hand, though they might look Blacker and sound Blacker than *The Tonight Show with Jay Leno* or *Late Show with David Letterman,* these two distance themselves from being designated as "Black." And they make obvious forays into Whiteness in hopes of boosting ratings among the eighteen- to thirty-four-year-olds who are coveted by advertisers. Like Wayans's last television project, *In Living Color,* and *VIBE* magazine, on which the eponymous show is based, the programs appeal to young Whites as well.

With interracial or predominantly White audience members pumping their fists for such performers as rappers Bone Thugs-N-Harmony, the shows have offered an image of integration, an image of one nation under a groove that defies this country's cultural segregation. In a sort of reverse forced busing, *Vibe*'s first guests were President Clinton on video and, in person, actor Anthony Edwards from *ER.* Compare them with the guests on *Late Night with Conan O'Brien,* and it just goes to show that, while these shows avoid being too Black, you can never be too White.

"Black culture is a highly commodifiable thing. It can call up certain viewers," says Herman Gray, author of *Watching Race: Television and the Struggle for Blackness.* "These shows have the strategy of using Black popular culture to go after that late-night viewership. They're playing with who's left after *Late Night, Leno, Politically Incorrect, Charlie Rose,* and *Nightline.* Think about who is left. It's not unlike what's going on with UPN, WB, and Fox."

Both of these late-night shows take pages from *Arsenio, Oprah, Def Comedy Jam, In Living Color,* and music videos—and warm them over. Kind of like yet another way to fix chicken. To dig in, you click the remote. You tune in.

Out here, if you want to find the recipe, the kitchen secrets, you visit studios and offices. You search for late-night soul.

Toil and Trouble

All over Los Angeles, Keenen Ivory Wayans's head—a trendy baldy, urgent eyes, smiling, just shy of handsome—appears on billboards. In the back lot of Fox Studios, his name is repeated on a tiny sign swinging on Building 9.

Inside, the bustle of primarily White young staffers gives no hint that the show has been in turmoil, with firings and resignations almost from the start.

During this week in September, Charlie Parsons, an executive producer known back in London for creating cutting-edge shows, will depart. The official line is that Parsons intended to leave all along, once the show got up and running. But studio insiders say that Parsons and Wayans clashed, just as Wayans has clashed with other producers. The result, insiders say, is that the collective energy required to produce a nightly one-hour show has been thwarted. But despite the turmoil, Wayans's ratings have consistently been higher than those for *Vibe.*

It is minutes before the four-thirty taping of Wayans's show. The audience is in place. Names of that night's guests—Brian Austin Green, Carl Lewis, T'Keyah "Crystal" Keymah, and the Lost Boyz—appear on a makeshift movie theater–style marquee. The backlit yellow and lavender fiberglass walls of the set look either cheesy or very hip, depending on your taste. The entire front row of the audience is occupied by women of various ethnicities who look like they stepped out of music videos: slim, skimpy outfits, bare shoulders, and long hair of varied textures and colors—blond, a red dye job going brown at the roots, braids, straight, curly.

"It's important that you're animated when he's out here," a man in wire-frame glasses tells them. "Not like now, with everyone sitting with their legs crossed!"

A standing crowd has been positioned by the door where Wayans will enter. The announcer announces. The all-female band, which never seems to play a complete song, strikes up the show's rock theme music and—whoosh!—here comes Wayans, running, giving highfives. Everyone is on his feet, clapping, yelling.

His wardrobe has calmed down. No more clothes like the pants and shirt he wore at the premiere, clothes that looked as if they were cut from a sheet of black plastic. He reaches the stage and basks in the noise. He is a symphony of browns. From his leather jacket to his hightop boots, he is a picture of overstated understatement.

He goes into his monologue—relationship and woman stuff. "Just give me the cheeseburger," he says, describing the modest order of a woman out on a first date, compared with a year later when she always orders lobster. He does a bit about women being bad tippers in restaurants. He rolls his eyes, playing the role of some imaginary Sapphire: "I'll give her a tip," he says. "My beautician's phone number."

Everybody laughs. Wayans is at his best doing this mini-stand-up. He comes across like he's lived a little and, at thirty-nine, is old enough to be knowledgeably risqué. He has less success as an interviewer. Instead of engaging in conversation with Carl Lewis, Wayans airs a lame segment taped earlier of Lewis racing around the exterior of the studio. Then we get to watch, in slow motion, a close-up of his athletic butt.

The Talking Game

"It doesn't matter who the host is, the color of the skin anyway," says Chris Spencer, a stand-up comedian and host of *Vibe*. "Bryant Gumbel was on *Today* all those years. Was that a Black show or a White show? Is Jerry Springer a White show or a Black show? I'm just a Black bus driver with a whole lot of people on board going to the promised land."

Spencer has said that *Vibe* would be so inclusive that it would have everyone from "the Wu Tang Clan to the Ku Klux Klan."

Just now, Spencer is arguing with the show's producers about sex. Tonight's show will feature a clip from TV's *Hercules: The Legendary Journeys,* in which star

Kevin Sorbo easily gets a woman to take her clothes off, and Spencer has to come up with the right line to joke about Sorbo's on-screen mack-daddy proficiency.

But Spencer doesn't want to ask yet another guest about his love life.

"That's the one I'm running from," he says. "It seems like I'm only asking that. Everybody who's pretty, we ask that."

He loses the fight. After all, in the new late-night competition, the battle of the sexes rules as a topic of interest. Unlike the mainstream late-night shows, these rarely get into politics or other current events. *Keenen* and *Vibe* keep it sexy and frothy.

"The average viewer wants to hear about how Demi Moore likes to get off cleaning her ears with Q-Tips, rather than her opinion on what happened with the paparazzi and Lady Di," says a producer who prefers to remain nameless. "They've already watched the late news. They're laying in bed and they really want to hear something really stupid. In fact, producers prod the guests into coming up with the silliest, the most ridiculous, the most fluffy anecdotes that they can."

Spencer, at twenty-nine, is quick-witted but doesn't have a street edge. He's not a pretty boy. He grew up in the middle-class enclave of Inglewood in Los Angeles and graduated from UCLA.

Along with Wayans's brother Shawn, and another comedian, Suli McCullough, he has authored *150 Ways To Tell If You're Ghetto,* a joke book similar to others using the popular conceit, except that it focuses more on a presumed ghetto pathology than humorous resourcefulness. ("You know you're ghetto if you have the numbers to several prisons on speed dial.")

A lot of viewers think Spencer looks like he's trying too hard. Maybe he feels he has to. Unlike competing late-night hosts, he doesn't get his name in the show's title.

"I grind myself into the ground trying to perfect the next show," he says in his dressing room. "You're always thinking about doing a better show the next day. It's just like playing ball. Some days, you might hit three free throws in a row, the next day, you might make six or seven."

He pads around in socks and massage slippers. He's thinner and more athletic than he appears on camera.

"Everybody's a critic," he says. He has heard the assessments that he seems nervous, unfocused, and overly reliant on cue cards. Even some guy he saw in the park said to him, "You gotta just relax and talk to the people on the show like you talk to us in the park."

He adds sarcastically: "Everybody has had a talk show before, so everybody knows how to host."

The Color Line

While we enter the worlds of *Vibe* and *Keenen* through Black hosts, they are fronting for predominantly White staffs of writers and producers.

T. Sean Shannon, head writer for *Vibe,* has worked on such shows as *Leno, House of Buggin',* and *In Living Color.* He doesn't think it's a stretch for him to write for a show whose core audience is African-American.

"I don't think it's a different part of my brain," he says in his offices housed in a trailer on the production lot. "You can make references that you wouldn't on *The Tonight Show.* Chances are, if I mention Lil' Kim, the Notorious B.I.G., or the Wu Tang Clan, our audience will know who that is. I wouldn't necessarily call our show a Black show or call *Keenen* a Black show, but I would say that they have a Black point of view."

Producers want it both ways. They want the ultimate crossover Black talk-show host, the equivalent of a Mariah Carey or Michael Jackson. Producers want to draw a core Black following, then go as "broad" as possible. Or, as the rules of crossover dictate, the only African-American culture shown has to also be palatable to Whites.

Producers who preach the host-as-god dogma will also claim that there are a few guests—Madonna, Jim Carrey, maybe Robin Williams, maybe Demi Moore, maybe Sylvester Stallone—who will get you a spike in the ratings. Maybe that's the case on *Leno* or *Letterman,* but none of these mega-guests are Black, and their appearance as guests in the early episodes of *Vibe* and *Keenen* did not boost ratings, causing much surprise among the producers. Then again, the list of the ten most-viewed television shows among African-Americans—topped by *Living Single,* which Fox nevertheless nearly didn't renew for the fall—is almost totally different from the ten most-viewed list among Whites. Only on late-night shows catering to African-Americans do producers want to pretend that the lists are the same.

Magic Moments

Talk to the executives and producers of Johnson's *The Magic Hour* at Fox's executive offices in Century City, and it's obvious they believe they literally have some magic in hand—the ultimate crossover man—despite the fact that Johnson is not a comedian like his late-night peers.

"What we see with Magic is not only someone who has an unbelievable amount of credibility with that constituency [African-Americans] but also someone who we believe can cross over like no one in late-night television," says Rick Jacobson, president and CEO of Twentieth Television, which is developing the show. "If you don't get big ratings, you can't generate the revenue to support production of the program. So it's important to be broad-based. But you always start out with a core audience."

Johnson's longtime associate and the show's executive producer, Lon Rosen, sits across the table and dismisses any idea that Johnson might distance himself from his own culture in the quest for higher ratings. After all, Rosen reminds, this is the man who is investing in the construction of movie theaters in Black communities where few exist.

"Earvin, by no means, wants to be a sellout," Rosen says. "That's one of the words he's always . . . He doesn't want to be in a situation where we're telling him, 'We want you to be Jay Leno.'"

Crowded Playing Field

In the new world of talk-show TV, there are not only more late-night programs, there are more shows in general beckoning to celebrities to come and chat. They start early with *Today, Good Morning America,* and *Live with Regis and Kathie Lee.* Afternoons, in many markets, bring *Oprah, Rosie O'Donnell,* and, soon, Roseanne and Howie Mandel. Shows like *Entertainment Tonight* and *Access Hollywood* take over in the evening. It would seem that the world has become more varied. Or maybe it is just the same world, only fatter than when Johnny Carson was king.

"Everyone is trying to come up with the natural successor to Arsenio because he was true to who he was and the kind of entertainment his audience expected him to deliver," says Ken Smikle, president of Target Market News, a Chicago-based market research firm specializing in African-American media and marketing. "The more formulaic your decisions become, the less appealing the program becomes. You have to know what you stand for or else you can't challenge yourself, surprise your audience, or do the other things needed to become a winner. What would have happened to *American Bandstand* if a group like the Wu Tang Clan had showed up? All 'crossover' means is that you keep the same package and try to deliver it to more people. Shows do not cross over. Audiences cross over. Artists don't cross over. Audiences cross over."

Many people observing and working on the shows say that any one of them could easily survive despite its flaws. But since there is a battle for survival right now, let's hope that when the dust clears, the "winner" isn't just another clone of what already exists, that it doesn't only slouch toward *The Tonight Show* to be born.

Black Star–Keenen Ivory Wayans in *Most Wanted*

October 10, 1997

Wayans writes, produces, and stars in his own movie vehicle to expand into the action-hero genre. It doesn't work.

Jackie Brown

December 25, 1997

Director Quentin Tarantino creates a vehicle and ode to actress Pam Grier in this crime thriller that stars Grier and Samuel L. Jackson. Grier is Jackie Brown, a flight attendant who has been smuggling cash for an arms dealer, Ordell Robbie. But the feds are onto her and she must devise some scheme to survive both her boss and the cops. There are lots of twists and turns in the stylish production, which is propelled forward by our desire to see how things work out for Jackie (as in Foxy) Brown.

Black Star–Denzel Washington in *Fallen*

January 16, 1998

In this supernatural thriller, a demon has the power to turn humans into murderers with a single touch—a tough case to crack for Detective John Hobbes (Washington). This is a crazy movie but it keeps your attention until the twisted end.

Ruby Bridges

January 17, 1998

It would have been easy for Walt Disney to make a hackneyed mess out of *Ruby Bridges,* a two-hour movie premiering on ABC about a little girl who integrated a New Orleans elementary school in 1960. After all, how many movies allegedly about the heroism of Black people (*Mississippi Burning*) have been turned instead into stories about White heroes? How many others (*A Time to Kill*) have turned dramatic racial conflict into a mélange of clichés and cardboard characters?

But this movie doesn't make these mistakes. It is a bit brightly lit, looking at moments as if they might burst into animation. Some scenes, like one at the neighborhood church, look too stagy. But otherwise it is fine. Don't be afraid to watch it.

It works and it grows on you because it never wavers in its focus on little Ruby and her world. Her best friend, Jill, begins going to Catholic school and announces that, according to her father at least, this school makes her better than public school kids. Ruby slyly outreasons her pal, saying that no, *her* new school must be better because she has a teacher, a classroom, and, indeed, the whole school to herself. Therefore, her public school—which is being boycotted by Whites—must be the real private school.

Moments like this keep the movie fresh under the direction of Euzhan Palcy (*Sugar Cane Alley* and *A Dry White Season*). Ruby's parents, Abon and Lucielle Bridges, played well by Michael Beach and Lela Rochon, aren't hat-holding grateful to have their child walk the gauntlet of screaming and spitting racists every day. Abon, a Korean War veteran, is especially suspicious of the merits of integration. "I was in the army," he tells Lucielle. "I know about integration. I know all about it. It doesn't work."

He is also cautious about the educated, light-skinned professionals from the NAACP preaching to him about what a "privilege" it is for Ruby to be in the position she is. "How many of y'all put y'all six-year-olds up to this here privilege?" he asks them. His views are balanced by Lucielle, who wants Ruby to see in the lives of the NAACP people what a good education can bring in life. She wants her daughter to see a nice house without being hired to clean it. The focus on Ruby is made complete through a peek at her sessions with a white psychiatrist who finds that Ruby does not fit the expected mental profile of a child under siege. It is through their sessions that we begin to see the impact of this time and event in history on a young child, and not on judges, lawyers, marchers, or anyone else.

The characters have enough complexity that they don't insult us—including Diana Scarwid as Ruby's teacher and Kevin Pollak as Robert Coles, the psychiatrist whose study of Ruby Bridges launched his monumental work on children in crisis that would make him a leading voice in the psychiatric world. The direction, acting, and screenplay by Toni Ann Johnson all combine to make a worthwhile snapshot of the little girl who inspired the famous Norman Rockwell painting—starched white dress, white sneakers, white bows tied to her plaits—being escorted into an elementary school by four burly White federal marshals.

Porgy and Bess: An American Voice

February 4, 1998

One thing can be said for *Porgy and Bess: An American Voice,* which airs at ten tonight on PBS. It provides an opportunity for that great American urban sport: talking back to the movie.

It's not just the opportunity to shout back at your television set: "Okay, enough with this *Porgy and Bess.* Isn't it 1998?" But more than sixty years after the debut of George Gershwin's Broadway opera—which has had several different productions and was eventually made into a movie—this two-hour documentary airs out some of its controversies. It lets Blacks speak back about a work made about them. It teaches us about how art speaks to us and how race can frame that speech.

At its very beginnings, *Porgy* was a product of a type of cultural voyeurism by Whites, an outsider's gaze. A White Southern aristocrat named DuBose Heyward, inspired by a newspaper clipping about a legless Black beggar who wheeled himself about on a cart, wrote a novella named *Porgy.* He made it into a play in 1927, and then granted permission for Gershwin to transform it into a Broadway production that would alter the conventions of the musical toward opera in 1935.

"My preoccupation with the primitive Southern Negro as a subject for art derives from the often unworthy quality of curiosity," Heyward wrote. "What, I wondered, was the characteristic in the life of these people who formed this substratum of the society that endowed them with the power to stun me unexplicably to tears and laughter. I saw the Negro as the inheritor of a source of delight that I would have given much to possess."

Gershwin, who visited Harlem clubs and spent time in Southern communities before writing *Porgy and Bess,* found inspiration in the jazz, blues, and spirituals he heard. In his head and in his music, the rich traditions of blues and gospel—art forms in their own right—were transformed into European operatic voice. The dope peddlers, gamblers, prostitutes, and other criminals of Charleston's slums would sound like Leontyne Price instead of Muddy Waters or Big Mama Thornton.

They also, of course, would be blasted as stereotypes at the time of their creation, when Blacks in Harlem and other urban centers had been experiencing an artistic and intellectual flowering—one of the critics was the father of the opera's original Bess, Anne Brown. He said: "Negroes had been pictured in the usual clichés as ignorant dope peddlers and users and criminals . . . we've had enough of that."

Despite mixed reviews, it ran 124 performances in New York, toured the West Coast, and was revived on Broadway in 1942 in a less operatic form, with much of the recitative replaced by dialogue. In the ten years after World War II, it played almost constantly. One version with William Warfield as Porgy and Price as Bess played before President Truman in Washington. The State Department, sensing an artistic weapon in the Cold War, sponsored tours of the musical in Europe—including the Soviet Union and Milan's La Scala Opera House (with the young Maya Angelou in the role of Ruby). In 1958, Miles Davis recorded the score with an orchestra directed by Gil Evans; in 1959, Samuel Goldwyn's movie production was released.

As America and relations between the races moved into the activism and militance of the 1960s, images of the production's happy-go-lucky characters would present a jarring juxtaposition to the real-world anger of writers of the Black Arts Movement such as Amiri Baraka, Nikki Giovanni, and Sonia Sanchez. Even the militant-chic of cheesy '70s blaxploitation flicks was preferred by a newer generation suspicious of any art like *Porgy and Bess,* which made servitude and ignorance look upright and heroic. In 1970, it was finally produced in Charleston, its setting, where earlier productions had been stymied by segregation. In 1985, it finally reached the Metropolitan Opera House. Productions in 1995–96 saw the opera's first African-American directors, Hope Clarke and later Tazewell Johnson.

Clearly, the issues of race, politics, art, and image aroused by the opera are still contentious ones.

By raising these issues, tonight's program allows those gazed upon to return the gaze. Many former cast members, including Diahann Carroll and Angelou, are interviewed.

Carroll, in particular, is remarkably candid in relating the conflict of being involved in the production. For so many actors and singers, the many successful stage productions and the Hollywood film were too big an opportunity to pass up. Even though Carroll, for example, had misgivings about participating or whether the film should even be made (as civil rights protesters were being jailed and killed in the South), participate she did, as did Sammy Davis Jr., Dorothy Dandridge, Sidney Poitier, and Pearl Bailey. Mary Moultrie, a labor organizer who in 1959 organized a strike of dozens of Black women fighting for equal wages and benefits with Whites, remembers the film version of the production—with its big-screen image of Dandridge as a stereotypical loose Black woman—as a slap in the face, a hindrance to the strikers' efforts to create a new dialogue with Whites.

Indirectly, tonight's show asks us to consider how art is created, how the privileged often have strong voices in that creation, how voices are raised and broadcast, even worldwide.

Just the fact that a two-hour documentary has been devoted to *Porgy and Bess* means that the debate over it has not ended, that it continues to provoke questions, criticism, and anger, to invite us to gaze and speak back at it. *An American Voice* is ultimately weakened by its failure to make this gaze, this voice, stronger. Promotional information about the program states that Harry Belafonte refused to appear in the film version, but his voice is not heard here. Neither is that of Poitier, who did appear in the film version but later said it was something he always regretted. The documentary offers a striking comparison of the content of *Porgy and Bess* to '20s Harlem Renaissance writer Claude McKay but fails to really portray the scorn directed toward the production, scorn uttered by Black writers and intellectuals like Langston Hughes.

Despite the production's longevity, there are still debates about its quality and importance. Is it just musical theater? Is it an opera? This documentary offers lots of perspectives but ultimately embraces its subject. As it erases some history along the way, it is forgiving of *Porgy and Bess.*

Black Star–Samuel L. Jackson in *Sphere*

February 13, 1998

In a sci-fi-horror thriller like this one starring Dustin Hoffman and Sharon Stone, we usually wonder how long the Black star, usually a man, will survive. He usually doesn't make it to the end, that's all I'll say. As a crew of scientists explores an alien ship and mysterious golden sphere at the bottom of the ocean, the story has its moments of intrique but is kind of a snooze.

The Wedding

February 22, 1998

Halle Berry stars in this well-written TV movie adaptation of the Dorothy West novel about a mulatto who chooses between Black and White suitors.

Black Star–Wesley Snipes in *U.S. Marshalls*

March 6, 1998

This is really a follow-up for the Tommy Lee Jones performance in *The Fugitive* when he played a U.S. Marshall in relentless pursuit of Harrison Ford. This time, he is hunting Snipes, who plays a convicted murderer with more to his story than meets the eye.

Always Outnumbered

March 21, 1998

In this likeable TV movie based on the Walter Mosley novel, Fishburne stars as an ex-con who has a profound effect on his neighbors as he seeks his own survival in a Los Angeles neighborhood.

The Player's Club

April 8, 1998

The fascination of the hip-hoperati with strip clubs gets the full dramatic treatment in *The Player's Club,* which also marks the directorial debut of rapper Ice Cube. He also stars in the movie, which tells the story of the ups and downs of one strip club through the eyes of a college coed (newcomer LisaRaye) who can't resist the easy and large money that "dancing" pays. But, of course, there is drama brewing behind those glass heels. This is a breakout role for LisaRaye, who gets to show body through the production. This film also fuels the idea that your average young stripper is actually working her way through school.

He Got Game

May 1, 1998

In this deft depiction of a complex father-son relationship, Denzel Washington stars as an ex-con temporarily freed from prison to persuade his son, the nation's number-one high school basketball recruit, to attend the governor's alma mater.

Woo

May 8, 1998

I am always on the lookout for decent depictions of Black women in this era of Black film, but *Woo* just doesn't cut it. In fact, it is one of the craziest films I have ever seen. Darlene "Woo" Bates (Jada Pinkett) is a scorned and jaded young woman intent on putting her new suitor (Tommy Davidson) through some serious paces. I'm all for a free spirit and varied depictions of who we are but, most of the time, it seems as if Woo skipped her meds.

Black Star–Halle Berry in *Bulworth*

May 15, 1998

Berry makes me cringe in her role as Nina, the around-the-way girlfriend of a White suicidal politician (Warren Beatty) who has taken out a hit on himself and decided in the meantime to totally speak his mind—usually by rapping. I think this is a very strange flick.

Black Star–Samuel L. Jackson in *The Negotiator*

July 29, 1998

In this fast-moving summer action flick, Jackson is a police negotiator accused of corruption who takes hostages himself in order to buy time to prove his innocence. F. Gary Gray (*Set It Off*) is the director.

How Stella Got Her Groove Back

August 14, 1998

I'm not totally sold on Taye Diggs as a younger leading man opposite Angela Bassett, but, all in all, this is a very likeable adaptation of Terry McMillan's novel about middle-aged Stella, who finds young love in the Caribbean. The direction by Kevin Rodney Sullivan keeps the story moving and takes advantage of the moments of poignancy and humor. And I like Whoopi Goldberg in this touching role as Stella's best friend.

Black Star–Wesley Snipes in *Blade*

August 21, 1998

In his fiercest and most memorable role to date, Wesley Snipes plays a half vampire–half mortal who is a day walker with the power to withstand sunlight. When a horde of evil vampires declares war on humans, Blade—aided by his friend Whistler (Kris Kristofferson)—is humanity's only hope.

Why Do Fools Fall in Love?

August 28, 1998

Halle Berry, Vivica A. Fox, and Lela Rochon all star in this tale about three women who claim to be the widow of singer Frankie Lymon and therefore eligible to receive some of the millions from his estate. Larenz Tate is the boyish Lymon.

10

Fight the Power

OPM—*Family Name*

September 15, 1998

Family Name, a PBS documentary, is a complex reminder that how we react to matters of race depends on who we are and where we come from.

Like Edward Ball's book *Slaves in the Family,* Macky Alston's *Family Name* tells the story of a White man's search for the connections between his family's slaveholding past and the descendants of African-Americans he suspects were once held as family property. He says it wasn't until he was a young adult, when his father—a civil rights activist—handed him a history of the family, that he learned the Alstons were one of the largest slaveholding families in North Carolina.

With that knowledge, Alston approaches the subject and search with a degree of sincerity and energy. It is not clear, however, what his point is or what this film is trying to say. It doesn't have an overarching message about race today (other than the point, perhaps, that slavery is handy grist for a debut film).

At various points in the film, Alston confronts the aimlessness of his mission, asking himself such questions as, "What am I really trying to do?" The unpretentious quality of the film, which is part of the *P. O. V.* series, turns out to be a source of both weakness and strength, depending on, again, who we are. It may be possible for some of us to identify with Alston's quest, his natural curiosity, and seeming good intentions. (*Rolling Stone* called *Family Name* a "moving, unforgettable film." Siskel and Ebert gave it "Two thumbs up, way up.") It may be possible to understand how

Alston equates the need to come out as a gay man with the need to uncover the secrets of his family's slave dealings.

Still, others might be taken aback by his naive assumptions that Blacks as a group are seething with ready anger about the past, that they'd gladly rip open badly healed sores for the sake of one White man's intellectual curiosity. He seems never to have given much thought to the facts that—wonder of wonders!—Black female slaves were actually raped by White men, that many African-Americans have skin about as light as his. Sometimes the film stops just short of those moments many African-Americans have experienced when White people approach them and say, "Both our names are Jones [or Marriott or Curry]. My family might have owned yours!" (Ha-ha.)

If you can survive Alston's lack of knowledge about the world he has chosen to explore, then keep watching. The real strength of this work rests in the actual quest. It becomes a mystery.

He comes across information about the prominent Harlem Renaissance painter Charles Alston and is immediately intrigued by the painter's light skin. He watches films the painter made for the Harmon Foundation in which he talked about his childhood, his father, his family. It is obvious from Charles Alston's work that he carried a consciousness and loathing for American racism. The interviews conducted with Charles Alston's sisters by Macky Alston and an assistant are valuable for their insights into the heyday of the Harlem Renaissance and how the women—light-skinned enough to "pass" for White if they had so chosen—survived.

Macky Alston's research, which proceeds in fits and starts, takes him repeatedly to North Carolina—to former plantations, to cemeteries overgrown with weeds, to libraries, church archives, and countless troves of public records, to the town of Pittsboro, where everything and everyone seems to be named Alston. Before the film concludes, he has found his answers.

Reactions of both Blacks and Whites to his search begin to fill in the film's meaning. A White descendant of notorious slave owner Jack Alston, or "Chatham Jack," talks about how she believes he was well liked by his slaves. Another offers as proof of this slave owner's compassion the fact that he often went about accompanied by two slave boys and used them as foot warmers in bed.

A group of Whites stands outside their church. One of them tells a story of how Chatham Jack killed a slave boy. The others react with nervous and uncomfortable laughter to the story of how the boy's ghost still haunts Chatham Jack's "big house."

Macky Alston's quest to ascertain ownership or blood relationship obviously strikes older African-Americans as odd. They sometimes explain to him patiently how the history of racial mixing during slavery is known and obvious but, at the same time, not something people sit around discussing.

"Nobody likes to say, oh, my mother was raped," offers Aida Winters, a sister of Charles Alston.

These various notes of discomfort, ambivalence, and curiosity give the film its texture. They swirl around Macky Alston's camera lens. They are a chorus saying, in effect, "Yeah. What about it? What now?"

Beloved

October 16, 1998

Based on Toni Morrison's award-winning and highly acclaimed novel, this haunting film, produced by Oprah Winfrey's Harpo Productions, tells the story of a Black woman, Sethe, who escapes slavery and is haunted by the ghost of the infant girl she murdered rather than see her returned to the plantation where murder, violence, and sexual molestation were the norm.

This film deserves more than it gets. The performances by Winfrey, LisaGay Hamilton (*The Practice*), Kimberly Elise, and Danny Glover are powerful. The recreation of the era and memory is startling. Especially moving is the open-air "church" service held in a clearing in the woods. Presided over by Baby Suggs (Beah Richards), it is one of the most powerful film scenes that I have ever seen.

Belly

November 4, 1998

As could be expected, music-video director Hype Williams has produced a film with many visually stunning moments, including, I must add, lighting of actress/singer Taral Hicks in such a way to make her appear as a deep ebony beauty who is a trophy companion. The bigger story line, however, is thin, predictable, and falls apart. It centers on two thugs (DMX and Nas) who have an attack of conscience.

Black Star–Denzel Washington in *The Siege*

November 6, 1998

The Siege approaches the subject of terrorism on American soil—no doubt reflecting on the 1993 bombing at the World Trade Center in New York City and the 1995 bombing of a federal building in Oklahoma City. In broaching the possible declaration of martial law in this country, it wanders into rare political territory for a Hollywood release. Washington is the conscience here, aware of the racial component to the drama, which involves the United States secretly abducting a suspected terrorist of Middle Eastern descent.

Black Star—Will Smith in *Enemy of the State*

November 20, 1998

The casting for this film of a young Black man (Will Smith) as Robert Clayton Dean, the young attorney who winds up in the crosshairs of a malevolent NSA official, seems perfect. It recalls the name of the hip-hop group Public Enemy sardonically meant to refer to the sociopolitical status of Black men in the United States. But while such racially specific realities are only hinted at throughout the movie, the larger meaning of the title warns about the ease, proliferation, and illegality of government surveillance in the United States—something that COINTELPRO and other such surveillance during African-American history have already taught us. During a chance encounter with an old college buddy, Dean winds up, unknowingly, with proof that an NSA official was involved in a political murder. Using everything from miniature tracking devices to satellites in space, the NSA hunts Dean, destroys his life, and even murders his friend—until he gets help fighting fire with fire. This is a riveting and sober warning about government corruption and abuse of power.

Down in the Delta

December 25, 1998

Maya Angelou's directorial debut is a comfy, innocent film that does not make any big mistakes but is not very fresh or revealing. I appreciate the story of one family attempting to heal its own wounds and solve its own problems, but much of the action and dialogue puts me to sleep.

Black Star—Laurence Fishburne in *The Matrix*

March 31, 1999

In this groundbreaking film by the Wachowski brothers, Fishburne plays Morpheus, leader of a band of human rebels who try to keep an evil computer program from destroying human life as it is known. The film is making a name for itself because of its highly stylized and tightly choregraphed fight and action scenes that combine martial arts, special effects, and a bleak futuristic tableau with human-hating killer machines. All hail, Morpheus. Fight the power, baby.

Foolish

April 9, 1999

This is at least the sixth film produced or written by the rapper Master P., who has developed a cottage industry with low-budget dramas that are publicized by word of mouth. Telling the story of Quentin, who wants to set up a comedy showcase for his brother (Eddie Griffin), *Foolish* gets a much-needed lift from Griffin's stand-up act.

Life

April 16, 1999

Eddie Murphy and Martin Lawrence are likeable in this mixed prison comedy and drama where they play the part of two lifetime inmates framed for a crime they didn't commit. The two have a genuine rapport and chemistry that shines through the uninspired production.

OPM–*Star Wars: Episode I–The Phantom Menace*

May 19, 1999

This highly anticipated first prequel to the 1980s *Star Wars* trilogy was especially notable for the high-profile character of Jar Jar Binks, a native of the planet Naboo who is loud, clumsy, annoyingly inept, and has the voice and exaggerated mannerisms of a Black caricature (among all the brave *Star Wars* heroes and fighters). In the story, the evil Trade Federation takes over Naboo, and Jedi warrior Qui-Gon Jinn and his apprentice Obi-Wan Kenobi try to save the planet. With them on their journey is the young queen Amidala, Jar Jar Binks, and the powerful Captain Panaka. Their nemesis is Darth Maul, a fearsome fighter with the light saber. Samuel L. Jackson makes a sharp, brief appearance as the Jedi knight Mace Windu.

Black Star–Will Smith in *Wild Wild West*

June 30, 1999

There is not much to say about this Western theme park movie, or Will Smith's appearance in it opposite Kevin Kline. They team up to stop the evil plan of a Southern inventor intent on assassinating the president and restarting the Civil War. Maybe the best part is Will Smith's title cut on the soundtrack.

The Wood

July 16, 1999

In songs, music videos, and film, the hip-hop generation is acknowledging marriage as a possibility in a culture dominated by images of forever single players. *The Wood,* set on the wedding day of one of three best friends, is one of the first of this generation to seriously take on an actual wedding.

We meet Mike, Slim, and Roland on the day that Roland is supposed to marry. But, three hours before the ceremony, Ro is nowhere to be seen and Mike and Slim must track him down and get the reluctant groom to the altar. It is during these three hours that Mike has a series of flashbacks to their coming of age in Inglewood, California, a Black working- and middle-class suburb of Los Angeles.

Just like the neighborhood, the experiences of the three boys straddle between hood and upwardly mobile. They go to the store to get some snacks and wind up witnessing a store robbery. On the other hand, they meditate over such mundane issues as the best breath mint to use before talking to girls, the agony of asking someone to dance, and the embarrassment of a public woody. Through the flashbacks, we get to know something about the lives of the friends and they allow the story to avoid the flaw of too little backstory that affects so many movies.

Omar Epps, Taye Diggs, and Richard T. Jones are likeable in the roles of the friends as adults, but the actors in the flashback scenes, Duane Finley, Trent Cameron, and Sean Nelson, give these scenes charm. The movie couldn't work without them. Newcomer director Rick Famuyiwa (yes, he's Black) has written and directed a young romance (produced by MTV Films) in a setting where young people are not so obsessed with survival and can concentrate on the great American teen sport of having sex. I also enjoyed the performance of Malinda Williams as the young Alicia.

I do tire of the drama of the reluctant groom as a standby plot device and I would like to see some really chocolate women be honored as fiancées, brides, and wives on the big screen.

Black Stars—LL Cool J and Samuel L. Jackson in *Deep Blue Sea*

July 28, 1999

When a businessman (Jackson) invests in a cure for Alzheimer's disease, two scientists discover a cure in the brains of sharks and, unknown to their colleagues, genetically modify the sharks to make them bigger to extract more of the enzyme. The sharks also get smarter, find a way out of their holding pen, and turn their attention to the scientists, who become shark bait. Not exactly a cat-and-mouse game—more like a shark-and-human game.

Introducing Dorothy Dandridge

August 21, 1999

Halle Berry executive produces and stars in this noteworthy but uneven biopic of actress Dorothy Dandridge, the beautiful Black female star of '50s cinema who faced racism, was the first Black actress to be nominated for an Academy Award, and then died from an overdose of pills.

Urban Menace

September 7, 1999

In a crazy little movie, Snoop Dogg plays the part of a crazy preacher out for revenge from local thugs.

Blue Streak

September 17, 1999

Martin Lawrence stars in this sometimes funny movie about a jewelry thief and ex-con, Miles Logan, who poses as a detective in order to retrieve his loot hidden in the building that now serves as a police headquarters.

The Best Man

October 22, 1999

Matrimony drama goes into overdrive in this very macho tale about the hidden secret between a highly conceited pro football player (Morris Chestnut) and his chosen best man (Taye Diggs), a writer who recklessly reveals the secret in a novel. Terrence Howard solidifies his rep as a light-eyed devil.

Black Star—Denzel Washington in *The Bone Collector*

November 5, 1999

In this gripping crime thriller, Washington plays a quadriplegic homicide detective paired up with Angelina Jolie.

Adwa

November 20, 1999

Haile Gerima's documentary is not fancy, big-budget moviemaking, but it tells the epic tale of Ethiopia's defeat of Italy at the battle of Adwa in 1896, when the Italians tried to colonize Ethiopia. Emperor Manalik and Empress Taitu are the heroes, who are seldom mentioned in the Western chronicles of world history.

11

Let The Good Times Roll

The "New Wave" at the Millennium

Feburary 7, 2000

As the "new wave" of African-American cinema rumbled its way into the new millennium, it was possible to see a new Black film or a film featuring Black actors almost every week.

Whether it was a late run of *The Best Man, Any Given Sunday, The Cider House Rules,* or more recent releases such as *The Hurricane* or *Next Friday,* there was no shortage of opportunity to see Black images and hear Black voices on the big screen.

It appears that this wave of film, an energetic movement launched unofficially by Spike Lee's *She's Gotta Have It* in 1986, shows no sign of rolling to a halt. Indeed, what we see on the screen from Hollywood represents only the most visible part of this swell of talent, which is high and wide.

A combination of forces—including the sprouting of the Urbanworld and Acapulco film festivals, better access to direct-to-video deals, made-for-cable productions, and digital technology—are combining to make this a prolific and pivotal era for African-American cinema. At the same time, eternal issues remain—including racism within the industry, lack of distribution opportunities, and the often very wack marketing of Black films. Did you see those weird commercials for *Beloved?* What was up with that?

"It's definitely not necessary to rely on the Hollywood channels to get films out to the people," says St. Claire Bourne, a veteran filmmaker whose documentary on Gordon Parks will premiere on HBO this year. "You can make a film in digital video. You don't even have to make a print. You can have a really good video, distribute it through a satellite, and people can download it.

"The question really is," he adds, "are the people ready for the films we want to make, and are they ready for the new ways of seeing them?"

Well, it remains to be seen if Black audiences are ready for the new film world in its entirety. But certainly no young African-American coming of age in the last decade can imagine those dark days of the late '70s and early '80s. We had all but disappeared from Hollywood offerings, save for the meager and increasingly mindless roles created for Eddie Murphy or Richard Pryor.

Anyone remember *The Toy?*

Well, remember and weep.

The New Wave

This generation, perhaps like no other in our past, has been more likely to think of filmmaking as a possibility. The original new wave of Spike Lee, Robert Townsend, John Singleton, and others has spawned a second and third new wave. Now a twenty-seven-year-old filmmaker named Robert Hardy, who would have been about fifteen years old when Lee's *School Daze* was released in 1988, feels confident bypassing traditional Hollywood and is independently distributing his new feature film, *Trois.* The film, an erotic drama, is scheduled for release February 11, starting with theaters in the Southeast.

"What really did it for me was *School Daze,*" says Hardy, who is based in Atlanta. "That was something big for me. I wanted to see what a Black movie was all about. Then there was *Boyz n the Hood, New Jack City,* Matty Rich and *Straight Out of Brooklyn.* But *Menace II Society* just pushed me over the edge. I went home that night and started writing my first film. That was my motivation—looking around and seeing what others were doing and I wanted to be a part of that."

Just like the Black literary community has changed from just a few well-known Black authors, so the Black film world has changed. It is no longer a small (gentlemen's) club. Chances are, you never even heard of Robert Hardy.

Hollywood

When considering the Black film universe, it's tempting to divide it into Hollywood films and those produced outside of the studio system in the independent film community. The reality, however, is a little different. Most of the films we think of as

"Black" films coming from Hollywood are actually independent ventures that have, after they were completed and perhaps screened at a film festival, landed a distribution deal with a major studio. In 1999, *The Best Man* was produced by 40 Acres and Mule Filmworks and had a distribution deal with Universal.

Or to put the new wave into a more human metaphor, imagine hundreds of Black filmmakers standing on each other's shoulders knocking on the big Oz-like doors of the major studios. Despite the high-profile careers of actors such as Denzel Washington, Whoopi Goldberg, or Wesley Snipes, Blacks do not have a collective foothold of power in the big studio system. That has always been the scenario, even back in the days of Paul Robeson or Oscar Micheaux. Because of this lack of power, Blacks have complained during the past decade that, though numerous scripts are being written, there are no Blacks in power at the studios to "green-light," or approve, the films. They say that Hollywood backs known quantities based on its timeworn formulas. In the case of Black films, that formula usually involves an "urban" (read ghetto/hood) drama, action, or comedy.

"Distribution and publicity of the films are the biggest issues," says actress Cynda Williams. "I've seen a number of films that nobody went to see because of the way the film was marketed. [The big studios] are putting the money in for publicity and they think that to sell a movie it has to come off as something that an eighteen-year-old might want to see—a gangbanger type of thing. It's so amazing what they can make a movie look like in a commercial."

Talk to Doug McHenry, director of *Jason's Lyric,* and he'll explain that Black films are viewed as having a limited audience—a potential of about six to seven million viewers compared to forty to fifty million for a "general release" film. Studios are more interested in films that would seem to have a crossover appeal. So Denzel Washington, who has such crossover appeal, stars in general releases such as *The Bone Collector, Courage Under Fire,* and *Crimson Tide.* We love Denzel but we wouldn't call any of those films a "Black" film. His Black presence in these big-budget films makes them crossover films, just like all of the ebony-and-ivory buddy films with Martin Lawrence, Chris Tucker, Danny Glover, or Wesley Snipes are crossover films. Hollywood has been tinkering with this crossover thing for a while and now the stakes are higher. African-Americans make up at least 25 percent of this country's moviegoing audience.

"As an actor, the single most influential person has been Denzel Washington," gushes Wendy Davis, a young up-and-coming actress who left Maryland and headed west a few years ago. "I believe his talent is far greater than DeNiro,

Pacino—all those so-called icons of the acting world. In terms of art, he's who'd I'd like to be as an actor."

And the new wave rolls on.

Black Independents

Imagine that Black human wave pounding on Hollywood's door. The door never really opens wide. There may be a crack opening every now and then and a Black film squeezes through and gets picked up in a distribution deal. Until recently, the rest of the filmmakers left out in the cold had nowhere to go. Sure, there are those who never knocked to begin with. But the fact is that most independent filmmakers want a big distribution deal. They want a national audience for their work and, until recently, the studios seemed the only way to get that. But now there are other avenues for some degree of success and recognition as a Black filmmaker—and new ideas are being hatched every day.

The Urbanworld Film Festival and the Acapulco Black Film Festival

In 1997, two film festivals aimed at catching some of this wave of film were launched. Both the Urbanworld Film Festival and the Acapulco Black Film Festival include star-studded premieres and receptions, screenings, panels, and award presentations. Urbanworld, held in New York City, is a grassroots festival with more screenings and lots of people—last year, ten thousand festivalgoers converged on Manhattan. The Acapulco Film Festival is a smaller affair designed as a retreat for the Black film community. This year it will be held June 5–10 and the registration will be limited to fifteen hundred people.

"The festivals are critical because they did the obvious—they provided a showcase for all these films," says Bridgett M. Davis, a college professor whose independently produced feature film *Naked Acts* received some exposure through Urbanworld. "They distinguished themselves because they are really national Black film festivals. The others have been city film festivals."

In 1997, four hundred people went to Acapulco. The next year it was eight hundred, and last year sixteen hundred made the trip. Its organizers say they don't want it to get larger than that.

"This has become Black cinema's annual retreat," says Jeff Friday, president of Uniworld Films Inc., organizers of the festival. "Because we're outside of the country, we're like camp. We wanted to be a market for Black independent film and we wanted to celebrate the achievements of Blacks working in Hollywood right now—like Halle Berry, Morgan Freeman, Denzel Washington, Bill Duke, Debbie Allen, Samuel Jackson, and Pam Grier."

Both festivals have suffered growing pains. Some say Urbanworld is too big and has struggled to solve logistical blunders. Others say Acapulco legitimizes the Hollywood system at the expense of building an independent film community. But regardless of these problems, few doubt the importance of providing national and international forums for Black film.

"I get tired of living in America where we make up 25 percent of the audience going to the movies but it's like we don't exist," says Stacy Spikes, a former marketing executive at Miramax Pictures and October Films who is founder and executive director of Urbanworld. "I saw too much product coming across my desk that nobody would give the time of day. You could say that Urbanworld is for my sanity. If I can make a few more filmmakers happen and make a few more films happen, then if God put me here for that reason, then that's why I'm here."

Direct-to-Video

Many of the films that do not get picked up by studios go directly to the video market—which means that they might be offered to you at your local video rental store or a chain like Blockbuster. A variety of research indicates that African-Americans, though only 12 to 15 percent of the population, also account for 25 percent of the video-rental market.

"Black people are basically the number-one consumers of video," says Joe Brewster, one of the partners of Delta Entertainment, a video distribution company with offices in Miami and New York that focuses on Black filmmakers and urban themes. It is also committed to the filmmakers being generously compensated for their art.

"You can't take a film and earn millions of dollars by taking it straight to video, but there are lots of people who make a living by taking products to video stores for Blacks," Brewster adds. "I would go so far as to say that if you take Blacks out of the video-store market, it [meaning the video-store market] may become unprofitable."

Since its launch last September, Delta has distributed two films—*Winner Takes All,* an urban drama starring Bones Thugs-N-Harmony and directed by Daniel Zirelli, and the director's cut of *Pimps Up, Hos Down,* a documentary by Brent Owens (you may have seen a portion of this on HBO). Coming up over the next several weeks is *Naked Acts*, written and directed by Bridgett M. Davis; *Divided We Stand,* a political drama/action about the takeover of a college campus directed by J. R. Jaxon; *Blood and Tears,* about a man wanting to get away from thug life by Jose

Quiroz; and *Night Runs Red,* a modern-day film noir set in the South Bronx, directed by Edward Holub.

Davis sees the deal as providing more exposure for her film, a drama about a young woman learning to love her body. It was completed a few years ago but did not land a distribution deal. "This kind of opportunity didn't exist before," she says. "And Black films do very well on video."

Joe Kelly Jackson, one of the three partners of Delta, got his start in the video business eleven years ago selling gospel videos of groups like the Mississippi Mass Choir to mom-and-pop stores in the South. He said that all the major video chains, including Blockbuster, had purchased *Naked Acts* and that he anticipates that it will do well enough for Davis to get started on her next film.

Brewster, a psychiatrist turned filmmaker, said he learned about that shut door in Hollywood when he completed his 1994 film *The Keeper,* which won an award at the Seattle Film Festival. He searched for a studio distribution deal but found none. He ultimately wound up with Kino International, theatrical and video distributors of Julie Dash's 1991 *Daughters of the Dust.* He said that, while White independent filmmakers have more freedom to work in a variety of genres and can take advantage of the overseas markets, independent Black filmmakers are limited to two or three genres like action, comedy, or ghetto drama if they have any hope of being picked up by Hollywood.

Cable Television

Tim Gordon, a radio producer and film writer based in Washington, D.C., annually polls Black film critics for their favorite Black films of the year. For 1999, made-for-cable productions were among the favorites. HBO's *A Lesson Before Dying,* directed by Joe Sargeant and starring Don Cheadle, received the most nominations in this category, followed by Showtime's *Love Songs,* a trilogy of films. And many don't know that *Down in the Delta* was an original Showtime production that had a theatrical release before it was shown on the channel.

"So many of these good movies are coming from the cable channels," says Gordon. "There are so many of them. A&E, Bravo, Showtime, BET—and HBO is really doing it."

You could say that, unlike Hollywood movie studios, cable companies more readily recognize the strength of Blacks as consumers. Just as we are big moviegoers and video renters, we also watch a lot of TV.

From the filmmaker's point of view, cable provides a couple of opportunities.

First of all, you could be tapped to develop an original film funded by the channel. Second, they might be interested in buying your independent film.

A third kind of opportunity has been created with the launch of BET Movies, the twenty-four-hour cable channel devoted to Black film and the development of BET Pictures, which operates a micro studio in downtown Los Angeles. (Both are divisions of BET Entertainment.) BET Movies has produced four original productions. There were two documentaries, *Scandalize My Name: Stories from the Blacklist,* and *Melvin Van Peebles' Classified Acts.* The channel's first feature was *Funny Valentine,* directed by Julie Dash and starring Alfre Woodard. They have also purchased *Loving Jezebel,* directed by Kwyn Bader.

Since it launched in the fall of 1998 in SoHo-type lofts in a very gritty area of downtown Los Angeles, BET Pictures has produced ten romance movies, based on the Arabesque line of romance novels that BET now owns. These have been shown on the BET channel. In the process, more than 200 African-Americans have been employed behind and in front of the camera.

"The launching of our micro studio I think is important. It's one of the most cost-effective bases of production that we've had control over," says Roy Campanella, executive producer for the Arabesque film series and director of two of the films. "We've historically lacked an independent base of production and distribution. We're laying the groundwork and providing films for television and theatrical release and that's exciting. You know the term 'show business'? Well there's a lot of business in that show."

Nina Henderson, vice president of marketing and distribution for BET Pictures II, said that BET Pictures is also planning four theatrical releases each year, starting with three for this year with budgets of about $3 million each. Some may be produced from a script or treatment, while others may be independently produced.

"We have a low budget but I think we will be able to do a tremendous job," says Henderson, who is based at BET's corporate office in Washington, D.C. "We're trying to tell stories involving African-Americans. We want whole stories where the people have all kinds of sides to them. Independent film has always been where you go to get more complex stories, more complete characters."

Cynda Williams, who stars in one of the Arabesque Films, *Hidden Blessings,* and was recently seen in a showing of Spike Lee's *Mo' Better Blues* on the BET Movies channel, said that cable exposure makes a big difference in an actor's career. She said it can make a special difference for those not in the current clique of popular actors constantly receiving big roles.

"People think I'm the busiest actress in the world because I might have seven films on cable," she says. "So cable can keep you alive. People really watch this stuff."

Digital Video

Just as cable has provided more opportunities, the hope is that digital video—which produces high-quality images at a fraction of the cost of the traditional filmmaking equipment and materials—will bring a greater degree of freedom to filmmakers. There even exist Web sites such as www.atomfilms.com, www.thebitscreeen.com, and www.ifilm.net that do nothing but play digital video shorts.

Kenny Blank, known to many as Michael Peterson on the WB's *Parenthood,* is one young African-American taking advantage of this new media. At last year's Urbanworld Film Festival, his experimental short subject video, *Manifested Intent,* was screened and he dazzled the audience with his knowledge of the technology. He shot, directed, wrote, scored, and edited the video himself. He thinks that new computer software for film editing can do for films what desktop publishing software did for print publications.

"Because the medium is very inexpensive to shoot with, there is a lot of experimenting that you can do that you wouldn't do with film. With the editing software that exists now, you can create whatever look you want—high tech, glossy and colorful, or dark and gritty with no light."

Blank, twenty-two years old, was introduced to music and video technology while young. He was born in Manhattan, and lived for a time in New Jersey before moving to Stamford, Connecticut. His stepfather, Bob Blank, is a music producer, and he let the younger Kenny experiment inside his state-of-the-art recording studio there. By three, Blank was playing with a video camera, and he began making his own videos by the age of nine. All the while, since a baby, he has appeared in commercials for products such as Pampers, Bubble Yum, Kodak, and Jell-O pudding (one of those too-cute kids talking with Bill Cosby). Since the age of nine, he has also scored music for television shows and acted in films. Phew! No wonder he's ready for the new technology!

He is currently working on his first feature-length film, *Desygn,* which is being shot entirely with digital video. In it, three characters experiment with supernatural events. He describes it as "kind of *X Files*–ish."

What's Next—Independent Distribution

Festivals, direct-to-video, cable, digital technology. All these outlets seem promising as an alternative to knocking on the big studio door that never opens. But more and more folks in the African-American film community are deciding to directly challenge the studio's hegemony over theatrical releases.

Oscar Micheaux independently released his films early in the century. Melvin Van Peebles independently released *Sweet Sweetback's Baad Asssss Song,* and most recently Haile Gerima says he "footwalked" his film *Sankofa* around the country to reach audiences that lined up to see it. On a smaller scale, Gerima is distributing his new documentary, *Adwa,* about the Ethiopian colonial war victory over the Italians.

"We feel we are making the last stand in the cultural struggle," Gerima says. "That is the struggle to make our own image."

This month, Robert Hardy is embarking on an ambitious plan to independently release his film *Trois.* Beginning on February 11, it will be shown in twenty cities in the Southeast, from the coast to as far west as Chicago and as far north as North Carolina. If sales are strong, he will leave the film there and expand to other regions.

"I look at films the way that Master P looks at music," says Hardy. "He tried to do the majors and couldn't get a deal so he did it himself and built community support. A lot of people saw him large in 1997 but he had paid a lot of dues before that. Some people want to see their names in big lights right away."

Hardy tried hard to get a studio deal. He said he even tailored his film to include those features—recognizable talent, a good story, subject matter that might be controversial and create a buzz—that he was told would appeal to those in a position to green-light his film. But the most the studios offered him was a direct-to-video deal. He'd already been there and done that, though, with his cheapie first film, *Chocolate City,* which he shot while a student at Florida A&M. Ultimately, he wound up making more money on the film by selling it directly over the Internet than with his video deal.

"We were told they didn't know how to market it," Hardy says. "They still considered it a no-name cast [even though he cast former Miss America Kenya Moore and Gary Dourdan of *A Different World* fame—the fine man with the locks]. A lot of people in Hollywood considered *The Best Man* a no-name movie, even though it had Taye Diggs and Nia Long."

Those in the film community will be watching *Trois* closely. It has been the traditional wisdom that this type of large-scale distribution to first-run theaters such as AMC, Carmine, Regal, and Magic Johnson Theaters was nearly impossible for a filmmaker to do independently. The conventional wisdom has been that smaller filmmakers couldn't compete because the big studios have such clout with theater chains. (Like, if you don't take my film, I won't give you my big blockbuster next year.)

But perhaps such doomsday logic isn't entirely correct. What theaters need, more than a studio name, is a guarantee that a film can fill the seats in their theater, and most independent filmmakers don't have the marketing budgets to guarantee that anyone other than their momma will even know about their film.

"If you can show them that they are going to have butts and feet in their theater, that's all they care about," Hardy says. "You raise the marketing money and show them your marketing plan. That's the trick—can you raise money to make your film? *And* can you raise money to market your film?"

Alisa Starks and her husband, Donzell, own the Chicago-based Meridian Theaters, the biggest chain of African-American-owned theaters. She agrees that the problem is not with theater owners or exhibitors, but rather with distribution. From where she sits, she thinks that many theater owners serving Black populations know what their clientele wants and would be more than happy to serve up more Black films. The catch, though, is that most of these films have no distribution plan or money.

"Yes, there is a tenuous relationship between the theaters and the big studios," she says. "We want to get the best film product and they want to release all their films. We're both out to make money.

"The distributor puts money behind films. They know what kind of money they are going to put behind that film in each market. The issue becomes then who is picking up that film. No one is picking up Black films.

"I've seen films that I think will do very well in our theaters but I don't have the funding for marketing," she says. "How do we break this gap? What I think we have to do is break the distribution code. We don't have anyone distributing. Until we crack it, we're going to have films—and that's it. Most filmmakers, they know very little about the distribution game—they just wanted to make a film. They know very little about the exhibition game—they just wanted to make a film."

Hardy's film was shown by Meridian because he was able to show them an extensive marketing plan that showed he was prepared to spend several times more than the $1 million he spent to make his film on its marketing.

"Now that you have exhibitors, you have people who will fight for Black films," says Starks. "We have the theaters. We have the films. . . . I know there is a lot of talk out there. People say they are going to do it, I just haven't seen it done yet."

It makes sense that much of the buzz about distribution is occurring around the film festival scene. Executives at both the Acapulco and Urbanworld festivals see the setting up of some type of distribution business as the logical extension and next step to what has already begun. The festivals are where the filmmakers come all dressed up and ultimately have no place to go.

Next month, Friday, director of the Acapulco Film Festival, is launching Black-FilmFestAmerica, a traveling show of three Black independent films—*Park Day,* directed by Sterling Macer; *Personals,* directed by Michael Sargeant and starring Malik Yoba; and *Invited Guest,* audience winner at last year's Acapulco Festival, directed by Timothy Folsome and starring Mekhi Phifer. In a partnership with Loews Cineplex Entertainment, the festival will launch March 2–14 in Manhattan, before traveling to Atlanta in April and Washington, D.C., in May. The plan is to have no less than a two-week run for the films and hit one market per month. They are marketing their festival at www.goseeblackmovies.com.

"Filmmakers are filmmakers. They're not distributors," says Friday. "The studios have mystified what it takes to distribute films but it's really not that complicated. Music promotion has been somewhat demystified but film has not."

Spikes is in the process of building a Black film distribution company that he says will take advantage of mall theaters and community theaters that are often left in the shadow of the mega-multiplex theaters.

"It's the hardest thing in the world and it's the easiest thing in the world because you can bet that no one is doing it," he says. "That's our goal—to be the Motown or Def Jam of the Black film industry.

"There are a good number of films being made but they're not getting out," he adds. "People in the positions aren't giving them the break. It's the lack of distribution. I'm actually happy the dog is asleep because I want it to wake up when we arrive.

"A theater owner who builds something based on race will not survive," he adds. "You need marketing. If you put it in there because it's a Black movie, it won't necessarily make money. When *Beloved* came out, I went to see it and more Black people were lined up to see *The Bride of Chucky.*

"If I'm going to try to get you to a smaller, not as clean theater, I have to market to you even better. You're going to want to go to a nice theater, one that is clean and modern, where your feet are not going to stick to the floor.

"I have to ask myself, how do I get you to like it?"

Interview—Vin Diesel

February 18, 2000

This is a big weekend for Vin Diesel. He's a star of two movies opening tomorrow—the sci-fi action thriller *Pitch Black* and the Wall Street drama *Boiler Room.*

It is also his Hollywood debut as a "man of color."

The first time you saw him in a big movie, he played a young, brave Italian in *Saving Private Ryan.* And then in the next flick, *The Iron Giant,* he performed behind the scenes as the basso, gravelly voice of the animated star.

But he's Black enough in *Boiler Room* for the White boys to make references to him and "niggers." And *Pitch Black* offers a long, close look at the thirty-two-year-old native New Yorker. (And the looking isn't bad, ladies!)

That's not just a deep tan. Look at that nose and those lips. And maybe those Steven Spielberg folks knew how to work wonders with a razor and a combat helmet, but the clincher here is the hair. It's not that crew-cut White boy fuzz on the sides. It's not that Puerto Rican curly-type thing. It's that close-cut grain, that fresh-from-the-corner-barbershop grain, that Vincent Carter grain, your brother's grain.

Vin Diesel is living La Vida Multicultural, which, it turns out, might be the same as La Vida Loca.

"I've been presented with some interesting offers—like to play a skinhead [in *American History X*]" he says, sitting in a room at Washington, D.C.'s Four Seasons Hotel. "There's something cool about this kind of ambiguous, chameleon-like ethnicity. I try to think back to what actor has played all these different kinds of roles and I can't think of any, can you?

"It's very fascinating," he adds. "A man of color is being exposed to so many different opportunities. Hopefully it says something about my acting. Hopefully, ideally, that's what I want it to do."

Diesel was raised by artsy parents in New York. He doesn't like to get too specific about his background. He's Italian and a lot of other things. He's never met his biological father but was raised since the age of one by a Black stepfather.

"We're going to get to a place in our culture where I think there will be a lot more ambiguous people," he says, adding a quote here and there from Sidney Poitier or Martin Luther King Jr. to reinforce his point. "I've noticed that people feel comfortable with me or they feel uncomfortable with me. They either adopt me—whether it's any kind of nationality—Italian, Latin, Black, or you name it," or they don't.

It's not like Diesel is trying to pass. Pass as what? Himself? He doesn't consider himself Black or White. He's in that multicultural zone. He rejects that "one-drop" rule of this country. And when it has come to acting, he has had to sort of go White to be able to come back to being Black. Maybe one unanswered question is this: Once seen in this country as Black, can he go back?

A few years ago, he wrote, directed, and starred in a funny and poignant film, *Multifacial,* about a young actor of mixed-race heritage who goes about the task of auditioning for parts. At the first gig, he dons a hat (to hide that grain!?) and plays a Brooklyn (or New Jersey or Philly) thuggy Italian. At the next audition, he's rejected by a Black casting agent as "too light." Some other Black folks are looking for more of a "Wesley type." Then he plays a Latino but gets caught ass-out when he can't speak Spanish. It goes on and on, ending, finally, with the young actor sitting in a diner where the White woman behind him orders a coffee that's "not too light, not too dark."

His own personal story picks up from there. Director Steven Spielberg saw *Multifacial* and wrote a part for Diesel into his epic, award-winning film about World War II. Since then, opportunities have continued to come Diesel's way.

"I think that we're at a point in society so that if you look at a person on the screen and say that is a person of color, then that is a person of color," he says. "You know what I mean? If it's someone who is Aryan, then you don't say that."

Of course, there is the matter of his name. He wasn't born Vin Diesel.

"Well, the name is really simple," he says. "It's not the name on the birth certificate. Honestly, it's in line with how so many of my idols changed their name just a little bit, just enough to feel comfortable with where they are, to feel comfortable with how they're talked about.

"It's unnatural to have your name be that big, that larger than life," he adds. "There's a reason why so many actors, like Tom Cruise, why their names have been altered a bit. I think it gives you just a little breathing space. It doesn't put your whole history—like what hospital you were born at, the whole thing, on record. It doesn't make your mom a public subject. It gives you a little space. And also, being an actor and having your name up on the screen or a big poster is a little impersonal in a way. Unless you're born Jesus Christ, you don't need your name that big."

Diesel grew up in Lower Manhattan with his sister, an artsy dad, and a mom who worked as an astrologer. (He's a Cancer with Scorpio rising.) His stepfather taught theater when he was young. He was riding his banana-seat bicycle around one day with his friends when they decided to stop at an old theater, go inside, and start tearing up things. A woman in the building stopped them and wound up giving him a part in a play about dinosaurs. And though he's plied other trades—like being a bouncer for ten years at New York clubs like The Tunnel, 1018, and The Grand—he's had the acting bug ever since. And, probably like every little boy back then riding his banana-seat bike, he's always wanted to be an action star.

Well, this weekend, Vin (or Vincent or Vinny or whatever your name is), you got it, brother. Be an action star—in big, bold, living color.

Black Star–Vin Diesel in *Pitch Black*

February 18, 2000

You might not want to roll into *Pitch Black* by yourself.

Director David Twohy plays here with the fear of darkness, the fear of all kinds of darkness, and comes up with a pretty scary movie.

When you think about it, scary stuff in the movies rarely happens in bright light, unless it is that Big-Brother-Is-Watching-You/Nazi scary, when they actually prefer to kill you while everyone can see. But the fear starts in blazing hot sun here. In the not-too-distant future, a group of earth space travelers is forced to crash-land on another planet. With three suns that never seem to set, the planet is brutally hot. In this light, the dark, scary thing is Riddick, the convicted murderer (Vin Diesel). In this movie you can see that Diesel—bronzed, muscled arms, short haircut, and one of those Paul Robeson deep well voices—is not a White man.

Riddick is being transported by lawman Johns (played by Cole Hauser). While the band of earthlings figures out how to survive, they fear Riddick like he's some Hannibal Lecter–Jeffrey Dahmer demon just waiting to slice them up and enjoy them with a nice Chianti. And while they are busy fearing him, they slowly realize they have a bigger problem on their hands—they have landed on just the wrong planet at just the wrong time. It is time for the planet's suns to be eclipsed, turning the planet pitch black. And now they really need to be afraid—of giant, swarming batlike creatures that work with more collective precision than Hannibal Lecter ever did.

All of which doesn't necessarily have to be scary. Once you've figured out the scare tricks that Hollywood has up its sleeve, many of these movies seem boringly similar. But Twohy keeps our attention in this one, first of all, with the jarring crash of the ship and camera work that keeps us bouncing and zooming around the bright, bleached-out landscape. The travelers, for the most part, don't act like silly lambs who you wish would be slaughtered. As a matter of fact, Twohy makes a point of trashing much of what is ordinary and expected. Lots of things here are not what they seem. The planet seems empty but is not, a man who is supposed to represent the law is really kind of skanky, a male turns out to be a female, and—most important—the dark man considered a demon is the one whom everyone must learn to trust.

Diesel, who has the kind of face that can take him from the hip-hop club to the heavy metal show, plays his part with a kind of I've-been-to-hell-and-back nonchalance. He's an action hero for the new millennium—not as smart alecky as Bruce Willis and much cooler than Arnold Schwarzenegger. He easily conveys the fact that Riddick is so far out there that it's no big deal to grab a giant bat and try to beat the crap out of him. Since he's killed, he's not afraid to kill again, especially if he's fighting for his life.

He is aided by special night-vision eyes. Good thing, because on this planet, seeing the light is not an option. It is a matter of survival.

Freedom Song

February 27, 2000

The test of all of these movies that claim to show the Black experience is the humanity test: How well do they really show all of us? Do they really include all the wrinkles and inner beauty—weakness, strength, ugliness, and radiance—in our portrait?

We've been disappointed so many times by films that take defining moments of our history and turn them into clichés and turn us into two-dimensional dummies. Or our history of suffering, survival, and triumph is turned somehow into a story about White people.

Thankfully, *Freedom Song,* premiering on TNT, does not fall into these familiar traps. It tells the story of the civil rights movement coming to a small town in Mississippi in 1961 and the turmoil, danger, and change that follows. But it is not a true story, nor does it claim to be based on a true story that we are forced to match for historical accuracy or faithfulness to our collective memory.

Of course, given the sad precedent, this manufacturing of fiction could've produced a disaster. But this taut little drama unfolds nicely and it stands on its own. Only later, you might think about how—when it comes to the civil rights movement—we have been almost compelled to focus on true-life stories. The civil rights era wasn't that long ago. Even those of us who were babies or not even born then have seen the water-hose and attack-dog footage; the video of stern-faced students in sunglasses being stronger than we ever were in high school, or in college. Presented as docudrama or documentary, these scenes—though historically meaningful—have become very familiar: The church is focal point for change and danger, there is the vulnerability of women as wives and victims of rape, there is the late-night drive to the lynching tree, and then come the fire bombings and screaming babies. The fear and violence strike a collective chord and produce the effect of a story we feel we know. But do we? Do we know the people and see ourselves?

In this movie, writer, director, and executive producer Phil Alden Robinson has the freedom and power to create a town and breathe life and feelings into characters of his own making. And it probably was a major benefit that he had as his consultant several former civil rights activists, including Vincent Harding, the distinguished historian who is a professor of religion and social change at the University of Denver.

The effort, first of all, was not to tell the whole story of the civil rights movement. The focus here is on one little Mississippi town and a few of the kids who decided to change things in their little world—little things like sitting down at a lunch counter, going to the "public" library, or registering to vote. Making a new fresh story out of the cement of history, oddly enough, provides the opportunity to focus on the humanity and not the tremendous sweep of history taking place under their feet. Sure, there were daddies like the one played by Danny Glover who, through the pain of experience, wanted nothing to do with all the rabble-rousing. Sure, there were sons like the one played by Vicellous Reon Shannon who thought their daddies were punks. (In this picture, Shannon speaks normally, not like in *The Hurricane,* when it sounded like his Brooklyn accent was created with a mouth full of marbles.) Sure, there were organizers like the one played by Vondie Curtis-Hall who were soft-spoken and were not afraid to admit openly to children that the goals they were fighting for had to be weighed against the possibility of death. There is flesh, bone, complexity, and contradiction here.

But there isn't a barrage of violence—especially early on.

There is, instead, fear and all the other emotions within a family and a community when change and danger come. There is one young man—an ordinary, kind of chunky brother—telling his story about growing up in the American South (in Mississippi Goddamn!) and how that made him into a fighter. As odd as it might seem, given the wonderful documentaries like *Eyes on the Prize,* we don't hear enough about the big contribution made by all the small people, the people who risked their lives just to register to vote—just regular humans.

3 Strikes

March 1, 2000

There are enough films such as *Friday, Next Friday, Blue Streak, Life,* and now *3 Strikes* to form a new sub-genre of Black film. Let's call this type of film a "lockdown comedy."

They all focus on young Black men in jail, recently released, or running to stay out of trouble. There is no job or vocation visible or on the horizon. Days or weeks are spent in a haze of weed, women, getting beat down or the fear of a beatdown. The ultimate goal is usually getting over. Winding through a series of ridiculous situations, the young protagonists run the race and class gauntlet. We, the audience, are expected to laugh along and cheer their ultimate victory, even if it is a marginal victory.

We laugh with them; we laugh our two-souls laughter, aware of the pain and hilarity of the moment. We smile at the comedy of real-life survival and the recognition of survival skills that we claim as our very own. (Like Richard Pryor demonstrating a Black man skipping over a snake in the woods.)

These movies hit their high moments when the writers, juggling a series of time-worn hood jokes, manage to come up with enough twists and turns to keep us laughing anyway. The comedies also are given a turbo boost by talented comedians like Chris Tucker (*Friday*), Mike Epps (*Next Friday*), and Martin Lawrence (*Life* and *Blue Streak*). All three comedic actors are able to convey that brother-on-the-edge insanity, verbal quickness, and any number of physical qualities that no doubt have spontaneously improved on the original scripts while the films were being shot. All three actors have played leading characters whose street-survival skills include a lot of loud talk. Since most of them are slim, slightly built men, part of the comedy usually involves them writing a verbal check that their bodies can't cash.

There are a number of problems that writer and first-time director DJ Pooh has run into with *3 Strikes.* He starts with a good premise—the ordeal of a young man facing his possible third conviction and, under a "three strikes" rule, twenty-five years in prison. But Pooh, who cowrote *Friday* with Ice Cube, hasn't come up with enough fresh jokes or situations for his own movie. Poor David Alan Grier. He doesn't seem to be finding many vehicles for his acting. Playing the part of police detective here, he jokes about some White cop still being angry about the O. J. trial and the joke falls as flat as Gwyneth Paltrow's ass. It's like Pooh has forgotten that there is nothing inherently funny in the story line and that the comedy has to be created along with it.

Yeah, there are those who will think it is the funniest thing in the world to crack a bottle of malt liquor over someone's head, to hear several long-winded farts throughout the film, to be shot in the butt, to fear homosexual rape, or escape the sexual advances of a fat woman. There will be even more who will enjoy the sophomoric depiction of women-as-hos throughout the flick. In the film and video version of South-Central L.A., it seems that Daisy Duke shorts/panties have never gone out of style.

The other problem is that, while Brian Hooks (*Phat Beach*) is obviously a fine actor, he doesn't have the zany comedic edge here in the leading role that has made these films work better in the past. Comedian and actor Faizon Love is funny and adds a certain street authenticity to the film, as does rapper E40. They play brothers making it through the race and class gauntlet without being on lock down—at least not at the moment anyway.

Ghost Dog: The Way of the Samurai

March 17, 2000

Thanks to the TV hit *The Sopranos,* Hollywood's long-standing affair with the mob movie has gotten an injection of Viagra. Cropping up in the new spate of mob stories is an irresistible idea: to bring together the old-school Mafia (or Asian gangs in the forthcoming *Romeo Must Die*) with gangstas (real and studio models) of the hip-hop nation.

Ghost Dog: The Way of the Samurai, starring Forest Whitaker and featuring music by the RZA, takes the mob theme and spins it in a totally different direction. A man called Ghost Dog (Whitaker), living in a rooftop shack with a trained flock of pigeons, has adopted the code of samurai warriors—Japanese soldiers who fought at the behest of a feudal baron under the shogun, or military governor of the country.

Rather than feudal Japan, this movie is set in poor, urban, capitalist America. It looks like some bombed-out section of Newark or East Orange, New Jersey. Rather than soldiers and feudal barons, we have Ghost Dog (Whitaker), who has devoted his life to following the directions of an Italian mobster named Louie who, many years ago, saved his life in a street attack.

In this modern world of predator and prey, Ghost Dog has become a hit man for Louie. He has killed at least a dozen people. When we meet him, he is preparing to execute his next victim. But the hit doesn't go as planned and Ghost Dog winds up in the dog house. He becomes predator and prey, and he makes the same of the mob.

Director, writer, and coproducer Jim Jarmusch saves his improbable story line by combining a stylish production, quick violence, and a sardonic wit—like old Mafiosos who quote Flava Flav and watch Looney Tunes. With his droopy eye, cornrows, and thick body, Whitaker creates a hip-hop samurai who is brooding, analytical, and slow-moving. He is eerie in his machine-like approach to murder. (Eerie like a crazy man who lives on the roof with a bunch of pigeons.) The RZA, who makes a cameo appearance in the film, has terrific screen presence.

The story doesn't offer much insight into when or why Ghost Dog has adopted the samurai way of life—if this occurred before or after Louie saved his life. We only know that he has evolved to the point where he believes he must kill and always be prepared to die. The movie asks us to accept his obedience to a code that has nothing to do with our accepted notions of human behavior. In the end, it asks that we not think of Ghost Dog or anyone in the movie in those familiar terms.

By juxtaposing the code of the samurai with the code of a modern, urban Black man, Jarmusch offers a different vision of what the streets can do to you. Ghost Dog is a street soldier not immersed in the business-as-usual drugs or gangs. He is not portrayed as mindless, testosterone-driven, or ignorant. His murders are driven by what he feels his options are.

But the film doesn't offer a simple hero. And despite its ending, it certainly doesn't offer the samurai code as an answer to surviving modern life. If anything, it says that this ancient code of honor might be better left in the past. The strongest idea it leaves is a question: What do you kill for every day? And is it killing you?

Black at the Oscars—*The Hurricane, The Green Mile, The Cider House Rules,* and *The Matrix*

March 20, 2000

From *The Hurricane* to *The Green Mile* to *The Cider House Rules* to *The Matrix,* movies about or featuring African-Americans are a big part of this year's Oscar race.

Denzel Washington is vying for Best Actor for his lead role in *The Hurricane,* based on the life and ordeal of boxer Rubin "Hurricane" Carter. Michael Clarke Duncan is up for Best Supporting Actor for his eerie and controversial portrayal of a prisoner on death row who possesses supernatural powers in *The Green Mile.*

But you might not know that Best Film nominee *The Cider House Rules,* about a boy who comes of age in a New England orphanage, focuses in large part on a group of Black migrant workers. The head of the migrants, played by Delroy Lindo, and his daughter, played by Erykah Badu, figure prominently in the film's story line concerning childbirth and abortion. And finally, though it has only been nominated for technical awards, *The Matrix* is dominated by an intense performance by Laurence Fishburne. He plays Morpheus, the leader of a band of revolutionaries that is fighting an evil cyberintelligence that has taken over the world. *The Matrix* also grants a special place—and appearance—for the wisdom of Black grandmothers through the role of the all-knowing oracle, played by Gloria Foster.

The films nominated this year—an eclectic bunch dominated by productions that were not box-office smashes—are meaty examples of the power that modern directors have in bringing their original voice, vision, and worldview to the screen. Competing for best picture with *The Green Mile* and *The Cider House Rules* is *American Beauty,* a twisted look at middle-class suburban life that cavalierly tosses cloaked homosexuality, masturbation, and murder into its mix. *The Insider,* loved by critics and a flop at the box office, probes the inner workings of television journalism. *The Sixth Sense* tells the story of a young boy who sees and talks to the dead.

Whether or not we individually prefer any of the films, there is no denying the power of cinema to shape how we see the world and how we see ourselves. The Academy Awards ceremony provides a ripe opportunity to explore this power and the power of the stories we see. Whose stories are being told? Who gets to tell the story? Whose view is expressed? The answers to all of these questions have a lot to do with who "wins."

For example, *The Hurricane,* which gives a Black man the best chance of bringing home the Best Actor prize since Sidney Poitier won it in 1963, is a story with an African-American man at its center. It is expressed, in large part, from a Black point of view and offers one of those rare opportunities for a Black actor to tackle a meaty lead role.

Since its December release, *The Hurricane* has been the subject of controversy. Articles written by some journalists who covered Carter's actual case have charged that the movie glosses over facts—Carter's criminal record, his philandering, his temper—that might make him look less like a heroic martyr and victim of racism. Because of this fight, some film writers began speculating as soon as the nominations were announced that Washington—who has already won the Golden Globe Award for Best Actor in this film—could see his favorite-son status jeopardized for the Oscar. Some film writers have gone further to state that *The Hurricane* probably would have gotten a best film nomination if it were not for the fuss.

Both points are debatable. It could be argued convincingly, for example, that the script and direction for *The Hurricane* was far less inspiring than Denzel's performance. Critics of all stripes, professional and armchair, cited this flaw in the movie early on. But on the other hand, since when have Hollywood films had to be historically accurate? How many White people have been prettied up by Hollywood? How many of us had to grow up seeing, on the big screen, slave owners as benevolent? Italian and Jewish mobsters as brutal but handsome and honorable? And all kinds of White people as attractive who, in real life, are not?

But, more importantly, such arguments mask the underlying problem, which is the historical rejection by those who choose the Oscar winners of any film with Black people at its center or with a firm African-American sensibility. The singular Best Actor win for a Black man was for *Lilies of the Field,* in which Sidney Poitier, playing an unemployed construction worker, helps some Eastern European nuns build a church in the desert. While Black men have been nominated for roles that had Black life at its center—for example, James Earl Jones in *The Great White Hope* (1970) or Paul Winfield in *Sounder* (1972)—none of them won, just like Diahann Carroll didn't win Best Actress for *Claudine* in 1974 and Whoopi Goldberg didn't win for *The Color Purple* in 1985. No Black woman has ever won for Best Actress.

The two wins for Best Supporting Actress have also been for roles that included a Black presence in a larger drama about Whites. Whoopi Goldberg won in 1990 for *Ghost,* starring Patrick Swayze and Demi Moore, and way back in 1939 Hattie McDaniel won for *Gone with the Wind,* which has to be at the top of my Makes Me Wanna Holler list.

When Louis Gossett Jr. won in 1982 for *An Officer and a Gentleman,* he played in a film that was really about a White officer (Richard Gere) and his woman (Debra Winger). Of course Cuba Gooding Jr.'s 1996 win was for *Jerry Maguire,* which focused on Tom Cruise and his blonde love interest. The one award won for a film about Black people was perhaps the Best Supporting Actor award picked up by Denzel Washington in 1989 for *Glory,* though even that film had as its center the White Civil War regiment leader played by Matthew Broderick.

The point is that this year's flack over the "accuracy" of *The Hurricane* is only the most recent proof that when it comes to seeking recognition from Whites for a film (or any art for that matter) with Black people and Black sensibilities at its center, there will always be a problem. Even if the problem is that White people don't get it or don't view the Black story as comparable to stories of their own humanity, there will be a problem. (Like you strongly suspected, after you saw the list of nominees, that Spike Lee's *Four Little Girls* was not going to win against another documentary about the Holocaust.)

When you think about it, our history in this country is too fraught with deep racial strife, violence, and death not to produce artistic strife of the same magnitude. There is a reason that the Pulitzer Prize was not given to Toni Morrison for *Beloved.* Instead, she had to go to Europe to collect a Nobel Prize. The fight is good because it is evidence of the struggle to create our own images and stories, which become markers of our identity and survival.

Somewhere, right now, a Black spoken-word artist is crafting a poem about the Amadou Diallo case. She is comparing the Black community, the community she lives in, with the firing range where police practice. The dark human outlines the officers shoot at are like the dark bodies that pass her on the street every day. Her poem is different from the poem of the White police officer. One day, if the poet creates a film about the incident, it will be very different from one created by someone who does not view Diallo as a victim.

The postmodern art age that we live in demands the assertion of our own voices. If the new millennium brings anything, hopefully it will bring to our arts community this idea of assertion without seeking the approval of Whites. It makes no sense to annually wring our hands over how voting members of the Academy judge films about us, compared to those about themselves. There is no science to this nomination process. It is subjective and the members respond to those things that they know and can identify with. (The same thing happens with traditional music awards, if you've wondered how Barry White can win over D'Angelo or Maxwell.) They support things they are comfortable with and since when is anything to do with race relations comfortable? The Academy Awards should remind us to commit ourselves to developing better and better stories and films that illuminate the fullness and complexity of Black life. We should develop those stories for us, without expectation that Whites will necessarily "get it" or approve of them. If they do, that's fine, but they should not be setting any criteria.

Expecting that is like expecting a stranger to be able to use your prescription glasses, like expecting someone to fit your shoes.

Did folks back in the '60s wait for White people to raise their White fists and declare Black is beautiful?

Romeo Must Die

March 22, 2000

Despite its promotion, *Romeo Must Die* is not a love story. It is also not a sleek stylistic mob movie. If after *New Jack City, Hoodlum,* and *Belly,* you're still waiting for your hip-hop *Godfather* to come along, you'll just have to keep waiting.

But *Romeo,* starring Jet Li (*Lethal Weapon 4*), is a martial arts flick with some pretty tight fight scenes. If all the punches, kicks, and sounds of snapping bones aren't enough, director Andrzej Bartkowiak supplies the occasional cinematic MRI of a pierced heart or shattered vertebrae. Also, singer Aaliyah gets to play the purty-purty girl and there is one scene that might satisfy everybody out there waiting for another dramatic death plunge like Frank Nitti's in *The Untouchables.*

The story, about rival African-American and Chinese-American gangs, is set in present-day Oakland—which should unsettle all those would-be West Coast gangsters out there. Never before on the big screen have so many Black men been beat down by the Chinese so often. Beat down at the garden apartments. Beat down in the factory. Beat down at the (Black-owned!) club. Even those concerned with excessive violence in rap lyrics might find themselves calling on Dr. Dre, Snoop Doggy Dogg, or even M.C. Ren to come out of retirement and take up arms.

The key to remember is that this is a martial arts flick, a vehicle for Li, in the role of Han Sing, to once again show his awesome physical talents. And, very often, in these fight flicks, there are the hordes of hapless fools who keep putting their arms, legs, heads, and guts in the path of the star's fast hands and feet. In *Romeo Must Die,* the hordes of hapless fools are Black. With the exception of the ever-dignified/ever-scary Delroy Lindo and that mucho-fine Isaiah Washington, the Black men here serve as martial arts fodder. They are not cool street soldiers like Nas in *Belly* or Wesley Snipes in *Sugar Hill.* They are more like replicants of Biz Markie, acting a fool.

If everybody in the movie were a fool—like the characters in *Analyze This* or *Mickey Blue Eyes*—these comedians would fit right in. But for most of the film, the Chinese are shown as reserved, dignified, organized, and full of honor. Even at the end, when we see that the Chinese are just as crooked as the brothers are painted to be, the Chinese still are shown as better organized in their crookedness.

This movie is not a comedy—in fact it lurches awkwardly forward in an identity crisis. Sometimes the messy script takes itself too seriously and, at other times, not seriously enough. Explosions and murders happen and, in the end, we are still not sure why.

Some more editing could have been done. For example, it really wasn't necessary to have Aaliyah do a little singing and dancing.

Since this picture is supposed to be based on a forbidden liaison between Trish

O'Day (Aaliyah) and Han Sing, it would have helped to establish at least an ounce of romantic chemistry between them.

Finally, the film could have made better use of hip-hop beats and lyrics to aggressively drive its rhythm and mood—as did the recent *Boiler Room.* But it does not. In more than one sense, hip-hop—its beats, its promise, its people—exists on the fringes of *Romeo Must Die,* not at its heart.

Erasure at the Oscars

March 27, 2000

Watching the Academy Awards show can give a Black person an out-of-body experience. You watch the parade of film "excellence"—Best Picture: *American Beauty*; Best Actor: Kevin Spacey; Best Actress: Hilary Swank; Best Supporting Actor: Michael Caine; Best Supporting Actress: Angelina Jolie.

And it is all very White.

The dashes of color come as we arrive in service as presenters or performers. Vanessa Williams is tanned and lovely. LL Cool J looks bored. Samuel Jackson is solemn. Billy Crystal jokes about missing Oscar statuettes being found in Erykah Badu's "hat." There is occasional film footage of Laurence Fishburne fierce as ever in *The Matrix.* Isaac Hayes sings "Shaft" surrounded by bikini-clad women in frosted afro wigs.

Kingly Morgan Freeman is grave as he strides to the podium and reminds the worldwide audience—without blinking or cracking a smile—that only some of what Hollywood has produced has been historically accurate. The audience laughs nervously, knowing he is referring to charges that the movie *The Hurricane,* starring Denzel Washington and based on the life of boxer Rubin "Hurricane" Carter, is historically flawed.

Yet, despite these appearances, the 72nd Annual Academy Awards offered a first-row, close-up view of our erasure at the Oscars. This isn't a year when there were no Blacks nominated behind closed doors. There were two high-profile, larger-than-life nominees in front of our faces. And more, Denzel's nomination for *The Hurricane* was for a movie and story about the Black experience.

None of the films we've ever won an Oscar for in the past—*Jerry Maguire, Ghost, Glory, An Officer and a Gentleman, Lilies of the Field,* or (can you believe it?!) *Gone with the Wind*—had the Black experience at its center. Not to take anything away from the fine winning actors, but these performances were also in service to a larger story line and show about Whites. Just like every other time an actor has been nominated for a film about Black people, Denzel didn't bring home the prize this year, either. Yet his portrayal of Carter was so excellent that it makes the competing acting jobs, though fine, seem ordinary. Freeman and every other Black actor in Hollywood have every right to look grave: If Denzel could not win with for this tour de force performance, can anyone ever win for portraying the Black experience?

When members of the Academy of Motion Picture Arts and Sciences voted for Kevin Spacey's portrayal of another White man in midlife and moral crisis, they were once again voting for themselves, their stories, their version of what is important, their history—even if we have seen different versions of that same movie over and over and over. They also voted for a documentary about the killing of Israeli athletes at the Olympics over *The Buena Vista Social Club,* about octogenarian musicians in Cuba, and over *On the Ropes,* which tells stories of struggle and triumph of Black youth through sports.

If, while in the middle of watching this year's show, you are still not convinced of your Black invisibility, it is reinforced during a short film about how film has depicted history since the beginning of time. Here is *One Million Years B.C., Clan of the Cave Bear,* the Elizabeth Taylor–Richard Burton version of Egyptian and Roman history, all kinds of flicks about Europe—the Dark Ages, Renaissance, as colonizers. Then there is American history punctuated most often by stories of war.

And it is all—save some dashes of color—Very White.

Forget for the sake of being "accurate" about the majority of people of color in the world. There is no Chinese or Japanese cinema, African or South American cinema. This is truly his story. It certainly ain't ours.

Finally, you get that feeling of being stabbed quickly as Spacey's name is called out for Best Actor. Unlike Michael Caine, Spacey is not gracious in acknowledging the excellence of his competitors. He acts just like the fool he plays in *American Beauty,* so maybe his "acting" wasn't really acting at all.

Denzel is all gentleman, clapping with the rest of the crowd. His face barely registers the blow to the body. As for the rest of us—the larger body—this is a total out-of-body experience.

It's like we're not even here.

Black and White

April 5, 2000

A cinematic bumrush is underway. *Black and White,* written, produced, and directed by James Toback, is certainly the most provocative of a new batch of films by White directors, producers, and writers with a feel or fascination for hip-hop.

All of them, including *Boiler Room, Ghost Dog,* and *Romeo Must Die,* offer a vision of the hip-hop nation in the popular imagination. Ever posed nude for a group of artists? Probably not. But, if you can imagine, the effect is the same in this crop of films. Others gaze at and paint you. And none of the resulting paintings are necessarily how you would paint yourself.

But they are interesting.

Black and White is, all at once, funny, tragic, unsympathetic, and flawed as it tells many stories. Wealthy, White, teenage New Yorkers adopt a hip-hop lifestyle imagined from music videos and celebrity interviews. A college basketball player (Allan Houston of the New York Knicks) gets caught up in love and greed. A fledgling filmmaker (Brooke Shields) tries to make a film about Whites adopting a "Black" hip-hop lifestyle. All of these stories are interconnected with the story of a Harlem gangster and his boys (assorted members of Wu-Tang Clan) who are aspiring rappers.

Toback won an Oscar nomination for his screenplay for the mob film *Bugsy,* and this film also has lots of outlaw flavor. It jumps around, with a freestyle feel, among the interconnected subplots and allows characters to improvise what they say. Of recent films, it is the most courageous attempt to examine the ugliness, brilliance, and contradictions of that place where gangster street culture and hip-hop intersect. It is the only one to explore the idea of making it in the lucrative world of hip-hop, and the people and personalities inhabiting that world. While it crowns young Black men as princes of this place, it reserves a high pedestal for Whites with power and for the availability and influence of White women and White p#$*y.

It has some twists and surprises—like Mike Tyson playing himself very well—so that you might not think until the end about what Toback is saying about this Black and White world. His version of the hip-hop world is a brutal place where you get what you want only through thuggery, intimidation, and the threat of violence. (Sounds like a good old American movie!) Here, you pay the ultimate price for betraying loyalty to those from your hood.

And here, White women are variously portrayed as some version of teenage mutant chickenheads or as educated, curious hos flirting with the raw-real-animal-whatever of Black men. In most cases, the Black men here act like most men will when tail is constantly thrown in their face—they grab it. There is very little room here for a Black and White relationship, or any relationship, that is not somehow dysfunctional.

And, finally, here, Black women are almost nonexistent. It's as if this film imagines that Black women have been pushed out of the hip-hop world. I'm not sure that's the case. Those of us who attend or attended big-name jock colleges might identify with the notion of seeing Black men dragged by their ankles away from Blacks and into a lily world of White men and women. Maybe those of us who exist in hip-hop entourages might know the extent to which Toback's version of life is true.

This is one point that will surely be debated.

Toback makes a few more points: that nothing good comes from any of this; that Black life is cheap; that it's easy to become a ho or a commodity and not even know it; that in this world of predator and prey, White men still have the biggest guns even if Black men are believed to have the biggest personal guns. Finally, he says in the end, nothing matters but who survives.

Maybe these points will be debated, too.

Third World Cop

April 14, 2000

Third World Cop is an entertaining remake of cops and robbers, with a dash of Jamaican rum. It recalls the slickness of *Shaft*—a smart, lean Black man fighting the bad guys. Like early movies in the recent wave of Black film, such as *New Jack City, Juice,* and *Sugar Hill,* the bad guys aren't all bad and the good guy isn't all good. It plays on our sympathy for the brother we all know—he has a good heart but has gotten caught up in some bad decisions. Finally, like the other famous Jamaican export—*The Harder They Come* (1972, starring Jimmy Cliff)—it tells about corruption through the poverty of a developing nation.

But the most fascinating thing is that *Third World Cop* achieves all of this while looking like a TV soap opera. Amateurish lighting and cinematography render it handicapped, appearing less realistic than old police and private-eye series like *Mission: Impossible* or *Mod Squad.* Forget for a moment what we are accustomed to seeing in theatrical releases, even independent ones. You need only think about the professional production quality of current TV shows like *The Sopranos, NYPD Blue,* or *Once and Again* to find better examples of lighting and production without a big movie–sized budget.

Though so handicapped, it nonetheless keeps our attention. Director Chris

Browne does keep the action moving. The thin story line follows police officer Capone (Paul Campbell) when he receives a new post in Kingston, his hometown. As he investigates a gun-running scheme, he realizes that a slain friend's brother—whom he had also embraced as a younger brother—could be the head of the crime ring.

Shot in Kingston, the film's scenes of ghetto shanty towns give it authenticity, as do scenes inside homes and the dialogue. Even though Jamaicans speak English, the heavy accent, dialect, and Kingston slang prompted the filmmakers to subtitle this film, so that it is clear to outsiders exactly what the fast-talking Jamaicans are saying. And Campbell is a first-rate leading man.

Like blaxploitation films of the '70s, there is gratuitous sex (right at the start). There is also plenty of shoot-'em-up, machismo, profanity, (too few) reggae club scenes, and a tight soundtrack, as well as humor. My favorite funny scene is when a crime boss with a metal hook for a hand tries to escape in the woods with his gangster hat and gangster pose and gets twisted up in vines. (And maybe it is cheap humor to have an obese woman trying out as an exotic dancer, but it is still humor.)

Without a lot of preaching and fanfare, *Third World Cop* says that, for many of us growing up in poverty around the world, a life of crime becomes an easy option. Without developing its characters very much or making excuses for them, it offers a simple morality tale. It offers two simple paths and shows the risk, hard decisions, and violence associated with both.

Finding Buck McHenry

April 16, 2000

The camera loves Ossie Davis. For a lifetime, it seems, there hasn't been a more endearing old Black man on the screen—be he pops, pop-pop, or the neighborhood drunk. *Finding Buck McHenry,* a family movie directed by Charles Burnett and premiering on Showtime, gets a big boost from the immortal pairing of Ruby Dee with Davis. He stars in the role of Mack Henry, a school janitor who becomes the subject of a mystery and a lesson in Black history. Dee appears as his wife.

Unintentionally, this film offers an idea of how the craze for Harry Potter–type mysteries might be translated into something a little more multicultural for young people. A young boy named Jason, who is a baseball fanatic but doesn't have skills, gets cut from his community team. At the same time, two more talented ball players come to town, including Aaron, the grandson of Henry.

The story unwinds as the players look for a coach for the new team they are forming. After Henry agrees to do it, Jason becomes convinced that the kindly janitor with an eye and feel for baseball is really Buck McHenry, a legendary pitcher from the old Negro Baseball Leagues. Then Jason has a mystery on his hands, a mystery that is not solved until the very end.

On the plus side, this movie offers a great history lesson, obviously aimed at young Whites as well as Blacks. Shots of the actual Negro League Museum of Kansas City give the film some substance, as does historic footage of the league, which had its heyday before Jackie Robinson broke the color line in modern baseball. Television hasn't offered many family-friendly, made-for-TV movies with as much to say about this sports era.

This is also a boy movie. It might be of particular interest to parents who grapple with their male child's obsession with sports, or their belief that sports glory awaits them just past puberty. (The film is also loosely based on Alfred Slote's novel of the same title, which my normally noncommittal seven-year-old loved and devoured in a few days.)

On the minus side of this made-for-TV flick, some of the scenes and dialogue are stagy and the Muzak-like soundtrack sounds best when it is barely heard. Also, the Black and female characters could have been better developed. Aaron, for example, has lost his parents in a car accident, but we don't hear his feelings about the tragedy or learn much about him. Kim, the female ball player who is also new to town, is simply rendered a snob and we don't know where her mother is.

These less-than-stellar moments are overshadowed by those when Davis gets to do his thing. For his moments and the history it tells, *Finding Buck McHenry* is more than worthwhile.

The Corner

April 16, 2000

Don't be fooled when tuning into *The Corner,* HBO's newest original miniseries. It is not a look at the hard-rock existence of most urban African-Americans—the solid working class and working poor, who pass the corner every day to run copy machines, flip burgers, care for the sick, or fill mall jobs. It also does not depict the male bonding, doo-wop singing, or playful macho posturing of the romanticized "corners" of yesteryear.

Based on the nonfiction bestseller *The Corner* by David Simon and Edward Burns, it is, instead, a riveting depiction of the violent, dead-end world of a Baltimore drug market and the tattered lives revolving around it.

In six episodes starting this week, *The Corner* is raw and unsparing as it explores the ravages of the drug world—from old-school heroin addicts to new-jack crack dealers "slinging rock" and shooting up the streets.

If you're prepared for this, jump right in. This series, directed by Charles Dutton, examines corruption, decay, and promise gone sour. In this world, the young are prematurely aged. Faces, necks, and arms are covered with abscesses, lesions, scabs, or blotches. Bodies are unwashed. Abandoned buildings that have no running water, that have rats or that reek of urine, serve as dwellings or hiding places. Empty lots are filled with garbage, discarded mattresses, and, occasionally, a corpse.

This series provides an alter reality to the glamorous drug culture shown in music videos and action movies. This reality is from the perspective of the user. Entire families are on drugs. There is a lot of hard work as well as misery involved in being a drug addict. People spend hours on end trying to score a few dollars for a "blast" of drugs. And then the cycle starts all over again. Street dealers are shown for real. They don't have money to buy Benzes or Bentleys. There are no diamond-studded hotties in the back of a limo or fancy dinners dripping with Cristal. Dealers maybe earn enough to buy new sneakers or a pair or jeans. Maybe.

Though a host of characters revolve in and out of the plot, the primary focus is on three people who once formed a family. There is Fran, a drug addict (Khandi Alexander); her former husband, Gary (T. K. Carter), who is also a drug addict; and their teenage son, DeAndre (Sean Nelson), who divides his time between dealing drugs and trying to go straight.

The acting is first-rate. Alexander, in particular, should garner award nominations for her stellar performance. The direction and set deliver an up-close, realistic portrait that you don't doubt for a minute. The dialogue, drawn in part from the book, is convincing, even if the actors lack the Baltimore/D.C. Black accent that, for many, borders on a Southern drawl.

Reflecting the experience of the book's authors and true-life people they followed, each episode begins and ends with an interview. The concluding interview at the end of the series features some of those who really lived the story these shows are trying to tell. They remind us, as one character does, that drugs take some of our humanity away each day. And they remind us that, no matter how much humanity is taken away, we are still human.

Love and Basketball

April 21, 2000

Love is a rough-and-tumble sport. Relationships are negotiated, massaged, prayed over, postured, and rejected. Seldom do they go smoothly like a perfect baseline jumper, hitting nothing but the bottom of the net.

Until recent films such as *Love Jones, Sprung, Waiting to Exhale,* and *The Wood,* few films focused on any substantial relationship between a Black man and a Black woman—be it smooth or stormy. *Love and Basketball,* the fine feature debut of writer and director Gina Prince-Bythewood, is, first of all, a part of this welcomed genre of new African-American romances. Second, it touches on complex relationship issues that emerge in this era as feminism, postfeminism, and antifeminism battle for turf and credence in the Black community.

Love of basketball is the vehicle though which Prince-Bythewood, an athlete herself, tackles the gender sport. Quincy McCall (Omar Epps) and Monica Wright (Sanaa Lathan) grow up next door to each other in a middle-class section of Los Angeles. They are fast friends and basketball buddies after young Monica proves that she can hang on the court with the fellas. The early kid scenes are a little clunky but, overall, Prince-Bythewood handles shots of both play and intimacy with a lot of finesse.

Lathan (who appeared in *The Best Man* and *The Wood*) steps out strong as an up-and-coming film diva to be reckoned with. She relies on her ability to be emotionally convincing, as well her considerable screen presence and acquired basketball skills, to handle this complex lead role. Epps is good, as it seems he plays slight variations of the same tough-cool cat in every film.

More of *Love and Basketball,* however, focuses on Monica and her struggle to find professional fulfillment with romantic happiness. So Monica is really a Black woman for the modern era. The soundtrack, a mix of '70s and '80s hits and new tunes, helps to pace and date the film. Depending on your taste, a pumping Al Green's *Love and Happiness* at the start will either get you in the mood, or seem like too much love too fast.

Though both Quincy and Monica develop into star student athletes, they are of course tracked by gender. Quincy, whose dad was an NBA player, sets his sights on an NBA career, too. But nothing of similar magnitude awaits Monica. Even in high school, as Quincy enjoys media attention, offers from prestigious colleges, and propositions from gaggles of girls, Monica is ridiculed for still being a tomboy with no fly hairdo, long nails, tight dress, or high heels. She tires of her prim mother

(Alfre Woodard) harping on her and—in a comical moment—declares herself to be a lesbian, just to shut her up.

When Quincy and Monica's friendship develops into a romance and they head off to college, their different gender tracks—as well as the complexities of modern Black relationships—develop as well. This film, like others, warns Black women that a focus on career and personal development can block their chances to get a man. It tells us that there is always a woman waiting in the wings ready to snap up an attractive Black man, but stops short of preaching to women to pursue or hold onto a man for dear life.

And, like recent films, it says that women must be the ones to make the relationship happen. Monica has to play a game—literally, in this case—to get a man. This potentially corny or misogynist point in the plot only works because, it turns out, Quincy is also forced to think about and play for a woman in his life. The prefeminist wisdom of Monica's mother combine with Monica's modern female sensibilities, including her athleticism, to create an ending that lets everyone win something worthwhile.

Black Star–Djimon Hounsou in *Gladiator*

May 5, 2000

Spring fever is underway. High-action summer blockbusters are rolling out. And male hormones have loomed large in the news lately. So it is difficult to write about the movie *Gladiator* without thinking about testosterone.

From its high-pitched war scenes, to its brutal Coliseum battles that evoke *Ben-Hur,* to its juxtaposition of manly courage with spineless cowardice, it is a movie that highlights the energies that drive men to either glory or destruction. Russell Crowe is burly, handsome, and convincing in the role of Maximus. (Could you find a more macho name than Maximus? It must be the Latin equivalent ofThe Notorious B.I.G.) Crowe embodies the idea of the fierce and wise warrior, the soldier who fights for family, honor, duty, country—all the stuff that we're told, and told again, in this movie, defines manhood.

Better Hollywood movies, like this one, force us to ignore any real-world questions we have about such easy truisms. The characters, action, and story wrap us up so tightly that there is little room to wriggle free. And we don't want to wriggle. We want to stay, fixated on the big screen, and see the story until the end.

Gladiator draws us in, first of all, with a tight story. Though set in the Roman Empire, and based loosely on actual historical figures, it offers up a tale primed for modern corporate America. Army general Maximus has sacrificed years of his life in service to Rome. In the process, he has earned the respect and fierce loyalty of both the dying emperor Marcus Aurelius (Richard Harris) and of his soldiers. But when Aurelius dies, Maximus suddenly finds himself betrayed by Aurelius's flaky and unstable son, Commodus (Joaquin Phoenix), who takes over as emperor and destroys Maximus's life. We watch to see whether Maximus's skill and integrity will serve his survival, his sense of honor, and notions of revenge.

And who wouldn't root for Maximus? Who, in this world where people are being downsized, laid off, hit with the glass ceiling, blackballed, whatever . . . ? Who, in this world where all kinds of folks—white collar, blue collar, pink collar—regularly "go postal"? Crowe makes it easy to root for the hero. Like his Oscar-nominated performance in last year's fine film *The Insider,* his performance here is first-rate. It is also easy to cheer him because Phoenix plays the egomaniacal villain so well. (Actually, Phoenix's character is just slightly over the top.) To seal the deal for me, Maximus eventually befriends and fights alongside an enslaved African named Juba, played superbly by Djimon Hounsou.

This movie doesn't insult our intelligence. If anything, it makes clear the relationship between Western "civilization" and barbaric brutality. The real-life Commodus was also very wack. Instead of commanding the troops fighting at Rome's far-flung borders, he was more interested in staging gladiator fights for the amusement of his increasingly restless subjects. Instead of fighting himself in war, he preferred fake sword duels. Ultimately, his warped notion about battle led Commodus the emperor, to the horror and shock of those in Rome, to seek public adulation and respect by fighting in the ring himself.

Gladiator sets up a macho match that is real, ancient and modern, and more complex than it seems. It says that real men fight, while weak men don't even know what real is.

From Mammy to Mama

Mother's Day 2000

Mammy, Castrating Mammy, Foxy Mama, a Real Mother for Ya, Mamasita, Mamma Jamma, "Welfare Mother," Hoochie Mama . . .

Watching Black film images is sometimes like watching the minute stages of human evolution, its greatness and pathology, up close. And nowhere is this slow change more apparent than in how we depict Black mothers on the screen.

Finally, in *Love and Basketball,* for example, we have portraits of, ultimately, three Black mothers who are drawn with some complexity and sensitivity, without the mask of comedic sexuality or mocking parody that prevent us from really seeing them. In this current film, Nona McCall (Debbi Morgan), Camille Wright (Alfre Woodard), and Monica Wright (Sanaa Lathan) are a trifecta for Black mothers. Their respective roles—the wife of a former NBA player, a middle-aged housewife, and a budding basketball player—represent the newest stage in this evolution that has only recently allowed Black women to be even featured in any substantial relationship with Black men.

Have you seen a mother like YOUR mother in a movie, television show, or video? Have you seen an image like yourself as a mother? Recently, I had a conversation with a young White woman. She was desperately trying to get pregnant and, somewhere in the conversation, I mentioned my then six-year-old son. "You're a mother?" she asked in obvious shock. She had just never thought of any Black woman—young, not matronly, and, by her standards, hip—as a mother.

We all suffer when we don't see ourselves in our full complexity and beauty on the screen. Yes, the mammy image was vicious and demeaning. But is it any less demeaning to have our identity narrowed to the ever-childless girlfriend/sex object? A steady stream of music videos and movies like *The Player's Club* and even upstanding fare like *The Best Man* show us more prominently as hoochie mamas, rather than real mamas. They are squeezing our brains and bodies into a giant thong. It's as if Sisqo's hit is the theme song for our trapped identity as nubile nymphs forever swishing our booties to the beat.

Why does this happen? Well, for a number of reasons. First of all, since the 1960s, our films have sold what most Hollywood pictures sell—action, violence, and, whenever possible, sex. Surely, in the popular imagination, fewer things are less sexy, violent, or action-packed than motherhood.

Also, just as with Black music, Black films have been very adolescent-driven. And, just as adolescents, the films themselves simultaneously ridicule and fear the role of parent. You only need to check out Ice Cube and his pals in *Friday* and *Next Friday* to feel a loss of hope for the progeny of our community. Despite its underdeveloped story and acting, at least Hype Williams's *Belly* portrayed a young mother (T-Boz) of the hip-hop generation.

Finally, the simple fact is that most filmmakers, Black and White, are men. The Hollywood fantasy is funneled through male sensibility, so along with the blazing guns and gangsters come the big boobs and bikinis. Sometimes misogyny comes, as well as the particular worldview of these males—single mothers abdicating responsibility in John Singleton's *Boyz n the Hood,* deceased mothers in Spike Lee's *Crooklyn* and *He Got Game,* the deep-fried ghetto moms of anything made by the Wayans clan.

Not suprisingly, *Love and Basketball* is written and directed by a woman, Gina Prince-Bythewood. A quick glance back at recent films focusing on Black mothers—*How Stella Got Her Groove Back, Down in the Delta, Beloved,* and *Waiting to Exhale*—shows that all were either written originally or directed by women. Sure, these movies have their weaknesses, but they also show that it makes all the difference in the world to have Hollywood fantasy funneled through female sensibility. The end result, instead of a shootout, is a family. Instead of more stereotypes about our legendary and matriarchal "strength," there is a glance at our fragility and vulnerability.

We grow up and give birth. So films should, too.

Milestones in the Journey from Mammy to Mama

Mammy: Louise Beavers in the television series *Beulah* (1950s)
Single Mama: Diahann Carroll in *Julia* (1960s) and *Claudine* (1974)
A Real Mother for Ya: Esther Rolle in *Good Times* (1970s)
Middle Class and Gorgeous: Claire Huxtable (Phylicia Rashad) of *The Cosby Show* (1980s)
Mamasita: Rosie Perez in *Do the Right Thing* (1989)
Mamma Jamma: Regina King in *Enemy of the State* (1997) and *Jerry Maguire* (1998)
Mad-As-Hell Mama: Angela Bassett in *Waiting to Exhale* (1995)
Hoochie Mama: any woman in a Wayans flick
"Welfare Mother": See Hoochie Mama
Foxy Mama: Sheryl Lee Ralph on *Moesha* (late 1990s)
Hip-Hop Mom: T-Boz in *Belly* (1998)
Castrating Mammy: Melissa DeSousa as Shelby in *The Best Man* (1999)
Female Basketball Player: Monica (Sanaa Lathan) in *Love and Basketball* (2000)
Old-Fashioned Housewife: Alfre Woodard in *Love and Basketball*
Aging Wife of Former NBA Star: Debbi Morgan in *Love and Basketball*

Held Up

May 12, 2000

The biggest victim in the movie *Held Up* is its audience. For ninety unrelenting minutes, you are held hostage to a flimsy story, unfunny jokes, and tired characters. You might find yourself crying for mercy into your popcorn—unless, of course, you are one to just give up and walk out of the theater. The story is about Mike Dawson (Jamie Foxx) and his fiancée, Rae (Nia Long), who are on vacation at the Grand Canyon. Rae learns that Mike has taken money they both saved to buy a house and spent it on a vintage sports car. She gathers up her luggage and leaves him at the convenience store, where all kinds of robbery and mayhem occur. You know a film is stale when all the jokes seem to come in slow motion. (Maybe this is a film for people on ecstasy or weed.) The eight-track tape of Tony Orlando and Dawn—big funny. The fast-food–induced diarrhea—big funny. Nia Long holding her butt for what seems like an eternity because she thinks this will somehow prevent that diarrhea from, uh, coming forth—ha ha. It only goes downhill from there.

Dinosaur

May 19, 2000

Just like the king-sized beasts it portrays, *Dinosaur* is both grand and plodding. It's not flimsy, sentimental, or filled with too-cute characters. With its battles between fierce creatures and a realism that may make young children flinch, it is a Disney film for the Pokemon generation. It's easy enough to figure out what is good about this movie. Of course the animation is superb. The film starts as a stray dinosaur egg is dropped by a pteranodon into the lair of a family of lemurs. Plio, the mama primate (Alfre Woodard), wants to keep the hatchling, while Yar, the dad primate (Ossie Davis), sounds more timid than the cowardly lion. Young Aladar grows up with the lemurs serving as his family. Everything seems to be going along in giddy Disney fashion until a killer meteor falls from the sky, laying ruin to all of the family's known world. The family is saved by jumping into the ocean and then joins a herd of dinosaurs looking for someplace on Earth that is still green. Along the way, the group meets drama, danger, and hope.

But if only the animals could have, at some point, also met some better writing. These Disney stock characters are *too tired:* the young buck fighting to be brave, the wise mother with the purring voice, the one clown who can't get a date. The (White) hot girl who gets her man in the end. And unfortunately, Disney has stayed true to its form of making Black-voiced characters (always animals, never people) either villains or buffoons. Plio's character is innocuous enough, but Yar is a monkey version of an Uncle Tom who is laughingly cautious. Eema, voiced by Della Reese, is a female Tom, an aged, plodding, big-butt Styrachosaur, who urges the young not to fight authority. You could say that these character flaws are seen by a discerning eye, seen by an adult who perhaps went looking for trouble. But movie images are powerful. And our children are smarter than we think. Pacing and character are the places where *Dinosaur* lays a big egg. It's as if the folks over at Disney had such a good time making the animals look great that they forgot to give them, and the story, more substance.

Black Stars–Thandie Newton and Ving Rhames in *Mission: Impossible 2*

May 24, 2000

No doubt. Director John Woo knows how to serve it up!

Even in a genre as timeworn as the summer action thriller, Woo delivers enough surprise and suspense to make *Mission: Impossible 2* well worth several dollars and two hours of your time. When you think about it, it makes sense that after *Face/Off* Woo would direct this film, which, like the vintage television series, also has spies and villains peeling off face disguises.

Of course, all these action films rely on healthy doses of machismo. And, of course, you could reel off a dozen Hollywood bad boys who might better provide that than Tom Cruise. Despite the movie-industry hype, I for one have never been able to see him as some fine, dashing roughneck. But, to give credit where credit is due, he does a better job this time of being convincingly macho. Seems like old Tommy boy has been eating his Wheaties, doing push-ups, and learning how to climb jagged cliffs. Maybe life has just given him a little more seasoning. What is required for a Mission: Impossible spy is this physical authority combined with a little finesse—enough finesse to throw an explosive while trying to get a rap on.

The summer mixture of action, danger, and romance is all very entertaining when wrapped around a decent script. Here, the story is that secret agent Ethan Hunt (Tom Cruise), aided in part by Luther Stickell (Ving Rhames), must prevent a deadly virus and its antidote from falling into the hands of the bad guy, Sean Ambrose (Dougray Scott). To get to the bad guy, Hunt recruits Ambrose's ex-girlfriend, Nyah Nordoff-Hall (Thandie Newton). But before Hunt and Hall can get to the business at hand, they have romantic business of their own to tend to.

Newton looks fabulous and plays the role of a skilled thief–trophy girlfriend fabulously. Her part, meaning the portrayal of women period in this film, has its problems. She's a pro and she is brave, but she's also irrational and reckless. Her role, however, is probably not worse than we've come to expect in these male fantasies. Most importantly, this is the first blockbuster film where a Black woman has played the beautiful and adored trophy, sought after by not just one man but two.

This is as close as Hollywood has allowed a Black woman to get to one of its big-box-office White males ever. This is also the first time that a relationship between said big White star and the Black leading lady has been unquestionably romantic and sexual. But that's as far as the filmmakers let it go. The much-hyped, steamy love scene between Cruise and Newton—a little jungle-fever-swirl-hype to peak the interest of the moviegoing public—has obviously been cut. It's possible that any steamy sex scene would be on the editing floor to ensure a PG-13 rating (and increase the box-office draw on this breakout Memorial Day holiday weekend). But you know how it is. The swirl added a little too much steam to that steam.

Too bad they threw water on Tom and Thandie, but the rest of the film sizzles.

Big Momma's House

June 2, 2000

Martin Lawrence would do well playing the role of a mad wizard with the ability to turn candy necklaces into gold chains or Now and Laters into multi-carat chunks of ice. While there is little in Lawrence's latest film, *Big Momma's House,* that can be honestly compared to gold or diamonds, his comedic talent takes a weak script and messy directing and creates moments that are hilarious.

To get to the laughs, though, we have to get past bathroom humor made a bit too visual, and the skewering of the Black grandmother as icon. (We can expect more of this in *The Nutty Professor II: The Klumps*.) I don't think any of us want to see our grandmothers loudly using the toilet or, for that matter, see them naked on a fifty-foot screen. As much as this film has its funny moments, it also deconstructs and ridicules the tired and triumphant bodies of elderly Black women to make the plot work.

Fat, elderly women are brought into the plot because FBI agent Malcolm Turner (Martin Lawrence) is investigating the prison escape of Lester, a notorious bank robber and murderer (Terence Howard) and whether he was aided by his former girlfriend Sherry (Nia Long). When Sherry learns of the escape, she flees her apartment and seeks refuge at the home of Big Momma in Georgia. To find out whether Sherry is innocent and to catch Lester, Turner transforms himself—with the help of a mask, bags of peanuts, and layers of fabric—into Big Momma. While the real Big Momma is away, he moves into her house.

In the process of solving his case in disguise, there is plenty of opportunity for big funny. In one moment, Turner's mask is peeling and he fixes it with a wide swatch of duct tape on the side of his face. In another moment, he is in a self-defense class for elderly women and he takes the opportunity to kick the butt of the bully instructor.

Moments of poor directing, editing, and lack of continuity in this film could be considered as just another facet of its humor. For example, the duct tape just disappears in the next scene with no explanation. Later on, there is no explanation as to how an elderly woman goes into town wearing a dress and winds up, a few minutes later, in workout clothes ready to take karate. It also seems that, by the end, the scriptwriter totally ran out of ideas.

This is a new comedic role for Lawrence. Only once does he do his old neck-rolling Sha-nay-nay female. Nia Long plays a straight woman with a lot of finesse, asking Big Momma in the one inevitable bed scene what is the hard thing poking her in the back. And each time I see him as the menacing bad guy, I like Terrence Howard more and more.

This film has a lot to offer but also asks a lot of the viewer. Go if you need a laugh, and you're in a generous mood.

OPM—*Me, Myself & Irene*

June 15, 2000

There are always unnatural acts in these Jim Carrey comedies.

In *Ace Ventura: Pet Detective,* he was an abnormal investigator. In *Liar, Liar,* he struggled to say something other than the brutal truth. In this newest film, *Me, Myself & Irene,* he plays Charlie, a Rhode Island state trooper who wrestles with a split personality brought on by a failure to express anger.

In other words, Charlie is mentally ill because he is a chump.

What has humiliated him to the point of chumpdom? Well, not only did his wife leave him, she left him for a Black midget genius (Tony Cox) who once whipped Charlie's butt. Not only did the midget whip his butt, he also apparently got busy with Charlie's new genius bride. How else do we explain Charlie and the bride's triplets, who are as chocolate as Tootsie Rolls? To top it off, the midget and the bride leave their genius Black children with Charlie to raise, and leave him with the scorn and contempt of the entire town.

So, if I get this right, if Mr. Charlie had just stood up like a (White) man, kicked the poop out of the (Black) midget, and told him to get off his wife, he'd probably be mentally healthy. Right?

Phew! This is a bit too much for me in these times we live in. Sure. It's easy to laugh at Jim Carrey acting like a fool, but the subtext for this film makes for very uneasy laughter, if not nausea.

Parodying Black people comes naturally for Carrey. He learned from the king of race parody as a regular on Keenan Ivory Wayans's *In Living Color*—the show that brought Black babies' mamas and inarticulate prisoners to TV. As racist as some might paint Carrey's latest flick, would they find it offensive if the Wayanses did exactly the same thing? The difference, some might feel, is that Black comedians are laughing with us, and White comedy is laughing at us. You be the judge.

Carrey works hard in this mindless movie, transforming himself from scene to scene into either of his dueling personalities. The plot, a combination of chase scenes and tasteless personal interaction, provides ample opportunity for Carrey to contort his face and limbs. It provides opportunities for bathroom humor, the exploration and display of sex toys, and a wacky pursuit of romance. Renée Zellweger plays the clueless pretty girl caught up in the mix. She is so vulnerable. Somebody help her!

Depending on your taste, this film effortlessly drifts between the hilarious and the foul. There is no better way to describe a chicken head buried in someone's rectum. The Black thing is used as another part of the freak show, as the three boys grow up into genius homie versions of the three stooges, brothers who cuss up a storm and refer to women as bitches, while solving complex algebraic equations.

They (We) are unnatural acts—a part of the sideshow. This is the Jim and Renée show. Read the title of the movie one more time.

Shaft

June 16, 2000

There is a part of Samuel L. Jackson that was born to play Shaft—the part that is old-school tough in a new century of posturing thugs, the part that is just as crazy as the eccentric gunmen he plays so well, the part that walked center-stage, nearly twenty years ago, in *A Soldier's Play*. At the close of Charles Fuller's World War II drama, when it was clear that Black soldiers would be allowed to go to war in Europe, Jackson's character declared: "LOOK OUT, HITLER. THE NIGGERS IS COMING!"

It is precisely the legend of the bad nigga (shut-yo-mouth!) that Jackson carries on in this high-powered, entertaining, though troubling, update of the 1971 classic. John Shaft for the twenty-first century, a nephew or play nephew of the old

Shaft (Richard Roundtree), is a New York City police detective. He is tall, has a cool baldie, wears leather coats and turtlenecks (designed by Armani), confronts racism, is not intimidated by Whites, and declares that it is his duty to "please that booty." (Though, perhaps out of character, he gets no swerve on in this film.) The bad nigga (shut-yo-mouth again!), whether he is Shine, Staggerlee, Dolemite, Trouble Man, the Mack, or Blade, is always, first and foremost, a screen wonder.

While Jackson carries this film as far as he can in updating the legend of Shaft, the script takes several questionable turns. It works, perhaps, that Shaft is a cop rather than the private detective in the earlier flick. Since that time, African-Americans have gone into many areas of employment previously closed off, including police departments. And the main story line certainly works: Shaft is obsessed with seeing that justice is done in a case of racial violence that left a young Black man dead.

But beyond that, it is really unclear who Shaft is, except a man with a passion for his vision of justice-by-any-means-necessary. (And maybe that is the only hero these action flicks can offer.) Shaft's passion leads him in one scene, as he grabs a shotgun and prepares to mow down some Latino bad guys, to declare: "It's Giuliani time!" (If this reference is unfamiliar to you, it is what Abner Louima said New York City police officers said to him in 1997 while beating and sodomizing him in a Brooklyn precinct station.) Would Shaft say this?

Just as in the first *Shaft,* the writer this time (John Singleton, who also directs) wants to make it clear that White people aren't the only bad guys. The villains (with thick foreign accents), who are in collusion with the White racist, are Latino, probably Puerto Rican. Shaft spends a lot of time shooting Puerto Ricans and the arch villain, Peoples Hernandez, is played superbly by Jeffrey Wright.

Even the original Shaft was not what you might have expected him to be. At the height of the Black Power movement, Shaft was not a consummate race man. He slept with White women and took a scolding tone with revolutionaries. He was cinema's Black playboy, a bon vivant and citizen of the world taking advantage of newly available cash, sass, and ass. Shaft's character was a big, audacious statement in 1971. The same character would not be so big now, especially in the post-soul, hip-hop bad boy, crack-Reagan-Bush-Clinton-Million Man March-O. J.-new economy world that we have survived.

The new *Shaft* is fast, slick, doesn't spare any bullets, and is funny as hell. Jackson makes this film like whoa, and Busta Rhymes is totally off the hook!

But, of course, it's up to you if you can totally dig it.

12

Acapulco 2000 and Summer Madness

Acapulco Black Film Festival—*Dancing in September*
Acapulco, Mexico
June 5-10, 2000

You gotta love *Dancing in September.* It looks at a potent issue in the African-American experience: our images on television, the behind-the-scenes struggle to create those images, and how human ambition, greed, and vulnerability get mixed in the fray.

Reggie Rock Bythewood, who wrote the screenplay for *Get on the Bus* and has been kicking around Hollywood since his days of writing for *A Different World,* doesn't take a preachy approach in this, his directorial debut. He tells his story through an up-close look at a young writer, Tomasina Crawford (Nicole Ari Parker), and her eventual relationship with a network executive named George Washington, played by Isaiah Washington. Though the plot is fictional, both Bythewood and his wife, Gina Prince-Bythewood, director of *Love and Basketball,* had plenty of experience in the world of television to stoke the writer's imagination.

The film looks great. It doesn't have that cheap, unconvincing veneer that plagues so many independent projects. And the writing is first-rate. It's obvious that Bythewood took his time in formulating dialogue and scenes that do more than just get us to the next point in the plot.

He serves up dialogue that sounds like how Black people really talk about things, think about things, agonize over things, get pissed off over things that other people don't give a second thought to. He offers dialogue about something other than assorted crimes; somebody's budding, static, or dying love jones; or about subjects that are supposed to be funny but are, instead, very tired. He offers a good love scene that is tender and real, not just a bunch of awkward or comical humping.

The characters are not perfect and they don't have perfect endings. They are complex enough to add depth to the plot. Bythewood gives us that complexity by letting us know a little about who these grown-ups were, and what they faced, as children. So many films by emerging artists, including many screened at this festival, could give their characters more dimension simply by adding more personal history.

As if relishing the opportunity to play different kinds of characters, Washington, Parker, and Vicellous Reon Shannon (*The Hurricane, Freedom Songs*) give excellent performances. I may be biased when it comes to Isaiah Washington, but he plays the buppie here just as well as he's played the thugs and solid family men in the past. Parker has an ease in front of the camera that draws us into her character, and Shannon is losing more of his stiffness and awkwardness with every part he plays.

As independent filmmakers continue to explore serious themes in their work, the question is whether they will have success selling their works. Can they interest Hollywood distributors? Can they distribute independently? And, finally, will an audience accustomed to the latest action flick, ghetto crime drama, or comedy turn out to see a story like this? It does not focus on violence, martial arts, or lasciviousness—but it is a story well told.

Acapulco Black Film Festival 2000–*Simeon*

This film is a feast for the eyes and spirit.

In the tradition of many filmmakers from other parts of the African diaspora, Palcy, a native of Martinique, makes culture the biggest star of this movie. From the beginning until to the end, music, myth, dance, language, religion, and spirituality are central to the plot, and serve as metaphors for the vitality and persistence of African life and culture.

Like her wonderful film *Sugar Cane Alley, Simeon* is set in Martinique, where one town's children are taught music by the beloved and gregarious Simeon (Jean-Claude Duverger). Simeon is a tall, ebony-skinned and salt-and-pepper-haired man who loves wine, women, and song. He loves strong drink so much, in fact, that one night, after a huge community festival, he drunkenly stumbles and falls to his death.

His transformation into a spirit is a catalyst for the culture. Spurred on by his legacy, the town's musicians, who played alongside him in a band, are encouraged to explore their art more fully. Isadore, a close friend to Simeon and one of the most respected of the musicians, makes the timeworn trek to Paris to sell the sounds of the island, a former French colony. In the process, he hawks his talents as a composer, guitarist vocalist, and bandleader to a European audience. Isadore's young daughter Orelie, who loves Simeon dearly, is forced—even though she is quite young—to consider how love and culture persist past death.

Palcy sets some island portions of her film almost as if they are on a stage, like an old-style Hollywood musical. The brightly lit scenes brim with so much life that they resemble a modern fairytale. Her use of low-tech special effects to evoke the idea of the supernatural reinforces the idea and feel of a modern fable.

Foreign films often flow at a slower pace than what we're accustomed to in the shoot-'em-up, car crash, scary movie culture. This film is driven as much by on-screen performances as by narrative. Through Simeon's death we are, in effect, given a tour of the time he spent in Paris. As a spirit, he accompanies Isadore to Paris and returns to his old haunts. He sees that the music played during his time lives on in a very real sense. He is able to create a link between the legacy of his aging musical peers and the music of the future coming from his island. Along the way, Palcy makes a statement about cultural preservation in the face of European influences, tastes, dilution, and appropriation.

There is a woman named Roselyne in this film who sings about returning home and embracing her roots. That singer sounds like she is a voice for Palcy, who has never forgotten her roots and never failed to make her people's culture a star.

Acapulco Black Film Festival 2000—*For Da Love of Money*

The comedian Pierre is genuinely funny. He has that around-the-way, guy-you-grew-up-with kind of humor that works without the need for vulgarity. In this, his first feature-length movie, he uses his considerable comedic talent to spin a hood tale about how wack folks can get when they think a brotha has maaad loot. As these crazy comedies go, this one is pretty good. It's funny in precisely that light, breezy manner that you hope for from a stand-up comedian writing his first feature-length film. It has jokes.

Pierre is given a big assist by fellow stand-up comic Ralphie May, a rotund White man who has his Ebonics and quick wit down pat in the role of the mailman. Reynaldo Rey, the wiley old veteran, is convincing in the role of Pierre's absent father. Pierre's script injects a lot of humanity into his characters. As funny as the film is, it also has its tender moments. Check this one out when it hits the streets.

Acapulco Black Film Festival 2000—*Nothin 2 Lose*

Add *Nothin 2 Lose* to your list of new hip-hop films that take on love, romance, and marriage. It's described in promotional materials as "*Friday* meets *Four Weddings and a Funeral*." (Hint: You know it's a hip-hop movie because there is a numeral substituting for a word in the title. Variations on this rule include using "Da" for the word "The" or using the latest slang from hip-hop records.)

It's okay as these situation comedies go. There is some good dialogue between the two main characters, Kwame (Brian Hooks) and Yasmine (Shani Bayete). There is enough of a story and comedy within that story to keep it flowing until the end. There is a good subplot and scenes that capture the energy and club scene that swirls around emerging musical artists.

The story is this: Kwame and Yasmine have been seeing each other for a couple of years and are living together. When Yasmine's best friend gets married, she starts thinking about her desire to be married and be a mother, too. And, of course, as these stories go, Kwame is reluctant to marry her, even after she gives him thirty days to get to the altar or it's splitsville. It would be wonderful if just one of these films that focus on male phobia about marriage at least made a stab at exploring the fear: It could come out in a conversation with a buddy. It could be a flashback to his childhood or the fact that he didn't have a father in his life or has never seen an intact family. Any plausible explanation would help. Even comedies need a little deepening to make us feel the characters more. We might even laugh a little harder.

Acapulco Black Film Festival 2000—*Love the Way*

Love the Way, by Christine Swanson, winner of the 1998 HBO Short Film competition, takes a mature look at a young woman seeking love and commitment. Swanson is onto something here. There is some good writing. The characters are not one-dimensional, and the presence of Lisa Raye and Chris Spencer, formerly host of the *Vibe* television show, makes for some funny moments. The story follows Nicole (played by Renee Goldsberry), who has been working hard for her relationship and is ready for a commitment from Robbie, her boyfriend. He works as an attorney at the firm where she is a paralegal. It is obvious, however, that he's not as hot-and-bothered over her. She throws him an elaborate surprise party and he treats her like the hired help. With this conflict set up, the movie starts out fine.

But *Love the Way* needs to shake off the feel of a made-for-TV movie. As much as Swanson should be credited with making her young protagonist more than one-dimensional, there is something missing. We need a little more of Nicole; good portions of it need better lighting and a better set. A musician and his love songs need to be better set up in the plot: Sometimes the music goes on too long and sometimes it seems sort of corny. While the singer and actor Terron Brooks—a sort of Brian McKnight type—is obviously talented, it takes a special effort on the part of directors, producers, and writers to successfully incorporate musical numbers into a drama. Finally, in order to be successful, these love dramas must maintain the ring of emotional truth. Perhaps if we get to know Nicole a bit better, we will be better able to accept her transition from the walking wounded to a woman who is ready to walk away.

Acapulco Black Film Festival 2000–*Under Suspicion*

Under Suspicion takes apart a man and woman's social facade and strips them down until they are totally naked. In this sense of gradual exposure, it functions well as police drama. You'll love it for that. And you'll hate it for leaving you hanging with too many questions in the end. The movie looks great. At a film festival, you only need to see one movie like this with decent cinematography to make most of the independent offerings look like caca. But the problem here seems to be the script. Despite the fact that Morgan Freeman executive produces and appears in *Under Suspicion,* it unfortunately falls into the lesser vehicle trap. Somebody please bring Freeman some roles.

Acapulco Black Film Festival 2000–*Same Difference*

This little film, from one of the fledgling film companies debuting at this year's festival, takes an ambitious look at how AIDS and street violence are raising the death toll in African-American and gay communities.

Writer Don Mays, who also directs, has the outlines of a good story. In a Providence, Rhode Island apartment, a young woman juggles the drama of a White cross-dressing gay roommate, her roughneck ex-lover who has dropped in with a serious gunshot wound, and the tragedy of her roommate's ex-lover who is dying of AIDS. But without more depth, the film looks too much like a video—a series of visually arresting impressions—without the underpinnings needed to really draw us into a full-bodied story. This is a great start. Hopefully we'll see more of this film and more films in the future from Mama's Reel Black Market Films.

Acapulco Black Film Festival 2000–*Box Marley*

This film runs neck-and-neck with Melvin Van Peebles's *Bellyfull* as the strangest offering at this year's festival. Consider *Box Marley,* Christopher Scot Cherot's second feature, as Exhibit B in the case proving his odd comedic talent as a writer and director. The first exhibit was his romantic farce, *Hav Plenty,* in 1997. Also consider this film as more evidence that some Black filmmakers are trying, by any means necessary, to make movies they want to make, and to break out of the box of predictable comedies, romances, or hood films. The subject here is boxing, with all its possibilities for humor—mountain-sized men pummeling each other for sport; thuggy promoters; and air-brushed, calculating women circling the cash. It is also, as is many of these comedies, an exploration of that place that might be called Loserville. In this world, we are introduced to Wade "Soul" Ross, played by Hill Harper, most recently of *City of Angels* and *The Skulls.* To call Ross skinny, uncoordinated, or untalented would all be understatements. He alone sees his potential as he pursues his dream with a logic that is also understandable only to him. Despite his need for improvement, his training regimen does not include training or working with a real trainer. This movie isn't for everyone, but it deserves to reach its audience and its audience deserves to see it.

Acapulco Black Film Festival 2000–*Field Guide to White People*

There are so many good White-people jokes. If there was a slave comedian, he or she probably had fellow cotton pickers in stitches over the ways of White folks. Certainly in the last century, comedians like Redd Foxx, Richard Pryor, Eddie Murphy, and Chris Rock have served up a bounty of jokes that allow us to ridicule the owners of skin and social privilege. So it is almost a mystery why the *Field Guide to White People* is such a failure. Even if the writers had simply revamped old jokes—the way White people walk, dress, smell when wet, dance, gang up on one Black man, and shoot up high schools—it would have been funnier than what has been produced here. Go figure.

Acapulco Black Film Festival 2000–HBO Short Film Competition

Short films presented at this year's competition were strong contenders and represented a wide range of styles and subject matter—from satire to horror fantasy to suicidal drama. The winning film, chosen by a panel of African-American directors and an HBO programming executive, was *My Father's Hands.* It paints a picture of a West Indian family—the mother who works hard as a nurse, the father who owns his own butcher shop, and the son who is an aspiring dancer. The son, though he continues to work in his father's store, is a vegetarian. The father has never gone to see his son dance. But tragedy forces them to communicate with and hold onto each other.

Acapulco Black Film Festival 2000–*Something to Sing About*

Consider this film, which has "made-for-TV" written all over it, as a Black Christian response to thug life in African-American cinema. Its message is simple: You need Jesus. This type of religious appeal is unusual. We are all more accustomed to seeing religion in a documentary, or in yet another fiction about the life of Christ. We are confronted with all kinds of supernatural wonders on the big screen, but we usually don't see evidence of the extraordinary faith of our parents and grandparents. Even if the religion is presented in a way that is not over the top, we think we hear preaching. *Something To Sing About* doesn't preach too much and it has some excellent singing by the star, newcomer Darius McCrary. Kirk Franklin even makes a cameo—and his appearance is appropriate. This film is the cinematic equivalent of a CD by Franklin or Yolanda Adams. It's a contemporary mode of delivering religion.

Acapulco Black Film Festival 2000–*Bellyfull*

This is a crazy flick.

If you think that the Simpsons, Al Bundy and company, or *Malcolm in the Middle* paint bizarre pictures of family life, then *Bellyfull,* an eccentric art film, ups the ante considerably. Along the way, the film also spins a twisted tale about postcolonial realities and attitudes in France. This is a different kind of story. Check it out for its take on French hypocrisy and racism—if you can also take two hours of weirdness, sarcasm, and watching a young, vulnerable Black woman do a mean postcolonial shuffle.

Scary Movie

July 7, 2000

Parody only works if it's funny. *Scary Movie* has a few chuckles but it doesn't have too many big jokes. Even if you're a big fan of this summer's abundant gross-out humor, *Scary Movie* falls short in that category, too.

It's a great idea to satirize horror movies—all those flicks that have left us forever peeking out of our shower curtains. Recent offerings in the genre, such as

Scream, have already added humor to the horror equation. In a sense, Keenen Ivory Wayans is parodying the parody.

And, unlike his hilarious *Don't Be a Menace* and *I'm Gonna Got You Sucka,* this effort just fails. Don't get me wrong. I'm glad he can make movies. I'm glad the brother and his brothers are getting paid and are able to handle their business. That's all good. One love.

But Keenen, who directs this project, needed to work on some sharper humor for it. I know he is capable of it. He is not credited as the writer here. His brothers Shawn and Marlon, who also star in the film, are listed as two of the film's writers. This team has delivered a script that rests on clichés, the run-of-the-mill, and the been there, done that.

Of course, it doesn't help that this is just the latest sorry film this summer. I'm tired of vulgarity and shock used as a substitute for humor. I'm tired of "comedy" that isn't funny. I'm tired of stupid movies. I'm tired of feeling like I've wasted a perfectly good two hours of my life. It's bad when I walk out of the press screening and say, "Well at least I didn't have to pay to see this."

This film, like many of the horror flicks, follows a group of teenagers, who fall victim to a mysterious crazed murderer dressed as the grim reaper. This movie does a decent job of both playing on our fear of the psycho murderer and making him the butt of jokes. One moment he steps out from a hiding place and looks scary and unmoving, in the familiar movie pose of the killer. We're supposed to look on (him) and quake. In the next minute, he's smoking blunts with a bunch of guys so stoned they don't seem to notice their new buddy's ghost face and hook-shaped hand.

The grim reaper, and the artist who created his masks, is actually the star of this movie. The reaper has a regular ghoul face—the mouth is opened wide in a perfect O, in a silent howl. Then he has a face like he's stoned after he's been smoking blunts. He has an amused face. He has an entertained face when he's watching one of his victims do Irish step dancing in midair. (Don't ask.)

This movie is scary. It's so scary I forgot to laugh.

Black Star–Halle Berry in *X-Men*

July 14, 2000

Berry stars as Storm, who in the comic book series is a fierce leader of the X-Men but is reduced in this big-budget film adaptation to mainly controlling the weather by rolling her eyeballs up into her head.

The Nutty Professor II: The Klumps

July 28, 2000

I have newfound respect for Eddie Murphy as an actor. He's successfully taken assorted characters from his ancient stand-up act and created a whole movie about them in the flesh—lots of flesh. In *The Nutty Professor II: The Klumps,* he plays five members of the Klump family, the same fat, flatulent folks introduced in his first Nutty Professor movie. But this time, it's all Klump—there's papa and mama Klump, two brothers Klump, and a very horny grandma Klump. These people know how to get their eat on. And you could call grandma a man-eater.

It is this multiplicity of roles that makes this movie entertaining. (But one strong warning: It is not for children.) The makeup team does an incredible job of making Murphy's many faces. Director Peter Segal and the special effects and editing teams create realistic group scenes of the Klumps when only one person actually exists. All in all, it is enjoyable, if you can get past the bathroom humor, the repeated bashing of elders, and if you allow yourself to suspend some common sense.

It's not that I don't believe Murphy and his costar, Janet Jackson, could really be geniuses. It's not that I don't think the cherub-faced Jackson could actually marry a doughy blimp. But in the hustle-and-bustle of Murphy's madness, it's obvious that the writers are playing fast and furious with basic science. But maybe you can only laugh at the idea of creating a human being from some blue slime and a single strand of dog hair.

This sequel's writers (who do not include Murphy) are, literally, obsessed with the human body—its genetic code, its corpulence, its decay. When painting the Klumps, their overuse of clichés and weak jokes is tempered somewhat by a stroke of humanity given to them. The main character Murphy plays is Sherman Klump, a biology researcher at Wellman College in California. For a bumbling, uncool guy, Sherman has a lot on the ball. He has stumbled onto a formula that may reverse the aging process and his fellow professor Denice Gains (Jackson) thinks he's just wonderful. She'd rather have a big guy who is kind and has integrity than a svelter version of eventual disappointment.

But Sherman is dogged by his alter ego, Buddy Love, a foul, fast-talking hustler who is actually part of Sherman's genetic makeup. Sometimes Buddy controls Sherman's personality, leading him to say uncouth things—he suggests to Professor Gains that he could put "some beef" in her "taco." To protect his love affair from Buddy's foul tendencies, Sherman decides to extract Buddy's gene from his body.

The extraction results in Buddy taking human form and creating havoc once more. As Sherman tries to keep together his love thang, he must also, once again, protect his scientific secret from falling into the wrong hands—Buddy's.

At its best, this movie hilariously combines a comedic rendering of complex science with basic animal functions: eating, waste elimination, mating, and sleep. The giant hamster is the bomb. This latest comedy-in-overdrive this summer is almost surreal in its foolishness.

A House Divided

July 30, 2000

When it comes to slavery dramas, we think we've seen it all—sweating, degradation and death, whips and chains, sorrowful singing in the high cotton, rapes, torture, and overwhelming terror. Who needs to see the same take on the same terror again? And so many of us run away, as if some slavery ghost might jump from the screen and shackle us here in the year 2000.

But, just as surely as the African-American experience is deep and wide, there are many more stories to tell. *A House Divided,* premiering on Showtime, is a slavery-era drama worth your time. Starring LisaGay Hamilton, Jennifer Beals, and Sam Waterston, it is based on the true story of Amanda America Dickson, the mixed-race daughter of a Georgia slave owner who fought in Southern courts to keep the inheritance left to her by her father.

This little film deals in a straight-ahead manner with the often complex and heartbreaking relationships on a slave plantation. It has moments that don't quite work, but even then the effort is interesting. Imagine a slave owner attempting to discuss with a slave how he was wrong to molest her, or imagine the family of a Black child supporting the Confederate Army. Without melodrama, *A House Divided* shows how the peculiar institution created houses of deception and contradiction.

Though the film was obviously shot on modest means, the production and direction combine to create scenes that are realistic and dramatic. This tightly written film is driven by a compelling narrative and dialogue that is both natural and revealing. This film shows that violence is not always loud or visible in the life of a slave. Sometimes it happens quietly. Sometimes it happens during events that are supposed to be happy—like childbirth.

13

Urbanworld 2000 and Black Women on the Verge of a Film Breakdown

Urbanworld Film Festival
New York, New York
August 2-6, 2000

The Urbanworld Film Festival is proof positive of both the tremendous vitality and the ongoing struggles of the Black film movement. More than sixty films, including independent features, documentaries, and short-subject works, gave festivalgoers a bounty to choose from, and made this year's competition the most difficult to judge in the New York festival's four years.

The Visit, a riveting drama about family and prison starring Hill Harper (*Hav Plenty*), Billy Dee Williams, and Marla Gibbs, won the audience award, while *One Week,* the powerful AIDS drama that picked up several awards at the Acapulco Black Film Festival in June, was awarded Urbanworld's prize for best feature.

"I don't usually like to go to film festivals or put my work in them," said Jordan Walker Pearlman, writer and director of *The Visit*. "Most of them are marketplaces. Urbanworld is one of the few festivals in the world that is still about a celebration of movies."

A work in progress, *30 Years to Life,* demonstrated ably that there are plenty of buppies out here who can out-talk, out-funny, and out-quirk that popular *Friends* cast. Director Vanessa Middleton proves that you can't go wrong with good writing and a script laden with comedy and drama.

Documentaries also showed a tremendous range in vision and style. *Legacy,* directed and produced by Tod Lending, follows the journey of one Chicago family as they move from public assistance to independence. *Scottsboro,* directed and produced by Daniel Anker and Barak Goodman, chronicles the infamous case of the Scottsboro Nine, a group of African-American youths who were wrongly convicted and jailed in Alabama for the alleged 1931 rapes of two White women. *Scottsboro* shared the documentary award with *Freestyle,* a lively, no-holds-barred look at the hip-hop world by Kevin Fitzgerald.

Another documentary, *Voice of the Voiceless* directed by Tania Cuevas-Martinez, is a vivid account of the international movement to free journalist Mumia Abu-Jamal, sentenced to Pennsylvania's death row for the murder of a Philadelphia police officer. *House on Fire,* directed by Mustapha Khan, is a documentary designed to raise awareness of HIV/AIDS in the Black community. Though Blacks comprise only 13 percent of the U.S. population, we represent nearly 60 percent of those infected in this country.

Though energy was high, the festival does continue to experience growing pains. Some screenings were oversold, while weekday screenings and informative panels, which covered everything from the nuts and bolts of filmmaking to distributing films on the Internet, were sparsely attended. But despite such glitches, the festival gave Black filmmakers an audience and a vote of support.

"We were at Urbanworld in 1997, and we said we weren't coming back without a film," said Carl Seaton, director, cowriter, and coproducer of *One Week.* Kenny Young, cowriter and coproducer of the film added, "We're building our own power base in film."

Myla Churchill, who won the festival's screenwriter's competition, her first award ever, said that Urbanworld (despite its inclusion of films by Whites with a Black theme) is a place that allows Black artists and Black people to have voice. "The work that everyone is doing is for us and about us," the Brooklynite said. "And that type of work hasn't always been apparent in the mainstream."

Urbanworld Film Festival 2000–*The Visit*

Even at its start, *The Visit* feels like the return of long-lost friend. It is far from a perfect film. But it is moody and full of the pathos of modern life. It is moving in a manner that does justice to our emotional and psychological lives.

The gossip is that *The Visit* is struggling to land a distribution deal so that we can see it in theaters. Well, shame on Hollywood—and shame on us. This film has ten times more human feeling than the June box-office hit *The Perfect Storm.* At some point, our serious stories about the African-American experience will need to be fought for, not only by the movie industry, but by us.

This film tells the story of Alex Waters, incarcerated after a rape conviction, and shows us Alex's bond with his mother, father, brother, and community. Hill Harper (*City of Angels, The Skulls, In Too Deep*), who plays Alex, is really getting the chance to flex his acting muscles in this year's crop of Black independent films. I saw him in June as the star of *Box Marley,* Christopher Scott Cherot's latest quirky film, which previewed at the Acapulco Black Film Festival.

In *The Visit,* Harper portrays a man angry at injustice, angry with his family, and angry about AIDS wreaking havoc on his body and spirit. His eyes are deep pools, his stare is intense, and he acts like a man running out of time.

Much of the film rests on Harper's superb performance, flashbacks to Alex's childhood, and the dialogue during his family's visits in prison. Very few films that explore the African-American experience do so with this much texture and sensitivity. It's almost understandable why Jordan Walker-Pearlman has gotten caught up in the atmosphere a bit too much, at the expense of the plot.

This movie could move quicker. It could answer more of the questions it raises—like what was the turning point for Alex? What made him the younger, drug-using, self-destructing brother? Do all the childhood scenes have anything to do with who he is today? How did he get AIDS? Was he given a death sentence, in effect, by being raped in prison? We don't know the answers. Instead, we're offered psychological drama, which includes Phylicia Rashad in the role of a sympathetic prison counselor. She purses her lips in such a way and is shot at camera angles that make her look a bit spooky.

Obba Babatundé, with his deep-circled eyes and droopy jowls, is convincing as Alex's pained and perplexed older brother, Tony. Billy Dee Williams is strong in the role of Alex's father, Henry Waters (a straight-no chaser type), who insists that Alex be responsible for his decisions and shows no pity. Maybe this film is like Alex's father. It offers no excuses, and it offers few answers. It gives all the caring that it can then leaves us to make our own decisions.

Urbanworld Film Festival 2000—*Voice of the Voiceless*

Mumia Abu-Jamal is the most visible and controversial inmate on death row. The Philadelphia Police Department and the widow of the officer he is convicted of murdering clamor for his execution. A wave of national and international supporters—convinced of the racism of Philadelphia's police and judicial system—demand a new trial and call for his release.

This documentary does a good job of chronicling the events and atmosphere in Philadelphia that led to the conviction of Abu-Jamal, a journalist and former president of the Philadelphia chapter of the National Association of Black Journalists. Some of its technical aspects, especially the sound, need improvement. Much of the interview with Abu-Jamal, conducted inside a prison visitation area, is inaudible. But as a Black native of the City of Brotherly Love, I appreciate the effort made here to portray the tension and hostility existing between the police department and the city's Black community. Philadelphia's police took a special interest in Black political groups, such as the Black Panthers and, later, the naturalist group MOVE.

When I was a young child, there were vivid news accounts of the police forcing members of the Black Panthers to strip naked and stand spread eagle on a public street not far from my parents' house. As a teenager, and then young adult, I watched as members of MOVE were first evicted from one house and then in 1985 bombed out of another, the latter action resulting in nine deaths and the fiery destruction of dozens of homes.

Abu-Jamal, as well documented in this film, was marked by the federal government and the local police as early as age fifteen. As a teenager, he wrote for the Black Panther newspaper. When MOVE was in the news, he was one of the few journalists who offered in his dispatches the perspective of MOVE in addition to the perspective of police and government officials.

By focusing on Abu-Jamal's supporters, *Voice of the Voiceless* delves into myriad related issues, including the rise of the prison-industrial complex and the disproportionate number of Black men on death row. It has its messy moments, but Tania Cuevas-Martinez has the talent to tell a story with force.

Urbanworld Film Festival 2000—*30 Years to Life*

Don't be fooled by the title.

30 Years to Life is not some dreary courtroom or prison drama. In fact, it is one of the funniest comedies I've seen about that rite of passage, turning thirty years of age. It has the hilarity of *Sex and the City,* the friendship and bonding of *The Wood,* and the just-can't-get-it-right reality of *Love Jones.*

Bright writing is the key. It shows that writer and director Vanessa Middleton has paid her dues (TV writing credits include *Saturday Night Live, Cosby,* and *Hangin' with Mr. Cooper*). Her multifaceted characters make us laugh at life's oddities, like having a foot with six toes.

The ensemble of men and women, all of whom turn thirty in the course of a year, are an interesting and strange lot. They include a comedian, a high-powered executive (Melissa DeSousa of *The Best Man* and *Ride*), and a man (Allen Payne) who chucks a big promotion to pursue his dream of becoming a supermodel. They're not all beautiful and perfect. In fact, I have to give *big props* to Paula Jai Parker (*Friday, Woo*) for donning a fat suit and Klump-esque makeup. She plays the part of a plus-size sister who spends her nights devouring large bags of nacho chips. Not many thin-obsessed, itty-bitty Hollywood actresses would be so bold.

I like how Middleton mucks with conventional wisdom. In her script, it is a man who is a bit age-obsessed as he watches a younger, obviously less talented, comedian get breaks because of his fresh-faced youth.

Like many of the gender comedies arriving in the shadow of *The Wood,* the battle of the sexes is part of the equation here. One woman doesn't understand why she's not married. She looks good and has a great job. Why hasn't Mr. Right shown up on her doorstep? One couple has been living together for a few years and the woman in the union (Erika Alexander of *Living Single* and *The Cosby Show*) is starting to think that enough is enough and that it's time to get married. The rest of this crew seems to have problems in the love department as well.

Middleton's female sensibilities are obvious. Much of the story is told from the perspective of women, and there is obvious sympathy for them. They are living in a world where they care deeply about having a relationship, yet most of the men around them fear commitment like they would fear a world without beer. To be fair, maybe the men do get a rough deal in this film. Though it may seem that way, not all guys are selfish, self-absorbed, passive-aggressive jerks.

But at least Middleton makes them funny jerks.

Divided We Stand

August 8, 2000

The popular image of the college experience, in countless television shows and movies, is one of lazy days, liquor- and sex-filled parties, and cursory attention given to classes and exams. But just think about our portrayals of college life, notably Spike Lee's *Higher Learning.* For African-Americans, college is often a trial by fire in race consciousness and identity. This movie, shot at Columbia University in New York City, attempts to deal in an up-front manner with Black radicalism on campus. There is sincerity and passion here, as well as the outline of a good story. But the plot is sabotaged early on as it reveals too much too soon about pivotal events. It's as if scenes and story building are treated as less important than performance. In several scenes, you get the sense that *Divided We Stand* functions best as opera. The only thing missing, perhaps, is loud choruses by The Last Poets and Public Enemy. There is plenty of high drama—dramatic poses, melodramatic acting, and dramatic situations. On the face of it, that sounds fine. But ninety minutes of high drama like this will wear you out.

The Original Kings of Comedy

August 18, 2000

The success of *The Original Kings of Comedy* tour is proof positive that Black comedians are the superstar preachers of African-American secular life. Funneling the world's sins and idiosyncrasies through their crazy, down-home, or salacious humor, they fill huge arenas and—more than singers, dancers, or actors—elicit moans, shrieks, and tears from the crowd.

In this live concert, the four self-proclaimed kings, Steve Harvey, D. L. Hughley, Cedric the Entertainer, and Bernie Mac, make the Charlotte Coliseum their pulpit and make the audience roar with laughter.

Each of the four, who stride on stage in tailored suits, offer modern parables: the President and his stank ho intern, the man who does not want to cuddle in the summer because it's *hot*, the two-year-old tyrant who looks down on a grown man, the particular art of Black people running en masse. They see us as we see ourselves—our families, friends, neighborhoods, and U.S. survival skills. They allow us to laugh at ourselves, knowing full well that the man on stage is laughing with us, not at us.

No doubt, this film will draw comparisons to concert flicks by Richard Pryor, Eddie Murphy, and Martin Lawrence. The big difference, of course, is that there are four men here in the place of one. Each one contributes a distinct style. Harvey, the West Virginia country boy who grew up in church, most evokes the Southern preacher with his country drawl and sage, finger-wagging style of telling jokes. While his live act is peppered with profanity, he is not blue.

Hughley's dead-aim humor is drawn from his family experiences as a child and now as a husband and father. Perhaps most in the tradition of Pryor here, he is a storyteller and is able to convey his amazement and amusement with everyday life (though he was able to stretch out more on his HBO special).

Cedric the Entertainer, who steals the show here, is a master of timing, inflection, and facial expressions. Of the four, he is the one we're most likely to laugh at before he even opens his mouth. Mac is the bad boy, leading the congregation down the paths of oral sex and adultery, all the while making his eyes pop out like some rerun of a Stepin Fetchit flick.

Because all four acts had to fit into the show and film, this format favors quick-hit funny versus storytelling. Each comedian comes out and must keep the energy high. They both challenge and feed off of one another. Director Spike Lee adds another dimension with scenes backstage and scenes of the funnymen at a basketball court (of course, Spike!), playing cards, and riding their tour bus. Cedric fusses over what suit to wear, while Bernie Mac makes the sign of the cross on himself before he goes out to cuss up a storm.

Like sermon time at most churches, a total male energy and viewpoint is presented here. Despite the overload of testosterone, misogyny doesn't rule the day. The Kings of Comedy represent an old-school, pre-hip-hop sensibility in the culture. There is little or no bitch and ho talk in this film. Harvey does a long segment extolling the virtues of old love songs and vintage soul acts like Earth, Wind & Fire. The audience, particularly the women, jump up at the start of each new song, dancing and reveling in memories of younger days.

For the moment, just like in the moments we see them take pictures in front of those cheesy concert backdrops, the women dancing in place are the queens of these kings. And the night has renewed everyone.

For a moment, everyone feels sane and like it's Sunday morning.

Catfish in Black Bean Sauce

August 24, 2000

There is a Vietnamese man named, of all things, Dwayne. He grew up in Los Angeles, adopted by a Black family. So he has some of the Black talk, is accustomed to his mother's combination soul food–Vietnamese cuisine (catfish in black bean sauce?), and he dearly loves a Black woman named Nina (Sanaa Lathan). He also has a White roommate with a cross-dressing girlfriend/boyfriend.

Phew! Dwayne has a lot going on. Director and star Chi Muoi Lo certainly can't be faulted for a lack of plot in his feature-film debut. He packs a lot of story into his funny and flawed movie that explores life on the edges of the American melting pot.

Dwayne and his sister, Mai, were raised by Harold and Dolores Williams, played tenderly by Paul Winfield and Mary Alice. Mai is obsessed with finding their real mother, who it turns out is more interested in Dwayne than her. Not only does Dwayne grapple with the meaning and direction of his life, his love life leaves him confused and insecure about being short. Even indoors, he stays glued inside a pair of thick-heeled boots that add inches to his height.

Chi is full of good ideas and he has a lot to say. He knows that people of color lead interesting and funny lives without being buffoons or caricatures. Much of the underlying comedy comes from our voyeuristic look at the melting pot as it simmers. Only we voyeurs can see the hilarity and idiosyncrasies of members of the Williams family, who are just living their lives as they always have.

But the problems here seem to be with writing and direction. While Chi takes pains to show the rift between Mai and Mrs. Williams, he does not help us to understand the distance between the two women. Similarly, while we know that Dwayne is obsessed with his lack of height, we don't learn much else about him. And we need to know. It seems like a wasted opportunity for either comedy or drama to not explore more fully how Dwayne has come of age as a Vietnamese man in a Black environment, and then assimilated into yuppie Los Angeles.

As it is, this film makes us care about Dwayne, but only marginally. It seems that Mai is an ungrateful heifer and poor Nina is given about as much personality as a Black Barbie. Obviously, the problem is not Lathan's acting. She just needs something to say and do, other than offer the camera that Sanaa Lathan pained expression.

At least Chi is tackling something different and fresh. He is writing in part from his own experience as one of the Vietnamese "boat people" resettled in Philadelphia after leaving his homeland in 1975. As he matures as a writer and director, he may create scenes that are shorter, as well as more pointed and visually interesting. But this is an ambitious debut. In opting to bypass the easy out of easy entertainment, he's one more filmmaker insisting on the need for and value of telling our own stories.

Black Star–Wesley Snipes in *Art of War*

August 25, 2000

Sure. Wesley Snipes has done and said some disappointing things. He has managed to turn off much of the very constituency—Black women—that catapulted him into the realm of sex symbol and movie superstardom. But since, for me, he has ceased to exist as a real person—only a screen persona—I must admit that I do enjoy the South Bronx street energy he brings, the ebony profile he cuts (as long as he's not dyed blonde or wearing a dress). And, no doubt, there's still something about Wesley and his big . . . Black . . . gun. (What did you think I was going to say?)

It seems as if the creators of *Art of War* were determined to make a mediocre movie, and Wesley Snipes saved their butt—at least a little. If you can get past its clumsy start; cartoonish, Cold War depictions of China and North Korea; and its muddled plot, then this movie has something in store for you: a high-action, suspense-filled, and entertaining shoot-'em-up. This is a guy flick. The bad guys are jumpin' and the body count is high.

Snipes plays Neil Shaw, an undercover agent for the United Nations. He's so undercover that he officially does not exist. I'm sure of this much. Beyond this, the story gets cloudy, so here is a mini-primer for following this film: The first action-packed scene, set as North Korea (I think) celebrates the new millennium, shows that Shaw is a bad-mutha-shut-yo-mouth but the scene has little to do with the rest of the plot.

When a container of murdered Chinese refugees is found at the New York harbor, it sets off a series of events designed to make China look like a "rogue nation" and bring on the downfall of the United Nations as it prepares for a historic free-trade summit with China. Shaw must uncover the plot as bodies start to pile up around him. It doesn't help when he is accused of murdering the Chinese ambassador to the U.N. and must solve the mystery while on the lam. The only person he can trust is a translator, Julia (Marie Matiko), who helps him to figure out the bizarre happenings.

There is so much going on in this film that it's difficult to keep the bad guys and bad motives straight. In the meantime, Snipes gets his fight on. His martial arts moves look good. He has lots of fire power like big ole machine guns. He even has enough high-tech little gadgets to give James Bond a run for his money. In a less-racist Hollywood, Snipes would make a wonderful 007. They only thing he doesn't do here is peel off his face.

He also doesn't do Black women here. I'm just letting you ladies out there know so you won't get indignant like the sister sitting behind me at the screening. "Is he ever going to be with a Black woman in his movies?" she asked loudly. A friend of mine quickly chimed in, "He was with a Black woman in *Sugar Hill* and *New Jack City* and . . . ."

All near-ancient flicks. I guess the sister has to go back in time for some Snipes Black-on-Black love.

Orfeu

August 25, 2000

This remake of "Black Orpheus" brims with samba, hip-hop, and attitude as it tells the ancient Greek tale of the tragic lovers Orpheus and Eurydice. Orfeu, (Tony Garrido), is the music king of his ghetto hood in Rio de Janeiro. Eurydice, (Patricia Franca), is a woman of native Indian descent. Their improbable union becomes the center of controversy and tragedy during Carnival. From Carlos Diegues, director of the classic, *Quilombo*, the film looks good and sounds good. It comments on police brutality, the lost innocence of childhood, and grinding poverty amid the glimmer and shine of Rio.

American Pimp

August 31, 2000

As globally more women (and children) are forced into prostitution, the Hughes brothers' new documentary, *American Pimp,* feels almost like a throwback to another era. It does not focus on the new-style world of pimping: escort services, massage parlors, underground brothels, or "dates" set up on the Internet. Instead, it is consumed with the world of men, represented entirely by Black men here, who lord over the shrinking arena of streetwalkers, women on the stroll, or—as this movie describes them—women "on the track."

The horse-track metaphor is right on target. Told from the vantage point of more than a dozen men, prostitution is just another sport at which a brother might excel. Just like a gambler hopes to bet on winning horses, the pimp is betting that his "bitches" or stallions will bring home their earnings to him. The pimps here refer to hoing and pimping as "the game" and the game starts by "stealing a bitch's mind." Once her mind is stolen, she is convinced of the desirability of selling herself on the street and handing over her money to a pimp—for protection, for love, or for "guidance" and assistance in excelling at being a hooker.

Also, because men are the subject of focus, the ordeal of the women and, in essence, their dehumanization, is not emphasized. In one section, pimps like Fillmore Slim of San Francisco tell about women they have pimped who have been murdered, strung out on drugs, or admitted to "the crazy house." But even in this moving segment, it is not the women who draw our sympathy. Rather, the pimps get to tell their stories of loss, sorrow, or of how life must go on.

This eighty-eight-minute film, being shown at select theaters around the country and scheduled to be released on video in the coming months, takes pimps seriously and treats them with respect. It does not make them heroes but it does allow them, to some extent, to glorify and justify what they do.

Most of the men, with colorful street names like C-Note, Sir Captain, Gorgeous Dre, and Bishop Don "Magic" Juan, are talking heads being interviewed. They are able to represent themselves and their lifestyle—the fancy clothes, alligator shoes, and high-end automobiles—as they see fit. One D.C.-based pimp seems to perform for the camera, peppering his cell phone conversation with one of his women with profuse use of the word *bitch*. Snatches of the business life are shown but, unlike documentaries about prostitution in the past, this is not an up-close, cinema verité version of pimp life that might allow us to draw more independent conclusions.

It accomplishes a number of things: First of all, it brings full circle the fascination for Black pimps in that region of the hip-hop nation that has resurrected the likes of Dolemite, the Mack, and Huggy Bear as icons. In this region, pimping seems benign and almost benevolent, compared to selling drugs or mowing folks down with your Uzi. It's like a smarter version of being a player—you get paid.

It also begins to explore the big why and how of pimping. Not only do prostitutes depend on pimps for protection, many women also rely on pimps to be a man in their life and a lover. According to these pimps, many of the women come from abusive homes, foster homes, shelters, and other societal dead ends. The pimp, often after preying on those known to be vulnerable, becomes a rock, someone to hold onto, in an unstable life.

It all makes sense. But, then again, that's truth according to these men. And this subject is important according to the Hughes brothers. This documentary isn't for everyone, obviously—but neither is being a ho or a pimp.

Turn It Up

September 6, 2000

Turn It Up follows the story of emerging rapper Diamond (Pras) and his various struggles: getting out of the world of illegal drugs, finishing his first album, a troubling relationship with his parents, and tensions that develop between him and his girlfriend when she becomes pregnant.

He travels this maze of mishap and misunderstanding with his manager, Gage (Ja Rule), at his side. Gage is a hot-tempered man who is more wound up than bright. He might remind you of Bishop, the role Tupac played in *Juice*. He's the crazy nigga-for-all-seasons living and dying by the gun. There is a lot of heat here without humanity.

The emerging-rapper story line is starting to wear me out, but this film obviously had potential. The performance scenes are fun and both Ja Rule and Pras have some funny lines. Diamond is a thoughtful, driven man. He wants badly to succeed, even if it is unclear what special talent he has to offer the world of music.

But writers Chris Hudson and Ray "Cory" Daniels haven't taken the time to make Diamond a person who shows enough in the way of wit or conviction. Scenes aren't directed by Robert Adetuyi to maximize the emotional impact of success, struggle, or death. Finally, Pras, though he may be developing acting skills and looks good in the film, is woefully unprepared to play a lead role. This film requires that Diamond be it all: an artist, warrior, and lover. Even the veteran Samuel Jackson couldn't pull off two of those roles in *Shaft*.

We wind up here with the robotic rapper. Pras's range of emotion, on a scale of one to ten, stays at a steady four or five. There is no way of really telling what he's feeling. And the bad, bad White villain in this film looks so much like someone from 1973—only with an updated haircut.

OPM—*Nurse Betty*

September 8, 2000

In this crazy and funny synthesis of *Pulp Fiction* and Doris Day reruns, Morgan Freeman and Chris Rock play a pair of unlikely hitmen on the trail of a clueless soap opera fanatic (Renée Zellweger). This is a crazy flick precisely because it is a celebration of being crazy.

Backstage

September 8, 2000

Big blunts! Big cussin'! Big breasts! Bare asses!

The unspoken message behind any hip-hop documentary titled *Backstage* is a promise of the outrageous. How many MCs have boasted, bragged, and warned us about horny chickenheads, drugs, and off-the-hook parties? How many have basically told us that we're really not living if we're not living with a concert pass inscribed Total Access?

With this promise in mind, I have to say that *Backstage* delivers the outrageous, as well as the funny and bizarre. Not being an up-to-the-minute hip-hop head, I didn't know that DMX had eighteen dogs. (Do they all stay in his house?) I didn't know that after a concert only the dogs are allowed in his dressing room. I did not know that those around D.J. Clue openly describe him as a space cadet. I did not know that Method Man and Redman are often so blunted that they look catatonic.

But I digress. Any talk of drugs is not what is bizarre but—as I said—what is expected in a hip-hop documentary titled *Backstage*. This film takes a behind-the-scenes look at the wildly successful Hard Knock Life Tour, featuring Jay-Z, DMX, Method Man, Redman, Ja-Rule, Beanie Sigel, and others.

I must admit that I am suspicious of any homegrown documentary produced by a record company about a tour of its own artists and artists from other labels. (Damon Dash, CEO of Jay-Z's Roc-A-Fella Records, is the producer here.) It's like an edited home movie with more props. Doesn't it serve the international marketing of hip-hop to show smoke rising from fat rolls of weed? Doesn't it serve hip-hop celebrity to show a series of women willing to "show something," or bare their bodies in order to sneak backstage with a rapper? One woman shows her nipples and allows herself to be fondled, two others are completely nude, another unhalters a pair of massive breasts then eventually performs oral sex on someone in a public bathroom stall.

I almost hear the makings of another rap—"Chickenhead giving me head . . . ."

This isn't a concert film in the sense of *Purple Rain*. Performance off stage rather than on stage is the main idea here. One of the most interesting scenes features Dash and some poor representative from Def Jam Records who unfortunately purchased every performer on the tour a jacket with Def Jam emblazoned across the back. Dash takes extreme exception to this and basically admits how insecure he is about Def Jam's superior sense of marketing. It's superior enough to make many people think, to paraphrase Dash, that the concert tour is a Def Jam production, rather than a Roc-A-Fella production.

It's hard to believe that in this media culture of closely controlled images and sound bites any performer would allow himself to be caught off guard and real. But, then again, this is hip-hop and—even if it is faked—there's a high premium on being real. A fake real.

Backstage definitely doesn't tell the whole story, but it tells and shows some things that are real. You check it out and separate the cinematic fact from fiction.

Black Women on the Verge of a Film Breakdown—*Big Momma's House, Black and White,* and *X-Men*

September 9, 2000

Wondering at times if you are crazy is just part of being Black and conscious in America.

So this summer, and before I began to write this, I had to ask myself: Am I crazy?

Am I crazy, or has this been one jacked-up summer for Black women in film? Hollywood said, take your pick, Black girl: Be fat, be some other joke, or be invisible.

In an early scene of *Big Momma's House,* I lost my appetite for popcorn as I watched a very large, elderly Black woman use the toilet—with loud gas and feces sound effects. Then I squirmed in my seat as the same actress stripped naked—all of her big parts bigger still on the big screen—to take a shower.

A Black radio producer sitting next to me muttered in disgust, "I don't need to see this."

I'm not a prude. I have a sense of humor. I can even get with the idea of destroying Aunt Jemima and a host of stereotypes. But, looking at the scene, I felt ashamed rather than amused. I wondered why I haven't seen other people strip their elders for comedic effect. I've watched some funny-ass films and none of them went there. . . .

I realized, watching her, that the woman on the screen was not Aunt Jemima. This was supposed to be Big Momma, a common, heroic grandmother. She—all of her too-much-fried-chicken corpulence, flatulence, and fatigue—was the embodiment of the toll that life had taken on her and us. And when we stripped her, we stripped the best of ourselves.

In disbelief, I just shook my head in the dark.

By the point in late May that I went to the *Big Momma* screening, I was actually primed for this particular Summer of Added Insult to Black Women. In the hip-hop feast *Black and White,* White women were the babes of choice. I groaned at the big-butt styrachosaur voiced by Della Reese in *Dinosaur.*

There was some reprieve as Thandie Newton played the trophy woman in *Mission: Impossible* 2, but even then, hers was an erratic and crazy character.

Finally, off-screen, the Black women depicted as nasty, bald, toothless, or pitiful in Zadie Smith's novel *White Teeth* left me with a deep sense of despair. And then, of course, there's Lil' Kim's gradual transformation into a White girl.

Makes you wanna holla. Who you gonna call? Where can a cullud girl turn?

Not to the movies. (Thank God for Venus and Serena!)

By the time *Big Momma's House* was released, there were already commercials airing for *The Nutty Professor II: The Klumps.* The highlight of the promotion was the image of an elderly, toothless Black woman dropping her clothes in pursuit of a young man (we don't actually see "her" naked body, though, until the closing credits). The young man screams in horror. In another scene, she takes out her false teeth in order to perform fellatio on the young man underwater in a hot tub.

Just like in *Big Momma* (especially the scene with the dismembered "body parts"), or the wack moment in *Road Trip* where a spindly White man sleeps with a plus-size sister, these *Nutty Professor II* scenes made Black women's bodies the object of ridicule and scorn. The overweight Black woman has been a running joke for comedians, blues singers, and music video makers for some time. In the summer of 2000, she also became the running joke in film.

Take your pick. Be fat, another joke, or invisible.

What is the sister in *Scary Movie* other than another kind of joke? While the film's White teenage girls get regular attention from guys, the sister's boyfriend is really gay. His idea of sexual excitement is to dress her up as a football player—in full padded gear—and fake like he's hitting it from behind. So in *Scary Movie,* perhaps as in real life, the message is that even cute, shapely Black women do not get a love that honors who they really are.

As for invisibility, we're accustomed to that. Volumes are spoken by our absence. Was Halle Berry really in *X-Men?* I blinked and she was gone. The Black little man in *Me, Myself & Irene* was head over heels in love with a White woman. Couldn't he find a Black little woman? The White fishermen in *The Perfect Storm* had lives and women save for the Jamaican crew member, played by Allen Payne. Shaft didn't really have a Black woman. All he had was a weak promise to "please that booty." And, of course, Wesley Snipes had no Black woman in *Art of War.* When I see Snipes later this year, teamed up with Sanaa Lathan in *Disappearing Acts,* I'll be a happy soul. Finally, *Bring It On* really surprised me with the attention and props it gave to the tightness of Black, urban cheerleaders. But it reserved the most sensitive and in-depth character portrayals for the suburban White cheerleaders who are its stars.

Fall is here and all I have to look forward to is a new season of *Once and Again* and fresh episodes of *Sex and the City.* No wonder I feel crazy sometimes. It has to affect us down to our chromosomes—brain cells included—to constantly view our African-American female sensibility through the eyes, experience, and camera lenses of White women and the writers who create their characters.

Can Hollywood give me a real Black woman this fall? Can we pick up where Sanaa Lathan in *Love and Basketball* left off? Just one Black woman is all I'm asking. (In the manner of Chris Rock asking for "one rib" in *I'm Gonna Git You Sucka*.) Just one Black woman.

I'M WAITING!!!

14

We're Bamboozled *and Black Stars Rule*

Bait

September 15, 2000

After the misery of Jamie Foxx in *Held Up* last spring, you might not have high hopes for *Bait*.

But hold on.

This film is stylishly directed, surprisingly well written, and Foxx is genuinely funny—even with his habit of mumbling killer punch lines, and even as he plays the brother who writes verbal checks that his body can't cash. If this film had a lesser melanin and ghetto quotient, it would be hailed in the mainstream as "Supremely funny!" and "A must see!"

Advertisements for *Bait* promise another Blue Streak-Friday-Just-Outta-Jail thang, with young African-American men as the butt of the biggest jokes. But, thankfully, it is more complex than sheer comedy. While it may lure you with the promise of slapstick, *Bait* is really an action flick masquerading as comedy. (Or is it a comedy masquerading as an action flick?) It's hard to say. Director Antoine Fuqua (*The Replacement Killers*) and writers Adam Scheinman, Andrew Scheinman, and Tony Gilroy have managed to put together a film that combines lots of humor, high drama, and action.

It could not survive as an example of any one genre, but it is a great example of many things mushed into one. Just when the action starts to get old, the comedy sets in. Then, just when you're tiring of Mike Epps and his crazy-nigga routine, the drama starts—babymama drama with Kimberly Elise, the beatdown in the alley drama with Kirk Acevedo (who plays my man Miguel Alvarez on *Oz*), the crazy

White-boy computer genius drama. There is plenty of drama—and a little of that *Enemy of the State* satellite-computer thang, too.

Only this is more like *Bait of the State.* Foxx plays Alvin Sanders, a parolee with bad luck and an underdeveloped criminal mind. He gets locked up in a jail cell with John Jaster, who has just pulled off one of the biggest heists in history—robbery of the Federal Gold Reserve. Sanders only spends eight hours in the cell with Jaster, but that is long enough for the feds to believe that Jaster has told Sanders where he hid the gold.

After the gold thief suddenly dies, the feds decide to use Sanders as "bait" to catch the accomplice, who was stiffed out of his share of the gold by Jaster. They figure that the accomplice will also want to get at Sanders. A high-tech tracking device is planted inside poor Sanders. He doesn't know it, but he is walking, talking bait for a very mean man, Bristol. This role of the criminal psychopath with the demeanor of Anthony Hopkins's Hannibal Lecter is played by Doug Hutchison (the sick little prison guard from *The Green Mile*). Bristol is pursued by a federal investigator, Edgar Clenteen (David Morse), who is equally nasty.

In fact, Clenteen contributes mightily to making this film a striking study in extremes. While he is brooding, mean, and obsessive (almost to the point of unbelievability), Sanders is chilled out. Bristol is a very bad, bad guy and, on the other hand, this film has the cutest baby I've ever seen in a movie—ever. Finally, the look of the film—dark and sometimes grainy—acts as a palpable counterpoint to comedic silliness.

After the reviews of *Held Up,* I'm sure Jamie Foxx wanted to tell everybody to kiss his butt. Well, after this film, maybe Hollywood will. And maybe they'll kiss Fuqua's butt too!

Uninvited Guest, Asunder, and *Shafted*

September 22, 2000

There is a crop of Black directors out there who've decided that they can run with Hollywood's big dogs and write "thrillers" that are not very thrilling. (And I'm not just picking on small, independent films. *What Lies Beneath* was a big-budget-thriller dud.)

For a while now, perhaps starting with the forgettable *Juice,* we've all gone to violent Black films where the drama and violence spin out of control. It gets so out of control that it becomes over the top and meaningless. Major characters are killed. We react to the loud popping sound and the actor's body jerking to the faked impact. But we don't really care about them.

We need to be given more to care about in these films—and that brings me to *Uninvited Guest.* I am not sure what writer-director Timothy Wayne Folsome is trying to say in this mishmash of a film. The story is about what happens when an ex-con shows up at the door of a middle-class home and is invited in to use the phone. There are interesting twists and turns in the plot but much of it is not believable. A stranger shows up at a house. Next thing you know he's playing cards with the guys and having sex with the wifey. Next thing you know, people start dying. Shock value comes from the popping noise of the gun, rather than from a masterful culmination of suspense.

The explosion in Black film means that there are a lot of scripts floating around and that more and more people have the knowledge and skills to turn an idea into a walking and talking movie. But certain rules must still be followed like good writing and creative direction, production, and photography. The best films still have something to say. Too often now, our films are saying very little and what little is said is clichéd or tired.

We don't need to make films that prove we can produce the same hackneyed Hollywood formulas. Someone could make a lot of money, or at least perform a great community service, by teaching the art of creating characters and scenarios that are believable and that can draw our sympathy.

Folsome lost me here, despite the remarkable performance by Mekhi Phifer and the notable film debut of Wanya Morris of Boyz II Men fame. Morris managed to create a character I cared about. He offered a moment of something real, even inside an awkward script.

Soap Drama

If *Asunder* were a soap opera, I'd start watching the soaps again.

There is drama, drama, and some more drama. The principal actors—Blair Underwood, Debbi Morgan, and Michael Beach—provide solid performances. Collectively, they contribute mightily to getting this Black *Fatal Attraction* off the ground and keeping it moving.

But the problem with soap operas is that they don't feel, look, or sound quite real. We watch them as is if they are unfolding on stage. We don't really experience them. As fresh as some of the writing and dialogue are in *Asunder,* it still spirals downward into melodrama like much of what we see on TV. (Currently traveling to theaters around the country, it is scheduled to appear on cable in the coming months.)

It does not give us enough suspense, mood, or insight into each character so that we really feel for the three people caught in a vicious love triangle. Ultimately, it turns into another formulaic thriller with a crazy person carrying a knife.

The story is this: Chance (Blair Underwood) and his wife, Roberta, are expecting a child when Roberta and the baby are killed in a freak accident. In his grief and rage, Chance grows to blame his best friend, Michael (Michael Beach), for the accident and begins to obsess over Michael's wife, Lauren (Debbie Morgan), with whom he once had a secret affair. His grief forces his "dark side" out and he begins to stalk Lauren, who learns she is pregnant, too.

The stank twist to this fatal attraction, though, is that Michael and Lauren's marriage is on the rocks and it seems like Lauren still has the hots for Chance. If pushed enough by Chance, and pushed in the right spots, it's hard for Lauren to say no. As she wavers between Chance and her husband—sleeping with both of them at one point—it is difficult to feel much sympathy for her. She's not a person who made one single mistake on one single night. We also have to grow to love Michael, who, we learn, has been having an affair himself.

As for Chance, we need to know something more about what makes him tick so that his major meltdown makes sense. People lose loved ones all the time and sometimes the circumstances are messy. But most of these survivors do not lose their minds and turn on their friends. In *Fatal Attraction,* we understood the crazy mind-set of Glenn Close's character when she said, "I will not be ignored." We need a similar hook for Chance, who is played to a frightening tee by Underwood.

Based on a novel by Eric Lee Bowers (who also wrote the screenplay) and directed by Tim Reid, this film is perhaps an attempt to transform more of our books into film. Features like *Beloved* and *How Stella Got Her Groove Back* show that sometimes literature makes for more in-depth characters, better-written dialogue, and stories with more substance. But if novels are simply transformed into Hollywood formula, as seems to be the case here, why bother?

We Can't Dig It

I really had high hopes for *Shafted,* a direct-to-video release. The premise is hilarious: A White man believes somehow that he is John Shaft (the Black private dick who's a sex machine to all the chicks, can you dig it?). In a time-warped way, this White man lives his life like he's in a '70s blaxploitation flick.

But, boy, is this a disappointment. The big problem is that the filmmakers, including the White director, Tom Putman, fail to deliver on the premise. Rather than capture the humor of a White man trying to emulate the over-the-top slickness of Shaft and other film heroes of that era, it works too hard, and unsuccessfully, to mock the heroes, the genre, and '70s style.

When Steven Byzinsky (that's the White man's real name in the movie) dons an afro wig, it is not funny that he is wearing an afro. Rather, the afro itself is funny. It's so funny, in fact, that it's used to sop up urine, and a urinal refresher cake gets stuck in all the frizz. Funky theme music plays when Byzinsky picks his hair. Ha-ha. Byzinsky writes his name as Shat, which I think is sometimes used as a past tense of the slang word to have a bowel movement.

Even with all the mocking, *Shafted* does not recapture the humor, melodrama, or bad-ass attitudes of '70s action movies. There is a woman playing a Pam Grier–Foxy Brown-type character. There are guns and plenty of bad guys but not much sense to it all. Byzinsky is a mental patient accidentally released from the crazy house. After watching *Shaft* movies in the hospital, he really thinks he's Shaft. Somehow he manages to secure a full set of '70s clothes and accessories in the '90s so he can't be but so cracked. While looking for "action," he meets a Japanese man (who is really a woman) who has come to the United States to avenge the murder of his brother.

In the process, they find themselves in a variety of situations that range from dumb to dumber. The scenarios might have had potential but are not very funny.

Putman better call the Kings of Comedy. This film needs a story, some acting, and a reason for existence. Most of all, it needs some jokes.

Remember the Titans

September 29, 2000

In recent years, the most moving films about the African-American experience—including *Beloved* and *The Hurricane*—have been based on real people and real human drama. It could be that our actual rugged history provides the best plots for works depicting Black people's struggles and victories.

I really enjoyed *Remember the Titans.* It's not perfect or nearly perfect but it is touching, funny, and packed with hard-hitting football action. It is another story that comes from the dynamic era of the civil rights struggle—which was full of racial revelation, heroism, destruction, violence, and hope. It is the real story that saves this movie when it wants to descend into Disney corn and spam. And, thankfully, it is a movie we can take children to see.

It tells the story of what happened to high school football in Alexandria, Virginia (a suburb of Washington, D.C.), when Black and White high schools were ordered to desegregate and join into one in 1971. In Virginia, one of the Southern states without a major league professional sports team of any kind, high school football is king. And, in 1971, forcing these young White and Black players to become a team was like forcing Elvis Presley and Angela Davis to marry.

But marry they did. Black and White players competed with each other for spots on the school's team, the T. C. Williams High Titans. This is where Denzel Washington comes in. He plays the role of Herman Boone, a winning Black coach brought in from South Carolina and given the position of head coach over Bill Yoast, the existing coach who enjoys enormous community support.

As always, Washington is masterful. (And, of course, I don't say this because he befriended my son at the film's premiere in Washington.) Perhaps, more so than in his other roles, you can see Washington tapping into something in his personal life to play Coach Boone. For years, he has coached his children's sports teams and, while in real life he is not as salty a coach as he portrays Boone to be, you can still see the genuine coach come out of him—that only-in-football mix of daddy, personal trainer, sadist, and motivational speaker.

The writers do a decent job of portraying the uneasy process of integration as the team retreats to a summer football camp and then returns to a city and school wracked by racial strife. Genuine friendships are slowly developed. Stock characters like the funny fat guy, the Martin Lawrence–like clown, and the is-he-gay hippie White boy don't go too far over the top. The drama culminates in a series of intense games as the Titans try to maintain a winning season—or Coach Boone may lose his job.

Unlike Hollywood stories about the Black experience that are told through the eyes of Whites, *Remember the Titans* is told primarily through the story of a Black man, Boone. It does falter, however, with the limited development of Boone's wife or children as characters, especially when compared to the full treatment, almost to the point of nausea, given to the character of Yoast's young daughter, Sheryl (Hayden Panettiere). The trick here is that, while much of the focus is on Boone, it is also on Yoast (Will Patton). And it is actually Sheryl who introduces and ends the story—perhaps to draw in Disney's young White audience.

While we learn snippets about many of the White football players and see some of their families, we learn less about the Black players. Wood Harris does an excellent job in the role of Julius Campbell, a leader among the Black contingent of players. It is largely the power of his acting that keeps his role from becoming a caricature of Another Angry Young Black Man.

Still, I enjoyed this film and I know an eight-year-old boy who insists that it is the bomb. Er, uh, excuse me. He says, "It's tiiight!"

The Ladies Man

October 13, 2000

A real "ladies man," according to mythology and legend, whips a woman into such a state that she literally doesn't know whether to scream, laugh, or cry. I am here to report that the new movie starring Tim Meadows had a similar effect on me. I didn't know whether to scream, laugh, or cry—though I was nowhere near a state of ecstasy.

The Ladies Man might need some Viagra.

This movie has some funny moments. I particularly liked the musical dance routine and the Internet site for Victims of the Smiley Ass (don't ask). But it has difficulty sustaining itself with one joke, repeated over and over, until it mercifully ends.

The character that Meadows has created on the television show *Saturday Night Live,* a '70s-styled player-sexoholic who offers bedroom advice and is irresistible to some ladies, seems like good material for a comedy. But, to sustain a feature-length movie, he needs more jokes.

How many times are we supposed to laugh at the legend of the big Black penis? How many times can we laugh at immature references to anal intercourse? How many times is it funny to see White women throw themselves at an unemployed, though well-endowed, Black man? (I guess as many times as we can tune into Jerry Springer!)

Leon Phelps, the Ladies Man's real name, is best enjoyed as a bumbling, uneducated stud who has parlayed his well endowment into the semblance of a life, and a career as a sex-show radio host. He is laughable and pitiful with his dated clothes, old-school afro, Bama mannerisms, and a speech impediment that makes him sound like Moms Mabley on crack.

With all these accoutrements, Phelps should be the Black comedic equivalent of Austin Powers. Just as Mike Myers, also a *Saturday Night Live* alumni, parodied the '60s James Bond spy, Meadows updates and makes light of the '70s player–modern-day buck. But in *The Ladies Man,* the comedy is not as fresh or utterly silly or as rib-tickling.

Not only does Meadows need more jokes, he needs to decide whether he is laughing with us or at us. This film walks a tightrope of racial and sexual tension that it pretends does not exist. Just as Phelps is a super stud-buck, all the White women are uninhibited, swinging love bunnies. Phelps's longtime friend, a Black woman (Karyn Parsons), is a loser at love, and we assume at sex as well, and is living at home with her parents.

The film looks great and Reginald Hudlin's direction makes it visually interesting and flowing smoothly. But *The Ladies Man* needs a little more somethin'-somethin' to leave us satisfied.

Love Beat the Hell Outta Me

October 19, 2000

Love Beat the Hell Outta Me is best appreciated as an eccentric meditation on male bitterness and misogyny. As four men—Glenn, Chris, Wesley, and Samuel—sit around a patio table playing dominoes, each privately and publicly obsesses over a rocky, lost relationship. If the attempt is to make these four seem like regular, professional brothers kicking it with the fellas, it fails. On some important level, they all seem like losers. No wonder their women left. This might not be a great date flick unless you're the type that likes to make up after a fight. Obviously a low-budget effort, this film would have been helped by more imaginative direction and better editing. It tends to go on and on with much of the same thing. And where the movie goes especially wrong is in its horrible depiction of women. If women are going to be made simply into bitches, then they should be made at least into interesting bitches. If the ex-girlfriends and wives had been given the same quality of dialogue and thought as the men, the film would have worked better. It would have fulfilled the requirements of an evenhanded, eccentric riff on relationships. As it stands, it is just an interesting and long-winded riff with very disturbing conclusions.

Bamboozled

October 20, 2000

Race, no doubt, will loom large in most debates about *Bamboozled*. But just as important is its surreal and otherworldly portrayal of corporate media and corporate greed. If modern-day TV minstrels in blackface—tap dancing and shuffling to a soulful Terence Blanchard riff—isn't surreal, then nothing at all is.

It offers the outrageous as utterly conceivable: that in the year 2000 there could be a mad-racist vaudeville television hit, *Mantan: The New Millennium Minstrel Show,* and that folks would actually buy it. By beating us over the head, Spike Lee makes the point that you can sell people anything. In the process, he combines the sardonic tone of *American Beauty,* the eccentricity of playwright Suzan-Lori Parks, the social commentary of Amiri Baraka's classic dramas, and, to top it off, he asks what the Last Poets asked: "Nigga, can you kill?" *Bamboozled* makes regular life surreal, which is precisely what most corporate-produced images of Blacks can be—even today.

Inspired by the 1940s performances of the comedic buffoon Mantan Moreland, the film's minstrel show is created as a bluff by Pierre Delacroix, a highly affected Black television executive with a Black assistant (Marlon Wayans with Jada Pinkett Smith) based in New York City. But then *Mantan* is gleefully approved by their boss, a Blacker-than-thou-because-my-wife-is-Black White television executive (Michael Rapaport). The entertainers chosen to star in the show are named Mantan and Sleep'n Eat (Savion Glover and Tommy Davidson).

Mantan is certainly over the top and, as a necessity, *Bamboozled* must be also in its satire about the recycling of old stereotypes. At a time when Black popular culture is a hot commodity and lots of people—more non-Black than Black—have a say in its ultimate content and distribution, Lee reminds us that there is often a difference between the culture we create and what culture is sold back to us. He wonders aloud if a parading of stereotypes is a refutation of them, rather than a reinforcement of them.

As a native New Yorker and a student at New York University so long in the heart of Greenwich Village, Lee is acutely aware of how all manner of images and words are recycled and hyped as new and hip. But when these images and words involve race, the hip game becomes more complex. Blacks may draw the line and consider the content insensitive and racist. But, of course, these are generalizations. Lots of Blacks will find a reason to laugh, too, and protest loudly to the "Mau-maus" that it's "just a show" and that they need to lighten up—especially if folks are getting *paid*.

In the process of telling this story, there are great breakout performances. Wayans jumps out of his comedic pigeonhole and funnels his talent into the role of Delacroix. Pinkett Smith brings a smooth, relaxed sophistication to the role of Delacroix's assistant, Sloan Hopkins, and I really enjoyed Mos Def in the role of Big Black, leader of a group of radical poets who fiercely oppose the airing of *Mantan*. Rapaport is so great that you have to hate him.

Lest we forget, the film reminds us that everyday people sell their souls for what they mistakenly believe is the natural progression of money-power-respect.

Speaking of money-power-respect, in *Bamboozled*, there are lots of references by omission to the minstrelsy in today's Black popular culture. At some point in the film, when there is a long montage of old offensive images of Blacks, you wonder if the timeline will continue to the present and include music videos, comedy shows, and much of what passes as Black film. But it doesn't.

Spike is a little long-winded in making his points. Just when you think you've seen your last blackface scene in the film, here comes another. But, in the process, there are lots of bright, funny, or riveting moments. Particularly spooky is the Jolly Nigger Bank that Sloan gives Pierre. It's an old piece of Americana, a blackfaced man with big red lips. When you put a coin inside, the eyeballs go back in its head. The blackfaced man can't see, just like Pierre—who is getting paid—can't see either.

Interview—Spike Lee

October 20, 2000

Spike Lee, on a national tour to promote *Bamboozled,* his controversial new film about modern minstrelsy, sat down recently with a roundtable of journalists in Washington, D.C. Following are excerpts from this mini–press conference, where I was in full effect!

Question: When you look at Blacks in the media today, what are the minstrel shows that you see?

Lee: Well, where are you from?

Question: I'm here for BET.com.

Lee: Oooh. You guys show a lot. The videos you guys show. A lot of the gangsta rap videos—I think that's another form of a modern-day minstrel show—bling bling!

Question: Are there any videos in particular? Can you give me an example of a particular video that really set you off?

Lee: I can tell you the ingredients—the Bentleys, the ever-flowing Cristal, the standard shots of throwing one-hundred-dollar bills at the camera, the scantily clad, quote-unquote-not-my-words hos and bitches gyrating. Bling bling!

Question: What are the standard comedy shows, networks shows, that might be minstrel shows?

Lee: There are some TV shows that might be minstrel shows. What we hope that this film shows is that in the twenty-first century, in the new millennium, you don't have to wear blackface to be a minstrel performer.

Question: You don't want to be specific?

Lee: I think that's as specific as I need to be.

Question: Who do you blame for the current state of the minstrel show? Do you blame the Black actors. Or do you blame White Hollywood?

Lee: I think there's enough blame to be spread around. The greatest thing about doing this film for me is that I have a greater understanding of performers like Mantan Moreland, Stepin Fetchit, Hattie McDaniel, Butterfly McQueen, Bill "Bojangles" Robinson, whereas in the past I've totally dismissed them.

But doing this film has made me come to the realization that they didn't have a choice. They basically had to do that stuff. At the same time, it's made me a lot more critical of us—and I include myself—of what we do now because we have a lot more choices than they did.

What has to happen is that there needs to be more diversity in the people writing these roles, these television shows, these films, these scripts. It's going to have to come down to that.

Question: Talk a little bit about your thought process for including the amount of violence that's in the film. Did you have any reservations, second thoughts about the violence in the film?

Lee: No. Because I think the violence in the film is a comment on violence. It's not exploitation of violence. I don't think we're promoting violence.

Question: What made you decide you had to pull the trigger?

Lee: What happened is that when I wrote the script, three-quarters of the way in, I wanted to change the tone. I really wanted to stop all the laughs and have the characters pay for their consequences. Consequently, that's what you see. For me, anytime I do a film and somebody has to get killed, for me it's not fun and games. That's always hard when you have to shoot somebody in a film.

Question: You're considered the father of the new wave of Black film and there was a point, early on, when you, Robert Townsend, and the first crop of new Black filmmakers were doing films that were creative, designed to challenge people, that were different from what people had seen in the '70s. When do you think it turned? Did it turn with *New Jack City*?

Lee: No, not *New Jack City*. I think that John Singleton's film, *Boyz n the Hood,* which is a great film . . . When that blew up, everybody tried to jump on this "hood" thing and that's when it got really stagnant.

Question: Not necessarily the film but the reaction to it and the trend it started?

Lee: Yeah.

Question: In an interview, I believe, with Soledad O'Brien, she asked you where does this go, what are the solutions. You said that you don't have a solution to racism. She didn't mention racism. Can you explain why you went directly to the issue of racism?

Lee: Because I've seen this before where *Do the Right Thing* was criticized because Spike didn't have the answer to racism. They're starting the same thing with *Bamboozled*—this film doesn't mean anything because at the end of the film, he doesn't give us an answer, he doesn't lead us out of the wilderness or tell us how we can turn this thing around. I think it's just a cop-out—to diminish the work.

Question: Were you inspired by Reggie Bythewood's *Dancing in September?*

Lee: No. That didn't inspire me, no, not at all. . . . *Hollywood Shuffle* was about the same thing. *Putney Swope* was about the same thing . . . *Drop Squad.* One of my films at NYU I did back in 1980 was about a young Black screenwriter who is hired to write and direct a big remake of D. W. Griffith's *The Birth of a Nation.* So you can have similar ideas.

Question: Mos Def, did he add to, improvise the script?

Lee: Oh yeah, Mos Def did. Those rap guys aren't too structured. . . . He's a good actor. But he's going to say exactly what he [wants]. So that's fine because what he did is great.

Question: Has there been any TV show in recent years that has served African-Americans pretty well?

Lee: I liked *Homicide* when it was on. But I want to go back to another question: I never felt like every Black person in my movies has to be 100 percent angelic, godlike—like you can't have Black people look like crackheads, or this and that. To me, that's not really truthful. But I just think you need to have a balance. So if it's well written, I don't have a problem with a Black villain—as long as it's not one-dimensional. As I've said before, a lot of time those villains have the best parts.

Question: Do you have a definition of when [a show] crosses into a minstrel act?

Lee: I think that's something that people have to make up their own mind about. It's not something you can look up in a book and say, "This is it. This is the law." It's something you feel inside. What you feel might be borderline, I might not feel, or vice versa. It's knowing and trying to understand whether an audience is laughing with this person, or at them. To me, that's the difference.

When I look at a show like *The PJs* and the caricatures of those claymation people—the lips and stuff—[rolls his eyes] that's why we did that stuff in *Bamboozled* at the beginning of the show. That was really computer animated. But that was a take-off on *The PJs.*

Question: The Jolly Nigger Bank—is that an actual piece of Americana?

Lee: Yes. That was a very popular bank. I didn't make that up. Someone pointed out to me today that the Jolly Nigger Bank was also in Ralph Ellison's *Invisible Man*. And a lot of that stuff you see in the film is from my own collection—Black collectibles.

Question: Why do you think our parents wouldn't have touched things with blackface, wouldn't have touched mammy dolls, and now this generation is starting to pick it up?

Lee: It was too painful. I understand that. It grows more acceptable as the distance grows greater. And I can perfectly understand if there's an African-American person or a White person who says, "These things are too offensvie and I don't want them in my house or whatever . . . but, for me, I use it as a reminder."

Question: How large is your collection?

Lee: About twenty pieces.

Question: Do you know what your next project is?

Lee: Yeah, I'm working on a script on Joe Lewis, the Brown Bomber.

Question: In a recent interview, you hinted that you're going into television. What are you going to do in television?

Lee: An announcement is going to come out very soon about a deal that I'm going to do. I hope to put on an entertaining, thought-provoking show on television. It will be an hour-long, dramatic series. I think we have enough sitcoms already, so I want to do something else.

Cora Unashamed

October 25, 2000

Okay. It's probably time to get over the fact that Regina Taylor plays so many maids. She's a fine actress and she has to eat. Her characters have not only dignity, but intelligence as well. And the fact is that, even into the 1940s, the majority of African-American women were forced to earn a living as household servants. When we groan at another rag-on-the-head, up-from-slavery saga, many of us are groaning at the simple act of facing history.

But, to be fair, many of us also groan at stories of our history that don't quite ring true. A new film adaptation of Langston Hughes's short fiction *Cora Unashamed*—premiering on PBS—has lots of moments that don't ring my bell. Despite the painstaking care the filmmakers take in re-creating life in a turn-of-the-century Iowa town, the emotional landscape is only half-painted. Despite its drama, good acting, and direction, something just ain't right.

Part of that something is the fact that Cora is a woman who, after tragedy, receives the emotional meaning in her life from Whites. There is no historically true place of sustenance. The relationship with her mother is cold. There is no extended family, neighborhood, or church that we see. She has lived all of her life in the small town of Melton, with her mother and young daughter, Josephine. When her parents moved to the town, they were the only "colored" people there. From the looks of things in the film, it doesn't seem like too many more Blacks have arrived since. Cora's siblings have all moved away and she says, in one scene, that Black men can't get work in the town. But there is plenty of cooking, cleaning, and laundry for any Black woman to handle.

The lack of brothers around is perhaps the reason that Cora takes up with Joe, an itinerant White union organizer for the International Workers of the World. Despite the tenor of the town and times, the film presents this union as totally natural. It tells us that a Black woman in the Midwest at the turn of the twentieth century would not have been at least reticent about approaching a strange White man out in the woods and easily taking up with him.

Because their love is shown only in snatches, it is difficult to determine whether Joe is really sincere in his feelings for her or whether he simply ran a game—sweet words to the lonely Black girl—to snag some quick chocolate love. Whichever the case may be, the fact is that Joe tells her he has to leave town. Cora is left pregnant with their child. Joe does not come back for her. He does not send for her. She does not leave for the big city and there is no one else around for her to date. So she becomes the asexualized, noble mammy, mother to all, lover to none—except in her dreams and memories that she relives and relives to the point where it's just plain sad.

There is a lot to recommend in *Cora Unashamed*. Taylor is great. Her hair looks great. She gets to be strong. But it would be great if the story—no doubt marred by Hughes's own awkwardness in relationships—was also more rooted in reality.

Loving Jezebel

October 27, 2000

Based on the promos, you might think that *Loving Jezebel* is simply about a brother who's a player, daddy mack, ladies man—whatever you call the species. But, really, this very funny film is a missive from the "multicultural" minority among us: the biracial or Black males who grew up in White suburbs, had mostly White friends, listened to White rock bands and are comfortable gravitating to White women as potential romantic partners.

If you have a sensitive jungle-fever antenna, you might groan at the start of this flick. But I guarantee, in the end, you'll stare at the screen with a silly grin on your face. Just when you're ready to dismiss the main character, Theodorous Melville, as simply another hopelessly vanillafied brother, debut writer and director Kwyn Bader ups the comedic ante.

Actually, let's say that Bader works a little sleight of hand. He approaches these interracial relationships so unself-consciously and with enough humor to derail the type of reaction that, for example, can transform Black women into Sha-nay-nay. (You know what I'm taking about: that, even if subtle, eye- or neck-rolling, teeth sucking, or talk-to-the-hand dismissal.)

Like the best funny films, *Loving Jezebel* relies on the humor in little things, like vintage schoolboy eyeglasses, to make us laugh. Bader also uses screwball humor to build a case in support of Theo (Hill Harper), the blundering, suburban product of an interracial marriage between a Black mother (Phylicia Rashad) and White father (John Doman).

Nothing that the very White-identified Theo does seems filled with self-hatred or malice. He is simply living life as he knows it. Bader tells Theo's story with such honesty that you can't help but like him more and more—for the most part. Once we see young Theo jerking spastically around his room playing air rock guitar, we want to paraphrase former Texas governor Ann Richards: "Poor Theo, he can't help it. He was born with a white-bread spoon in his mouth!"

You've heard of a wigger. But what would we call Theo? A backer? He is definitely a poster child for the uncool Black man. The one speech he makes about race, a declaration to a White woman about how he does not care about whether she is Black, White, Red, Yellow, or whatever, actually reveals his blind spots. It reminds us that Theo's "multicultural" universe of lovers includes no women, as they say, darker than a paper bag. No women as dark as his mama.

Hmmmm . . .

I appreciate Bader's take on the eccentricities of women—though it would have been helpful to have one sane woman of color. Starting with, perhaps, Paul Robeson in *Body and Soul,* Black films have certainly presented their share of womanizers. But this film, as well as other recent Black independent features, have offered a whole new take on the man eater. As lovers drift in and out of poor Theo's life, this film also reminds us of the romantic wasteland. There must be pretty slim pickings if all these gorgeous women are crazy over goofy Theo.

Finally, I can't say enough for Hill Harper. This is the third independent feature I've seen him in this year and all I can say is, right on brother! While *The Visit,* which was screened at the Urbanworld Film Festival, put Hill's dramatic skills on display, *Loving Jezebel* and Christopher Scott Cherot's *Box Marley* have allowed him to show his gifts as a comedic actor.

As young Theo, Harper is as goofy as Jerry Lewis or Pee-Wee Herman. He transforms his face into a mask of wide-eyed tension and angst that slowly relaxes as he matures and goes through the rites of passage of '80s haircuts: high-top fade, baldie, dreads . . . .

Theo spends a lot of time as a loser at love, but at least he's an amusing loser.

Miscegenation has never been this funny.

Black Star—Will Smith in *The Legend of Bagger Vance*

November 3, 2000

Any legend that *The Legend of Bagger Vance* aims to tell gets lost in a swirl of sports, war, romance, and blonde ambition. As this film settles into the ambience of early twentieth-century Savannah (and gives that warm and fuzzy feeling to a violent period for African-Americans in the South), it is great for atmosphere. It is also a decent love story. But it misses its intended mark—that frequent Hollywood obsession—of somehow combining sports with the supernatural.

It definitely misses the mark with Bagger Vance, a golfing caddie played by Will Smith. One night, Vance appears out of the darkness as Rannulph Junuh (Matt Damon), a one-time golfing champion, is trying to regain his golfing swing. Junuh had given up his game after he came back from World War I as the shell-shocked survivor of a battle that killed all the other men in his fighting unit. Years later, Junuh returns home and lives in a house that looks abandoned. At the height of the Depression, he shares meals, card games, and alcohol there with a bunch of Black hobos.

As Bagger Vance, Will Smith is supposed to be a mystical type of cat, a sort of guardian angel. But director Robert Redford seems unsure of how to develop the right spiritual vibe. (I suppose since the story involves White people, they couldn't just do the usual and pump in some gospel music!) There are only hints of Vance's supernatural insight and wisdom, which help Matt Damon chase his demons and heal his soul. Vance is not given the scenes or voice to become more than an annoying counselor who is shaken off more than once by Junuh, who enters a major golf tournament.

There are several moments when the mysticism rubs hard against the reality that Bagger is really just a caddie, a young Black man living in the South early in the last century. And, let's face it, Smith isn't the mystical type. His roles, including those in the blockbuster films *Independence Day* and *Men in Black,* might best be described as reluctant alpha males—aggressive but with enough angst and paranoia to make us laugh.

Because this film jumps all over the place, it's also difficult to feel much for Junuh—who is really the central character—and his romantic interest, Adele Invergordon, a feisty blonde played to a tee by Charlize Theron. The film, perhaps in an effort to be faithful to the novel by Steven Pressfield, quickly summarizes much of Junuh's early life and triumphs as a young golfing champion. Then he's off to war battles that we only glimpse. Then he's back. In the beginning, this film jumps around more than a *Soul Train* dancer.

The film is told in flashback, through the eyes of a young boy, Hardy Greaves (J. Michael Moncrief), who befriends Junuh and Vance and eventually works as Junuh's caddie as well. With this type of storytelling, we should feel as moved by the storyteller's memories as he is. The sports story, which is obviously what excited Redford, is well told. In fact, it looks like there was so much excitement over the sports story—the White gentlemen's game of golf—that the brother, and the spirituality he was supposed to bring, got lost in the Hollywood shuffle.

The Invisible Soldiers: Unheard Voices

November 9, 2000

Few events reveal the soul of the African-American experience as does World War II. Few of us in the spoiled post–civil rights generation can fully imagine the degradation our parents and grandparents experienced to simply stake a claim at equality and full citizenship. The thought of Black men and women fighting in a war and risking death for a country that denied them basic liberties—the same liberties they were fighting for abroad—is beyond simple comprehension. Words like dignity, pride, strength, character, and will don't seem up to the task.

Television journalist Tom Brokaw calls the World War II generation the world's "greatest." But, unlike Brokaw and the countless war documentaries repeated on the History Channel, *Invisible Soldiers: Unheard Voices* on PBS recognizes the contribution of one million Black soldiers.

Blacks fought on two or three fronts: against fascism abroad, and against virulent racism at home—and in the armed forces. Black soldiers returned from battlefields to face White racist mobs that wanted to keep them in their place. They returned to states in the South where they could not vote, eat in restaurants, or use public toilets or water fountains—not to mention get a job.

Invisible Soldiers is a good attempt at beginning to set the record straight. Through the simple act of telling a fuller history, it reveals how African-Americans have been written out of this pivotal era by most historians and, certainly, by Hollywood. As a matter of fact, indignation over films like *Saving Private Ryan, Patton,* and *Sands of Iwo Jima* is readily apparent here and seems to have been a mighty motivator to executive producer William H. Smith.

The documentary, comprised of rarely seen original black-and-white footage and interviews with veterans, details the bravery of Black men fighting in the Battle of the Bulge and other victories. But it notes how the film *Patton,* which included this portion of the war, only included one Black man—Patton's personal valet. Interviews of Black men who participated in D-Day are included, along with the fact that *Saving Private Ryan* didn't even have Black soldiers in the background.

But *Invisible Soldiers* isn't simply a critique of media images. The Hollywood saga is raised to simply provide proof of the deliberate exclusion of Black men from the larger history. This one-hour show makes it clear that America did not want and has not wanted to see Black men in the role of fighting heroes. It even includes an interview with a Jewish survivor of the concentration camp at Dachau and a Black soldier, one of an arriving unit of Black soldiers, who were the first to arrive at and liberate the camp. Also fascinating is footage of Black engineers and construction workers who built the Stilwell Road from India to China.

This program isn't a slick production. The interviews are harshly lit and the graphics have the look of a school filmstrip. But the content overwhelms these shortcomings and, in its own way, helps to erase the ways the Black soldier has been erased from World War II history.

Men of Honor

November 10, 2000

Again, a true story of the African-American experience has produced a good film. *Men of Honor,* based on the life of navy diver Carl Brashear, is moving and genuine. It forcefully weaves together one Black man's experience with racism in the military and the strength passed down through generations of poor Southern Blacks. It is ripe with a sense of time, place, human courage, and human frailty.

It uses the bond of military service to throw the spotlight on two men on either side of the racial divide: Brashear and his foul-mouthed alcoholic superior, Billy

Sunday, played by Robert DeNiro. It is the tension between these two men, along with Brashear's manic ambition, that form the basis for this story.

At first it is what you expect. In 1948, the son of a poor Black sharecropper joins the navy and soon learns that all he is expected to be is a cook. Because of his excellent swimming ability, he is eventually saved from kitchen duty and allowed to join a water-rescue team. Later, he gains admittance to a previously segregated navy training program for divers. At the school, he falls under the charge of Sunday, who initially blocks his admittance but, slowly, comes to respect Brashear's will and tenacity.

Then much of the story is what you don't expect: Sunday, also the son of a poor White farmer, realizes that he and Brashear share, in addition to a passion for diving, a love for their tough fathers. Though they go their separate ways, years later they are reunited when Sunday helps Brashear to prove that he can still dive even though he was crippled during a ship accident.

The environment of the film is convincing, from the dust of Southern films, to northern Black neighborhoods, to the diving school in Bayonne, New Jersey—one of those New Jersey towns that might just as well be in Alabama. DeNiro makes an excellent redneck, spitting profanity and epithets with the skill of DMX.

Gooding's face, taut with determination and anticipation throughout the film, is not a mask that grins and hides. His best performance is as an older, seasoned Brashear. While playing the man in his youth, Gooding projects a confidence and impatience more in keeping with prep-school children of privilege. It doesn't help that his character, though from Kentucky, sounds like he's from San Diego.

Billy Sunday is not a real person. Screenwriter Scott Marshall Smith created him from an amalgam of White officers who Brashear worked with in real life. Compiling all these men into one character does not diminish the film's depiction of Brashear's career triumph. It does, however, alter the truth enough to give perhaps too much credit to the impact, benevolence, and transformation of an avowed racist.

There is a powerful scene at the end when Brashear and Sunday are together again, and they fall very naturally back into the roles of drill sergeant and recruit. At that moment, you might wonder if Brashear is calling on strength his daddy taught him, or on strength from Sunday, the kind of man that his daddy knew would test his son's strength to the end.

What's Cooking?

November 17, 2000

Here we are at Thanksgiving—the perfect blend of family delights and family drama. In *What's Cooking?* director Gurinder Chadha takes the most American of holidays—Thanksgiving—and investigates the function and dysfunction of four American families: one African-American, one Latino, one Vietnamese, and one Jewish.

It's a lot of challenging ground to cover, and, at the start, the film jumps around, family to family, scenario to scenario, somewhat awkwardly. But it finally settles down and delivers the humor, warmth, devotion, bad blood, and stupidity that make up what we call family life. Its strength is an honest realism that makes us laugh out loud at the little things—like winding up with a bucket of fried chicken to replace your burned-beyond-hope turkey.

The wealthy Williams family, headed by Dennis Haysbert and Alfre Woodard, must come to grips with the cracks and fissures in their seemingly perfect bourgeois lifestyle. Vietnamese emigrant Trinh Nguyen (Joan Chen) tries to understand her new homeland and new family traditions. At the Avila household, pots are boiling with more than just holiday dinner: Add to the stew male adultery and the fact that mama has moved on to a new man. Meanwhile, the Seligs must learn to accept the fact that their daughter is never going to meet a nice Jewish boy and settle down—with him at least.

Chadha, who describes herself as a Kenyan-born Englishwoman of Indian descent, and who directed the critically praised film *Bhaji on the Beach,* has a keen eye and ear for the ways ethnic differences color our family lives and holidays. She takes great pleasure in presenting the bounty of foods served at each home: how the turkey is prepared, whether the side dishes are candied yams, tamales, or shiitake mushrooms. Food and the hearth become potent and tasty metaphors for those things that remain wholesome and nurturing in our lives.

The further we get from the food, the closer we get to the drama. Without giving that corny We Are the World feeling, Chadra shows that racial differences can mean very little to the humanity we all share, or the ways that we can be alienated both within our families and from our community.

Women, guarders of the hearth, take center stage. Mercedes Ruehl plays another feisty, big-bosomed, big-attitude woman without creating a Latina cartoon character. She seems the perfect match for Dennis Spain, the womanizing dog who is suddenly apologetic and contrite. Like her role in *Love and Basketball,* Alfre

Woodard plays another doormat wife stuck in a boring marriage to a stiff jerk. She is totally convincing, totally brilliant, and totally depressing. Juliana Margulies (formerly of *ER*) is a sweet-faced lesbian who looks as good, and plays as natural, on the big screen as she did on *ER*.

Don't go to *What's Cooking?* feeling cynical or feeling hungry. A whole lot is cooking up in here.

Boesman & Lena

November 17, 2000

Now wouldn't it be something if, instead of Jerry Springer, Judge Judy, or Ricki Lake, folks tuned into drama as written by Athol Fugard? He's the prize-winning White South African playwright who brought us *The Blood Knot* and *A Lesson from Aloes* before completing what is probably his best-known drama in the United States, *Master Harold and the Boys.*

His 1969 play *Boesman & Lena,* now released as a film starring Angela Bassett and Danny Glover, seamlessly combines the heated, interpersonal drama of an old married couple and the wrenching social, political, and personal violence wrought by apartheid.

Fugard gets in the middle of emotions and all types of human imperfection. Those of us more comfortable with bolder political statements might conclude that he is never hard enough on apartheid, that he never billboards quite large enough the evils of institutional racism and genocide. But he manages to get to politics through the lives of his intricately drawn characters—and they have a lot more going on than what passes for television entertainment here.

In *Boesman & Lena,* Boesman (Glover) and Lena (Bassett) find themselves living on the muddy banks of a river in Capetown. As Lena laments, they have "the sky again for a roof." Just evicted from a ramshackle squatter camp that was suddenly bulldozed by the police, they have wandered to this desolate place. This is the same place they have returned to in the past as housing and livelihoods have passed through their fingers again and again.

It is here that their life drama unfolds for us. It unfolds as Lena tries to remember, painstakingly, how they have come to this place again. She tries to piece together the meaning of her life. Film, as opposed to the stage, allows these memories to unfold before us. She tries to remember all the places and the routes they have taken to each. Of course such homelessness is a metaphor for Black life under apartheid. And the wandering has taken its toll.

They are "colored," or of mixed-race ancestry, looking every bit as cocoa brown as most African-Americans. Yet—even in rags and without a pot to piss in—they sneer at "Blacks," referring to them as "kaffirs," a word that is comparable to "niggers." But colorism is just one fact of their complexity. Boesman can be cruel and abusive and is very bitter over their being childless. He berates and tortures Lena in the tried-and-true way that a kicked man will kick his dog. Lena, paraphrasing the song, tries to be gay for her sad, old man. She loves to dance and sing, and misses her pet mutt, who was lost when the camp was bulldozed. Both seem to be alcoholics.

Bassett plays this part of a lifetime with a clear command of regional language, gestures, and physical space surrounding her. She is high-strung, emotionally complex, an emotional wreck, and positively brilliant. So is Glover, though with similar crusty-old-fart roles under his belt, it is less impressive to see him play a variation of the same mean man.

This is an opportunity to see film art starring two talented Black actors. It is a film that pays respects to the emotional complexity of Black people outside the realm of American ghetto pathology or Hollywood melodrama.

Half Past Autumn

November 30, 2000

Any portrait of the true artist is complex. Any portrait of the Black artist is complex to the tenth power. A new documentary on the life of Gordon Parks includes enough detail about this brilliant photographer, filmmaker, writer, and composer to make it worthwhile viewing.

It leaves some important ground uncovered, yet manages to tell about the struggle of all artists, and, in particular, about the Black artist in the White world. In some ways, Parks's life is a metaphor for integration and the possibilities of a "color-blind society." So your reaction to his life and this story will depend mightily on your view of assimilation and racial identification.

Half Past Autumn, premiering on HBO, reminds us that not long ago a Black man or woman's chance at "success" in American society was tied to the acceptance and benevolence of Whites. It also reminds us that the art world is a place of exclusivity and privilege that can, from time to time, be bumrushed. Given an inch, it was almost the responsibility of Blacks to take a mile in places that were previously off-limits. Repeatedly, Gordon was given an inch in the rarified circles of corporate media, photography, fashion, film, literature, and classical music and showed that he could run a mile.

He ran these miles, perhaps unconsciously knocking down barriers for generations afterward at newspapers, magazines, and television stations. At the same time, because he worked for "White folks" and was not radical in thought, he was viewed with less than total trust by some in the Black community—especially during the 1960s and 1970s, when more strident visions were the norm. Writer Nelson George, interviewed for this documentary, notes that, while Parks is admired, few in the Black community would consider Parks a cutting-edge artistic figure. At a time when the debate was over "the ballot or the bullet," Parks's weapons remained his lens and pen.

Aside from George's brief interview, the discussion of Parks's life in this context must be gathered between the lines. This ninety-two-minute documentary, written by Lou Potter, directed by Craig Rice, and produced by St. Claire Bourne and Denzel Washington, feels more like a respectful tribute. It acknowledges Parks as a Renaissance man who achieved professionally while his career and ambition helped wreck three marriages. Two ex-wives, two children, and one grandchild are interviewed. While clearly he was not a husband and father at home, Parks defends his role in his families, citing the fact that he gave his children everything and that they enjoyed privileged lives.

He was born in 1912 in rural Kansas and was living a hardscrabble life to support his wife and children when he bought his first camera in 1938. The sales clerk at a film shop in Minneapolis was so impressed with his work that he offered Parks a one-man exhibit. Parks eventually landed a job taking photographs for the federal Farm Security Administration.

After the FSA was folded in 1943, he followed his supervisor there, Roy Stryker, to work for the Office of War Information. After this stint, during which he recorded images of Black pilots and soldiers, he landed a job at *Vogue* magazine in New York City. In 1949, he became the first Black staffer for the then extremely influential *LIFE* magazine. He remained with *LIFE* for twenty years.

He went on to write the best-selling novel *The Learning Tree,* which has been translated into several languages and became the first Hollywood studio film directed by a Black man. After directing *The Learning Tree,* he went on to make more films, including *Shaft,* and published more books, and composed music, songs, and poems. Parks turns eighty-eight on Thursday and he is still working. This year, a book of photographs and poems, with a CD of his music, *A Star for Noon,* was published. The retrospective of his work after which this documentary is titled, which was organized in 1997 by the Corcoran Gallery in Washington, D.C., is expected to travel the country for at least three more years. The companion book to the exhibit, as well as *A Star for Noon,* are published by Bullfinch Press.

This chronology is skillfully woven in with interviews, his words, and, of course, his striking images—including the well-known portrait of the impoverished Washington, D.C., cleaning woman Ella Watson, portraits of Malcolm X, the Black Panthers, and—almost incongruously—dreamy images of fashion models.

Missing is a meditation on Parks's artistic process. You come to the conclusion of *Half Past Autumn* still wondering about how the music played in his head, and how the words and images danced there. Perhaps such insight cannot be easily squeezed into a sound bite, but a documentary about such a full life should give us a fuller sense of his thoughts and who he is. We should know what Parks felt when he looked through the lens.

Love Song

December 1, 2000

Oh please.

I never thought I would have to sit through *The Bodyguard* again! I honestly believed that the story of the rich, spoiled Black diva falling for her blond, salt-of-the-earth Prince Charming and savior would forever be banished to the place of eight-track tapes, jheri curls, and Vanilla Ice.

But here it is again. This time, instead of Whitney Houston looking droopy-eyed and Barbie stiff, we have her pop-heir wannabe, Monica, tiptoeing through the celluloid as haughtily as she can, eliciting about as much sympathy as Cruella. This film, designed as an acting vehicle for Monica, may play well on MTV. It may, as it is hoped, deliver high ratings. (Originally, Justin Timberlake of 'N Sync was supposed to costar. So MTV was going for theirs.) But this is a cinematic replay that even the young and restless can do without.

The story is that Camille Livingston (Monica), daughter of a wealthy New Orleans physician and an undergraduate at Xavier University, has a fly wardrobe, fly haircut, and a boyfriend named Calvin—also from the local Black bourgeoisie—who is headed to medical school. Of course, Camille's father loves Calvin, more so because Calvin is considering Dr. Livingston's alma mater, Morehouse College, as his place of study.

But while Calvin dreams of "M.D." behind his name, Camille meets Billy Ryan (Christian Kane of *Angel*). Billy Ryan is White. His hair is wet and stringy. He is working at a gas station. Quite frankly, Billy looks more like a stalker than a lover. Though he gives Camille the eye and semi-mack, no relationship seems likely in the land of the sane. But, as it turns out, old Billyboy is also a talented blues musician. You know how White boys be rocking some blues! And he is also persistent (and played very well by Kane). Calvin had barely hit the highway before old Billy was knocking at Camille's door.

As for her part, Camille falls slowly for Billy. She needs a man who is more down than Calvin. And, in this MTV movie, the White man is more down than the wack brothers around. Billy will sing for some young sisters from the hood, who Camille counsels, while Calvin never had time to visit them. Billy will help her discover her true self and tap her unrealized gifts and potential. Billy leads a band with gospel and Afro-Cuban riffs. Billy even explains to the sister what mojo is, and how she can get it working for her. In other words, like Dunwitty in *Bamboozled,* he's more down, more Black than most of Detroit. Meanwhile, Calvin and her father want to simply railroad Camille into a staid life of fulfilling their bourgeois expectations.

With all this craziness, you are probably wondering how such a film could be directed by Julie Dash, creator of the fine modern classic *Daughters of the Dust.* Well, as far as I can tell, the final version of *Love Song*—sliced and diced in pre- and post-production—is not the same film that Dash signed on to direct. The original script by Josslyn Luckett, a Black woman who has written for *The Steve Harvey Show,* was cut in several places to meet the time restraints of television. In the process, richness of several characters and situations—that might have balanced the White-man-as-savior-vibe—fell onto the editing floor.

Too bad. The story, though perhaps too sophisticated a vehicle for a neophyte actress, obviously had potential. You can see and hear snippets of bright writing despite the editing.

Well, at least there are no Dolly Parton songs.

Interview—Julie Dash on *Love Song*

December 1, 2000

Iverem: How did you first get involved with *Love Song?*

Dash: I got a call from Maggie Malina at MTV to meet with David Guillod, whose company is Handprint Entertainment. They manage Monica and this project was written for her. It was originally written for her and Justin Timberlake of 'N Sync. Well, we started in preproduction while 'N Sync was on tour and he just didn't feel he was going to be able to do it. He pulled out and we cast a young man,

Christian Kane, who's a singer, guitar player, and a really great actor. He's a regular on the *Angel* television series. There's a whole cult following behind that show. He was really the best choice. We also had Rachel True—people remember her from *The Craft*—and Essence Atkins, the middle sister from *Smart Guy*.

Iverem: This is such a change in mood from *Daughters of the Dust*. Was that difficult for you?

Dash: I've done other films since *Daughters of the Dust*. When I choose a project, I love to do things about African-American women at pivotal periods in their lives. It has to be something smart, clever, witty, and with dynamic characters. That's what I look for—and I saw that in Josslyn Luckett's script. These are college girls [Camille, Toni, and Renee]. They go to Xavier College in New Orleans. But we lost a lot of the story. Originally, one woman was writing a thesis on the blues and another was like an Internet geek—she was into electronics. The lead character was a psychology student who was moving into social work. These were strong, vibrant young women, and so that attracted me to the story.

[Losing much of the story] was very, very difficult but it happens all the time in television. It was too much story for the time allotted. It was too full. Some of the story lines had to come out so the others could blossom fully. The A-story was the love story, so we had to stick with that. Originally, there were class differences, cultural differences, and I found that something exciting to work with—all within the African-American experience.

Iverem: Is there a portion that you regret cutting the most?

Dash: Yes. There was a conversation between Camille's mother and [another] mother that really pushed the whole envelope in terms of the class differences between the girls—Camille, Toni, and Renee. Calvin's mother was looking at them with disdain because they weren't the right class. They wear more makeup. They were very free with their bodies. They weren't stiff.

Iverem: Was it difficult directing a singer with little acting experience?

Dash: No. Monica's a professional. I understand that she's been working since she was fourteen or fifteen. When she steps on "stage," she hits her mark and follows directions. I would torture her, though. We would shoot takes three or four times at three in the morning. The ground would be wet because I prefer that for shooting. She would say, "My feet are cold!" She's only, like, nineteen. Without all the makeup, she really looks like a baby, a little kid. She'd come in the morning with her little do-rag on. And I'd say, "Is that you?"

Iverem: Was there much discussion about the direction that this interracial love story should take? Did the writer have the final say or did the rest of the crew have input?

Dash: I tried to maintain the integrity of Josslyn's script, although I didn't cast Ryan as an Italian as the script suggested. I chose to cast someone who looked more like a straight-up White boy. I wanted a real contrast. She meets him. He's pumping gas at a gas station. It was written for a man with dark hair. But Christian looks more like a country-and-Western singer or a surfer. Christian doesn't look like what you would see in most interracial love stories.

Iverem: Tell me, what were the challenges of doing a film about interracial romance?

Dash: Surprisingly enough, we had a preproduction meeting so Monica and Christian could meet. Well, ten minutes into the meeting, they were leaning into each other and poking each other. They really got along well and had good chemistry. Monica was so much more relaxed than we expected.

I would have loved to build in a stronger African-American male character. Because after the cutting, [one Black male character] Malik becomes too flaky and [another] Calvin, is kicked to the curb. . . . Those are the minefields you find yourself in when you do projects like this. I would have liked to do more with Tyrese's character, Madd Rage. There was more written for him in the script but that got cut. . . .

There were low days. I felt like, Oh my God, like I was in the middle of a minefield, having set up all these things and not having them play out as they ought to. Then you have to go tweak something else to keep the balance in line. The struggle for all of us is keeping balanced images.

Iverem: For so long, you've been pointed to as *the* Black female director. Now there are more, like Gina Prince-Bythewood. Are there more opportunities opening? Are there more avenues?

Dash: I think yeah, there are. The doors are opening . . . slowly, but not enough. There should be ten more Ginas by now. It's really exciting to see Gina's work. I'm really looking forward to seeing *Disappearing Acts.*

Iverem: Are there opportunities to do your own projects or the projects of others?

Dash: I have not been able to direct my own projects since *Daughters of the Dust.* I have not been able to get anyone to finance what I would like to say. I have no problems getting directorial assignments. I've directed films, commercials, music videos. . . . But it's still very hard to have that other voice heard. I felt really blessed to work on Josslyn Luckett's script. She's a young Black woman.

She's the one who really suffered with the cuts. I look forward to working with her again.

Iverem: Are Black women getting to tell their stories? Are Black people getting to tell their stories?

Dash: No. I don't think we're getting to tell our stories. We're being assigned stories. *Love and Basketball* is a great story Gina was able to tell and now with *Disappearing Acts,* she's telling someone else's story. It's the same situation with Kasi Lemmons. We still don't have the same access and opportunity. It's about access and opportunity. The last time I saw that—that kind of voice that you recognize—was with *Living Single*. The same producer, Yvette Lee Bowser, is doing it now with *For Your Love*.

Iverem: How much of an impact are the new Black independent productions having?

Dash: So far it's been Wesley (Snipes) and his Amen-Ra Productions. He's done some important documentaries and he's produced films like *Disappearing Acts* and *Blade*. He's very quietly doing his thing. He's doing his thing and he's doing it well. St. Claire Bourne has been working with Wesley for several years with these projects.

Iverem: What are you working on now? I heard you were working on a novel. . . .

Dash: I dropped the novel to do this film. It's supposed to go to print in May 2001 so I'd better get to work making these spelling corrections. It's my second novel. It's *Vetiver, Jasmine and Zen,* a love story.

Iverem: An interracial one?

Dash: Nahh . . . But she has three different lovers at three different times in her life . . . .

Iverem: Is there anything else that you wanted to mention that we haven't discussed?

Dash: Yes. We need to have some creative people in development. Kimberly Ogletree produced with me on my Arabesque films and I brought her in to produce for this one. I suggested her. We need people to fight to maintain the integrity of the story we are trying to tell. When someone says I don't recognize the names of the medical schools, Howard or Meharry, we need to have someone in there to say that these are important Black colleges and that it is important to use their names. We need to have our own developing staff, set-up producers, executive producers.

For example, I brought up a story line about color discrimination in the Black community and executives from MTV had never heard of it and didn't care. One said, "No one will know what you are talking about because I don't know what you are talking about." There's a story line where Camille's mother grabs a brown paper (and shows that she's darker than it). That stayed in only because Monica's people stepped up and said, "That's how it really is. . . . "

Snatch

December 6, 2000

Despite its tired parading of White toughmen, Black bumblers, and extreme cynicism, there are moments that will make you laugh out loud. This is *Pulp Fiction* with a twist. It is transatlantic, based in London, so part of its allure is as a British freak show: a pitiful would-be thug named, of all things, Turkish; his more pitiful sidekick Tommy; a corrupt fight promoter who feeds corpses to hungry pigs; a big ole Black man in black leather; and a band of indecipherable gypsies that are the English equivalent of trailer trash.

Because everybody is living on the criminal edge, there is lots of shooting. Killing and corpses happen easily in this zone of the mob world. The body becomes a joke, and so does the corpse. This film asks a lot and, then again, nothing at all. To watch it comfortably, we must suspend our belief in what we are seeing. Director-writer Guy Ritchie plays a lot with the quickness and strangeness of life with fast-forwards, quick edits, and repetition. He knows how to build a joke, and then build upon it some more. He frames the odd and bizarre and forces us to decide whether we will laugh at it or be grossed out. You could say that *Snatch* simply reflects the absurdity of these times. In it, as in the real world, all kinds of outrageous crap is happening. For example, George W. Bush is actually going to be inaugurated as president!

15

Pimps, Hos, Brothers, and Sisters

Disappearing Acts

December 9, 2000

Even post *Love Jones* and *How Stella Got Her Groove Back,* Black relationships beg to be treated with some sensitivity and depth on the big and small screen. In *Disappearing Acts,* premiering on HBO, Black love has a fighting chance in the hands of Gina Prince-Bythewood, the director who earlier this year brought us *Love and Basketball.* In one year, Prince-Bythewood has done more for Black romance on the screen than nearly twenty-five years of the "new wave" in Black film—though this is not a call for her to be pigeonholed as the "love director."

The secret is that she has successfully delivered the Black female romantic heroine—beautiful, emotionally vulnerable, and worthy of our empathy. Of course, in both pictures, she had the fine acting of Sanaa Lathan to fill the role of heroine convincingly. Together, both Prince-Bythewood and Lathan have broadened the cinematic reality for Black women. To the list of sad Black woman film personas—mammy, sapphire, female buck, castrating mammy, hoochie mama, and one-dimensional diva—we can now add real deal—for-real Black woman.

Silly monikers aside, this business of looking at the screen and seeing something real is serious business, which is why this film is also worth checking out. Based on Terry McMillan's novel of the same name, it tells the story of Zora, a music teacher and aspiring singer played by Lathan, and Franklin, a construction worker played by Wesley Snipes. They fall in love and the relationship must bear up under their fragile and flawed humanity. We get to see the startling beauty, as well as the terrible stupidity, involved in this and many love affairs.

This is arguably McMillan's best novel, which explores some level of interpersonal complexity as well as some of the social dynamics of the 1980s in New York City. Her story, told from Franklin and Zora's point of view, nevertheless still portrays Franklin—not quite divorced, needing a GED, unpolished, and insecure—as troubled and a troublemaker. As far as relationship material, he had red flags all over him. The same sensibility has been transferred to this film. So part of your reaction to the film, especially if you are a man, might depend on your view of Franklin. Love stories require both female and male heroines. This story is from that 1980s era of dominant Black women's fiction often sorely criticized for its depiction of Black men. That depiction is not invisible here, though the screenplay by Lisa Jones softens the rough edges of Franklin's character and offers more hope for Zora and Franklin as a couple.

Wesley Snipes plays his part convincingly. He is great as an around-the-way brother, and even as a lover of Black women. The honey-colored lighting of the film does not always compliment his mahogany complexion, as did the dark, bluish light of *Art of War.* (Or it could be that, at this point, Snipes looks more fierce than fine?)

One critic, writing about McMillan's novel, called it "a love story waiting to explode." The same can be said of this film, and the state of most Black romance in film. But for a meantime experience, *Disappearing Acts* is rich, moving, and worthwhile. It is a human story.

OPM—*What Women Want*

December 15, 2000

I was fully prepared to scoff at and hate *What Women Want.* Mel Gibson as the Mack has never worked for me. He was most convincing as the obsessed genius in *Conspiracy Theory.* The idea, given by the trailers, that what women want is Mel Gibson, was only amusing because Loretta Divine, the high priestess of homegirls, made an appearance talking about his ass. (Now c'mon. What is the probability that Gibson has an ass worthy of the high priestess's admiration?) But despite my bias, this movie has a lot going for it—even though it is as melanin challenged as George W. Bush. *What Women Want* has chick flick written all over it. But it is not sappy or melodramatic. It is a chick flick for smart chicks—and their dates, too.

Finding Forrester

December 19, 2000

Some movies work because, despite their flaws, they tell a moving story. For me, *Finding Forrester* is one such film.

It starts rather awkwardly in the way that Hollywood usually fakes the funk when it comes to Black culture, but then it recovers and offers a realness, warmth, and humanity. Jamal Wallace and his boys from the Bronx shoot hoops and hang out at a little coffee shop (yeah, right). Overlooking the court where they play is an old prewar building standing in the middle of what looks like a sea of boxy public housing projects. From a corner window of the building, a White man, who never leaves his apartment, spies the world through binoculars. They notice him. He's been there all of their lives and they have built a mythology around him. (Is he a killer? A freak?)

On a dare, Jamal goes up to the man's apartment and, after being confronted as an intruder, he flees and mistakenly leaves his schoolbag filled with his precious writing journals. He eventually strikes up a relationship with the spooky but learned old man, John Forrester (Sean Connery), who, after reading and editing every one of Jamal's journals, takes an interest in the boy's writing and academic talent. Around this same time, Jamal scores very high on a standardized test and is admitted to an expensive private school. Jamal's relationship with the old man proves pivotal as Jamal faces new challenges in a racist and elitist environment, and must balance his academic talent with his identity as a Black jock.

There are several pitfalls that director Gus Van Sant and writer Mike Rich have avoided in this updated, urban version of the wizard and the apprentice. First of all, this interracial friendship is not corny or fake. This is a difficult, edgy relationship between two males who, though separated by generations and ethnicity, are both proud and stubborn. Importantly, it is clear that Forrester, though wiser, has his own human fragility and shortcomings. Jamal's friendship helps him, too. Forrester's vulnerability keeps the relationship balanced, creates a sense of reciprocity, and helps us to steer clear of the great White father trap. Jamal has a family—a mother and a brother—that gives him roots. Though he is helped by the old man, the old man does not remake him like Tarzan tames a savage.

Connery is not a stylized toughman here. He gets to growl and unfurl his velvety voice and accent, but his face is softer and he actually looks like a fragile human. Newcomer Robert Brown, a native of Harlem, is amazing as Jamal. He really makes this film with an honest and open relationship with the camera, and a dead-on portrayal of a young and gifted Black man constantly battling society's assumptions and low expectations. Anna Paquin, the little girl from *The Piano* all grown up here, has a case of chocolate fever. My man Busta Rhymes, as Jamal's brother, peppers his sentences with "yo" and "dog." One thing is for sure, with Busta around, you can be sure that all the funk here is not faked.

Pimps Up, Hos Down—The Director's Cut

January 15, 2001

In *Pimps Up, Hos Down—The Director's Cut,* director Brent Owens runs out of steam in his cottage industry of making documentaries about the seamy world of prostitution. This version of the popular documentary, which aired often on HBO, includes thirty more minutes of footage. And all I can say is, "For what?"

Owens's other documentaries on HBO, like *Hookers on the Point* (Parts 1 and 2), were sometimes fascinating cinema verité glimpses into the world of sex-for-sale that piqued our prurient interests. But with this newest version of *Pimps Up, Hos Down,* now for sale to the public, Owens seems to be squeezing the last bit of mileage he can from a subject that seems anachronistic in the new millennium. The tone, beyond respectful, is pimp-as-demigod. The garish outfits look like clown suits. The real story—what makes a prostitute in these times?—is not touched.

For some time now, we've been tired of seeing maids, mammies, and coons, right? Well, if I don't see another processed brother wearing a big hat, gator shoes, fur coat, and thick ice, I'll be just fine. I suppose many men in the hip-hop generation do not put the pimp into the same category of tired, offensive stereotypes. Instead, with the popularity of '70s movies like *The Mack,* the pimp is viewed by many men as an icon of power and status.

How skilled, how powerful he must be to get a woman to sell her tail on the street and hand over her money! And besides, selling p#$*y seems so benign, almost natural, something that the women would be doing anyway. As painted in this documentary, the pimp is simply a smart guy able to go along for the ride.

As for icons, I wish we'd resurrect El-Hajj Malik El-Shabazz. Anybody still got their X hat?

Like the drug dealer, the pimp is a hood hero, able to parlay his ability to "steal a bitch's mind" into big cars, fancy clothes, ridiculous jewelry, and, perhaps, a nice place to live. He has found a way to beat the system, which asks that most of us get a regular job. Another problem with this desperately narrow way of thinking, and with this documentary, is that it does not reveal the ultimate price paid for this lifestyle—AIDS, sterility, drug abuse, child prostitution, mental illness, and death—and who pays it (women).

According to the men interviewed here, a pimp is just a natural extension of being a player, and a ho is just an extension of being a sexually active woman. One particularly wack pimp, Pimpin Snookie, says that if a woman has had sex with more than one man, she is a ho. So, according to this man, most women are hos, in need of only the proper grooming to hit the track.

The vicious misogyny of many of the pimps makes matters worse. Snookie's prostitutes follow behind him, always standing or sitting with their eyes downcast. Mr. Whitefolks, the sole White pimp included, talks about the natural order for men to control women. Bishop Don "Magic" Juan recounts the whippings administered to hos with clothes hangers and sticks.

If there is anything fascinating here, it is the subservience of women, the acceptance of themselves as chattel. It reminds me of stories (told by White folks) that, upon Emancipation, some slaves ran to their master asking to stay and remain on the plantation. To me, the incomprehensible mentality is the same. I come to the end of this documentary interested less in the pimps and their ability to capitalize on the bodies of women than in the women who choose this as an option for life's work, who choose the world order—Pimps Up, Hos Down.

OPM—*Traffic*

January 5, 2001

There are no cookie-cutter plots or people in *Traffic,* Steven Soderbergh's new film about the "war on drugs." It is not simplistic or, though more than two hours long, boring. There is no Mafia (or Black Mafia) mystique, or Schwarzenegger–Harrison Ford toughmen coming to save us wretched crackheads.

Set in Mexico, Washington, D.C., California, and Cincinnati, *Traffic* is full of detail, complexity, and seduction. The seduction comes from a cast of imperfect characters, including Don Cheadle as a DEA agent named Montel Gordon; Michael Douglas as judge turned federal appointee Robert Wakefield; Catherine Zeta-Jones as Helena Ayala, the drug lord's naive wife; and Benicio Del Toro as Javier Rodriguez Rodriguez, a police officer in Tijuana, Mexico. In four separate but interconnected plots, none of these characters are painted in Black or White. All evolve in some remarkable way and acquire the strength to do whatever is necessary—good or evil, brave or foolish—to preserve their existence.

What will Javier do to improve his substandard pay and move up the ranks of a corrupt bureaucracy? What will Helena do when her wealthy husband, presumably a successful "businessman," is suddenly arrested and thrown in jail? What motivates Montel to continue fighting a seemingly futile battle against drug trafficking? And can Robert actually be appointed as the nation's drug czar when, unknown to him, his daughter Caroline and her preppy friends are heroin heads?

If I say, of course Michael Douglas is painted as the most integrity-filled, it will sound cynical. And maybe I am cynical, or maybe the film is. This story requires that you think long and hard about prejudices and expectation on all levels. On the other hand, it requires that we think long and hard with limited information. There is no arch villain; the closest that we get is an old man who just wants to slam Salma Hayak and, also of course, a young brother slinging rock and heroin with a gun at the ready. There is no innocent victim; the closest we get is a precocious White girl who ends up as an upscale version of a crack ho.

It could be that by painting police officers as somewhat bumbling, Soderbergh is just being realistic, not cynical. It could be that by having a social butterfly housewife suddenly evolve to the point where she hires a hit man is not cynical, but, rather, a realistic look at what she will do to survive. It could be that a man selling out on his best friend to get ahead is not cynical but, rather, what this man will really do in order to survive—even if it means his friend will be killed.

Prostitution, literally and figuratively, is a major theme here. Drug trafficking requires all kinds of people to sell their bodies for cash. Police, drug addicts, drug dealers, and families of drug dealers are all putting their bodies on the line.

Is this cynicism or reality? Hard to say in this so-called war.

Jazz

January 8, 2001

Wynton Marsalis rightly notes in the new Ken Burns documentary, *Jazz,* that the reason this music is often so controversial is because it is the soul of America. Similarly, this massive, ten-part series (premiering Monday, January 8 and ending Wednesday, January 31 on PBS) reflects both that soul and controversy. Spanning from the start of the twentieth century to the present, it tells the story of jazz from its bluesy origins in New Orleans right up to today's musical styles.

But what story does it tell? How do you investigate the soul? Jazz manages to incorporate the most sorrowful blues with improvisational ecstasy. It mixes Black and White, and rich with poor. A true jazz history, therefore, tells many different stories because the music means many different things to different people. While this series obviously tells well-crafted stories—complete with startling vintage black-and-white footage and archival photographs—it is not clear based on the eighty-five-minute sampler reel sent to www.bet.com that it tells the story of what the music has meant to the African-American community.

There is an energetic emphasis on the wild popularity of the swing era and that moment when jazz was America's popular music, and when it rescued the country from the doldrums of the Depression and World War II. This part of the program feels like a continuation of the ongoing tribute to that generation of Whites who came of age during the war, fought abroad, and returned to a deeply segregated and racist country.

It acknowledges in interviews the birth of swing in Black communities and the music, for example, of Duke Ellington and Chuck Webb, which was happening years before the rise and coronation of Benny Goodman. But unlike news accounts and reviews from Whites voiced over as a historical record, there are no comparable Black voices, either from the Black press or Black authors, to take us inside the clubs and juke joints on the South Side of Chicago, in New York's Harlem, or on Central Avenue in Los Angeles.

Also, as it presents a series of experts, such as critics and historians, musicians and writers, it is clear that much of jazz "history" is jazz as it has been studied, critiqued, and crafted into a narrative by Whites. And, for this, Burns cannot be totally faulted. To some extent, he is just reflecting reality, which includes the fact that many key Black jazz figures have died. On the other hand, he could've included more Black critical and community voices. There are Black jazz critics and writers, younger and older, who could have offered insight and pointed the way to historical writings from early in the last century. For much of it, Marsalis and Stanley Crouch (yikes!) serve as master representatives of musicians and Black people. They make lots of good points. But I sure would have liked to somehow go inside a New Orleans joint where the music was being born.

Postscript: Jazz *is obviously worth watching. The series, seen in its entire ten parts, filled in many gaps in the narrative, included more Black voices, and told a fuller story of the African-American community and its classical music.*

Bojangles

February 4, 2001

Recent films based on real life, including *The Hurricane* and *Malcolm X,* all prove the difficulty in making an autobiographical movie. How much of the story will be based on real life? How many real-life details will be included? Who tells the story and how will it be told?

All of these questions swirl around *Bojangles,* based on the life of Bill "Bojangles" Robinson and premiering on Showtime. Born in Richmond, Virginia, in 1878, Robinson became one of the most famous and highest-paid African-American entertainers of the early twentieth century. Appearing in vaudeville, on Broadway, and in Hollywood films, some consider him the greatest tap dancer ever.

This made-for-cable version of his exceptional life amounts to a theatrical production on film. Performances, conversations, and even love scenes transpire as they would on a stage. Characters sometimes face the camera and speak to us directly, reinforcing the fact that they are players in a drama. Rather than being immersed in a cinematic world, we watch a play.

The result is mixed. This movie is colorful and the narrative and scenes are creatively constructed. The overall production is pushed forward mightily through solid performances by Gregory Hines in the role of Robinson and by Kimberly Elise in the role of his second wife, Fannie Clay. But from almost the beginning, when Robinson's longtime White manager turns to the camera to speak to us, the narration and perspective is suspect. Also, there is not enough focus given to the inner man to allow us to gain much feel or sympathy for Robinson as a man. Autobiographies don't have to be glowing puff pieces, but they should allow us to feel their subject. Surely there was something ticking beneath Robinson's exterior of hard gambling, drinking, ego, and mad talent.

How did the South shape him? How did he reflect on the death of his parents when he was only seven or eight? The film excludes his early collaboration with comedian George W. Cooper. Seemingly important milestones in his life, such as his tour of Europe, are not even mentioned.

Such shortcomings don't help Hines very much as he portrays a man who was about ten shades darker and obviously walked through a different world very differently. But despite this handicap, Hines does what he can and does what he does best—he dances his butt off. One of the most interesting sequences of the film comes during the closing credits when original footage of Robinson performing his signature *Stair Dance,* up and down a set of stairs, is juxtaposed with Hines's detailed and masterful copy of the original footwork and performance.

Bojangles flows and it is entertaining. But as it both makes a claim to and ignores history, it also makes the viewer aware of its flaws. We are reminded of what it shows and what it says—as well as what it doesn't.

Double Take

January 12, 2001

In tone, *Double Take* fits into that Hollywood netherworld where minstrelsy, senseless violence, and busty-lusty women feed a frantic and frenetic humor. Sure, depending on your taste, you might laugh at Eddie Griffin with his crazy self, doing a poor-man's imitation of Martin Lawrence. Or you just might look at all the mayhem on the screen in utter disbelief, like you're watching a music video featuring, all at once, Biz Markie, Weird Al Yankovic, and Lil' Kim.

In less than ninety minutes, it offers a twist in the usual "brother-on-the-run" plot, familiar to us in lockdown comedies like *Blue Streak* and *3 Strikes,* which gave us visions of brothers en route to or recently released from jail. *Double Take* takes the action out of the hood and, like *Blue Streak,* even has international aspirations. The brother runs all the way out of the country!

The brother this time is Daryl Chase (Orlando Jones), a Harvard-educated investment banker with all the trappings of an outrageously wealthy life. I think he pays more than $15,000 a month for his spot, which I hope he owns. He has a trophy girlfriend who looks like she fills a D cup. He is book smart and so puffed up with himself that he doesn't know that he's dorky, uncool, and couldn't survive five minutes on the street without handlers.

Chase finds himself suddenly embroiled in a conspiracy involving murder, drugs, Mexican outlaws, and money laundering through one of his accounts. Taking advice from those he thinks he can trust, he flees the country. But the problem with his plan is that he doesn't know whom to trust. There are more cops and agents in this film than there will be at George W. Bush's inaugural. Poor Daryl. Out in the real world, all that Ivy League education gets him is a dog bite and a cheap motel room next to a smelly emu farm.

Of course, this is the plot apparent, which is merely a backdrop for the real purpose of the movie: for Griffin, in the role of a man named Freddy Tiffany, to take his turn as the wild brother on the edge. Dancing, cussing, lying, and jiving, he carries the plot from one crazy scene to the next. For most of the film, we don't even know who Griffin is. Is he a hustler? Murderer? FBI agent? A Black native of Malibu? All of the above?

In this film, there are two Black men on the run but they seem to serve as symbols of the same Black-man-in-society, who receives good or bad treatment based on whether he is wearing an expensive suit and has the blessings of the right circle of White people. As the two men trade clothes and "identities" on the run, each moves seamlessly into the role of the other. Freddy becomes immediately highly affected and a stiff butt. Daryl suddenly wants to wash down his dinner with some Schlitz Malt Liquor.

All of it is enough to make me get a drink myself.

OPM—*Save the Last Dance*

January 12, 2001

Though in most Hollywood films the heroes and heroines are White, African-Americans have learned to root for them anyway. We identify with Tom Hanks, Meg Ryan, Kevin Costner, Susan Sarandon, Mel Gibson . . . and whatever cinematic world they inhabit at the moment. We have learned to see and interpret humanity through a White face.

Sometimes, like in the case of the new movie *Save the Last Dance,* Whites are taken out of their world and plunked among us, the dark masses. Because we are shut out of so many flicks about personal triumph, we might be simply grateful to see ourselves in the context of the great humanity story and feel that it is a movie about us. In reality, though, it is not. We are simply a backdrop, a sort of exotic locale, for the familiar story of White triumph.

It would be harsh to call *Save the Last Dance* a sort of hip-hop *Tarzan,* with Jane in the leading role. The film is actually well written. It has moments of depth and insight as it recycles the plot of *Beat Street* to tell a new-millennium tale of interracial romance. But even the underdeveloped love story is not the main story

It is unswerving in its focus and sympathy for Sara Johnson, a seventeen-year-old aspiring ballerina who, after the death of her mother, leaves her Midwestern town to live with her estranged father, a poor jazz musician, in a Chicago slum. She is enrolled in the area high school, which is predominantly Black, and is befriended by the popular and precocious Chenille Reynolds, who is the sister of Derek, Sara's eventual love interest. Derek is the smartest boy in the graduating class, the boy who is hoping for an acceptance letter from Georgetown University. And the new White girl gets him.

Sara's new friends introduce her to the world of hip-hop dance at a night club they use fake ID cards to enter. Though it is never explained how, Derek has a knack for teaching Sara to dance hip-hop style. Through hours of often comical coaching sessions, they build a friendship, trust, and romance. Derek learns that Sara is actually a talented ballerina and that she has stopped dancing because she is wracked with pain over her mother's death.

Sara is written as a White girl who has learned to accept people on their own terms. She is smart but dorky when it comes to street dance. Julia Stiles plays the part with a face that is stoic or dimpled with confusion and pain as the scene requires. Sean Patrick Thomas shows talent in the role of Derek. He is not a convincing dancer but delivers an emotional honesty. Kerry Washington is also sassy and on point in the role of Chenille. Their performances, plus some good dance scenes, make this movie more likeable than you might think.

The Queens of Comedy

January 27, 2001

There is a particular sista thang. It's hard to describe other than we know it when we hear it. No one can tell you off worse than a Black woman. No one else can get down with it and take no prisoners. At its best it's speaking truth to power. On its coarser level, it's speaking truth about our raw humanity, which usually involves beatdowns, jail, sex, physical imperfection, and the comedy of oppression. How else can we laugh *hard* at someone being called an illiterate motherf*****?

It is the coarser sista thang, the salacious tradition of Moms Mabley and Millie Jackson that fuel the often hilarious *Queens of Comedy* special, premiering on Showtime. If you like nice, polite comedy, maybe you shouldn't tune in. Comedians Mo'nique, Adele Givens, Sommore, and Laura Hayes cuss up a storm and describe in raunchy detail most sex acts you can think of. If regular raunchy jokes are called blue, then these ladies' jokes are deep purple.

But it is high raunch with a decidedly sista-thang twist. There is something about the way that Givens struts across the stage in her high heels with mannerisms not far from those of an R&B diva or a church evangelist. Before she even gets to a punch line about Jenny Craig diet plans, we are rolling with laughter, anticipating a flood of righteous female indignation that may well involve beating someone's ass.

Wearing a pop-tart outfit, funny homegirl facial expressions, and dropping easily into the stance of a corner fight, Mo'nique (*The Parkers*) is a master at turning the tables on our ridicule of fat women. Playing both cheerleader for big women and harsh judge for "skinny bitches," she does for Black female comics what Martin Lawrence does for the men—she brings an around-the-way energy that is as neurotic as it is funny.

Sommore's girl thing is the most physical and involves making a lot of faces and holding her body in comical positions. As the host and elder stateswoman of the group, Hayes sets the tone with jokes about grandchildren and growing up in a family of girls. Of all the stand-up routines, Hayes's act needs the most polish. The regular on BET's *Comic View* takes a while to warm up both her act and the audience. She does warm it up, though, and ends with the audience roaring.

Like in *The Original Kings of Comedy* movie, director Steve Purcell intersperses show footage with scenes of the comedians as they arrive and travel about Memphis. Unlike the "kings," these queens get up close and personal with the people of Memphis—inside a beauty salon, general store, soul-food restaurant, and on one street that Givens suspects to be the "ho stroll."

Women might laugh at these comedians more than men. The audience at the Orpheum Theater in Memphis is made up largely of females, who cheer loudly when Givens looks out at them and declares them to be queens, too.

Black Films at 2001 Film Festivals

February 12, 2001

The Caveman's Valentine, directed by Kasi Lemmons (*Eve's Bayou*), and *Kingdom Come,* starring Whoopi Goldberg, are among the Black films representing at the kickoff of this year's film festival season. The early round of festivals-with-melanin include the Hollywood Black Film Festival, which concluded February 4; the Pan African Film and Arts Festival, underway in Los Angeles through February 19; and FESPACO, the huge biennial Pan-African festival held this year, February 24 through March 3, in Burkina Faso.

"We're witnessing the rise of the new Black film industry on the planet," says Ayuko Babu, executive director of the Pan African Film and Arts Festival. "Now, you get a chance to get in on the front line of this new culture. It's like being at Minton's Playhouse in 1947. Seeing the work of these filmmakers is the equivalent of seeing Charlie Parker or Dizzy Gillespie."

The largest of the Black festivals, the nine-year-old Pan African Film and Arts Festival, kicked off February 8 with a special presentation of the new comedy by Fox Searchlight, *Kingdom Come,* with LL Cool J, Jada Pinkett Smith, Vivica A. Fox, and Cedric the Entertainer. Over twelve days, seventy-five films by African-Americans and from throughout the diaspora will be shown. About twenty thousand people annually attend the film portion of the festival, held at the Magic Johnson Theaters in South-Central Los Angeles. Another 150,000 stroll through the visual arts portion of the show at the adjacent Crenshaw Plaza shopping mall.

International highlights include *Bàttu,* starring Danny Glover and directed by Mali's Cheick Sissoko; *Faat Kiné,* a new film from Ousmane Sembene of Senegal; *Boesman & Lena,* starring Angela Bassett and Danny Glover; and *Brother,* directed by Japan's action master Takeshi Kitano and starring Omar Epps. *Lumumba,* the latest offering from the Haitian filmmaker Raoul Peck, will also be shown.

The Pan African Festival is the sister festival to FESPACO, which has become a mecca for those interested in cinema by Africans from around the globe. "Here's an opportunity to see, over twelve days, different aspects of the African personality," said Babu. "Here's a chance to see things you're not going to see anyplace else—love, politics, all of it. You don't have to get on a plane to go anywhere. You can come to our festival. If you really want to understand who we are, you celebrate our diversity. You've got to see our stories from the Caribbean, from Papau New Guinea, from the Continent. Your mind is blown."

The three-year-old Hollywood Black Film Festival opened with *The Caveman's Valentine,* which is an adaptation of the 1995 novel by George Dawes Green. In it, Romulus Ledbetter, a Juilliard-trained musician, succumbs to schizophrenia and lives in a cave at the edge of Manhattan. Samuel L. Jackson, who also appears as a brilliant but mad man in last year's critically acclaimed *Unbreakable,* continues his crazy streak as this film's star.

In total, HBFF offered forty-nine films in its competition. There were two special presentations: *Long Night's Journey Into Day,* a riveting documentary directed by Deborah Hoffman and Frances Reid, about the South African Truth and Reconciliation Commission that investigated crimes under apartheid, and *Chalk,* directed by Rob Nilsson, about a skilled pool player who is forced to play the game of his life. The festival closed with *Lockdown,* directed by John Luessenhop and written by Preston A. Williams, about a competitive swimmer who tries to get his life back on track after dropping out of college.

The Jury Award was presented to the South African film *Chikin Biznis,* written by Mtutuzeli Matshoba and the Audience Award was given to *Amour Infinity,* written and directed by Jerry Lamothe.

"We have actually doubled the number of panels and workshops," said LaTisha C. Green, a member of the HBFF steering committee and spokesperson for the Hollywood festival (which is actually held in Culver City, California). "Since we've been able to double our number of participants, we hope to double our attendance as well."

If you are wondering, the Hollywood Black Film Festival and the Pan African Film and Arts Festival—two festivals in the same month, in the same city, with the same audience—do have an uneasy coexistence. Babu said that he welcomes the newer Hollywood festival and any additional opportunity to showcase Black film, but doesn't understand why organizers of the Hollywood festival scheduled it during the same month as Pan African. He said back-to-back festivals can create confusion and conflict.

"Our position from day one has been that there should always be more outlets for Black film—the more the better," said Babu. "We just wanted them to have their festival during another part of the year. But they decided to do it right next to ours."

Green acknowledged that the Hollywood festival does draw from the same pool of films and audience as the Pan African Film and Arts Festival. "There are some overlaps," she said. "Sometimes we screen some of the same films. But I think we're attracting two different audiences. They're attracting more people into culture and the arts. They get more African films. And we're attracting more people just interested in making films."

Even at the recent annual Sundance Film Festival in Utah, more Black films were screened than ever before (though none of the Black films were among the festival winners). Those familiar with the selection process said that the increase was due to more Black staff input during the planning process.

Some of the Black features and documentaries screened at Sundance are those we reviewed last year at the Acapulco and Urbanworld film festivals. These include the funny and irreverent directorial debut of Vanessa Middleton, *30 Years to Life,* which focuses on a group of friends who all turn thirty during the course of a year, and *Dancing in September,* directed by Reggie Rock Bythewood and starring Isaiah Washington and Nicole Ari Parker. Bythewood's directorial debut, which centers on the challenges of Black folks in the television industry, won a spot in our 2000 Top Ten list and is being shown on HBO this month.

The Black list at Sundance also included: *3 A.M.,* directed by Lee Davis, about the wanderings of the New York City cabdrivers; *Lift,* directed by DeMane Davis and Khari Streeter, about a salesclerk who supplements her earnings by boosting; and *The Middle Passage,* by Guy Deslauriers, about the horror of a slave-ship voyage. The documentaries *Marcus Garvey: Look for Me in the Whirlwind,* directed by Stanley Nelson, and *Ralph Bunche: An American Odyssey,* directed by William Greaves, were also offered.

As Black film festivals continue to draw crowds but often don't produce distribution deals for filmmakers, many Black artists have become discouraged and wonder if they are worth the effort. But Babu said that the festivals remain a viable outlet.

"It's a problem Black people have whether it's film, whether it's practicing law. Whenever Black folks try to carve out a place for themselves within these industries, these institutions, these societies—they run into marginalization. They run into marginalization, dismissal, all the things that the dominant society throws at you—and that is the situation in film. They are only interested in their stories, or their cultural family's stories—and that is one reason we developed this festival.

"I'm not pessimistic," he added. "I'm optimistic. Sometimes you've got to look at progress over forty, fifty years. It's a long process and you have to be in the game for the long run. Black folks want to be in films and they want to tell our stories all over the planet."

Down to Earth

February 16, 2001

When he's really on, Chris Rock can bring down the house. Smart-assed irreverence, spiced with a taste of wild-eyed craziness, is his style. Unlike Martin Lawrence or D. L. Hughley, he doesn't bring an around-the-way flava. Rather than the brother from the corner, he is the kid who went to school with White kids. He is your basic class clown all grown up—widening his eyes, twisting up his face, and bucking his teeth to within an inch of looking like Goofy from Disney.

All of which comes together nicely for him in the surprisingly funny *Down to Earth,* a takeoff on the 1978 film *Heaven Can Wait.* Rock, as executive producer and cowriter, has crafted a series of punchy stand-up routines surrounded by a crazy plot. This movie is surprising for a few reasons: Its promotion leads us to groan at the possibility of seeing another tired ebony-ivory, formulaic movie. Second, we have become accustomed to most of these comedian movies somehow involving a brother on his way to or recently released from jail. Thankfully, Rock has found humor outside of the lockdown. Finally, since Rock is doing stand-up, he doesn't look crazy like he did on HBO, looking sideways trying to read the cue cards.

And, thankfully, this movie doesn't mute Rock's irreverence. In fact, he uses it as a vehicle for deft humor on the racial divide. He plays the role of Lance Barton, an aspiring comedian who is killed in a bike accident. When Barton gets to heaven, though, it turns out that he has died before his time. To compensate him, the angels—one who looks like he's from *The Sopranos* and another who looks like a

Jewish booking agent—give him the opportunity to inhabit another body. There are slim pickings for corpses and Barton winds up inside the body of a rich White man named Charles Wellington. Barton continues to see himself as himself. But everyone else sees him as a portly, pink-faced man in expensive clothes.

He decides to become Wellington in part so that he can help Sontee (Regina King), a pretty health-care worker who is organizing opposition to Wellington's plan to privatize the Brooklyn hospital where she works. From here on in, the plot revolves around the comical and improbable pairing of Wellington and Sontee. To help their cause, the filmmakers play a little sleight of hand. Except for a few brief scenes, we continue to see Barton as he sees himself. We are given enough reminders that others see him differently, but we don't see King slobbing some old White man. We continue to see Rock.

Wanda Sykes, the hilarious regular from Rock's cancelled HBO show, appears here as a maid. The versatile Frankie Faison plays Barton's manager. Though not as funny as Robert Townsend's vintage comedies *Hollywood Shuffle* and *Meteor Man, Down to Earth* also does not rely on pathology for humor. It's funny without getting too funky.

The Caveman's Valentine

March 2, 2001

It is a remarkable thing to watch director Kasi Lemmons paint pictures and release poems. This girl can paint! And boy is she a poet, of the visual sort. Her patient, moody, and fresh rendering of a bourgeois Black family in spooky ole Louisiana was startling for her debut feature, *Eve's Bayou.* In her new film, *The Caveman's Valentine,* she turns her focus to the netherworld between genius and mental illness. Straddling the last film and this one is her seeming obsession with mystery, easy and hidden crime, taboo, curses, and lifetime consequences.

Taking the story from a novel by George Dawes Green, Lemmons explores the world of Romulus Ledbetter, a Juilliard-trained classical pianist who succumbed to schizophrenia and is now homeless, living in a cave in a city park. As we "see" through his eyes often in the film, Ledbetter views the world differently than we do. Sometimes he sees in black-and-white. Sometimes his surroundings move in slow motion. Much of his obsession is with someone named Stuyvesant, an evil power whom he believes resides in the art deco pinnacle of Manhattan's Chrysler building. Ledbetter looks up and imagines the building is emitting Gatorade-yellow beams of light aimed directly at him.

This is all good. But, of course, there is the necessity of meeting poetry with storytelling. This is where *The Caveman's Valentine* suffers a bit. For much of the film, Romulus goes about investigating the death of another street person whose body he finds outside his cave. His investigation, such as it is, carries him into the monied and morally bankrupt circles of New York's art elite. He focuses his attention on a celebrated photographer who specializes in sadistic images. During his sleuthing, Ledbetter zips back and forth between Manhattan and upstate New York, where the artist lives, more than the state governor. He functions very highly for a man who hasn't made his way out of a cave. You can't help but think that, if he is this lucid for this long, surely he could take a regular bath.

The versatile Aunjanue Ellis (*Men of Honor* and *The Practice*) shows more of her depth and range as Ledbetter's daughter and a police officer. Samuel L. Jackson has played a good crazy man for so long now that, I believe, there is a good chance he may not be acting anymore. As Ledbetter, Jackson dons a full head of long gray locks that, combined with his wild and talking eyes, make him a poster child for insane genius. What's next? Othello? We're not really sure, though, why, how, or when Ledbetter sank into his current mental state. There are hints. Tamara Tunie plays his estranged wife with a cool, icy finesse that makes her look like Exhibit 1 in possible triggers for craziness. But, of course, as the film is quick to remind us, schizophrenia may evoke images and poetry, but it has no rhyme and no reason.

Blacks at the Oscars 2001

March 20, 2001

True. The fine folks at the Academy of Motion Picture Arts and Sciences did not deem any Black performance or film worthy of an Oscar nomination this year. But it's not as if there was no Black presence among this year's Best Picture nominees, which were an assortment of modern and ancient fairy tales, with one true story thrown in just to sort of keep it real.

Take *Traffic,* for example. Of course Don Cheadle plays the narc and Benicio Del Toro won for Best Supporting Actor. But you might not know that, in this film, the worst of America's drug problem is epitomized by a thinly muscled, young Black drug dealer towering over a White teenaged addict in sexual intercourse.

When I caught this film in January, at a theater just outside of Washington, D.C., a collective gasp arose from the Whites around me. I was mesmerized, trying to absorb the complete impact of the powerful scene, which highlighted the brother's ebony complexion against the white light in the dilapidated room and, of course, against the teenager's pale skin. The scene screamed: 1) that illegal drugs will bring you down, even bring down a privileged daughter of a judge to the point of selling her body to a ruthless ghetto animal; 2) America, maybe this will get your attention, even if stories of "inner-city" drug wars don't; 3) that the image of the Black, sexualized man can still be used in this millennium to strike a note of horror, especially if it is in connection with a White female; and 4) that the Society of Crack Hos has equal-opportunity membership.

Appearances in the other films, such as they are, are not so menacing. Djimon Hounsou is strong and brave in the role of Juba, an enslaved African in the film *Gladiator,* set during the time of the Roman Empire. He befriends and aids Maximus, the main character played by Russell Crowe, who won for Best Actor. When Hounsou gets screen time, he is smart, fast, and very human. In the end, he is determined to make his way back home to Africa.

There's not much more in the other films. No Black man, enslaved or free, makes his way to ancient China in *Crouching Tiger, Hidden Dragon.* In *Erin Brockavich,* there is a sister who works in Erin's law office and is one of the little women who doesn't like Erin, with her skanky outfits and salty language. The sister is one of the common women who are not fully realized like the daring and audacious Erin. In *Chocolat,* set in a small French village, there is a startling and brief Black presence—only by accident. The chocolate maker, played by Juliette Binoche, sets up a display in her shop window to celebrate female fertility. Because the nude, female figure she places in the window is made of chocolate, she certainly looks Black. I swear she looks a little like Jill Scott. Then the poor chocolate lady is hacked to pieces by the crazy village mayor. How do you like that? Let's call the NAACP!

Seriously, though, the absence of a Black nominee this year really only underscored the travesty of Denzel Washington's loss last year. It's not only that his performance in *The Hurricane* was superior, it's also that the kinds of Oscar-caliber roles that can put a Black actor in line to win do not come that often. Sure, the members of the academy are White, affluent, and are not feeling Black people. But we also aren't going to get many Oscar nominations with films like *Big Momma's House, The Nutty Professor II,* or even *Shaft.* Some of the best films of last year, with great Black performances, had very limited distribution, or are not getting distribution deals at all.

Let this year of absence and dissing remind us to seek out and support real Black films in 2001. That's an award we can give ourselves.

The Brothers

March 23, 2001

Call it the *Exhale* backlash.

Watching *The Brothers,* the highly anticipated beefcake fest, you get the feeling that writer-director Gary Hardwick took all those Terry McMillan dramas too much to heart.

In a script that dances on the surface between comedy, drama, and the surreal, Hardwick gives the big payback. Rather than four women wandering a wilderness of no-job-hygiene-challenged-spineless-or-otherwise-sorry men, Hardwick tells the story of four young, professional Black men in the desert of dizzy dames. While they wander, Jackson (Morris Chestnut), Derrick (D. L. Hughley), Terry (Shemar Moore), and Brian (Bill Bellamy) are also getting it thrown at them.

Despite their flaws—most notably Jackson is commitment phobic and Brian is an unrepentant misogynist—they are all portrayed with some sympathy as average Joes who gather for clichéd games of basketball, huddle around bars, and perform unremarkably at their jobs. In contrast, the (primarily Black) women in their lives seem to exist in some permanent state of PMS—they tote and shoot guns, have problems in bed, can't hug their sons, and, in general, don't have much of a life outside of games and drama in relationships.

Maybe this would have worked better as slapstick comedy. Had Hardwick pushed harder, he might have wound up in that wickedly hilarious zone where nothing makes sense because it is not supposed to make sense. As this film stands, it is only mildly amusing. There are some jokes but, after a while, the same lines about oral sex or exclamations about the booty get stale. It is not clear whether the viewer is supposed to take this film seriously or not.

When we try to take it seriously, we are confronted with an annoying lack of emotional consistency and truth. Who are these brothers? Chestnut's character, a doctor who is seeing a therapist to cure his dysfunction, is given the fullest treatment. Yet, in the end, we still don't understand his phobias, his anger with his father, or his immaturity in relationships.

It is difficult to judge acting when the script offers so little, but all four of the main actors do a decent job in their roles. Though we know very little about his character, D. L. Hughley—playing the married man among the bunch (a role he also plays in his stand-up routine and on his television show)—actually comes across as the most genuine. Jenifer Lewis is great in her Sapphire-esque stint as

Jackson's mom. The film's bright light is Gabrielle Union in the role of Denise Johnson, a photographer who becomes romantically involved with Jackson.

Denise and Jackson's mother are allowed, in spurts, to play the traditional role of wise women. But not much other wisdom is allowed here. In place of tender affection, wild passion, or even humorous mating ritual, there is anger, pettiness, and male backlash. It doesn't quite undermine the little progress cinematic Black romance has made with films like *Love and Basketball* or *Sprung,* but it reminds us that the struggle for convincing stories and characters is not easy, and continues.

16

Challenging the American Culture Machine—And Not

Et Cetera–Blackbuster: Haile Gerima's D.C. Store Rents a Different Kind of Black Film

April 9, 2001

Just north of Howard University's campus in Washington, D. C., amid vegetarian eateries, a neighborhood bar, and a typewriter repair shop, a different kind of video store has opened, and it is much more than just a place to rent movies.

"We feel we are making our last stand in the cultural struggle—that is the struggle to make our own image," said veteran filmmaker Haile Gerima, whose movie *Sankofa* was an underground hit. He was speaking from the porch of the building he purchased to house his company, Mypheduh Films, Inc. and his Sankofa Video and Bookstore—which specializes in a select group of works by and about people of African descent.

At the store's grand opening four years ago, such grandiloquence was poignant. On that brisk spring day, Gerima was addressing a crowd of his fellow cultural soldiers—local writers, musicians, and filmmakers—gathered in the front yard of the building. Balloons tied to the front fence danced in the wind and a red Howard Centennial banner flapped overhead. A Yoruba priestess poured a libation for the ancestors, intoning: "It is because of their sacrifices that we are here, that we have not died, and that we shall not die."

Gerima's "tough Detroit wife" and business partner, Shirikiana Aina, was at his side, pregnant with their fifth child. Standing behind him were fiery poets from the 1960s generation of Black writers, Haki Madhubuti and Sonia Sanchez. With graying hair and weary, smiling eyes, the three looked like veteran warriors who easily fashion the language of war to fit what is a social and cultural fight.

"I respect this place we have here very much," Gerima said in the accent of his native Ethiopia, gesturing to the two-story building behind him. "That's why I call it a liberated territory."

Since then, Sankofa has taken on and struggled with its mandate of selling independent and foreign films to a Black filmgoing population more accustomed to Hollywood fare such as *Big Momma's House* and *Scary Movie.* To Gerima's generation of activist artists, it is that rare thing: a concrete result of "institution building" and the efforts of these artists to challenge the American popular culture machine. While the store wants to be a gathering place for artists and thinkers, it must make money or go the way of many such well-meaning but cash-starved free territories.

"No doubt," said Kwame Alexander, publisher and president of the Alexander Publishing Group, an Alexandria, Virginia–based company that presents poetry and music slams in the Washington, D.C., area. "A lot of people might tend to gather in the store because Haile and Shirikiana have created this family-like atmosphere," he says. "But to a certain degree that can go overboard where people are enjoying the intellectual vibe—you know, they like talking to Haile, and discussing the plight of Black people—but nobody's buying anything.

"You want to create a balance between economic support and cultural appreciation," he says, adding, "My favorite expression is, 'Everybody's conscious. But how we gonna eat?'"

Maceo Williams, a native of Sankofa's neighborhood, is just the kind of customer the store wants to attract. Until he transferred to Howard a few years back, he was a graduate student in film at the University of Southern California. Visiting the store, Willis plunked down a credit card on the rear glass counter and filled out an application for a video-rental membership. "I think the store should attract people who are looking for films that aren't readily available elsewhere," he said.

He walked over to shelves stacked with videos to rent and pointed to several of them: "Films like *Sweet Sweetback's Baadasssss Song* [by Melvin Van Peebles], *Putney Swope* [by Robert Downey Jr.], and *Dark City*—that's an African film—they won't be available at your average video store," he said.

The store feels more like a living room, with carpeted floors, a couch, a television, and warm wooden shelves. Those shelves are also stocked with Hollywood hits like *Menace II Society* and *Juice,* which are more popular with the general population of the neighborhood.

But it is the task of the store to "make it normal," as Gerima says, for more African-Americans to view foreign, independent, and little-known Hollywood films from the Black diaspora. Open from 11:00 A.M. to 8:30 P.M., the store is renting 100 to 150 films a week, up from just 30 to 40 a week when it opened. About fifteen hundred people have joined as members. Most of its business comes from sales of books and videos, said Tesfu Gerima, a manager at the store and the owner's younger brother.

One woman who worked next door said that because she has cable she rarely rents movies. "Foreign films don't appeal to me," she said. Another area resident, Adrienne Waheed, a photographer and student of film, said that she hadn't developed a taste for foreign films, either. But, she added, she is interested in renting the store's English-language films. Both agree that foreign films need to be better marketed to the Black community.

"I guess a lot of people who don't go to see foreign films don't know a lot about them," says Waheed. "If there was more advertising for them, they would go to see them."

In a sense, Mypheduh Films and Sankofa Video and Book Store came about as a result of marketing—with a healthy portion of stubbornness thrown in. When Gerima's film *Sankofa,* about African-American slavery, was turned down by movie distributors and theaters around the country, Gerima "footwalked" it to thirty-five cities, and ended up grossing $3 million. When Blockbuster Entertainment declined to stock his film on their shelves, he decided to open his own video store. Gerima used some of the *Sankofa* profits as a down payment on the commercial property on Georgia Avenue, which cuts through the Black neighborhoods north of downtown D.C.

The building houses a conference room, business offices, and editing facilities, used by Gerima's wife, Shirikiana Aina, the company's vice president, to finish her first feature, *Through the Door of No Return.* The film tells two stories: one about Aina's search for the history of her father, the other about African-Americans who visit West African slave castles. Gerima also used the space here to edit his 1999 film *Adwa,* named for the region where the Italians were defeated in 1896 in their attempt to colonize Ethiopia.

The director/entrepreneur sure can talk. He holds forth on his passions—film distribution, the evils of Hollywood, young filmmakers with big studio deals but no vision, sex comedies that he calls "booty up–booty down" movies—and barely takes a breath. It's all about war.

Yet, here in the building, home to the institution he is building, he shows a mellow side as well. When school is out, his five children have the run of the building. They like watching videos in the conference room.

Gerima recalls that, when he came to the United States in the '60s as a college student, he didn't know Black people here had come from Africa. Soon he was caught up in the decade's nationalism and, through the African-American embrace of Africa, he was able to embrace his own African roots.

Although he was called Haile, the formal name given to Gerima by his father was Mypheduh, from the Ethiopian Geze language. Gerima interprets the word to mean "sacred shield of culture." On the sign out in front of the video store, there is just that—two fierce warriors carrying a shield, frozen as they advance. Gerima thinks that, by distributing a wide range of films and making his facilities available to independent filmmakers, he has made his store into a sort of base of operations for the cultural war being fought. "Here in our own building, we're cultivating those kinds of ideas," he says. "It is our children, and all children of African descent who must take up the battle from here."

Kingdom Come

April 11, 2001

Think of the crazy Slocum family in *Kingdom Come* as a Southern hurricane of madness, humor, and love. This assortment of flawed and neurotic characters spins around the death of one of their own, Bud Slocum, and come out of the ordeal for better or for worse. In this film, as in real life, death is the catalyst that brings family together in this small Southern town named Lula. And with all these half-cocked personalities involved, you know you're in for a major twister.

Hell, just sit back and enjoy the ride. This isn't DMX walking up walls or Shemar Moore taking off his shirt, but this is really an enjoyable movie. As Sting says, they're all here—Bud's high-strung daughter-in-law, Charisse (Jada Pinkett Smith), who is about one nerve pill away from total collapse; her blubbery husband, Junior (Anthony Anderson), who blew the family's house on an invention that cleans parking lots; and Junior's brother, Ray Bud (LL Cool J), who is emotionally repressed and turning to the bottle. LL is one rapper turned actor whom I can't begrudge a film role. He's able to turn all that hip-hop swagger into a tight performance as a level headed mechanic who, along with his wife, Lucille (Vivica A. Fox), aches for children.

In general, this ensemble cast acts its butt off. Loretta Devine raises her sugary, high-pitched voice as Bud's stern, Bible-quoting sister, and Cedric the Entertainer does his preacher thing. In the midst of the storm is Bud's widow, Raynelle (Whoopi Goldberg), who acts as the voice of sanity and reason while everyone/everything swirling around her is crazy. (So in this human version of *Twister,* the Slocum family is the flying cow and Goldberg is Helen Hunt.) Raynelle calls it the way she sees it. While Charisse is ready to climb into Bud's coffin, Raynelle tells everybody that her husband wasn't anything but mean and surly.

What also keeps this crazy story from spinning off its axis is a tight script by David Dean Botrell and Jessie Jones (Botrell authored a play, *Dearly Departed,* on which this film is based). Despite an unnecessary dip into bathroom humor, Botrell's script offers interesting story lines and dialogue, rather than shallow jokes, disjointed logic, or hollow action. It blends comedy, tragedy, and simple humanity in a believable fashion. Some of its characters are rather stock in a humorous way, but they are familiar and real.

Director Doug McHenry (*Jason's Lyric*) gets up close on these people. I'm so glad he's gotten an opportunity with this film. He stays up close on their drama—through pregnancy tests, intestinal distress, and living-room brawls. People and places aren't prettied up with lights and bright colors. The Slocums and the people in their world are just as tacky, fat, overly made-up, poorly dressed, mentally challenged, uptight, flatulent, horny, scheming, and sorry as they wanna be. But that's okay. Because they are in the whirlwind of life.

And they are family.

Filmfest DC 2001–*Lumumba*
Washington, D.C.
April 17–29, 2001

Lumumba is a powerful and important film that seeks, with some difficulty, to tell the heinous story behind the rise and execution of Patrice Lumumba, the freedom fighter and first leader of the newly independent country of Zaire. The documented complexity of what happened in the Congo—including chaos among the country's soldiers, intervention by the U.S. Central Intelligence Agency, and the presence of more than four hundred foreign correspondents—means that it is challenging to tell an all-encompassing story in two hours. Complete books have been written, for example, focusing on solely the United States's role or the experience of the men who ultimately cut up and burned Lumumba's corpse.

Director Raoul Peck, who also produced a riveting documentary on the same subject in 1992, has focused on the crisis from the perspective of Lumumba. Peck, who received a standing ovation after the screening at Filmfest DC, said he made his film in part because there are few movies that show history and Black heroes through the eyes of people in the Third World.

Featuring a brilliant performance by Eriq Ebouaney, the film makes an important contribution to understanding what Lumumba saw and experienced in his short tenure as leader before his murder. It is unsparing in its portrayal of the residual pathology of a country under eighty years of colonial domination by Belgium. It is all laid out here, in all its sickness, for us to see: the conditioned response of a people trained to hate themselves and trained to trust Whites, trained to betray each other to get ahead, trained to be suspicious of radical thought. Peck does not flinch from the issue of African complicity and rises above nationalism and even Pan Africanism to embrace the global importance of a liberated Africa.

While the film's finale is its strength, its beginning is its weakness. There is no narrative—not even a flashback—about Lumumba's formative years. We are given no clue about the influences—familial, social, or educational—that shaped him into an important thinker about African independence. There is another gap in explanation when Lumumba arrives in the capital as a postal employee, winds up selling beer, and then makes the seemingly sudden transformation into a political leader. Finally, while depicting the heat of political combat, it seems as though it was easier for Peck to dramatize the brutality toward Whites by the country's Black soldiers than it was to dramatize the cumulative effects of colonialism on the Congolese people, or the plotting and scheming by Whites against the young nation and leader.

Peck has created a human hero, one with a wife and child. But the focus is more on the external political crisis than Lumumba's family or emotional life. The first cut of this film was three hours in length. I can't help but wonder what nuance and detail was sacrificed for the sake of cutting it down to a conventional running time. Despite its flaws, *Lumumba* is the must-see Black film of 2001.

Filmfest DC 2001–*Samia*

I vote *Samia* the Black girl flick of the year. And I vote young actress Lynda Benahouda as Homegirl of the Year. This unembellished, plotless yet engrossing film maintains unswerving sympathy for a young teenage Algerian girl growing up in Marseille, France. Samia, who swishes through the world with a thick ponytail and much attitude, could easily live in North Philly or the South Side of Chicago. She is a poster child for roll-your-neck Black girl defiance. Samia is defiant of racism in the streets and of her dysfunctional family at home. And, to top it off, she has the regular teenager funky surliness.

Director Philippe Faucon tells a complex story in a very unadorned fashion, yet he manages to cover lots of turf: a young girl's disdain for the school system and for the prospect of dead-end jobs, her budding interest in boys, the conflict between Muslim traditions at home and the decadence of Western life. Most of all, it shows Samia's determination to make her own way in a world dotted with minefields. Skinheads in the streets aren't afraid to curse her and her mother, calling them "dirty Arabs." At home, she must contend with a household where women are subservient to men. She is expected to clean her brothers' rooms and serve them at the dinner table.

The major tension and story line, such as it is, is the relationship Samia and her sisters have with their older brother Yacine. Big brother Yacine takes it upon himself to safeguard the honor and virginity of his sisters against French men who "take all the pretty" Algerian women. He is painted as a rabid, obsessive, and angry young man. He is unable to find work and morosely suggests that if, perhaps, his name was François, a job might be easier to come by. He takes his place in a French version of the brothers on the corner—out of work, angry, resentful, and sometimes exercising their limited sense of power over those at home.

In his home excursions, Yacine is sometimes given support by their mother, Halima. Plump and always in motion about the small apartment, Halima is a bundle of thickening frustration as she tries to play referee in a household where her daughters are restless and rebellious and Yacine is bullying and sometimes physically abusive.

This little movie, based on a true story, goes a long way to depict the emotional and social texture of the Algerian community in France. There is fasting at Ramadan, a bridal shower, and a wedding. There is the trip to the doctor to determine if the virginity of the daughters is still intact. And, just when everything seems to be bouncing along and building to some kind of finale, the film ends. We are left with a story and a life as a work in progress. And perhaps this ending is as it should be in a tale about a teenager, who has her work cut out for her.

Filmfest DC 2001–*Cuba Feliz*

I must admit that I had a bit of an attitude watching *Cuba Feliz*. I couldn't help but wonder about the underpinnings of the film, in light of the commercial and critical success of the 1999 documentary *The Buena Vista Social Club*. In *Buena Vista*, a Black musician, Compay Segundo, guides us to the aged Afro-Cuban musical masters of the Buena Vista Social Club. In *Cuba Feliz,* director Karim Dridi follows Miguel Del Morales, a White musician, across Cuba. Along the way, Del Morales acts as a guide to various Black musicians and musical traditions of the big island.

Don't get me wrong, I'm no raving nationalist. I just have little tolerance for the way that African cultures are more often selected, filtered, or edited by others. Second, my trip to Cuba last year has left me acutely aware of the racism on the island. I couldn't help but wonder if this new film, with the elderly, white-haired White man as guide and interpreter, was just another example of Afro-Cuban culture being co-opted and exploited by Whites to bolster their sense of cultural authority, and not for the empowerment of the Black population.

I tired of Del Morales going to various houses where musicians seemed to suddenly burst into song. As it tries to be both impromptu and filled with artistry, this ninety-six-minute work can't help but feel staged in moments. People just don't sit around making music all day, even in Cuba. And I'm not quite sure how I, as a Black woman, am supposed to respond to the scene where Del Morales sings to an aging Black blonde: "Oh my Black girl . . ." or something like that. Yuck.

On the other hand, the plus side of this flick is that, unlike the *Buena Vista Social Club* set in old Havana, *Cuba Feliz* covers a wider swath of the island—Havana, Santiago de Cuba, Guantanamo, Trinidad, and other cities—and includes a rich variety of musical styles and rhythms. Despite several on-screen performances by the veteran master Morales (I am not saying I cannot give the man some props), the star of the film is Pepin Vaillant, a talented vocalist and free spirit who steals several scenes in Santiago. During one, Vaillant shows his versatility by singing in one moment a classic ballad and then pairing with a trio of young rappers. As they rhyme, he vocalizes and wails in some Sun Ra-esque moment of creative possession. Vaillant is clearly a rare being. At home, the camera catches him, in his aged body, doing a series of physically challenging stretching exercises, including a full split down to the floor. We all need whatever this Vaillant guy is taking.

Cuba Feliz presents a road less traveled. For that it is good. It just could have used a tour guide from around the way.

Filmfest DC 2001—*Brother*

Cultures all over the world have their version of the Mafia, gangsta life, thug life—whatever you want to call it. And, along with this variety of world thuggery, there is a global variety of the gangster flick. In these flicks, high-octane criminals are drawn in bold relief. Be they smart, stupid, evil, or inwardly virtuous outlaws, they are usually glamorous.

Brother, from Japanese director Takeshi Kitano, is no exception. Over the past several years, Kitano has been a prolific producer of stylish and eccentric takes on Japanese organized crime, or the *yakuza.* As in many of his other flicks, in *Brother* he stars as a member of the *yakuza*—in fact, he is the primary character, Yamamoto or Aniki. Here Kitano also continues his tradition of combining virulent violence, comedy, and a jazzy musical score into a high art form.

But while *Brother* contains the common elements of the gangster flick, it also reminds us about the genre's cultural specificity. We want to identify with the tough guy, the outlaw, because he is bucking the system, living life on the edge by his own rules and wits. So Black folks could probably identify with Wesley Snipes as Nino Brown in *New Jack City* or Laurence Fishburne as Bumpy Johnson in *Hoodlum* more than with Al Pacino in *The Godfather* or than with James Gandolfini in *The Sopranos* (especially since Tony Soprano flashed his racist card this season).

Brother is designed, first of all, to appeal to Japanese audiences. Aniki, the slick gangster in *Brother,* is unemotional and methodical as he shoots and cuts up his enemies. His young lieutenants seem to all be wearing Armani. As he is displaced from Japan to Los Angeles, he mows down his new adversaries, all the while displaying the true gangster's ability to survive.

When we first see Omar Epps (which is why we are writing about this flick) in the role of a two-bit drug dealer named Denny, he is woofing and bassing in Aniki's face before he is promptly struck by Aniki with a broken bottle. While Denny holds his bloody eye, Kitano settles at the outset the matter about who is tougher. Black gangster Denny/ebony-hued Omar Epps of *Juice* and *In Too Deep* pedigree is quickly put in his place. In this Japanese version of gangster cinema, the threat of the African-American male is neutralized. Even gangsta rappers wouldn't have anything on the *yakuza.*

Other culture-specific matters are the traditions of the *yakuza,* which apparently include suicide and self-mutilation to prove one's honor and devotion. This do-it-yourself bloodletting might feel a little out of character for those of us weaned on fare like *Scarface.* In our American gangster flicks, people get done, they don't do themselves.

I actually thought *Brother* was just as believable and entertaining as any other shoot-'em-up. It's taken a lifetime of conditioning to accept twisted codes of gangster honor that manage to accommodate, all at once, respect, murder, and romance under one umbrella. But the (Black) brother who saw this flick with me, who is from a certain Northeast city where shooting is not uncommon, dismissed it as totally unrealistic. His disbelief started with Epps making peace with a man who had gouged his eye and was reinforced when a gangster shot himself in the head.

A fundamental rule of our culture-specific American gangsterism is to survive, not die.

Filmfest DC 2001—*Bob Marley Live in Concert*

We can never get enough of Bob Marley. This longing is what happens when one of our prophets is snatched away prematurely. Partly because they have not finished their lives, they become larger than life. What they left us in the way of words, songs, action, and spirit we want to see over and over again, and see in new ways. We want fresh insight into and interpretations of the social and human drama that we already have seen. We want one more look.

Hence the interest in *Bob Marley Live in Concert,* a sixty-five-minute documentary by Stefan Paul from Germany. Most of this previously unseen footage comes from a 1980 concert that Marley and the Wailers played at the Dortmund Westfalia Hall in Germany, less than one year before his death. Some portions of it are grainy and obviously poorly lit but the uneven quality gives the film a historical, very low-tech feel by today's standards. Also included is some footage of Marley performing at the 1979 Reggae Sunsplash festival in Jamaica and scenes from Marley's funeral in Kingston with the eulogy from Prime Minister Michael Manley.

Watching Marley posthumously, his songs and stage energy take on added meaning. When he starts the concert with the rolling and hypnotic *Exodus,* it sounds as if he is foreseeing another time when Africans across the globe will rise up against slavery and injustice. When he sings *Zimbabwe,* it is easy to remember the optimism and pride felt for the last African country to break the chains of colonialism. Also included are performances of *Coming in from the Cold, Lively Up Yourself, Get Up, Stand Up, Natural Mystic, I Shot the Sheriff, War/No More Trouble, Jamming,* and *No Woman No Cry.*

In Germany, Marley gave his all in performance, singing lead, of course, on all of the songs and dancing up a stream of sweat in a blue denim shirt and jeans. Sometimes he holds his head and you can't help but wonder if he is feeling the effect from the brain cancer that would take his life in May 1981. The camera pans occasionally to the back-up singers, including Rita Marley, and the band. The White audience is packed into the large hall cheering, clapping. I always wonder if these audiences understand the lyrics or are just rocking to the beat.

With the concert mood established, the switch to Marley's funeral about halfway through comes out of nowhere. I have no doubt that Paul wrestled with the best way to include this footage. Perhaps he wanted to end the film on a note of celebration and not bereavement. But as it is edited, the effect is jarring. When the film returns to the concert for several songs, the mood has been broken. It is almost like we are seeing a ghost.

And we never want to think of our prophets quite like that.

Filmfest DC 2001–*Andanggaman*

Andanggaman centers on the African slave trade without ever leaving Africa and without ever showing a White person. Director Roger Gnoan M'Bala's focus is squarely on the foul treatment and enslavement of Africans by other Africans. Europe's initiation and domination of the transatlantic slave trade is only referred to in small ways. The focus of this story is on the dangers at home.

On the one hand, I thought of settling into my seat and dismissing *Andanggaman,* which like many African films was funded in Europe, as part of a revisionist history. On the other hand, I was willing to see if the film told the other side of the story that we also know is true: that many Africans were complicit in cooperating with Whites to capture and sell other Africans—usually members of rival ethnic groups and nations. What I got, though, was neither naked revisionism or a narrative about African collaboration. Instead, M'Bala tells a simply produced story that is fascinating, gripping, but still troubling. The emotional intensity is high. The social upheaval is palpable.

Set in the seventeenth century, the story centers on Ossei, a young man who, over the fierce objections of his father of noble blood, loves and wants to marry a slave girl in their village. The father and other village elders have another bride in mind and they try to force the young man to have and marry the chosen woman. But rather than give in to their demands, Ossei runs away from the village. As it happens, on the very night that he leaves, the village is set upon by a group of fierce slavers from the tyrant Andanggaman. The slavers are highly trained, fierce and merciless warriors who are all women. The women wear bright orange clothing (I guess they weren't worrying about camouflage!) and masklike painting on their faces. Wielding spears and machetes with confidence and skill, they aren't afraid to take on men one-on-one.

In the raid, many are killed and the rest are marched off in shackles and chains. As he leaves the village, Ossei hears the commotion in the far distance and hurries back. But when he arrives, the captives have been taken. He determines to find the group, but when he does, he winds up a captive himself.

From here, *Andanggaman* echoes a theme familiar in many African films—life under a crazed tyrant. Andanggaman demands tribute and slaves from various provinces and sells slaves to other Africans. One man sells for something like a few sheep and bottles of rum. And, it is at this point that the story takes a twist to show us more possibilities of life under slavery for those who never made the voyage through the Middle Passage.

Andanggaman feels more like a fable than realism. It presents moments of courage and even romance. Though it does not deal directly with the transatlantic slave trade, it points Africa in that eventual direction. At the same time, it focuses on the destruction of Africa more from within than from without.

Filmfest DC 2001–*Faat Kiné*

Ousmane Sembene, the seventy-eight-year-old father of African cinema, has shown the tenacity and perseverance of African women in many of his films. The village women of *Emitai* stand up to French colonizers, the widow in *Guelwar* has her angry say. In *Xala,* the young daughter of a bureaucrat is sassy and outspoken.

But in *Faat Kiné,* Sembene gives full focus and attention to the African woman in postcolonial society. Faat Kiné (Venus Seye) is a woman who must straddle the traditions of her parents' generation and the demands of the modern world, where traditions have either broken down or are certainly hostile to an unwed mother like her.

Faat Kiné is placed squarely on the divider between colonialism and independent Senegal. When we meet her, she is forty years old, which means that she was born in 1960, the year of the country's independence from France. When she was twenty, she was seduced and impregnated by her teacher, who then refused to marry her. A few years later, she was abandoned by a rogue fiancé, who made off with her money and wound up in prison. Her father felt shamed by her single-mother status, called her children "bastards," and tried to burn her to death. Her mother, who shielded her from harm, nonetheless wished that she would die.

Betrayed by her teacher, who denied her a high school diploma, Faat Kiné has had a rough road. She started work as an attendant in a gasoline station—an unusual position for a woman that subjected her to mockery and ridicule—and, defying the odds, has worked her way up to be a manager of a station. The job pays well and, by Senegalese standards, Faat Kiné is living phat. She has supported her children so that they can finish school and she owns a large, well-furnished home.

Having accomplished so much, we might think that Faat Kiné would be held in esteem by her family and community. But no. Apparently, the lack of a husband and being a woman who works at a gas station is reason enough for folks—even her own children—to sneer. She presses on, both bemused and hurt by the perceptions of others.

Her story and emotional life unfold in Sembene's conversational style wherein most of the action takes place through storytelling. Through dialogue about personal history and current events, and the occasional shot of modern Dakar's skyline, this film style fills the role of the African griot. Initially, the pace might seem slow and scattered for those of us weaned on Hollywood fare, but Sembene's story builds in momentum and complexity. His dialogue is filled with human drama, pain, and comedy. One minute, we're horrified by the physical abuse from Kine's father. A few scenes later, we're laughing out loud at the sexually frank talk between Kine and her girlfriends.

As much as Sembene focuses on women, he also, as a result, comments on the role of men. It might be more accurate to say he gives men a backhand slap while showing what "survivor" really means.

Two Souls at the Acapulco Black Film Festival
Acapulco, Mexico

June 4-9, 2001

If the Acapulco Black Film Festival ever decides to rename itself, it might try the Two Souls Black Film Festival. For nothing better than W. E. B. Du Bois's famous description of the African-American condition—"two warring ideals in one"—better sums up the state of the Black film community on the fifth anniversary of this gathering.

On one hand, many Black filmmakers want the wide distribution and big-bucks promotion that Hollywood studios can provide. At a panel titled Black Hollywood 2000, established directors like John Singleton, Gina Prince-Bythewood, and Reginald Hudlin told an often-fawning audience how they have made it. (Even if "making it" for Hudlin means directing the likes of *The Ladies Man*.)

On the other hand, with such studio deals few and far between—no major studios show up here, for example, to shop for films they way they do at Cannes or Sundance—the movement is continuing to build for an alternative distribution network to handle independent Black films that never make it to your theater. The big news this year is the formation by Jeff Friday, cofounder of this festival, of Film

Life, which will provide theatrical distribution for independent Black films. Film Life's first release on October 5 will be last year's big film festival winner, the powerful drama *One Week,* directed by Carl Seaton.

"We want to release classic films—the way *Cooley High* was a classic," says Friday. "We know there is a market for these films. When the studios are ready to do a 'Black film,' they're looking for the widest audience possible. They don't know our culture."

Last year, Friday kicked off BlackFilmFestAmerica, a fledgling tour of Black independent films that visited a few cities but suffered from poor promotion. He said that Film Life will invest $1 million to promote *One Week* and, taking a cue from music promoters, will use Black radio and street promotion to get the word out.

Films in the Hood

As for the movies, let's just say that the hood film is back with a vengeance. In addition to providing a sneak peek at John Singleton's upcoming *Baby Boy,* the festival offered three films in its U.S. competition—*Blue Hill Avenue, Lockdown,* and *Lift*—that dealt to varying degrees with crime, drugs, violence, and murder. *Blue Hill Avenue,* which had its world premiere here and chronicles the rise of a group of drug dealers in Boston, won the audience award over the other two, and also won over *A Huey P. Newton Story,* starring Roger Guenveur Smith and directed by Spike Lee.

Love Come Down, while not exactly ghetto but dealing with drugs, race, and family conflict, was inexplicably voted by the audience as best International film over Raoul Peck's powerful epic *Lumumba*. A story about the consequences of crime, *Jacked,* was considered the best work in progress over three others, including *Voice of the Voiceless,* Tania Cuevas-Martinez's worthy documentary about death row inmate Mumia Abu-Jamal. Saving the day and, as far as I'm concerned, saving the reputation of the festival, was the selection by attending filmmakers of *Lumumba* as best film.

Acapulco Black Film Festival 2001—*Love Come Down*

Sometimes a film possesses a depth of emotion and is superbly acted but, ultimately, does not work. Its flawed message only becomes apparent about halfway through the plot. *Love Come Down* is just such a blessed and cursed creation.

Director and writer Clement Virgo's story of interracial family conflict, drug abuse, and emotional chaos centers on two half brothers, one Black and one White.

The youngest and darkest brother, Neville (Larenz Tate), is an aspiring comedian who works as a store clerk to support himself. At night, he loves to dance at the local club where the women are willing and the drugs are free-flowing. In fact, Neville has a drug problem, and the film is punctuated in several places with his arrival and departure from a rehabilitation program run by nuns.

The eldest brother, Matthew (Martin Cummins), is an aspiring boxer who seems to spend much of his time working out, wrecking his personal relationships, and protecting Neville from himself. He is the one who repeatedly rescues his brother from the men's room at the nightclub where Neville is always melting, injecting, or sniffing something. It is Matthew who comes time and time again to pick his brother up from rehab. In a pivotal moment in the plot—fraught with biblical intensity—Matthew rises up in righteous indignation against his brother and we wonder if he might actually kill him.

There is certainly nothing wrong or unprecedented in the displaying of Black pathology in film. But in *Love Come Down* it is the repeated and multilayered theme of Black pathology versus White strength and indignation that ultimately beats up the conscious viewer. Not only is Matthew forever saving his little brother from himself, their relationship echoes the twisted relationship their White mother had with Neville's Black Caribbean father. As it turns out, dad liked to smoke a joint from time to time and he sometimes forced the weed onto the boys. Neville complied (and ultimately wound up a drug addict) while the eldest boy, the White one, rightly resisted. And, of course, once mama found out about these little drug sessions she was furious and rose up against a man stupid enough to give his own children drugs.

The same pattern of pathology versus strength is repeated in Neville's relationship with a Black woman who was "adopted" by a White couple. In that situation, the (great?) White father looks on in disgust as his daughter, now grown, brings home a series of boy toys. As it turns out, the real reason for his resentment of the girl and her existence only underscores further the theme of Black pathology. In this film, Whites are constantly cleaning up the messes of their Black brethren, and cleaning up themselves after some regrettable contact with a dark body. Whether he intended it or not, Virgo's poetic and moody story works only as a warning to Whites of the consequences of their love coming down in a dark direction.

Acapulco Black Film Festival 2001–*Blue Hill Avenue*

Each gangster flick must have its own gimmick and edge. It must be entertaining and it must have something that sets it apart from the legions that have gone before it. *Blue Hill Avenue* has an edge in Allen Payne, and it has scenes that are entertaining and action-packed, but, unfortunately, it is not all that fresh. To those of us with even a cursory repertoire of film viewing, it will recall *Sugar Hill, Hoodlum,* and perhaps even *New Jack City.*

But not all reruns are bad. In this case, writer-director Craig Ross Jr. sets his story in the Roxbury section of Boston where four boys quickly graduate from street games to street crime. Their rise and transformation from b-ball loving kids to gun-toting drug dealers is swift. One moment, they are almost afraid to look at a gun, the next minute they are blowing cats away—boom!

As adults they become Boston's biggest ring of crack dealers. Tristan (Payne) is the leader. E. Bone (William L. Johnson) is hotheaded. Simon (Michael Taliferro) is the very big bodyguard and enforcer. Money (Aaron D. Spears) is the nondescript faithful soldier. Much of the plot shifts between the rise of these gangsters and the moral dilemma that Tristan feels as he confronts the community impact of what he is doing. A series of incidents—a break-in at his uncle's barbershop, the physical deterioration of his junkie sister, the dysfunction in his marriage and in the relationship with his parents—all seem to lead him away from his chosen life of crime.

It is through the voice of Tristan that this story is told and it is his character that receives any semblance of development. Good thing, because the story provides an opportunity to wax poetic about Allen Payne. Ever since his role in *New Jack City*, he has made us root for the gangster. He speaks volumes with his increasingly chiseled and mature face and especially his eyes. One minute, he appears hardened and cold, ready to kill. The next, he is introspective. You never forget he is a human being with a past and connections. And while the script does help him in this regard, Payne takes the role further than the dialogue.

There is a scene here when Tristan comes upon his wife, whom he has just seen conversing with the police in front of their home. Behind her, he stands in the doorway, silent in a flawless suit (I should have added that the clothes in gangster flicks have to be all that). At this moment, Payne looks menacing and spooky and he plays the scene straddling the line between menace and tenderness toward his wife.

Though obviously working with a low budget, Ross nonetheless does a decent job with pacing, creative scenes, dialogue, and the soundtrack. He earns a plus for avoiding the obligatory, gratuitous, and usually tacky sex scenes in these g-flicks.

Blue Hill Avenue could be a great flick for a new generation of filmgoers who see all the fine thugs wearing fine suits and toting guns for the first time. But for me, it's too much been there, done that.

Acapulco Black Film Festival 2001–*One Week*

In his feature film debut, director Carl Seaton capitalizes on the recent rush on Black romantic comedies and springs off into drama. Serious drama. When we first meet Varon Thomas and Kiya Parker, they are in bed seven days before they are to be married. Varon takes a phone call that rocks his world. The health counselor on the other end of the line tells him he must come into a clinic to speak to her. When he finally does, he learns that he has been listed as a recent sexual partner of someone who is HIV positive. He is advised to get tested for the virus but the results won't be available for one week. Seaton and cowriter Kenny Young, who is also the star, have woven a tale that skillfully blends the giddy anticipation of nuptial bliss and the uncertainty, dread, and mounting crises as Varon awaits his results. In the process, they tell a story about modern relationships and the role men and women are playing in making AIDS a leading killer among young African-American men and women.

The film says all of this without preaching. Telling the story primarily through Varon's experiences, it allows us to get to know him—his mundane-looking desk job, his modest house where Kiya will move after the marriage, his philandering, and his almost-corny obsession with being one day like Cliff Huxtable from *The Cosby Show.*

Newcomer Kenny Young delivers a convincing performance in the role of Varon. He is supported superbly by Eric Lane, another up-and-coming actor who is a natural in front of the camera. Lane plays the role of Tyco, Varon's roughneck best friend. Tyco has been crashing at Varon's spot, where he spends his days playing video games, eating large bowls of cereal, hunting women, and planning Varon's bachelor party. Every one of these new marriage films and music videos has the bachelor party–stripper scene. Poor men. It's like, if they are going to make a film about marriage, they have to at least put some ho action into the mix.

It is through Varon and Tyco's relationship that the plot turns and we learn more about attitudes toward AIDS. As it turns out, Tyco has received the same kind of notice and has been tested. But he has no intention of going back for the results. He tells Varon point blank: "Man, if I got that sh**, I don't want to know."

The filmmakers play very deftly on the Black film audience's expectation of laughs. They manage to blend humor into the story of the man whose world is falling apart. I'm not sure why we laugh but maybe it is because so many of us have been in that hard place and it is easier to laugh at misery than it is to silently contemplate it.

The film could allow us to know Kiya a bit better. A shortcoming of most of these recent romances is the cursory treatment of female characters. Also, perhaps a larger budget might have allowed them to give some scenes a more professional look and sound.

Overall, though, *One Week* takes a hard story we don't want to hear—and tells it well.

Acapulco Black Film Festival 2001–*Van Van: Let's Party*

I almost didn't give *Van Van: Let's Party* a chance. Besides the corny disco-sounding title and previews that showed lead singers doing some comical pelvic-thrust thing, I was, momentarily at least, through with movies about Cuban and Latin music (after *The Buena Vista Social Club, Cuba Feliz, Calle 54,* and counting . . .).

But if you have any of the aforementioned prejudices, I'm here to persuade you to lay them aside. This movie, about Cuba's most popular band, Los Van Van, is pure pleasure, even for those who are not aficionados of Latin jazz, salsa, or whatever name is being used. The filmmakers, directors Liliana Mazure and Aaron Vega, want to explain why Los Van Van is so popular. They follow the group on tour in Cuba and on an international trip that includes Miami, where Los Van Van is embraced by fans and denounced by placard-carrying demonstrators of that city's right-wing Cuban-exile community.

Though the band's founder and leader, Juan Formell, is White, the band's leading members are Black and many songs refer to the island's African heritage, as well as the popular African-derived religions practiced there, including Santeria. Though embraced by the Cuban government, which gave financial support for the making of this film, the band has also had its differences with Castro. At one point, one of its songs honoring a supreme faith in God was banned from Cuban radio. In eighty-four minutes, this film covers performance, interviews, personal stories of artistic challenge, and straightforward discussion about the African roots and history of Cuban popular music.

Acapulco Black Film Festival 2001–*Lift*

In chronicling the world of a professional shoplifter (or "booster"), the film *Lift* concerns itself with the frivolity of fashion accoutrements. It is a decent attempt at revealing an important aspect of the culture of poverty: the importance of being "so fresh and so cle-clean" with the latest gear, expensive jewelry, and fancy cars—but having no real wealth, as in real estate or a savings account. Even an honest vocation leading to personal satisfaction rather than jail is an asset in short supply in this world.

You know the sentiment. The same sentiment that allowed us to identify with the suit-wearing felon played by Eddie Murphy in *48 Hours.* When Nick Nolte calls him a worthless con, Murphy seems to agree with the assessment and responds, "Yeah. But I *look good*." Consider the scene Exhibit 1 in defining ghetto fabulous. *Lift* does not provide a deep look at our often twisted consumer consciousness. Most of it is concerned with the surface of the matter. Niecy, a cherub-faced young woman (Kerry Washington), works in a department store and moonlights as a very sophisticated thief. Though it is not clear, it appears that her con jobs include the use of fake credit cards and bogus checks. Sometimes she simply steals the old-fashioned way—by lifting goods and stashing them in a bag or under her shirt.

The thieving scenes are shot with much artistic effect. As she strides through store aisles, drawing the eyes of White salespeople and security guards to her dark skin, Niecy acts more like a model on a runway than a thief. The filmmakers return to the theme of the fashion runway again and again for comedic effect. Niecy knows the necessary veneer. She knows how to exude the confidence of an NBA wife, someone who *belongs* in a store with tremendous mark-ups on designer goods. As she glides though the stores, giving all the eyecandy an appreciative once-over, the sound of an operatic soprano drenches the scenes in mocking irony.

The directing-writing team of DeMane Davis and Khari Streeter does make an attempt to go beneath the surface here. As the story is set up, it is possible to accept some connection between Niecy's crimes and her sense of obligation to her abused and deprived mother. It is far more difficult to accept familial bonds as a total excuse—especially without more information about the shared history between mother and daughter. To really understand what drives Niecy and to really feel her character, I wanted to hear her talk about her values, how her desires cannot be fulfilled on a store-clerk salary. I need the issue to begin and end with Niecy, not with her mother.

In part because of these omissions, it is also difficult to know who Niecy is or to truly accept the superficial romantic relationship she has with a recovered booster, Angelo, who keeps encouraging her to give up her life of crime. I really wanted to root for Niecy. And I did sometimes. I just wanted the filmmakers to give me more of a reason to do so.

Acapulco Black Film Festival 2001–*A Huey P. Newton Story*

The 1960s—with its politics and prophets of social change—remains fertile ground for artists seeking to tell stories of contemporary significance.

As always, the battle is over what stories will be told and who will tell them. How, for example, will the Black Panthers be remembered? Members of the Black Panther Party for Self Defense have been successful at turning first-person accounts into books. There was, of course, Hollywood's brief, superficial flirtation, with the film *Panther* in 1995. Last month, former Panther Kathleen Cleaver was sponsor, along with filmmaker St. Claire Bourne, of a Black Panther Film Festival in New York City. It is in this tradition of Panther narrative that I place *A Huey P. Newton Story,* a powerful if sometimes plodding film based on Roger Guenveur Smith's one-man stage play and directed by Spike Lee. (Premiering June 18 on Black Starz!)

In Smith's veteran and imaginative hands, Newton—the Panther's minister of defense—is drawn in warm relief. There is no beret, no rounds of ammunition slung over his shoulder. He is dressed simply in a black shirt, pants, and shoes, sitting in a chair on an otherwise bare stage. The set represents the Oakland high-rise apartment where Newton lived in the later years of his life. It is from this position that he ruminates on his life, all the while nervously bouncing his right leg and chain-smoking Kools. With a Southern-boy charm, Smith disarms the audience, which looks on in silhouette behind a tall, chain-link fence. While he is being so affable, Smith looks both as if he is on stage and as if he is in prison.

Smith uses humor and references to current events to make Newton just a regular guy, one with obviously a few physical ticks and dependencies. This Black Panther is an around-the-way brother, the youngest of seven children of a minister, the one who was a slow learner, the one who hated to be teased with chants of "Baby Huey." It is in this homespun style that Newton's Panther pedigree seems natural rather than radical. Who can argue with the right to housing, jobs, an end to police brutality, and trials before a jury of your peers?

This production has evolved considerably since its beginning in 1996. Now Newton refers to the 1997 murder of the Notorious B.I.G and calls the Oval Office the "Oral Office." Both comments are references to events that occurred well after Newton's 1989 shooting death on an Oakland street, after an alleged drug-related altercation.

The dialogue is a lot funnier than the original stage play. While Smith doesn't approach the feel of stand-up comedy—the closest thing to a one-man show in the Black film tradition—he gets his share of laughs. One joke is J. Edgar Hoover's assertion that the biggest threat to the internal security of the United States was the Panthers' Free Breakfast Program. On stage, Newton finds humor in the subversive power of "grits."

This version of Smith's performance also downplays the original play's emphasis on Newton as a drug user. The result, you could say, is a more "positive" portrayal of Newton, but "positive" isn't really what is projected. Here is a painful and complex humanity.

Historic footage and photographs break up the visual monotony of the bare set, though they cannot fully save it from its slow moments. It is almost inevitable, despite Smith's significant acting feat, that the minimal action will be cause for squirming—especially when viewed on a small screen. Thankfully, the challenge of filming one man sitting does not overwhelm the power or substance of this important interpretation of '60s history.

Black Star–Halle Berry in *Swordfish*

June 8, 2001

In this slick but soulless heist flick, Berry plays the sexy babe (who gets topless) in a crew trying to get its hands on billions in unused government funds.

Baby Boy

June 29, 2001

John Singleton's latest film is a scathing and at times hilarious critique of male immaturity and our dysfunctional relationships. He asks us to consider, how is a man made? And what, exactly, is he supposed to do with himself?

The macho veneer of many film roles for Black men is replaced in *Baby Boy* with a more complex persona that reveals the fear, lack of direction, and lack of education plaguing so many young brothers. The main character, Jody (singer Tyrese Gibson), is twenty years old, jobless, and still living at home with his mother, Juanita (A. J. Johnson). Yet he has two children by two different women and drops in like a hotel guest to see his main babymama, Yvette (Taraji P. Henson).

Yvette is also young, and maybe not so smart, but she is mature enough to keep a clerical job, pay for a small garden apartment, take care of her son, and make a car payment. It is primarily through Jody and Yvette's relationship that Singleton explores the multilayered issues of unwed mothers, absentee fathers, and how the

Black family and, in particular, Black women, have become competitive fodder in the hunt for "getting a man." As Exhibit A, Singleton presents a man who particularly does not seem worth the fight, especially since it takes a life-or-death scenario for Jody to summon the will to protect his woman and child.

Tyrese brings just the right vacant swagger to the crises confronting his character. Singleton, perhaps rightly, has been criticized for continuing (and perhaps even initiating) Hollywood's choice of Black singers and rappers over studied Black actors for such lead roles. I think while Tyrese scores in this role, other upcoming and seasoned actors could have made a slam dunk. Henson is an expressive, around-the-way sister without all the neck- and eye-rolling. She plays to a tee in one of the very energetic sex scenes here, as does Ving Rhames, as the new man in Juanita's life. After the low-level libido of his past films, including last year's hit *Shaft,* Singleton has finally gotten himself some (on screen).

But even the sex here, in all its delirious hoopla, seems only to underscore the fragile and very human predicaments the characters find themselves in—up until the very end—as they try to live their lives, and try to love.

Pootie Tang

June 29, 2001

Pootie Tang is an unlikely crime-fighting superhero, who is also an actor, recording star, dancer, and all-around celebrity. With his hair slicked back into a ponytail, yellow-tinted lenses, and a wardrobe that includes rabbit fur and feathers, his aura is part pimp, part drag queen, and many parts Bama.

Based on the character from *The Chris Rock Show* and played by Lance Crouther, Pootie is a languid and slow hero, dodging bullets per *The Matrix,* but with the minimalist movements of Richard Pryor skipping over a snake. He records a CD that is absolutely silent. And, last but not least, he speaks in a language indecipherable to all outside this film.

With such indications, you might assume that Pootie Tang is a superhero on drugs. But the plot says otherwise. In fact, Pootie Tang—despite his name that seems to play on both the derogatory term for a woman's sexuality and for that of a no-account cream puff (pootie butt)—is a squeaky-clean hero who warns kids about the dangers of liquor, cigarettes, and too many hamburgers.

Pootie Tang has a '70s flavor. Pootie lives his life to a funky beat: He hangs with his partners, including one played by Chris Rock, and his girlfriend, Biggie Shorty (Wanda Sykes), dresses very ghetto. He battles a combination of villains, including

Corporate America (made up of evil White people) and street crooks, including a hygiene-challenged criminal named Dirty D.

While much of it is poorly written and predictable, this film does have its funny moments, and it does present an interesting mockery and critique of celebrity and the power of corporate marketing. It is a subtle satire challenged even more by its subtle, indecipherable hero.

Scary Movie 2

July 4, 2001

Only years after my breakup with an older boyfriend, who regaled me with recordings of '70's funk, jazz, and fusions of the two, did I realized that much of what he played was what you might refer to as reefer music. Lush instrumentally, thick with beats and imagination, the music suited the altered state in which this particular self-absorbed brother strode through the world.

Cut to the year 2001, fifteen years into the new wave of Black film, and let's consider the advent of chronic cinema. *Scary Movie 2,* riding the financial coattails of last year's *Scary Movie,* is a solid contribution to this genre of film, seemingly created to be viewed by those smoking weed and offering tribute to the world of the weed-induced.

As in last year's film, being stoned (Marlon Wayans as Shorty) or being so stupid that you might as well be stoned (Anna Faris as Cindy) is the central theme. Lush only in bathroom humor, profanity, and cheap-thrill sex, it is the kind of movie made in particularly for those who are full of testosterone, and who act stoned even if they're not.

It does have its share of laughs, especially at the very start. In fact, the prologue of this film—a send-up of the '70s classic *The Exorcist*—seems to have been written by an entirely different team than the rest of the film. After its frenetic start, it slows down into another mediocre story that follows last year's high school students who are now (inexplicably) enrolled at a college.

Fascinated with the group's experience with the supernatural, an evil professor at the college lures the students to a haunted house where he hopes to conduct an experiment. At the house, a series of scenes, inspired as much by recent films such as *Hannibal* and *Charlie's Angels* as by '70s horror flicks, unfold in all their sophomoric, frequently disgusting, and predicable glory. This humor is not deft or imaginative, but when you're a film on drugs, you don't have to be.

OPM–*The Score, Made,* and *Sexy Beast*

July 13, 2001

A Mafia boss who talks to his shrink on HBO's *The Sopranos* is obviously making a big impact on filmmakers. This summer, for example, you can see all kinds of neurotic thugs on the big screen.

In fact, both *Sexy Beast* and *Made* concern themselves more with fickle personalities than with any organized crime. In *Sexy Beast,* which interlaces tension, brutality, and humor, Ben Kingsley delivers an award-caliber performance as a feared gangster named Don Logan. Kingsley is such a tornado of bile, rage, and evil that he threatens to tear through the screen.

Made is funny and exasperating as it follows two best friends, Bobby and Ricky (Jon Favreau and Vince Vaughn of *Swingers*), in the world of organized crime. Ricky is one of those best friends who keeps getting in trouble because he has a big mouth and a big foot inside his mouth. This film also marks the acting debut of Sean "P. Diddy" Combs, who, sad to report, does not do much acting beyond that required for a music video.

The Score, with Robert DeNiro, Angela Bassett, and Marlon Brando, and the widest released of these flicks, actually focuses on the crime rather than wacky personalities. It is easy to praise all three lead stars, as well as Edward Norton, who plays a young accomplice. But the sleek direction by Frank Oz is a star as well.

One thing *The Score* does have in common with the other films is a main character who decides at some point that he is giving up his life of crime. Though the characters in *Made* and *Sexy Beast* are nuts and DeNiro's character (Nick Wells) is not, they all share predicaments that stress their humanity—even though they are thugs and criminals.

OPM–*Planet of the Apes*

July 27, 2001

In his rendering of *Planet of the Apes,* director Tim Burton combines a WWF Smackdown for primates, Dickensian urchins, and startling images of what might be called Burton space gothic. This film does not, however, give us much to care about in the mix of talking and leaping monkeys.

This remake, which is based on Pierre Boulle's classic science-fiction novel, follows Leo Davidson (Mark Wahlberg), an astronaut who crash-lands on a planet. Quickly, Davidson realizes that humans are being hunted and enslaved by apes.

Bands of scraggly White folks (with one token brother) run though thickets of misty forest, where they are pummeled, stomped, and eventually herded onto a truck. They cross a black, glistening terrain that looks like an onyx desert. From a distance, the city where they are headed is very Burtonesque—dark, stylish, and spooky. But inside, it resembles an extraterrestrial version of muppet land. Little apes even play b-ball.

Here, animal brutality exists alongside notions of civilization. The apes growl, screech, and fight like animals then sit down at the dinner table, served by their human chattel. Bristling with thuggish ruthlessness is the leader, Thade (Tom Roth). And then there is Ari (Helena Bonham Carter) who is a "human rights" activist. All of this social drama is supposed to make us think about the film's larger issues of equity and the tyranny of one species over another. But any message it has gets lost as its initial momentum gives way to a Cowboys and Indians fight.

Even back in the '60s and '70s, these ape flicks were points of political contention, with their depiction of Black brutish apes and White intelligentsia. This time around, I'm not feeling the one lone-brother vibe or the no-Black-women-at-all vibe. I am definitely not feeling that Ari character who is supposed to be an ape hottie. I'm not feeling Mark Wahlberg as the cocky, conquering White hero. Nor am I feeling the White chick with the skimpy, slave-girl outfit that for some reason has sequins and a plunging neckline.

Maybe this is a film for all those folks I see rushing to the primates house at the zoo, or for all those folks who say "awwwww" every time they see a chimp. Maybe these same folks were unfazed by Michael Clark Duncan's role as a Black freak show in *The Green Mile,* and will be equally unbothered by his role in this film as the biggest, Blackest ape in service to a smaller, Whiter one. It seems that Hollywood's Black sidekick syndrome even extends to the animal world.

Movies for Black Children

July 1, 2001

As difficult as it is to find quality films about the Black experience, it is even more difficult to find them made for, and appropriate for, our children. So as the hot landscape and lazy days of summer stretch before you, peep at our list of eleven worthwhile Black and kinda-Black flicks available on video (and some on DVD) at your local rental store or public library. (Chosen with the assistance of my film-savvy eight-year-old boy, so this list may be heavy on the testosterone.)

Remember the Titans (2000)—Denzel Washington stars as the coach chosen to head the football team at a newly integrated high school in Virginia.

Meteor Man (1993)—A musician and teacher (Robert Townsend) gains superhuman powers after being struck by a meteor in this classic and overlooked flick.

Finding Forrester (2000)—Newcomer Robert Brown makes a breakout performance in this film starring Sean Connery about the relationship between a teenager from the Bronx and a recluse writer.

The Lion King (1994)—The awesome animation, humor, songs, and the voice of James Earl Jones as King compensate for the wack hyenas. Hopefully you didn't O.D. the first time around.

Men in Black (1997)—Science fiction meets hip-hop and the action hero—with Will Smith in a starring role.

Sounder (1972)—A superbly acted film, with Cicely Tyson, Paul Winfield, and Kevin Hooks, about a family of Southern sharecroppers and the maturing of a young boy.

Seventeen Again (2000)—Fans of *Smart Guy* and *Sister, Sister* will love to see the Mowry clan in this entertaining flick about grandparents who suddenly find themselves seventeen years old again.

Cool Runnings (1993)—Hey, hey, stop that moaning. This isn't about what you think is corny, it's about what kids like. And they like the story of Jamaican bobsledders.

Cinderella (1997)—The classic fairy tale updated with singers Brandy and Whitney Houston.

Finding Buck McHenry (2000)—This baseball flick, about a boy discovering the history of the Negro Baseball Leagues, is made worthwhile with performances by Ossie Davis and Ruby Dee.

Return of the Jedi (1983)—The most action-packed of the original *Star Wars* movies includes Billy Dee Williams as a soldier in the fight to save the universe.

Happy summer viewing! Don't burn the popcorn!

Black Star–Chris Tucker in *Rush Hour 2*

August 3, 2001

As the name implies, *Rush Hour 2* is hectic, fast, and full of the road rage of furious kicks and punches. It is a metaphor for how most of us see movies—in the weekend rush to get a laugh, a jolt, and, for ninety minutes, to not think, especially not about cheesy race humor.

This is also, very much, Chris Tucker's movie. He is a rush. Depending on how you view him, he is a lethally funny comic-to-the-bone, a buffoon, or some twenty-first century combination of bad boy, Stepin Fetchit, and pitiful ladies man. In this sequel to 1998's *Rush Hour,* Tucker again plays LAPD detective James Carter and is paired with Detective Inspector Lee (Jackie Chan) on a vacation in Hong Kong.

While there, both are lured into solving an international crime and Carter's sleuthing tools are always the same: insane logic, wacky body moves, and his mouth almighty-tongue everlasting. Tucker's voice—loud and edgy—might best be described as a Black man imitating a ghetto parrot. He could never *ever* deejay a *Quiet Storm* radio show.

Almost by accident, Carter goes about the business of being a cop. It takes his brand of street savvy and sleuthing ability to do what he does. As the pair travels from Hong Kong to Los Angeles to Las Vegas, Carter counsels Lee that behind every crime there is a rich White man. He finds clues in a South-Central L.A. Chinese food joint owned by a Chinese-speaking Black man (Don Cheadle). He warns Lee that he should never jump in front of a Black man in a buffet line.

As they fight the bad Chinese guys, Chan supplies logic as well as fighting muscle, while Tucker supplies most of the laughs. Tucker's on-screen performance here of his classic Michael Jackson imitation is one of the funniest moments for us who appreciate Tucker's humor.

On the other hand, what he provides throughout much the rest of the film is one more opportunity for an international audience to see a Black man—raw, open, and frequently ignorant on race matters—who does not garner respect or even intrigue. While we might think of Denzel Washington, Wesley Snipes, or Laurence Fishburne as premier Black actors, Tucker is actually the best-known Black actor around the world, largely due to the phenomenal success of the first *Rush Hour.*

The fight moves here are complex and energetic but, of course, must pale in comparison to the tour de force choreography in *Crouching Tiger, Hidden Dragon* and Jet Li's acrobatic performances in films like *Kiss of the Dragon.* Ziyi Zhang, who played the talented fighting protégé in *Crouching Tiger, Hidden Dragon,* makes her debut here in an English-language film as a mysterious and evil villain with a penchant for delivering bombs. In her limited fight scenes, she shows she can not only hang with the guys but can also beat their ass. Rounding out the we-are-the-world casting is the performance of relative newcomer Roselyn Sanchez as a shapely Puerto Rican U.S. Service agent who happens to undress with her curtains open.

There are more laughs here than I expected, especially at the end. If you go, don't skip the credits for the hilarious outtakes, which will not only make you laugh, but might also make you think. . . .

17

Epic Lives and Fantasy

Urbanworld Celebrates Five Years of Building Black Film
New York, New York
August 1–5, 2001

The Urbanworld Film Festival celebrated its fifth anniversary in New York City by showing more than sixty films highlighting the range of creativity existing outside mainstream cinema and television. With film screenings in Times Square and in Harlem, as well as panels, parties, and an upgraded awards presentation, Urbanworld showcased the vitality of the independent film movement.

Unlike the Acapulco Black Film Festival, which has a stronger emphasis on feature films, Urbanworld also presents a variety of short films, as well as several strong documentaries. One of the noteworthy documentaries, *Beyond Tara: The Extraordinary Life of Hattie McDaniel,* is showing on AMC. While the nucleus of Urbanworld is Black cinema, it also includes films made by others about the African-American, Latino, Asian, and urban experience.

"It is really difficult being an independent filmmaker," said Craig Ross Jr., while picking up an award for Best Director for his gangster flick *Blue Hill Avenue.* "Sometimes I wonder if the path I've chosen is the right one. I'm thankful for recognition at Urbanworld because it makes me believe that maybe I've done the right thing."

Both Acapulco and Urbanworld are celebrating their fifth anniversary this year, patting themselves on the back for creating truly national festivals for the Black film community and for distribution deals. (Recognizing this lack, each organization has formed an independent distribution company to bring these films to theaters near you.)

This year, Urbanworld Films made its first theatrical release with *The Visit,* the powerful prison drama starring Hill Harper and Billy Dee Williams. The film's promotion, distribution, and box-office receipts were spotty, but the film garnered good reviews. Urbanworld Films is also planning five new releases, including *For Da Love of Money,* starring the comedian Pierre.

Jeff Friday, founder of the Acapulco festival, has formed Film Life, which will have its first theatrical release this October with *One Week,* a riveting story about AIDS in the African-American community, directed by Carl Seaton, which won awards at both festivals last year. "We're able to release our own films. We don't need to rely on Hollywood," said Stacy Spikes, founder and chairman emeritus of the Urbanworld festival. "It's our responsibility as a people to get the work out."

In addition to *Blue Hill Avenue,* a variety of films received awards at Urbanworld this year. *Lift,* a complex drama about a young shoplifter by DeMane Davis and Khari Streeter, won the Best Feature award. A prize for Artistic Achievement went to *Love Come Down,* a drama about interracial relationships and the strength of family ties. The New York–heavy crowd gave the Audience Award to *Harlem Aria,* a drama written and directed by William Jennings about a mentally challenged man who dreams of becoming an opera singer.

Two documentaries won awards: *Raisin' Kane: A Rapumentary,* about the world of hip-hop, directed by Alison Duke; and *Fidel,* an up-close chronology of Cuba's revolutionary leader, directed by Estela Bravo. Also emotionally complex, *The Life and Times of Little Jimmie B.,* based on the writer James Baldwin's childhood and written and directed by Alison McDonald, won the award for Best Short. Beresford Bennett, an actor based in Brooklyn, won the screenplay competition with *Mood Indigo,* concerned with three sets of people with romantic entanglements.

Urbanworld Film Festival 2001—*Beyond Tara: The Extraordinary Life of Hattie McDaniel*

As children of the post–civil rights era, exposed to big-screen images a lot more diverse than those presented to earlier generations, perhaps it is easy for us to dismiss the predicament of pioneer Black actors who played roles of mammies, coons, and buffoons. I have to admit, until I saw *Beyond Tara: The Extraordinary Life of Hattie McDaniel* (premiering on AMC this month), I'd always viewed McDaniel as a sort of pitiful character who loved the actor's payroll too much to opt for dignity.

Even her famous quote, "I'd rather make $700 a week playing a maid than earn $7 a day being a maid," while bona fide Black-girl reasoning, still sounded to me like an old-school version of the new excuse for lameness: Well, the brotha or sista is getting paid. I dismissed her receipt of an Academy Award for the role of Mammy in *Gone with the Wind* as just another example of Whites rewarding a Black for being a good nig.

But this one-hour show, directed and coproduced by Madison Davis Lacy and narrated by Whoopi Goldberg, widens the perspective on McDaniel and the times she lived in. Most of all, it provides a snapshot of the cultural environment in the first half of the last century, the particular choices she faced, and how she tried to make the best out of what she was given to create a more sophisticated image of African-Americans in film.

Okay. I can hear you scoffing at the term "sophistication," but this show reminded me that there are gradations to the role of mammy. Using *Gone with the Wind,* the pinnacle of McDaniel's career, as an example, the program shows us how McDaniel raised the level of the character from a dumb, subservient big mama to that of a smart, opinionated woman who took very seriously the running of these White folks' household. She could warn Scarlet that a lady shouldn't eat like a pig in public and she could try to adjust Scarlet's dress so she wouldn't go out in public looking like some antebellum hoochie mama. McDaniel had the word "nigger" removed from the script and refused to make references to "de Lawd" in her dialogue. At the end of her career, playing the role of a maid on the radio show *Beulah,* she insisted on complete control over the script. Before she took the Beulah role, it had been played by a White man.

Beyond Tara also reveals the ways in which McDaniel's hands were tied because of her Hollywood contract, which not only kept her typecast as a maid but also forbade her to lose weight. Finally, it explores the idea of success. What McDaniel thought was achievement as a creative artist was not necessarily appreciated by many in the African-American community who, especially after World War II, were insisting on more uplifting images—despite their artistic interpretation—than those of Black maids and slaves.

Black Star—Mekhi Phifer in *O*

August 31, 2001

Oh, Please . . .

I ask you this: What if Othello was a White man? Would Shakespeare's play work? Would the sundry spin-offs and adaptations make more sense or less sense? Even though for centuries White actors have worn dark makeup to play the part of the Moorish king, the story line is that a Black man is so smitten by the White woman Desdemona, so homeless and so totally played by some White boy, that he really loses it. Would this story line work with a man who is presumed to be smart, savvy, and sane?

I can't help but consider these questions as I ponder the movie *O,* which is loosely based on the classic play, stars Mekhi Phifer opposite Julia Stiles, and is often exasperating. Phifer is Odin James, star of the basketball team at an elite prep school somewhere in these United States. Stiles is Desi, the daughter of the school's dean of students. As the film opens, the two—one ebony-hued and presumably street smart, the other a dead ringer for Rebecca of Sunny Brook Farms—have been together for about four months. (Stiles was also half of the Black-White couple in *Save the Last Dance.* Is she, uh, the type that brothers are going for these days? Let a sister know!)

Despite his street pedigree, poor Odin is treated like a chump in an elaborate scheme of lies and deception by Hugo (Josh Hartnett), a teammate who is also the coach's jealous and psychopathic son. Perhaps this plot and film could have worked as a deft narrative about the isolation of Black athletes on all-White campuses. Instead, with a series of early soap opera–quality scenes, it falls flat on its face as it fails to establish Odin as a multidimensional young man and fails to convince us that a brother, who should know a hustle when he sees it, would be so easily duped.

In an effort to make their stories work, the writers of both movies, *Othello* and *O,* create the illusion that the Black star lives in a world where, because of the privileged position that he has been granted, he never feels the stings of racism, and that even the plot against him is motivated by something other than race. And when the Black star becomes wary, he is suspicious first and foremost of the woman who has given him her love, trust, and body. But as a Black person watching this, I found the presumptions of this illusion to be absurd and full of racist arrogance. It's almost as arrogant as the insistence that the issues of slavery, colonialism, and reparations be off the agenda at a conference about racism.

Both *Othello* and *O* are also about the fraternity of men, more specifically a false fraternity where a man chooses the word of his "boys" over that of his woman. In this world, women are outsiders and cannot be trusted. All of this deceit and misappropriated trust leads us to a tragic and bitter end.

Phifer, Hartnett, and Stiles turn in fine performances and Tim Blake Nelson has moments of startling direction. There is enough concluding fireworks here to make us believe that we've witnessed a straight-forward and powerful narrative about race. But if we believe that, we're the ones being played in the end.

Two Can Play That Game

September 7, 2001

At least *Two Can Play That Game* knows what it wants to be—another comedy on that seemingly inexhaustible subject: the battle of the sexes. And sometimes it succeeds, with a big assist from Anthony Anderson on the male side of the net, and an assist on the woman's side from the big, beautiful, ghetto-fabulous Mo'Nique. (You must give homage to Mo'Nique's size or she might declare you a "skinny bitch" enemy and beat you down.)

With two current stars of Black comedy pushing it along, the film has some hilarious moments. Some. For most of it, we're captive to prim lessons in a charm-school-teacher tone from Vivica A. Fox, here playing Shante Smith, a marketing executive. Shante, an around-the-way sister from Compton who now drives a jag and lives in a mini-mansion, is famous among her friends for knowing all the rules when it comes to catching and keeping a man. The only problem is that she has problems making her rules work for herself as she tries to keep her man, Keith (Morris Chestnut), a successful attorney, in line.

The narration goes throughout and it is literally in our face, as Shante turns to speak directly into the camera at us, again and again, so much so that we might be tempted to turn away. Watching folks as they bug out in relationships is fun. Getting a diagram and lesson about the process isn't as much fun. The best comparison I can offer is that sometimes the movie seems like an extended TV talk show on the subject "How to Whip Your Man into Shape," with actors and actresses at the ready to illustrate the lessons being taught.

Like many of the recent Black romantic comedies, it leaves us suspended in an emotion-free zone where real love expressed on the screen is replaced instead with gaming and scheming, and passion is replaced with expressions of lust. This backward way of approaching human intimacy can be funny and sometimes this film is funny, when it is not resting on clichés and too much been there, done that. What Black middle class means in most of these films is having a successful career but no emotional depth. What being a woman means in most of them is seeking an engagement ring like a heat-seeking missile finds its target. And, of course, there is always the commitment-phobic man who views women, literally, as booty in the war of the genders.

Even though the cardinal rule is that a romance needs a romantic hero and heroine, it is also true that romantic comedies need lead actors who are funny as well as romantic. As much as I appreciate both Chestnut and Fox as romantic ideals, they're not all that funny. On the other hand, I would pay good money to see Anderson and Mo'Nique square off in a romantic tussle. Whew! What fun and how funny that would be.

Glitter

September 21, 2001

Those shimmering, metallic bits that we call glitter provide an easy and cheap sparkle. Pour glue on paper, sprinkle the glitter, and—just like that—you have a shining thing.

The same glue-and-scissors approach seems to have been taken to the rather pedestrian script for *Glitter,* the new movie starring Mariah Carey in her big-screen acting debut. Sprinkle in a little late-'80s New York City club scene, or some semblance of it. Sprinkle in dozens of wardrobe changes for the star and dozens more hair and makeup changes. Sprinkle in a comic-book love story (Sob! He's such a jerk!), and you get a shining thing. This movie is a flashy blur, carrying you along on a ride that is sometimes entertaining. Yet, all the while, it eludes its soul.

The soul is the relationship between the biracial rising star, Billie Franklin, and the alcoholic Black mother who abandons her at age ten or so. The first scenes introduce us to the mom, drunk on stage at a nightclub. She calls up her young daughter who looks White but sings like the lead soloist from a Black Baptist choir. The mom appears at the door of the seemingly wealthy White daddy begging for money. Like some bad flashback to the '70s, mom repeatedly falls asleep while smoking and her foolishness starts a fire that puts her and her daughter out of their ramshackle apartment. Soon after, Mom is forced to give up her daughter to the foster-care system but promises to look for her once she gets cleaned up. But she never comes back for little Billie, who, ten years later or so, is discovered as a singing talent and becomes an overnight star.

Imbedded in the conflict with the mother is the fact that Billie is biracial and has been abandoned by both of her parents. But the film does not allow her or the viewer to explore her search for identity, place, and security in the world. And, it is probably no coincidence that the biracial aspect is one that is transferable to Carey's real life story. What else have we seen from Carey since her 1990 debut other than a public search for identity, place, and security? Poor baby. Her considerable talents have been squeezed and mauled by the entertainment-hype complex, the changing tastes of the music-buying public, her own crossover lack of identity, and her own bold ambition.

The same search for and lack of identity plagues this film. It is not clear what Billie feels or wants to be. Her pain is masked beneath dozens of close-ups that offer only Carey's perfect cheekbones and expertly arched eyebrows. Clearly, this novice actress was not up to the emotional demands of this lead role. But this loss or lack of mission is all a part of modern youthful celebrity. Why should a twenty-year-old know who he or she wants to be? And are we supposed to care? We just want them to sing and dance. Sprinkle on a little glitter, and watch them shine.

Life and Debt

September 27, 2001

In the wake of the terrorist attacks on the World Trade Center and the Pentagon, the best TV news shows have gone beyond our borders to give viewers some much-needed background. They've shown dire suffering in other parts of the globe, the United States's role in that suffering, and the resulting antipathy sometimes directed toward us and the world order this country controls.

Now comes a timely new documentary that examines how the island nation of Jamaica is being strangled by globalization and $7 billion in loans from the International Monetary Fund and the World Bank. In *Life and Debt,* filmmaker Stephanie Black deftly shows how policies designed to lift people out of poverty have the opposite effect. The country, which won its independence from Britain in 1962, winds up paying off debt rather than providing even basic needs for its people.

Without being didactic, preachy, or whiny, *Life and Debt* offers a devastating analysis of how capitalism works for wealthy Western nations, but often not for the former colonies that make up most of the world. Slave labor and free natural resources from colonies were used, starting centuries ago, to crank the capitalistic engine of today's wealthy nations. Now those same former colonies are told to run behind the car and catch up.

With their new freedom, countries like Jamaica must now compete on a supposedly even playing field with their former rulers, who control banks and banking rules. Black manages the complexity of the topic by juxtaposing White tourists in a resort with the life and work of the country's largely impoverished Black population.

She mixes up a personal narrative written by author Jamaica Kincaid, news-show talking heads, and interviews with native farmers and business owners. Haunting images of the island's beauty and degradation and poetic visual effects are interfused with the island's reggae rhythms and voices.

Africans around the globe are routinely forced to absorb stories and histories told by those outside our world. *Life and Debt,* which is playing in select cities around the country, is a rare and fine accomplishment. Against the odds, it manages to give space to another history. It challenges not only the usual histories, but also how we are living.

Africa

September 27, 2001

I can't think of another series that has shown the motherland so startlingly beautiful as *Africa,* which is in the midst of an eight-week run on PBS. Eight one-hour episodes carry the viewer through the vast continent, from the horn to the cape, from the Sahara to the rain forests, from Lake Victoria to the Sahel.

Cinematographers have turned a loving eye toward their subject matter, which includes some of the last remaining unspoiled landscapes on Earth. Lush hills in steep, carved mountainsides in Ethiopia, a beautiful Fulani woman in the Sahel with gold and jewels woven through her hair, a shoe-billed stork in Tanzania that looks like a direct descendant of the pterodactyl. A particular joy is shown in the wide, open skies. So wherever we are in this Africa, and whatever episode you watch, you will see a mini-show overhead. In elapsed time, fat clouds pirouette across the blue backdrop; purple clouds hover over dense foliage in the Congo basin.

Presented by National Geographic, Nature, and Thirteen/WNET New York, the series's tone is similar to that of traditional nature shows, but the approach is not academic, dry, or ethnocentric. Each show focuses on two close-up stories of individuals within their family and community. These stories, mostly about men but including some women, do not frame African lives wholly within contexts of war, famine, political crises, or disease, as is so common to Western media. Also, they lack the type of historical anchoring that includes the great social upheavals that have decimated the continent, including slavery and colonialism. Depending on your view, these omissions might be either a relief or highly suspicious.

After wrestling with this question of viewpoint, I feel confident recommending these shows as inoffensive, thoughtful, and meaningful documents of how life is lived in little pockets all over Africa. Added to the spectacular scenery, extended sequences about wildlife, and dramatic storytelling is a soundtrack filled with indigenous music that contributes to the poetic texture of the project. To top it off, our Forever-Brother-from-Another-Planet, Joe Morton, is the narrator.

Training Day

October 5, 2001

Like no other actor, Denzel Washington has brought a range of Black men to the screen who we can identify as real, not wholly Hollywood creations. Yet, almost without exception, all of his characters, including Malcolm X, a defiant ex-slave in *Glory,* a military man in *Courage Under Fire,* and boxer Rubin "Hurricane" Carter, can be plotted somewhere in the realm of race men, flawed-but-good guys, and even Prince Charming.

But his artistic realm shifts in *Training Day.* As rogue cop Alonzo Harris, Washington plays another kind of brother we know very well: one who spews bile and bullets with a smile. Harris could be any kind of thug—a drug dealer, a pimp, a conman, a hit man, or carjacker. He could be any of those who have discovered how easy it is to get ahead, legally or illegally, on the backs and misery of others. But it just so happens that he is a crooked narcotics cop.

Washington plays the part convincingly, with the right amount of wicked swagger that is the norm for our hood-grown thugs. Harris's evil confidence, no doubt, involves a smiling deal with the devil, a quick measure of who is predator and prey, and a game of Russian roulette with death. Maybe the likes of Harris—suave, alluring, and yet totally unredeemable—have not shown up in prime time. He is too scary and, besides, he routinely preys on only his own kind—us. (So this Denzel performance will not get the praise in some quarters accorded to, say, Ben Kingsley in *Sexy Beast.*) This is a poem sent up from Harlem, or North Philly, or "the Jungle" in Los Angeles about the brothers whom we have lost, but we still pray have retained some of what their mommas taught them. This is also a poem, a bloody and unresolved one, about getting lost in the corrupt judicial system.

Harris's rookie-in-training, Jake Hoyt (Ethan Hawke), also makes this story about the relationship of one innocent, good White man to the most animalized Black thug. Hoyt badly wants to join Harris's narcotics squad. He wants to make detective. He wants a house like detectives have. But he has no idea that Harris's unit is all about graft and robbery and murder. He learns, eventually, on his first day of work—his training day—that he is simply a pawn in a scheme that has nothing to do with fighting crime. Through Harris and Hoyt, there is an old-fashioned fight of good versus evil that is played out on the streets. The tension and turns in the plot are thickened by the question of whether there is still honor on the street, and whether there is honor among thieves.

The poem here is created by director Antoine Fuqua (*Bait*), who creates atmospheric scenes of the street that don't look like those Hollywood ghetto sets made from dirty plywood and dated graffiti. By simply appearing and scowling, Dr. Dre and Snoop Dogg add their thug personas to the L.A. mix. As in *Bait,* this film is dark. The light is often cold with a greenish tinge, as if the world is literally full of bile. In one scene, the rookie is told to smoke what he doesn't realize is angel dust and the world melts before his eyes. All this detail serves the exploration of modern, casual evil among us, and, as we all have recently learned, how much your life can change in just one day.

Bones

October 24, 2001

Let me admit, right off the bat, that I am not a big fan of horror movies. A true-to-life film with suspense and danger usually wins hands-down over one that just grosses me out with cheesy scenes of blood, guts, and—in the case of *Bones*—oodles of maggots.

Having confessed, I must give credit to *Bones* for being, as was *J. D.'s Revenge,* a story about the supernatural in the hood. The evil in *Bones* comes from the small-time, street-level hustlers who spread crack on the streets of Black America in the 1980s. Not all horror must involve suburban White kids wandering around the woods or winding up, predictably, in some dark basement. And not all of it must involve abstract evil. Certainly, there is enough concrete evil in our lives to go around.

There is a basement here, a dark, nasty, rat-infested joint, but it is in some no-name hood, U.S.A. It is in the abandoned stone mansion of a long-dead numbers runner named Jimmy Bones, who is played by the very bony Snoop Dogg. Folks in the neighborhood swear that the house, one of those decaying, ornate architectural gems, is haunted by Bones's ghost. A jet-black dog with glowing eyes lives there and periodically chases people. The neighborhood psychic, Pearl (Pam Grier), warns her daughter, Cynthia (Bianca Lawson), to stay away.

The middle-class suburban kids show up, but they are the Black, White, and mixed offspring of people who do not live in the hood. The leader of the group, Patrick (Khalil Kain), has just purchased the building in order to turn it into the latest funky dance club. With him are his brother, Bill (Merwin Mondesir), their stepsister, Tia (Katharine Isabelle), and a friend, Maurice (Sean Amsig). Soon, they hook up with Cynthia, who is supposed to be like the hottie girl in this flick. As a band of too-hip and too-arrogant explorers (the arrogant ones always die, right?), they set about fixing up the dump. But, little do they know that the house has a spirit, a history that they share, and a date with destruction.

Director Ernest Dickerson juggles a lot of balls, pies, and flaming batons (not to mention pimp gear and severed heads) to keep the story going. In the beginning, the plot jumps back and forth between the present and past so much that I had to keep adjusting between Pam Grier's afro wig and fake dreadlocks. There are some inconsistencies, like the fact that the filmmakers tried very hard to evoke a '70s vibe even though crack really didn't make its debut until the '80s. Once the story settles down, it follows a somewhat predictable pattern, appropriately humorous in spots, as Jimmy Bones seeks revenge on all those connected with his death.

With the exception of the fine work of veterans—including Pam Grier and Clifton Powell—there is not much to say about the acting here. Snoop definitely has screen presence. This role allows him to do more than scowl as he did in *Baby Boy* and *Training Day.* As a rapper, he has mastered a fluid verbal delivery that adds to the silky pimp aura of Bones's character. With his wide brim, Mack-length coat, and bone-straight do, Snoop is the glue that binds the '70s, '80s, and present day together in a flawed, often yucky, but entertaining flick that tries to do the same.

The Wash

November 14, 2001

The now-classic videos produced for Dr. Dre's album *The Chronic* presented South-Central Los Angeles as a hyper-reality of impromptu street parties with free-flowing malt liquor, weed, low-riding cars, gang members, and scantily clad women bouncing to the beat of sampled George Clinton riffs. Images conjured for "Dre Day," "Nuthin' But a 'G' Thang," and "Let Me Ride" have had a profound effect on typecasting South-Central, and on building a hip-hop hood aesthetic in videos and film.

This same aesthetic has taken on a life of its own in scores of videos from West Coast rappers and in the mad-funny 1995 movie *Friday,* starring Ice Cube and Chris Tucker. Since then, the coproducer and cowriter for *Friday,* DJ Pooh, has followed his debut with decreasing returns—the disappointing *Next Friday* and *3 Strikes,* both of which badly needed a Chris Tucker–type comedic talent. Now he has brought us *The Wash,* an uneven, mildly amusing comedy starring Dr. Dre and Snoopy Doggy Dogg, the pair who mainstreamed West Coast gangsta rap in 1992.

In *The Wash,* which DJ Pooh also directs, the emphasis is away from "lockdown comedy," stories about brothers in or recently released from jail. Instead, DJ Pooh turns his attention to two struggling young men, Sean (Dr. Dre) and Dee Loc (Snoop Dogg), who are roommates and wind up working at the same car wash. But the influence of the original *Chronic* aesthetic is still strong—so strong, in fact, that some scenes involve both men partying with weed, assorted girlfriends, and George Clinton music in their two-bedroom spot. In another fantasy scene, sisters in thongs or spandex vacuum and wash cars and then hand over their money to Dee Loc, who stands there like a big ole pimp.

There is some semblance of a plot here. The owner of the car wash, Mr. Washington (ha-ha), played by George Wallace, is receiving anonymous threatening calls, which are actually some of the funniest moments in the film. And even though Washington's employees openly loathe him, they all pull together when their job survival depends on Washington's survival. There are some subplots going on—such as how Sean starts acting like the HNIC when he is made assistant manager and how Dee Loc is really caught up in the life of selling weed and running women.

But it is not very funny. There are some good lines, like one dope asking the question, "What's the number to 911?" And, it seems, I could spend at least two hours listening to Snoop Dogg's crazy speech where everyone is either his "nephew" or a "bitch-ass nigga." Or how he says Sean needs to bring some "chips and dip," meaning some cash for his half of the rent. It is also a scream to see a really grown man like Snoop tripping over the mechanism in his ancient, low-riding Coupe DeVille.

With such idiosyncrasies in the story, I thought that perhaps the filmmakers were taking a quirky, sophisticated approach to comedy, but Pooh's obligatory toilet humor made me reconsider that idea. Taken as a whole, *The Wash* is an interesting piece of hood travelogue—from the spot, to the car wash, and back to the spot again. Okay. Okay. I'm riding along. I'm definitely down with the George Clinton. But where are the jokes?

OPM—*Harry Potter and the Sorcerer's Stone*

November 14, 2001

With a slick, Brit version of magical realism, *Harry Potter and the Sorcerer's Stone* is an amazing journey to the place where dreams meet possibility. It is this young generation's *The Wizard of Oz*—a tale that combines the longing for love, courage, and home with a hair-raising battle against bad witches.

Young, wide-eyed Harry becomes the latest and certainly one of the most likeable great White heroes, ever. Though orphaned and abused in his aunt's home, where he is forced to sleep in a closet, he possesses at age eleven a nirvana and cool that is due, no doubt, to the fact that he has special powers. No need to get off-balanced when you can turn your enemies into snake food.

This modern Oz where Harry Potter lives is not a lily-white place. Unlike many of the classics, even recent ones, accepted as perfect children's fare—such as *E.T.* or *Home Alone*—the protagonist here operates with a backdrop that is at least somewhat multicultural. Just as in the best-selling series of books by J. K. Rowling, on which this film and others will be based, there is a dab of color here and there in the throng at Hogwarts. Most prominent is the role of Lee Jordan (Luke Youngblood), who announces in a crisp British accent the fast-paced games of Quidditch, played on flying broomsticks.

And it's okay for this to be Harry's story, not Hakim's. Generations of us have grown up seeing bravery and courage only through big-screen faces that do not look like ours. Or we watched how, after protests, a movie series like *Star Wars* added a little melanin to the mix. With added examples of our own stories and Black characters that we must provide ourselves, the children—especially the boys—will be okay. After all, look how well we all turned out. At least *Harry Potter and the Sorcerer's Stone* has a little Black in its magic.

Black Knight

November 21, 2001

African-American popular culture has been exported to the four corners of the world—to Japan, Brazil, Paris, and South Africa. So why not to twelfth-century England? This loony collision of cultures and centuries forms the basis of *Black Knight,* the latest crazy comedy from our favorite Martin, as in Lawrence.

The film's insane premise and even more insane action yields some laughs, just some. These laugh-out-louds come because of Martin's comedic talent rather than because of any particular strength in the general script or direction. Only the likes of Martin (and that would include Chris Tucker) could suggest to a nubile maiden that he could take a pair of her old drawers, "cut the ass out," and create for her an instant thong. Few films would dare begin with a comedic rendition of a man flossing his teeth and pulling the hair out of his nose.

For its ninety-five minutes, *Black Knight* is both a we-are-the-world declaration of faith in integration and a swaggering, shameless plug for the resiliency of Black culture. The clownish antics of its star aside, it practices a sort of fake evenhandedness. Sure, Jamal easily fits into the role of a Moorish court jester, but he is also savvy and fast on his feet. Sure, the White folks are either evil or clueless, but the good ones are also full of honor and honorable struggle. Like so many of these Martin efforts, you are better off just enjoying him despite his trappings. At least here, in Old Europe, the requisite toilet humor and cheesy sex scenes are given a whole new setting. And here, there are no naked Black grandmothers.

Et Cetera: Talk Show Mammies?

December 11, 2001

During one day in August 2001, I saw the premiere of Iyanla Vanzant's new talk show, followed by Queen Latifah's talk show, and, of course, in the afternoon, *Oprah*. There were also the cohosts, Star Jones on *The View* and Bo Griffin on *Mars and Venus*. In September, another Black woman, Ananda Lewis, from MTV fame, debuted her self-titled syndicated show. Taken as a whole, and added to the revolving crop of Black TV judges—Judge Joe Brown, Judge Mathis, *Divorce Court, Curtis Court,* etc.—there is certainly no shortage of daytime Black presence on broadcast television.

But beyond the realm of individual opportunity, what does all this on-camera melanin mean? First, it does not equal a safe space for the articulation of Black "talk." Decades of *Oprah* and years of Lewis on MTV certainly have shown that a Black host does not equal a "Black" show. Rather, these women become vehicles for conveying a staid brand of women's programming aimed at White Middle America—interviews with movie stars or Jerry Springeresque tackiness. Also, more and more, talk shows present "expert" authors on individual or relationship misery. So, more and more, the Black woman sitting in the host seat begins to look a lot like mammy.

In this media burlesque of television therapy, assorted couples or individuals take the stage to confess their dysfunction or inadequacy, while the camera pans to the Black host—caring, uttering words of comfort, and, sometimes, hefty in size. With a quick change of wardrobe, add an apron and a rag on the head, and it is not hard to imagine mammy—and yet, this perception is complex and, in many ways, unfair.

I believe that if the audience, both in the studio and in the perceived viewership, were Black, the host would be a big sister, mama, aunt, grandma, or girlfriend. We have been mammies in connection with caring for White people—cooking their food, cleaning their house, washing their dirty clothes, even nursing and raising their children. So it is not outrageous for the conscious Black viewer to be rattled by the TV mammy's new calling to heal White people and, perhaps, give them some soul. I think that the context creates the appearance of a mammy more than anything that the host does. Maybe if the Irish indentured servant was a national icon and historical servant to us all, Rosie O'Donnell would be in a similar boat.

Many of us are unprepared for something we consider a "Black" thing, a safe place to heal ourselves from the ravages of the White world, to be suddenly transformed and taken away into the unforgiving mainstream. Yet, this is what has been happening since the first "crossover" musical act. Global media and celebrity culture seek the widest audience possible. So just as defunct late-night shows like *Vibe* and *The Keenan Ivory Wayans Show* did, or just as the UPN and WB networks did, these talk shows with black hosts bank on support from a Black "core" audience, then seek to go as wide as possible. When the transition occurs, sometimes the Black audience feels used and discarded, but, most of all, we suddenly find ourselves minus one voice and space that we thought was ours. Our mama-aunt-grandma-girlfriend done left the building.

In this context, *Iyanla* is an interesting case. Because she has been steeped so long in the spiritual life and good graces of the Black community, it is easier—even while seeing her in the surreal TV host box—to envision her as our wise mama and not their mammy.

Yet this version of a Yoruba priestess, hair-weaved and permed, outfitted and airbrushed for mass consumption, is really fascinating. But it is "disappointing" for Black women like my friend Kimberly. At one time, Kimberly was a regular follower of Vanzant in a group of Black women who regularly met for a sister circle in the Washington, D.C.–Maryland area.

When she looked at Vanzant's premiere week, with mostly White women in the audience and Whites as guests, she felt the same way she felt one day when she showed up at the sister circle and there were White women there. While she agreed intellectually with the explanation by Vanzant's handlers—that the White women were our sisters, too, and that they, too, needed healing—she still left, disgusted that her refuge was taken away. There was no doubt in her mind that the group's conversation would change and that the circle would no longer be a healing from her pain, which was caused often by White women in the first place.

The same we-are-the-world sensibility is evident on the episode of Queen Latifah's show that I saw that day. It focused on four rather dysfunctional relationships where the men are either mad jealous, mad possessive, and, in general, mad crazy.

One man said point-blank that his wife was his "property." Sometimes you wonder where they get these talk-show guests. Is this an act? Do they just want to be on TV? On the plus side, by the end of that week, Latifah dealt with the serious issue of shortcomings within the criminal justice system.

Latifah, wearing a pantsuit, handles them all like a big sister who just might kick their ass. If she is anybody's mammy, she is a new-styled hip-hop variety who might give you a beatdown. The show also reminds me how angry I am that the entertainment-industrial complex has taken Latifah away from me as an artist (substituting Foxy Brown, Lil' Kim, and Eve!). It has left me with only Latifah as a talk-show host, which is far down on the totem pole of artistry. We need her art again, and we need her voice.

Only recently did I have the chance to see *The Ananda Lewis Show,* which like the others has become even more crucial as a place for therapy after the terrorist attacks of September 11. This show was billed as a discussion about racial attitudes, but it was one of those skewed, damaging, one-sided affairs that are best not done at all rather than further twist the already emotionally fraught subject of race. As usual with these types of talk-show race discussions, the interviews and discussions are designed to proceed without any historical or current context about White privilege or racism —internalized, institutional, or cultural. Everything is reduced to emotion and personal proclivity, using the most extreme examples that can be found.

The show started with a Black man who had fathered two girls with a White woman yet did not want his daughters to date White men. His feelings set the tone early. This would be a show that would reveal and mock serious contradictions within the Black community yet not give the community any historical footing for its pain or pathology.

The next set of interviews focused on two mixed-race teenagers who disliked the fact that their eleven-year-old sister "acted White." The younger mixed-race sister did not associate with Black girls, disparaged Black people, and openly identified herself as White. Yet much of the questioning from the host did not focus the young girl's obvious self-hatred. Rather, it chastised the two older girls for their concern. It did not explore the fact that the teens were angry with their sister for choosing to identify with a culture that they recognized as hostile to their identities as young Black women.

When I catch the tail end of *Oprah* on my day of watching talk shows, a youthful White couple with two little boys is trying to cure what ails their relationship. They have been on the show before and received advice from the ever-present and arch

Doctor Phil. This time around, there is a lengthy segment about how the wife has learned to get out and play driveway hockey with her husband and the boys. It is all quite warm, nicely shot, maybe it is the best that daytime TV has to offer. As a divorced single mother, I identify with the loneliness the wife felt in her marriage. I cheer at the path the couple has found to healing. But, in the end, this is another story about some White person's humanity. The video ends and there is a shot of Oprah, welcoming us back after the commercial.

And the audience applauds.

Ali

December 12, 2001

Legendary soul singer Sam Cooke figures prominently in the opening scenes of *Ali,* the new film about ten whirlwind years (1964–1974) in the life of boxing great Muhammad Ali. Think of Cooke's suave image, smooth rum vocals, and barely contained heat as powerful metaphors for these turbulent years of Black America, when Ali rose to fame as a light-footed boxer, and then became a spokesman for Black resistance to a racist status quo.

There are many such metaphors and mediums in this energetic movie, which tells a story about the '60s as much as it tells about Ali. The champ's life is a prism through which the decade unfolds: the flowering and assassination of Malcolm X, a civil rights movement in crisis, anger in urban streets, and the rise of a Black (economic, social) power movement—embodied ridiculously in the ambitions of big-haired boxing promoter Don King. As much as we see and hear Sam Cooke, there is a dissonance here worthy of Thelonious Monk or Sun Ra in both the film's era and style. There are interwoven images and competing sounds that we are unaccustomed to seeing in Hollywood's building of African-American narrative.

Neither the creative direction by Michael Mann, the story by Gregory Allen Howard, or the fine acting job by Will Smith idealizes Ali. Perhaps the dissonance, which borders on disjunction at times, allows all of us to see what we desire. Fans might focus on Ali's outspokenness, his dialogue at one moment—worthy of an August Wilson soliloquy—when he states his opposition to fighting in Vietnam for a country that doesn't fight for him at home. The indifferent might detect in the champ a vacant space as he displays his womanizing, his blind eye for the shortcomings of the Nation of Islam, and a simple country-boy slowness that contrasts with his fast tongue, feet, and fists. Here, Ali is a man unfolding himself and living in the moment, often simultaneously displaying and fighting his weaknesses.

There is an impressive lineup of talent that contributes to the symphony. In his best role to date, Mario Van Peebles plays a confident and down-to-earth Malcolm X. Joe Morton fills every inch of the role of Chauncy Eskridge, Ali's attorney who guided him through the legal process after Ali was stripped of his boxing license and title. As Drew "Bundini" Brown, Jamie Foxx breaks up some of the heaviness with his grits-and-sausage humor. Though Ali was married three times during the time period roughly covered by this film, the wives and children are stray chords in this composition, serving as window dressing to help us understand the flawed champ. This is very much a man's flick and the boxing scenes, enhanced with audio that makes punches sound like explosions, do not disappoint.

There are times when it is difficult to keep track of where the action is taking place, as well as the passage of time. The viewer is required to keep up the pace without too much explanation. This is not a play-by-the-numbers Ali. And the resulting composition, while not always flowing smoothly, gets better and gains power as it goes along.

OPM–*Piñero*

December 13, 2001

A heady mix of drugs, sex, and creative genius has become required in films about artistic icons. Combine this mix with criminal life and the needle goes way off the stimulant chart in *Piñero,* the new film about Miguel Piñero, Latino literary icon and one of the founders of the Nuyorican Poets Café, an incubator for today's popular spoken-word movement.

In this story—which includes snapshots of his tumultuous upbringing on the Lower East Side of Manhattan, his introduction to hustling, prison, stardom, and, ultimately, death—the swirl of these warring aspects of his life are painted in bold, seedy, and energetic relief. Written and directed by Leon Ichaso, this film is the perfect fit for Piñero's alternately inspiring and self-destructive life dramas and Ichaso's iconoclastic direction, honed on the sets of *Miami Vice* and on the feature films *Azucar Amarga, Sugar Hill,* and *Crossover Dreams.*

In the hands of Ichaso, Piñero's world becomes a pastiche of time, memory, fiction, reality, black-and-white, color, and tension. Piñero's overflowing and troubled talent, along with a seamless, salsa-spiced performance by Benjamin Bratt, pushes the film forward, covering all the bases, which are only in rough chronological order.

The eldest of five children, Piñero endured the pain of his father's abandonment and remained close to his mother, who read poetry to him and tried, but ultimately failed, to keep his interests away from the streets. The young Piñero is seen here as a victim of sexual abuse and as a young sex hustler. We see him in Sing-Sing but not as the petty thief who landed there. Out of prison, even as his genius spilled from him and he became an overnight success with the drama *Short Eyes,* he could not tear himself away from a criminal way of thinking. And even though his liver steadily deteriorated, he could not tear himself away from cocaine, heroin, and whatever other drugs were included in his habit. In one of the film's most poignant moments, Piñero likens his drug binges to diving the ocean for pearls and sponges. At first, the experience hurt, he says, just like diving can hurt your ears until you are accustomed to it. But after a while, he says, he preferred the depths. "I like it down there," he says.

His lifelong friend, Sugar, a struggling actress, would not tear herself from him and remained until his death. Miguel Algarin, still going strong on the Nuyorican literary scene today, was his best friend and mentor. Joseph Papp, the late founder of the Public Theater (now the Joseph Papp Public Theater), brought Piñero to fame by staging his plays. This is an unsparing portrait of a man, and of a particular time, when the voices of people of color were being raised with power and pain.

Black Star—Danny Glover in *The Royal Tenenbaums*

December 14, 2001

Maybe Ollie North and the whole warmongering crew have done *The Royal Tenenbaums* a favor. When they attacked actor Danny Glover for stating his antiwar and anti-death-penalty beliefs, flooded his offices with threatening calls, and called for a boycott of this film, they certainly raised the film's profile much higher in the Black community than it would have otherwise been. The organized response, a campaign to support Danny "Can-a-Brother-Get-a-Cab?" Glover, may wind up bringing out Black viewers who might have dismissed it, saying, "Tenenbaum Schenenbaum." Because this is one of those strange movies about strange White folks. One of those quirky tales about dysfunctional people who are rich, famous, and usually only deal with coloreds who are the hired help. (And, on cue, a little Indian man named Pagoda appears as the loyal servant.) Face it, this might not be our first choice for entertainment.

But hang in there. With a sly wink and nod, director Wes Anderson (*Rushmore*) ridicules societal achievement, wealth, celebrity, literary commerce, the concept of genius, and perhaps racism. A big perhaps on that last one. The whole plot turns on the fact that Etheline Tenenbaum, long estranged from her sleazemeat husband, Royal (Gene Hackman), is considering a proposal of marriage from her accountant, Henry Sherman (Danny Glover). Though Mrs. Tenenbaum has had suitors call in the past with no reaction from Royal, the idea of a man he calls the "big, Black buck" with Etheline sets him into action. Even if you find the Tenenbaums a rather narcissistic, sardonic, and white-bread bunch, you might enjoy sitting in the dark, full of contempt, laughing, and snickering your head off.

OPM—*The Lord of the Rings: The Fellowship of the Ring*

December 19, 2001

Along the way to its fierce finale, *The Lord of the Rings: Fellowship of the Ring* will take your breath away with moments of awe, power, and terror. The question remaining, though, is whether you can make it to the end.

At three hours in length and containing a sluggish fairy-tale narration and corniness near the start, this film proceeds with an air of languid privilege reserved for a classic of Europe's literary canon. We are expected to be obliging and patient, just as we were expected to be obliging and patient as schoolchildren if asked to read the heavy, British (very White, very male) tomes of author J. R. R. Tolkien, on which this film and its sequels will be based.

Beginning with images of fiery creation and ancient, epic battles, it tells the story of how the rings of power were forged by elven-smiths and distributed to would-be rulers. Secretly, the evil Lord Sauron also forged another ring, a sort of mother of all rings, which allowed him to rule over all the others. But, in battle, he loses the ring and, ages later, it is found by Bilbo Baggins, who belongs to a race of small, furry-footed people called hobbits. On his 111th birthday, Baggins leaves the ring for his favorite nephew, Frodo Baggins (Elijah Wood), who is told by the wizard Gandalf that he must travel across Middle-Earth to the land of Sauron and destroy the ring by tossing it into the fires of Mount Doom, where it was forged. It is the perilous journey of Frodo, who is accompanied by friends and pursued by dark, murderous horsemen and monsters, that shapes this adventure.

Just as Tolkien created an oversized world of good versus evil in his novel, director Peter Jackson creates a world of imagery and drama that is, at turns, spectacular and terrifying. Of course, evil is represented always as black, scary, and hideous. Here, evil is in the person of black-cloaked ringraiths, creatures who are neither living nor dead, who ride powerful black stallions in pursuit of Frodo. Evil is in the trolls, the orcs, and the uruk-hai who work for Sauron or his cohort, Saruman, an evil sorcerer who was once the ally of Gandalf.

On an epic scale, this story and film certainly enlarges the pantheon of black, evil monsters, while, of course, reserving the good for Frodo and his gang. An ally along the journey, for one scene, includes Galadriel (Cate Blanchett), who is shot with so much light, she positively glows with paleness. Gandalf, with his long white beard and wrinkles, and played with gusto by Ian McKellan, is the wise elder who can face off with evil and beat it down.

If you and your family can be patient and obliging with this typical dark imagery on such a huge scale, if you can survive the inaneness of hobbit land, and if you can make sure everybody is ready to sit for three hours, this rendition of Tolkien's work provides moving entertainment, as well as interesting insight into one Western vision for making and remaking the world.

Sins of the Father

January 2, 2002

Tom Cherry lives in a narrow place, between a prison of bigotry and freedom, between the past and present, and between the embrace and scorn of a parent. For four decades, federal investigators have believed that his father, Bobby Frank Cherry, was one of five men who in 1963 bombed the Sixteenth Street Baptist Church in Birmingham and killed four girls in the explosion. During the same four decades, Tom Cherry has wrestled with memory and lots of questions.

It is Tom Cherry's tumble of emotion and memory that is explored in *Sins of the Father,* a revealing film with no conclusions that premiered on FX Networks this month (only three days after a judge ruled that the real-life Bobby Frank Cherry is mentally fit to stand trial for the bombing). Memory in this film is rendered by director Robert Dornhelm as a pastiche of images, and lots of jumping around in time and events. The fact that Tom Cherry (Tom Sizemore) never remembers, or reveals his memory of, his father's participation in the bombing means that the film also takes no firm stand one way or another.

Instead, through memory, it presents strong evidence that perhaps Bobby Frank Cherry (Richard Jenkins) was involved—or wasn't. He was a member of a group called the Cahaba Boys, a violent offshoot of the Ku Klux Klan that set explosions at scores of homes, businesses, and places of social gathering in Birmingham's Black community. At home, he was a brutal man. He beat his wife and beat Tom, too.

He was an unabashed racist. He never shied away from proclaiming his hatred of Blacks. He told his son, however, when confronted about the bombing, that he had only hurt two Black people in his life: a young boy who had taken a ball of string from Tom, and the Rev. Fred Shuttlesworth, a local minister and civil rights activist. Because of his need to believe his father and because of a lack of physical evidence, Tom Cherry holds onto the belief that his father was not involved in the crime.

While he claims he doesn't fully remember his father's whereabouts on the night before the bombing, Tom Cherry does eventually say that his father's alibi—that he was home caring for his sick wife—does not square with reality. Tom Cherry remembers that his mother was sick with cancer only after the bombing and that he, and not his father, cared for her when she was ill.

This is what Tom Cherry tells investigators. Afterward, the movie version of Tom Cherry washes his hands of the case and of the burdens of his father. In this film, Tom Cherry is a man who has learned to embrace Blacks. Ving Rhames plays Garrick Jones, a Black man Tom Cherry hires to help him build a house for his father.

It is not clear if this part of the movie is either accurate or reflective of the attitudes of Tom Cherry, who briefly flirted with the Klan himself as an adult. Though he obviously owns a different set of beliefs than those of Bobby Frank Cherry, he has been described by relatives as still protective of and torn by the relationship with his father.

18

Battling Words, Beats, and Story

OPM–*Black Hawk Down*

January 18, 2002

Hollywood has honed war to a science. War, that is, of the American variety. Past generations were weaned on black-and-white images of actors like John Wayne as brave, courageous, and somewhat sanitized soldiers, even in battle. Of course John Wayne and crew were fighting The Good War, World War II, when no one had any doubt about the need to defeat Nazi Germany and halt fascism in its tracks. More than fifty years later, that war provided the setting for Steven Spielberg's *Saving Private Ryan,* which ratcheted up the intensity of cinematic combat with its on-the-ground, shaky, and chaotic lens, piercing audio, and unsparing, close-up carnage.

Black Hawk Down, the second war film to be released since the September 11 attacks on the United States, owes a lot of its bloodletting intensity and sense of moral certainty to *Saving Private Ryan.* With moments of slow motion and an almost balletic choreography of flying Black Hawk helicopters, director Ridley Scott also evokes moments of boding in *Apocalypse Now.* Conversely, however, when it comes to mowing down hundreds of faceless Somali militia, Scott turns to the art of the video game.

While nineteen American servicemen died in the 1993 raid in Mogadishu to capture that country's most powerful warlord, between one thousand and ten thousand Somalis lost their lives. With lots of text explanation at the start, this film builds the case that these Somalis were responsible for the continuing starvation in their East African country, which had already resulted in three hundred thousand deaths. The American, United Nations, and international aid presence was designed to end the cycle of civil war and starvation. There is no time given to explain why many Somalis would hate the United States and consider this country as a contributor to its problems, rather than a savior.

Black folks, "the skinnies" as the soldiers call them, are the bad guys here, and they are killed with both a ferocity and detachment typical of fight maneuvers on Nintendo, PlayStation, or X-Box. Can Black Hawk Down—The Game be far behind? The scene of one blue-shirted, not obviously armed, Somali being shot dead as he crossed a war zone evoked a burst of laughter at the promotional screening I attended in Washington, D.C. And in a pivotal moment, the only Black woman shown killed is shot by the only Black soldier featured in the film.

While Somalis are largely faceless, stars of this film fare only marginally better. Ken Nolan's screenplay does only a cursory job in the crucial beginning scenes to build a sense of the soldiers, including the staff sergeant played by Josh Hartnett, as believable. The idea, it seems, is to get to the main character, the combat, as soon as possible. In the heat of war, the soldiers bloom into shells of the World War II heroes this country has come to know and love.

As Somalia has been mentioned as the next possible target in the United States's "war on terror," *Black Hawk Down* is a powerful reminder that film and fiction are powerful companions, and that Hollywood's version of war, however convincing, is not the same as the real thing.

Middle Passage

February 7, 2002

Though the true horrors and consequences of the Atlantic Slave Trade and Middle Passage have not been made the stuff of popular culture (outside of *Roots* and the film *Sankofa*), we do know from many sources that the hull of a slave ship is a place of terror and death. It is a place we do not want to visit or stay. Even a static reproduction of a slave ship makes children scream and run at the Great Blacks in Wax Museum in Baltimore. The insistence that we stay down there is what gives *The Middle Passage* (playing on HBO) its grip on our psyches.

But once it gets us down there, it doesn't quite know what to do with us. Patrick Chamoiseau's French script, a poetic rumination adapted to English by Walter Mosley, is plodding and draining as it takes us on this voyage without new insight or depth of emotion. The only voice we hear is narration by a dead African captive (Djimon Hounsou), who speaks under the weight of less-than-inspiring text.

For such a visceral experience, there is an odd and somber detachment here.

Sadness is understandable, but referring to your fellow captives as "the slaves" sounds very strange. Did Africans boarding these ships already think of themselves as slaves? Especially since, at one point, the narrator tells us that some believed they were being carried away to be boiled and eaten by cannibals? Would a man captive in the bowels of a ship address himself and his community as "they" as opposed to "we"? The same questions hold true even if the narrator is speaking as an ancestral spirit.

The detachment is furthered by the silence of all other voices. Of all the sound effects—the toy flicks of a whip, the repeated fiddle music provided for the Africans' dancing, the moaning of the ship and the whoosh of the ocean—it is singularly the slip-splash of bodies into the ocean, as the dead are thrown overboard, that provides both an aural and visual sense of mounting horror.

Director Guy Deslauriers treats the action on the ship in a fairly benign way. There is a sense of unwashed bodies but not of a feculent atmosphere ripe with human waste of all sorts. The narrator speaks of the sailors' rape of women, girls, and boys, but this abomination is not even hinted at visually. The poetic meditation lends an air of calm to the story and a sense of passivity to the captives who seem to offer their wrists to be shackled. Long close-ups on faces of women, children, and men (whose fresh shape-ups and baldies never grow out on the four-month voyage) are designed to evoke emotion but do not. Little rodents scampering the hull look like white lab mice painted gray for effect. The scrawny rat that never bites anyone and the single pile of maggots on the floor also looks hokey and staged.

If filmmakers are going to take us on this voyage in 2002, or even in 1999 when the original film was made, it needs to be worth the trip. And still, for some among us who have never seen or heard the history, maybe this is worth it.

Monster's Ball

February 8, 2002

All of art tries, on some level, to convince us of its truth.

Monster's Ball tries to convince us, in a raw, depressing Southern Gothic style, that a Black woman in a small Georgia town will turn to a White man, who is an open racist, for sexual comfort and companionship. It also tells us that a racist will release his hatred when confronted with personal tragedy and the unexpected attention of a pretty, young Black woman. Beneath these two ideas is the old theme that love—even if it really is something else, like neediness or convenience—redeems and conquers all.

The "truth" of the woman is established through her misery. Leticia Musgrove (Halle Berry), who works as a waitress, is about to be evicted from her tiny house. Her husband, Lawrence (Sean "P. Diddy" Combs), has been on death row for eleven years for killing a cop. Her grossly overweight but kindhearted son gets sweetness in his life by devouring chocolate candy bars. She prefers to suck down miniatures of strong whiskey. She is seemingly without family or neighbors who care. In fact, the Black community, particularly the Black male, is depicted here as a complete failure in her life—her husband, her son, the boss who fires her, the sheriff who comes to evict her.

Important to Leticia's world, as presented here, is the fact that she does not know her new man's attitudes, or the fact that he just supervised the execution, the "monster's ball," of her husband. She doesn't seem to care. What she wants is to "feel better," so she throws herself at him. What she knows is that this man, Hank Grotowski (Billy Bob Thornton), has assisted her when she needed it and when no one else would.

It is fairly clear, at some point, that Hank knows who Leticia is but he never discusses the other connection between them. His transformation from a man who scares Black children from his property with a shotgun into a man head over heels in love with a Black waitress is not marked, understandable, or believable. Your gauging of this transformation will greatly influence your reaction to the much-hyped sex scene between these two. Leticia is clearly needy. But what is Hank feeling and acting on? Is this hot and raw? Disturbing? Both?

When Leticia discovers the past of her new guardian angel, her reaction is probably the closest the movie gets to emotional truth, which is not the same as resolution. Time and again, this film asks us to consider how we see a person's soul and what we see. It asks us to define "monster" but is clueless about the antenna and caution African-Americans, particularly Black women, have developed to survive within the monster of racism. In the end, Leticia is forced to confront the former hate-filled soul of her new man as seen by her dead husband. Through his own tragedy, Hank is forced to look inside himself and consider human beings in a new way.

On some level, *Monster's Ball* is similar to histories that attempt to recast or ignore the history of rape of Black women by White men, and how that legacy still reinforces a strong racial barrier. (Think of stories of Thomas Jefferson and Sally Hemmings that depict Sally as the sexual aggressor.) Berry, the product of an interracial relationship, who says she "begged" for the part, may not be representative of the impulse or truth of most Black women.

But Berry gives an able assist, an Oscar-nominated one, in helping the writers and director to convince us of the truth they want told.

Black Star—Denzel Washington in *John Q*

February 15, 2002

If in some future world we can only imagine, the Academy of Motion Picture Arts and Sciences creates a "Saved Your Ass" award, there is no doubt that Denzel Washington would be a winner year after year. How many times have we seen Denzel spin gold (and an Oscar nomination) out of straw? How many piddling to simply less-then-perfect films (no need to name names here) has he raised from the realm of so-so?

His latest amazing recovery is *John Q*, in which he plays John Quincy Archibald, a factory worker who, when failed by the nation's unforgiving health-care system, takes matters into his own hands to save his dying child. Primed by previews and commercials, there is no mystery here in the first half of the film. Add to the lack of surprise the fact that Hollywood often doesn't do working class very well. It can do the middle class, the rich, and the beautiful. But the average Joe, with the possible exception of tough cops and soldiers, always comes off a little fake.

Here, the dialogue set up between Washington, his son, Mike (Daniel E. Smith), and wife, Denise (Kimberly Elise), is skimpy and forced. John, struggling on a part-time salary, lives in a White community, is best friends with a White couple, and attends an integrated church. Boy, John Q is a statistical wonder. It's as if this story were originally intended to focus on a White family but Washington was chosen to plug the hole and transform the film into something we will want to watch. Elise has to be given a lot of credit for bringing a sense of emotional truth to the film as a waitress confronted with the imminent death of her only child. Elise can project a lot of pain without saying a word. And here, as in other projects, she doesn't mind looking real and a little torn down on the big screen.

As John does the unthinkable and uncharacteristic for a simple family man, and takes over the local hospital to save his son, the drama gets better but still has a quality reminiscent of quirky episodes of *ER*. There is the callous cardio specialist (James Woods) and the icy-cold hospital administrator (Anne Heche) who you just want to slap. An assortment of average Joes create a whole other drama and comedy as they are holed up with the gun-toting John Q in the emergency room.

Out on the streets, the bad police chief with a political agenda (Ray Liotta) thinks the best way to diffuse the situation is to kill John, while a good (or better) cop (Robert Duvall) works as a hostage negotiator to convince John to turn over his captives. A rowdy crowd gathers behind barricades to rally around John, making him a folk hero and his situation a rallying point for the reform of the nation's health-care system.

Whew, there are a lot of stock characters and situations here. Despite the debris, Washington still manages to strike gold.

Queen of the Damned

February 22, 2002

Based on what we learn from *Queen of the Damned,* it seems that Dracula would have no problem melting into the punk or goth crowd of Hollywood Boulevard, Times Square, or some seedy district of London. The star here, the vampire Lestat, visits our century and quickly transforms himself into a rock star with one of those musical bands that wear all black, apply lots of dark makeup, pierce assorted body parts, and have a ready-made paleness suitable for the undead.

By the time Aaliyah makes her stunning appearance as Queen Akasha, the mother of all vampires who hails from ancient Egypt, Lestat and crew have clearly established the film as theirs, not hers—even though she plays the title role. With a sense of irony, frequent melodrama, unintentional humor, too much narration, and souped-up editing, the story and visuals proceed with a rock-band pace and sensibility. This is vampire chic for the MTV set.

Based on Anne Rice's novel, much of the story unfolds in fits and starts, telling the tale of how Lestat came to be. We meet his "host," the ancient vampire Marius. We visit castles, private islands, mansions, and Hollywood hideaways for the rich. If you don't know, you know now: Vampires live large. They don't seem to need money or maybe, appropriately, vampires are all descendants and heirs of the super-rich.

Lestat meets Jesse (Marguerite Moreau), a half vampire and half human, and it is obvious that the two of them are supposed to do the vampire nasty at some point. *Queen of the Damned* stretches to an almost comedic extreme the experience of blood sucking, with the vampires reveling in it like it is the bomb weed or sex. Hearing Lestat, with his British accent, cry out for "more" recalls Austin Powers exhorting, "Oh yeah baby!"

The slumbering Akasha is awakened by Lestat's vampire rock music circling the globe. She aims to find Lestat, make him her king, and once again rule the world. Lestat's outlandish openness, contrasted with the traditional secrecy preferred by vampires, scares and enrages vampires around the globe and they want to beat him down. But they will have to deal with Akasha first, who will blow up the spot—poof!—if you try to hurt her man (who really doesn't look the part). The stage is set for a showdown. The whole world is, quite suddenly, against the evil but beautiful ancient Egyptian vampire. The scene of her battle royal is one of the most disturbing scenes I have seen featuring a Black actress.

As with most adaptations of novels, there is an attempt here to tell too many stories in the short space allotted for a film. On the one hand, it is too bad that Aaliyah doesn't get more screen time. Killed in a plane accident in September, Aaliyah gives a striking final performance in this film. She uses her limited appearances to establish presence; a mean, queenly swagger; a wicked glare; a flair for playing the villain and for eating bloody human hearts. On the other hand, from the moment she makes her video-queen entry—all glowing like she's been eating her queen Wheaties—she sticks out like a chocolate chip in vanilla gelato among all these sunken-eyed creatures of the night.

Interview—Alice Walker

February 28, 2002

A writer must always live with his or her own words—especially if they wind up on the big screen. And there is no better example of this idea than Alice Walker and her 1982 novel *The Color Purple.* In 1994, Walker dedicated an entire new volume, *The Same River Twice: Honoring the Difficult,* to chronicling her complex journey as *The Color Purple* was made into a film. And now, more than twenty years after the novel's release, she is back on the trail talking about it again, as well as the firestorm that greeted the 1985 film directed by Steven Spielberg. Why? Because an enhanced *The Color Purple* DVD recently hit the shelves.

"The DVD, I think, is really special because you have some additions to the film itself that I think will really help people see how much commitment went into creation of the film," Walker said in a recent interview with www.seeingblack.com and other journalists. "I think that there were a lot of questions early on about how it was made. And a lot of those questions will be answered. And I think that it will be lovely for people to just see what a family we created on the set."

When it was published in 1982, *The Color Purple* raised a stir in the Black community because of its depiction of a brutal and soulless Black man who abused his young wife, Celie, in the rural South. At the time, the book's portrayals of Black men, described as "often negative" by Mel Watkins in the *New York Times Book Review,* were seen by many in the Black community to be a part of a general trend in fiction by Black women.

Books by authors including Terry McMillan, Gloria Naylor, Toni Morrison, and Walker, all with contracts at major publishing houses, included less-than-shining examples of Black manhood. Who can forget trifling Franklin in McMillan's *Disappearing Acts*? Or the buzzard Luther Nedeed in Naylor's *Linden Hills?* When Walker won both the Pulitzer Prize and the American Book Award for *The Color Purple,* many took it as validation of a Black feminist voice, while others said that the awards only proved that Black women writers were being rewarded for bashing Black men. "I got tired a long time ago of White men publishing books by Black women about how screwed up Black men are," wrote Courtland Milloy, in his column for the *Washington Post.*

In *The Same River Twice,* Walker acknowledged such critics and quoted them. And now, even while promoting the DVD, she still says *The Same River Twice* closed the chapter on that part of her life.

"I looked at all of that controversy and criticism, and I put it to rest," Walker said. "But, you know, criticism comes, it goes. And, you know, you're lucky if, after they get through with you, you're left standing. And I'm very much left standing."

Since the book and film, Black film has undergone a renaissance, and now there are a greater variety of images of both Black men and women on the screen. Walker says that she enjoys the work of many in this "new wave" of filmmakers, including Spike Lee and Robert Townsend, and is working with one of the producers of last year's critical hit *Frida* on a film version of her book *By the Light of My Father's Smile.*

"I think that the book did help to bring in greater freedom for people to express how they view life," she said. "And, I'm very happy about that. Because you really can't, you know, be a good artist if you can't say what you really feel. And people may be offended, but that's how you feel, and that is your right, and that is your gift as well. . . .

"From the writer's point of view I think that [*The Color Purple*] has had a really good impact, especially on literature. And I think also on film. Even if you don't like it, you have to see the incredible acting and just amazing beauty of the people. I mean, I think that you would just have to feel that you want to have more of these people on-screen. I know that's how I feel."

Walker said that in *The Color Purple,* as in other works, she worked for and in honor of her ancestors. "I always felt their help. I always felt supported. I have never felt alone in that sense, you know? I mean, even when I was alone with all the people doing whatever they do, I always felt my ancestors. And, over time, I guess, it just got really clear that they are the most honest and reliable critics and appreciators of one's work. . . .

"And when things like that are right, the synchronicity, you always feel your way to be the right way. I mean I felt like I was really on course, and that if I went off of it, they would let me know. . . .

"How many of those ancestors had to do whatever they had to do to make it possible for me to get educated, to actually end up sitting at a desk writing about them? I mean [when I was writing the book], I was just crying and laughing, and just really feeling love. You know, just love for them, their love for me.

"Love is big. Love can hold anger, love can even hold hatred. I mean, you know, it's all—it's all love. It's about the intention of what you want it to do. It's about what you're trying to give. And often when you're trying to give something, you know, it has a lot of pain in it. But the pain, too, is a part of the love."

She offered special support for women of color who need to forgive: "Well, you know what? Actually, some pain is so severe that there's nothing else you can do. I mean, forgiveness is the only remedy. I mean, unless you want to just worry it to the grave. Because ultimately, it hurts you, you know. The person that you are going on over, often they don't even remember. So there you are with your heart all hard and not forgiving. And, you know, wishing they'd fall over dead or something. And they don't even know.

"So the best thing is to really work on yourself and opening your own heart and just letting all that stuff go. And it is possible. It sometimes takes a lot of time and a lot of sitting. You know, just sitting with yourself and trying to work with your own heart. And this is one of those areas where Buddhism is very, very good."

Finally, Walker affirmed her sense of activism as a writer, and this sense of activism circles its way back to her voice in works such as *The Color Purple.*

"Oh I, you know, talk at rallies, I march, I write. In fact, eleven days after 9/11, when the president was talking about retaliating by bombing people in Afghanistan, I made an address in which I talked about how we really do not want to be bombing children and women and people and donkeys and whatever else people have over there. You know? We don't want to be bombing the earth itself. It's wrong.

"I mean, when we're attacked and we suffer, what that's supposed to teach us is not that we want to attack other people to make them suffer. What it's supposed to teach us is that we don't want that to happen. You know? War is so obsolete. . . .

"We are a family," she said. "And we have all the different representations of humanity in the family. And, within this family, there has to be total freedom. There has to be the freedom to be yourself. You have to be free to express your views."

Joe and Max

March 3, 2002

Before Muhammad Ali became the greatest, there was Joe Louis, the Brown Bomber, who fought at a time when African-Americans looked to a Black heavyweight champ to potently symbolize our fight, might, and possibility of victory.

Joe and Max, premiering on the Starz movie channel, is a better-than-decent attempt at telling the story of Louis's life as it intertwined with that of Max Schmeling, the German boxer with whom he fought two pivotal fights during his career. Schmeling and Louis battled during a tension-filled time in the 1930s when the United States and Germany were almost, but not yet, fighting each other in World War II. At the same time, both boxers had to contend with being used for national propaganda purposes but ultimately abused within their home country. Remarkably, despite the tensions of the times, the two established a bond as athletes and men.

In the United States, open racism was the order of the day. Even though the country gave lip-service support to the undefeated Louis during the first fight with Schmeling in June of 1936, many in the crowd at Yankee Stadium turned on Louis and cheered for his opponent as Schmeling began to pummel and, ultimately, knock out Louis. In the stadium, there were fights between Black and White spectators. Nearby in Harlem, Black folks rioted after listening to the bout on radio, convinced that the outcome was somehow rigged.

In Germany, Hitler and his Nazi crew used Schmeling's victory in the first fight as a propaganda tool to support Nazism. The icy minister of information wanted Schmeling, who was also the European champion, to say that he "detected a weakness in the Negro" that allowed him to win. Schmeling became the toast of the country, which was slipping further into Nazi rule and stepping up persecution of Jews and political opposition. When Louis knocked out Schmeling in a rematch, fortunes changed for Schmeling, who was ultimately sent to the frontlines to fight Allied soldiers itching to claim his dog tags as a prize.

Leonard Roberts (*He Got Game, Hoodlum, Love Jones*) ably handles the role of Louis as he matures from a baby-faced youth to a weary old man. Roberts rocks a sort of crazy afro, which was not exactly how Louis carried it in 1936 but certainly gives Roberts a dated look for this part. Til Schweiger (*The Replacement Killers, Driven*) is given more to work with in the more detailed tale told of Schmeling's personal and professional life.

The boxing scenes are well staged and edited. And while care was taken with scenes in Germany, most moments in the Black community, in Harlem or the South Side of Chicago, look like a movie set or backdrop for a stage play. Similarly, the story, though worthwhile overall, could have benefited from more description about the social conditions among African-Americans during the time that Joe Louis was in his prime.

All About the Benjamins

March 8, 2002

Ice Cube should kiss the ground in Miami, kiss cowriter Ronald Lang, kiss Mike Epps, and maybe jump back and kiss himself, too. *All About the Benjamins* is no stellar feat, but it is fresh and funny enough to save Cube from his camp of diminishing returns with DJ Pooh, who, with Cube, cowrote the 1995 hip-hop cinema classic *Friday*.

None of Cube and Pooh's comedies have been quite as good since then. Chris Tucker, who provided the comedic spark for *Friday,* has moved on to making Jackie Chan movies. The same South-Central Los Angeles backdrop and characters have become cliché and Cube is too old to keep playing a juvenile delinquent.

In this film, instead of playing a brother heading to, just out of, or in imminent danger of jail, Cube plays Bucum Jackson, a bounty hunter increasingly frustrated by his piddling salary and the high-risk nature of his work. A maturing Cube looks the same as he always has—thick, short, a little dumpy but athletic enough here in a Miami Heat jersey to chase bad guys and punch their lights out. He is a good shot and, in what could be a cynical reference to Los Angeles, knows how to handle a stun gun.

One of his targets is Reggie Wright, a petty criminal played by Mike Epps. And there couldn't be a better target. Guess what? Mike Epps is hilarious. Chalk it up to better writing, better jokes, more on-camera experience, or something. But Epps, just like Tucker once was, is the spark that drives much of the comedic insanity here.

Bucum and Reggie wind up as partners as they try to track down $20 million in diamonds and a misplaced lottery ticket. Along the way, they run, get shot at, and trade insults with White people. The plot gets predictable here and there but it also has enough unexpected bright spots to keep you interested. One of the bright spots is the bit performance by Roger Guenveur Smith, in the role of a crook masquerading as a fashion photographer. With the sunny art deco backdrop, Smith's performance is signature Miami, something that would not be possible in the usual humdrum hood flicks.

The budget for this film, at $18 million, is small by Hollywood standards but large compared to the miniscule budgets of Cube's other around-the-way comedies (*Friday* was made for $3.5 million). And you can see the additional money on-screen. Novice feature director Kevin Bray and editor Suzanne Hines take an imaginative approach to many scenes that allow the action to proceed with whimsy and a degree of sophistication usually missing from hip-hop comedies. We all probably would like to study, second by second, the faces of two broke-ass folks who've just won the lottery. We probably want to see how crazed someone looks when locked in a car trunk.

There are enough funny moments here to keep Ice Cube and Mike Epps in the comedy business, and rolling in the Benjamins.

Black Star—Eddie Murphy in *Showtime*

March 15, 2002

Showtime, the new Robert DeNiro–Eddie Murphy collaboration, works best as a mildly amusing critique of the television industry—its superficiality, deft maneuvering between fact and fiction, and powerful grip on our imagination and lives. Here we have two big film stars playing police officers who, in turn, are featured as TV cops in a doctored reality show.

Working with this premise, it is easier for someone, especially someone who is not a big Eddie Murphy fan, to stomach Murphy's role as a clueless, vapid jerk who plays at everything and masters nothing, especially not character or integrity. The police officer he plays, Trey Sellars, is a failure and a joke. As an aspiring actor dying for his big break, Sellars is a miserable failure and a joke. While he wants desperately to be a star, he is a walking-talking billboard for the emptiness and comedy of celebrity culture. He is so empty, it is painful to watch him.

It is especially painful to watch him opposite the Man of Honor Himself, DeNiro, who is the straight man here as Detective Mitch Preston. And I mean really straight. Preston is serious about his work, good with his work, and always on point. He's a man's man, as much as Sellars is no man's man. The only things crooked about Preston are the lopsided ceramic pots he struggles to make as a form of anti-anal therapy.

While the "real" man Preston is grumpy and grumbling in his role of TV star, Sellars embraces the frill of celebrity and is loved by fans, including one sister who offers that she could take care of Sellars, um, physically. The cop team becomes a hit as they try to track down an all-purpose crook named Vargas who has come into the possession of a gun so powerful that its blasts can level a house. In the process of solving the crime, the incongruity of "real" police work and fake TV police work is glaring and often funny.

The ways in which the African-American community, which watches more television than Whites, is often caught up in TV culture becomes part of the plot. There are references to and appearances by Johnny Cochran, who is the lawyer for a young, sort of pitiful brother who is caught up in the drug world. Said same pitiful brother is featured in one scene, one of the most insightful about the power of television, where he is duped into believing that he is conducting an interview for a nonexistent TV show.

Moments like this, some killer one-liners by DeNiro—very few by Murphy—some wild action sequences, and an appearance by Mos Def make *Showtime* a decent diversion. It at least has some substance beneath comedy that heats up here and there, but never gets too hot.

Black Star–Wesley Snipes in *Blade II*

March 22, 2002

Blade II cannot be accused of lacking anything, except perhaps some restraint. Following new exploits of the half-human, half-vampire Blade (which is, by far, Wesley Snipes's best role), this film is a mixture of Jet Li–type martial arts, *Alien*-type horror, James Bond gadgetry, and a few WWF Smackdown! moves thrown in for good measure, and for a good, gory time.

This vampire business can get nasty, though, so if you're not prepared for doughy-faced creatures with expanding mouths, splattering blood, or scenes of internal organs, maybe you'd better stick to something more on the order of *E.T. The Extra-Terrestrial* this weekend.

In this story, shot entirely amid decaying, industrial areas of the Czech Republic, Blade is still battling the Vampire Nation, which wants to rule the world and use humans for food. But Blade is persuaded to join forces with this "nation" to help them fight a new breed of vampires suffering from a virus that gives them super strength, allows them to infect other vampires, and is, ultimately, deadly.

He is aided again by Whistler (a very wrinkled Kris Kristofferson—they don't let women look like this in movies). At the start, Blade rescues Whistler from the nation, which had held him captive for years. It turns out that Blade needs all the help he can get from his old pal. These new super vampires can fight like *Crouching Tiger, Hidden Dragon* to the fifth power. They are even impervious to the silver bullets in Blade's assorted big guns. Though Blade is assisted in this quest by a band of fighter vampires from the nation (most notedly Donnie Yen from *Iron Monkey*—yay!), it is Whistler who ultimately is Blade's right-hand man.

This is definitely a vehicle for Snipes, who stars in all the big fight scenes and adds a vampire twist to the development of the Black superhero in film. He rocks a wicked vampire fade cut, complete with a funky widow's peak and some very 1980s designs shaved onto the back of his head. He is the commander here, striding to a hip-hop beat. He is in charge, even when others think they are. This ain't no Black sidekick flick.

One question for all you fashionistas: Who will win the war of the long black coat this year, Blade or Morpheus? (My *main* man, Laurence Fishburne, is coming at you again in *Matrix II*.) Based on the previews I've seen, I pick Morpheus, but maybe I am biased. I think that whole baldie thing with the right-shaped head and dark shades give Morpheus an advantage, whereas Wesley sometimes looks more like a vampire pimp. But you be the judge, if you care at all about this very inappropriate diversion.

As if conscious of its over-the-top super-hero genre, *Blade II* is not above a little self-mockery. Toward the end, when Blade has kicked the butt of one of the bad guys, Whistler tosses him something we assume to be a weapon to continue the fight. But the item in question is his pair of black shades, which he promptly sports, en route to the next beatdown.

Not All of Us Are Oscar Happy

March 28, 2002

While in this moment, the beauty and power of two Blacks winning Academy Awards for Best Actor and Best Actress cannot be denied, maybe we will realize eventually that what has happened is really business as usual. The Academy of Motion Picture Arts and Sciences has still managed to avoid giving any big award for a film or performance centered on the Black experience. What's more, similar to the 1939 Best Supporting Actress award given to Hattie McDaniel for *Gone with the Wind,* this year's Best Actress award (and to a lesser degree the Best Actor award) was given for a role not only controversial in the Black community but openly despised by many.

We talk about it among ourselves, out of range of the microphones, TV cameras, and reporters' notebooks of corporate media—lest we be accused of hatin' or raining on our thespian moment in the sun or, worse, being ignorant of the potential resulting gains in Hollywood. And, of course, how the Black community feels about our portrayal in film is usually waved off as insensitive whining about the creative process. In the oh-so-sacrosanct world of critical authority and voice, we lack credibility given by said same corporate media. But still we know, with the kind of authority that we claim over our own history, story, and lives, that Denzel Washington "won" the Oscar for Best Actor when he starred in Spike Lee's *Malcolm X* in 1992. We know he "won" it again when he played Rubin "Hurricane" Carter in the movie *The Hurrricane* three years ago. (And if he didn't win, Kevin Spacey damned sure didn't!)

Not only were Denzel's performances phenomenal, not only did he, establishing a pattern, make flawed films into decent ones, these stories were important ones for illuminating the Black experience. They not only told a story about history and race, but also about racism (after the *New York Times* "race" series, I'm beginning to understand the difference) and our complex existence in a racist society. But just as Sidney Poitier did not win for *In the Heat of the Night* (but instead for the sappy *Lilies of the Field*), just as James Earl Jones did not win for *The Great White Hope,* just as Cicely Tyson and Paul Winfield did not win for *Sounder,* and just as Diahann Carroll did not win for *Claudine,* Washington did not win for his roles in films about our journey.

It has not escaped the attention of even the most casual observer of Black film that Washington has finally won the Best Actor award for playing a crooked LAPD narcotics detective, a thug so without heart that he risks the lives of his mistress and son to save his own (and who provides cinematic counterbalance to images of four White LAPD officers beating Rodney King senseless). Don't get me wrong. I give large props to Washington's performance in *Training Day*. I am not one of those who cried foul just because he was not playing the usual upstanding good guy. It is just striking, and to many of us more than a coincidence, that he is awarded for playing one of our thugs we know so well, rather than for playing our "shining Black prince." Sure, some White actors have also gotten "make-up" awards, where the actor is seen as having been passed over and wins later on as a sort of compensation. But none of those actors and performances have the same social resonance that Denzel Washington has when he plays a thug versus a race man.

We have won Oscars for playing bit parts in stories really about White folks—Cuba Gooding Jr. in *Jerry Maguire,* Whoopi Goldberg in *Ghost,* and the list goes on. And while every performance was wonderful and deserving, they still required the Black actor or actress to fit into a role and story centered around White folks and written from their perspective. And this fitting into a role outside of our experience is the problem many folks have with *Monster's Ball.*

In the film, deftly written and filled with thought-provoking images and scenes, the writers try to convince us that a poor Black woman in a small Southern town (Halle Berry) will turn to a White man (Billy Bob Thornton), who is an open racist, for sexual comfort and companionship. Only through this prison guard, whom we see (but she doesn't see) chase Black children from his property with a shotgun, call his co-worker a nigger, and execute the woman's husband, does she find peace. We are also to believe that the racist's own personal tragedy, coupled with the Black woman's desperation and neediness, will cause the racist to make an about-face. Ultimately, *Monster's Ball* uses the legacy of racism in an unconvincing manner to belittle its impact, and historical and present-day consequences.

I think the only reason there hasn't been a bigger outcry is because, unlike the premiere of *Gone with the Wind,* which was a national event, not many people—especially Black people—have even seen *Monster's Ball,* a low-budget flick playing on a limited number of screens. And, based on comments on the message board at www.seeingblack.com, many Blacks, particularly Black men, have determined not to see the movie and support it financially.

"I simply find the premise of *Monster's Ball,* in which a character played by one of our most prized beauties, falls in love with a racist White prison guard who led her husband to his execution, deliberately insulting," said Miles Willis of Houston. "With its profanely incongruous and utterly implausible scenario, the plot of this film is a sneering, in-your-face taunt to all Black men. Imagine the seething indignation that a Jewish man might feel while watching a story in which the widow of a Nazi concentration camp victim has an intimate relationship with the SS officer that shoved her husband into one of those ovens at Auschwitz!"

Others posting on the board, men in particular, said they would not go to see the film. "I refuse to support the movie with my hard-earned dollars," said MrUnitesUs. "When we start recycling more of our Black dollars we will be make more of own movies and be in control of our own future."

It is the sentiment of these men and women, which was not felt by the largely White male cadre of film critics who praised the movie and are quoted in print ads promoting it. Their sentiment has not been heard as part of discussion, gossip, and hype concerning Oscar contenders. Though none of these filmgoers question the quality of Berry's performance, they are questioning the film's plot and message as a way of questioning an image of race and racism in these times.

I also do not belittle Berry's performance, but like the writers and thinkers of the 1930s who raised their objection to our continued depiction as maids, butlers, and slaves, I want to leave this record of thought in the year 2002. We are all not bowled over by the Academy's recognition and supposed validation of "us" as artists. We are all not accepting of and happy for roles that turn the complexity of our history into a twisted joke much more heinous than anything in *Gone with the Wind.*

Not all of us equate "making it" in Hollywood with the uplifting of Black people. Not all of us, as Ms. Berry said in her very moving, positive. and respectful acceptance speech, want a time when they "won't see our color." Some of us do want our color seen, as well as our history and stories told from our perspective.

Some of us want something more than business as usual.

Black Star—Morgan Freeman in *High Crimes*

April 5, 2002

This is a whodunit with a military court twist in the tradition of *A Few Good Men* and *Rules of Engagement*. In contrast to the current spate of war glory films, *High Crimes* takes us into the messy world of U.S. military covert action during the 1980s when we called the rebels in El Salvador terrorists and fought to defeat them. And El Salvador is a world away from Claire Kubik (Ashley Judd), a high-powered attorney in San Francisco who wins cases and is trying to get pregnant. But this super lawyer apparently hasn't been cross-examining her husband, Tom, very well. One day he is arrested and whisked away to face charges in military court that he executed nine civilians in a raid on a village in El Salvador.

This is definitely Ashley Judd's film. From start to finish, Judd is the center of attention and the primary object of our attention and worries. Despite her tough lawyer getup, she is presented as a pale, frail thing, the pretty wife, the damsel in distress. And this focus does not waver, even after Morgan Freeman makes his entrance as the scruffy, struggling lawyer whom she turns to for assistance on the case. The two of them, in a relationship that accentuates his salty wisdom and her yuppie courage, try to defend Tom against the usual insurmountable odds. They have an assist from a very green court-appointed lawyer (Adam Scott) and Claire's flaky sister, Jackie (Amanda Peet), who has a white stripe in her hair like the mean chick from *Josie and the Pussycats.* Violence and fear, or the threat of it, keeps our eye on the ball until the very end, and makes us wonder which way it will bounce.

Black Star–Samuel L. Jackson in *Changing Lanes*

April 12, 2002

While the promotion of *Changing Lanes* leads you to expect two hours of high-testosterone vehicular assault and a suped-up battle between a yuppie and another Angry Black Man, it is actually a surprisingly sensitive portrayal of modern moral dilemmas. It is also well worth it to watch Samuel L. Jackson rock another crazy hairdo. He's chucked the crazy 'fro from *Unbreakable* and the locks from *The Caveman's Valentine* to look like an insurance salesman, corny eyeglasses and all. If we didn't all look alike anyway, Jackson could play a secret agent!

Here, Jackson again plays a man on the edge. Doyle Gipson, a recovering alcoholic, is trying to make it in New York City selling insurance. By purchasing a rickety-looking house, he is making a last-ditch effort to save his marriage and keep his wife from moving across country to Portland with their two sons. On the way to the divorce hearing, he is involved in a car accident with a young lawyer, Gavin Banek (Ben Affleck), also heading to court to finalize a multimillion-dollar deal.

Gipson wants to exchange insurance information. He wants to take the time to handle the matter correctly. But Banek is in a hurry—he leaves the scene of the accident and will not offer Gipson a ride, setting in motion the disintegration of everything Gipson has been working to save.

Things don't go so well for Banek, either. At his important hearing, he realizes that an important document he needs was dropped on the highway and that it is probably in the hands of Gipson. Banek goes about trying to find the man he has just dissed. As the day proceeds, and the need for revenge between these two men spirals out of control, Banek is also forced to confront an ever-multiplying series of his own moral crises that cause him to question his values and life. The racism that Gipson confronts is as matter-of-factly presented in the film as it is normally presented to us in real life. Racism operates convincingly as a thick subtext rather than the direct point of the conflict.

Chap Taylor's screenplay is filled with complex, believable characters and meaningful dialogue that offers more than the usual same-old lame morality blather. In a story about fast-paced lives and life-changing decisions, director Roger Michell creates a sense of intimacy amid chaos. He makes good use of pace, dialogue, and close-ups on folks who look real and never too pretty, except, of course, Affleck.

What makes the movie a surprise is the extent to which chaos is showed to be internal as well as external. Banek is inhabiting a vacuous world full of charades. Though Gipson tries mightily to overcome his past inconsistency as a father, his rage is fed by events that seem to rob him of what he has worked hard to achieve. Affleck and Jackson turn in more then solid performances in a film that offers more than the sum of its obvious parts.

Filmfest DC 2002–*La Tropical*
Washington, D.C.
April 17–28, 2002

The story of La Tropical, Havana's popular outdoor dance hall, is told like a love story in the hands of director David Turnley. In an atmospheric swirl of black-and-white, the regulars of the hall loom large in weekend dramas of romance, passion, lust, the transforming power of music and dance, and the triumphs and travails of Cuba's Black population.

The focus here is on sensuality, sexuality, and African-inspired dance that emphasizes movement of the pelvis rather than the feet. The camera moves close up on shaking butts, grinding hips, graceful arms, and a joyful sense of purpose that completes the performance package. Turnley, a White Pulitzer Prize–winning photojournalist who in recent years has turned to documentary, takes the role sometimes of an informed commentator and, at other times, of a giddy voyeur, treating the dancing Black female form like eye candy.

The video starts in slow motion, with a shot upward of a young, smiling woman churning her hips opposite a dance partner. It captures the frenzy of two wild women on stage, rubbing their crotches, with their panties visible, hard against Pedrito, the fine lead singer for the band Los Van Van. It winds down with shots of the entire hall visible through a pair of flapping Black thighs.

Often positioned in the midst of gyrating bodies, the ninety-six-minute documentary captures the impersonal intimacy included in many Caribbean dances, which take bumping and grinding, or "winding," to the limit. Debate, if you want, issues of origin and cross-pollination, but it is clear that dances at La Tropical have much in common with your average performance on an average rap video from these United States.

What sets this video apart from other good-time concert flicks is the extent to which it goes outside the concert hall and gives voice to dancers and performers. Here, on the streets and in the homes of Havana, moving bodies become people with histories, aspirations, challenges, triumphs, and tragedies. There is the poor young man in love with a girl from the other side of the tracks. There is the family of performers caring for a teenager with disabling cerebral palsy. There is the seventy-seven-year-old dance-hall diva, a real character who goes by the name Tikitiki, who swears her Sunday visits to La Tropical keep her alive.

It is through these stories, as well as through a series of fruitful interviews, that *La Tropical* empowers the voices of those being featured and becomes less about typical Euro-American voyeurism. It also becomes a story about race in Cuba. Most of the hall's patrons are working-class Blacks; very few Cubans who consider themselves "White" go there. While the revolution has vastly improved life for the island's majority Black and "mulatto" populations, entrenched race divisions that are also class divisions still remain.

Toward the end, a carload of elderly Black Cubans, leaving La Tropical after a rainstorm, praise the social changes seen on the island in their lifetime. But a young White guitarist for a troupe of flamenco artists—obviously not as popular as the bands of La Tropical—rails against the lot that fate has dealt him. He wants to go to Florida. He sings a morose song that can remind you of Ricky Martin's "La Vida Loca," as if he is imagining how, with his White skin and musical ability, he could be living large in another place. Through an engaging mix of such voices and ideas, Turnley manages to tell a story bigger than La Tropical, one that is as timeworn and winding as Old Havana's churning streets.

Filmfest DC 2002—*Karmen Geï*

Energetic traditional music and dance, featured often in African cinema, provides the spark for *Karmen Geï,* loosely based on Bizet's opera *Carmen* and a novel by Prosper Mérimée. Carmen's story line, about a determined, free woman with free thoughts about love, has proven adaptable to the African-American experience in productions like *Carmen Jones,* featuring Dorothy Dandridge in 1954. The African experience, or more specifically, the Senegalese one, proves as accommodating here as well.

Djeinaba Diop Gai, in the lead role, is sensual and playful. She commands all her scenes and dialogue, and sometimes sings in the rhythmic monotone associated with griots. There are also some scenes where everyone present joins in, creating a chorus of African call and response. This African Karmen casts a spell and charms through her intense gaze and swiveling hips. The dance here is a modern dance of seduction, not the dances we know related to custom or ritual. It functions as an aphrodisiac. It's not a striptease, but more like a hypnotic boom-shaka-laka that entrances those around her.

When we first meet Karmen, she is in prison, for what we do not know—but we do know that Karmen is a *baaaad* girl. In the prison's open-air yard, she dances everyone into such a frenzy that the female (presumably gay or bisexual) warden summons Karmen to her bed. After that sexual favor, Karmen is freed.

Director Joseph Gai Ramaka wastes no time in making subtle commentary about official corruption and dishonesty. If this Karmen is cast as a sexual maverick, she is also cast as a political dissident who dares to mock and challenge the military and government. Not only are wardens doing it with inmates, military men are cheating on their wives. When Karmen is released, she dances at a public event attended by a local official who is smitten with her. Well, the man's wife, sitting next to him, doesn't take too kindly to Karmen shimmying her ass in front of them. The wife stands up, ready to engage in a dancing duel with Karmen. Shapely and bejeweled, but obviously no match for Karmen, she winds up on the ground with Karmen swinging on her. Karmen is no joke.

Karmen has an affair with the soldier—basically ruining his life in the process—and then can't get rid of him. She secretly loves an older man, Samba, also a social outcast. She indulges a handsome suitor, Massigi, with some attention but is not very interested. In all versions of *Carmen,* there is always the question of whether the woman is ultimately portrayed as so foolish and coy that she somehow deserves what she gets, or whether she is simply a free spirit that others, specifically men, want to cage for their own tired purposes. *Karmen Geï,* like many *Carmen* productions, straddles between the two extremes, making the protagonist both a hero and villain.

Filmfest DC 2002—*Ali Zaoua*

In a desolate corner of Casablanca, Morocco, a young boy named Ali is killed when a gang member strikes him in the head with a rock. Over the next few days, his three friends, young children living on the city's decayed streets, work to give him a proper burial. With this premise, director Nabil Ayouch hurls us into a world of stark contrasts: of childhood innocence existing despite harsh brutality, of security alongside precarious existence and, worse, complete destitution.

Ali's friends, Kwita, Omar, and Boubker, are a childishly salty, humorous, and heartbreaking crew. The actual street children playing these roles, Mounim Kbab, Mustapha Hansali, and Hicham Moussoune respectively, turn in awesome performances. To say they are convincing is an understatement as well as a misstatement. They are, after all, what they are—smudges, scars, rags, and all. Kwita, the oldest of the three and the leader after the death of Ali, tries to steer the trio clear of the major street gang and its leader, Dib, an obviously mentally challenged man who lords over young ones with terror and brute force.

The film is unsentimental but not graphic in presenting existence in a poor developing country. Life, as it is lived here, offers a set place and station for these boys. There is not even an illusion of upward mobility to a higher class or standard of living. The children are homeless "glue sniffers." Ali's mother, though a prostitute, at least has a home that includes a room for her son. She has repaired his boombox so that it will play loudly and drown out activity in her room next door. A pretty student, loved by Kwita from a distance, enjoys a security he can only imagine.

Ayouch tells a story true in much of the world today—even in our own communities—of discarded children and futures, but still manages to wrap in dreams those without apparent possibilities. Ali and Kwita once imagined living in the "twin towers," two large apartment buildings in the modern downtown Casablanca. Before his death, Ali had taken the first steps to fulfill his dream of being a sailor. He had arranged to work as a cabin boy for a local fisherman. He was a talented young artist who created happy-ever-after drawings of himself with his future love. It is these childish images that form a thread throughout the film, allowing sweet imagination to literally float over a world that promises little hope.

Ali Zaoua premiered two years ago and, since then, has won more than thirty awards at international film festivals, including the grand prize at last year's Pan African Film and Television Festival in Burkina Faso (FESPACO). It was also Morocco's submission to the Best Foreign Film category for the 2001 Academy Awards. Distributed by Arab Film Distribution, it is scheduled to have a limited theatrical release in several U.S. cities this year before being released on VHS and DVD.

OPM–*Star Wars: Episode II–Attack of the Clones*

May 16, 2002

If, like many Black folks, you are ambivalent toward the *Star Wars* phenomenon—and you have not camped out on the sidewalk to be the first in line—the latest installment in the series is unlikely to change your mind, despite the presence of Our Man Sam. Let's just say that "the force" is not strong with this one.

Episode II—Attack of the Clones is entertaining in spots but, overall, suffers from a case of lethargy and split personality. Not quite an action flick, not quite a drama, and not quite a love story, it spirals into that netherworld of dawdling entertainment usually reserved for soap operas and the Disney Channel.

It's too bad, really. It starts out fine with the loud, victorious soundtrack, with the prosaic scrolled text that sets up the plot. (The Republic is being threatened by a growing separatist movement.) Throughout, there are whimsically constructed alien creatures and, of course, there is Samuel L. Jackson in the role of a chilled-out jedi knight. The story doesn't give Samuel L. all that much to do, though, aside from offering a noble presence. Just when you think good old Sammy has been relegated to talking-mannequin status, he is suddenly out there for a moment with his shiny baldie, brandishing his light saber and kicking alien ass.

Also made more noble is the freaky Jar Jar Binks, who, as in *Episode I,* still speaks in some rough parody of Ebonics and walks in some rough parody of the urban stroll. There are some fast-paced chase and fight scenes but, in all honesty, the biggest comedic moment goes to the robots when R2-D2 pops off C-3PO's head.

Black Star–Morgan Freeman in *The Sum of All Fears*

May 31, 2002

The approach to evil in *The Sum of All Fears* shows the sheer banality of evil. And this approach is probably very close to reality. The wicked can appear very plain and unremarkable. Look at photographs of convicted Nazi criminals or brutal slave owners. They don't always look like movie villains. Evil, in this movie, is not that ugly or menacing. There are just dull, old fascists sitting around plotting the start of World War III. Yeah, Morgan Freeman is in the movie, but his role, as director of the CIA, is designed to blend into the national security scenery as much as possible. None of the characters here are drawn to be memorable, though Freeman gives as much to the role as can be given. This is a good story and a decent, but not great, film. It might better hold the interest of spy-novel fans but, even then, don't expect to be thrilled.

19

Big Laughs and the Unkindest Cut

Undercover Brother

May 31, 2002

Right On!

Don't be fooled by the corny commercials. *Undercover Brother* is not another jive installment of Weak Ghetto Cinema, filled with the usual clichés and recycled jokes. From start to finish, it is unsparingly funny and works in everything from "Black man's kryptonite" (White women) to the Godfather of Soul, who paralyzes villains with fancy footwork. The writer here, John Ridley, has a brain and a degree in wit. And director Malcolm D. Lee (*The Best Man*) is not faking the funk. On a rating scale, I give *Undercover Brother* four afro puffs.

There must be some '70s hallucinogen that periodically invades the water supply of people who make movies, music, and sneaker commercials. And in the case of *Undercover Brother,* I'm not mad about it at all. Even Eddie Griffin is funny. He plays the role of a nickel-and-dime private investigator, permanently stuck in the aesthetics of big afros, platform shoes, bell-bottom pants, Black Power fist medallions, and Cadillacs. Undercover Brother is dedicated to saving the Black community from the social and cultural losses since the 1970s. As the rollicking intro reminds us, between the '70s and now, we've gone from *Shaft,* Pam Grier, and Jim Kelly, to Urkel, Mr. T., and a blonde Dennis Rodman wearing a white wedding dress.

But Undercover Brother not only cares about images and cultural messages, he is willing to rob the rich to give to the poor. He hooks up with The B.R.O.T.H.E.R.H.O.O.D., a Black secret organization dedicated to fighting The

Man, who loathes the spread of Black music, language, dress, and dance, and plots to keep a popular Black general (Billy Dee Williams) from becoming the first Black president of the United States. Undercover Brother soon finds himself really going undercover, trading his funky '70s attire for khakis and penny loafers, at a multinational corporation that is a flimsy front for The Man's operations.

While the plot matters here, it does not matter as much as the absurdity that the filmmakers create and ride like a wave, all the while poking fun at popular culture. In this crazy world, James Bond–like famous gadgets are funkified—platform shoes and pimp jewelry can do amazing feats. Eating the wrong fried chicken will turn you into Sambo (you can get a Nappy Meal complete with a bottle of malt liquor). And a *Jaws*-like shark attack comes out of nowhere.

Chris Kattan is mad funny here, as is Dave Chappelle in the role of Conspiracy Brother. This film raises the level of our comedies back to the standard of classics like *Hollywood Shuffle* and *I'm Gonna Git You Sucka.* Along with *All About the Benjamins, Undercover Brother* makes 2002, so far, a good year for laughs.

Mama Africa

June 7, 2002

Three short films presented in *Mama Africa* are compelling and insightful about the lives of young people growing up in modern, urban Africa. The compilation, featuring the work of three talented female directors, is not romantic or sentimental. There is not a focus here on village traditions or customs. This is postcolonial Africa set to the beat of the West, where young people are torn between the counsel of elders and the lure of a glamorous "better" life, which challenges their developing sense of identity and integrity.

So, even with their African twist, these coming-of-age sagas might seem familiar to us. *Uno's World* tells the story about a young woman who thinks she's grown and is, therefore, forced to grow up well before her time. Uno lives in Windhoek, the fast-paced capital of Namibia. She is pretty and strikes a tall, slender, sophisticated pose with long-braided extensions in her hair, figure-flattering short skirts, and fashionable knee-high boots. Preferring to hang out in nightclubs with her friends, Uno speaks to her mother in a tone of contempt as she heads out of the door for what she describes flippantly as "music . . . dancing . . . fun . . . life."

As it turns out, "life" brings Uno a quick lesson in the form of a jive-talking man named Kaura, who leaves her pregnant and thinking about what being an adult is all about. Writer-director Bridget Pickering of Namibia tells the story with creative scenes and lighting. Actress Sophie David delivers the right combination of youthful arrogance, immaturity, and resolve to carry off the part.

Kwame (Brian Biragi) is also dealing with his own arrogance and frustration in the film *Hangtime,* directed by Ngozi Onwurah of Nigeria. A college basketball scout will arrive soon to watch him play and Kwame does not want to play in his tattered sneakers. His desperation for new athletic shoes, which he thinks will both improve his performance and his chances of receiving a life-altering scholarship to the United States, leads him and his family to both tragedy and continued hope.

Onwurah is a talented storyteller. All the characters here, including Kwame's grandmother and sister, are multidimensional and speak a dialogue that does not sound canned. *Hangtime* is so compelling that it literally leaves you hanging, waiting for the Hollywood ending that never comes. Of all three films, *Hangtime* seems the best candidate to be expanded into a feature-length film.

In *Raya,* director-writer Zulfah Otto-Sallies (South Africa) focuses on a young woman who has rebelled against her strict Muslim upbringing but has been met with nothing but trouble. When we meet Raya, she is being released from prison. We learn eventually that she probably served time for dealing drugs with her friend Joe, who is still peddling packets of white powder on the street.

Faced with the choice of living under her mother's rules or surviving with her old crew, Raya chooses to leave home with her daughter. She wants to find a legal means of supporting herself but, until she gets on her feet, she lives with Joe and that decision changes her whole world—again.

Promotion of *Mama Africa* has been aided a great deal by the association of the project with Queen Latifah, who narrates at the beginning and end of the presentation and in between each film. Latifah's narration gives *Mama Africa* the packaging of an instructional project, one designed to be shown to young people in schools, on cable television, or on one of those network after-school specials. And this packaging isn't all bad. It just isn't the feel of a theatrical release. These three films, strong efforts from burgeoning talents, are potent enough to carry the show without so much additional explanation and talk. The film world could use more voices like those of these fine artists.

Black Star—Chris Rock in *Bad Company*

June 7, 2002

Bad Company is what you call a summer action flick, with plenty of shooting, car chases, casual profanity, and cheesy allusions to sexuality. A notch above most films of its type, it is very entertaining, beautifully shot, and has some killer one-liners, obviously contributed by Chris Rock. And it is very much a Jerry Bruckheimer guy flick. Women are in the margins as husband-seekers, either clad in Victoria Secret–type lingerie, bound and gagged as wilting hostages, or carrying a torch on the DL for old Anthony Hopkins (please!). The surface plot, to keep all the action going, is that Jake Hayes (Rock) is asked by the CIA to stand in for his dead twin brother, who, before he was murdered, was on the verge of buying a nuclear weapon, to keep it from falling into the wrong hands. Like *The Sum of All Fears,* this film seizes upon our fear of terrorism and the threat of annihilation—and creates a nuclear-bomb movie with jokes. Like Bruckheimer's *Black Hawk Down,* it places the ultimate task of saving the world into the hands of the White men who run the U.S. military and "intelligence" communities.

But, in this case, a brother is asked to come in and save the day, too, and, in the process, provides the texture for the subplots: "Whose is Bigger?" and "Hip-Hop and CIA: United We Stand." Rock gets to stretch as an actor here. There is one moment, in a scene with actress Kerry Washington, where the comedian has totally left him. He is broken, not laughing, and not trying to make us laugh. For this moment alone, I found *Bad Company* worth the time.

OPM—*Sunshine State*

June 21, 2002

I admit it. Ever since *The Brother from Another Planet,* I've been a huge fan of the work of director John Sayles. He doesn't step away from the plate of relevance. He always reminds us of the grander potential of film to reveal and rock our world. But he never lets us forget the absolute absurdity of much of what we see and say every day.

He is one of the few White directors who is able to portray the Black community realistically, and incorporate African-Americans into "all-American" stories in a manner that is not cliché. So it is not surprising that his latest film, *Sunshine State,* which explores land speculation and development in Florida, does not ignore the centuries-long occupation of land in that state by Black people. Without waving a flag or petition, *Sunshine State* reminds us that African-Americans are losing property at an alarming rate, all over the country, but particularly in the South, in shady dealings that sometimes involve the complicity of government agencies.

The story of change is told through two women in a place called Plantation

Island. (I told you dude didn't step away from the plate!) Marly Temple (Edie Falco) is tired of running the family's aging motel and restaurant for her father who is blind, crotchety, and wary of all land speculators. In a nearby enclave, Desiree Perry (Angela Bassett) has come home for only the second time since being packed up and sent off as a pregnant fifteen-year-old. In addition to sorting out her own past, Desiree is confronted with the fact that land dealings could threaten her mother's beachfront home, in a community that was once the only beach that Blacks could visit for miles around.

The story of community is interwoven with that of two families and two women in a series of layered and overlapping narratives that stretch on for more than two hours. There are moments when the film seems to bog down with too many pieces, but the stories are absorbing and absurd rather than bland. A great cast, which includes James McDaniel (*NYPD Blue*) as Desiree's husband; Mary Alice as Desiree's mother; and Jane Alexander as Marly's mother, infuses the stories with humanity and an oddball realness that marks Sayles's films but is elusive in much of what comes from Hollywood.

Speaking of oddball realness, I have to say that few actors can evoke, with just a look, that "my life ain't been no crystal stair" sense like Bill Cobbs (*Enough, Random Hearts*). The wrinkle and furrows in his brow must hold secrets. He seems to be perpetually squinting in the sun or squinting at White folks like they're crazy. In *Sunshine State,* that look, and all the race-man attitude behind it, is the perfect antidote for greedy land-grabbing developers. His character provides the expression and words to go against development-as-gospel that comedian Alan Silver delivers in a series of comedy routines notable, too, for their oddball realness.

American Black Film Festival 2002–Fun, Films, and Fans in the Sun Miami, Florida

June 26–30, 2002

As soon as I check into my Miami Beach hotel for this year's American Black Film Festival (ABFF, formerly the Acapulco Black Film Festival), I click on the television and there is Miss Cleo, the TV psychic, who is in Florida facing charges that she is a fraud. What a welcome, I think. How appropriate a greeting for film festivalgoers, who are attracted to the realm of storytelling, entertainment, illusion, and fantasy.

I see no more news about Miss Cleo for the duration of the festival, but I do see lots of films that delve into the inner mind. Most noteworthy is *Crazy As Hell,* a psychological drama directed by Eriq La Salle and starring Michael Beach, about a psychiatrist who winds up wrestling his own demons. *Karmen Geï,* Joseph Gai Ramaka's sensual and energetic remake of *Carmen* set in Senegal, does not draw huge crowds but well represents the continent, along with *Daresalem* by Issa Serge Coelo and *Ubuntu's Wounds,* a powerful short film about South Africa's Truth and Reconcilation Commission process, written and directed by Sechaba Morojele.

Preferring homegrown products and talent, the audience awards go to *Civil Brand,* a female-prison drama directed by Neema Barnette; to actress Monica Calhoun (*The Best Man, The Player's Club*) for her role in Rob Hardy's upcoming erotic feature, *Pandora's Box;* and to actor Clifton Powell (*Bones, The Brothers*) for his role as a crooked prison warden in *Civil Brand.* The Lincoln Filmmaker Trophy, an award chosen by Black filmmakers, is awarded to *The Riff,* a jazz drama set in New Orleans, and the winner of the HBO Short Film Competition is *Quest to Ref,* a comedy written by and starring Benjamin Watkins.

At the ABFF Awards Show on the final night, the intense young actor Mekhi Phifer is on hand to receive the Rising Star award, and the festival presents Career Achievement awards to costume designer Ruth Carter and to its longtime supporter Robert Townsend—the versatile artist who, along with Spike Lee, ushered in the "new wave" of Black filmmakers. "It's not about a Black thing, it's a human thing," a tuxedoed Townsend, who is the MC for the evening, tells the audience gathered inside the gracious Jackie Gleason Theater. "All I want to do is create something that speaks to people."

Townsend, visibly moved by the surprise award, confides to the audience that he is going through a "horrible divorce" and thanks his longtime friend Keenan Ivory Wayans, who is on hand to give him the award, for helping him in his difficult time. Megastar Chris Tucker is also here on Townsend's behalf, grateful to pay respects to the man who he says gave him his first film role, though he complains with comedic bitterness that he was "cut out of the film."

Actors like Tucker and Phifer have made this first stateside ABFF more star-laden than those recently held in Acapulco. Actress Sanaa Lathan (accompanied by actor Omar Epps) is on hand to present the Career Achievement award to Carter. Director John Singleton, whose short film *Drama,* about domestic violence, is screening here, is also an awards presenter. At one festival party, I witness a Phifer fan, obviously drunk and overcome when Phifer smiles at her, slowly slink to the floor and weep.

Overall, South Beach—which remains a work in progress with pricey art deco hotels and condos ajacent to vacant storefronts—seems a bit more hospitable to

ABFF than Acapulco. Real estate in the area has been hard-hit since September 11 and local merchants seemed appreciative of the influx of business. Mayor David Dermer says the festival is pumping $10 million into the city's economy.

The heat here is just as intense and even more humid than in Acapulco (but while many of the locals prefer to speak Spanish, they can also usually speak English). In Miami, the festival is able to draw on the resources and interests of the community in a manner that was impossible in Acapulco. Jeff Friday, producer of the festival, has announced plans to expand the mission of the festival to include the Latino community. There are more nightclubs playing danceable music, more restaurants serving edible food, and, here, we can drink the water.

"We outgrew Acapulco," Byron Lewis, founder of the festival, says before a small TV crew from Ohio after a morning press conference. "Here we have more access to a larger body of filmmakers and better technical facilities—and I'd rather be home" in the States.

It could be that festival organizers, intent on demonstrating the festival's economic impact on the city, spread functions and programs out to as many varied venues as possible. But this decision makes for some disappointing "official" parties and much scrambling for better alternatives. The cruelest blow comes on the final night, after the wonderful awards program filled with images of Black beauty and excellence. Well, off we head down the noisy main drag of South Beach to a club called Liquid, where we are greeted by two blonde chicks standing on high pedestals on either side of the entryway wearing nothing but *I Dream of Jeannie* ponytails, bikinis, and knee-high boots. Inside, high above the middle of the dance floor on another high pedestal, is another bikini-clad ponytailed chick, dancing in a way that might be described as a mix between '70s go-go girl and '80s techno. She reigns over the dark crowd, which wanders around, bewildered. "I'm a smart person," one Los Angeles entertainment attorney says earnestly, glancing upward and sipping champagne. "But I don't understand this. Do you?"

I have no answers for her. I don't understand it myself.

I think this might be a job for Miss Cleo.

American Black Film Festival 2002–The *Riff*

The jazz movie is a special genre. It brings together our classical music with the particular rhythms of cinema. Films like *Round Midnight* or *Bird* manage a fine marriage of music and images, with each driving the other forward, and driving the story forward in the process.

The Riff, written and directed by Mark Allen, is an interesting take on the jazz genre but falls short of the required magic. Set in New Orleans, it centers on the relationship between a longtime talent scout/manager, Adam Goodnight (Cameron Smith), and his drug-addicted friend and client, the once-great trumpeter Shoop Summers (Antonio Fargas). There is a slowly unraveling mystery in Goodnight's and Summers's past that binds them together and piques our interest, the photography sets the right nightclub mood, and Antonio Fargas lends scenes the right tortured presence, with an unfocused gaze, a crooked sneer, jive talk, and a frequently nasty disposition. But these strong points aren't enough to save the film. Most disturbingly, music is not at all a driving force in the film. Throughout, it relies on a weak score of what is commonly called "cool jazz," that insipid, zippy Muzak-like stuff that lacks any semblance of soul. There is the skeleton of a decent story here. Too bad there isn't the meat, muscle, and music to make this film really sing.

American Black Film Festival 2002–*Crazy as Hell*

The best film I saw at this year's ABFF was *Crazy As Hell,* a complex psychological drama directed by Eriq La Salle, known to most of us as Dr. Peter Benton on the television show *ER.* Produced with an eye for convincing visual detail and a flair for the dramatic twist, this film is one that will make you think twice as it interrogates the meaning of good and evil and the devil. Centered on a psychiatrist named Dr. Ty Adams (Michael Beach), the film takes us into the harried wards of a mental institution where Adams hopes to prove, once and for all, the success of his controversial methods of treating the mentally ill. The film builds a sense of tension and anticipation by showing us two competing visions. First, it shows what only Adams sees—visions of his laughing daughter, his knowing wife. Then it shows us what everyone but Adams sees. A documentary crew is at the hospital producing a program about Dr. Adams's controversial methods. Hidden cameras placed all over the building catch Adams in repeated, heated discussions with the thin air. Who is crazier, the patients or Adams? Can Dr. Adams be both successful and troubled?

Men in Black II

July 3, 2002

Men In Black II has jokes, action, and lots of funky aliens—including a seven-ton worm, a two-headed man, and a snake lady—that give new meaning to the phrase "get your freak on." But the film does not have an ounce of tension. (Hey, even

Ghostbusters had tension.) Not for a moment do we believe that Will Smith and Tommy Lee Jones are really saving the earth from anything more dangerous than a rolled-up comic book. And not for one moment do we really believe that they might lose their paper fight.

In the summer of a tough, flying Spider-Man, a saber-wielding Yoda, and a crime fighter with removable eyeballs, *Men in Black II* comes off as a parody of itself, self-conscious and mocking of its own silliness. And that's not all bad. At the same time that it seems designed for the thirteen-year-old male, it also holds some amusement for adults who enjoy a film with no pretension that it is about more than entertainment. From its first scene, a fake TV show with 1930s special effects about the Men in Black agency, this movie lets us know that it's all jokes.

Without tension, we're left with a series of visually interesting scenes that, depending on your investment in them, will either amuse you mildly or a great deal. The story here is that Agent J (Will Smith) has not given up his good government job and is still working for the Men in Black, a secret agency that regulates alien life on Earth. When a new alien plot that could endanger the planet is uncovered, Agent J is sent to find his old partner, Agent K (Jones), and bring him out of retirement. Together the two must face the evil and determined Serleena (Lara Flynn Boyle), a slithering Kylothian monster who has transformed herself into a Victoria's Secret model.

Ha-ha. So go the jokes, with Sarleena, having just landed and devoured a man whole, strutting through Central Park in her lingerie, with a belly the size of a planet. So goes the movie—entertaining in spots, mainly frothy, not riveting.

In the four years since we last met Agent J, he has developed more confidence and competence in his work but he is still foundering in the shadow of the legend, Agent K. Smith brings some hipness and energy to the flick but is confined by his character's lack of cool and action skills. Several scenes are supposed to be funny because aliens toss Smith's character around like a ragdoll, in a manner that they never toss Jones's character. Agent K might be wrapped up in snakelike vines. He could be about to be eaten. But he is always cool. Good thing, because Agent K's coolness helps to mask the fact that Jones sleepwalks though the movie.

Aside from the talking dog, the real acting standout for me is Boyle who, with her best steely stare and demeanor, shows that there is not too far a leap between the assistant district attorney she plays on ABC's *The Practice* and a control-freak alien from outer space who can eat you alive.

Like Mike

July 3, 2002

Step aside, Harry Potter. Or maybe we should just tell Harry to get off the court. *Like Mike* has enough magic, in real time, with real people, to do for audiences what wizards, muggles, and Hogwarts have done for the witchy crowd. In place of magic wands, potions, and spells, insert the allure and captivation of the NBA, rich ball players, and the wondrous transformation of a cute orphan—and there you have a magic we want to believe in most definitely.

Calvin Cambridge (Bow Wow) is living in an orphanage in Los Angeles, befriended by the cute, bespectacled Murph (Jonathan Lipnicki, the kid from *Jerry Maguire*). He is tormented by the crooked guy who operates the orphanage and some big kids, namely one beefy White dude that everyone at my screening wanted to see beat down very badly. He also has his own kid demons—he's afraid of the dark, afraid of geometry, and afraid of never finding a family that wants to adopt him. But all those fears are pushed to the background when, with the help of a pair of special sneakers, he suddenly has the ability to play "like Mike." Suddenly the four-and-a-half-foot kid finds himself playing for the Los Angeles Knights and showing the NBA what a short dude can do.

But the strength of *Like Mike* is that it is more than just another sports glory story, even though ball players Jason Kidd, David Robinson, and Vince Carter make funny cameo appearances. It replays the admittedly stale orphan saga with enough freshness to pass the smell test. Childhood negotiation of bullying, phobias, responsibility, and dreams give the story more texture and laughs. Finally, it is a human story, without all the violin melodrama, about the challenges of adults as well.

Bow Wow is a solid player here. We already know from music videos that the camera loves him. But he shows here that cinema has a reason to love him as well. I'm glad our children have this movie to see. Who would've thought that hip-hop would produce such a sweet marriage of magic and phi slamma jamma.

Black Star—Vin Diesel in *XXX*

August 9, 2002

If you think that the image of Vin Diesel standing on the rear of a red Corvette as it plunges off a bridge is way over the top, you ain't seen nothing yet. Watch him outspeed an avalanche on a mere snowboard or turn a dirt bike into air transportation.

With these high-wire stunts in mind, Diesel's new flick, *XXX,* as often silly and testosterone-charged as it is, is best appreciated as his big-splash arrival into the realm of action hero. The first baby step came more than two years ago in the underappreciated cult classic *Pitch Black,* a futuristic flick in which he played an outlaw who uses his wits, will, and grit on a far-off planet to survive an attack by scary, predatory creatures.

Since then, in *The Fast and the Furious,* Diesel has made a name for himself as Hollywood's new bad boy. With a street toughness and an authenticity lacking in Arnold, Tom Cruise, or even The Rock (stuck, so far, in ancient Egypt), Diesel is able to bring an urban sensibility to a realm until recently only populated by the likes of James Bond or White mercenaries.

Along with his New York attitude comes his deep, commanding voice; a wiry, muscular body that translates to pumped on the big screen; a cute shaved head; and biracial looks that make him an action hero for a global era. He is part of no particular place and, at the same time, able to go anywhere and be anything, especially in Hollywood.

But while his presence might bring a new flava to the action flick, it does not change the nature of the flick, or its obvious appeal to teenage boys. *XXX* takes the stunts, gadgets, guns, explosions, jingoism, and freaky women of the genre and synthesizes them through an aesthetic more closely associated with rock music videos, '70s chic, and fashion-conscious anarchists.

Diesel plays Xander Cage, an extreme-sports athlete coerced by the government into going undercover to nab a ring of car smugglers who, he discovers, are also planning to foment worldwide anarchy through the use of a bioterrorist attack. The action shifts from California to Colombia to Prague, which must be the new favorite place of movie producers. Must be the centuries-old architecture spared by Hitler in World War II and all the people who look, in films anyway, like a mixture of punk, goth, and vampire.

Diesel melts into the scenery here easily. As in *The Fast and the Furious,* he exists in an almost totally White environment. With the exception of rapper Eve, who plays someone vaguely connected with him, another brown woman who seems to be mute and slithers into his bed like a snake, and Samuel L. Jackson, who plays the NSA agent in charge of the operation, Cage's world, including his main love interest, is pretty vanilla. And so the movie makes Diesel pretty vanilla, too. Jackson, who couldn't be expected to do much with the pro forma dialogue given, does serve in the film as someone who really sees and believes in Cage (and, we might imagine, is able to see in him, in a way that only we can, that "that boy got some Black in him").

In this, our season of fantasy entertainment, *XXX* is loaded with action, craziness, some corniness, and pathetic attempts at being meaningful. (At a key moment of heroism, Cage floats from a huge American flag parachute.) But, really, *XXX* is just as entertaining, and maybe even more so, than most of the James Bond flicks I have endured in misery or perplexity since girlhood. For the right crowd, *XXX* will be tight.

The Adventures of Pluto Nash

August 16, 2002

The good news is that Eddie Murphy is back. He's back with all that swagger, gun-brandishing, and wannabe mack-daddy vibe that made him a favorite draw back in the days of *Beverly Hills Cop, Coming to America,* and *Boomerang.* I'm not a huge Murphy fan and I'd almost forgotten how much he can shine like a piece of pretty, polished mahogany. After sitting through the misery of *Showtime* and the various Nutty Professor and Dr. Dolittle projects, I'd forgotten that there is a real leading man underneath all those parrot feathers and layers of fake fat.

Here, Murphy plays Nash, a Black man who apparently grew up on the moon. (If for nothing else, you gotta love *Pluto Nash* for this brother-in-outer-space thing. We be in the future, too!) A former convicted smuggler, Nash has rehabilitated himself and transformed into a successful club owner in a section of the moon called Little America. His Club Pluto is the most happening lunar spot there is until the Mafia tries to force him out of business.

Unfortunately, the club is where the bad news comes in. All that polished Eddie cannot improve the film's script, which needs better jokes. All that polished Eddie also cannot improve the production values. Some of these scenes look like they were shot as an afterthought in someone's backyard. But this film's cheesy scenery and weak humor give it a certain charm. If you consider the B-movie as a likeable, comfortable genre all its own, then you will find plenty to smile at in this movie.

Honestly, I will take *Pluto Nash* over *Austin Powers* any day. Pick the corniness you like. Pick the humor that best suits you. I'll take mine with a Black leading man and lady, a big red gun, and a wacky plot. I suppose Warner Brothers, the studio releasing *Pluto Nash,* didn't have as much faith in their film since they did not make it available for a press screening and reviews in Washington, D.C. Most of the films released this summer have been made for teenagers and *Pluto Nash* is no different. But even *XXX* and *Blue Crush* were screened for critics.

We all go to films for different reasons. But, very often, our reasons involve escape, fantasy, and comedy. *Pluto Nash* succeeds on the first and second score. It falls flat on its face on the third. It could be that Hollywood is only comfortable with Murphy if he is making comedy and if they can laugh at him. I'm looking at him in a different way and I am happy not to see him be a buffoon. *Pluto Nash* is the kind of offbeat, silly action film that creates a new possibility for a Black hero on-screen. I think I will buy the video. I think I will like to have in my collection this rendering of a Black man on the moon.

Undisputed

August 23, 2002

A boxer played by Ving Rhames in the new film *Undisputed* hits home when he describes all boxers as gladiators, and not athletes. An athlete plays games but no boxer plays boxing, he says.

The same could be said for a boxing film. A real boxing flick, like last year's *Ali,* makes its fighters gladiators with hearts as well as muscle. It is visceral outside the ring, as well as inside of it. By the time the final bell has sounded, we've seen and felt something about a human struggle, too. While *Undisputed* has great fight scenes between two convicted felons, played by the muscular Wesley Snipes and Rhames, much of what occurs outside the ring only plays at being human.

All of which is hard to fathom because *Undisputed* has the additional "advantage" of being set in a prison, which certainly is one of the more visceral environments on Earth. The story is that Monroe Hutchens (Snipes), a serious former contender on the outside, is undefeated boxing champ at California's maximum-security prison Sweetwater. But when the arrogant heavyweight champion of the world, James "Iceman" Chambers (Rhames), is convicted of rape and sent to Sweetwater, the two men find themselves on track for a world-class boxing match—inside the prison.

All action leading up to the big bout is handled in a choppy pastiche of styles, one of which you might call "*Oz* Light." Instead of the brooding, danger-tinged mood set up by better episodes of the television drama, *Undisputed* has a cool distant quality, as if we are supposed to look at its scenes, instead of be inside them. Aside from the fight scenes, with punches that sound like explosions, there is little realness here.

***Barbershop*'s Unkindest Cut**

September 13, 2002

It was easy for me to see and understand both sides of the *Barbershop* controversy. As a journalist, I framed the controversy as one over free speech versus a dire need in the African-American community for defense against the daily onslaught of media that denigrates our existence, struggles, and victories.

I don't think Jesse Jackson and Al Sharpton were wrong, self-serving, or promoting the protection of "sacred cows" when they publicly denounced a scene in the film that belittled Rosa Parks, the Rev. Martin Luther King, the idea of reparations, and police beating victim Rodney King. The statements in the film are made not by one of the regular misguided young men who frequent the barbershop. Rather, it is made by the shop's wise elder statesman, the one who shows the others how to properly shave a customer, the one who contains the history of the shop and neighborhood. Sure, he is rebuffed after he makes his comments, but he is rebuffed by younger men who the film tells us do not have the credibility to really refute what the old wise man is saying.

Film is powerful, and the filmmakers made the intentional decision to include these comments, which I personally did not find funny, and thought were not helpful to anyone struggling for our liberation as Black people. Not only did the filmmakers have the power to disseminate their ideas through the film, promoters of the film made a calculated decision to use these comments to promote the film, spilling the message even to those who did not see the film, and providing comfort to those in the larger community who hold racist ideas. I realized that such a marketing strategy was successful when I saw two middle-aged White critics praising the film because it allowed them to be voyeurs into an inner sanctum of the Black community that they couldn't usually access. I realized that Whites heard the talk coming from this barbershop, and in particular from this wise old barber, as the real talk that real Black people talk when out of the earshot of Whites.

If we are not to be passive consumers of culture, we all have a right to raise our voices about those items of mass culture we find offensive or dangerous. Where Jackson and his crew went wrong was in the demand that the scene be altered or deleted from the film. Dissenters have a right to freedom of speech but so do the filmmakers. We should not be promoting censorship as a remedy to ideas we don't like. We have to use the same media and all forms of media to present alternative views. Raising the controversy was good enough. It got folks to talking and thinking about issues.

It was personally helpful to me as a film critic that the controversy occurred just before the airing of *The Rise and Fall of Jim Crow* on PBS. Documenting the violence and murders that routinely fell upon African-Americans until the midst of the civil rights movement, it was a refresher course for me in how much King, Parks, and others sacrificed. No, they may not have been perfect people. But they put their lives on the line for us. Black men and women were routinely mutilated and lynched for doing far less than what they did. Parks did more than "just [sit] her Black ass down." Can't we, their children, do more, do something else, other than spit on them?

Snipes

September 20, 2002

The new crime thriller *Snipes* is a case study in how so much of hip-hop suffers from bipolar disorder, a sort of manic depression. Either the mood is high, everybody is going to get paid, and is boasting about what ice or cheese or panties are coming their way, or the mood gets down real low, into the realm of dealing drugs, cappin' somebody, or some other nastiness.

The good thing I can say about *Snipes* is that it at least shows why the manic depression exists. It reminds us how, for so many aspiring artists, there is a thin line between the two worlds, and how, for so many young brothers in particular, few options present themselves other than the very high and very low.

But to get to what the film has to offer, you have to survive a story of steadily diminishing returns. The setting is Philadelphia, which to us illadelphians is always a good thing. There is Erik (Sam Jones III), who has decided to blow off his classes at Overbrook High and spend his nights "sniping," putting up those promotional posters you see wrapped around poles, fences, on abandoned buildings, or any available surface. He is promoting a new hip-hop artist named Prolifik (Nelly) and, at the same time, trying to help his buddy Malik finish a demo tape. A late-night session at a "borrowed" studio leads the two young men deeper into the rap game than they ever expected to be when they discover a corpse. From then on, *Snipes* becomes a whodunit that Erik tries to solve in order to save his own life.

There is an interesting plot here that will keep you wondering what will happen next and to whom. And for a low-budget flick, the production values and direction aren't bad. But the development of Erik, Prolifik, and the others as real characters, and not just placeholders in the plot, is what's missing here. Forget all the shoot-'em-up, the thug atmosphere, the crazy White guy (there's always one). If the film and dialogue does not take the time to develop its characters as real people—the high school dropout, the record company buppie who is suddenly packing a gun, even the crazy White guy—it is very difficult to believe much of what is going on. We start watching the movie, as opposed to being inside of it.

And, no doubt, what we need in a hip-hop movie, even more than a big star like Nelly (he's as good as the movie will let him be, and looks great on-screen), is that tight connection between the audience and what's happening on-screen. Otherwise, it seems kind of fake. It's just not keeping it real.

OPM—*The Four Feathers*

September 20, 2002

Here I was, all prepared to hate *The Four Feathers.* I had no doubt that the subject of brutal English colonization of the Sudan, combined with yet-another-story-of-dashing-pale-Brits, combined with any peek at a noble savage, would be enough to make me hurl my popcorn and Raisinets.

But I was wrong. In the hands of director Shekhar Kapur (*The Bandit Queen*), whose homeland, India, certainly knows a thing or two about English colonization, *The Four Feathers* has both a depth and epic scale that many movies only fake. The latest adaptation of the 1902 novel by A. E. W. Mason, it is multidimensional, treats African peoples and cultures with respect, and tackles big ideas and questions such as what it means to be a soldier, to be brave or a coward, to be loyal or a traitor. And certainly, these are ideas that resonate now, one hundred years later, in our own country, the last remaining world empire.

The Four Feathers is set in the era of the far-flung British Empire when young privileged sons at an English military academy are called to fight in the Sudan. But this call to war sets into motion a crisis for Harry Faversham (Heath Ledger), who is the son of a decorated military officer and the fiancé of Ethne Eustace (Kate Hudson), whose father died in battle. Unwilling to fight for a cause he questions, Harry resigns from his regiment, bringing disgrace upon himself and the delivery of four feathers, each symbolizing cowardice, from his friends and fiancée. His desire to prove them wrong and his desire to fight for his friends (even though these points are not well explained in the film) takes him into the heart of the battle he first tried to avoid, and to the limits of self-sacrifice.

Along the way, he is rescued and assisted by Abou Fatma (Djimon Hounsou), a sort of wandering warrior whose ferocity, heart, and wisdom is the glue that holds this story together. For me, Abou is more fierce than noble in the derogatory sense. He does not cower, buck his eyes, or look with reverence upon Whites. He sizes up Harry as a man and nothing more or less, even though in the desert and with no shaving Harry does start to get that White Jesus look. (Somebody look that up, I'm sure Ledger has played Jesus.)

Abou's balance in temper permeates the entire sense of the film. There are moments when the relationship between the two men starts to get tired—I mean how many times can a White man go off track and how many times can a Black man save him? Similarly, the story could have given us a little more reason to believe that Harry would hurl himself into war and then, repeatedly, arrive at just the precise moment to save his friends. Ultimately, the film walks a fine line, keeping Harry's courage just on this side of believable.

Aside from these shortcomings, *The Four Feathers* is worth seeing, even if for Hounsou alone. These Brits aren't all unbelievably dashing. They may think they are but then they quickly learn the limits of human empire.

LaLee's Kin: The Legacy of Cotton

September 26, 2002

In much of today's media, poverty is depicted as a fast-running spigot of misery—fallen-down neighborhoods, drugs, out-of-control children, and easy murder. But poverty in the Mississippi Delta, as depicted in *LaLee's Kin: The Legacy of Cotton* (repeating on HBO), is like a slow drip that has been dripping for decades, even centuries.

By tying together the legacy of slavery and sharecropping with inferior education, illiteracy, and poverty, the filmmakers—Susan Frömke, Deborah Dickson, and Albert Maysles—make the case that dire community conditions faced today are a result of the past as well as the present. They remind us that not all slavery ended with the signing of the Emancipation Proclamation. Consider *LaLee's Kin* as Film Exhibit A in the argument favoring reparations.

I'm sure there will be some who find LaLee Wallace's world—her excitement over a better trailer home, the lack of running water, her aimless adult children, and the struggle for survival amid tumbledown surroundings—shameful or clichéd. Indeed, as Wallace recounts the large numbers of family children born, starting with her great-grandmother and down to the present, you could also ask yourself if the family's legacy was really created by too little family planning and too many men who left their children. But can it be that illiteracy and poverty also played a part in these domestic dramas?

Also, ever since George C. Wolfe's *The Colored Museum,* which satirized sorrowful matriarch dramas, and with the rise of a hip-hop aesthetic that renders non-youth-oriented and non-urban-oriented narratives as irrelevant, stories like this one have become unfashionable. But because *LaLee's Kin* (which received an Oscar nomination) is a documentary, it is less concerned with fashion and more concerned with reality, and covers that reality with scenes that are inspiring, and moving.

The documentary shifts between two primary locations: the trailer where Wallace lives with many of her grandchildren and great-grandchildren, and the local public schools, part of the West Tallahatchie School District, where student performance is so low that the state is threatening to take over. Links are made between the two spaces through interviews and a bright-yellow school bus. Wallace's great-grandmother, grandmother, and mother all worked in the cotton fields, received little education, and had large numbers of children. Cotton was king and picking cotton was the only way that area people made "a living."

At the school, an administrator explains how, not too long ago, the school year didn't even start for Black children in the area until the final cotton crop was picked during the fall. "It has become ingrained that getting an education is not important," says the district superintendent, Reggie Barnes. Educators are still fighting to change that mind-set. At the same time, they have the daunting task of educating children of the illiterate, if the cycle of poor education and poverty is to end.

There is also some hope presented here, and much of it involves a decision to leave the impoverished Delta. Even if illiterate parents are able to push their children to learn, it may be necessary for younger generations to leave in order to make best use of their diplomas and desire for achievement.

The Rise and Fall of Jim Crow

October 1, 2002

The new documentary series *The Rise and Fall of Jim Crow,* airing on PBS this month, seems tailor-made for these times of war, violence, and rhetoric. In four taut, often harrowing segments, the producers correctly refer to the one hundred years between the Emancipation Proclamation and the thick of the civil rights movement as a time of "domestic terror" for African-Americans, especially in the South. Analogies between America's social reality and South African apartheid are as clear as day. Comparisons some Blacks made between Adolf Hitler and certain rabid Southern politicians are clearly not hyperbole.

Starting with the betrayal of Blacks after the Civil War, and ending with the birth of the modern civil rights movement, *The Rise and Fall of Jim Crow* tells a story that your whole family should see. Even those of us who think we know do not recall it all. We might not remember that the term Jim Crow derived from a derogatory minstrel characterization of a dancing darkie.

We might have a vague notion about disenfranchisement during the era of post-Reconstruction in the South but we might not remember that this frightful era was fully supported by the U.S. government. We might remember some contributions of Booker T. Washington but not remember that his famous or infamous Atlanta Compromise speech was a signal to some Whites that their system of social apartheid was supported by a Black leader. We might know in some way that horror of lynching but not remember the story of Mary Turner, a woman nine months pregnant who was tortured, burned, and lynched before her unborn fetus was cut from her body and crushed.

Obviously, this subject matter is not for the faint of heart, but the producers, Richard Wormser, Bill Jersey, and Sam Pollard, also make the story of Jim Crow one of hope. Early heroes include educator Charlotte Hawkins Brown, who saw the need to provide education in impoverished Southern communities; W. E. B. DuBois, who used his pen and piercing intellect to wage war against the dehumanization of an entire people; and Ned Cobb, a farm owner who fought for better conditions for exploited Southern sharecroppers.

The battlefronts were many, including employment, the criminal (in)justice system, education, public accommodations, and the simple right over your own body and life. The four episodes also make very clear the overarching power of news organizations and institutions of popular culture—which we still do not control even in the post-civil rights era—to shape not only our present but also our future. Time and time again, all four episodes illustrate how lynching and race riots—including the infamous burning down of the Greenwood section of Tulsa—were precipitated by an erroneous and inflammatory news article or cultural presentation that depicted Black men as murderers or rapists.

Though this series ends with the landmark Supreme Court decision in *Brown vs. the Board of Education*, it also makes clear that the power over information and culture has shaped Black history as much as politics, the legal system, or the educational system. This is a tour de force of history that reaches us here in the present.

20

Sanaa Rules, Drumline Beats, Denzel Directs

Brown Sugar

October 11, 2002

If you can imagine that making a good film is a little like making a hearty stew, then think of *Brown Sugar* as enough good acting, writing, and direction to make you feel full and warm. Following the relationship of hip-hop writer Sidney (Sanaa Lathan) and hip-hop producer Dre (Taye Diggs), *Brown Sugar* uses the music passion shared by both to thicken this romance that, once again, has a Black woman checking her watch and patting her foot. (Oh Lawd! How Long? Will Sanaa Ever Get Her Man?)

Lathan, our first true Black romantic heroine (aside from Tisha Campbell in *Sprung*), is the glue that holds this energetic production together. True, she doesn't muster any type of New York accent, but she does portray a sensitive, creative soul. Her work, combined with fine contributions by Diggs and the rest of the cast, keeps *Brown Sugar* from becoming the next predictable hip-hop romance. There were the adolescent beginnings (*The Wood*). And then the heavy drama or marriage (*The Best Man, The Brothers, Two Can Play That Game*). Now there is something else—a film that renders its men and women with more depth and empathy.

Writer Michael Elliot (*Like Mike* and *Carmen: A Hip Hopera*—oops), along with director Rick Famuyiwa (*The Wood*), frames this film as a love story from Generations X and Y. It starts out with a series of interviews with hip-hop artists who tell when they first fell in love with hip-hop. Then it flashes back to Sidney and Dre as children growing up in the Bronx, where hip-hop was born.

As grown-ups, Sid and Dre have continued their friendship. Dre has somebody, in fact, a woman named Reese (Nicole Ari Parker) whom he has decided to marry after dating for a few months. But poor Sidney can't seem to find anybody whom she really vibes with—except for Dre, of course. But Dre is, as Biz Markie said, just a friend.

Likewise, Sid is Dre's pal. He even, to her momentary shock, affectionately refers to her as his "dog." Eventually they both must decide whether it is better to be married to a best friend or to someone else who holds a different type of attraction.

There are a lot of surprises here, including more cameos by more rappers than ever seen before. Did they film *Brown Sugar* after The Source Awards? Mos Def is irresistible in the role of an emerging hip-hop artist. Queen Latifah adds to what is already a script full of irreverent observation and funny lines. I'm not sold on Taye Diggs as a leading man, especially opposite Lathan, but he does have the capacity, like Lathan, to infuse his role with an emotional complexity. He's in the big mix here, a mix with enough substance, love, and flava.

Knockaround Guys

October 11, 2002

The most interesting thing about *Knockaround Guys* is that it serves as a snapshot of Vin Diesel before his transformation into a high–octane action hero. Made a few years ago and now released to cash in on Diesel's success with *XXX*, consider it the last time in a while that you might see Diesel without the accoutrements of big stunts, explosions, and fawning women. Enjoy watching the king in waiting. Watch him work out with a crowbar on some unsuspecting gambling machines. Check out his precision at beating the crap out of some small-town bully in Montana. Note how fierce he looks firing two guns at once. See? This guy will be (is) a star.

Paid in Full

October 20, 2002

There is certainly no shortage of films focused on the culture of drugs and drug-dealing in the Black community. Blossoming as a genre with *Superfly* in 1972, and continuing with the likes of more recent works such as *New Jack City* and *Training Day*, drug-dealer films are the African-American contribution to the gangster cinema that Americans, particularly men, love to love. How many brothers do you know who will watch and rewatch every rerun of *The Godfather?*

With this brief history in mind, the new film *Paid in Full*, first screened at the

Urbanworld Film Festival in August, might unfairly be put into the category of been there, done that. And that dismissal would be too bad. What gives *Paid in Full* a different twist is the extent to which it shifts its focus from tough-guy posturing and violence chic to a more human and gritty realm. If it feels more real, maybe that is because it is based on the real-life story of 1980s Harlem drug dealers A. Z., Alpo, and the late Richard Porter. As it follows one man's transformation, from a clerk at a dry-cleaning store to a major drug lord, it follows a human being forced to make choices that will impact his life forever.

Wood Harris, the talented actor who portrays a Baltimore drug kingpin on HBO's *The Wire,* is also an unlikely and un-Hollywood face of a drug dealer in this film. In the role of Ace, he is not slick, ruthless, or cruel. He almost falls into the trade. All the while, it seems as if he would rather be doing something else if life had dealt him a different hand. Harris's portrayal reminds me of the Biggie rhyme that says that many young Black men during the 1980s felt they had only two ways to escape the ravages of their hood—either by playing basketball or selling drugs.

In a subtle manner, *Paid in Full* depicts the devastation of many Black communities as drugs, especially crack, flowed freely. But the story is ultimately one that focuses on relationships within families and between friends, and the fragility of those relationships. Mekhi Phifer has some electric moments here as Mitch, Ace's longtime friend. Rapper Cam'ron also steps up remarkably well in his feature film debut.

Charles Stone III (of "Wassup" beer commercial fame) is also making his big debut as a film director. In his hands, *Paid in Full* benefits from an imaginative re-creation of '80s cultural energy—hip-hop as an emerging force and gilded '80s fashion—Kangol hats, big gold chains, watches, door-knocker earrings, and fur coats. There is a very energetic, stylized scene at the beginning and end of this film that looks like a segment of a music video. On a street corner, outside a bar or neighborhood hangout, everyone is ghetto fabulous. The women look a little slutty. A lot of cash is being flashed. There are expensive cars and guns. It is the glamour of the high life, "big balling," and gangsterism of our imagination. In a sincere but uneven effort, *Paid in Full* reminds us of the difference between film imagination and reality.

I Spy

November 1, 2002

Move over Beavis and Butthead, Kenan and Kel, and Homer and Bart Simpson. The duo in *I Spy* wins hands down in the realm of the ridiculous and the embarrassing. This distinction may not be a good one, especially to those of us who squirm in the face of too much stupidity. But for about ninety minutes, it makes for a slow-starting but fairly entertaining movie, especially if you can stand Eddie Murphy playing another over-the-top fool.

8 Mile

November 8, 2002

For his big film debut, rapper Eminem is given the full rust-belt treatment, or as much rust and funk as his story can stand. The world of *8 Mile,* the area where Eminem grew up, which separates Black Detroit from the White suburbs, is a world of abandoned buildings, trailer parks, has-been businesses with faded signs, and folks steered hard into dead ends. We first see Eminem in a nasty public restroom at a spot where local rap battles are staged, perfectly comfortable in his ambient filth, trying to gather his nerve among Black rappers who don't respect him. If we didn't know it, we know it now: Eminem is real. Eminem is hard. Eminem has a lot of heart.

It is from this spot and premise that *8 Mile* creates a stage for Eminem as both a rapper and actor and is only somewhat successful. The biggest star here is the film's relaxed and unexpected humor, and the cinema of funkiness created by director Curtis Hanson (*The Wonder Boys, L.A. Confidential*) along with cinematographer Rodrigo Prieto. (Kim Basinger is also excellent in the role of Eminem's broke-down trailer mom.) Surrounded by all this grit, Eminem need only play himself, which is not such a hard task. And he does that just fine. In the role of Jimmy Smith Jr. (aka B-Rabbit or Rabbit), he is a perfectly likeable screen presence but is not an actor who emits a lot of emotion. As a matter of fact, he always has pretty much the same expression, whether in a beatdown, in his big rap moment, or in the most uncomfortable sex scene every filmed. Eminem as an actor is kind of like one of those paintings in *Scooby-Doo* where the face stays the same and only his big blue eyes move or fill with expression.

His performance here as a rapper will be judged based on whether or not the viewer is a big Eminem fan and, even then, big fans will have to admit that at no point does he really wreck the mic. This isn't some hip-hop version of *Purple Rain* (which also had a funkiness about it in a sleazy Prince sort of way), which also served as a concert and distinct musical moment. *8 Mile* is only a distinct hip-hop moment for the story it tells, not for the performances it contains. Eminem's big moment of triumph on the mic is not a clear or clean victory. Verbal skills aren't so much at stake at his rap battle as is the turf of credibility and toughness—and, as previously mentioned, the filmmakers have already, predictably, given the star, Eminem, a leg up in that category.

In the rap world of *8 Mile,* Enimen wears his White skin like a scarlet letter. B-Rabbit is forced to be the minority and pull himself up by his bootstraps. And he is allowed to. Less believable are some of the street scenes, including a couple of fights and a very hokey verbal street battle at the factory where he works during the day. In *8 Mile,* Blacks make an issue of race. B-Rabbit never does, and neither do the trailer park White people he comes from. How real is that?

Standing in the Shadows of Motown

November 15, 2002

How do you recapture a musical moment from the past? How do you let it breathe and walk in the present? These are some of the challenges tackled with finesse by the makers of *Standing in the Shadows of Motown,* an energetic and human documentary about the Funk Brothers, musicians who played on all of the hits from Motown's Detroit era—and collectively played on more number-one hits than any other group in history—but are unknown by name to most of the public.

The fact that so many musical artists, Black artists in particular, have not been given their due by the music-industry is a fact. And we're accustomed to hearing these stories in various somber tones of gray and blue. But director Paul Justman, an early pioneer in the music-video scene, scores a serious thumbs up here with his decision to make *Standing in the Shadows of Motown* a celebration and not a funerary dirge. Footage from a joyous Funk Brothers reunion in Detroit is interfused with poignant and funny interviews (did you hear the one about the bassist and the rancid pig feet?), dramatic renactments, vintage footage, still photographs, testimonials from admiring artists, and moments that place these musicians back at the scene of their greatest triumphs: Studio A, in the basement of Hitsville USA, where Motown's founder, Berry Gordy, changed music history.

The story is bitter and sweet. During the time of Motown's biggest hits, these artists, including Richard "Pistol" Allen, Jack Anderson, Bob Babbitt, William "Benny" Benjamin, Eddie "Bongo" Brown, Johnny Griffith, Joe Hunter, James Jamerson, Uriel Jones, Joe Messina, Earl Van Dyke, Robert White, and Eddie Willis, still struggled and scraped as artists, playing all the extra gigs they could find to feed their families. An especially moving story is told of Robert White, who created the famous intro guitar lick for *My Girl*. Years later, on hearing the song in a restaurant, he almost told the waiter that the guitarist playing was, indeed, him. But then he stopped suddenly, embarrassed that the waiter would think he was just an old fool.

And the sweetness cannot be denied. Just watch the musicians, those surviving all gray with age, get down in an impromptu jam. Watch them back up today's stars like Gerald Levert, Meshell Ndegeocello, Chaka Khan, and Montell Jordan on hits like "Ain't No Mountain," "Reach Out I'll Be There," and "Shotgun." The biggest scream of these performances includes Bootsy Collins, in a huge purple top hat, gold tights, and gold boots, singing "Do You Love Me?" Watch their easy laughter at precious history. Depending on your age, these guys will remind you of your pops or pop-pop, and how previous generations expressed themselves musically and verbally without disrespecting themselves or the people around them. These musicians may have stood in the shadows but they stood as creators and artists and men.

Friday After Next–Who You Callin' a Ho?

November 16, 2002

Oh no they didn't.

It is one thing to sit through another inane TV commercial for the latest movie in the *Friday* series. (You know the drill by now: Comedian John Witherspoon in another toilet scene; some broke-down chick in heat; Ice Cube, momentarily grossed out, saying "ill!") But it is quite another thing for the film's promoters to superimpose the word "Ho!" over pictures of three young Black women on national television.

Oh sure. They are trying to be cute.

Friday After Next, which looks to be very funny, has a holiday theme. The "Ho! Ho! Ho!" is supposed to be some witty double entendre that both references the sound of Santa and engages in ghetto speak and terminology for women. Well, there is nothing jolly or playful about the result. Imagine watching *Monday Night Football*, consistently one of the highest-rated shows in the country, and seeing, during a commercial break, these young women labeled this way. Imagine that it is the night before the national elections, that many children do not have school the next day and are being allowed to stay up late and watch the game. Imagine that maybe many of the children interested in watching the game are young Black males, who get to see, once again, Black women insulted and denigrated. And it is all part of a joke told nationally to a large audience of men . . . .

Oh, am I supposed to laugh?

The insult is only aggravated, of course, by the fact that this is a "Black" film with all the appearances of being totally created and promoted by Black people. And the insult is aggravated by the fact that this is another Ice Cube movie that promotes itself by insulting the Black community. Much of the controversy about the scene in *Barbershop* failed to mention the fact that the same scene was actually used to promote the film. The promoters, at least, were fully aware of the scene's controversial nature, and the power of the scene to pique the interest of filmgoers, particularly Whites. In the process, they spilled the film's ridicule of the Rev. Martin Luther King Jr., Rosa Parks, the reparations movement, O. J., and Rodney King to those who did not even see the film, and provided comfort to those in the larger community who hold racist ideas. I realized that such a marketing strategy was successful when I saw two middle-aged White critics praising the film because it allowed them to be voyeurs into an inner sanctum of the Black community that they did not usually access.

I realized that Whites heard the talk coming from this barbershop, and in particular from a wise old barber, as the real talk that real Black people talk when out of the earshot of Whites. There is a trailer for *Friday After Next* on the film's official Web site that does not include the insulting segment. But, for some reason, this is not the trailer being shown right now on national television. Repeated calls to New Line Cinema were not returned.

Oh, it's so entertaining.

The promotion of this newest movie, though handled by New Line Cinema as opposed to MGM for *Barbershop,* provides the same sense of Black voice: that this is a Black film made by Black men, which can take the liberty of calling Black women "hos" because it is being said by "us" about "us." Obviously, then, it must be okay. Well, it's not okay. Even cable music video stations and many radio stations force artists to edit out words like "ho" and "bitch." Why is this okay for national broadcast television? The filmmakers may have the bigger voice on the big and little screen. But Black women also have a right to speak truth to this kind of media power, and to raise our voices about, once again, being called out of our name.

Rabbit-Proof Fence

November 29, 2002

The wiry fence that traverses thousands of miles in Australia serves as a mighty metaphor in *Rabbit-Proof Fence,* a powerful film that tells the story of how, from

1900 to 1970, the White Australian government kidnapped young Aborigine girls and trained them to be domestics for Whites. The brutality, racism, and genocidal agenda of the British-controlled government sits on one side of our metaphorical fence, while the Black natives of the island, along with their basic human rights, certainly sit on the other.

The girls taken were called "half-caste" because one of their parents, usually the father, was White. There is no explanation of how the initial relationships were sparked but none of the Black women whose children were taken had a White husband standing at her side. The government reserved the right to determine if interracial marriages were "legal" and also hoped to engineer the eventual erasure of the Aborigine people by assimilating "half-castes" and continually mixing them with Whites. The Black people of Australia call these kidnapped children, many of whom never saw their mothers again and who are estimated to number in the thousands, the "stolen generations."

Adapted from the book by Doris Pilkington Garimara, Christine Olsen's screenplay gives power to this heinous chapter of history. It focuses on the true story of Molly (played by Everlyn Sampi), her litle sister Daisy (Tiana Sansbury), and her cousin Gracie (Laura Monaghan), who in 1931 were kidnapped from their mothers in Jigalong, a remote Aboriginal community in Western Australia. Driven twelve hundred miles south, a part of the way locked in a cage, the children eventually fled on foot from Moore River Settlement, the government-controlled mission where they were forbidden to use their language and told that they did not have mothers. As the children try to find their way home, *Rabbit-Proof Fence* offers powerful ideas about mother, family, and the defiance of wicked power.

It does not flinch from telling the story: how Aborigines referred to White government officials as "Mr. Devil," the inconsolable grief felt by mothers and grandmothers when their children were snatched away. As the wailing girls are taken away in a police wagon, Molly's silver-haired grandmother beats herself repeatedly in the head with a rock, almost as if to kill herself.

Filmed in the Australian Outback by director Philip Noyce (*The Quiet American, The Bone Collector*), *Rabbit-Proof Fence* has a visual poetry that highlights the links between the awe-inspiring and harsh landscape and the people. As she journeys home, Molly uses her knowledge of the earth and nature to outwit the wise Aborigine tracker, who was forced by Whites to hunt down and return the girls to Moore River Settlement.

African-American audiences, exposed to more stories about our own slavery and less to stories about other people of the African diaspora, will find much to identify with in this story about far-off European colonialism. Just as startling as the story is Samperly's portrayal of a young, clear-eyed Black woman who is certain the world is wrong, that she is right, and that she has the power to fix her world.

Black Star–Taye Diggs in *Equilibrium*

December 6, 2002

There is a coldness and sterility that infuses the violent environment of *Equilibrium,* so much so that it is possible to conclude early on that the filmmakers have failed to give their production a real sense of place and humanity. But then it becomes apparent that we are not dealing with human life and space as we know it.

Set in the near future, *Equilibrium* paints the picture of a society where feelings and enjoyment of the senses are strictly forbidden. The reasoning, if it can be called that, for such laws is that human emotions give rise to war and inhumanity. Taye Diggs arrives on the scene here as an enthusiastic soldier for the state named Brandt. His role, which he plays in a somewhat genial way—I don't know if he can look really menacing—reminds me of the scene in *Outland* (1981) when the final enforcer for the corrupt state is a Black man who straps on his space gear and battles the hero.

Equilibrium is *Minority Report* without all the flash, dazzle, and big budget of Dreamworks, and with a little bit more to say that is relevant. (So that must be why I haven't seen much promotion for it.) Director and writer Kurt Wimmer has given this world gray hues and stone and metal surfaces. Christian Bale is steely perfection in his role as another enforcer of the law. The chiseled edge of his cheekbones matches the hard edge of the production precisely. Like in *The Matrix,* executions are grisly, bloodless, and unseen by the drugged populace. Even if the people did see them, they are programmed not to care. There are a lot of bullets here and each one counts more than in the mindless bullet orgies of 007.

Leguizamo's Latino *Empire*

December 6, 2002

Beginning in the 1980s with his New York stage hit *Mambo Mouth,* and continuing with the 1998 TV special *Freak,* John Leguizamo has built a reputation as a grating and controversial comedic actor who takes a hard look at the complexities of his life, identity, and community. Like Whoopi Goldberg, Lily Tomlin, and perhaps Jerry Seinfeld, Leguizamo's strong suit has been his ability to tell a story in the first person and have us really believe him; to create characters and have us really believe them.

He brings the same strengths to *Empire,* his first real leading role in a feature film, for which he also serves as executive producer. Writer Franc Reyes has produced a script that allows Leguizamo to tell a first-person story of a South Bronx heroin dealer, Victor Rosa, and Rosa's effort to leave the life of hustling. In this role, one that he surely had to find and build for himself, Leguizamo has climbed out of the often embarrassing comedic hole that he has fallen into during the past decade. *Empire* offers Leguizamo a measured opportunity to transform himself into a serious film actor. You have to be a damned good actor to convincingly go from Fox's *Ice Age* to playing a New York City heroin dealer.

Leguizamo carries the film as far as he can. After that, it survives on above-average writing and direction, and good performances by Delilah Cotto, who plays his girlfriend, Carmen, and an around-the-way cast that includes rappers Treach and Fat Joe. *Empire,* like Charles Stone's recent *Paid in Full,* tells the story of drug dealing on a gritty street level that acknowledges how the 1980s spawned a new generation of hustlers and attendant street violence. With Leguizamo at the helm, *Empire* does not suffer the fate of so many of our gangster flicks. Here, the lead character is full of humanity and complexity, and those qualities allow us to accept some of his shortcomings and stupid life decisions.

But we can't accept everything here. *Empire* has a '70s blaxploitation feel to it, with some stock characters, including the standard stock White villains. It also fails to convince us that an otherwise savvy street hustler would totally lose his common sense when it comes to dealing with a slick investment banker. When Victor finds out that Carmen is pregnant, he reevaluates his life and decides that he wants a clean break. He decides to invest with the banker some of the various millions he has stashed in safes around the Bronx and then he decides to invest it all. When things don't go exactly as Victor expected, we are left to wonder why all his street smarts went out the window. Giving the filmmakers the benefit of the doubt, perhaps we might guess that they are offering a subtle message about the insecurity lurking beneath the macho of street hustling, about the thin line between "legal" and "illegal" moneymaking (Enron, anyone?), and how race and class overpower "street cred" in the battle for social and moral legitimacy in this country.

Drumline

December 13, 2002

Drumline is a clean, fun movie you can take your whole family to see. (How often do I get to write those words?) The story centers on a cocky but talented Brooklyn college freshman named Devon (Nick Cannon) given a full marching-band scholarship at a Black college in Atlanta, where we follow his successes, challenges, failures, and budding romance. The acting and sounds are energetic and keep the so-so story moving to its musical finale. Finally, Black college bands—which are a lot more talented than the New York cast of *Stomp!*—get their due. I hope you see *Drumline* in a theater with a better sound system than the one where I screened this movie near Washington, D.C. I assume director Charles Stone III invested in top-quality recording. Without the booming rhythm, watching a college drumline is somewhat underwhelming. The theater should be rocking!

Antwone Fisher

December 19, 2002

In *Antwone Fisher,* Denzel Washington demands as a director what he has always demanded as an actor: that a Black man be rendered on-screen in his full complexity and humanity—and the result is a startling success. His directorial debut is filled with so many quiet horrors, miracles, demons, and angels, with what is blessed and cursed inside us, that it is a cinematic metaphor for our community. So, to the things that Denzel Washington is credited with being—a fine actor, a man who is fine, a family man, and a Black man of some consciousness—add the title of poet.

Based on a true story written by the real-life Antwone Fisher, it follows Fisher (Derek Luke), a young navy recruit with a short temper and a big heart who is forced to see a Navy psychiatrist, Jerome Davenport (Washington). Over time in sessions with the doctor, Fisher gradually peels back layers of accumulated shame, confronting his sense of abandonment, of being from nowhere and from no one. Born to an imprisoned young woman, he was last with his mother when he was two months old, before being sent to an orphanage and then a foster home, where he was emotionally, verbally, and physically abused. His father was shot to death by a girlfriend before he was one year old.

As Fisher remembers and dreams, we see his visions in a series of startling flashbacks. Central to Fisher's experience and his fitful rites of passage is his mistreatment at the hands of Black women—the mother who never came for him, the evil foster mother, another young woman who abused him. But it is the open-hearted love from a female fellow sailor that helps him on the road to healing and home.

Scenes between the two young lovers and between Fisher and Dr. Davenport are greatly benefited by the real-life Fisher's script, which feels like real conversation, real pain, and real moments of unexpected joy and laughter. There are no pat answers to anything. One of the most powerful "conversations" occurs between two people, one of whom never utters a word.

Of course these scenes of introspection also rely on the knockout performance by Luke, a novice actor with a dark berry complexion who cannot be called a diamond in the rough. Honed by this process of working with Washington, he shimmers from deep inside. Washington does his thing, of course, and makes us believe everything he says and does. He draws his young charge into a warm on-screen rapport that is the muscle driving the story forward.

What is apparent to the viewer is not Fisher's rage but the deep pain, sensitivity, and, yes, humanity, that he has retained despite his ordeal. The honesty of this film will grate on the nerves of cynics in need of more edge. There will be those who ignore the pain and ugliness it bares and declare it too sentimental, especially since it talks about Black pain. This film reminds us that the abandoned child doesn't ask, "What was wrong with the people who left me?" Rather, the abandoned child—as many children in our community are—asks, "What was wrong with me?" With these painful questions and answers, Washington offers a heartbreaking and joyous poem.

OPM–*Gangs of New York*

December 20, 2002

The nineteenth-century filthy slums of Lower Manhattan held within them all the seeds of the budding New York City and nation: grisly violence, crime, corruption, racism, and a bitter clawing for survival, all of which is vividly portrayed in *Gangs of New York,* the big-budget Martin Scorsese epic that has been years in the making and handled with kid gloves by Miramax since the September 11 attacks.

Scorsese and his writers could have gone anywhere with this period of the Civil War leading up to the city's bloody draft riots of 1863, in which dozens of Black people were beaten to death, lynched, or burned alive. Taking the title and legends of Herbert Asbury's 1928 cult classic book, they have boiled the era down to a barbaric street struggle among White ethnic gangs and between two men. William

Cutting, also known in the story as Bill the Butcher (Daniel Day-Lewis), lords over the Five Points area of Lower Manhattan with his "Nativist" or ironically called "Native American" gang, which abhors the starving Irish arriving by the droves. At the heart of the Five Points, where a brutal battle takes place between the Nativists and Irish, the Butcher kills a priest and then, years later, faces the vengeance of the priest's son, Amsterdam Vallon (Leonardo DeCaprio).

As the Irish eke out a living, they and the Nativists hate with a passion the "niggers," most especially the idea that so many of them have been called to fight and die in "Mr. Lincoln's war" that will free the "niggers." As depicted here, Northern unity for the war effort is a myth. There is much support for the Confederacy, especially since the specter of more free Blacks in the city means more competition for the menial jobs fought for by the newly arriving Irish.

The larger racial dimensions of this era's struggle, however, is held at the periphery of this story. One Black man makes a regular on-camera appearance as, for some historically questionable reason, part of Amsterdam's Irish crew. Only in passing and marginally do the writers and director allow us to fully grasp the collective hatred by Whites toward the Black population. This is not a story about Black history, pain, or inclusion in the building of the United States. This is Scorsese's story and, like some of his past celebrated films such as *Taxi Driver* and *Raging Bull,* it serves up the underworld and poor Whites as the salt and builders of America. Their racism, though depicted as virile and ignorant, is ultimately depicted as less important than their own fight for survival and the supposed quest to be an American.

DeCaprio gets top billing here, but because he plays the role of a man who has come through hell still with some morality, his character and performance cannot compare in intensity with that of the Butcher, who is infused with an animated evil by Day-Lewis. The portrayal of twisted souls has been popular at awards time in recent years and, no doubt, Day-Lewis will continue to gather nominations in the coming months.

As bodies drop in Lower Manhattan, there is something honest and prescient in the bloodletting and barbarism of this film—hence, no doubt, the kid-glove treatment. For some of us, it will be a reminder of the karma of violence and hatred. *Gangs of New York* may not be for the fainthearted or for those still needing to heal after September 11. For everyone else, it provides another type of understanding of the bedrock underlying our country and our times.

21

Who's Zoomin' Who?

Interview—Spike Lee to Black Audiences: "Grow Up!"

January 10, 2003

Iverem: *25th Hour* felt to me as much a meditation on New York as a story surrounding one man. Was it that for you? And if so, how much of that comes from Berlioff's novel and script? How much of it is your vision as a director?

Lee: The script came from David Berlioff's fine novel, which was written before 9/11. I added the references to 9/11. So we're basically taking on Monty's last hours of freedom in a post-9/11 city.

Iverem: How did you get involved in this project?

Lee: I was sent the script. Berlioff has an agent and he sent me the script and I was drawn by the writing and by the characters. You don't see a script like that very often. I don't read a lot of scripts. You know, I mostly write my own stuff. What I do get sent is usually terrible. . . . I'm not going to direct a script if I can't be comfortable with it. It has to be something within my own sensibilities, and that I can personalize.

Iverem: Did it feel odd to approach New York City from outside the African-American culture for a story like this? I see this as being different from *Son of Sam,* which was particular to an historical event, person, crime spree.

Lee: No. I'm a New Yorker and New York is a diverse city and that diversity has been in my films since way back in *Do the Right Thing. Son of Sam* focused a lot on Italians living in the Bronx.

Iverem: How do your projects happen now?

Lee: It really happened the same way they always happen. You have a script and you try to get money for it.

Iverem: Following up on that, is that process harder or easier for you now? People know who you are.

Lee: It depends on how much money I am trying to get. *Bamboozled* was a very difficult film to try to get made because of the subject matter. We wound up at New Line because no one else was interested. Mike Deluca was very instrumental in getting that film made. *25th Hour* was a lot easier to make. It cost $15 million but, remember, the average Hollywood film is costing $50 million so there is a definite difference there. . . .

Iverem: I've always thought of you as a maverick Black independent filmmaker who didn't care about big budgets, who wore as a sort of breastplate of honor that you do not need a big budget. But is Hollywood's budget disparity beginning to bother you?

Lee: It depends on what you're trying to do. This film should not have cost more than $15 million, but there are two epics I want to make that I have not been able to get funding for—at least $75 million—one on Jackie Robinson and one on Joe Louis. One, they think baseball films don't make a lot of money and that Black baseball films definitely do not make a lot of money. But Jackie Robinson marked a seminal moment in American history. Hollywood still has a limited viewpoint on the type of Black films they'll make. Gangster, hip-hop, shoot-'em-up, or low-brow comedy. Recently there have been two films that have broken that mold—*Drumline* and *Antwone Fisher*—but, for the most part, these are exceptions. It's hard to get the studios to think outside of those ghettos. And the African-American audience has to support films that are outside of those boxes.

Iverem: But the African-American audience is no different from the larger one. It goes to the movies for entertainment. We want to laugh.

Lee: Yeah. We want to laugh but if that's all we want to do then we can't be complaining all the time—look at these movies Hollywood is putting out—when films are made outside of these ghettos and we don't support them. Look at *Antwone Fisher.* It did okay but it should have done much better. Black people should have come out and supported that film.

Iverem: But *Antwone Fisher* did not open initially in very many theaters. Here in the Washington, D.C., area, a women told me that she and her husband went to see the film at a theater where it shared a screen with *Lord of the Rings,* which also had three other screens in the same theater. So *Antwone Fisher* had only three screenings the whole day. At the show she attended, there was a line of Black people that stretched around the corner and most of them could not get in because that show was sold out. So the audience isn't always to blame.

Lee: I think that's an isolated case. . . . When a film gets a limited release you gotta drive the extra two miles to see it. We're trying to do films outside the regular thing and the audience doesn't come. . . . I was on Tom Joyner yesterday and a friend called me from Atlanta. He said, I heard you on the radio and it made me think, Why did I go to see *Chicago* before I went to see *Antwone Fisher?* So I said to him, Yeah, you have to answer that question for yourself. . . .

Iverem: Okay. But I still say you can't fault the audience if the film isn't playing where they are. The same thing happened with *Bamboozled.*

Lee: These are totally different situations. *Bamboozled* was marketed very badly. There is a world a difference between how *Antwone Fisher* is being marketed and how *Bamboozled* was marketed. . . . Do you think *Antwone Fisher* is going to make as much money as *Barbershop?*

Iverem: I think it could.

Lee: You really think so? How much money you got?

Iverem: Not very much. Well. Maybe it won't make that much, but it could. I don't see how you can compare the two movies. *Barbershop* opened on so many more screens and it was marketed to pique the interest and voyeurism of Whites. . . .

Lee: Well, *Antwone Fisher* is going wide this weekend. We'll see.

Iverem: Are you able to do the things you want to do? Do you have to trade off between projects you want to do and those you have to do that are more commercially viable, meaning palatable to White folks?

Lee: No. I've done everything I've wanted to do. I've been able to make sixteen feature films in the last seventeen years.

Iverem: Is Hollywood more comfortable with statements about race made in movies that are not Black?

Lee: Of course. It makes White people uncomfortable—some—when race rears its ugly head.

Iverem: At the time when *Bamboozled* was released, you spoke a lot about minstrelsy on television and film. Do you see Black independent film as a way to still change that, to make a difference?

Lee: It's not going to be a one-prong approach. The one way to change everything is to get Black people into those gatekeeper positions (where they have the power to green-light films). That's how you change things, not with Academy Awards.

Iverem: Well maybe you're more optimistic about this strategy than I am. I think that if studios put a Black person into that kind of position it will be a Black person who they know thinks like they do and who will do things just as they have always done them—kind of like the Hollywood version of Colin Powell.

Lee: That's a valid point but there's also the chance that it is going to be someone visionary and the studios will think, hey, that guy can make us some money. As long as you appeal to their bottom line you can do some work. But I agree that just because someone is African-American doesn't mean that they're going to be—you know what. The example you gave of Colin Powell is apropos. . . .

Iverem: What is most important to you right now?

Lee: To just continue to master my craft. Good directors are good storytellers.

Iverem: You're a father, right? Do you ever think about doing something for children?

Lee: This past November, my book came out, a children's book titled *Please, Baby, Please, Please, Baby, Please* that my wife, Tonya, and I cowrote, so maybe that's the first step in doing something for children. . . .

Iverem: When *Bamboozled* was released, you said you were working on a TV program. Whatever came of that?

Lee: I'm still working on it.

Iverem: Can you say anything about it?

Lee: No. It's a jinx to talk about it before it happens. [On that night's *Charlie Rose* show, Lee offers that he is working on a drama—maybe for ESPN—based on his film *He Got Game.*]

Iverem: It's a drama?

Lee: Oh yeah. I'm not doing any sitcoms. No, no, no. . . .

Iverem: What is the most important development for Black filmmakers now?

Lee: I think there are more Black films being made now. The last time they were making this number of films was during the Black exploitation era. The challenge is how do you navigate this world where we're still relegated to those three ghettos. You don't see movies about Sojourner Truth or Matthew Henson or Black science fiction or a Black thriller. The studios say, We're not buying that. They say, Do you have something with drugs or a rapper, something we can put Nelly in?

Iverem: So you believe it's all about the studios? Can't we make our own films?

Lee: There's not one way to do it. It's not an either-or situation. You can make the film yourself. *My Big Fat Greek Wedding* was not made by a studio and it was one of most profitable films last year. . . .

Iverem: What's next?

Lee: Don't know yet. Hopefully we'll be shooting something in the spring.

Iverem: I had no idea you were so superstitious.

Lee: Oh yeah. Don't put a hat on a bed, and don't split the pole.

Iverem: Where do you spend most of your time now?

Lee: Still in New York, in Manhattan. . . .

Iverem: Anything else?

Lee: Just the fickleness of the African-American moviegoing audience. . . . I have nothing against entertainment but there are different kinds of entertainment. We're still in that buffoonery thing. I'm not against those types of films but we have to have more than that. It's not about the budget, it's the vision, and calling Martin Luther King a ho and saying all Rosa Parks did was sit her fat, Black ass down is not visionary. But this year, when the studios consider what movies to fund, they will see what *Barbershop* made and what *Antwone Fisher* made and that's why you'll see *Barbershop II* and *Barbershop III*.

Iverem: So those two films, with entirely different screen situations, will be compared like that?

Lee: I'm telling you, I'm telling you. I talk to these studio people and that's how they think.

Black Star–Busta Rhymes in *Narc*

January 10, 2003

The dizzying opening sequence of *Narc* has done for the police drama what the opening of *Saving Private Ryan* did for the war flick: It has forever ratcheted up the bar for how we experience the danger of battle. But instead of mass carnage on a foreign shore, the opening of *Narc* presents the frenetic chase of a crazed junkie by a crazed narcotics officer. This is a different kind of battle in our own homegrown war.

It is from this unsparing and intense point of departure that writer and director Joe Carnahan launches us into a cold and gritty Detroit winter. The subsequently suspended narc, Nick Tellis (Jason Patric), must fight for his own personal and professional survival while investigating the murder of another undercover officer, found shot in the head inside a tunnel walkway. Along the way, Tellis is paired with officer Henry Oak (Ray Liotta), a volatile veteran on the force who initially investigated the murder and has found no suspects. Director Joe Carnahan tells a tightly plotted story that mixes, in an intentionally disconcerting manner, the grit of the streets—heroin dealers, junkies, and various sordid players—with the fragility of families and the innocence of children. The young Black hustlers, including Big D Love, played by Busta Rhymes, enter into the story as a part of the grit and danger of the streets and, to Carnahan's credit, are used to do more than offer a moment of ridicule and laughs. For all its focus on the struggle of Tellis, *Narc* also explores in a brutal scene the relationship between White cops, Black suspects, and the idea of justice.

City of God

January 17, 2003

Life is cheap in the sprawling Black slums, or favelas, of Rio de Janeiro, Brazil. It is this cheapness, not only in terms of easy, quick death but also of pitiful wasted life, that is at the heart of *City of God,* a brutal, sometimes brutally honest, and troubling film by Fernando Meirelles that tells the story of one man's way out.

There are multiple layers of story and meaning here: First, we can listen simply to our hero, Rocket (Alexandre Rodrigues), tell the violent and entertaining stories of three generations of neighborhood hoodlums, complete with petty stickups, random shootings, and naked people caught in the wrong bed. Told in a manic, souped-up style, with lots of creative camera work and fast-paced editing, this trendy, edgy layer of the film is what grabs us and makes us laugh at the young men and boys whose lives are as disposable as a condom.

Second, we might see through the story how dehumanized these young men are. Through our giggles at their trigger-happy antics, perhaps the film asks that we think about whether it is easier to laugh at them than to face who they really are and how their world and our "global" world has shaped them. And finally, maybe Americans might wonder if, in the push for edge, attitude, and rawness in film—except of course when it comes to important films about White folks—ghetto people must always be made so animal-like to both entertain us and justify their miserable life station.

City of God, somewhat similar to *Gangs of New York,* offers the entertainment of dehumanization and senseless, cheap killing. Coming from Brazil, a country more blatantly racist than the United States, with the largest population of African descendents outside of Africa, *City of God* contains this animal-like behavior within the slums where the majority of people, if they lived in the United States, would be categorized as Black. It hints that there are racial divisions: a few of the lighter-skinned poor folks call darker ones "niggers" and there is a true sense that the City of God is a Brazilian version of a South African Bantustan. But, except for these instances, Meirelles deals less with his country's paranoid obsession with race, color, and classification and more with Black ghetto pathology and self-destruction as a fascinating yarn.

The villain, L'il Zé (Leandro Firmino da Hora), is a very Black, "ugly" man with a broad nose and full lips. Our hero, Rocket, is also very Black with African features and, like L'il Zé, has not had much success with the opposite sex. This failure in the mack-daddy department is a running joke throughout the film and allows the audience to feel both sympathy and pity for Rocket. He chooses to hang with a crowd where he is the only Black person. He loves a White girl who gives him no rhythm but falls for a lighter-skinned Black man who dyes his curly hair blond. As always here (and as the longtime hype has gone in Brazil), the way out is to get as White as you can, get with some White folks—because, after all, they have all the houses, wealth, and education—and get the hell away from all these shooting, senseless Negroes.

The Murder of Emmett Till

January 20, 2003

An adage from journalism school goes like this: "If you have a story, tell it. If you don't have a story, write it." Meaning that if you have news, give it straight and quick. If you don't have any, give the reader the most well-written narrative that you can. I'm reminded of this rule after screening *The Murder of Emmett Till,* the latest and most riveting documentary by Stanley Nelson, a recent MacArthur Fellowship recipient who has accomplished himself by chronicling African-American history.

There is nothing fancy in this documentary—no tricks or expensive recreations—and there is no need for any, because what Nelson has here is a story. In a lean and gripping one hour of telling that story—of the grisly murder of a Black fourteen-year-old boy in Mississippi in 1955—Nelson convinces us that Till's murder was an important catalyst for the civil rights movement that changed the course of the United States.

This is in-your-face history for those of us who run from it, who weren't born in 1955 and wonder why we have to go there, for everybody who doesn't understand that less than fifty years ago in Mississippi, a Black boy could be tortured, shot, and drowned because he whistled at a White woman. And for those who remember the case well, Nelson offers, probably for the first time, interviews with witnesses who have never spoken publicly about the case.

By allowing these voices to be heard, Nelson and writer Marcia A. Smith have allowed this important moment in Black history to be told and interpreted by the Black people who lived it. And they have told the story in the context not of misery but of eventual triumph. It reminds us that one hundred days after Till's death, Rosa Parks refused to give her seat to a White man in Montgomery, Alabama, sparking the Montgomery bus boycott.

Says Mamie Till Mobley (who recently died on January 6, just days before this television premiere), "When people saw what had happened to my son, men stood up who had never stood up before. People became vocal who had never vocalized before. . . . Emmett's death was the opening of the civil rights movement. He was the sacrificial lamb of the movement."

Brother Outsider: The Life of Bayard Rustin

January 20, 2003

On PBS affiliates is *Brother Outsider: The Life of Bayard Rustin,* a candid portrait of the life of the civil rights and peace activist who was openly gay during a time when the United States was less open-minded about homosexuality. Directed by Nancy Kates and Bennett Singer, the eighty-three-minute program is lively, informative, and chock-full of interesting footage and interviews, including those with Rustin's White lovers. It traces Rustin's life from his childhood in the segregated town of West Chester, Pennsylvania, to his powerhouse years as a mentor to the Rev. Martin Luther King Jr. and as the organizer of the historic 1963 March on Washington.

Rustin is shown as a smart, committed man who, partly because of his homosexuality and onetime arrest on a "morals charge," was a political liability to the struggling civil rights movement. In many instances, he was made an outsider in the movement to which he dedicated his life. The producers attempt to make the case that if it weren't for Rustin's homosexuality, he would have been a leader on par with King, but *Brother Outsider* does not make this case convincingly. If anything, it shows that Rustin's outsider status was just as much a product of his lifestyle, which was as decidedly outside the spiritual and cultural mainstream of Black culture as was his sexual preference.

Biker Boyz

January 31, 2003

This is the first film to try and capture the energy of the world of Black motorcycle clubs. Those in that life have their own technical issues with the film—apparently some of the street racing isn't as challenging as it would be in real life, etc.—but, for me, the problem is the rather simplistic and predictable story (which stars Derek Luke and Laurence Fishburne). To its credit, it is also a father-son tale, which we don't have enough of outside the usual context of absentee fathers and sons running amok.

Unchained Memories: Readings from the Slave Narratives

February 5, 2003

Premiering on HBO is *Unchained Memories: Readings from the Slave Narratives,* a powerful seventy-four-minute program that highlights the life stories of enslaved African-Americans, as told in their own words during the 1930s. At that time, there were approximately one hundred thousand men and women still living who had been born into slavery and many of their narratives, collected by journalists and others employed by the federal government's Works Progress Administration, are housed at the Library of Congress. For this program, which is narrated by Whoopi Goldberg, excerpts are read by eighteen actors, including Samuel L. Jackson, Angela Bassett, Ossie Davis, Ruby Dee, Roger Guenveur Smith, Courtney Vance, and CCH Pounder. Each actor, shot close up, speaks directly into the camera, creating an intimate portrait of the dehumanization and resilience of the human spirit—backbreaking toil, freezing winters with no shoes and little food, the tearing asunder of families, the rape of Black women, and the neutering of Black manhood. Readings are combined with actual photos of the men and women who offered their stories, other historic photos, and footage of Southern Blacks.

Deacons for Defense

February 5, 2003

The cadres of Southern Black churchgoing men who armed themselves to protect Black communities during the civil rights movement have been all but forgotten as narratives about nonviolent protest and strategy predominate in books and films. But a new film on Showtime tells the important and little-known story of the Deacons for Defense, which formed in Bogalusa, Louisiana, in response to virulent regional Ku Klux Klan violence that was not yielding in the face of desegregation law.

It is so refreshing and impressive to see this type of story, which has something new and real to say about Black history, that it is easy to forgive the film's deficiencies. Forest Whitaker does a decent job starring as Marcus, a factory worker who evolves from a compliant Negro into a gun-toting race man, intent on protecting civil rights protesters, desegregating his workplace and public accommodations, and ending lynchings, beatings, and other intimidation.

The story, based on a book by journalist Michael D'Antonio, puts at the heart of Marcus's transformation the physical assault on his daughter, who is struck by a police officer during a downtown student civil rights protest. During Marcus's defense of her, he physically restrains the police officer with a chokehold and lands in jail. When he emerges, he bears the signs of a brutal beating. In *Deacons for Defense,* men become militant after they have been personally brutalized by racism, rather than because a neighbor or the larger community has been wronged. In this sense, Marcus's big transformation, which is somewhat sudden and needs more foundation, is better understood in the context of his role as a protective husband and father.

Similarly, the characters of two White civil rights workers who have been dispatched to the town need a little bit more flesh to be believable. We need to hear and see more to understand why two young, northern White lawyers are risking their lives in the Deep South, and why they are so gung-ho about nonviolence, and apprehensive about the deacons, even though the deacons protect them from sure danger or death.

Director Bill Duke and his editors make creative use of a mixture of color and black-and-white footage to re-create the sense of real history. Neighborhood and protest scenes shot for this movie are edited along with actual historical footage of civil rights demonstrators—not necessarily originating from Bogalusa—being attacked and arrested by police. Similar use is made of actual or re-created news broadcasts that detailed the growing danger in the town.

As in real life, many of the Black men who took up arms with the deacons—which ultimately had many chapters across the South—were military veterans who had fought in World Wars I or II, or in Korea, but were still denied basic rights in their own country. This story is one of the few that shows how Black veterans were still intent, long after the end of World War II, to score that "Double V" for victory, both abroad and at home.

Good Fences

February 5, 2003

Thank God for *Good Fences,* both the kind between good neighbors and the new film by the same name on Showtime. Sure, it has its made-for-TV moments—some choppy editing and an uneven tone—but these deficiences are outweighed by the compelling and artfully told tale of one upwardly mobile Black family during the 1970s.

Set during a time when the civil rights and Black Power movements had given birth to many individualistic achievers, *Good Fences* poses questions about the definition of achievement and "making it." In this case, a success-obsessed attorney, Tom Spader (Danny Glover), is determined to make his way out of the legal research basement and up the career ladder, even if it means working in opposition to his own people and community. Standing by Tom's side is his silent wife, Mabel (Whoopi Goldberg), who knows better and sometimes challenges her husband's decisions but largely does not, as the family moves from a middle-class neighborhood in Hamden, Connecticut, to the nearby wealthy and WASPy community of Greenwich.

Director Ernest Dickerson gives the story, based on a novel by Erika Ellis and a teleplay by Trey Ellis, the oddball texture of a twisted '70s fairy tale. The feel is more surreal than funny as Tom is willing to literally "tom" his way to the top, as Mabel endures endless meetings with chattering, neurotic PTA wives, and their daughter, Stormy, evolves into a Black Farrah Fawcett wannabe. But, as seen primarily through the eyes of Mabel, the whole world is loopy. She runs into an old boyfriend, for example, the one her father wanted her to marry, and discovers that he is just as nuts as her husband but less socially successful. His latest scheme involves mail-order pork.

When a Black recent lottery winner from Florida (Mo'Nique), with obvious around-the-way credentials, moves in next door to the Spaders, all hell breaks loose. Tom believes his family will be blamed for "inviting" her and he thinks his upward mobility—he hopes to make it to the state Supreme Court—is about the end.

Throughout, *Good Fences* gets into the hearts and minds of Tom and Mabel. While Tom isn't afraid to sell out in order to "make it," we learn that he is not simply foolish but has adopted a twisted response to his own terror at the hands of Whites. And while the story sets him up as the primary boogeyman, it is obvious that Mabel is complicit in her silence while she battles her own demons as well. What a treat, so soon after the stellar *Antwone Fisher,* to have another film that gives attention to the ways African-Americans struggle within while struggling with the outside world. *Good Fences* adds a dimension to the manner in which film has depicted Black families, class conflict, and the 1970s, a decade that continues to define us today.

Deliver Us from Eva

February 7, 2003

Eva is a bad-mother-shut-yo-mouth. The kind of sista who can cut a man down so low he'll be looking up at his shoes. The kind of sister who will remind a brother, who delivers meat for a living, that it's his job to cart around a "pig's ass." And while Gabrielle Union sometimes goes a little over the top in her portrayal of the bitch-on-wheels, there's no denying that it is her performance that makes *Deliver Us from Eva* one of the more oddball and refreshing films to come out of this genre of Black romantic comedies.

The story is that her three younger sisters, who are either married or about to be, are very dependent on her. They are all very close and she is the one who, at age eighteen, took care of them and held the family together after their parents died in a car accident. Well, the men in her sisters' lives want Eva and her sharp-tongued influence to go away, and they concoct a scheme to have a local player, Ray (LL Cool J), sweep Eva off her feet and away from them. The result is a funny, fast-paced romp. I kind of think that LL looks a little like a fathead here, that beauty parlor scenes are a little tired, and that Kim Whitley's persona as the hefty slut is very, very tired, but these weak links didn't prevent me from having a sorely needed laugh in these very insane times.

Interview—Dan Haskett, Master Animator

February 7, 2003

Dan Haskett, a veteran animator with three decades in the business, designed the character Belle for *Beauty and the Beast* and Ariel for *The Little Mermaid.* He won an Emmy for his work on *The Simpsons* and has credits for *Toy Story* and *The Prince of Egypt,* as well as for commercials and cartoons for *Sesame Street.* Yet the Harlem native, who now resides in Burbank, California, is still humble enough to be self-deprecating. The fifty-year-old master animator describes himself as "heavyset and nearsighted" after so many years of up-close, intense drawing about his journey.

Iverem: How has being African-American impacted your experience?

Haskett: One of the things that has been helpful about being Black in this business has been [my] lack of pretense. I often have told people that animation is the nigger of the movie business. It's the thing that has been the most scorned and, at the same time, it has been remarkably successful. Animated films are remembered longer, they have a longer shelf life, they make money years after their release. At the same time there is still a stigma about them—they're for kids, they're not taken seriously for whatever reason. Being Black in this business I didn't have any illusions about that. I was twenty-five when I first came out to Hollywood. A lot of people had not had the type of background I came from. Their concept of making it in Hollywood was very different from mine. . . . Black people that I grew up with didn't even consider anything like this as a career. You know, if we do any type of art, it's performing art. It was interesting that I was even able to get a foot in the door.

Comparatively speaking, it still hasn't changed all that much. There is still only a handful of us. Not that long ago, a young animator working on *Batman* wanted to have a gathering of Black animators; he called around and reserved a table at a soul-food restaurant near the Warner Bros. Studio. Soon the table was filled up. People just kept coming in and coming in. We filled up the place! But you know . . . [*laughs*] if someone had dropped a bomb on that soul-food restaurant, it would have killed the entire population of Black animators. It's still an exotic thing.

Iverem: What are the challenges to getting more Black characters in animated movies?

Haskett: We have to make our own movies. I don't want Disney to do the Black characters. I've already seen what they do with the Asian characters and the Mexican characters and the Hawaiian characters and I don't like it. There's your image up there but what are you doing with it? What are you saying with this image? I remember during the making of *The Little Mermaid* there was an idea, wouldn't it be funny to make Sebastian the crab be a Jamaican? And basically what that meant is give him a big, fat lower lip and popping eyes—and that's what they had in the film. A lot of our folks think that because it's a cartoon that it's harmless, that you can put a coon image in a cartoon and it will be harmless. But it's very important . . . people remember those images.

We have to make our own stuff; we can't depend on Hollywood to make better pictures. Hollywood is not interested in you. They've made allowances but it's nowhere near where it ought to be. There is still a lot to be done in American animation in multicultural representation.

Iverem: Tell me how your upbringing led you to animation. Were your parents artists?

Haskett: I think I inherited my talent from my mother and her mother, but I'm the first one able to use it professionally. My mother had the talent because when she was in high school she won a fashion design contest sponsored by a department store, but they took away her prize when they found out she was Black. She worked as a clerk for the Department of Hospitals. I definitely did not grow up rich and I definitely did not grow up middle class, either. But living in New York City was a definite advantage. It has so many places like museums that are free. I actually enjoyed going to the library. We lived at 154th Street and Eighth Avenue in Harlem and one block away there was a tiny little library on Macombs Place heading toward Yankee Stadium. I wasn't an enormous reader but I just loved the atmosphere.

At the library I found my first book about animation. I took it away and kept it. I paid for it. It was *The Technique of Film Animation*. . . . I must have been about fourteen. By that time, I had already tried animating some things on my own. My folks did like to read. Our place was full of magazines and newspapers—and so it was also full of cartoons.

My first attempts at animation were on 8-by-10 sheets of paper folded into sixteen squares with sixteen little pictures—one was a Christmas story with mice, another was a *Looney Tunes*–type dog chasing rabbits. The dog was named Spotty and the rabbits were Pierre and Horace Hare. The first time I saw any explanation of the process was on a program by Walter Lance, who created Woody Woodpecker. At the end of the *Woody Woodpecker* show, he would do a show explaining the process. That was the first time that I'd actually seen the process at all. At that time on TV (in the 1950s), they ran every cartoon that had ever been done to fill up the time. So I had an education about the actual history of the craft. I would watch cartoons and fantasy films and commercials. Saturday morning cartoons really didn't start until the '60s. Before then, CBS ran *Mighty Mouse* on Saturday. NBC started running Hanna Barbera's *Ruff and Reddy* series.

Iverem: Tell me how you wound up as an animator.

Haskett: I attended the High School for Art and Design at Fifty-seventh and Second Ave. and took the course in cartooning and animation. I was a good student. I had a high B average. The whole experience is what did it. It was the first time that I had been with a group of artists of all ages. They were all people who either had or still had a career in commercial art going while they were teaching at the school. They were in the nuts and bolts of it every day. Just being around teachers and students who were all on the same wavelength with what they wanted to do with their lives was unique and had a lot to do with me going into this full-time. It's where everybody was insane. I started working right after I graduated and started college at Pratt Institute for two years, left college for a few years, and then went back to the New York Institute of Technology, where I took TV, radio, and communications. Six months shy of graduation, I took a job setting up an animation department that did commercials and corporate films. It was a place that did low-budget work but we had some big clients like Procter & Gamble and Kellogg's. I stayed there two years. Up to that point, I'd taught myself how to put a film together. While there, I learned some finer points. The biggest thing there was learning to supervise a group of people.

Iverem: What happened next?

Haskett: I was twenty-three when I left. My co-workers told me about this man, Richard Williams, who would later go on to make *Who Framed Roger Rabbit,* who was coming to New York to make a feature-length animated film. I told myself, if there is a chance of working with this guy I've got to take it. We made *Raggedy Ann and Andy.* Fox released it. I worked on it for one year and it was a very important experience for me. I met the people who would be my animation family for several years.

After that, thanks to Williams, I got an audience at Disney with Frank Thomas, a master animator, one of the original animators, and I had to choose between going to Disney and going back to London with Richard Williams. I went to Los Angeles. I came in as a trainee and animated two pictures: *The Small One* and *The Fox and the Hound.* I drew some images of the hound as a pup. . . . Everything was done by hand. Each individual plate. There are 1,441 frames in one minute and just about all of them have to be drawn. You do the math. . . .

Over the last twenty-five years I've worked at Disney at least once a year. I'm a freelancer. The biggest change has obviously been computer-generated imagery. Now the animation drawings, the drawings that make characters move, and the backgrounds are being done on computer and the computer enables you to get a three-dimensional effect that you couldn't do before. It remains to be seen what kind of effect it will have on an audience. *Shrek* and *Toy Story* really haven't changed things a lot. It's just a different look. It hasn't changed the initial design of the characters or settings. It hasn't changed storyboarding of the films or the visualization of the script.

Iverem: Isn't a lot of animation now being done in Asia?

Haskett: Yes, and that's a sore spot here. The actual animating of the figures is not done here anymore—so if it is your true desire to do that kind of work, you can't do it here. That's the part of the process that Americans consider "manufacturing" and so they ship it out to get the cheapest price. At the very beginning some of the main countries were Mexico, Japan, Korea, and China. Now the main countries would be China, Korea, the Philippines—and India is starting to make a big inroad as well.

Iverem: What are the exciting things happening in animation?

Haskett: On the horizon is the Internet and how it could change the movie business altogether. It could change the distribution. The Internet has helped a lot of people get into animation who would not have otherwise tried it. A computer allows them to work solo and not form a studio. Combined with the Internet, the computer allowed a lot of kids to come in and make films without selling their ideas to studios. Right now it's still in the baby-step stage. It could be that they can change everything.

There has been a blossoming of interest in animation during the past ten years. With shows like *The Simpsons* and *South Park,* we're reaching an older audience. People aren't ashamed to say [*laughs*] that they actually watch cartoons. Animation has even acquired a cachet of sorts.

Iverem: How would you characterize your career? It sounds very impressive. Are you at the top tier of animators? Are you now a master animator?

Haskett: Yes, I am considered a master animator. I would say that I am at the top of the old game. Things are changing quite a bit. There are types of stories that I'd always wanted to do in animation but I could not do commercially and that might finally be changing. I've done about all I can do with what has been given me, I have the reputation within the business, and now I have to go into my own thing, do my own thing. . . .

Iverem: What do you feel is your most important work? What has been most gratifying?

Haskett: I've been able to influence a lot of young talent. A lot of people like what I do and they like how I do it and they want to learn. And it's very important to me to create characters that have a life of their own—and apparently I've been successful at that.

Lockdown

February 14, 2003

For at least the immediate future, all prison dramas will draw comparisons to *Oz,* the popular television series that has created a compelling prison burlesque of brutal violence and sleek melodrama. Of course, Hollywood has raised "jumping on the bandwagon" to a high art form and, in recent years, there have been reportedly several new prison dramas in the industry incubator.

Lockdown has the violence and raw power—and then some. It centers the prison experience among the lives of Black men, who are disproportionately represented in today's prisons—one of the nation's largest "growth industries." Some have even called prisons "the new plantations."

It states, simply, almost in passing, how easy it is for Black men to become caught up in trouble and land in prison. Three friends from Los Angeles who wind up locked down are innocent of the murder of which they were convicted. And one of the men, Avery (Richard T. Jones), is a talented swimmer who has just lost the possible opportunity to attend college on an athletic scholarship.

More focus and more sympathy is given to Avery and his story. His friend, Cashmere (Gabriel Casseus), is a drug dealer and was seemingly headed to prison anyway (especially, as the plot has it, since Cashmere shoots a police officer in retaliation for the officer shooting at his dog). The third prisoner, Dre (De'aundre Bonds), a quiet man making an honest living at a dry cleaners, is the most vulnerable of the three. He shudders as the bus makes its way to the prison. Obviously, the bus scene prepares us for Dre's lack of toughness and how he is ill-suited for the life ahead—if anyone ever is.

Though it is not adequately explained, childhood and lifelong friendship is what binds the three men together. None of their characters are finely drawn. Once inside the prison, each is defined by the one-dimensional persona given him: Avery is tough, hotheaded, and physically able to defend himself. Cashmere is criminal to the bone and lives inside the prison by the same street rules he knows. Dre is an innocent and, in prison, becomes a sacrificial lamb.

Despite the deficiencies in the script by Preston A. Whitmore II (*Fled, The Walking Dead*), the performances by Jones, Casseus, and Bonds are first-rate. Also worthy of mention is Clifton Powell, who plays Malachi, a seasoned and mellow con who offers Avery tips for survival.

The violence is unsparing and exhausting. If only the filmmakers had been as unsparing in their effort to fully draw these characters, they would have a better movie on their hands. *Lockdown* wrings you out with its rawness, which comes from its raw action, not from its raw passion for the lives of three Black men.

Amandla!: A Revolution in Four-Part Harmony

February 19, 2003

During that momentous era of Nelson Mandela's release from prison, his election in 1994 as South Africa's first Black president, and the end of that country's vicious system of apartheid, the moving anthem "Nkosi Sikel' iAfrika" ("Bless, O Lord, Our Land of Africa") became an anthem for people who care about freedom on the continent and the world over.

And though the anthem's worldwide popularity came on the heels of other exported South African freedom songs, through the musical *Sarafina!* and through artists such as Miriam Makeba and Hugh Masekela, it still represented only the tip of a larger body of songs that helped build and sustain the antiapartheid movement. This history of music and struggle in South Africa is at the heart of *Amandla! A Revolution in Four-Part Harmony,* a new documentary, years in the making, being screened in theaters around the country.

First-time director Lee Hirsch, along with producer Sherry Simpson, both Americans, have artfully combined storytelling and music. The emphasis of *Amandla!* (which means "power" in Xhosa) is not on the horrors and genocide of apartheid, a brutal system under which the country's twenty million Blacks were ruled by a tiny White minority. But it does offer an overview about major changes in the country, starting roughly with the all-White national Party coming to power in 1948 and bringing with it a new level of repression of the Black population.

This history merges with music in the little-known story of composer and activist Vuyisile Mini. After the election of the National Party in 1948, Mini wrote the famous song in South Africa "Beware Verwoerd," which warns Hendrick Verwoerd, the architect of apartheid, that one day he would get his comeuppance. Mini was ultimately imprisoned and executed for his songs. The story of the brave and victorious manner in which Mini went to his death, still singing defiantly and with other prisoners joining in, is one of many moving narratives in the film. His story is told amid stunning scenes of his bones being unearthed in a crude grave, and then reburied in a hero's ceremony.

Equally important is the fact that *Amandla!* serves as an archival record for many indigenous folk songs that have been passed down verbally, and are a part of Black South African oral history, but have not been recorded until now. (One bittersweet segment includes Mini's family singing "Beware Verwoerd" as we know they are also reburying him.) Songs sprinkled throughout the film are sung by people in their homes, in meetings, and at stadium gatherings, such as the new government's victory rally in 1995. Interviews with surviving activists, almost all associated with the ruling African National Congress, bring the narrative through the decades and up to the present. Footage of artists such as Masekela, Makeba, and pianist Abdullah Ibrahim fill out the story, making *Amandla!* a story about a music and people that touched and changed the world.

OPM–*Dark Blue*

February 21, 2003

I am really tired of films that ask me to sympathize with racists. Last year I was supposed to believe in Hank Grotowski's amazing transformation in *Monster's Ball.* At Christmas, there was Bill the Butcher in *Gangs of NewYork* spewing a special (Oscar-nomination worthy) bile at "niggers." And now there is Sgt. Eldon Perry Jr. (Kurt Russell) of the LAPD in *Dark Blue,* which tells a story based on the era of the Rodney King beating and resulting Los Angeles riots, largely through the eyes of a very cinematic White rogue cop.

This isn't to say that racists shouldn't have their day or that they do not deserve treatment as anything other than one-dimensional villains. Too many films offer us cardboard bigots and that is not the answer. But it is also not the answer, for this Black woman anyway, for a film to reflect on one of the most pivotal eras involving race in the last decade solely through the eyes of a racist. It's the same effect as only listening to reactionaries on Fox News defending Trent Lott (or saying anything, really). To hear Perry tell it, if the lethal LAPD chokehold had not been outlawed, none of this King beating, captured famously on videotape, would have even been necessary.

To make matters worse, *Dark Blue,* like *Monster's Ball* and *Gangs of New York,* offers the loud voice of the bigot and the silence of those Blacks murdered or injured. We know that Perry has killed about a dozen people in the "line of duty," and we know those deaths are questionable. But that is all we know in a vague sort of way. What we are shown powerfully is how hard it is to be a cop in such a sprawling, dangerous place full of young Black men standing around on corners, drinking malt liquor, maybe selling drugs and jonesing for a Fatburger.

What we hear is Perry and his buddies talking about law enforcement as a way of life passed down from their daddies, about how there is a sense of honor even in the dishonorable. We see that crooked, racist cops are funny and look nice in their jeans and unshaven faces, that their tradition cannot be disgraced without also disgracing so much on which they stand. (Does anybody else remember the episode of *All in the Family* when America's beloved Archie Bunker waxed nostalgic about how he got most of his views from his daddy? He then wondered out loud how anyone could ask him to believe that his daddy could be wrong. Consider said scene an early appeal for our understanding and sympathy for bigots.)

In *Dark Blue,* we don't hear much from the Deputy Chief Arthur Holland (Ving Rhames), a Black man who is promoted as a sort of counterpoint to Perry in the story but who is really not given much of a role or a voice about the important issues so viscerally explored by Whites. To counter vile racism within the LAPD, the filmmakers offer us career-minded colored folk who glare at Whites while patiently and quietly plotting victories. And, yes, after Michael Michele's performance here, where she sleeps with a young White cop, I think we can call it: The Berry-ization of Hollywood is in full effect. There will continue to be more half-baked Black women characters climbing all over White men (who they don't even know) in bed.

Sure, it can be argued that *Dark Blue* paints Perry as a total mess, personally and professionally, and not as a hero. But I know that tortured-hero treatment when I see it, hear it, and feel it rumbling in Dolby sound.

Just don't expect sympathy from me for such a powerful mess.

Bringing Down the House

March 7, 2003

Queen Latifah has never been anybody's mammy. And she is not a mammy in *Bringing Down the House,* a film to which she brings the same in-your-face, hip-hop style. In fact, I think of this movie as a Black woman's anti-mammy manifesto and a hilarious exploding of racial stereotype and taboo.

Latifah plays Charlene Morton, an escaped ex-con who forces her way into the life of a divorced tax attorney, Peter Sanderson (Steve Martin), whom she met in an Internet law chat room and whom she believes can help her prove her innocence. Peter thinks he is chatting with a slim blonde with whom he can begin his first postdivorce relationship. Charlene's entry into Peter's life, of course, is unrealistic, filled with an initial denial of who she is and very awkward. It is a White middle-class nightmare of the nig invasion, unfolded with a wink and a chuckle. And much of the movie offers this same wink and chuckle at White people, too, as well as an overall absurdity.

Depending on your taste in race jokes and this kind of absurdity, *Bringing Down the House* will either work or bomb. I think it works. Not only does the film offer equal-opportunity jabs at everybody, in the process it also shows the ignorance of racism and racists. When Sanderson's White neighbor, played by Betty White, makes her various loopy statements, the audience can laugh at her ignorance. Sure, there will be some in the audience who do think like the neighbor and laugh because of that, but, then, they are also laughing at themselves.

All along the way, there are many funny jokes about America's racial divide and many assumptions and (mammyisms) are torpedoed. Charlene is, literally, free here to make her own life. There is a big difference between the conscious choices made by Charlene and the doting slavish image and responses of a mammy. And it is about time that Black women get a crack at racial spoof, just as Black male comedians Chris Tucker, Martin Lawrence, and Eddie Griffin get it. On some level, it is all buffoonery, even the act by Steve Martin, but no one calls a White comedian that. This film is not perfect, but what Queen Latifah has done here also is expand the cinematic options for Black actresses—without taking off her clothes—just as Gabrielle Union did last month in *Deliver Us from Eva.*

Long live the queen.

Tears of the Sun

March 7, 2003

Tears of the Sun fills us with the extreme horror and hope born of war. Despite its setup of the great White savior, and troubled depictions of women, Muslims, and dissenters, it is a remarkable, riveting film that gives images and voice to African pain and suffering. It is the first film that I can think of that has made its focus the brutal civil wars that have torn asunder countries throughout the continent.

Set in Nigeria, this film tells a fictional story about a civil war between the Muslim Fulani rebels and the Christian Ibos. The Ibo president and his family have been assassinated by the Fulani rebels, who are moving across the country on a campaign of genocide and "ethnic cleansing." In one Christian mission, there is an American doctor, Lena Kendricks (Monica Belucci), and the Pentagon orders Navy SEAL Lieutenant A. K. Waters (Bruce Willis) and his team to go in and retrieve her. When Kendricks refuses to go without the refugees at the mission, the soldiers, doctor, and refugees set off on foot on a perilous journey to refuge in neighboring Cameroon. In the process, the group engages in lessons of survival and humanity.

As he did in *Training Day* and *Bait,* director Antoine Fuqua proves that he is a master of suspense and nonstop motion of a story. And even though battle scenes are highly charged and unsparing, the most heartrending moments are those that stop to consider the innocent victims of war—murdered and tortured men, women, and children.

Of course we largely approach this conflict through the eyes of White Americans, more specifically the military establishment, and this means that we come into Africa with people who have contempt for her. Waters declares that "God left Africa a long time ago," and his attitude is probably representative of how most White Americans view Africa—as a problem place full of problem people.

An American perspective is even more troubling because the United States has not actually acted as "a savior" in the recent bloody civil wars, particularly those in Rwanda. Also, the setup of Muslim villains is suspect given Hollywood's declared intention to support the U.S. government's "war against terror." (This is the first of several war, terrorism, or spying flicks coming out this month. Be on the lookout for *The Hunted, Buffalo Soldiers, Basic,* and even a kiddie spying flick, *Agent Cody.*) *Tears of the Sun* does not feel like naked propaganda, as did *Black Hawk Down,* but it does paint supposed Muslims as heartless murderers, torturers, and rapists.

It also sets up Kendricks as an impetuous woman who puts herself and others in danger. Time and time again, the film makes her into a complainer and troublemaker, a film version of a "bleeding-heart liberal," who must eventually concede to the wisdom and strength of the military. There is a subtle interrogation of patriotism, loyalty, and heart here, and all the answers aren't easy or pro-war. Even though Kendricks is shown as somewhat of a reckless ditz, Waters must also confront the issue of "following orders" as he veers from his original mission and escorts the refugees. The film allows for the possibility that sometimes for soldiers to do the right thing, they must disobey orders. Waters, ultimately, is shown as a man and soldier caught in the middle, between stern orders and the dictates of his conscience. This internal conflict, even with questionable images of female fickleness and African hopelessness, makes this a film that does not outright preach flag-waving militarism.

Early scenes of refugees find them languid and listless. It is only later in the story that we see Africans fierce and determined to fight for their own survival. A sense of African solidarity is powerfully depicted by Ellis "Zee" Pettigrew (Eamonn Walker), a Black soldier under Waters's command. Pettigrew declares that the people they are fighting for are "his people" and that he fights on their behalf.

Black Star–Morgan Freeman in *Dreamcatcher*

March 21, 2003

Folks who like to talk film are calling *Dreamcatcher* just another version of *The Thing*

(1982) or *The Thing from Another World* (1951). And while this adaptation of Stephen King's novel does involve men and aliens, you could also consider it just one extended beer commercial, with very scary monsters thrown in for special effect. What other than the beer-ad aesthetic could produce so many scenes of grown men belching, farting, cursing, obsessing over their johnsons, going for their guns, and—above all else—bonding? Beer commercials, which have become pop-culture sign-posts, are always filled with funny guys doing funny guy things. In *Dreamcatcher,* even when these same guys are about to be gobbled or neutered, they still have a smart-ass remark, a middle finger held high, and one last yell of "eat me" at the monster who will, literally, eat them.

Morgan Freeman gets top billing here, but quite frankly, it's not clear what his role is all about. He plays Colonel Abraham Kurtz (must be some diversity casting!), a specialist in hunting aliens, all of which he calls "E.T." Like Taye Diggs in *Equilibrium* or the nameless brother from 1981's *Outland,* Freeman gets to be the dark spoiler in a sci-fi world. A Black man, ever the efficient soldier for the state, winds up challenging the White hero and the right side of history.

22

Truth Be Told

Head of State

March 28, 2003

So, what were you expecting? A buffoon?

As silly as Chris Rock's *Head of State* can be, it is not as stupid as it is irreverent and sardonic toward all things White, wealthy, or government-related. In this ninety-five-minute romp, which could have been titled *The World According to Chris Rock,* sure, he takes jabs at Black men who sell stolen meat, at Black women who are husband hunters, and at Black folks who have straight-up gone crazy. But he reserves his sharpest darts for the White powers that be who declare "God bless America, and no place else."

He makes this mini-political manifesto—in terms of career path, a step similar to Richard Pryor's *Blue Collar*—through the comedic story of Mays Gilliam, a struggling, nonconformist alderman representing a low-income area of Washington, D.C. (But it will be obvious to many folks in the Baltimore-Washington area that much of this was shot in Baltimore and not D.C. And since when does D.C. have aldermen instead of city council members?)

Anyway, the point is that Mays Gilliam represents a hip-hop-styled public official and vision of government. As he goes about his day-to-day, not wearing the obligatory suit and tie and not playing by the rules, he really believes that government should be representative of the people and that he can make a difference. When Gilliam is improbably tagged to run for president of the United States, he takes his hip-hop style, vision, and idealism with him—and there is an ensuing comedy of errors and absurdity that has special overtones given these politically turbulent times.

For some, the idea that Gilliam's candidacy is mocked might be proof positive that this film is degrading to Black people and that Rock is playing a buffoon. But, especially in light of the serious candidacies of the Rev. Jesse Jackson and others, Black people aren't being laughed at here. What is funny is the improbability of a funny hip-hop presidential candidate wholly committed to the culture's dress, language, music, and dance, who might actually take a Nelly aesthetic to 1600 Pennsylvania Avenue. It is also the idea of a culture that prides itself on being raw and honest merging with the world of politics, which is all about the makeover, the cloak, polish, and all kinds of deception. It would be just as improbable—and not considered racist—if Adam Sandler was a presidential candidate.

And besides, part of the beauty of this tale is that Gilliam and his cohorts, especially his brother Mitch, played by Bernie Mac, seem totally committed to keeping it real—and no campaign manager, news anchorman, or political dirty tricks can intimidate them. So the new world order meets the ghetto world order.

In these new comedies that focus on race with interracial casts (for example, Rock's *Down to Earth* and the current hit *Bringing Down the House*), taboo and stereotypes are fair game and are made large on the big screen. The jokes in *Head of State* aren't as outrageous as they can be, but the level of discomfort in the audience, Black or White, seems to stem from whether these movies joke more on White people or Black people, and whether the audience feels the filmmaker is laughing *with* them, or *at* them.

This movie might not be enjoyed by all the White folk who began loving Rock after he made his joke, much heralded in reactionary circles, about how he loves Black people but hates "niggers," who always mess it up for Black people. If it helps at all to do any type of scorekeeping, *Head of State,* just like *Down to Earth*—both collaborations with the same writer, Ali LeRoi—enjoys digging at old, rich White folks. LeRoi and Rock like positioning the ruling class to ape hip-hop culture in a manner that evokes laughter but is getting a little tired. As much as I might laugh, I'm sure White folks are tired of being reminded how stiff, un-hip, and uncoordinated they are. What if it was a running joke in movie after movie that some Black folks can't speak proper English or that some Black people hate their natural hair?

Rock saves himself in *Head of State* by going after a bigger fish than culture and style. In his own way, he speaks truth to a greater power. As he talks about economic injustice, which cuts across lines of race, he is cutting more than joking.

And not everyone will laugh.

Black Star—Delroy Lindo in *The Core*

March 28, 2003

There are some fast-paced scenes and very good jokes in *The Core*. One eye-popping sequence involves scores of pigeons that are whipped into the kind of cinematic frenzy not seen since Alfred Hitchcock's *The Birds*. And one of the best jokes, among many little jokes tucked into the script, revolves around the lanky postadolescent named Rat (D. J. Qualls), who is compensated for expert computer-hacking with *Xena* tapes and Hot Pocket snacks.

But, alas, a movie that purports to tell a story about the possible end of the world needs more than wow action and some laughs. At some point, a doomsday flick has to convince us that we are supposed to take it seriously and, unfortunately, *The Core* isn't consistently convincing. You know a script and production have problems if Alfre Woodard even comes off as not quite real. Brazleton (Delroy Lindo), who is at least likeable, is an oddball scientist dedicated to building the tunneling craft that carries the crew to the center of the earth where they must jump-start the earth's core so that it will start spinning again and restore the earth's electromagnetic field. Other than the children's TV show *Smart Guy*, this might be the first time I've seen a Black male play the brainiac scientist, and Lindo, better known for being menacing or thuggy, plays a convincing nerd.

Most impressive in *The Core* are kamikaze birds, the amazing images of Rome and the Golden Gate Bridge, the suspenseful shuttle landing, and the often imaginative creation of what the earth's interior might look like.

A Man Apart

April 4, 2003

After the high-powered silliness of *The Fast and the Furious, XXX,* and the reprised *Knock Around Guys,* Vin Diesel has landed in a movie that has at least the semblance of seriousness. In the larger scheme of things, *A Man Apart* is not an important movie with big ideas, but it is important to the grounding of Diesel's career, and to getting director F. Gary Gray back into the game of action-packed flicks. Antoine Fuqua can't have all the fun.

Gray makes this story, focusing on two DEA agents played by Diesel and Larenz Tate, into such a display of brutality, ruthlessness, and gore that, at moments, I'm hard-pressed not to compare it to ultra-macho video games such as Grand Theft Auto. This business of creating violence that will still "shock and awe" blasé American filmgoers (who, to think of it, are nightly watching real bombs being dropped in Iraq) has been ratcheted up so high that these films can literally take your breath away. Add in a few naked women, a sketchy love story, and goo-gobs of cocaine and we have a flick that combines the gangster flick, the cop flick, and the action-hero flick.

Diesel plays the role of Sean Vetter, a high-octane DEA agent who can, on foot, chase down a car and, in general, be a one-man hell-raising machine. In the ever-unfolding display of Diesel's many cinematic faces, *A Man Apart* marks a return to his portrayal of a man of color, as he was in *Pitch Black.* All he basically has to do is show that hair grain (here, he also shows some facial hair) and change the company that he keeps. Diesel is having the time of his life making millions of filmgoers deal with the reality of his multicultural existence—what it means for them, but, most important, what it has meant for him all his life, especially in those pre-*Saving Private Ryan* years when he didn't fit in anywhere.

In spite of the intensity in *A Man Apart,* there are enough laughs, some unintended, to give it balance and let us take a breath. Maybe Vin Diesel is somewhere right now taking a breath, too, wondering who he will be next.

Dysfunktional Family

April 4, 2003

Eddie Griffin is raw and unsparing in *Dysfunktional Family,* a pastiche of stand-up comedy and family documentary that surely must surpass any movie for lack of shame. Even the word outrageous doesn't adequately describe a film that shows a comedian joking graphically about sex in front of his mother. How many times can you say, "Oh no he didn't!" as Griffin makes light of excruciating details in his life for the consumption of a mass audience? This is one of the craziest comedy shows in recent years. How funny you think it is, or how tasteless you think it is, will be based on your personal meter for material that is very, very blue.

Race: The Power of an Illusion

April 24, 2003

Slowly, in movies and books, it has become the norm to talk about race without talking about racism. De-fanged of its institutional nature in works such as the 2001 *New York Times* "race" series, race becomes a benign topic about individual prejudices and personal discomfort. Reactionary pundits have actually begun using the famous quote by the Rev. Martin Luther King—about people not being judged by the color of their skin—to justify attacks on affirmative-action remedies.

It is in this atmosphere of race doublespeak that *Race: The Power of an Illusion* is one of the most important, sweeping, and groundbreaking documentaries in recent memory. Taking full advantage of scholarship documenting how the United States invented modern ideas of "race" and "Whiteness," the producer—California Newsreel—illustrates how racism has been used institutionally, socially, and politically to create an affirmative action for Whites.

This is not fancy moviemaking—interviews with scholars are juxtaposed with historical footage and photos with narration by CCH Pounder—but it is powerful. Airing in three parts on consecutive Thursdays, the series will either build its reputation over three weeks or see its impact diluted by this questionable scheduling. Hopefully, it will experience the former scenario. The first episode, "The Difference Between Us," follows the progress of a DNA workshop for high school students and illustrates how scientists have proven the lack of genetic difference between human beings classified as being from different races.

But while the show proves that race isn't real on a biological level, it segues into how "race" is very real as a social construct. A history is given of how "scientific" research was used to justify enslavement and attacks on people of color in this country, as well as the violent takeover of Cuba, the Philippines, and Hawaii during the era of colonial expansion. These same scientific theories from early in the last century were also used abroad, for example by Hitler in Germany, to build support for ideas of Aryan superiority and the extermination of other populations.

The series really kicks into high gear in the second episode, "The Story We Tell," airing May 1, with a history of the creation of race and Whiteness in the United States. It was easy and convenient, for example, to create a system that equated Black people with slavery and inferiority, and that built a sense of cohesion and new national identity among Whites. Moving beyond Blacks and Whites, this show details the demarcation created between those from Europe and Native Americans, Chinese, and Mexicans. This divide would define who would be considered really "American." White settlers would receive land forcibly taken from Native Americans and would be the only ones granted the full rights of citizenship. Even New Deal legislation of the 1930s, considered a step forward for all Americans, would discriminate against domestic workers and agricultural workers—who were almost all people of color—and against skilled people of color banned from all-White labor unions that could bargain collectively for better wages and work conditions.

The final show, "The House We Live In," airing May 8, goes a long way to illustrating why, in the United States, the worth of the average White family is ten times that of the average Black family. Moving beyond the violence of slavery and Jim Crow laws, it details how the federal government, particularly through the Federal Housing Administration, set in motion a series of laws that allowed for the creation of wealthy White suburbs and impoverished Black communities.

By initiating a system of appraisal whereby White communities were automatically given a higher value than Black or "mixed" communities, and by providing federal grants and tax incentives for the construction ofWhite suburbs that excluded people of color, the federal government not only segregated much of the country's housing, it set in motion a process through which White families have become wealthier, because their homes are worth more. In addition, the equity in these more highly valued homes, and the wealth passed on from previous generations, snowballs into more opportunity, including money to pay for a college education, to start a business, or to assist family members.

Race may not be "real," but, when it comes to opportunity and survival, cold, hard cash is no illusion.

Black Star–Morris Chestnut in *Confidence*

April 25, 2003

There are plenty of clever people saying clever things in *Confidence,* the latest but not the greatest flick about the age-old art of the con game. As a matter of fact, even with Doug Jung's script taking some clever turns and James Foley's direction having some clever moments, it never adds up to much more than that—a sort of clever movie. Sadly, *Confidence* is not as clever, as slick, or as believable as all the movies it tries to imitate. Speaking of the unbelievable, who told Morris Chestnut that he could play a thug? Okay, for a hot second here, I bought the mean stare and the gun pointed at Jake's head. Chestnut also sounded good as he cursed and made like he would pistol-whip Jake a little bit. But, you know, maybe Chestnut needs to change his appearance to play a tough man, just like Vin Diesel changes his look (and "race") in every movie he plays. I'm sure there must be some henchmen with the look of smooth skin and hands, who look buffed and massaged, but how many pretty hit men can there possibly be? And why, without a little help, am I supposed to believe that Chestnut, who epitomizes the buppie/pretty-boy aesthetic of Hollywood, is suddenly ready to bust a cap in somebody?

Black Star—Halle Berry in *X2*

May 2, 2003

There is no doubt that *X2* is an entertaining flick, but it is probably most entertaining for fans of the original comic book/animated series about mutants here on Earth. If you're not a fan, you can enjoy the freaky doings of the mutants such as Wolverine, who has the metal claws, Jean Grey, who can move objects with her mind, or the white-haired Storm (Halle Berry), who creates all kinds of weather weirdness every time her eyeballs disappear.

Also, most striking is the stunning entrance of Nightcrawler, a blue-black mutant with a devil's pointy tail (an image of Lucifer), who gets the party started, in the opening scenes, with an attack at the White House. You put it together: a very black mutant, who moves in a wispy puff of black smoke, invading the very White White House. It is intriguing, to say the least.

This sequel to the 2001 *X-Men* is larger in scale and scope as it tackles a brewing war on Earth between mutants and humans. As the mutants go about reining in the loose canon Nightcrawler and averting a world war, they find out who is really behind the warmongering. This story line is also interesting, given our war-torn times. The motives for "war" are not always what they seem and, just like in Nazi Germany, it is very easy to manipulate a gullible people into hatred of a group that is really not the enemy at all. It is especially easy to whip up hatred when the targeted group is different.

Daddy Daycare

May 9, 2003

Eddie Murphy has finally claimed adulthood, if not middle age.

In *Daddy Day Care,* all the brash cockiness of youth, which has been Murphy's trademark since the 1980s, gives way to a kinder, gentler maturity. And the result is fine for those of us who don't expect him to be a bug-eyed caricature until he dies. As he plays the part of Charlie Hinton, a suddenly unemployed father who learns to care for his son at home, Murphy joins legions of males within the hip-hop generation who have abandoned Peter Pan personas and decided to grow up.

Geoff Rodkey's script doesn't rely on Murphy acting a fool. There are enough quirks in characters, dialogue, and, of course, the antics of the children, to add to the mix. Little Khamani Griffin offers a mighty-mite performance and is mighty cute. Garlin is most hilarious running around a playground with a dead mouse, and

Steve Zahn, playing the part of a science-fiction geek named Marvin, steals scenes with his many talents, including the ability to speak the language of Vulcans. Unlike some Murphy movies, that have been promoted to appeal to children but have been filled with mature subject matter, *Daddy Day Care* is actually a film you can take young children to see. It is quite a change to see Murphy as a sensitive dad. But maybe it is time, for both his sake and ours, for such a change.

Only the Strong Survive

May 9, 2003

What's not to like about Wilson Pickett?

It seems foolish, if not sacrilegious, to badmouth any effort at giving props to 1960s soul singers, many of whom have seen their hits become classics while they have gone uncompensated and become sidelined as artists. But overshadowing issues of form and fashion are the very real questions documentaries such as *Only the Strong Survive,* currently in limited release, bring up—they demand we undertake the very serious business of looking at history. What history is being told? Who is telling it? And what, exactly, is being said?

Once we examine these questions, the ninety-five-minute documentary, directed by Chris Hegedus and D. A. Pennebaker, begins to seem less than the sum of some very nice parts. The movie functions best as a slice of time in 1999 when these filmmakers, along with journalist Roger Friedman, filmed performances by and interviews with Sam Moore (of Sam and Dave), Mary Wilson (formerly of the Supremes), Wilson Pickett, Rufus Thomas, and his daughter Carla Thomas. A few others are included, most notably Isaac Hayes, Jerry Butler, and the Chi-Lites. There are some early references and connections made to the Rhythm and Blues Foundation, which has championed the cause of many performers who, unlike songwriters and producers, do not get paid royalties every time their song is aired.

But the documentary does not really explore the history—and economics—that help explain why such a foundation is necessary, or why so many of these now sixty- and seventy-something peformers are still on the road. I suppose it could be argued that by avoiding the fray, *Only the Strong Survive* avoids painting these artists into victims. Maybe, but by avoiding the topic, the film is allowed to appear to be mainly about a love of the artists, and not be accused of having an "agenda." Into this seemingly benign void, however, emerges a portrait of important Black artists now surrounded by, "saved" and appreciated by, good-hearted White folks.

The Matrix Reloaded

May 15, 2003

Everything in *The Matrix* has gotten bigger the second time around.

Everything—the last underground refuge of humans called Zion, the power and repression of the matrix (and of the notorious Agent Smith), the love, the sensuality, the humanity, and even the range of Neo's powers—has blown up big-time in *The Matrix Reloaded.* Laurence Fishburne even looks thicker (in a good way) and, just as suspected, he has beat Wesley Snipes in the contest of who is the baddest Black man to wear a long black coat and shades in '03.

The directors, Andy and Larry Wachowski, have tackled this bigger-budget sequel with bigger ideas, a bigger sense of seriousness, and probably the biggest sense of a multicultural future ever seen in a science-fiction flick. This time, the fate of all surviving humans is at stake as a crew of freedom fighters, led by Neo (Keanu Reeves), Morpheus (Laurence Fishburne), and Trinity (Carrie-Anne Moss), battles a huge advance on Zion by the machine army. There is a vision here of humanity at the edge of its existence, holed up inside a massive cavern powered by machines, and seemingly built of crudely fashioned metal and rock. In Zion, located near the center of the earth, everybody is kind of raw and funky. Everybody is a little sweaty and clothes aren't always Tide-fresh. People are pierced, they wear ankle bracelets, and their hair is nappy.

Yes. Nappy. In this vision of the future, Black folks have survived and they are fierce and in the leadership. Morpheus retains his position as the sage visionary and believer. Niobe (Jada Pinkett Smith) is the captain of her own ship. Harold Perrineau Jr. (the brother in the wheelchair from *Oz*) drives the mother ship, and Nona Gaye appears as his lover and friend. A council of leaders meets, and who but scholar Cornel West sits among them, and who but boxer Roy Jones,, Jr. sits and listens. Of course actress Gloria Foster (who died during this filming) returns as the all-knowing Oracle, and it is a momentary hoot when Neo searches for her in a place that looks like a Brooklyn housing project. There is a stunning sequence, on the eve of the fight against the machines, when all of Zion seems to dance, writhe, shake, or have sex, as if to raise warrior and life energy with the stomp of human feet and the merger of spiritual and carnal powers. This scene is filled with lots of beautiful, postapocalyptic Black folks who are rendered with spirit and humanity, not as stereotypes. Think of the cover of Marvin Gaye's *I Want You* transported light years to funky science fiction. It is stunning.

The Wachowskis go heavy on the human here, so much so that the robotic and military emphasis of the first film melts into flesh and blood. Scenes in *The Matrix Reloaded* have a pulse and sometimes the pulse slows to a crawl. There are fierce fight scenes, but in a film that most will expect to be wall-to-wall action, there is also much stillness and quiet dialogue. You must listen to this film, as well as watch it, to understand it. Because a sequel to this sequel, *The Matrix Revolutions,* is expected in September, there is a literal sense of "to be continued. . . . "So, along with waiting to learn the fate of Frodo and Sam, after this film you will also be waiting to know what happens in Matrixland. Being left hanging might be very upsetting for some fans but this limbo is the price we pay for an idea that has gotten so big it cannot contain itself.

Black Star—Don Cheadle in *Manic*

May 23, 2003

There is such raw pain in *Manic* that it can't help but spill from the screen. Adolescents holed up inside a mental institution are the players here and their assorted illnesses provide the wrenching drama of angst, anger, horrible violation, extreme longing, and extreme violence. It is in the exploration of turmoil that Don Cheadle stars as staff psychiatrist Dr. David Monroe, who is in charge of helping young people to identify and manage their rage. Cheadle handles this role as he has others in the past—with a simplicity and subtle command of scenes that has allowed him to be, variously, a cop, a teacher, a beggar, or a thief. I am not a huge Cheadle fan, so I'm not trying to blow kisses or smoke, but it is impressive how he projects a Black male sensibility and perspective into this film, which, for the most part, focuses on young Whites in a predominantly White world.

Black Star—Morgan Freeman in *Bruce Almighty*

May 23, 2003

Even if you don't like Jim Carrey, or have shied away from him since the omniracist *Me, Myself & Irene,* it's hard not to like *Bruce Almighty,* a funny film that tackles big issues of godly omniscience, human weakness, and, indirectly, the neurotic state of American corporate and media life. (But I temper these remarks for those who can't stand seeing another Black man pushing a broom.)

Bruce, a television news reporter, is brought into contact with The One, not Neo of *The Matrix,* but the man upstairs who comes in the person of Morgan Freeman, who is a very chilled-out God. As a matter of fact, his motto throughout seems to be that humility and modesty is best, so when Bruce first meets God,

God is pushing a broom in a huge, empty warehouse. Of course Bruce gives God the disdainful half-acknowledgement accorded to a servant. A few minutes later, God is doing building repairs and then, moments later still, he peels off his overalls to reveal a gleaming white suit. God does it all and even "he" is subjected to our assumptions based on appearance and wardrobe. His point to a slow-to-believe Bruce is that since Bruce thinks that God is doing such a lousy job that maybe Bruce should try holding it down for a while. He is not, as in some blast from the cinematic past, doting or fatherly toward this somewhat pitiful White man. He offers Bruce do-it-yourself salvation.

2 Fast, 2 Furious

June 6, 2003

In tone, *2 Fast, 2 Furious* seems to take its cue from last year's *The Fast and the Furious.* Miami's car culture is multicultural with many light-hued, model-thin women with long, straight hair. In the opening scenes, a lone chocolate woman walks through, another is given some Sapphire-like lines to deliver with an attitude, but, really, this is one of those environments that is multicultural in a sense that it is definitely not Black. Instead, Blacks (the Sapphire sister, a big fat man, the first crash victim) serve as not-so-subtle butts of jokes as the film begins.

Rapper Ludacris makes a benign appearance as a hustler named Tej, and singer Tyrese is somewhat of a counterbalance to the initial mockery. (Looks like Baby Boy has been pumping iron and polishing that ebony skin!) Tyrese is charismatic and funny and definitely shows his leading-man potential but his character, Roman Pearce, gets justhisclose to being a serious stereotype. Roman is a going-nowhere-fast sort of brother from a small town in California. When we meet him, he has just been released from prison, is forbidden to go more than one hundred yards from his house, is wearing a monitoring device on his ankle, and is a habitual, though not very slick, thief.

The story is that Roman's old high school buddy, Brian (Paul Walker, who reappears from *The Fast and the Furious*), is in trouble himself for street racing. Paul has been recruited by the feds to help intercept a shipment of "dirty" money. Roman and Paul are some of the best street racers around and Roman is convinced to participate after being told that, if he does, his criminal record will be cleared and he can rid himself of the ankle accessory. The various predicaments of the duo, including one scene of homoerotic fighting and wrestling, are entertaining. It would have been cool if Roman could have been as slick and smart as he is fine and funny.

Fast cars are good. Smart men are better.

Wattstax–The Special Edition

June 13, 2003

Wattstax, the 1972 Los Angeles concert preserved through documentary and a recording, was far more about the people than the music. *Wattstax—The Special Edition,* in limited release this summer to mark the documentary's thirtieth anniversary, further bears out this point. Sure, the new and improved version includes the Isaac Hayes performance cut for legal reasons from the original film, but even a chain-clad Black Moses pales beside the funky parade of globular afros, hot pants, yay-wide apple caps, non-concert snippets from comedian Richard Pryor, and much funky Black attitude and voice.

In a liberating era when "express yourself" was a societal mantra and African-Americans were leading the charge in cultural revolution, *Wattstax* was surely the first theater-released documentary to focus so intensely on the social life of a Black community. Commemorating the 1965 Watts riots, it included interviews and other footage throughout the community. Director Mel Stuart got up close and personal commentary from the average Black man and woman on the streets, on subjects ranging from unemployment to White women to the meaning of the blues.

These folks interviewed are not middle class or necessarily educated—and that's all good. One brother with a thick scar down the middle of his chest speaks about how he learned in Soledad that prison is not the place to be. At some points, though, you feel like the White filmmakers share that canny knack with some White TV reporters of finding the craziest Black folks to put on camera.

The tenor is Southern California Southern—all those direct transplants from Arkansas, Alabama, Mississippi, and Texas who make South Los Angeles, really, one of the more down-home (can we say Bama?) places in the country, especially in 1972. So South Los Angeles was really one of the better big-city venues for Wattstax, which featured artists from the Memphis-based Stax record label. Hayes, in his post-*Shaft* fame, was Stax's biggest star at that moment, followed hard by the Staple Singers, who rode high on the charts that year with "I'll Take You There" and "Respect Yourself."

Most of the acts on the concert, however, such as Rufus Thomas, Carla Thomas, Johnny Taylor, and Albert King had seen their heyday. By 1972, they were running hard against Black artists with a more urban sound—folks like Stevie Wonder, Roberta Flack, Al Green, Billy Paul, and, of course, Motown or Motown-derived acts like the Temptations, Diana Ross, and Michael Jackson who topped the charts. Black folks were digging their roots music but wanted it with an edge that was either smoother (the Stylistics, Al Green), funkier (Parliament), or more Soul Train popping (the O'Jays) than what most Stax artists offered.

Without these artists on the lineup, the concert portion of this film is best described as a showcase of Stax talent during a time of expanding Black musical tastes, while the rest of the film serves as a mind-blowing time capsule of Watts. This is not to say that the artists here don't have their moments. Some of the best performances, by the Emotions in a neighborhood church and Johnny Taylor in a nightclub, occur away from the concert, which was held at the Los Angeles Coliseum and attended by 110,000 people. One indication of the changing musical times is that, when Rufus Thomas performs his big dance-based hits, "The Breakdown" and "The Funky Chicken," more of the young, enthusiastic crowd was popping and locking, a la Soul Train, rather than doing the then-dated breakdown or funky chicken. The Bar-Kays, in their weird gear, signal the emerging popularity of groups such as Earth, Wind & Fire and a fully constituted Parliament-Funkadelic.

Wattstax—The Special Edition will remind or educate about the power and promise of the '70s, a time when there was plenty of pre-hip-hop bling-bling and hoochie mama clothing—how many people remember the sizzler with the matching panties?—and a time when a stadium full of Black people raised their fists and chanted, in unison with the emcee, a young afroed Rev. Jesse Jackson, "I am somebody!"

This Far by Faith: African-American Spiritual Journeys

June 19, 2003

The extraordinary role that spirituality has played in the lives of African-Americans is given a thoughtful and compelling exploration in *This Far by Faith: African-American Spiritual Journeys,* a six-hour documentary series premiering on PBS.

Though historical in scope, spanning from African beginnings to this new century, the series avoids labeling itself as a documentary about *the* African-American spiritual journey. Rather, by focusing on individual "journeys," the show's producers—Blackside Inc. (creators of *Eyes on the Prize*), the Faith Project, and the Independent Television Service—have built rich narratives around individual people and the intimate relationship between the human being and spirit. *This Far by Faith* is the last project conceptualized by the founder of Blackside Inc., Henry E. Hampton, who died in 1998.

This Far by Faith doesn't tell all the story, but it tells much of it with informative interviews, colorful footage from today, and a lively inclusion of historic images and documents. It could use fewer talking heads and it could use more stories about Black women and faith.

Harriet Tubman wasn't called Moses for nothing.

Black Star—Bernie Mac in *Charlie's Angels: Full Throttle*

June 27, 2003

Near the merciful end of *Charlie's Angels: Full Throttle,* Bosley, the character played by Bernie Mac, declares, "It's raining White women!" Wow, who would figure that a throwaway line could epitomize both the superficiality of this action flick and Bernie Mac's pitiful role in it. All the subversive feminist promise of the original TV *Charlie's Angels* has been distilled into a frenzy of kick boxing in high-heel boots.

These three super-fem investigators, created for the 1970s hit television show, are given a super injection of adrenaline for this sequel to the 2000 film. *Charlie's Angels* has always been about this girl thing—not Bosley. He has always been, at best, a nerdy straight man to all the hormonal wildness of the angels. His character, now made Black (because Mac is supposedly the brother to the last Bosley, Bill Murray), has morphed into a different caricature. Bernie Mac has a limited, though entertaining, range to his acting. His trademark big and rolling eyes, set in his ebony skin, take on a whole different meaning outside the setting of a Black narrative and community, where we can laugh with him and not at him. In this film, he trips over himself with silliness while babysitting the angels. Who knows? Perhaps, if this series continues, they will have Bosley go back to school. Maybe he needs to go back and get his G.E.D. to make a more meaningful contribution to society—or at least to this film's dialogue.

23

Film Can Be Fierce

Unprecedented

July 1, 2003

While the 2004 presidential election looms on the horizon, it must still share the spotlight with the contentious race of 2000. Few have forgotten the controversial balloting in the state of Florida, which disenfranchised tens of thousands of voters, prompted an overhaul of the nation's voting system, and ended with a divided U.S. Supreme Court deciding, in effect, the winner of the presidential race.

Just how so many Floridians, particularly African-Americans, were disenfranchised, is recounted dramatically in the award-winning documentary *Unprecedented,* which is being screened around the country. Including scores of interviews and original footage from news organizations, the hour-long documentary details the concerted effort by Republicans to deliver Florida—governed by George Bush's brother, Jeb Bush—to the GOP.

Much of this hour-long video is based on reporting by investigative journalist Greg Palast, who is author of the book *The Best Democracy Money Can Buy.* For Palast, the issue in the Florida election is one of basic voting rights. "We thought the issue of race and voting was settled . . . after the Voting Rights Act of 1965," Palast says in an interview on the documentary. "Now we're back to the basic issue: Do Black people have the right to vote? Except, this time, it's not George Wallace standing in the doorway of a schoolhouse, saying, 'segregation now and forever.' Now, it's done quietly, and with computers."

The extraordinary events of the 2000 election revealed by *Unprecedented* have raised questions about the integrity of all U.S. elections now and in the future.

Case in point: Now, four years later, thousands purged illegally from Florida's roll have yet to be reinstated.

Black Star–Naomie Harris in *28 Days Later*

June 27, 2003

Move over, Jada. (Sorry!)

There is another fierce Black chick battling those evil nasty-nasties and she's appearing in one of the better edge-of-your-seat flicks to hit U.S. screens this summer. It's called *28 Days Later,* it's from London, and it's flying under the radar of Hollywood's big-budget slam-and-bam action movies.

Consider it a warning from across the pond, to match the many current warnings here about the dangers of weird science, especially if coupled with military madness. Jim (Cillian Murphy) awakes about a month after being in a coma from an accident on his bike. He leaves the empty hospital and walks the streets of a deserted London in total shock. It is only when he happens upon a church filled with corpses that he realizes that he has awakened to a nightmare. It is also shortly after this that he meets Mark (Noah Huntley) and Selena (Naomie Harris), seemingly the only other survivors of a deadly virus that has transformed those infected into savage beasts, wiped out much of the British population, and spurred evacuation of all those lucky enough to escape.

Selena, more than any other film role that I've seen, is a remarkable vision of a postapocalyptic Black warrior. With a bandana on her head and a long machete at the ready in her hand, she could just as well be a fierce escaped African of any quilombo in Brazil, maroon colony in Jamaica or the U.S., or settlement of cimarrones in Cuba. But in *28 Days Later,* she is the last woman standing in these times (wearing the requisite sharp, long leather coat). At the same time, she is an embodiment of the first woman standing, an original Eve trying to survive.

Harris is a remarkable newcomer to the screen. She looks great. She does not render Selena as a cardboard or comic-book heroine. Anyone who has to slice the heads off carnivorous attackers should be expected to be at least a little hard, but Harris (and the script by Alex Garland) does not make Selena into a super Sapphire or any neck-rolling stereotype. Serena is written and rendered as tough and smart, but also as tender and able to cry and smile. She is also caught in London's racial-sexual politics through the eyes of these White filmmakers and it is interesting to watch as her character unfolds. Like the story told in Zadie Smith's *White Teeth* (Harris starred in the television adaptation of that novel), *28 Days Later* tells the story of a London where Black folks, most especially Black men with White women and, to a lesser extent, the left-alone Black women with White men, do melt into the melting pot.

The director/producer team of Danny Boyle and Andrew Macdonald (*Trainspotting, A Life Less Ordinary*) are smart enough to craft this production so that it takes big advantage of suspense and the fear of the sudden attack (usually in the dark, in the basement, in a tunnel, you know the drill). The low-tech, grainy feel of many of the opening scenes do look a little cheesy but they also put us in the mind-set that we are watching something true unfold on television news. At the very start, we literally are watching TV scenes, of repeated and barbaric incidents of violence of humans inflicted on other humans. The film asks us in a horribly believable way to visualize a world where barbarism and rage is distilled into a virus that could kill us all and, yet, where there can be innocence, sweetness, and survival.

Whale Rider

July 4, 2003

Do yourself (and a child) a favor. Turn away, for a moment at least, from all the booming summer blockbusters and head to see *Whale Rider.* Set among the Maori people of New Zealand, this film artfully combines ancient myth with modern life, and mixes ideas about humanity and special powers in a far more natural way than another flick about super heroes or super freaks.

The Maori, who range in skin tone from cocoa to café au lait, have seen their people and culture decimated by war, European settlement, and colonization. Like *Once We Were Warriors,* a powerful 1994 film by Lee Tomahori about a Maori family's struggle to survive amid violence and poverty, *Whale Rider* deals primarily with conflict within the Maori community and family, and focuses on gender relations, rather than race or ethnicity, as a point of strife.

The script by director Niki Caro and the performance by Keisha Castle-Hughes infuses Pai's character with a powerful and right mix of sweetness and defiance. Gender roles are also explored through Pai's relationship with her grandmother and through the relationship between both grandparents. There is a wonderful scene at the start of the rites-of-passage program when Pai is, as usual, the leader of the group and singing. She sings in a rhythmic and soaring call and response with her grandmother who seems to beckon her, in this public ceremony, to greatness and to shatter the limitations forced onto her because of gender.

Bad Boys II

July 18, 2003

Despite the fact that in *Bad Boys II* there are more cars crashed than I've ever seen crashed in any movie ever, it is by far the best of the big action, fun flicks so far this summer. Will Smith and Martin Lawrence put the "whoa" factor back into going to the movies. Too bad the filmmakers, toward the end, ruin a perfectly good movie with a nonsensical reference linking Cuba to the U.S. drug trade.

After *Black Hawk Down,* I don't really expect any better from producer Jerry Bruckheimer. Maybe since the Ku Klux Klan also takes it on the chin early on in the story, the filmmakers figured that our sovereign socialist (and majority Black) neighbor to the south was fair game. But as far as enjoying the movie, the shoddy Cuba link occurs so late in the process that, by then, we've laughed at so many jokes and been so wowed by the loud music and zippy editing that it's easy not to let such ignorance totally spoil a good time.

In this sequel to the 1995 hit, Smith and Lawrence reappear respectively as Miami narcotics detectives Mike Lowrey and Marcus Burnett, who are tracking the import of large amounts of the designer drug ecstasy into the city. The investigation leads them to a ruthless drug kingpin, Johnny Tapia (Jorda Molla), who wants to take over the entire city's drug market. The detectives' intense and dangerous work, combined with the fact that Mike has developed a romantic link with Marcus's sister Syd (Gabrielle Union), bring the two into such conflict with each other that they are in danger of blowing the case and putting themselves and Syd in danger.

On the job and off, this duo is funny and has serious jokes. Some of the credit has to be given to John Lee Hancock's screenplay, which despite the lame Cuba bashing has good running jokes about anger management in the police department. But much of the big funny here, including the hilarious scene when a young suitor arrives to take Marcus's daughter out on a first date, is obviously cooked up by Smith and Lawrence. When, in the middle of a dangerous car chase in his Porsche, Mike suddenly starts bugging over minor damage to his car, all you can do is look at that Black man on the screen, laugh, and say, "true."

Watching *Bad Boys II,* it is easy to see why Will Smith was made into a star. He has the looks and presence and skills. It is also easy here to glimpse Lawrence's continued promise and talent as an actor, if only he has quality material to work with. He still is not forgiven for *Big Momma's House,* and his stand-up film *Runteldat* was only marginal, but *Bad Boys II* at least puts Lawrence back in the game.

Dirty Pretty Things

July 18, 2003

Part immigrant saga, part love story, and part thriller, *Dirty Pretty Things* is a seamless portrait of the civilized West as soulless and spiritually barren. In London's world of illegal immigrants, where a Nigerian named Okwe lives, human beings, especially the dark others, have been reduced to fleshy cogs in society's money-making machine. They give their labor, their bodies, and their minds but are officially nonexistent. Here, much of the action happens in the dark and the daylight is cold.

This is an immigrant story told through the eyes of director Stephen Frears (*Remains of the Day, Dangerous Liaisons*) and writer Steve Knight that is not sentimental or sparing. Once again, Frears commits himself to exploring the moral and emotional texture of lives. *Dirty Pretty Things* is so unwavering in its bleak focus that, even when it makes us laugh, it is an uneasy laugh. The life of Okwe (Chiwetel Ejiofor) is tightly confined. He is razor sharp and is a trained doctor but, in London, he drives a cab during the day, works a hotel front desk all night, and chews potent leaves to stay awake. A maid at the hotel, Senay (Audrey Tatou), who is from Turkey, is allowing him to rent the couch in her tiny flat. Both are subject to deportation at any time and are therefore subject to the evil intentions of those who treat them like cornered animals. As the story unfolds, both Okwe and Senay must decide what they will do, and not do, to survive.

In this story, not only does the West show its ugly backside to immigrants, it also shows its ignorance. There is a hooker, Juliette (Sophie Okonedo), who, despite her dark racial mix, keeps asking Okwe questions as if there is no drop of Africa in her veins. She wants to know if he comes from a place with lions. Has he ever seen a lion? She is oblivious to the fact that he comes from a place where some people have more self-respect than she has. She is definitely not making any connection between their dark skins.

With Juliette, however, we dark beings are once again presented on-screen with the contrast of the dark whore with the light (can pass for White) virginal woman in the person of Senay. Okwe adores Senay, even though she is slow to acknowledge any feelings for him. She eventually admits that she does have love for him but, in this netherworld of immigrants, mutual love does not guarantee a happy ending.

Frears makes sardonic comments here about affairs of the heart and, indeed, about the loss of heart, as well as loss of spirit. In their place, he presents the corrupted body with its various diseases, fluids, and deep wounds. He presents people who do not really "exist" in society and who can easily disappear into back alleys and inside hotel rooms. He presents a coldness but, for those who haven't given up, the possibility for warmth and the warm sun.

OPM—*Lara Croft Tomb Raider: The Cradle of Life*

July 21, 2003

At heart, Lara Croft is an old-fashioned adventure hero—wealthy, White, privileged, well educated and daring in a weak world that is, after all, hers to conquer. In *Lara Croft Tomb Raider: The Cradle of Life,* she is not more obnoxious than, say, James Bond or Indiana Jones but just a lot less believable and a lot more hokey. She is not unbelievable because she is a woman. Her girl status is only a footnote anyway. Her screen appeal is that she is just as rough, heartless, and ruthless as any man, and that she is able to kick a man's butt—and she does kick much butt.

But, sadly, even Croft's curled-lip toughness has the air of a rich girl trying too hard. Star Angelina Jolie pulls such a steel curtain across her emotions, and the script gives Croft such little humanity, that she might as well be that blond robot that kicks Arnold Schwarzenegger around on *Terminator 3: Rise of the Machines*. It is only toward the end, in a key scene, that you sense any emotion sloshing around beneath the curtain and, by then, the viewer might be too numb to care.

Like the first movie in this series, in which Jolie plays the only child of a slain expert in antiquities, there are heady and very silly moments of action. My favorite is when Croft punches a shark in the mouth and then jacks the shark, holding onto the big fin for a ride near the water's surface. See, if someone had punctured James Bond's air tank as goes the story line here, he would have had a little gadget that instantly generated more oxygen and another gadget that propelled him through the water to safety. (And we all would sit in the dark and say "Oooohhh!) Lara Croft needs to refinance that mansion and buy some better toys.

Usually in these flicks (*The Mummy,* etc.) the tombs, burial places, and history of some dark developing nation is ripe for plunder and destruction. This time, Croft sets her site on ruins left by Alexander the Great off the coast of Greece. She is in the search for a golden orb that, little does she know, tells the location of world's "cradle of life," (Africa, of course) and Pandora's Box. She must find and then secure the box before an evil bioterrorist gets his hands on it.

Of course the locations remain dark and exotic for the British heroine. China, Hong Kong, Tanzania, and Kenya. And, like in most of these flicks, the dark masses serve as a convenient backdrop of expendable villains or helpful sidekicks. Djimon Hounsou makes a brief appearance as one of Croft's helpers but does not fall into the trap of being a noble savage. These type of movies always acknowledge regions other than Europe as places of antiquity, and even as the birth of humanity, but then, in one fell swoop, make Whites into masters of the universe who ultimately decide *history*.

Lara Croft makes it *herstory* but it is still the same old tale.

Black Star—Samuel L. Jackson in *S.W.A.T.*

August 8, 2003

Breaking the mold of these high-octane flicks of summer, *S.W.A.T.* has the feel and pace of an old-fashioned cop movie, with more drama than eye-popping action. While this band of super cops works through hostage rescues, bank robberies, and prisoner escapes, the action unfolds at closer to real time and real life (and sometimes feels a little slow) but is not zipped along with hyper-quick editing or special effects.

For all of its plusses, which must include the script and dialogue, make no mistake, *S.W.A.T.* is also a slick promotion for the police as a quasimilitary force in the urban jungle. All of which is a very potent force against the urban hordes, depicted here as a largely criminal, insane, or unworthy element. Even the lowly homeless are made suspect and the audience is asked to laugh at police brutality and the possibility of prison rape for a hated suspect. While the urban masses are villified here, certain police elements don't fare much better. Pettiness and greed can be found in all quarters.

In the world of S.W.A.T., the path is narrow, the heroes are tough, and the bad guys are very, very bad. When you are S.W.A.T., there is not much room for error, weakness, or too much diversity. There isn't even room for a vegetarian who declines a good old American hot dog. Despite the inclusion of some kick-ass artists like Jimi Hendrix on the soundtrack, this is not a fancy musical video for the police.

Civil Brand

August 29, 2003

This favorite of the 2003 Black film festival circuit makes a foray into the nasty world of the prison-industrial complex, where those incarcerated in U.S. prisons are used as a super cheap supply of labor for corporations. The attempt to grapple with a serious and timely social issue is admirable and almost obscures the usual women-in-prison theme of at least seminudity or sexual exploitation of the cast. (Here, the attractive cast is LisaRaye, N'Bushe Wright, Monica Calhoun, Tichina Arnold, and Da Brat.) The many budget and production challenges faced by director Neema Barnette—including having her script, shooting schedule, and location slashed—are obvious, however, and the resulting film, reconfigured in the editing room, is only a shell of what it might have been. Despite the diminished potential, there are good performances, especially by Clifton Powell and Wright. Mos Def also makes a notable appearance.

The Fighting Temptations

September 19, 2003

Featuring Cuba Gooding Jr. and singer Beyonce Knowles, *The Fighting Temptations* feels like it was cut out and stitched together to fit the disparate talents of its two stars. Gooding plays a New York executive who travels south to collect an inheritance but finds that he must organize a gospel choir before he can get his cash. Once there, of course, Beyonce figures prominently in the singing and in the plot, which struggles to be mildy amusing.

Matters of Race

September 23, 2003

A more provocative title for the new PBS series *Matters of Race* might have been *Race: Beyond Black and White.* (But maybe someone's already tried that.) The four episodes, set in North Carolina, Los Angeles, South Dakota, Hawaii, and San Francisco, shift the starting point of the discussion about race away from the U.S. history of slavery and Jim Crow and toward race as it is experienced today by Mexican immigrants, young Native Americans, Hawaiians, and those who prefer to be called multiracial.

Not all history is cast aside, however, so the four episodes, shown in pairs, do have something substantial to contribute to the perpetual race debate, especially in light of the fact that those categorized as Hispanic now outnumber Blacks and are considered the nation's number-one "minority." The series, which has moments that are riveting, poignant, and funny, is also relevant because there are more people choosing to identify themselves as multiracial. Finally, *Matters of Race* gives voice to those, primarily in the Asian and Latino communities, who deeply resent the historical dominance of the Black-White race discussion and desperately long for more emphasis on how race impacts their communities. You can clearly hear this resentment in the comments of Angela Oh, a California attorney who is Korean, who bristles at what she says is a silencing of voices on the race issue "that are not Black or White."

The series begins in North Carolina, where one town, Siler City, has been dubbed by some as Little Mexico because of the tremendous influx of Mexican immigrants. Told primarily through the eyes of the newcomers, the show chronicles the impact on housing, jobs, education, churches, and, of course, race relations. Seen from the perspective of the immigrants to North Carolina, Black people are Americans with citizenship. There is no sense given here that the newcomers relate to Black people as another people of color. And, on the other side, it is clear that many Blacks trapped in low-paying jobs see the immigrants as competition for those jobs and as a force that will keep wages low.

A Black-Latino divide is also highlighted in the next story, which focuses on the King-Drew County Medical Center in South Los Angeles. The third episode, "We're Still Here," offers fresh insights into life on the Pine Ridge reservation of the Oglala Lakota nation. The final show includes three short, bright films directed by young filmmakers concerning the issues of being multicultural.

The Blues

September 28, 2003

The massive film project *The Blues* is an intricate study in the power of voice and perspective.

Interpreted freely through seven independent films by seven different filmmakers—Martin Scorsese, Wim Wenders, Richard Pearce, Charles Burnett, Marc Levin, Mike Figgis, and Clint Eastwood—the subject of the blues is handled with energy, creativity, and as the unique vision of each director or auteur, all of whom are men and only one of whom is African-American. The production was not designed to have a pure documentary approach, which might have made it more historically complete and comprehensive but, on the other hand, might have made it far less poetic.

As it is, we are privileged to witness through these full-length films young bluesman Corey Harris connect with roots of the blues in West Africa. We consider the mind-blowing fact that blues records were sent into space to represent earthlings to aliens. We go on the road with B. B. King and also experience the marriage of hip-hop to blues as Chuck D and Common jam with the oldheads of Electric Mud.

But as with any approach so freewheeling to a subject so important, the viewer might especially be conscious of what is included and what is excluded. Take, for example, the fact that the first image for the entire series, repeated each night in the introductory montage, is that of a Black woman bent over with her back to the camera, with her generous and jiggly derriere humping up and down in a booty dance performance.

Considering the fact that Black women are given scant attention in this series, dedicated to an art form launched by the likes of Ma Rainey, Ida Cox, and Bessie Smith, this image of a dancer for bluesman Bobby Rush is the strongest impression of Black womanhood presented, overshadowing brief appearances by singers Shemekia Copeland or Taylor. It completely obliterates those artists barely mentioned, if at all, such as Billie Holiday. (In contrast, an entire film, *Red,White and Blues,* directed by Mike Figgis, is dedicated to White British musicians who are credited with, in the 1960s, expanding the appreciation for blues artists among Whites in the United States.)

Another striking inclusion, at the start of Burnett's film, is an image of a lynching and of a prison chain gang. These images may be the most graphic attempt in the series to give some attention to why African-Americans sang the blues in the first place.

Sure, any blues project should highlight the brilliant, moving, and often funny performances (a favorite new blues lyric from Skip James—"I'd rather be the devil than be that woman's man"). We'd all prefer to hear Muddy Waters, B. B. King, or Howlin Wolf rather than a bunch of talking heads.

But the missing piece of the puzzle—why did we sing the blues?—proves important to countering the undercurrent of questions bubbling beneath the surface of such a massive effort: Are the blues dying or dead? Have younger generations of African-Americans let White people "steal" our music? Why don't we honor our roots?

Such questions are left echoing in the wind by *The Blues,* which speaks with great eloquence about the art without probing in too much detail the pain of the blues, and why younger generations of African-Americans might turn away from that pain or interpret it in a different way. (And why Whites might "embrace" it in a whole other way.)

The Blues (which has been trademarked as a phrase for this show—but at least it isn't *Martin Scorsese's Blues*) contains a wealth of information and inspiration. It ultimately serves best the vision of these filmmakers, who are interested in exploring their own questions and approach the subject matter with their own creative perspectives and voices.

Out of Time

October 2, 2003

With *Out of Time,* director Carl Franklin manages to recycle the tried-and-true thriller format into a fresh and likeable flick. In the beginning, there are some moments of awkwardness as the script sets up all the pieces that will come falling down later. But when the pieces do fall, the effect is—yes—thrilling, like a thriller should be.

Of course, it doesn't hurt that Franklin has a big assist from two of Hollywood's most likeable and, probably more important, believable actors—Denzel Washington and Sanaa Lathan. In setting up an extraordinary story of betrayal, at least Franklin has the charisma of these two, plus their easy chemistry, to smooth over the shortcomings. This issue of believability and charisma—and how each viewer relates to the actors—makes all the difference in a genre with so many twists and turns, and I think that Washington and Lathan pull it off. (And for the first time since, perhaps, *Devil in a Blue Dress,* Denzel has what appears to be hot sex in a movie. Kind of gives a new meaning to the term "thriller.")

OPM–*Kill Bill*

October 10, 2003

In his fourth film, which is the first of two parts, director Quentin Tarantino continues to dabble in his theater of the absurd. His theater is always profane, violent, bloody, and especially indifferent toward innocence or racial sensitivity. In this film, he continues to focus on the theme of the avenging angel/cowboy/hero and adds to the mix more martial arts, animation, and scene after spectacular scene of sprayed and splattered blood. The Bride (aka Black Mamba, played by the blonde Uma Thurman) awakes after being in a coma for four years, intent on killing a gang of assassins who tried to murder her on the day of her wedding. Meticulously working from her "kill list," she travels the United States and abroad in search of her victims. No doubt Black Mamba, who is a skilled fighter, must be added to film's list of kick-ass females. She must also be added to film's list of Great White Hopes, as she wreaks havoc with Vernita Green, played by Vivica A. Fox, and, in a big showdown, the entire Japanese *yakuza*, headed by O-Ren Ishii (Lucy Liu).

OPM–*Pieces of April*

October 17, 2003

Even as it ignores the stickier issues of interracial romance, *Pieces of April* offers so many moments that are genuine, funny, and poignant that it is difficult to complain that it is just another movie asking us to sympathize with another story of crazy White folks.

Scary Movie 3

October 24, 2003

Even though the *Scary Movie* franchise has passed on to new hands—David Zucker, Brian Lynch, and Craig Mazin—it is still as tacky as ever, only now the humor has veered in the direction of *Dumb and Dumberer* and other White-boy comedies. This switch simply means that in place of hip-hop jokes about getting blunted, the new *Scary Movie 3* offers a beer-commercial aesthetic. Consider early scenes when the twins from the Coors beer commercials are front and center and shaking their assets.

From there, most of the humor only goes downhill, although with fewer Wayans-style scenes of cheesy sex or toilet acts. In the place of these, there are vomit, jokes about women's bodies, corpses, and—really not funny to me—very flip abuse and violence against an admittedly obnoxious child.

Okay, I can hear some saying, gosh, it's only a movie. Some things are just a laugh. Yup. It sure is just a movie. But movies and images are powerful, and it doesn't hurt to stop and think about what and who is made into a joke. Sometimes the joke is on us.

OPM—*The Human Stain*

October 31, 2003

Even though the director, actors, and writers of *The Human Stain* do protest such a characterization, this film is very much about a light-skinned Black man's rejection and hatred of his Blackness. It is also about his overwhelming lust for White women, who dance nude across the screen as in some racist's vision of what a Black man's heaven would be. It is so lacking in sympathy or understanding of the connection between Black identity, pride, and love—and so intent on raising up only the limits of Black oppression—that it is like a big glob of derision in the face of the Black community.

This unfortunate quality of the movie, which is very faithful to the novel by Philip Roth, is not readily apparent. It is so beautifully shot and skillfully directed by Robert Benton (*Kramer vs. Kramer, Places in the Heart*) that its derision sort of sneaks up on you, like a bad flashback to *Monster's Ball.* But then little odd things are included, like a scene with a caged crow that "doesn't know how to be a crow," or another scene when the young, very fair-skinned Black protagonist pummels a darker Black man in the boxing ring as if to knock out the Blackness in his very own soul.

In looking at such a complex and painful subject from outside the Black community and with no kinship with Blackness, *The Human Stain* layers these insults like a frothy white icing over very bitter chocolate. Roth, who learned of "passing" from a friend in graduate school, says of his main character Coleman Silk: "All he's ever wanted from earliest childhood on, was to be free, not Black, not even White—just on his own and free." This is a nice but somewhat naive sentiment because the fact is that Roth created a character who equated that sought-after freedom with being White. Silk ultimately equates his identity and being "on his own" with rejecting his racial heritage and identifying with a community that, in the 1940s when this novel is set, still viciously and systematically attacked his own.

Perhaps film critics aren't supposed to reveal Silk's "terrible secret" in the plot of *The Human Stain,* but it is impossible to write about what works and what does not work in it without revealing this central aspect of the plot (and we know that www.seeingblack.com's readers care more about these issues than some faux standard for journalistic conduct). Also, not to talk about the racial dimensions of the film means that we also cannot discuss how the film handles race.

The story focuses on Silk (Anthony Hopkins), an eminent classics professor at a small liberal arts college in New England whose career is cut prematurely short when he is accused of bigotry. With his life suddenly in a shambles, he begins an affair with a young woman half his age who works at the college and at the local post office as a cleaning lady. She also milks cows in exchange for a room at a farm. The part of this down-and-out woman, who harbors demons and secrets of her own, is played by the delicate Nicole Kidman, who is about as believable as Spike Lee playing Shaquille O'Neal. There is something way off-kilter in scale with this bit of casting.

On the other hand, Anna Deveare Smith delivers a very moving performance as Silk's mother, who, though fair-skinned, tries to instill in her son notions of race pride and solidarity, but to no avail, and who grapples, really, with the loss of her son. Though he is still living, it is as if her son has died. He tells his White girlfriends that he is an only child and that his parents are dead. The final meeting between Silk and his mother is as poignant as the scene in *Antwone Fisher* between mother and son, only in *The Human Stain* it is the son who is guilty of abandonment.

I hesitate to use the word "guilty." Though Silk's life is referred to in this film as a "tragedy," the story works hard to absolve him of his choices, as if it is, of course, the most natural thing in the world for a Black man to want to be White, and as if he did not leave anything of value when he left his community. It sides with him against those who are silly enough to accuse him of bias. It acknowledges his self-hatred while, at the same time, ignoring all the possible consequences of that self-hatred. And, you know what? This story is true of some Black souls—we meet them now, even in a new century, but in the hands of Black people, their stories are clearly tragedies. As told here, the writers and director cheer on the Black man's "triumph" over group Black identity. They cry out to those who pass: Go ahead, free your inner White man!

Wow. What a definition of what it means to be free.

The Matrix Revolutions

November 5, 2003

The Matrix Revolutions, the third and final installment in the *Matrix* trilogy, builds to a futuristic final conflict between good and evil, with a knock-down-drag-out battle between Neo, the savior of the world, and his arch-nemesis Agent Smith. In it, Morpheus (Laurence Fishburne), Trinity (Carrie-Anne Moss), Niobe (Jada Pinkett Smith), and other remaining humans on Earth try to save their underground city, Zion, from the ravenous and powerful machine world. Regardless of whether the "wow" special-effects factor of the original *Matrix* has worn thin for you, this remains science fiction and fantasy filmmaking on a grand scale, both in technique and ideas.

To arrive at its big finale, the film connects a lot of dots from the first two films. And because of its complexity, with many jumps and shifts in the plot and extended dialogue, the first half might drag a bit for action fans. As in *The Matrix Reloaded,* the filmmakers, the Wachowski brothers, stop the mayhem for long periods and take time to talk. An elderly woman teaches a young girl to make cookie dough. A father talks to a stranger about saving his daughter's life. Agent Smith prattles on about the uselessness of human beings. Predictably, lovers declare their undying commitment to each other. This is all shot and stitched together to create a tapestry of apocalypse that might be more satisfying to those of us with longer attention spans.

Because Neo (Keanu Reeves) is the one with the power to save humanity, and because so much of the action switches to him and Agent Smith, portions of *The Matrix Revolutions* feel like a cyber version of an old-fashioned Western, with the showdown at high noon between two White guys. Even so, this film series has been remarkable for its inclusion of a diversity of humanity in a futuristic setting. That diversity is even extended further this time with the Chinese attendant to the oracle taking on a greater role, a man from New Zealand featured as a fierce Zion soldier, and the hint that the elderly African-American oracle is passing on her vision to a young Indian girl.

The role of Morpheus, which helped attract many of us to *The Matrix* in the first place, has decreased in importance as Neo has honed and developed his powers and as the script has highlighted the strengths of other people of color, particularly Niobe. In the beginning, Morpheus was the man, he was actually the one humans looked up to as they survived and searched for "the one." In the evolved story line and in the context of the bigger picture, Morpheus is viewed by many in Zion as a sort of eccentric man of faith, a believer in doubtful miracles. The Wachowski brothers resist this sort of tit-for-tat, however, in scenes between Neo and Morpheus. Whenever they bring the two men together, the meeting is always one of mutual respect, with one always giving honor to the other.

That mutual respect, a last bit of raw humanity, is an important underlying strength of the *Matrix* series. In this world, where so much has been honed to a hard edge of metal or computer chip, where nothing is easy or predictable, respect—even between sworn and equally matched foes—keeps us wrapped up in the intrigue, keeps us wondering whether we will all be saved.

Postscript: Sophia Stewart, a Black woman living in Salt Lake City, claimed in a 2003 lawsuit filed in California that The Matrix *and* Terminator *film franchises were based on her ideas. She says she sent a copyrighted short story titled "The Third Eye" to the Wachowski Brothers in 1986 in response to an ad they placed in a national magazine soliciting science-fiction ideas for a comic book. Though Stewart's case ignited a firestorm on the Internet—and a widely circulated but erroneous news article article stated that she was victorious with it—her case was actually dismissed in June 2005 when a judge ruled that she had failed to produce evidence of her claim in a timely manner. Stewart has announced that she will continue to pursue her case.*

24

A Troublesome Property

Tupac: Resurrection

November 14, 2003

The same camera presence and raw heart that made Tupac Shakur an artist to be reckoned with also makes *Tupac: Resurrection* an engaging, though somewhat drawn out and one-sided, narrative. On the positive side, it allows a young Black man to funnel important U.S. history of the 1980s and 1990s—including Reaganomics, crack, and the widening gap between rich and poor—through his own urban sensibility. On the down side, by excluding "outside" voices, it presents a simplistic account of many controversial episodes in Tupac's life, such as his role in the molestation of a young woman, for which he served prison time, or earlier run-ins with the police in California.

We are also not confronted with Tupac's opportunism or the extent to which he may have encouraged hype and controversy to serve his career. Tupac possessed both star quality and troubling demons. He could be infectious then exasperating, and—by his own admission—arrogant and egotistical to a fault. Like a favorite cousin, or a big or little brother, he oozed with an endearing imperfect humanity, both in film and on stage. His frequent bouts of insane or stupid behavior could be dismissed by fans as by-products of tortured genius. Then, in September of 1996, he was shot to death—and his murder remains unsolved.

These highs and lows are handled with detail and sensitivity in the film, which was produced by MTV Films in collaboration with his mother, Afeni Shakur. A mother's touch is obvious here; the entire film is told largely in his own words, as opposed to the words of journalists, critics, or even family or friends. When Tupac is not "speaking" through old audio or video footage, there are scenes from concerts or backstage clowning, or still images of him as a baby, young boy, teenager, and, finally, as a young man haunted by poverty, paranoia, and extreme anger.

As it recounts an important era in hip-hop, the rise of so-called gangsta rap, it does so from the eyes of the gangsta celebrity, which doesn't mean that the truth is totally glossed over. The producers include much footage of Tupac acting out, spitting at cameramen, and defending his use of the terms "bitch" and "ho" to describe women. We are forced to live though all the juvenile hype and media manipulation all over again from that era when MTV made hip-hop stars into Black "leaders," while, at the same time, further wresting control of the music away from the Black community.

As *Tupac: Ressurection* includes loads of MTV footage, especially of Tupac conducting an interview with a young White woman while strolling along the boardwalk in Venice, California, it is obvious to the media savvy what is happening: MTV, the original mass disseminator of many of the images and messages about gangsta rap, is back, ten years later, to interpret and analyze for us, and present the final and "authorized" word on Tupac.

Black Star—Djimon Hounsou in *In America*

November 26, 2003

There is something about the Lower East Side of Manhattan, or the romantic notion of it anyway, that is used to bridge the racial divide on the big screen. The latest contribution to the LES genre is *In America,* a sweet and touching flick, told largely through the eyes of a young girl, about a penniless Irish couple, Johnny and Sarah, who move to the United States with their two young daughters. The oldest girl, Christy, remembers the day they moved into their ratty apartment as the day they moved to the building with the screaming man.

That screaming man is a painter named Mateo (Djimon Hounsou), who lives among a clutter of art supplies and a big refrigerator that is empty except for large bottles of medicine. His door is marked crudely with paint to warn away potential visitors who aren't already turned away by his frequent shrieks and hollers. We do learn a very important fact about Mateo but we never learn much more. We see a snapshot of his parents and we can assume, along with the Irish woman talking to him at the time, that at one time he was rich. We can assume that he is tortured by his art because he tears his canvases to shreds with a knife. Other than that, he seems to be totally alone in the world, except for his newfound connection with the new family on the top floor.

This limited sketch of Mateo is noticeable in a story that so richly fills in the physical and emotional details of Johnny and Sarah's family. While we are drawn into the lives and story of the couple, Mateo is simply a bit player, just as Derek Luke played the somewhat anonymous part of Bobby in *Pieces of April,* which was also set on the Lower East Side and focused on the family of Bobby's (White) girlfriend. Both films draw these Black men as nearly blank slates that are "filled in" by their association with Whites. (The presence of the Black men also seems to serve as an illustration of at just how low a station in life these White people exist.)

Fortunately, *In America* also shows how Johnny and Sarah's family is enriched by their association with Mateo. He offers them African wisdom and sets Johnny straight about his racist assumptions and condescension. He teaches them to value their lives, no matter how humble. It would be easy to characterize Hounsou's role as an urbanized version of the noble savage but that wouldn't be fair. He infuses what little he is given with so much life, passion, and sophistication that perhaps he enhances what the script originally offered.

Life happens quickly in *In America.* Johnny pursues his acting career. His wife learns that she is pregnant, while the girls quickly adapt to the American rituals of Halloween and school plays. All the while, the family wrestles with their own recent tragedy. If Mateo is given no history, the family is given a troubled one. Together, they all form a tightly wound narrative that is full of sadness, struggle, and surprising joy.

Honey

December 5, 2003

Honey is a lot like its main character—lightweight, plastic in a benign sort of way, and, at times, somewhat likeable and entertaining. It is certainly one of the more well-intentioned urban films to come along in a while. You can take children to see it. There is no gratuitous butt-naked action. No gratuitous violence or profanity. Rather, it is a vehicle for the young actress Jessica Alba to star on the big screen. There are so many Alba close-ups in the beginning scenes you might think for a minute that you are watching a remake of *Glitter.*

Honey is sort of an updated *Flashdance.* But, in our MTV culture, Alba plays a New York dancer named Honey Daniels who aspires not to ballet or to the Alvin Ailey Company but, rather, to dance hip-hop moves in music videos. This aspect of the film, which illustrates the creation of TV illusion and the unscrupulous ways of some music industry professionals, is actually more interesting than others. It allows the filmmakers to critique the pop culture machine that it also promotes. It allows them to offer alternative models for what it means to be an artistic success.

Love Don't Cost a Thing

December 12, 2003

It's now official: The Nickelodeon/Disney Channel generation has grown up and bumrushed the movie studios. With the release of *Love Don't Cost a Thing* coming on the heels of *Honey,* it's clear that the steady stream of teen programming, regularly pumped out and aired on these types of channels, is making its way to the big screen for Black audiences.

Both *Honey* and *Love Don't Cost a Thing* are only notches in quality above the made-for-TV fare on these channels. The difference is that these two theatrical releases are seasoned with more Black attitude and ambience, and they are skewed older than movies such as *The Lizzie Maguire Movie.* The plots and dialogue are predictable. The performances are by young talents that are budding but not quite fully blossomed. But perhaps traditionally important staples of film are not make-or-break for this genre that emphasizes attractive crossover actors and features scenes with loud music and bikini-clad girls.

The story in *Love Don't Cost a Thing* is an update of the 1987 teen comedy *Can't Buy Me Love.* It features Nick Cannon, well known to the Nickelodeon/Disney crew long before *Drumline* because of his appearances on shows like *All That* and *The Nick Cannon Show.* He plays a science nerd named Alvin Johnson who seizes the opportunity to trade in life with good grades and geeky friends for a shot at being cool and part of the in-crowd. His opportunity comes through the most popular and beautiful girl in the school, Paris Morgan (Christina Milian), who agrees to be his girlfriend for a while in exchange for a car repair job. The trick is that Alvin also spends money on the repair that he had been saving for a scholarship science project.

The results of this little arrangement do provide some lessons and laughs but many of the jokes are well worn. There are the usual dumb and bullying jocks and catty girls. There is some effort to draw the interest of older viewers with a wacky appearance by comedian Steve Harvey. He plays the part of Alvin's dad, who is stuck in the '70s with oldies by Al Green and Earth, Wind & Fire blaring from an eight-track cassette player. The writers consider old-school Black culture as a place of weirdness where no cool person dare tread, as opposed to the very root from which all coolness originates. There is even some wack reference here to Alvin's afro, as if she is stating a generally acknowledged truth about the unacceptability of Black natural hair.

In fits and starts, *Love Don't Cost a Thing* clatters on awkwardly to its finale. Cannon does not play a very good nerd. Milian actually comes across as a three-dimensional character but her lively screen presence alone cannot keep the film afloat. Black teen movies don't have to be remakes of White teen movies. You can't just graft Black skin over the same formulas and, presto, make a Black movie that feels real.

Cinderella, the Bond Girl, and the Big Girl—*Maid in Manhattan, Die Another Day,* and *Real Women Have Curves*

December 23, 2003

Cinderella is alive and well in the new millennium. This fact will not come as a surprise to anyone who watches music videos, does nails, reads women's magazines, or watches TV shows like *The Bachelor.* This week, add to the churning Cinderella industry *Maid in Manhattan,* a new film starring Jennifer Lopez that updates the fairy tale with twists on race, class, and politics. Like the last big Cinderella flick, *Pretty Woman,* this film is often ebullient, funny, and aw-shucks cute in its tale of a poor woman rescued from her bleak existence by a wealthy prince.

Lopez plays an attractive single mother named Marisa who lives in the Bronx with her son, Ty. With a quick reference to him as *papi*, it is established early on that Marisa is Puerto Rican, but there are no other ethnic signs in the language, music, or general culture of the little family. Marisa has to say her last name, Ventura, to be identified to the larger world as a Latina. Ty is studying the 1970s at his elementary school and he readily fills his headphones with speeches by Richard Nixon and music by Simon and Garfunkel. (In this 2002 fairy tale, even a ten-year-old must get ready for society's ball!)

The ethnic and working-class burlesque continues at the hotel, where Marisa punches her card and joins other maids in the basement. Her fellow workers include a sisterly pal and a sizable Aunt Jemima–like Black woman who serves as a reminder of the gap in social mobility between fair-skinned Latinas and those from darker branches of Africa's tree. When, through a predictable cinematic trick of mistaken identity, Marisa gets a shot at snagging the presumably rich White Republican senatorial candidate Chris Marshall (Ralph Fiennes), who's staying at the hotel, her fellow maids rally around her, helping in whatever way they can to serve up their fairest one of all to the prince. And they cheer her on. What a feat! What a chance that must be grabbed—to be considered so fine, that one might be sucked from the literal basement and be placed beside the prince!

With a wink, the filmmakers ask us to believe, of course, that the story is really about the pure honesty of love, the power of love to overcome nasty man-made barriers to romantic bliss. But they leave powerful clues (wink-wink) that it really isn't about love and honesty at all. First of all, as much as Marisa is portrayed as a stand-up girl—she challenges the Republican a little about politics and policies—she is not stand-up enough to reveal who she really is (he thinks she's a wealthy socialite) or interrogate his politics. The omission amounts to her admitting that something is wrong with who she is and that Chris would not like her if he knew the truth. The promotional movie poster has J. Lo lovingly looking up at a vision of herself with Marshall as if she is glancing toward heaven (and of course, J. Lo's real-life pending nuptials to the "sexiest man alive" Ben Affleck cannot be left off the table).

Despite its inevitable fairy-tale ending—in which all is revealed, and accepted—it is the traditional aspect of Cinderella's disguise that makes *Maid in Manhattan* less about love and more about self-denial. As always, J. Lo is the official crossover chick who is able to pass even when, as in this flick, she is supposedly not really passing at all. She is able to flash her ethnicity, or, as always, her butt, like a stripper flashes her thigh. She charmingly peels back the layers, showing what a woman of color should be (certainly at least striving for the blue blazer of low-level hotel management) and what she should hide in order to be worthy of Cinderella's prince.

Berry Gets Behind (and Beneath) Bond

James Bond 007 never has to change. It may appear in *Die Another Day* that Pierce Brosnan brings us an edgier and grungier spy, but all this instant funk is just meant to fool us into thinking that things are different, especially since he gets beat up and gets down with Halle Berry.

The standard Bond props are still here. There is the tired, heavy-handed jingoism, with North Korea getting the villain treatment this time. There are the great gadgets, including a fly invisible car and a ring that shatters plate glass. There are the girls, girls, girls, who still find a more wrinkled Bond just absolutely irresistible. Speaking of girls, this film marks, of course, the debut of Berry as a (good) Bond girl. She does a serviceable job as an action hero but there is something wispy and unconvincing in her portrayal.

Watching Berry with a gun is a little like watching the comedian Mo'Nique suddenly skinny. Like all these Bond women, Berry's character, Jinx, is a little on the fast side. One minute she's speaking to a stranger, sipping a mojito, making sexy conversation, and the next minute she's fully mounted, swapping spit and, we are to assume, other bodily fluids.

Berry's fast-track sex is supposed to be seen less in the context of the stereotyped hot Black mama or Berry's aggressions toward White men in *Swordfish* or *Monster's Ball,* but all that history remains on the table. Here we are to assume that Jinx is just as smitten with Bond as every other woman has always been and just can't help herself. Some film-industry types, who measure success in terms of dollars and high-profile placement, consider Berry's role a real breakthrough. And, at one time, I also longed to see a pretty Black, romantic heroine on the screen loved and appreciated. But that idea isn't exactly what we get in the roles played by Berry and Thandie Newton (the other biracial actress allowed to go groin-to-groin with Hollywood's White leading men). Berry is less a prize and heroine here than an accessory in Bond's world of testosterone supremacy (not to mention White supremacy). Bond doesn't change, only the scenery, villains, gadgets, and girls around him do.

There are lots of fun action sequences and lots of unintentionally funny ones as well. My favorite such funny moment is when Bond stylishly pursues the bad guys in subfreezing temperatures, clad in his chic black turtleneck and no coat. Some things never change.

Curvy Comedy

If sappy-soap opera plots, on the big and small screen, have dulled your appetite for coming-of-age stories, take heart. *Real Women Have Curves* has enough attitude, drama, humor, and fresh air—as well as stellar performances—to make you savor the genre one more time.

Set in the Mexican-American neighborhood of East Los Angeles, the film follows Ana Garcia (America Ferrera), who, when the film opens, is preparing to leave her family's small, stucco home for her final day of high school. The story is propelled by the hilarious tug-o-war between Ana, the strong-willed baby of the family, and her mother, Carmen (Lupe Ontiveros), a matronly arch-critic. Carmen berates Ana's full figure and insists that her daughter live her life in the same way that women of the family always have: Get married and take care of a husband and children.

Ferrera carries the part of Ana, and the entire film for that matter, like a seasoned pro, making a convincing performance of adolescent despair, insecurity, willfulness, deceit, and determination. As she slides, marches, or stomps through her world, she reminds us of a time when even a girl's decision of how to walk is ridden with angst. Writer Josefina Lopez has infused this story, based in large part on her own life, with a warm brand of wit, humor, and eccentricity. Director Patricia Cardoso offers a fresh story from *el barrio.* It does not take us deeply into the subject of ethnic or racial identification. Ana tends toward assimilation in her attitudes. We do know that she believes that something else, probably something bigger and better, awaits her outside the reach and harsh glare of her mother. And we leave her to find that better thing.

OPM—*Cold Mountain*

December 25, 2003

When early trailers and press information began to circulate on the film *Cold Mountain,* I mentally rolled my eyes. Oh, now Hollywood wants me to sympathize with a Confederate soldier. In the same season that I was expected to accept Tom Cruise as a samurai warrior and Uma Thurman as a *yakuza*-killing machine, I felt a distinct bout of Western revisionism coming down upon me.

But such bouts are just par for the course. (Especially when it comes to the Civil War, which obviously some people have never gotten over. Did I ever tell you about the Dolly Parton attraction in Myrtle Beach, South Carolina, where they replay the Civil War and each side gets to win? Talk about revisionism.) Most films and TV shows do not really deal with race and racism. To cite a more contemporary example, even Eminem's *8 Mile* was a racial fantasyland filled with Black folks from the hood who love to hang with a White boy and, on the other hand, White trailer folks who don't have an ounce of bigotry. And we all know that more artsy fare such as *Monster's Ball* and *The Human Stain* are grossly racist. With so many other films out there, I decided that I didn't need to see *Cold Mountain.*

So it is from this perspective, of someone who reviews film for a living, that I considered the swelling controversy about the film. The first hint of it came in an e-mail forwarded from an "underemployed, under-appreciated" actor named Erik Todd Dellums. Ultimately calling for a boycott of the film, Dellums cited, in part, the fact that the film begins with the depiction of a decisive Civil War battle in which Black Union soldiers actually played a pivotal role and suffered high casualties. In *Cold Mountain,* however, these Union soldiers are White, not Black. Then I read William Jelani Cobb's piece *The Disappearing Negro,* which pointed out how *Cold Mountain* deftly avoids the fact that Confederate soldiers were fighting for a system that would, in effect, continue the enslavement of Black people. The writer Makani

Themba-Nixon also reminded me that films are, for many, the new journalism. There are scores of people, particularly young people, looking at films as real accounts of history and truth. And this is why it is necessary to throw the red flag.

But mine is not the impassioned protest of a frustrated Black actor, nor is it necessarily the same as that of a historian (who can, by the way, at Oscar time, talk about how *Cold Mountain* is "historically inaccurate" and, therefore, unworthy of an award, as Denzel was overlooked for *The Hurricane*). But my protest is against this steady drumbeat of images and revised histories that ask me, time and time again, to sympathize with racists, that proceed as if racism does not exist. I could just as well title this piece "The Disappearing Racist" because, when it comes to race, Hollywood has a hard time telling it like it is.

Protesting the slick revisionism of big-budget, beautifully made films like *Cold Montain* is correct but it's not enough. I am way past complaining about White people not putting Black history in their movies. There are exceptions like *Glory,* but most of the time when they do put us in, they get it wrong anyway. (When interviewed by the *Washington Post,* the filmmakers said that race was too raw an issue to put in their film.)

If I've learned anything in years of writing about art, it is that art is about someone telling their own story, and who gets the opportunity to tell their own story. We need to make sure that we tell ours. And support ours. It is just as important that Black folks support wonderful films, based on our history and literature, like *Beloved* or *Rosewood,* as it is to get upset at *Cold Mountain.*

Yes, all of media, film and journalism, too, is increasingly concentrated into the hands of big, White-run corporations that are, at best, often indifferent to our stories and histories. So we need to create our own means to create and distribute our stories. Yes, at first they will not have big budgets. Yes, at first they will not open on thousands of screens. Yes, filmmakers who continue to pioneer on this path (already blazed by others) will have to live without the description "millionaire," but, in exchange, Black people will be telling our own stories and history. *Cold Mountain* is less about the Civil War than it is a love story. Let's write, produce, and star in our own love stories. Let's not be content with bit parts in someone else's version of history. Let's write our own history.

The Battle of Algiers

January 9, 2004

If history does belong to those who tell it, then director Gillo Pontocorvo claims a fat portion of it for the Algerian people and the Algerian revolution in *The Battle of Algiers,* a taut, riveting film that recounts the 1950s Algerian resistance against French colonialism.

Distributed originally in 1965, this black-and-white classic has been rereleased just as the history it tells is strikingly relevant to current world events, namely the U.S. invasion and occupation of Iraq. Apparently, those at the Pentagon thought the film was so important that they actually held a private screening of it recently, promoting it with fliers that read, "How to win a battle against terrorism and lose the battle of ideas. Children shoot soldiers at point-blank range. Women plant bombs in cafes. Soon the entire Arab population builds to a mad fervor. Sound familiar?"

While we don't know how similar any of these described scenes from *The Battle of Algiers* are to the situation in Iraq, the film draws more meaningful parallels: There is the element of race, as White colonialists subjugate people of color, in Africa in this case. Set entirely in the Algerian capital, Algiers, the locals are called "dirty Arabs" and, after decades of occupation, many have been reduced to alcoholism, drug abuse, or prostitution. There is the National Liberation Front, or FLN, that, in nonmilitary terms, might remind African-Americans of the 1970s impact of the Nation of Islam, as it encouraged self-pride, sobriety, and the protection of Black women. Lacking a Pentagon-type budget, the FLN measures its success in bombings and individual shootings of the occupying police and soldiers, one by one. The French are the law and, therefore, resistance is outlawed. If you fight against the occupiers, you are committing a crime, so all resisters are criminals that are tortured and killed.

Finally, *The Battle of Algiers,* even by its rerelease—for years it was banned in France and has been largely unavailable in the United States—makes clear the supreme importance of information and media. Who gets to control what we read, see, and hear? How much of how we feel about the Iraq war is based on what media we listen to, watch, or read? This fact is brought home at many points in the film, most poignantly late in the narrative, when a young boy steals the microphone used by the French military to broadcast dispiriting messages into the Arab quarter. With the microphone in his hands, the boy yells messages of resistance and soon the forlorn crowd raises its fist in defiance.

Like Raoul Peck's *Lumumba,* which came many years after it, *The Battle of Algiers* was one of the first films, if not the first, to achieve the rare feat of telling history in large part from the eyes of the Black, Brown, and Yellow people of the formerly colonized world. Even so, Pontocorvo stands somewhat outside of the fray, neither making the French into stock evil characters, nor making the Algerians into saints.

The narration describes the scenes and players without emotion, as a newscaster might in a documentary, as powerful explosions of life, death, danger, and revolution quickly unfold.

Appreciation—Ron O'Neal

January 17, 2004

Actor Ron O'Neal, who died on January 14 at the age of sixty-six, may bear the distinction of being the actor with the briefest yet most influential career in Black film. In 1972, when *Superfly* was released, it was a time of rapid social change—for the upwardly mobile anyway—in the Black community. The Black Power movement had given birth to a Black-pride movement, and afros, afro puffs, dashikis, and fist medallions were the order of the day. "Even Diana Ross had to get an afro wig," quipped Nikki Giovanni in a poem.

At the same time, Hollywood was presenting another vision of Black life that appealed to Black pride by presenting Black men and women in roles as strong, defiant, proud, large, and in charge—but as criminals or other assorted street characters. In this environment, *Superfly* drew criticism from both the growing class of Black professionals who carried its images of hyper-reality into lily-white offices, and also from those in the Black Arts Movement who saw a film glamorizing a drug dealer as damaging for a people struggling to create accurate images of themselves.

Despite the criticism, the film grossed more than $6.4 million at the box office, quite a sum in those days, and put O'Neal on the map as one of a new generation of Black actors who got to do something different than clown and buck and grin for the camera. He had trained at Karamu Theater, a Black theater in Cleveland, and then appeared in the Broadway production *Ceremonies in Dark, Old Men* before winning an Obie and Drama Desk Award for his lead role in Charles Gordone's *No Place To Be Somebody.* In *Superfly,* whether he was putting out a contract on the deputy commissioner's life, stomping down some junkie who tried to rob him, or holed up in a Greenwich Village apartment with a naked White woman, O'Neal's character, Youngblood Priest, was no ordinary Negro.

With his thick mustache and eyebrows and straight hair brushed back from his high forehead, O'Neal brought to the screen a look of intensity and seriousness. His talent and understated performance created some balance with the over-the-top colorful leisure suits, floor-length coats, and custom-made Cadillac that completed Priest's aura.

While O'Neal enjoyed the celebrity that comes with such a starring role, his straight hair did not make him a ready heartthrob during an era of globular afros. And though his racially ambiguous look might win him points in the film market today, it did not during the 1970s. When he tried to get other roles after *Superfly,* he was often told that he just didn't look Black enough. Most of the roles offered were more of the pusher and pimp variety and he didn't want to do those anyway. He did take some parts. After the sequel *Superfly T.N.T.* flopped at the box office in 1973, he appeared in several films and television shows. In 1996, he appeared on-screen for the first time with other stars of the blaxploitation era, Pam Grier, Fred Williamson, Jim Brown, and Richard Roundtree, in the film *Original Gangstas.*

Citizen King

January 19, 2004

After the death of the Rev. Martin Luther King Jr., an autopsy revealed that the thirty-nine-year-old civil rights leader had the heart of a sixty-year-old. No doubt stress was the culprit, speculates historian Taylor Branch, author of the groundbreaking histories of America during the King years, *Parting the Waters* and *Pillar of Fire*. But this final physical evidence of King also tells us something that we already knew. By the time his short life ended on April 4, 1968, King had lived a lifetime.

We all know about his short, compact, world-altering life. We know its bold relief: the Montgomery Bus Boycott, the March on Washington, the awarding of the Nobel Peace Prize, his assassination on a motel balcony in Memphis, Tennessee. But a new documentary, *Citizen King,* on PBS, focuses on the smaller steps in between, the tremendous evolution in activism, and the measure of his mind, spirit, and heart during the final five years of his life, 1963 to 1968.

It would be a stretch to say that the filmmakers, Orlando Bagwell and Noland Walker, have produced a personal portrait—no family members are interviewed on camera—but *Citizen King* certainly offers, through archival footage and thoughtful interviews with associates and Branch, a startling close-up. More so than in other civil rights–era documentaries, which have recounted important history, *Citizen King* focuses more on what King was thinking and feeling as he carried out the work that he knew he had been chosen to do.

Citizen King makes his monumental life close enough to touch.

You Got Served

January 30, 2004

You wouldn't guess it, based on its weak promotional campaign, but *You Got Served* is actually an energetic and entertaining hip-hop dance movie, a youthful and worthy heir to classics such as *Beat Street* that captured the frenzy and human foibles of artistic street competition. At least, unlike the recent film *Honey,* this film includes actors who can actually dance.

The story, set in South-Central Los Angeles, focuses on the lively scene of dance crews who battle each other for cash and bragging rights. In spots, the plot is somewhat predictable and filled with stock characters like the (big, fat, greasy) drug dealer and thuggy henchmen. And there are immature flourishes by director Christopher C. Stokes, including one dance scene inexplicably set in the rain. The film is saved, however, by electric performances by dozens of talented dancers, superb editing, and musical artists Marques Houston of iMX and Omari Grandberry of B2K.

America Beyond the Color Line with Henry Louis Gates Jr.

February 3, 2004

These periodic television series that put African-Americans under the microscope are fascinating in the same way that it is fascinating to watch someone roll the dice. Is the player trustworthy or must we watch out for tricks? What is their throwing technique? And what number do they finally hit?

Similarly, how we respond to these series will depend largely on our assessment that the narrator is reliable, truthful, and somewhat in sync with our own racial views. With this criteria in mind, much of *America Beyond the Color Line with Henry Louis Gates Jr.,* premiering on PBS, is funneled through Gates's conservatism and seeming disconnection from the subject matter. Gates is the chairman of the Afro-American Studies Department at Harvard University who raised a storm of controversy in 1999 with his series *Wonders of the African World with Henry Louis Gates Jr.* Critics said at the time that Gates is not a specialist in Africa, that he overemphasized the African role in the Atlantic slave trade, and that the series was just another example of his tendency to join the White establishment in pointing a finger at Blacks in race debates. Five years later, *America Beyond the Color Line* could be just as controversial.

Gates is not a social scientist and throughout the series he is a somewhat unconvincing narrator as he focuses primarily on the very rich and very poor, leaving the majority of working- and lower-middle-class Blacks largely unrepresented. Like *Black in White America,* produced by ABC more than a decade ago, Gates approaches polar opposites in the Black community—primarily the wealthy and/or powerful and, at the other end of the spectrum, the impoverished underclass. Black women are also sorely unrepresented and somewhat dissed. If this is supposed to be a series that gives insight into important issues facing Black America, then it does not funnel these discussions through the majority of African-Americans who work as teachers, secretaries, bus drivers, retail clerks, government workers, or laborers. It seems that Gates is more interested in hearing what stars and executives have to say—and in lobbing softball questions at the likes of Colin Powell and Vernon Jordan. The result is a portrait of extremes and superficiality.

In the show's introduction, Gates draws parallels between this project and the scholarly work done at the start of the last century by the historian W. E. B. DuBois, who stated that the "problem of the twentieth century is the problem of the color line." Because this series is titled *America Beyond the Color Line,* the viewer is left wondering if Gates believes the color line no longer exists, or is not as important as it used to be. In a recent interview, Gates told PBS talk-show host Charlie Rose that he wanted this show to reveal the types of conversations that African-Americans have with each other. But seldom do we get the sense that we are hearing Black talk as much an explanation of our predicament to White people by one of their preferred explainers.

Finally, as far as reliability goes, Gates as a sort of Black everyman, wandering the streets to chat with the masses, kind of doesn't work. For the most part, he manages to keep his huffy elitism under wraps and does come across as a nice, avuncular guy, as he ambles around housing projects and Hollywood mansions with the assistance of a silver-handled cane. But there is also often a disconnection with those he is interviewing. After Morgan Freeman explains very eloquently why he has returned to his family's property in Mississippi, Gates concludes that if he didn't respect Freeman, he would think Freeman was "whistling Dixie." After an Atlanta couple states plainly their choice to live with other middle-class Blacks in the area, Gates concludes that couples such as them are not living out the dream of the Rev. Martin Luther King, who, he says, most of all, fought for integration. Well, maybe that is how Gates interprets King's legacy. Others might argue just as forcefully that King wanted equality and justice under the law, and equal access to housing, jobs, schooling, and transportation regardless of the color of our skin. It's not that we *had to* sit in the front of the bus; we just had to have *the right* to sit there. In one of the more amusing moments of the series, Maya Angelou chides Gates, reminding him of this different idea of progress that any "thinking" person should understand.

He interviews an interracial couple in Birmingham, Alabama—a Black man and a White woman—and allows the segment to end with the statement that the only real racial opposition that the couple, particularly the woman, has faced, has come from her husband's former Black girlfriends. Gates, whose wife is White, seems to funnel this aspect of the Black experience through his own particular circumstances. Similarly, later in the series, a discussion in Los Angeles about color discrimination within the Black community, with a group of aspiring Black actresses, seems disingenuous as well as disconnected.

Often, the issue is not disconnection as much as a failure to be totally honest about his agenda. He approaches the misery of Chicago's Robert Taylor Homes by rejecting what he describes as explanations for the community's pathology from both the left and right sides of the political spectrum. The left, he says, blames such problems totally on the legacy of slavery and racism and that the right puts all blame at the feet of individual irresponsibility. Gates says that neither set of answers takes into account the "human" factor, so he wants to know what the residents have to say. One grandmother cites the pervasiveness of drug addiction as the primary reason for the community's condition. A young man who used to sell drugs but now works at Popeye's says that individual choice is the key. So, based on these included anecdotes, it sounds like Gates is leaning very much to the right. Similarly, he concludes at the end of the third show that it is up to the Black middle class, which he never mentions is imperiled in the current economy, to bridge the gap between rich and poor Blacks, "or the class divide will become permanent" in our community.

When he goes to Hollywood in the final show, Gates mostly sticks with the stars. Though he has chided Blacks for not writing our own stories and histories when we are miffed with those of Whites, he spends little time focusing on the burgeoning independent Black film community, which is attempting to do just that, and which is often distinct from Black Hollywood, which is largely about the star system, the status quo, and someone else's story.

A lot of time and work obviously went into this series, but if you are already living in Black skin, little is revealed here, other than how powerful privileged voices can be in the age of information. This is a roll of the dice that Black folks just can't win.

Barbershop 2: Back in Business

February 6, 2004

As far as these sorts of comedies go, *Barbershop 2: Back in Business* is certainly likeable, and it is likeable without alienating half the Black moviegoing public with cheesy jokes. The filmmakers have gone full throttle with Cedric the Entertainer in the role of an aging barber who, day after day, cuts up more than he cuts heads. And, thankfully, they have eliminated the need for a minstrel sideshow that, in the first film, distracted from the in-shop entertainment.

There is much about this film that is more developed and mature. The writing and performances are better. Eve has softened her neck-rolling routine and Michael Ealy, in the role of Ricky, oozes with screen presence, as does Troy Garrity in the role of Isaac. I must admit, I am not a fan of Kenan Thompson's slapstick comedy, and his appearance here annoys me like a gnat. Queen Latifah's role is more like a brief special appearance, but she does trade beef with Cedric in all the scenes you have already seen in the previews. This is definitely a better barbershop. You can go and sit safely in the chair.

Sisters in Cinema

February 8, 2004

On cable television, Starz is premiering *Sisters in Cinema,* a fascinating and absorbing documentary about the inclusion and exclusion of Black women from the filmmaking community. Written and directed by Yvonne Welbon, *Sisters in Cinema* is the most comprehensive document to date about Black women who have worked behind the camera as directors of movies and television programs.

Welbon began working on the film in order to connect with other Black women in film, and the narrative switches back and forth between her own personal journey as an artist and interviews with the women, including well-known directors such as Maya Angelou, Euzhan Palcy, Julie Dash, and Kasi Lemmons. Welbon tells the history, beginning early in the last century, when Zora Neale Hurston, in pursuing her anthropological work in the South, made the first known films by a Black woman. The story of opportunity given and denied, winds on from there. Those interviewed concede that there are few women directors of any race in the very sexist world of Hollywood, but added that Black women face a double or triple jeopardy. "To make a Black film means to speak for a community," says Shari Frilot, a programmer at the Sundance Film Festival. "And those who are supposed to represent are men."

Mighty Times: The Legacy of Rosa Parks

February 8, 2004

This energetic forty-five-minute program brings the history of the 1955 bus boycott in Montgomery, Alabama, alive today with interviews of young members of Parks's extended family and of those who worked closely with the soft-spoken Parks to birth the civil rights movement. These interviews are interspersed with well-made black-and-white reenactments and actual footage of the city: empty buses, triumphant Black men and women walking to school and work, and of bombings carried out in an effort to terrorize the leaders of the boycott. You might think you've seen this story many times, but this telling is fresh.

Nat Turner: A Troublesome Property

February 10, 2004

Nat Turner: A Troublesome Property premieres on the Independent Lens series on PBS. Produced by Frank Christopher, Charles Burnett, and Kenneth Greenberg, the one-hour documentary reexamines, in a somewhat graphic fashion, the legacy of Turner, who led an 1831 slave revolt in Southampton County, Virginia, killing dozens of White men, women, and children. This show uses a variety of documentary techniques, including reenactments (some of which look a bit cheesy) and several provocative interviews with historians such as Vincent Harding and the writer William Styron, author of the controversial 1966 novel *The Confessions of Nat Turner.* The filmmakers creatively explore how Turner the man has been imagined and re-created several times over to suit the beliefs or tastes of many different authors. Harriet Beecher Stowe, for example, modeled a character after Turner but made her Black character into a kinder, gentler soul. Styron's book, in which he wrote of Turner in the first person and created a fictionalized romance between Turner and a slaveholder, elicited a torrent of fury from Blacks who consider Turner a hero. It certainly didn't help matters when Styron won the Pulitzer Prize for what many considered sacrilege.

A Place of Our Own

February 17, 2004

It could be that some longtime residents of Oak Bluffs, the Black coastal community on Martha's Vineyard, will see Stanley Nelson's new documentary, *A Place of Our Own,* as too close a gaze at the elitism and intrarace color discrimination that have existed there among the Black middle class. But, really, Nelson's story is a very personal one, in which the filmmaker turns the lens on himself and his family, which includes his sister, the writer Jill Nelson. He reveals how Oak Bluffs helped him find his "Blackness" during a childhood of being in many settings where he was the "only Black." This is a poetic and intimate study. Vintage family photos and video footage are interwoven into the narrative, which includes the recent death of Nelson's mother, and delves into the filmmaker's personal devastation over his parents divorce when he was a boy. During one recent summer visit to the family's oceanfront house, when the movie was made, Nelson's father joined him there and it was the first time in many years that the father and son talked in-depth. All of this very intense family drama unfolds against the backdrop of Nelson's colorful historical account of the community. In these segments, Nelson shows the experience he has had with documentaries such as the award-winning *The Murder of Emmett Till, A Dollar and a Dream: The Story of Madame C. J. Walker,* and *The Black Press: Soldier's Without Swords.*

Lost Boys of the Sudan

February 18, 2004

Despite its unfortunate title, there is much in *Lost Boys of the Sudan* that is illuminating and important. It tells an African story. It brings home the fact that civil strife, ongoing in the Sudan for twenty years, has left two million dead. Beginning in the late 1980s, twenty thousand young boys, many of them orphans from the Dinka cattle-herding people, fled into Kenya where they were housed at the Kakuma Refugee Camp. This film begins nine years later in the late 1990s as some of the young men have been accepted to travel as refugees to the United States.

As an African-American, however, it is easy to be put off by the title and premise of the film. Oh no, another film about some pitiful state of Black folks, and the White folks who help them . . .

Also, the "boys" documented are, in fact, young men. (Because no birth certificates were issued in their South Sudan village, their precise ages are often unknown.) I don't think I'm the only Black person who will have a problem referring to these refugees, most of whom are clearly men, as boys (or as "lost," for that matter). Finally, even those of us who understand centuries of colonialism and destabilization in Africa might still draw back from seeing the residue of that pillaging—with scant historical background offered—on the big screen.

If you can get past the film's framework and trappings, you'll find that the journey of the refugees, particularly two named Peter and Santino, is captured in moments that are genuine. Filmmakers Megan Mylan and John Shenk give viewers the sense that we are explorers, right along with Peter and Santino, of a whole new world. It slowly sinks in for us how quick-minded, resourceful, and hard-working these immigrants are. Most of us born in the United States, faced with a similar fate, would be truly lost.

The perspective here is not patronizing, mocking, or scornful. It is very much cinema verité, as if the camera is a fly on the wall making us privy to many intimate moments and conversations—many about race. Santino says he feels that he looks "odd" to Americans because his skin is so Black. African-Americans are brown, he says, and even many of us seem to look at him with wonder at his darkness. (And you know that's right.) Some of the Sudanese view all African-Americans as criminals. They wonder how to find a girlfriend.

As Santino settles into life as a factory worker in Houston, and Peter pursues an education in Kansas, the stories of both men make it clear that they are not sold on life in the United States as "better," despite so much war, destruction, and the death of family members in the Sudan. While most came with the hope of getting an education, they find themselves instead working furiously at low-wage jobs to pay their rent, feed themselves, and send money to Africa.

This is such a close-up portrait that it takes a concerted effort to remember that we are not seeing the stories of these men as told themselves. The view we see is framed, shot, and edited from the perspective and sensibility of the filmmakers. The insights of Mylan and Shenk also serve them well in capturing the texture of American suburbia, and the ways that American life has lost its way.

Against the Ropes

February 20, 2004

How do you tell the story of Jackie Kallen, the first female boxing manager, without really telling her story? This quandary is the biggest problem with *Against the Ropes,* which, while often entertaining, has a void at its middle. Thank goodness that Meg Ryan, Omar Epps, and Charles Dutton are likeable enough to make this a winner by a very close decision.

Perhaps those who aren't ready for Ryan to be anything other than a romantic heroine will blame the wispy blonde for failing to deliver a convincing portrayal of Kallen, who, in the late 1980s, worked as a boxing manager for clients including Thomas "Hitman" Hearns. Maybe Ryan is a bit low-keyed to play the brassy and sassy Kallen, but the problem here is really the script, which leaves out so much of the drama in Kallen's real life. The real Jackie Kallen was a mother while also trying to swim in the rough-and-tumble world of boxing. She faced extreme sexism and constantly fought off all kinds of nasty rumors, like the ones that claimed she was sleeping with her fighters. Ryan isn't given this kind of edgy material that might really draw us into the character and story.

Perhaps some of the film's void is a lack of panache. Director Charles Dutton said in an interview with reporters that the studio didn't want a very stylized movie. In other words, he said he couldn't deliver a *Raging Bull* type of film with creative, moody visuals, such as scenes in black-and-white or slow motion, that have come to be preferred for boxing films. Thank goodness that Omar Epps can box. At least the fight sequences look real. The script does not allow him to make the most convincing leap from street thug to professional fighter but he is able to act his way out of a box. Similarly, Dutton looks every bit the part of a boxing trainer but there is little in the story that really makes his character snap, crackle, and pop.

One good thing that can be said for the script is that it is not a Great White Mother story. Kallen is not portrayed as some sort of magnanimous soul who comes to the ghetto to save the souls of the wretched. She is as complex and flawed as she is tenacious and ambitious. She is not made "big" at the expense of someone else looking small. This is not a fancy movie, and though the story has some holes, it also has some soul.

Beah: A Black Woman Speaks

February 25, 2004

Beah Richards is the subject of the heartrending and triumphant portrait *Beah: A Black Woman Speaks* that premieres on HBO. Written and directed by LisaGay Hamilton (*The Practice*), the ninety-minute program is packed with the powerful life story of Richards, who, as an actress and artist, vowed never to betray her people. With a very dark complexion and full facial features, Richards overcame both discrimination from Hollywood and from within her race, and played many film roles, particularly in the 1960s and 1970s, with dignity and grace. Her career spanned more than fifty years in film, on TV, and on stage. She received a Best Supporting Actress Oscar nomination for playing Sidney Poitier's mother in 1967's *Guess Who's Coming to Dinner?* and earned three Emmy Awards, the last one coming shortly before her death in 2000, for a guest appearance on *The Practice.* Hamilton met Richards during the filming of *Beloved* and reconnected with her years later when she learned that Richards was very ill with emphysema. With a digital camera sent to her by director Jonathan Demme, Hamilton set about recording the final, precious months of Richards's life. This moving footage is the centerpiece of the film, which also includes segments from many of Richards's performances, including those in *Beloved*.

25

Those Bad Mother (Shut-Yo-Mouth!)

OPM—*James' Journey to Jerusalem*

March 5, 2004

With its unsentimental portrait of Israel's underground labor market, *James' Journey to Jerusalem* manages to be both attractive and repulsive.

Israeli writer-director Ra'Anan Alexandrowicz provides such a no-win scenario about the exploitation of undocumented labor that you cannot sit through its ninety minutes and not be taken aback by the ugliness of greed and desperation. On the other hand, acting newcomer Siyabonga Melongisi Shibe infuses the screen with such bright-eyed energy, and the process of money-scraping is so comically pathetic, that you cannot help but also laugh at one man's sojourn to the so-called "promised land."

With bold strokes, Alexandrowicz contrasts romanticism about Israel's biblical significance with the dog-eat-dog life, lacking anything spiritual, of some of its residents. He is also frank about the racism of many Israelis, who refer to Africans as "Blackies" and consider them obvious candidates for any sort of menial labor. Much of the story unfolds as James works day-to-day for Shimi's father, Salah, a white-haired crotchety fellow who lives in a shack and pines for his dead wife, Miriam. Salah holds on desperately to his land and fends off the plan of Shimi and Shimi's wife to move him into an old folk's home. It is through this story line that the filmmakers explore most ideas about the sacred and profane, and what is valued and not valued in James's life and the lives of those he has met in this new land.

African songs about James's journey interspersed throughout, along with close-ups of storybook-type paintings, lend *James' Journey to Jerusalem* the texture of a parable. The storybook feel is only enhanced by Shibe's chiseled good looks that make him a dead ringer for the handsome prince on a mission, the hero we all root for. This is an unsettling parable that might be unsatisfying for us accustomed to Hollywood endings, because it does not make complete villains of the exploiters, or total heroes and winners of the exploited.

Interview–Danny Glover

March 15, 2004

Lately, Danny Glover seems to spend more time in front of the camera as an activist than as an actor. The website www.seeingblack.com caught up with Glover recently in his role as chairman of the board of TransAfrica, members of which have been outspoken on the forced ouster of Haitian President Jean-Bertrand Aristide. Accompanied by TransAfrica's president, Bill Fletcher, Glover spoke to reporters about art and politics at the New African Films Festival in Washington, D.C.

Question: Relating current events to this film festival, do you think that the images that Americans get, either through film or through the mass media now, impacts our ability to empathize with people of color, particularly Africans of the diaspora?

Glover: Well, I think certainly so. And look here, you're not going to get all Americans to look at African films. But what you can do is build a constituency based on film and other related activities, in terms of organizing and setting in motion a different sense of what policy should be about, and what concern should be about. So they may form that critical mass that you need to not only affect how we view situations, how we view people, but also how we view the policies toward them.

Question: Is it the responsibility of Black artists to not only be artists but to be activists and advocate for causes?

Glover: I think that it is the responsibility of all of us to be activists, not just artists, and for us to frame the role of the citizen in that way. We all should see ourselves as citizens of the world. We have to be active. Wherever we are, whatever place in life we are, we have to be active.

I was just at a memorial yesterday for Edward Said at Columbia University—just an enormous individual. He's Palestinian. Edward Said is the one who made it possible for Columbia University to get [writer and political activist] C. L. R. James's papers. Edward Said was the cat who knew not only about his own struggle as a Palestinian but also knew about the struggle of African people and people of color around the world—and that's extraordinary. What he said was interesting:

We are not only artists and intellectuals. We have to rake muck. We have to create dissent. We have to question everything. We have to question power all the time, wherever that power comes from.

Question: Where do you see your future in film in relationship to your political activism right now?

Glover: I really don't know how to answer that [*laughs*]! I try to do films and I try to encourage films that I think are important . . . and hopefully, my work encourages young artists.

Question: Can you talk about your work with Carlos Santana and Artists for a New South Africa?

Glover: Carlos Santana is a wonderful man. I've known him a long time. We went to high school together in San Francisco. Carlos has made an extraordinary contribution to South Africa. ANSA has formed very strategic partnerships with organizations like Habitat for Humanity. We're focusing on the issue of AIDS, focusing on the issue of development. We began Artists for a New South Africa fifteen years ago during the height of the fight against apartheid. And to have it sustained makes a statement.

The first thing we have to acknowledge is the work that Africans are doing for themselves, right on the ground. From Senegal to Uganda to South Africa, and many other places. We have to acknowledge that work, and embrace that work, and uphold that work. Second, we have to campaign for the resources for them to do that work. We have to say that the work that we do, collectively do, works. It works. We need it to work. We're desperate for it to work. It must work.

Question: Can you talk about your work with [film historian] Manthia Diawara on the new documentary *Conakry Kas* [*The People of the Conakry*] in Guinea?

Glover: We talked to musicians, we talked to artists, we talked to people who have been influenced by the ideas of Sekou Toure and the ideas of liberation fostered by his movement. . . . What I take back from all my visits is the sheer, awesome dynamics of being there, being with people and watching their lives unfold before you, and watching them dance and enjoy music—whether it's a seventy-six-year-old tenor sax player, or a drum maker . . . or a young dance group . . . .

Question: How can we compete in the era of the $100 million film?

Glover: You don't want to do or compete with a $100 million film. You want to do a film that will allow you to build a culture, to build an idea, to place emphasis on the importance of film and its relationship to people's lives. Not just the entertainment piece but allowing people to see their own lives and have some revelation over that. That's what film is intended to do. When I say progressive film, I mean filmmaking that allows people a space in which they can be active.

Question: Do you think that Djimon Hounsou's Oscar nomination is a sign of change in Hollywood?

Glover: I don't know if the nomination is a sign of change, particularly in this industry. People make too much of Oscars and what they do and what they pretend to do. I think the sign of change will be when you see African films on television, African films at film festivals, and we feel just as comfortable with seeing African films as we are seeing European films.

Mind you, the heyday of seeing all kind of films—you used to be able to see Brazilian films, Bolivian films, Venezuelan films, Cuban films, Mexican films, Italian comedies, French films, and everything else. But what is happening is that this global monster has taken over and basically put many of the national film industries out of business because U.S. films dominate the screens—whether they are in Italy or in France.

Question: Why do you think it is important to be here tonight? [TransAfrica is a cosponsor of the festival.]

Glover: Let me begin by saying this: The first time that I saw an African film made by an African was probably thirty years ago. I watched African filmmakers, met with African filmmakers. Attended the film festival at Ouagadougou—the Pan African Film Festival. I was a founder of the Pan African Film Festival in Los Angeles. So I've been very, very close, actually, to African film—all over the continent. And well before so after doing *Mandela* (1987) in Zimbabwe.

So it was important for me to be able to help promote African film. We understand people through how they see themselves through their own fiction. It's as clear as that: Only they can tell their own stories. Their stories can't be told by *Tears of the Sun,* which was a film recently produced by Hollywood. Their stories can't be told by *Sahara,* which is another film that will be made by Hollywood, a big-budget film. They have to tell their stories, and you can learn so much about who they are, how they see themselves, and how they see their own transformation through their films. That's the exciting thing about seeing African films. Whenever I see African films, I'm just seeing another way in which people have identified themselves and stood on their own and told the stories that are important to them.

Question: What are the biggest challenges now for African film?

Glover: Certainly resources to do their films and distribution. But not only distribution. I think it's important on one hand and sometimes we overemphasize the importance. It's important on one hand to have distribution in the United States and the West but also distribution in Africa itself is important.

The first thing that Kwame Nkrumah did when he took office is set up the Ghana Film Festival and Ghana Films. Africans have always known the power of film. Ousmane Sembene's films—about the early transformation from colonialism to independence. So this way of telling stories in Africa is new. And they know they have been demonized in some ways by the previous films. One film that Paul Robeson did—*Sanders of the Rivers,* which he thought was going to be one thing but, in some sense, it turned out to be a glorification of colonialism. So the ways in which the powers of film—and we all know the power of film, particularly people of color here, African-Americans know the power of film, know how derogatory images are falsely created and sustained in film throughout the whole history of film over the last one hundred years. So it's important to us to see those stories. You understand so much about people when they begin to tell their own stories—even the smallest stories about family. And, what you find is that there is a place where you identify with each other.

Question: Is it the responsibility of Black artists to set up African art houses so you don't always have African films at a festival venue?

Glover: Well, we begin there [at a film festival]. I don't know what kind of structures ought to be set up but if we can get interest in showing African films on a consistent basis through film festivals, showing the films on a consistent basis—on places like Art and Entertainment or PBS—then you begin to have a creative dialogue about film. So we can understand what we are seeing. It's the idea that we can learn from these filmmakers.

Black Star–Ving Rhames in *Dawn of the Dead*

March 19, 2004

If we must watch another silly horror flick, or a remake of one, at least let us watch Ving Rhames in it. *Dawn of the Dead* gives Rhames the perfect opportunity to, once again, be the muscular tough guy who has enough common sense to save the world. (See Ving tote a shotgun! See Ving blow away cannibal creatures! This is what fantasy moviegoing is all about!)

He and an ensemble crew, including Mekhi Phifer, seem to be the only survivors of an attack of zombies, living-dead cannibals who have devastated some suburban community in Michigan. The viewer never knows where the zombies came from, whether they are really "living" or "dead," whether they have some kind of virus, or, in general, how all of this living-dead business got started in the first place. Where did it start? Did somebody rise from a grave? (Or leave their job at Halliburton?) What exactly is going on here? The only hint of an explanation we have comes from the promotional tagline: "When there's no more room in hell, the dead will walk the earth." But this doesn't explain much.

Apparently, such explanations aren't the point here. The point is to watch the gore, to watch the lightning-quick transformation of a human into a senseless creature, to watch our trusty band of survivors—who are holed up inside a shopping mall—try to outwit the zombies, and to be happily manipulated by the story. Has a living-dead gotten into the mall? Are there some among them who are secret zombies? What happened to the rest of the country and world? Why isn't anyone coming to help? Will the Black men make it to the end of the movie?

I'm no big fan of horror flicks but this one actually made me laugh two or three times, or maybe I laughed at the group of men behind me talking back to the movie, exhorting Ving to "shoot the m. . . ." James Gunn's screenplay, which adapts the original one from 1978 by George A. Romero, infuses moments of offbeat humor and sarcasm into what is supposed to be an apocalypse. Zack Snyder's direction includes equally offbeat timing that combines horror with the surreal and with comedy.

If we must watch another silly horror flick, or a remake of one, at least let it be one that does not take itself, us, or the apocalypse too seriously.

New African Films Festival—*The Silence of the Forest*

March 24, 2004

In *The Silence of the Forest,* actor Eriq Ebouaney continues to tackle the tricky terrain of Africa's postcolonial history and politics. He made such a huge splash in 2000 with his powerful portrayal of slain Congolese president Patrice Lumumba that this film, which is a meditation on social divisions among Africans, seems a natural next step for an actor dubbed the Denzel Washington of African film.

Here, Ebouaney plays the part of Gonaba, a man educated in France, who returns home to the Central African Republic to work as a school inspector. Though Gonaba acquires all the trappings of a well-off government official, he views the corrupt government rulers with contempt. He sits at official functions with a jaded eye, disgusted by the hypocrisy and superficiality surrounding him.

He is upset by the government's condescension toward indigenous cultures, particularly its treatment of the Babinga people (referred to in the West as Pygmies). In a major turn in the story, he turns his back on business as usual and decides to go live among the Babingas, and it is at this point that *The Silence of the Forest* leaves viewers behind. We lose some of our connection with Gonaba as the protagonist. We are not exactly clear of his mission. We watch him attempt to start a school. We watch him fall in love. Before we know it, he has been there for quite a long time and has gotten into trouble.

It could be argued that director Didier Ouenangare simply breaks out of the mold of simplistic Hollywood narrative and refuses to lead viewers along like sheep. We are given the opportunity to look at Gonaba from a different perspective. We are allowed to see him as not only a proud race man but also as a confused man who may harbor romantic notions about indigenous cultures that are condescending as well. On the other hand, any technique that causes us to lose connection with our main character weakens the film. Early in the story, Ouenangare makes extensive use of interior monologue to help us identify with Gonaba. It might have helped to hear his voice a bit more later, during his long period with the Babingas, so that we could stay in tune to what exactly the brother was thinking.

Despite these shortcomings, *The Silence of the Forest* is a fascinating story and an African story. It carries on an important conversation between African people about African culture and society without needing to place its action within the context of a relationship to Whites, or needing to explain itself to Whites. It is also the first film to feature so prominently the Babinga people as untrained actors. Through their unrehearsed contributions, Ouenangare continues the fine African film tradition of including cultural and artistic expression at the heart of the story.

Black Star–Don Cheadle in *The United States of Leland*

April 2, 2004

There aren't many movies such as *The United States of Leland* that tackle both murder and the middle-ground existence—between good and evil—of the killer. And there aren't many movies with a racially mixed cast that don't, at some point, rely on stereotypes and racist cynicism to hammer home their point.

But if there is such a rare film, you know Don Cheadle will find it and dive for the middle. This story, written and directed by newcomer Matthew Ryan Hoge, begins in the aftermath of a murder in Arizona committed by a smart, quiet, and sensitive teenager named Leland Fitzgerald (Ryan Gosling). Leland is White and suburban, and no one, including Leland, can believe or understand why he did what he did. Enter Cheadle as Pearl Madison (after Earl the Pearl Monroe), a frustrated teacher-writer at the local juvenile detention center who befriends Leland with the idea that the boy's story could be the meaty basis for a novel.

Pearl's selfish motives, which lead to genuine concern for Leland, keep his character from morphing into a male version of a doting mammy—especially with a name like Pearl. Cheadle's role as Pearl is very similar to the one he played in *Manic* (2001). In that film, he starred as staff psychiatrist Dr. David Monroe, who was charged with helping a group of young Whites to identify and manage their rage. You could say that these two latest roles are simply more of Cheadle giving the big assist to stories that are really about White people and their White-people problems. But, with the exception of *Mission to Mars,* Cheadle has landed fine roles in recent years that allow him to stretch as an actor and present portraits of Black men who aren't caught up in the drug life and are grappling with deep issues of crime, cruelty, and compassion.

Johnson Family Vacation

April 7, 2004

All those Cedric the Entertainer fans out there who believe that the roly-poly comic stole the show in *The Original Kings of Comedy* will love *Johnson Family Vacation.* This more soulful version of *National Lampoon's Family Vacation* (1983) allows Ced to strut his blossoming talents as a film comedic actor.

Of course, the film has its share of predictability and corniness. But the worst of these moments, an ill-advised sketch about Ced winding up nude in a hot tub, is fairly mild and not too offensive. He manages to joke his way out of, literally, hot water. The rapper and actor Bow-wow makes another film appearance here, but this time as the teenager that he is, and he absolutely shines. If this was the '80s all over again, Bow-wow would be the top candidate to do the *Fresh Prince of Bel-Air.* He has the camera presence, good looks, and fan base to carry the part. In *Johnson Family Vacation,* he adds to the comedic mix and helps to make this film a good laugh. In these days of weightier issues and concerns, chalk up *Johnson Family Vacation* as a lightweight, harmless, and funny distraction.

Filmfest DC—*Nina Simone: Love Sorceress*
Washington, D.C.

April 21–May 2, 2004

There is no better tribute to Nina Simone, who died last year in France, than to showcase the "high priestess of soul" in one of her recorded moments of musical brilliance, eccentricity, and comical diva excess.

Nina Simone: Love Sorceress, a sixty-five-minute film of a 1976 concert by Simone in Paris, is both a tribute and a priceless piece of performance history. By this time, Simone—fed up with both the American music industry and American racism—had already left the United States for France. In her early forties by this time, she is alternately regal and impishly mischievous, with her short afro, fitted black dress, and high-heeled pumps, as she regales the audience with a mixture of song, piano virtuosity, and much attitude.

This film captures not only a moment for Nina Simone, but also a moment for the 1960s Black Arts Movement, which she helped to export abroad. It is the free-form improvisational spirit of this movement that she represents here, with all of its bold willingness to use art to confront racism and White privilege. Produced by Rene Letzgus and released in 1998, *Nina Simone: Love Sorceress* is traveling to several film festivals in the United States, allowing those of us over here a glimpse of the priestess in rare form.

Filmfest DC 2004—*Soldiers of the Rock* and *Asshak: Tales from the Sahara*

About eighty thousand miners have been killed while working to extract gold and diamonds from the bowels of South Africa. This horrible fact, and the particular exploitation of Black miners, is the subtext of *Soldiers of the Rock,* a film made by students at the South African School of Motion Picture Medium and Live Performance. The story centers on a college student named Vuyo, who goes to work in a gold mine to experience what work was like for his father, who died in a mine and left all of his money for Vuyo's education. But what Vuyo intends to be a brief interlude turns into an important struggle when he joins an effort to organize the miners into purchasing their own mine.

Anchored by Vuyo's clear narration, this is an admirable effort at telling an important story about Black South Africans from their own perspective. The film suffers, however, from a story line and scenes of action that are often difficult to follow. The sound quality could be better; it may be a challenge for those of us outside of Southern Africa to understand some of the dialogue spoken in regional accents.

Despite these shortcomings and other production-quality issues typical of low-budget films, *Soldiers of the Rock* does attempt to deal in a serious way with difficult issues that confront a people trying to unshackle themselves from centuries of occupation and oppression.

At the other end of the continent, *Asshak: Tales from the Sahara* is a fascinating though slow-paced documentary about the lives in particular of the Tuareg people of the Sahara Desert. Produced by filmmakers in Switzerland, Germany, and the Netherlands, the film follows several individuals and families who live the same nomadic lifestyle that their people have lived for centuries. As the Tuareg people explain, "Asshak" and the fear of God are the same thing. It means the deepest respect for the rules of conduct between people, and to respect God and all living things.

This film has a simple, lyrical quality, and each story within it unfolds as if we a watching a scripted feature film. One man searches central Niger for a runaway camel; a grandmother tells of raising her grandchildren and other orphans; another elderly woman gives us her insight into the strength of Tuareg women: "With us, a woman accepts her life the way it is. She stays with her children and her animals and accepts her simple life. . . . Her agreement with God is what gives her strength. She takes on her duties and relies only on herself."

The dialogue is in Tamasheq and there are English subtitles. Much of the photography, of both the people and amazing landscape and sky, is wonderful. If you are interested in seeing real life in Africa, *Asshak: Tales from the Sahara* offers just that.

Man on Fire

April 23, 2004

Maybe the love of a child can save the soiled soul of a "U.S. operative" who has, on orders, killed people around the world. This big maybe, wrapped around themes of redemption, duty, self-sacrifice, and revenge, is at the heart of the gripping and violent film *Man on Fire*.

To lead us down such a morally treacherous path, there is Denzel Washington, the man we always want to root for on the big screen. Here, he plays the part of Creasy, a morose but functioning alcoholic who takes a job as a bodyguard to a wealthy family in Mexico, where kidnappings and murders are rampant. Creasy is killing himself slowly with shots of Jack Daniels. He is a soldier, trained in the ways of physical torture and death, now emotionally tortured himself. He is a man who has done horrible things and who wonders now whether God will forgive him. We don't know everything that he's done but we know that in some countries, he has killed "the insurgents" (the term, incidently, that U.S. media uses for those in Iraq who are fighting U.S. troops).

His primary duty is to protect the family's young daughter, Pita (pronounced like the bread), and so much of his day-to-day activity might remind you initially, depending on your generation's references, of *Driving Miss Daisy* with Morgan Freeman or some dusty Shirley Temple flick with Bill "Bojangles" Robinson. But with a character so tortured and morose, who is called "Mr." until he grants the child the privilege of dropping it, these comparisons are fleeting. And his hell-bent resolve to take revenge on all those connected with her eventual abduction makes it perfectly clear that he's nobody's subservient darkie—not in the typical sense anyway.

Creasy is, fundamentally, a killer, and you could say that he does what he knows best for the family that hired him. The twist that is different, from both the faithful servant or the soldier simply taking orders, is that Creasy is also fighting for himself and against forces that would hurt a young innocent who actually loved him. His incredulity and rage only makes sense if it is personal. Otherwise we are getting into Bojangles territory. *Man on Fire* forces us to accept, in one man, the impulses of both an assassin and a father and that's a lot to put in one man—even on mob shows like *The Sopranos.*

In this story, the viewer is expected to accept and understand this rich mix in a man that it doesn't bother to explain very well. We don't know much about him. It's as if the filmmakers believe that the few horrible tidbits that they do reveal should be enough. Instead of giving us depth, it offers, as if a substitute, a killing machine in ruthless action. This film goes from Denzel carrying a flask to Denzel as "the Terminator." There is so much cold-blooded killing that, in moments, the violence goes over the top, but then the film is saved by fancy direction and editing that gives it the feel of cinema verité. There is also a tight script, soundtrack, and sound effects that keep you listening as well as watching the complex and unpredictable drama.

The Agronomist

April 23, 2004

Those of us who toil in the so-called "free press," or any of us who benefit from it or value it, have been given the story of a new hero, thanks to the vision and sacrifice of director Jonathan Demme. His new, powerful film, *The Agronomist,* documents the life and work of crusading Haitian journalist Jean Dominique, who championed the cause of the country's poor majority and bravely challenged various corrupt rulers until he was brazenly shot to death in front of his radio station in April 2000.

Demme mixes face-to-face interviews with Dominique with archival footage, photographs, and audio to give the documentary a sense of the no-frills journalism that Dominique practiced. The resulting product is not fancy but it is very rich, moving, and profound. It presents an in-your-face reality of poverty and brutal power —and Jean Dominique's lifelong opposition to it—just off the coast of the United States.

Carandiru

May 14, 2004

Prison provides the perfect claustrophobic stage for dramas of human poverty and tragedy, and *Carandiru,* based on a true story of Brazil's infamous prison in Sao Paulo, adds some Latin American flava to this genre featuring murderers, thieves, rapists, the unlucky, and the doomed.

This is a Latin American *Oz,* based on the 1999 book *Carandiru Station* by Dr. Drauzio Varella, developed roughly at the same time that the groundbreaking TV series was still on the air. Its oppressive atmosphere of filth, human sweat, and disease surrounds each inmate, as well as the stories he has to tell. Much of the narrative spins out from the perspective of two characters. One is Ebony, a thief-turned-murderer who is the HNIC among the inmates; the other storyteller is a young doctor (obviously patterned after the book's author, Varella) who visits Carandiru to perform AIDS prevention work during this period, in the late 1980s and early 1990s. Both tell stories leading up to a 1992 uprising that occurred at the prison in which more than one hundred inmates were killed by riot police. Director Hector Babenco renders these tales in an engaging and immediate manner that adds dimension to each inmate. There is time here, in a feature film, to unwind the stories slowly: Deusdete, the boy who shot two men who molested his sister; Highness, the Black mack daddy caught between relationships with a White woman and a Black woman; another poor soul who shot his wife after learning that she cheated on him. They are all stories of human frailty, limitation, and imperfection—with a frequent emphasis on stupidity and comical circumstances. (One favorite moment is a homosexual wedding at the prison officiated by a transvestite who calls himself "the presiding queen.")

Poverty is the obvious undercurrent that is not commented on in any specific way. This film is not "political" at all in outlook and its avoidance of social commentary trips it up by the end. While there are fleeting references to the prison being severely overcrowded, and to the fact that many men are there for years awaiting trial, the riot happens out of the blue and the inmates seem to have nothing substantial to say to the authorities about their lives. Without a larger context to the violence, it becomes just a pitiful footnote in the lives of men who are rendered as colorful and interesting but who are made to look, ultimately, simply pitiful.

Brazil's color stratification is presented matter-of-factly, with almost all of those behind bars either Black or "pardo" in appearance. Babenco just can't resist one yarn that pits European and African standards of beauty against each other when Highness is asked to choose between his Black and White women. We never know the outcome of that decision but we do know that the White woman is painted as a woman of higher virtue because she works in a factory and is the mother of three of Highness's sons. In contrast, the Black woman, the mother of Highness's first-born, is a prostitute. Also, for this U.S. release, a character has been renamed Ebony. On the film's official site and in some press material, Ebony is still called by his original name: Black Nigger.

The portrayal of the physician by Luiz Carlos Vasconcelos is remarkable. He has a welcoming screen presence and smile that makes him, especially in contrast to Ebony, a sort of prison Marcus Welby nice guy. In the midst of a lot of pain and pathology, the physician reaches for what is human in each prisoner and holds onto that. He never reveals it to the inmates but the prison scares him; he shudders every time a metal door clangs shut behind him. The physician's ability to come and go, to be an occasional voyeur, gives *Carandiru* the feel of an exotic, bad excursion into a world that we can all leave and forget—as opposed to confront—whenever we want.

Control Room

May 21, 2004

In this information age, when powerful news organizations can foment war with stories later proven to be untrue, and when the press revises or ignores history to the point of absurdity, the new documentary *Control Room* is a like a moment of sanity in a whirl of media madness.

In it, director Jehane Noujaim (*Startup.com*) provides an up-close and detailed look at the inner workings of Al Jazeera, the popular Arab news channel that broadcasts to more than forty million people in the Middle East, and that rankles members of the Bush administration more accustomed to the lock-step reportage of Fox News. Bush has called Al Jazeera "the mouthpiece of Osama Bin Laden" for broadcasting images of killed and mutilated victims on both sides of the Iraq invasion. Hassan Ibrahim, a journalist for Al Jazeera, says in *Control Room* that the Bush administration "can't have their cake *and* eat it.

"You are the most powerful nation on earth—I agree," says Ibrahim. "You can defeat everyone—I agree. You can crush everyone—I agree. But don't expect us to love it as well."

There is important information here about the struggles and rag-tag nature of independent media. There is the disturbing and heartbreaking account of the murder of one of the network's reporters, Tarek Ayyoub, who, along with a reporter for another Arab network, was killed by an American military attack on a known media location in Baghdad.

But the most important aspect of *Control Room* is its interrogation of the ideas of "objectivity," "fairness," and even "truth" in journalism, especially in a time of war, and especially when it comes to journalists of color reporting and writing news that speaks to their own racial oppression.

Baadasssss!

May 28, 2004

In tackling a film about his father, Mario Van Peebles has, finally, lived up to his famous father's film legacy.

Baadasssss!, the phonetically aggressive new film starring and directed by Van Peebles-the-younger, is a fast-paced, well-directed, and funny docudrama that reveals important information about the history of both Black film and 1970s-era Black America.

In it, Van Peebles tells the story of the making of *Sweet Sweetback's Baadasssss Song,* the 1971 film directed by his father, Melvin Van Peebles, that created a precedent for Black independent film in that decade, shifted Black film images away from the buffoon and coon, and, some say, ushered in a new era of blaxploitation flicks filled with new urban images skewed toward pushers, pimps, prostitutes, and pathology.

But, to be fair, the brash and cocky Van Peebles-the-elder actually thought he was working with another "P"—for pride. His main character, Sweetback, does things that no Black man had been seen doing on the screen before. He is his own man. He defies "The Man" and lives to tell about it. The film, shot on a shoestring budget, depicts a man that the Black community knew very well but never knew in the movies.

Fast-forward more than three decades, and it is the rich story about the making of this film that makes *Baadasssss!* both informing and entertaining. In a Hollywood more comfortable with Blacks in comedies, like the *Watermelon Man* Melvin Van Peebles had himself just directed, his decision to break from that mold was a bold stroke that ended his career as one of the few Black directors of the time. His decision to create a Black character who killed crooked White cops, and exposed racism and abuse experienced by African-Americans, alienated the Hollywood establishment that was woefully out of step with the anger and restlessness of America at that time, especially of Black America.

Baadasssss! goes behind the scenes of making the film to the struggle to raise money, to the hardscrabble production, to the tribulations with distribution, to the fact that Van Peebles insisted on including in the crew people of color who would work alongside experienced Whites to get training. This crew also included the young Mario and his sister Megan. In one of the more discomforting scenes, a determined and somewhat crazed Melvin Van Peebles's insists that his son act in a scene depicting his character's loss of virginity. Sandra, Van Peebles's girlfriend at the time who is played by a sparkling Nia Long, laments that, in order to make his film, Van Peebles was "willing to sacrifice friends, family—even me."

There is a sense offered by Long and other actors of really enjoying and connecting with this film, as they play a part in telling a triumphant tale. Mario Van Peebles is a hoot to watch in the role of his father. And the production is filled with the type of details in language, demeanor, wardrobe, and environment that combine to be an excellent rendering of a particular, pivotal, and potent time.

Soul Plane

May 28, 2004

Seriously now. How many different ways can a film call me a nig? Will we ever learn the difference between a film laughing with us, rather than laughing at us?

Soul Plane, which we pray is not a hit, calls us stupid, drug addicted, not to be trusted, skank and stank. It makes a point to mostly laugh at Black folks in every which way that you can think of, and to use every stereotype that you can think of.

Believe me, I'm not hating on comedy. These days, living in Mordar, I need a laugh as well as anybody. But at what cost? Director and producer Jessy Terrero, as well as writers Bo Zenga and Chuck Wilson, obviously have very little clue about the fine line that Black comedy walks. And the must-be-desperate actors, actresses, and comedians who star here must not have a clue, either.

The story here, reportedly born when BET's Robert Johnson made an unsuccessful bid to launch the first Black-owned airline, is that Nashawn Wade (Kevin Hart) receives a ridiculously large award from a jury after an airplane accident kills his beloved dog. With his cash proceeds, Nashawn decides to launch NWA Airlines, the first Black-owned airline.

Some of these details are mildly amusing and place *Soul Plane* in the tradition of the *Airplane* movies of the 1980s that lampooned air travel to a much finer degree. But far more gags here are just straight unfunny, like the racism directed toward Arabs and Africans, the totally nasty bathroom humor, and the oh-so-tired caricatures of White people as corny and uptight "honkies."

Something the Lord Made

May 30, 2004

There is a boldness and subtlety to *Something the Lord Made,* premiering on HBO, that makes it one of the finest TV movies to come along in some time.

Its boldness comes in its telling of the little-known story of Vivien Thomas, a Black man who, though he never attended medical school, was a pioneer in the field of heart surgery. Its subtlety is born of exceptional production, fine direction by Joseph Sargeant (*A Lesson Before Dying*), and a performance by Mos Def that is most definitely excellent.

Something the Lord Made turns out to be about the intricacies of work, family, and opportunity (or the lack of it) at a pivotal period in African-American history, from the 1930s to the 1960s, when there were national struggles for equality and justice. Thomas's brother, who works as a teacher in the film, fights for equal pay, saying, "If I don't do something now, I'll be dead before I get paid like the White teachers do." He winds up as a plaintiff in the historic *Brown vs. Board of Education* case.

Mos Def, with his angular facial features and earnest eyes, fits the part perfectly of not only a humble, confident man, but also a man of this time period. He effortlessly fills fedoras, caps, and wool overcoats. He totes a pipe. He also wears well his white lab coat, which it seems no one at Johns Hopkins—Black or White—had even seen a Black man wear before. These finer points of Thomas's experience and the Black experience depicted make *Something the Lord Made* a cut above the rest.

The Chronicles of Riddick

June 11, 2004

The great Ray Charles (rest his soul) is on my mind while I write this review, so the first thing I think of is the title of Ray's hit *Look What They Done to My Song.* All us moviegoers smitten with the Black man with the sky-blue glowing eyes in *Pitch Black* will wonder, indeed, what the producers of this sequel have done to our fierce sci-fi hero.

From the just so-so computer graphics, to the meandering plot, to the oppressive direction, much of *Riddick* is lacking the intensity of both *Pitch Black* and that film's Riddick that we grew to know, love, and root for. For me, the letdown starts with the opening scene. There is this White guy running across jagged terrain while being pursued by some sort of space helicopter. Well, I wouldn't have thought it in a million years but the running man who looks like a Hollywood version of Jesus, complete with wet stringy hair, turns out to be Riddick, meaning Vin Diesel. Now, I know that part of the D-Man's thing is racial ambiguity, but even he admits that if we see him as a person of color then he is, indeed, a person of color. And he knows that the Riddick of *Pitch Black* had a visible Vince Carter–like grain in his haircut that would grow out to be more of an afro than a Jesus shag. (So maybe that is why, in order to continue with his racial ambiguity, Diesel maintains a baldie.)

The story is a bit jumbled but boils down to Riddick landing on the Planet Helion where he meets up with Abu "Imam" al-Walid (Keith David), a survivor from the last episode, and also seeks information on "Jack," the young girl who everyone thought, in that earlier episode, was a boy. Riddick, despite his protests that the planet's fight is not his, winds up joining the battle to save Helion, and the entire known world, against the advances of an army called the Necromongers, headed by the evil Lord Marshall.

There are some interesting special effects but none of them serve to enrich Riddick's character, or to give emotional depth to the story, which, based on the ending, is designed to proceed from here with more "chronicles." I only hope those episodes to come have more to offer than this one, and give us back the real Riddick.

Black Star—Ossie Davis in *Bubba Ho-tep*

June 14, 2004

A film intriguingly titled *Bubba Ho-tep* and marketed as a hip independent offering promises perhaps a story to pique the interest of us post–civil rights babies. We appreciate cross-cultural humor and have the capacity to laugh at both a "bubba," meaning a Southern redneck, and also a "ho-tep," a name sometimes given to a type of Black nationalist who knows more about ancient Egypt than he does about his own backyard. The idea that the two might come together in one human being could possibly produce new, hilarious cinematic race satire such as that offered in *Hollywood Shuffle, Brother from Another Planet,* or *Undercover Brother.*

But, sorry to say, this film by Don Coscarellli offers no such sensibility or humor for us. This is clearly coming from a different vantage point and set of references. To be sure, there is plenty of bubba here. The entire film focuses on Sebastian Haff, a pitiable former Elvis impersonator who is consigned to the Mud Creek Shady Rest Convalescence Home in Texas. Haff still has the swoopy hairdo, eyeglass frames as big and boxy as two television sets, and a bad case of self-delusion. He actually believes he is Elvis and when nurses and friends want him to settle down, they play along with his delusion. The only Black man here, and dangled for us enticingly in the promos, is actor Ossie Davis. He plays another resident of the convalescent home, Jack Kennedy, who believes he is another dead White man—John F. Kennedy. Kennedy prattles on about the conspiracy to assassinate him and states his belief that he has been dyed brown in order to keep his whereabouts a mystery.

26

Unbought and Unbossed

OPM—*Fahrenheit 9/11*

June 25, 2004

If you don't know it already, *Fahrenheit 9/11* will make it very clear that director Michael Moore takes the so-called "war on terror" very personally. In fact, he believes that one of the biggest wars, a war of fear and eroding constitutional rights, is being fought against the American people by the administration of President George W. Bush.

In his latest documentary, which he has had to fight to distribute and which won the highest honor at the Cannes Film Festival, Moore displays a naked antipathy toward Bush and the White House leadership of the past four years. He sounds a warning bell about the country's recent sweep of political history, from the rigged presidential election of 2000 to the use of the tragedy of September 11 to pass the draconian Patriot Act, to the illegal invasion of Iraq that has resulted in the death of thousands.

That antipathy is rendered in all of that Michael Moore sarcasm, humor, naked truth, horror, and pathos that you either love or hate. As for me, I'm not hatin' at all. One reason I'm not hatin' is because Moore doesn't forget in this film, just as he didn't forget in *Bowling for Columbine* or *Stupid White Men,* the pivotal role that race plays in this history. Early in the film, there is a startling sequence after the election of 2000 when, one by one, several members of the Black Congressional Caucus address Congress to raise official objection to the election, given the numerous election irregularities in Florida and elsewhere. Apparently, in order for these objections to be acted on, at least one senator would have to sign on—and not a single senator did so. The moment is raw in its exposure of American racism, of America's willingness to offer its African-American population no political redress.

When Moore isn't focused specifically on race and class, he is obsessed with demonstrating the power of image and illusion. He has gathered in one film an amazing array of footage that makes President Bush look, if not stupid, so superficial to the point of being a clear and present danger. Of course, there is the moment featured in the film's trailer when, out on a golf course, Bush offers a quick quote for the cameras about fighting terrorism, and then, in less than a heartbeat, asks those gathered to "watch this drive" as he swings his golf club. Moore is especially bugged by, and displays here, the seven or more minutes on September 11 that Bush sat at a photo opportunity in a Florida classroom reading *My Pet Goat* after being informed that airplanes had struck Manhattan's World Trade Center.

While powerful in its imagery, the classroom segment is actually one of the weakest, in that Moore goes overboard with his personal speculation about what Bush was possibly thinking while sitting there for so long with that weird expression on his face. The focus on image in this film is more powerful when Moore lets the power of image speak for itself—such as footage of Bush, Condoleeza Rice, Paul Wolfowitz, Colin Powell, etc. being enhanced with face powder before television appearances. (Is that Wolfowitz using saliva as a hair pomade? Yuck!)

Fahrenheit 9/11 also serves as a primer for some of the underreported stories in recent years, including the links between the Bush and Bin Laden families; and the business ties between those in the Bush administration, most especially Dick Cheney, and companies that are now making big profits from the war, including Halliburton and the Carlyle Group. The nation's security at home is shown to be laughably nonexistent while billions are spent to bomb other countries.

Moore looks at home as well as abroad here. In such a personal film, personally and passionately felt by Moore, it is no surprise that, as in previous films, he winds back to his hometown, Flint, Michigan, where some neighborhoods look as bombed as Iraq, where poor and working-class high school students are recruited in the cafeteria to join the army, where Moore finds in one mother an example of both blind "patriotism" and an example of fear and overwhelming grief.

Everyday People

June 26, 2004

Like an old couch, there is something familiar and comfortable about *Everyday People,* a movie debuting on HBO. But while retaining many of the tried-and-true elements of TV drama—an ensemble cast, young attractive actors, and immediate conflict—it also feels fresh as it attempts to tackle issues of race, class, gender, labor, and neighborhood gentrification.

The setting is a fictional restaurant called Raskin's located on a busy strip in the Fort Greene section of Brooklyn, where there is a mixture of Blacks and Whites, young and old, and a variety of income groups. Right away, we are confronted with the fact that the restaurant, which is an old-fashioned neighborhood institution, is facing financial difficulties.

One of the best things about the film is its conversations. Some of the dialogue by writer-director Jim McCay is right on. It doesn't sound canned or wooden. *Everyday People* also is a realistic-looking production that took advantage of an actual restaurant, Ratner's, located on the Lower East Side of Manhattan, for its primary set, and also includes real street shots of real people walking by in Lower Manhattan and Brooklyn.

One of the least-successful aspects of the pilot is its overall depiction of Black characters. Without exception, they are an unhappy, whining lot, with most wanting something from the White man.

Even though *Everyday People* is billed as a "slice of life" drama (that feels more like the start of a TV series than a fully contained movie), the film is trying to tackle serious topics and it should be commended for that. It would be an even better film if all the "everyday people" floating around Raskin's were more fully drawn and humanized. Like the lady said, "You can't wash out all the color and keep the flava."

OPM–*King Arthur*

July 7, 2004

Until a Black director like Antoine Fuqua can get funds to do a big-budget film on Shaka Zulu, Toussaint L'Ouverture, or my *main* man, Antonio Maceo (look it up), I guess we'll have to make do with King Arthur. But I have my arms crossed, I'm patting my foot, and I'm checking my watch.

Black Star–Will Smith in *I, Robot*

July 16, 2004

When it comes to beating down thug robots in the year 2035, you'd better call forth an emissary from the hip-hop nation, in this case Will Smith, who is *so* no longer the Fresh Prince of Bel-Air. In fact, in *I, Robot,* he is the Fresh King of Kicking Robotic Butt.

It's hard to believe that, not that long ago, a Black man would rarely be seen in a futuristic flick, even less often playing a major part, not to mention the starring role. But, as in *Independence Day* and *Men in Black,* Smith walks boldly—to a future Chicago where a Black man is the best candidate to keep the world safe for humans, the best candidate to turn a skeptical eye toward the excesses of technology—and the best candidate to survive a robot carjacking.

In a story inspired by the book of short stories by science-fiction writer Isaac Asimov, Smith plays Chicago detective Del Spooner who, despite the fact that robots have been thoroughly integrated into society, harbors deep suspicions and reservations about them. When Spooner is called to the high-rise offices of a major robotics corporation to solve an apparent suicide, he fears that the death is, instead, a murder and that a robot could be the murderer. Such supposition puts him, again, at odds with his commanding officer and everyone else, who believes that robots—because of their programming—could never harm a human being. His investigation leads him into a world of science gone mad and the survival of humans is at stake.

Director Alex Proyas (*Dark City, The Crow*) and a crack CGI team have created amazingly lifelike special effects, from a futuristic Chicago with lightning-fast traffic and sleek cars, to the very human characteristics of advanced robots who both aid and menace. The suspenseful scenes have real suspense, the action scenes are action-packed. None of this film looks amateurish, silly, or unbelievable. There is, realistically, also still a "hood" in the future, replete with run-down housing and graffiti. (Just a little commentary about the existence of poverty amid high-tech advances.)

A few more words about Smith: *I, Robot* allows him to really show his stuff, literally and figuratively. Even though this is an action flick, he gets to show more of his acting range, as he did in *Ali.* It gets hot and he takes off all his clothes, showing the world the effects of good bodybuilding. He serves as one of the executive producers and perhaps this role is one reason that Detective Spooner isn't the only spot in an otherwise White future. Spooner has a grandmother. He has a run-in with a hefty sister having an asthma attack. His Black boss keeps shaking his head at him in one of those expressions of dismay that we Black folks reserve only for each other.

There is lots of the futuristic and new in *I, Robot,* but some things never change.

Black Star—Halle Berry in *Catwoman*

July 24, 2004

Without the trappings of Gotham City or her worthy adversary, Batman, Catwoman in 2004 has been declawed. In this story, Patience Philips (Halle Berry) is a graphics designer for a cosmetics firm, which, she discovers, is intent on selling a new face product, despite the fact that it will disfigure its users. After Patience discovers this secret, she is drowned and then resuscitated by some cats—one of which is a magical cat that has been hanging around her apartment building. Patience goes from mousy to cat-quick with a new haircut, hair color, and some tight-fitting leather gear. She starts pouncing on furniture, eating canned tuna straight from the can, and eventually confronts the evil owners of the cosmetics firm, one of which is played by Sharon Stone. A drawn-out catfight between Cat-woman and the evil villainess is the neon cherry on an over-the-top production.

The Twentieth Anniversary of *Purple Rain*

Purple Rain Pimpology—The Missing Link Between *The Mack* and the Many Macks of Hip-Hop?

July 27, 2004

When the phenomenon known as *Purple Rain* burst onto the screen in 1984, it was still only a stone's throw away from the 1970s. Sure, long mack coats had given way to leather, and the "press and curl" had given way to the jheri curl, but there were still many land yachts—old Cadillac Eldorados, Buick LeSabres, and Chrysler New Yorkers—on the road. The faux fab aura of the pimp was still part of the pop culture imagination, and was taken to a whole new level in the big pimpin' decade of the 1980s, with its junk bonds, savings and loan scandals, and obsession with *Dallas*-like materialism and wanton greed.

In the larger context, the pimp aura (and, we should add, the "ho" aura as well) of *Purple Rain* is mild in comparison—but is startling nonetheless. Wardrobe is an easy mark. Minus the wide-brimmed hat, bandleader Morris Day is pimped out in his loud shiny suits, creamy white coat, two-tone wingtips, and straightened hair. He is vain and preening, as if accustomed to pampering himself with the proceeds of the pimpish music industry or, we could imagine, hookers on the track.

Day's self-absorption is rendered comically as he runs his hand over his hair like a girl and checks his appearance in a mirror held aloft by his manservant-sidekick-fellow performer Jerome. Prince is a whole other matter. He does sport the long coat, but his shirts with waves of ruffles, tight pants, pointy-toed boots, and curly locks make him look more effeminate or androgynous than pimplike. At some point, Morris Day, his worthy adversary, calls him a "long-haired faggot."

What really gives *Purple Rain* the aura of the pimp-hooker relationship is the inconsiderate and often violent interaction between Prince or Morris Day and

Apollonia and the other women in the film. Always couched in humor, albeit an immature type of humor, Day and Prince are, in one moment, abusive to women and, in the next moment, treating them like pet poodles with possible earning power. At a rehearsal for the new girl group he wants to form, Day grows increasingly irritated with two women executing the bump-and-grind dance moves that he has choreographed.

"Let's have some action!" he yells at them, both bent over in tights and high heels. "I want some asses wiggling! I want some perfection!" Pleased with his off-rhyme, Day smacks palms with Jerome before telling him outside, "This just ain't hapnin. The bitches are okay. But we need something more exciting." Just then, someone we assume is one of Morris Day's women jumps in his face about some slight she has suffered and, with one gesture from Day, Jerome picks up the woman and throws her into a nearby garbage Dumpster. The surly woman who dares speak back has, literally, been dumped.

In contrast, the relationship between Prince and Apollonia is more complex, with Apollonia playing more of a "ho" than Prince plays a pimp. Apollonia is a needy and ambitious aspiring performer who hopes Prince can give her the break she needs. On her very first outing with him, she accepts what she thinks is an initiation into the world of popular Minneapolis performers and strips down to her panties before jumping into a dirty lake. Prince laughs at her and pretends that he is going to leave her in the woods naked and wet. She has no money and is staying in a seedy hotel but she pawns a gold ankle chain to buy Prince a new guitar. Minutes later, when she tells him she is joining Morris Day's girl group, Prince slaps (as in pimp-slaps) her before she bolts from his basement digs in his parents' house. We are supposed to understand that, as depicted here, Prince has grown up in an abusive household, watching his controlling and domineering father repeatedly hit his mother. So the son has taken on the same behavior, which is the same behavior some pimps use to control the women in their lives.

Apollonia's ultimate decision to "sell" her sexuality as the lead singer for the new group Apollonia 6 is really what cements the pimp-hooker flava of *Purple Rain*. It is not her fault that men in the story look on her video-ready redbone looks and begin to lust, but it is entirely her decision to make that lust work for her career and monetary advantage. For her group's debut, she appears on stage in a cape and then peels it away to reveal only a black lace teddy, a garter, black stockings, and high heels—this moment is the cinematic intersection of the strip club, prostitution, and good old-fashioned girl-group entertainment. Men throw dollars onto the stage, perhaps they even reach to place one inside Apollonia's garter as she sings, "I'm a sex shooter, shooting out in your direction. Sex shooter, come and play with my affection."

Apollonia presents herself here as a woman confident of what her looks and sexuality should buy and cost. Appropriately for its superficial decade, *Purple Rain* was a precursor to many girl (and boy) groups that looked good on camera but could not sing. At the time of its release, *Purple Rain* was only the latest to tell young women that looks and sexuality can easily be sold, and to tell young men that maybe, just maybe, pimping is easy after all.

Black Star—Denzel Washington in *The Manchurian Candidate*

July 30, 2004

The new *Manchurian,* starring Denzel Washington and directed by Jonathan Demme, is a good movie for right now. First, in these perilous political times, any serious Washington, D.C.–based film must take itself seriously. Had Demme taken the same satirical tone of the 1962 version, how well would that play as body bags continue to arrive from Iraq? Second, it is refreshing, more than forty years after 1962's lily-white *Manchurian,* to see a film about America that shows a bit more American diversity, in Washington, D.C., New York City, and in the armed forces. For this fact alone, the film has to get big ups.

Demme takes the original story, about brainwashed Korean veterans, and grafts it onto more recent world events. In this version, Raymond Shaw (Liev Schreiber) is a member of Congress who has been tapped to run for vice president. Part of Shaw's allure is that he is a war hero, having won the Congressional Medal of Honor for his heroism in a decisive battle during the 1992 Gulf War. But details of that battle and Shaw's rapid political ascent have consistently troubled other survivors of that battle, most especially the head of the unit, Ben Marco, played by Denzel Washington, and Al Melvin, played amazingly by Jeffrey Wright. Washington soon gathers evidence that his military unit was brainwashed in an elaborate corporate scheme to create a "war hero," someone who could, in the future, present the perfect face for public office, all the while being privately manipulated.

Denzel Washington does a decent job with a script that does not paint him (or anybody else for that matter) as a fully realized character. I also enjoyed the performances by Meryl Streep and Schreiber. Wright does not appear for long in the movie but he is the star of the screen whenever he is there.

Though this film is set in the present, it has the feel of a futuristic sci-fi thriller, with evil science and evil scientists (from South Africa, okkaaaay?) taking center stage, and lots of background chatter about the dominance of Halliburton-like corporate power over our fragile electoral process.

It's something to think about.

She Hate Me

July 30, 2004

The story in Spike Lee's *She Hate Me,* about Jack Armstrong (Anthony Mackie), a corporate vice president who, when fired, turns to working as an in-person sperm donor for lesbians, covers the same themes of being a corporate sellout or "ho" that Lee covered in *Bamboozled.* But this time, the arena is the worlds of finance, politics, and sex (literal "ho"-ing), instead of entertainment.

Armstrong compares his situation to that of Frank Wills, the Black security guard who in 1972 discovered the break-in at the Watergate office complex in Washington, D.C. That break-in eventually led to the impeachment and resignation of President Richard M. Nixon, but Wills found himself unemployed and unheralded. He died at the age of fifty-two in 2000.

If Lee and writer Michael Genet do intend to make some commentary about the stereotype and history of the Black man as a stud, it is a subtle commentary buried beneath the unwavering sympathy they hold for Armstrong. The women depicted here do not fare as well. Fatima (Kerry Washington), Armstrong's one-time fiancé turned lesbian, and most of the other lesbians, are depicted as selfish and obnoxious. The movie's title, a play on the name of the former XFL football player He Hate Me (Rod Smart on the Carolina Panthers), asks us to believe that most if not all lesbians hate men, but Lee's bitchy depictions of women sometimes make this film feel more like *He Hate Her.*

But for me, a straight woman, the depictions feel more humorous than mean-spirited, just as humorous as Armstrong's pitiful friend who frets over his low and slow sperm count.

There is a fresh originality in *She Hate Me* that some folks might not be ready for. I say bravo for imagination, for taking a chance, for staying true to the reason we started to cheer our movies again nearly twenty years ago, for having a bold Black voice.

It ain't all about drugs and guns up in here.

Urbanworld's Tricky Pop Culture Terrain

August 4–8, 2004

From its star-studded premiere of *Collateral* in Harlem, with none other than Tom

Cruise walking the red carpet, to its screenings of provocative documentaries such as *Negroes with Guns,* this year's Urbanworld Film Festival continued to showcase films with an "urban" flair—however you define that tricky pop culture genre.

One hundred feature films, documentaries, and short films were screened at the four-day festival, which was held at several locations in Midtown Manhattan and at the Magic Johnson Theater in Harlem, and ended on Sunday with an awards program. Taking home top honors in the feature-film category was *Beat the Drum,* a moving tale from South Africa, directed by David Hickson and written by W. David McBrayer, about a young boy's navigation through the AIDS crisis. The jury prize for best documentary feature went to *Negroes with Guns,* directed and produced by Sandra Dickson and Churchill L. Roberts, about the civil rights leader Robert Williams and his philosophy of armed self-defense. The audience award went to *Cross Bronx,* directed by Larry Golin, about a group of friends who move into their first apartment together. A special jury prize for director to watch went to Kim Eui-Seok for *Sword in the Moon.*

"There are people out there getting it done," said Michael Boatman (*Law and Order: SVU, Arliss*) of the festival. "And that has been the most heartening thing to me."

"People are out here trying to fulfill their dream by any means necessary," said actor Andre Royo (*The Wire*). "I love being a part of that."

Both actors were on hand Sunday morning as presenters at an awards breakfast filled with lots of shining faces but often missing the winning filmmakers. Other winners included, for best short film, *Tap Heat* and, in the same category, special jury prizes for *La Milpa*; Morroco Omari, an actor in *Andre Royo's Big Scene*; and Monica Mallet, an actress in *Shooter.* Actress Cherine Anderson also won a special jury prize in the features category.

For a while now, the open secret of the Urbanworld Film Festival, which began as an earnest effort to showcase films by Blacks (or at least films by artists of color), is that so many, if not most of the films shown, are produced and directed by Whites. This year was no exception, but www.seeingblack.com did see several films directed by us. The first was *Fronterz,* directed by Courtney Jones, which told the frequently funny tale of three actors who decide to fake it as rappers so that they can, finally, land a film role. We also saw *Woman Thou Art Loosed,* a film adaptation of the stage play and book of the same name authored by the Rev. T. D. Jakes and directed by the veteran Michael Schultz. Not in contention for an award was a sneak preview of *The Seat Filler,* a romantic comedy about a law student who meets a celebrity singer while working as a seat filler for awards shows.

Films chosen for the festival were culled from five hundred films entered for consideration, said Stacey Spikes, founder and executive director of the festival. Screening work from around the world makes Spikes feel like he has "the best job in the world," he said, just before he added that many of the submissions put him in the mind-set of, "Thank God for fast-forward."

But there were obviously diamonds in the heap. In the documentary category, *The Sixth Section,* about immigrant union organizing, won for best documentary short, while special jury prizes went to *Juvies,* about juveniles caught up in the criminal justice system, and *I Promise Africa,* about orphans filmed in Kenya on the morning of the 9/11 attacks. An award for best screenplay was given to Casper Wong for *Babyface* and, in the same category, a special jury prize was given to Vernon Whitlock III for *Sugar on the Floor.* MTV2 was the sponsor of this year's festival and encouraged Spikes to include an award for best music video, which went to an artist who goes by the name of RT!, for *Time to Change.*

Black Star–Jamie Foxx in *Collateral*

August 6, 2004

In this season of movies, when the repeated theme is machine-like killing, director Michael Mann, with actors Jamie Foxx and Tom Cruise, has delivered a film that is almost operatic in its sweep and emotion.

Very few films about a psychopathic killer, like this one, manage to contain themselves from beginning to end, without veering into the realm of *Gothika*-like ridiculousness—with the wide-eyed boogeyman, with the cheap buildup of tension, with the monster jumping out of nowhere. But *Collateral* doesn't play us for suckers. Instead it offers an engrossing balance of storytelling, tension, action, horror, and even a little humor. (On the last point, how could it not with Jamie Foxx?)

But, for real, starting with his superb performances in *Bait* and *Any Given Sunday,* Foxx has proven himself to be more than just funny. Here, he plays Max, an L.A. native who drives a cab while dreaming of starting his own deluxe limo business. On one fateful night, he picks up a man named Vincent (Cruise), a hired hit man who orders Max to chauffeur him around on his killing spree.

Cruise holds down his part with a lot of mastery—illustrating the thin line between being the good-guy killer in *Mission: Impossible* and being the bad guy. Here he is the official Crazy White Man hired to kill people who are mainly colored and he terrorizes a Black cabbie with a pointed gun, plastic handcuffs, punches, and threats.

Of all the killing going on in movies this year, the violence of *Collateral* is certainly the most homegrown, and is certainly the most dramatic. All the action proceeds to a driving musical score that veers from rock to jazz to European classical to old-school soul. It is a hit-man opera.

The Cookout

September 3, 2004

Big-money sports is the subtext of *The Cookout,* the independent comedy produced and written by Queen Latifah and her longtime business associate Shakim Compere. The main ingredient that the recent *Mr. 3000* has that *The Cookout* doesn't have is a talented stand-up comedian and screen presence such as Bernie Mac who can at least carry a film and script that is marginal at best. *The Cookout,* while mildly amusing at times, has too many clichés and too many missed directorial opportunities by newcomer Lance Rivera to be consistently interesting or funny.

The big joke that the filmmakers attempt to set up is the collision between sudden sports celebrity and wealth for the young pro basketball rookie Todd Anderson (Storm P, aka Quran Pender) and the "ghetto" ways of his family in Newark, New Jersey. *The Cookout* attempts to capitalize on Black America's love affair with subjects and places near and dear to our community, such as *Soul Food,* the *Barbershop,* or the *Beauty Shop.* It's no surprise that this film has returned to the subject of home cooking and the promise of family life. The actual cookout, ultimately, takes a backseat to the sports drama. And, unfortunately, that drama is not very meaty, and overdone.

Black Star–Bernie Mac in *Mr. 3000*

September 17, 2004

It takes *Mr. 3000* a while to realize that it is a baseball movie. In those early moments, when the film has not found itself, it will be helpful if you are a big Bernie Mac fan. Only then will you weather its lapses into cliché, sloppy production (visible microphones and production crew), and a story that, only toward the end, allows its cast to be fully rounded characters.

But once it finds its identity, there's no denying its Bernie Mac humor and irreverence, or its snappy direction in the hands of Charles Stone III. Mac's "poppa don't take no mess" persona is right in sync with that of the cocky athlete—in this case, Stan Ross, the middle-aged, retired, and narcissistic baseball player he portrays in this film.

Adding another dimension to the film is the somewhat strained but fascinating relationship between Ross and an ESPN reporter (Angela Bassett) and the inclusion of sports talking heads such as ESPN's Michael Wilbon and Tony Kornheiser. As the assorted talking heads keep talking and talking about Ross, the film reminds us, larger social issues of race, gender, age, class, and aggression are played out under the guise of sports and "sports talk."

Chisholm '72: Unbought and Unbossed

September 24, 2004

The bold campaign for the U.S. presidency in 1972 by Congresswoman Shirley Chisholm (D-New York) is one of those facts of Black history that could easily be forgotten unless we tell the story. In the new documentary *Chisholm '72: Unbought and Unbossed,* which is being screened around the country, director Shola Lynch does just that: In a taut, well-organized seventy-six minutes, she chronicles Chisholm's campaign and how it fit into politically turbulent times that still shape the United States today.

When Chisholm announced her candidacy, she had already made history in 1968 as the first Black woman elected to the U.S. Congress. She represented New York's 12th Congressional District of New York in Brooklyn. At that time, she had broken a barrier not only in Congress, where she faced a cold shoulder and random insults from colleagues, but also in the Black Congressional Caucus, a boys-only club that included many representatives newly elected after the passage of the 1965 Voting Rights Act.

Lynch loses some of the strength of her film by not including more about the initial spark that motivated Chisholm's run, or details about Chisholm's plans for the country if elected. There is the hint that Chisholm was an advocate for government policies to strengthen families, including Head Start and day care, but there is little inclusion of her fierce opposition to the Vietnam War, or her championing of other social reforms. The absence of this information creates a void in the film that leaves Chisholm surrounded by questions, the same questions that dogged her campaign more than thirty years ago.

Woman Thou Art Loosed

October 1, 2004

Of the assorted stage plays, including bawdy comedies, morality tales, and interpersonal melodramas, that have frequented the chitlin circuit in the last decade, it's best that *Woman Thou Art Loosed,* adapted from a novel by the popular author Bishop T. D. Jakes, is one that has made it to the big screen.

But while most of these plays and, for that matter, a whole genre of our recent literature, is caught up in the aforementioned comedy, morality, and melodrama, at least *Woman Thou Art Loosed* concerns itself with subject matter of a bit more gravity—the unchecked sexual abuse of young girls who grow up to be troubled young women.

The real gems in this movie, who carry it and make it whole, are Kimberly Elise and Loretta Devine. They bring the right around-the-way flavor, and their performances are superb and lend depth and more meaning to what could be a run-of-the-mill story. Clifton Powell and Michael Boatman, the affable actor perhaps best known for his recurring role on *Arliss,* are also very good, though I am uncomfortable with the very dark and handsome Powell consistently being cast as a sinister bad guy, a literal devil.

Black Star–Will Smith (Voice) in *Shark Tale*

October 1, 2004

With Will Smith as its muse and guide, *Shark Tale* takes a wild ride into the uncharted world of multicultural animation. Pop-cultured and decidedly urban, message-filled yet rocking and fun, this cartoon is certainly the hippest and most hip-hopped—in all its positives and negatives—ever to come down the pike.

Hip, yes, but also familiar.

Writers Rob Letterman and Damian Shannon have basically taken the time-worn plot of owing money to the mob, added some reggae, '70s soul and '80s rap, and then submerged it under water. As much as the mob flick is a template here, so is the hip-hop music video. Smith peppers his manic voice-over performance with clips from MC Hammer and, of course, vintage Fresh Prince. There is the obligatory gold digger (Angelina Jolie). And there is an entire hip-hop dance routine, performed by competing groups of sea life, that mimics the drama of *You Got Served.*

The film is clean enough and visually interesting enough to keep young moviegoers interested, and it is sophisticated enough in its pop culture references to keep parents amused. *Shark Tale* is enjoyable enough and, for the most part, benign. It's difficult to be angry at the depiction of the fierce (White) Shark Mafia, compared to the weak and wannabe (Black) fish when that is precisely the power relationship set up by the hip-hop community, in its slavish adoration of mob and millionaire culture. (Gotti, Rocafella, anybody?) Despite the cheesy recycling, the movie also reaches for valuable lessons in societal climbing, and in the double-edged sword of being a feared predator.

Black Star–Queen Latifah in *Taxi*

October 8, 2004

First, when it comes to watching Queen Latifah on the big screen, I must make a confession. One of my sincerest wishes is to, once again, see her swaggering and fierce in the mode of that 1996 classic *Set It Off,* in which she played Cleopatra (as in Jones?), the tough girl in a quartet of female bank robbers.

Wrapped in the persona of Cleo, we had a rare Black female outlaw hero who carried just the right self-possession, irreverence of the *po*-lice, and tremendous facility with semiautomatic weapons.

No film role has offered us the same heroine again, though Naomie Harris as Selena in *28 Days Later* presented an across-the-pond variety of toughness, and Jada Pinkett Smith played the futuristic Niobe taking no prisoners in *The Matrix Reloaded* and *The Matrix Revolutions.*

Certainly none of Queen Latifah's roles, which have veered toward comedy rather than drama, have allowed her to return to the tough (lesbian, by the way) chick, who prompted the brother behind me in the dark theater to root for her at the top of his lungs. "Shoot him, Queen," he said, exhorting her to fire on her enemies. "Shoot him!"

I know that *Taxi* is another so-so comedy for Queen Latifah. But at least she has raised herself above the asinine script of *The Cookout.* At least here, in the role of Belle, she gets to drive the hell out of a car, show she's not intimidated by the NYPD, and wield lots of city-girl common sense—if not an AK-47.

Belle has just gotten her license to drive a cab when she, unfortunately, picks up a cop, Washburn (Jimmy Fallon), who is determined to regain his good name after a work fiasco. Together, Belle and Washburn decide to solve a series of bank robberies in the city—so he can hold his head high on the job, and she can continue driving a cab. In the process of all this mayhem, there are a few dead spots—for example a somewhat unsuccessful scene with Ann Margaret as a lush—but the writers and director keep us laughing enough to compensate for these lapses.

Black Star—Derek Luke in *Friday Night Lights*

October 8, 2004

A thoughtful and well-crafted sports flick that deftly turns over issues of class, race, and all sorts of American neuroses—sports and otherwise. Derek Luke gets a role that lets him do his thing.

Moolaadé

October 13, 2004

In Ousmane Sembene's films, you can't keep a Black woman down.

Moolaadé, the latest work by the eighty-one-year-old filmmaker, casts a harsh spotlight on the practice of female circumcision—some call it genital mutilation—which is still practiced in many countries on the African continent.

Set inside a small, remote village, the story focuses a woman named Collé, who invokes *moolaadé,* which means protection or sanctuary, when four young girls run away from the circumcision ritual and seek refuge in her home. Only she, among the wives in her husband's household, and among the women in the village, has spared her teenage daughter from what the girls refer to as the "cutting," and what the village elders refer to as "purification." And for this defiance of tradition, Collé is reviled, feared, and respected as a woman with her own strong convictions.

It is largely through Collé's defiance that this powerful and disturbing story unfolds, and that the impact of the circumcision ritual is made up close and real. Collé is a walking and talking symbol for the woman who is in possession of her own mind, but not of her own body. She is strong and determined, but she bears scars and deformation from her own cutting. We learn, through her story, how many girls who have been circumcised heal in such a way as to make sexual intercourse forever painful—sexual pleasure is out of the question—and to make natural childbirth impossible. We learn how, for some girls, the procedure is fatal.

Sembene, who is both writer and director, intertwines the issue of circumcision with commentary about the power of media and information, and, conversely, the power of ignorance. One result of Collé's defiance is the ordered confiscation of all radios belonging to women in the village.

This is the second part of a trilogy in which Sembene explores the lives of African women. The trilogy had been reported to begin with the 1999 *L'heroisme au Quotidien* (*Ordinary Heroism*). That film told the story of women from a small, remote village who are suddenly connected to the outside world through radio. In press materials distributed for the release of *Moolaadé,* Sembene says that the first film in the trilogy is *Faat Kiné,* which he released in 2000, and that he is working on the third part. *Faat Kiné* focused on a Senegalese single mother, an existence that is shameful and punishable by death in her society. Sexually and physically abused as a young woman, Faat Kiné straddles the traditions of her parents' generation and the realities of her postcolonial existence.

Aside from this trilogy, Sembene has long demonstrated a strong feminist streak in his work, beginning with his first feature-length film, *Black Girl,* in 1966, *Emitai* in 1971, and *Xala* in 1974. He has been unafraid to expose how traditions of gender inequality have helped to cripple African societies emerging from the yoke of colonialism.

In *Moolaadé,* Sembene makes powerful use of symbolism, mythology, and metaphors, as well as humor, music, and song, to drive along his narrative. As much as Collé's scarred and battered body becomes a symbol of her pain and perseverance, the radio and television are powerful symbols here of knowledge and education. In *Moolaadé,* Sembene raises an antenna as a symbol of information power, just as in the 1960s a fist was raised as a symbol of Black Power.

27

Big-Boned Cinema

Ray

October 29, 2004

Everything about *Ray,* the new film based on the life of musical icon Ray Charles, is big. Charles's life unfolds in a series of boldly drawn episodes that are bighearted and big-boned.

You know big-boned. (When the skinny low-rise jeans don't fit. When you can't get the Size A pantyhose . . . but I digress.) This movie, fifteen years in the making, is no delicate or wispy affair. The story of Charles's music, jumping the river divide between rhythm and blues and gospel, blows up the screen. The story of his impoverished childhood in Albany, Georgia, where he lost his sight at the age of seven, is so up close and personal that we might be tempted to turn away from the misery amid the sweetness, and the indomitable will of Aretha Robinson, Charles's mother.

But just when you think that the music and childhood flashbacks will be enough, there is an emotional complexity that renders this larger-than-life figure in all of his flaws and flashes of artistic genius. Musicians on the road curse and womanize and drink and do drugs (parents, be forewarned). And despite his fame and wealth, Charles (born Ray Charles Robinson) grappled with a deep-seated loneliness, was haunted by childhood tragedy, and was often felled by hallucinations and fears.

Everything good that you've heard about Jamie Foxx's performance is true. Watching Foxx morph into Ray Charles is amazing indeed. Maybe it's easier or maybe it is more difficult to play the part of someone without using the eyes to convey emotion. We'll never know. Foxx leaves nothing on the table for us to pick up and turn over in our hands. With every voice inflection, every twist and turn, every song and pounding of the keys, every sorry excuse offered to his waiting wife or girlfriends, Foxx is Ray Charles (who worked with the actor on the role before his death earlier this year). But for all of this Ray immersion, it's also a hoot to note how Foxx manages to find the point of intersection between himself and every character he plays. In *Ray,* that moment of intersection comes when a young Ray Charles lies to a bus driver, telling him that he was blinded during the invasion of Normandy in World War II.

Sharon Warren is excellent as Charles's mother, and Regina King, one of the Raylettes, always stands out on the screen. All the actors have to work hard in this film. Its scale and up-close scenes don't allow for slouching. Foxx, as the ball players say, carries the movie on his shoulders. Anything less than perfection in a story about such an icon would have made the movie look cheap and cheesy. They are aided by a script from James L. White that sounds like how people really talk, that pictures African-Americans with sensuality and energy as the community partied and shimmied its way into the civil rights era.

Director Taylor Hackford (*An Officer and a Gentleman*) has made a big movie, one that deserves big ups.

Black Star–Nia Long in *Alfie*

November 4, 2004

By all accounts, actor Jude Law is not a ladies' man off-screen, and he does not make a convincing one on-screen in this remake of the 1960s stage play and film about a playboy Brit. Law is, however, able to convince us that Alfie has a simplistic and naive outlook on life that does not allow him to really feel love relationships for what they are. Nia Long's return to the big screen here is notable for the depth and humanity she brings to a relatively small role. The writers put Long in the role of the Black temptress and treat tense race relations in the U.S. as if they don't exist. But, unlike Halle Berry in *Monster's Ball,* Long's character isn't unrealistic or pitiful. Omar Epps plays an even smaller role but uses those big eyes and every screw-face expression he can muster to portray a sensitive and aggrieved Black man.

Fade to Black

November 5, 2004

The high-flying and raw energy of hip-hop is captured, perhaps as never before, in this documentary featuring rapper Jay-Z and his sold-out show at Madison Square

Garden in November 2003. The movie gives Jay-Z the opportunity to reflect on his life and career and features performances by P. Diddy, Mary J. Blige, Beyoncé, Missy Elliott, Questlove, and others.

Black Star–Samuel L. Jackson (Voice) in *The Incredibles*

November 5, 2004

Masquerading as a kids' cartoon, *The Incredibles* is either the best parody of the cult of superheroism to come along in a while, or a tacky cheerleading film for the growing cult of White nationalism. You figure it out.

Black Star–Wesley Snipes in *Blade: Trinity*

December 8, 2004

The third installment of the *Blade* series, which follows the exploits of a stylish and fierce vampire slayer, luxuriates in its place as a cinematic comic book. In this place, people and events don't need to appear necessarily real. The over the top can be applauded. And its self-mockery provides some comic relief from the movie's marvelous pretensions. Blade himself, a day-walking half human and half vampire played by Wesley Snipes, is an amalgam of pretension: the comic-book hero, the martial-arts master who takes time to readjust his sunglasses, the vampire fashionista sprinkled, in this sequel, with a bit of the appearance of a drag queen. And here, for the first time, Snipes even incorporates something from Nino Brown, his breakout role in *New Jack City.* Blade gets all gangsta for a minute just to let us know that he has roots in the hood.

OPM–*Million Dollar Baby*

December 15, 2004

These days, when most sports movies proceed at a fast and furious pace, *Million Dollar Baby* has the patience of an old man. Clint Eastwood, the seventy-four-year-old director, has crafted a boxing film where the important action happens outside the ring. There are lingering conversations filled with life's regrets, common occurrences of spite and evil, and common occurrences of good.

The setting is a boxing gym where Frankie Dunn (Eastwood) is trainer and manager to notable talents. A waitress and aspiring boxer named Maggie Fitzgerald (Hilary Swank) starts hanging around the gym and pestering Frankie to be her trainer. After initially brushing her off, protesting that he does not manage girls, Frankie eventually agrees to be her trainer. Looking on is Frankie's longtime friend, a former boxer named Eddie Scrap-Iron Dupris (Morgan Freeman), who lives and works at the gym as a janitor.

As in last year's *Mystic River,* Eastwood includes lots of extended dialogue that adds personal history and dimension to the characters. But for almost the first half of the film, many of these boxing-gym quips and retorts slow down and add weight to the story. What is supposed to be perhaps witty sports banter falls somewhat flat. What is supposed to be wise reflection between the two veterans of the ring sounds clichéd and boring to me. (Who knows? Maybe it won't sound boring to movie viewers of another generation, or to big Clinton Eastwood fans.)

Thankfully, the pace of the story quickens once the boxing action begins. Frankie arranges several fights, and Swank acquits herself well inside and outside the ring. Maggie's growing success is juxtaposed with her roots in a trailer-park family. Through her story and through the hard-luck cases in the gym, *Million Dollar Baby* is a poem about the hillbilly and ghetto places that boxers come from, and the ways that boxing draws to it hard-luck stories and hard-luck outcomes.

Maggie is the epitome of poor White virtue, a hardworking girl from hardscrabble circumstances determined to work her way to the top. Though thirty-one years old, she is single-minded in an almost childlike way. She is not very smart but she has a good heart. In contrast, the Black folks in this film are either pitiable or evil. While Eddie has a good heart, too, and is a sort of father figure to the gym's various boxing hopefuls, he is cut down by Frankie as a man who has been reduced to "cleaning up spit." The evil female boxer in the film, Billie the Blue Bear (Lucia Rijker), who is Maggie's Apollo Creed, is a muscular Black woman with curving cornrows, arched eyebrows, and a reputation for fighting dirty. The narrator also tells us that she is a former prostitute. So if Maggie is a vision of poor White virtue, Blue Bear is a vision of poor Black vice.

Despite these stereotypes, Eastwood leaves room for what is mysterious, unexplained, and tragic in his characters, and in life. And he takes his time letting life, his cold version of it, reveal itself to us.

Hotel Rwanda

December 22, 2004

The first thing to recommend about *Hotel Rwanda* is its attempt to tell an important and ignored story—the civil war and genocide in the central-African country of Rwanda that left nearly one million people dead over the course of three months in 1994. Hollywood seldom deals with African tragedy and the mass loss of life as a subject matter worthy of respect.

The second thing to recommend is the performance by Don Cheadle. He stars as Paul Rusesabagina, who was manager of the country's upscale Milles Collines Hotel. The real-life Rusesabagina, who served as a consultant for this film, wound up saving the lives of hundreds—including members of his own family—who sought refuge at the hotel. He also saved the day through negotiating with military thugs, making personal sacrifices, and thinking fast on his feet in the midst of crisis. Cheadle morphs effortlessly into an ordinary African man who summons extraordinary courage. His accent, on my American ears anyway, is flawless. More than his other recent films, Cheadle fills up this film. He is not acting "opposite" anyone or anything, other than the horror. He is not the Black sidekick, or the one Black man in a sea of Whiteness.

And, fortunately for the film, Cheadle is like an anchor in a narrative that tends to drift. The script for *Hotel Rwanda* does not allow for a depth of character, the gravity of the moment, or for a full sense of the history that has brought the country to this horrific moment. The production lacks the atmosphere (and perhaps the budget) to portray the slaughter in its fullness. Cheadle's performance is a bright spot among a series of lesser ones. You could say that he carries the film on his shoulders.

Largely overlooked here is the role of colonialism in shaping Rwanda into a killing field. After Belgium colonized the country (it was made into a U.N. Protectorate governed by Belgium in 1918), the Tutsis, who generally were taller and lighter-skinned, were given privileges over the darker Hutu majority. Sporadically since the country's independence in 1963, there has been fierce fighting between the Hutu and Tutsi groups. Before a peace accord could be reached in 1994 between the two groups, Rwandan President Habyarimana was killed on April 6 in a plane crash planned by Hutu militia groups. Using its control of radio broadcasts, Hutu extremists blamed the death on Tutsis and urged the public to "cut down the tall trees." Mass killings began that night and did not stop for more than one hundred days, while the United Nations and the United States—headed by then-President Bill Clinton—refused to intervene.

It is this period in 1994 that *Hotel Rwanda* captures. It may not be a complete picture, but it is a snapshot of time, and the story of one brave man standing while his country descended into madness.

Coach Carter

January 14, 2005

There have been *so* many better-than-average sports movies (*Any Given Sunday, Friday Night Lights, Remember the Titans, Raging Bull*) that each new contender must clear a high hurdle. Thankfully, *Coach Carter* rises to the challenge in its gritty telling of the real-life story of Ken Carter, who coached a high school basketball team in Richmond, California, and challenged his young ballplayers to rise above poverty and dead-end expectations.

Like any movie about a Cinderella, up-from-the-grassroots team, *Coach Carter* had plenty of opportunity to be a clichéd mess. But a well-written script, realistic production, sensitive direction by Thomas Carter, and quality acting (and ball playing) by the cast makes this film probably one of the more meaningful films for our youth to come along in a while. At the same time, it offers lessons about education, priorities, and responsibility without heavy-handed preaching.

It seems as if Samuel L. Jackson has been in training for this role, as Ken Carter, for a lifetime. He straddles that fine line between street toughness and Black bourgeois upward mobility. He barks and he coos. He struts around the high school gym in a suit. While the story gives his ballplayers an ample amount of focus, his character is allowed to bloom most fully. The ensemble of actors/ball players who make up the basketball team are endearing and the singer Ashanti doesn't embarrass herself in her acting debut as a girlfriend to one of the jocks.

We don't see Ashanti very much. The thing about sports movies is that they are, primarily, male movies—the antithesis of the chick flick. Women are adornment here, mere sideshows in the larger male drama. The women in *Coach Carter* are really pretty annoying—Ashanti is a pregnant teenager who has no realistic idea of what having a baby will mean for her life. The principal of Richmond High School has accepted the poor performance of students at her school as par for the course. Cheerleaders bump and grind. Rich White girls from wealthy neighborhoods offer themselves up to the Black jocks. There may be a sports avenue offered here to the young men of Richmond but it seems the women are stuck in a pitiful (and stereotyped) rut.

Despite this shortcoming, *Coach Carter* redeems itself over and over in many little ways. Sure, we don't need another hero movie, but *Coach Carter* speaks more to the hero in each of us.

Unforgivable Blackness: The Rise and Fall of Jack Johnson

January 17, 2005

Jack Johnson, the first African-American heavyweight champion, was as mysterious and enigmatic as he was big, bold, and Black. And he will remain a mystery for viewers even after the premiere on PBS of *Unforgivable Blackness: The Rise and Fall of Jack Johnson,* the new unflinching documentary by Ken Burns.

Johnson's meteoric career during the early decades of the last century has been chronicled in near Shakespearean terms by scholars, and in the Broadway play and feature film *The Great White Hope.* At a time when theories of White supremacy were boldly pronounced and disseminated from the United States, Johnson mercilessly pummeled White men in the boxing ring. At a time when Black men were routinely murdered because of rumors that they had flirted with a White woman, Johnson openly took White women as lovers and wives.

What filmmaker Ken Burns does in this film, perhaps better than works on Johnson in the past, is assemble a visual narrative about the virulent racism that surrounded the heavyweight champ, and how that unrelenting racism dogged his career and personal life. Through this storytelling, which is fine and enhanced by startling vintage footage, the viewer is left with no doubt that, in the words of W. E. B. DuBois, it was Johnson's "unforgivable Blackness" that elicited such wrath and persecution.

Illustrations in prominent newspapers depicted Johnson as a monkey or ape. Johnson's biographer, Randy Roberts, says that journalists resorted to the worst stereotypes to cast Johnson's athletic achievements as proof of his subhuman nature. Roberts adds that if a Black athlete was tough and resilient, it was said that his skull was thicker, and that he was somehow more oblivious to pain. If the Black athlete was smart, he was said to be deceptive and devious.

When Johnson knocked out the biggest White hope, Jim Jeffries, in Reno, Nevada, on July 4, 1910, the *Los Angeles Times* made a point to warn African-Americans that they should not be too proud of Johnson's victory. "Do not point you nose too high," the editorial said. "You are just the same—as you were last week. No man will think a bit higher of you because your complexion is the same as the victor at Reno."

Before his historic bout with Jeffries, the *Chicago Tribune* said that the fight was "between the White man's hope, and the Black peril." The story of Johnson and race is riveting, and resounds even a century later as White America continues to play out its racial neuroses on the backs of unbowed Black athletes.

What has always been missing from accounts about Johnson, including this latest ambitious work, is a better sense of who Jack Johnson was, and what in the world he was thinking. There are snippets here of Johnson's words, read by Samuel L. Jackson, that inform us, for example, that he was a deep thinker, that he was conscious of the fact that others did not expect him to have thoughts beyond boxing. Author Stanley Crouch, one of the talking heads interviewed, offers that once, when Johnson was asked why a White woman would find a Black man attractive, Johnson is said to have responded with a straight face: "We eat cold eels and think distant thoughts," which obviously made no sense.

We learn so little here about Johnson's roots in Galveston, Texas (where he was born in 1878), that we get no hint about where he received his physical strength, his cockiness and swagger, his decided taste for "Miss Anne." What allowed him to smile in the ring as spit and shouts of the N-word landed about him? (And did Johnson cast the mold of the smiling Black athlete who is expected to never respond to abusive White fans?)

This absence of background creates a void for those of us who want to understand more about Johnson's relationship to his own Blackness—more about his relationship to a Black community that he did not pretend to champion in any way—as opposed to his relationship to White folks and how they could not forgive the color of his skin.

Black Star–Laurence Fishburne in *Assault on Precinct 13*

January 19, 2005

Laurence Fishburne will forever be able to play Morpheus, the sage revolutionary from *The Matrix.* In *Assault on Precinct 13,* Morpheus morphs into the form of Marion Bishop, a crime lord who finds himself in the custody of the Detroit Police Department. We know Bishop is Morpheus by the long black coat and shades; by the low, steady voice that hints of mystery; and by a deeper human knowledge than possessed by any of us mere mortals. And when Bishop starts kicking butt with that machine-like precision, we know our man Morpheus has, for sure, been resurrected. In this film, a remake of the 1976 John Carpenter movie, Bishop is holed up inside a precinct where he must join forces with other criminals and police in fighting some corrupt cops who are trying to kill him. Lots of bang-bang. John Leguizamo is brilliant (and funny) as the sage junkie.

Are We There Yet?

January 21, 2005

If you can stand that Disney/Nickelodeon kiddie humor, where children are obnoxious, rude, and have far too much agency in their dealings with adults, then you might be able to stand the first half of this comedy starring rapper turned actor Ice Cube and actress Nia Long. Nick (Cube) is trying to date Suzanne (Long) and so, to get into her good graces, he agrees to transport her children from Oregon to Canada where she is working as an event planner. The story (and children) do settle down in the second half into a workable tale about love and the single mommy. Hope you can make it to the second half.

Slavery and the Making of America

February 9, 2005

There is a wide gap between what Black Studies scholars have unearthed during the past decade about American slavery, and what most of us know through popular literature and movies. Thankfully, that gap narrows a bit with the premiere on PBS of *Slavery and the Making of America,* a four-hour program that adds new narratives and personal stories to the history we think we know too well.

Not since *Roots,* the record-setting 1977 miniseries, has a production added such an up-close dimension to America's peculiar institution. And these personal glimpses are not of the heroes most familiar to us, such as Harriet Tubman, Sojourner Truth, or Frederick Douglas. Rather, we hear the names of the first Black men sold into slavery in the United States in 1619. We meet Titus (Colonel Tye), a New Jersey slave who, with the promise of freedom, fought with the British in the Revolutionary War, then freed others from bondage. We meet David Walker, the free man who became a spokesman for abolition and wrote the famous David Walker "appeal" to end slavery. There is Frances Driggus, a free teenager who appealed to the courts when a White man repeatedly abused her and tried to enslave her. There is Harriet Jacobs, who fled slavery in order to save her children from harsh treatment, and became the first known person to pen a "slave narrative." There is Robert Smalls, who, during the Civil War, stole a Confederate ship and, after the war, became an elected representative in South Carolina, and then in the U.S. Congress.

Narrated by actor Morgan Freeman, these stories are spread over four one-hour shows—"The Downward Spiral," "Liberty In the Air," "Seeds of Destruction," and "The Challenge of Freedom." Together, they form a narrative that begins in

New Amsterdam, or today's New York City, in the 1530s, and ends after the issuance of the Emancipation Proclamation in 1862. While important in their own right, the narratives are placed in the larger context of how slavery and American racism was slowly developed legally and socially, how White wealth was built and expanded on the backs of its enslaved population, and how the young nation's contradiction of freedom and slavery almost tore it apart.

While the premise and even the title of the series seems to stress how slavery built wealth for Whites and the nation, it really does not offer as much concrete detail or analysis as, for example, *Race: The Power of an Illusion,* which aired on PBS two years ago. "The value of slaves was greater than the dollar value of all America's banks, all of America's railroads, all of America's manufacturing put together," says historian James O. Horton, who is an anchor of commentary throughout the program. But still, even with such insights by Horton and other experts, the program does not underscore the making of America as much as it does the poignancy of its stories, and the determination of enslaved African people to be free.

The historical re-creations are well produced and directed by a team working with Thirteen/WNET, the PBS station in New York City. The series producer—and producer, writer, and director for the first episode—is Dante Jones, who most recently was executive producer of *This Far by Faith: African-American Spiritual Journeys,* which aired on PBS in 2003. Episodes two through four each have a different writer, director, and producer—Gail Pellett, Chana Gazit, and Leslie D. Farrell respectively.

These producers prove the fact that when it comes to the subject of slavery, we haven't seen it all, and we certainly don't know it all. As scholars continue to unearth more about the past, it seems our documentaries are only beginning to scratch the surface.

Black Star–Will Smith in *Hitch*

February 11, 2005

In the role of a professional "date doctor," Will Smith ventures into the realm of serious romantic comedy—without a Black woman to be found within kissing distance. Still, despite the obvious reach for a larger audience with Eva Mendes as Smith's love interest, *Hitch* delivers enough of the quirkiness, queasiness, humor, and humiliation that accompany dating and mating in the modern age.

Sucker Free City

February 12, 2005

In *Sucker Free City,* which premieres on Showtime, director Spike Lee makes a foray into an aspect of Black film that he often criticizes—the drug–gang violence–hip-hop flick that dominates depictions of urban African-American life. In Lee's hands, these familiar themes are made more complex. No thug and nothing thuggish is painted as glamorous or slick. Rather, this film is a study of petty, marginal criminals living marginal lives.

Written by a newcomer, Alex Tse, *Sucker Free City* is set in San Francisco and alternates between the gang activities of a group of young Black men in the Hunter's Point section of the city; a hotheaded enforcer for the Chinese Mafia in Chinatown; and a young White man straddling the white-collar work world and street hustling.

Lee and Tse have a good time making fun of street-life stereotypes. Leon, second in command of the V-Dub street gang in Hunter's Point, is forever swigging from a huge bottle of malt liquor that resembles a cartoon rocket. Most of the V-Dub crew acts as if they are all on "liquid crack." The one exception is K-Luv (Anthony Mackie), who doesn't like gang violence and is more interested in making money by bootlegging CDs. Nick (Ben Crowley), a young White man who has decided to forego college, has a few hustles going, including credit card fraud, until he almost gets caught. In Chinatown, Lincoln (Ken Leung) is collecting protection money for Mr. Tsing, leader of the community's crime organization, and, at the same time, carrying on a secret and scandalous affair with Mr. Tsing's daughter. Lincoln oozes with insecurity and racial hang-ups. He tells his younger brothers to be like Yao Ming, the Chinese basketball player who can "dunk on Shaq" and challenge the Blacks.

As in most urban flicks of this type, *Sucker Free City* is a very male world and, unlike the usual thug flicks, the marginalization of women does not translate into an automatic propping up of men. Rather, the men are walking and talking examples of criminal and violent male behavior. They are the collateral damage of a city and national economy that has pushed them into the few remaining areas of San Francisco where poor people can afford to live. The women, for the most part, just aren't relevant. K-Luv has a girlfriend, the only young Black woman in the story, who is shuffled off screen in less than a minute, while his grandmother seems to suffer from dementia. Lincoln's love interest, Angela, is a spoiled princess who uses him for sex while pushing her preppie medical student boyfriend toward the altar. Lincoln's sister, Samantha, as well as his mother, are the only women depicted who might have a brain.

The varied story lines give the film a sense of layering and complexity, but, at the same time, the story jumps around quite a bit. In part to keep the various city neighborhoods straight in the film, a short paragraph giving some history about each area is flashed on the screen. Such setups make this movie feel like a pilot episode for a new urban TV series, perhaps something West Coast–based to rival the East Coast dominance of gritty cable dramas such as *The Wire, The Sopranos,* or *Street Time.* Nothing is tied up in a neat Hollywood ending. The story lines are a bit drawn out, but the characters are certainly interesting and could be developed.

28

State of the Union

Lackawanna Blues

February 12, 2005

From a bare stage production of only two men, a guitar, and an occasional harmonica has come a film bursting with more Black life than is often seen on the big screen. Ruben Santiago-Hudson's one-man stage show *Lackawanna Blues,* which won an Obie Award in 2001, makes its way to the small screen on HBO.

The setting is a boardinghouse in Lackawanna, a small Great Lakes town in New York State, where Santiago-Hudson grew up. He lived at the boardinghouse with its owner, Rachel "Nanny" Crosby, who watched and fussed over her motley assortment of tenants like a mother, therapist, and high priestess of the speakeasy. There were drunks, former felons, the crazed, the chronically unemployed—every hard-luck case you could imagine.

And of course there were hard-luck cases, the subtext of this rich tale reveals. The time period, during the 1950s and stretching through to the 1970s, was a time when segregation and limited opportunity—yes, even in the North—was giving way slowly to more opportunities and integration. But perhaps this progress did little for those already grown with little education, no skills, and no prospects beyond life as it had always been.

Nanny, a self-made entrepreneur who had only completed the third grade herself, drew to her struggling folks with names like Ol'lem Taylor, Mr. Luscious, and Small Paul. And, of course there was her husband, Bill Crosby, described as "a high yella Geechee seventeen years her junior." All of these characters that Santiago-Hudson had created so remarkably alone on stage are filled in this production by actors who deliver energetic performances. S. Epatha Merkerson strikes just that right balance of self-possession and worldliness in the role of Nanny. Of course Terrence Dashon Howard delivers a nasty rendition of Bill. The entire ensemble, which includes Hill Harper, Mos Def, Jeffrey Wright, Rosie Perez, Macy Gray, and Marcus Carl Franklin as the young Ruben, turn the movie *Lackawanna Blues* into an instant classic.

As in the play, much of the action in the movie takes place inside the boarding-house and so, as is the danger in many plays turned movies, there is, at times, a whiff of claustrophobia. In the heady and almost over-the-top opening sequence—when a woman gives birth, a jealous lover takes a razor to the competition, and another woman wraps her legs around someone else's husband—that tightness of space establishes the intimacy and intensity of life at Nanny's house. Director George C. Wolfe is obviously in his element, turning a discerning eye on the foibles and failings of African-Americans. Wolfe doesn't forget the blues, as the sounds of a blind bluesman provide the backbeat throughout the film, and underneath lives lived for the weekend.

Santiago-Hudson's original stories are like a rich vein that this film is able to tap into again and again. They are, once again, proof positive that our best films are still coming from our literature, which has been allowed to simmer to perfection away from the hot heat of Hollywood.

Unstoppable—In Ossie's Own Words

February 13, 2005

The great actor and activist Ossie Davis always offered the world his best, including a tremendous humility, and a very big heart. Davis, who was found dead February 4 at the age of eighty-seven in his Miami hotel room, shows the measure of his heart during one of his final interviews in *Unstoppable: A Conversation with Melvin Van Peebles, Gordon Parks and Ossie Davis,* on the Black Starz cable channel.

While Davis, with a lifetime of achievement under his belt, could have easily beat his own drum during the program, he was far more interested in subjects other than himself. Here are some excerpts from Davis's own words, on the state of Black artists, Black folks, and the world.

"We have, in the past, always been able to rise to the occasion presented to us by circumstance, whether those occasions were positive or negative, and even if sometimes they looked as though they might destroy us," he tells the show's host, Warrington Hudlin, while sitting with Parks and Van Peebles on a lemon-colored couch. "We live at this time, in a perilous time—on the international scene and here at home. We don't know exactly what step civilization itself is going to take. But we do know that it will take that step. And on the basis of what we have done in the past, and on the basis of how we do it, I'm calling on my own people to reach back into the pot one more time, and come out with the mojo, and the Brer Rabbit, and the magic . . . that it is going to take.

"What we need now is a new way to be Black, a new way to apply all that we have learned from the past," he says, dressed casually in a denim jacket, his white hair combed away from his square jaw and wise eyes. "And right now, there is a lot of spinning around, bumping into each other. It's night and we don't see very clearly, and a lot of things are happening that we don't thoroughly understand. As time goes by, we will pick up the beat. We will catch the keynote. Then we'll be able to put our instruments to our lips and add to the symphony. And I'm sure our addition will change the whole thing for the better. I can't wait to be as Black in the twenty-first century as I was in the twentieth."

At some point, Hudlin refers to writer Albert Murray's assertion that Black musicians are the "featured artists" of the Black experience, and Davis responds that this hierarchy within Black culture makes perfect sense for a people long denied access to literacy and ideas.

"Those who brought us to this country denied us our culture, our language, our heritage for reasons of their own," Davis says. "They made it impossible. Sometimes you could be put in jail for teaching a slave to read. They understood the importance of words and thoughts, and they kept those things from us as much as they could. And to some degree, we had to learn to communicate nonverbally. And a part of that nonverbalization of our culture led us to express in music what we could not express in words.

"The culture, which we inherited and in which we work, tends to de-verbalize us," he adds. "The musicians and the dancers got there earlier, and our writers and our word-workers came later to the process. But give us time and we'll catch up."

His wife of more than fifty-five years, the actress Ruby Dee, also offers commentary for the show. She says that their activism as a couple came naturally. "What does it take to be an artist?" she asks rhetorically. "It's being affected by everything in the universe that crosses your path. Both of us were formed by that kind of immature behavior of a country struggling to be intelligent, compassionate, sharing, and struggling for its identity," she says. "We recognized the task of helping America become what it should be. Was there anything else to be about?"

She says specifically about their personal life: "I've been fortunate to have been married to Ossie. We did a winner when we married each other, I think."

On the subject of women, Davis says that his life is so intertwined with that of his wife that they are inseparable. (He also adds that at the time of this interview in April 2004 that his mother is still with him and, at age 105, is still "a powerful influence" on him.) "Of course the most obvious connection is that I am married to an actress, to Ruby Dee," he says. "Ruby is my partner in the production company that we own. She's a writer and I'm a writer. She's an actress and I'm an actor. She has directed and I've directed. So it's a kind of extended togetherness. We do things together sort of automatically. She's an associate and a critic for me—and I like that. The advantage that I've always had being associated with Ruby is that from the breakfast table to the actual situation, there is always somebody to whom I can instantly relate. . . .

"And our life consists of continuing conversations, some of which have been going on for years. You know, things that we are concerned about, plans together, things that have to do with film, things that have to do with children, things having to do with what our people are concerned with. The whole total picture of my life, in all aspects, creative and otherwise, is so mixed up with hers that I really would find it difficult to say, particularly in creative activity, where her influence stops, and mine begins."

When asked, Davis says he most wants to do a movie on Haiti's revolutionary hero Toussaint L'Ouverture and the Russian poet and writer Alexander Pushkin.

"We as a people have had that kind of cultural capacity to, in a sense, either invent or reinvent ourselves," he says. "So, however we got here, we are here. Whatever the situation is, we are in it. I fully expect that our showing up in cinema will do as much as our showing up in music for America. . . .

"What is required is that creative spark. Part of our job is to remind young people of the importance of that spark—not to smother it, not to drown it, not to shove it aside. To nurture it."

Diary of a Mad Black Woman

February 25, 2005

Realism and quality drama are really not the point of Tyler Perry's popular stage plays. Perry frolics in the tepid waters of the melodramatic, where the morality tale meets Jesus and Bible. (All the better to keep those packed church buses rolling up to the theater!) In *Diary of a Mad Black Woman,* which has made the leap from the stage to the big screen, the action lurches back and forth between Perry's chitlin circuit comedy and the heart-wrenching saga of a soap opera. But don't get it twisted. In this story of one woman's tragedy and journey of self-discovery, there is plenty that is genuinely funny—especially if you like that pistol-packing grandma humor. And there is also plenty to make you as mad as the mad Black woman in the movie. Perry, who is a handsome gentleman, plays three roles, two to a comic tee, and Kimberly Elise has enough acting chops to keep Perry, and this film, out of the chitlin soup.

Interview—Ruben Santiago-Hudson

March 4, 2005

In addition to his stage play turned hit television movie, *Lackawanna Blues,* on HBO, Ruben Santiago-Hudson stars in *Their Eyes were Watching God* on ABC, and is an award-winning veteran of Broadway. Here, he discusses the fickle nature of fame, box-office receipts, and making Black movies that matter.

Iverem: Did you see Jamie Foxx win his Oscar? Do you think that Hollywood is finally able to accept complex and intelligent Black men on the screen?

Santiago-Hudson: Yes, I did see him. . . . I think they can accept them. Are they looking for those images to be projected? No. If someone comes up with a marketable star and project, I think they will accept that. But are they actively looking for that? I don't think so.

Iverem: In an interview, you once said that film just scratches the surface for you. Do you feel differently now that you've had a chance to work on these two substantive film projects, *Lackawanna Blues* and *Their Eyes Were Watching God?*

Santiago-Hudson: They're letting me scratch a little harder. They haven't opened up the absolute realm of what I can do. That happened with the character Nanny that I wrote about my mother in *Lackawanna Blues.* I wrote her as fully as I could as a human being. Has Ruben Santiago-Hudson been able to accomplish that on-screen as an actor? No I haven't. But I do see by looking at Don Cheadle in *Hotel Rwanda* that those possibilities exist. If I try to sell a story about Toussaint L'Ouverture the way that he ran the French out of Haiti, I can't sell that. If I try to sell the story of all the Harlem impresarios like Langston Hughes and Countee Cullen—when Russia came to recruit them and put them on a cruise ship, and took them across the ocean—when I try to sell that story and the complexity of that journey, I can't. If I want to sell Nat Turner, no I can't sell that. But I can sell *Diary of a Mad Black Woman.*

Iverem: It's always the same type of role that gets the Oscar win. And, up until the last couple of years, usually it was a Black character in service to a larger story about White people. So even though Jamie Foxx won for Best Actor, the movie *Ray,* a very moving story about the life of Ray Charles, didn't get that same consideration.

Santiago-Hudson: Taylor Hackford fought for something like fifteen years to get the story of Ray Charles done. A White man was struggling to try to get it done, so you know I'm in trouble if I try to get it done. It's especially hard to get anything done about the beauty and struggle and existence of the African-American community, overcoming all the obstacles in this country, going through all the [expletive] we do in this country.

Iverem: It seems nothing about our lives is ever good enough for the people who vote for these films. They're not feeling it. . . . They're just not feeling it.

Santiago-Hudson: In another venue, let's see what *Lackawanna Blues* does in the Golden Globes and the Emmys. Let's see these stories about our communities, about our families, about love, about mamma, about perseverance and integrity and dignity about us, making us look like, wow, they *do* want the same things, they do have the same emotions we have. They are just humans, they are just beautifully exotic and intelligent people.

Iverem: What does the horizon look like for you and those with similar talents? Will stories like *Lackawanna Blues* and *Their Eyes Were Watching God* be consigned to television?

Santiago-Hudson: Television is an easier market for these kinds of films because they think the paying audience—the audience that goes into their pocket and pays $10—is not going to pay to see these films. I think that is in their preordained notions. I've heard more than once that Black films don't have legs in Europe. White Europeans don't go to see films about African-Americans and their behavior and the way they survive. They want to see shoot-'em-up, action, hip-hop, yo-yo-yo movies with the down soundtrack, or Wesley Snipes jumping off a building with a sword chopping off three people's heads—that sells in Europe, they tell me. I look at the box office and see $27 million for *Diary of a Mad Black Woman.* Well, where is the $27 million for *Hotel Rwanda?*

Iverem: If these films are consigned to television, is that so bad if the stories are being told?

Santiago-Hudson: The thing about TV is that more people can see you in one evening. Twelve million people can see you in one evening. Three million people can see you in one evening—and that is wonderful in that respect. It touches so many people at the same time. Yet you have the censorship from General Motors. You have the censorship from Love My Carpet because they tell you what commercial time they will buy. They look at a film like *Their Eyes Were Watching God* and say yeah, we'll buy some time for this show. But if they see something they don't like, they'll say no . . . you're appealing to a Black audience and Black people don't buy Volvos—so we're not going to buy. But Black folks are buying Cadillacs so Cadillac will buy an ad. So, Ruben, you have to cut that scene where the people get their throats cut because nobody's going to buy commercial time if that scene is there.

See, with HBO you don't have to worry about that because nobody's buying commercial time. But then you have to deal with censorship from within. . . . Well, I think the story would be more powerful if you cut this character or made Nanny a ho. . . . Make your father retarded. Make him stutter, make him dumb. Whatever they say. Whatever their suggestions may be. But, fortunately, there is enough intellect at HBO to say, ah, I hear your voice. It's fresh. It's exciting. Bring it. Can you bring more? So that is exactly the place I want to be.

Iverem: Tell me what it's been like to juggle stage, like August Wilson's most recent play, *Gems of the Ocean,* as well as TV and film.

Santiago-Hudson: I'm a New York–based actor with no intention or motivation to move to Los Angeles. So if I was in Los Angeles, I could do one job—play the fat cop eating donuts with no family and no love and get rich, do that one little job and be rich. In New York, since there are so fewer jobs and they don't pay like they do in L.A., there are so many people out here who want those two jobs on *Law and Order* so they give you scale ten [a lower rate of pay]. I can't survive on scale ten so I do a lot of other things, which I enjoy.

Iverem: What process did you go through to rewrite the one-man stage show *Lackawanna Blues* for a whole cast of flesh-and-blood actors and actresses, and what was it like to see that production come to life in that way?

Santiago-Hudson: It's a much more meticulous way of writing. And the biggest difference was how many people I had to be approved by to go to the next step. In theater, I was the editor. I was the person approving, deciding if it was worthy to be presented. In Hollywood, so many people have to sign off on it.

Iverem: You have worked with the *Lackawanna Blues* material for several years now. Do you feel that you've finally seen the baby off to college?

Santiago-Hudson: The baby is just starting to walk. I'm going to come back out with the one-man show. I'm going to do *Lackawanna Blues* until I'm an old gray man and can't remember the words—and then I'm going to hand it to somebody else. *Lackawanna Blues* is going to live way beyond us. Any day that I get to celebrate my mother, that is a blessed day to me.

Iverem: Is it more difficult to get work as an actor, or to pitch your ideas as a writer and producer?

Santiago-Hudson: I've had no success with pitching ideas since coming out with *Lackawanna Blues* as of this point. No one has said, here's a green-light, or here's a couple of dollars to go ahead and write the first treatment—I want to be your partner on this. What they have said to me is, "Are you interested in writing this film about so-and-so-and-so?" And I say, "No I'm really not."

I wanted to get back to something—*Diary of a Mad Black Woman*—$27 million this weekend. We have to, as African-American people, recognize and understand the power of our dollar. That's big.

Iverem: And those are mainly our dollars.

Santiago-Hudson: Oh, ain't no White people go out and see *Diary of a Mad Black Woman.* But can we deliver that dollar to something significant? This kind of film is okay to get your laugh off, to get your jollies off. There are some incredible actresses in it—Cicely Tyson, Kimberly Elise. Cool. Cool. Cool. I'm happy to see them working. But can we deliver that dollar in a celebration of our strength, of our dignity, of our integrity, of our history, of our contributions? We have to or they will not allow us to show our films in their theaters.

We have to go to them and ask, "Will y'all run this film? Can we show this in your theater? Will you show this please? We think we can get some audience." And they respond, "Well you haven't shown that you can get any audience for these type of films. *Rosewood* didn't do anything. *Leadbelly* didn't do anything. . . . Yeah but they went to see *White Chicks.*"

Iverem: As a writer yourself who has worked with your own material for so long, how is it to work with a script written by others? Does your background make you more empathetic to the writing, or more critical?

Santiago-Hudson: I go and do the job I'm hired to do. If I'm hired to be an actor, I go in and I don't have a word to say about the writing. Of course, even as an actor, I have an opinion about the writing. . . .

Iverem: Considering both the genesis of *Lackawanna Blues* and some of the players in *Their Eyes Were Watching God,* is talent from the Black theater world making some gains in Hollywood? Something to counter, perhaps, the ready conversion of singers and rappers into actors?

Santiago-Hudson: You can't make them into actors. You can make them into movie stars—that's a whole different thing. I don't know what you have to do to make a person a movie star. I know what you have to do to make them into an actor. Everyone thinks that they can be an actor. This is the one profession that people can look at and say, "You know, I could do that." But, unfortunately, all you have to do is turn on the TV or rent a video and see that not everybody can do that. . . .

Everybody can play this one thing. It's taking Ice Cube and bringing him out of the snarl. Now they've finally made him comic a little bit. But throw him something deep. Throw him *Macbeth,* throw him *Henry the VIII.* Throw Ice-T a serious role. Throw him Martin Luther King in *Boycott.* You take a guy like Jeffrey Wright—an actor's actor—who can do Martin Luther King, and Basquiat, and then Bob Marley, and then Mr. Paul in *Lackawanna Blues* and then Peoples Hernandez in *Shaft.* Each time, he reinvents himself. He taps into another part of himself. That's an actor. When I'm working with Jeff, I'm having a ball. When I'm working with Jimmy Smits, I'm having a ball. When I'm working with Epatha Merkerson, I'm having a ball, or LisaGay Hamilton, Phylicia Rashad, or Louis Gossett Jr.

Iverem: Tell me a little about you. [He's forty-eight and lives with his wife, Jeannie, and their twins—a boy and girl. He also has two older sons.] Tell me about juggling being a husband and father with pursuing your career.

Santiago-Hudson: It's really no juggle. It's first. I have to take care of my family. I have the responsibility of leading by example. Of teaching, protecting, and providing. That's number one, and if I have to teach, or go drive a truck, or paint . . . I'll do that. Second, I'm an artist. It hasn't always been that way. Work was primary for a good part of my life but then I became a father, and I'm extremely blessed that God would give me the opportunity to take care of those responsibilities with art. I am doing both of them I hope in a way that not only sets an example for my family, but any person of color who comes up to me, I want them to be proud of what I've done. If more men were men, if more fathers were fathers, I think it would cure a lot of these ills in the African-American community.

Iverem: What's coming up next?

Santiago-Hudson: I'm looking to continue to attack the distorted images of my people. And when I say "my people," I mean Puerto Ricans, African-Americans, and Africans. My goal is to continue to tell stories about the beauty, integrity, and contributions of my people. I don't mean to do every historical story. I'm not going to do that but whatever stories I do, take the crooked with the straight. When I write my characters, I'm going to write them whole because, unfortunately, as an actor, I haven't seen that on TV and film enough. But with Jamie Foxx winning,

Denzel winning, Halle winning, hopefully things will open up more. Hopefully they will take the mantle and decide, Listen. Let's tell the stories about who we are. We've got to get paid. True. But let's get paid two, three times big and then this little bitty film over here is going to straighten some things out. It's a responsibility thing. People like Ossie Davis taught me that. People like Harry Belafonte teach me that. . . . So now I have that responsibility.

When do we all get together and say, Let's own some of this? That's what I'm waiting for.

Their Eyes Were Watching God

March 6, 2005

Zora Neale Hurston's lush, seamless 1937 novel, *Their Eyes Were Watching God,* is especially not suited for the cruel commercial interruptions of broadcast television. Nonetheless, a movie based on the book, premiering on ABC, retains enough of Hurston's Southern magical realism, deep empathy for Black women, and powerful love story to make this production a milestone for both Black film and television.

The movie is remarkable for its depiction of hot Black romance and sexuality. But it would be an understatement, as well as a cliché, to say that sparks fly between the movie's star, Halle Berry, and the last of her three husbands in the movie, played by Michael Ealy. These two can burn down the bed, and their chemistry is what makes the movie rise above the restrictions of its format and at least touch the level of Hurston's ebullient narrative.

Their Eyes Were Watching God, rescued from out-of-print status during the 1970s flowering of the Black Studies movement, tells the story of Janie Crawford (Halle Berry), a Black girl who grows up poor in rural western Florida but never gives up on the idea that life should be filled with deep, abiding love. Janie lives with Nanny (Ruby Dee), her grandmother, who, fearing that the teenager is starting to kiss boys, marries her off to an elderly farmer, Logan Killicks, who has "sixty acres" of land, and therefore can offer his young wife a step up in life. A weepy Janie takes this step up, but then soon finds herself stepping out on the old man. She runs away and marries Joe Starks (Ruben Santiago-Hudson), who, in the story, becomes the mayor, principal landowner, and businessman of Eatonville, Florida, the first African-American town to be founded and incorporated the United States (and also Hurston's hometown).

In her second marriage, Janie finds the higher social standing and wealth that Nanny always wanted for her. In the beginning she is showered with love, and then later, only showered with possessions. She realizes over the course of twenty years that she is also a possession. She is the mayor's trophy wife who is kept in her place—only a more highfalutin place. As fate would have it, life offers Janie yet another chance at love and a fuller definition of living. She meets Vergible "Tea Cake" Woods (Ealy), a migrant laborer with a taste for gambling and liquor, who is much younger. Janie cannot pass up this chance to see if she can, at last, find a fulfilling love.

This is a quality production by Oprah Winfrey's Harpo Films. The settings, which appear to be on location, don't have that made-for-TV cheesiness. The cast, which also includes Terrence Howard, delivers believable performances that keep us in the Deep South during the first half of the twentieth century. Berry has to be given props for a top-shelf performance, and so do Ealy and Santiago-Hudson. Berry has the star power to draw audiences but I wonder if she is miscast as a woman described in the book as "very dark" and therefore defying the typical barriers of color discrimination within the Black community, especially during this time period. Also, Berry's stylists may have gone overboard with a long, wild hair weave that contrasts to the book's depiction of Janie's hair worn in a long, thick braid. [After publication of this review, I was convinced by a friend, Kimberly Collins, then a graduate student at Howard University, that Janie was very light in the original novel but that the original Tea Cake, unlike Ealy, was very dark, further adding to the social scandal Janie created.]

Despite such troubling departures from the novel's fabric, *Their Eyes Were Watching God* is a worthy effort at adapting to the screen one of the great and classic American novels.

Can the Michael Ealy Era Begin?

March 6, 2005

The Wesley Snipes era is officially over. (I know you're saying, girrrrl, that's *been* over!)

Based on the promotion for *Never Die Alone,* which featured the chocolate chest, dripping in gold chains, of the story's drug dealer, you might think that the Snipes spot is being filled by rapper DMX, who looks best with his baldie and—like Snipes at his kingpin heights—with dark shades and expensive suits.

But no. It's not DMX. This pop cinematic shift is more dramatic. *Never Die Alone,* which came and went quickly at the box office, is wholly owned by the actor Michael Ealy. You could say that for Ealy, who first created a community buzz in the lukewarm *Barbershop,* this film marks a huge coming-out party, which continues with the world premiere of *Their Eyes Were Watching God* on ABC.

Both films are not only a coming out for him but for his generation of actors, which has yet to claim the same star and leading-man status of those, like Denzel Washington, Laurence Fishburne, and Snipes, who launched the new wave of Black film nearly twenty years ago.

But, of course, the biggest shift is, you know, the light-skin thing. Coming out of our precious Black Power and "Black Is Beautiful" movements of the 1960s and 1970s, the generation that launched the current Black film movement was loathe to create it with the same pre–Black pride ideals of beauty that included light-bright heartthrobs like Smokey Robinson and Dorothy Dandridge.

Snipes burst onto the scene, most notably in *New Jack City,* like an ebony lord and, with the persuasive power of the big screen, made very Black very much in vogue—for Black men, at least. Actor-comedian Joe Torre made the trend cinematically official in the film *Sprung,* when he told the character played by filmmaker Rusty Cundieff that very dark brothers like him were in style and that women were not checking for yellowboys like Cundieff anymore.

Snipes has been followed in the new generation by popular chocolate actors like Omar Epps, Mekhi Phifer, and DMX, who bridge the earlier generation's Black Is Beautiful stand with hip-hop's obsession with street authenticity and "keeping it real." As Dael Orlandersmith, the author of the stage play *Yellowman,* so poignantly reminds us, light-skinned men, though considered "pretty" by some, were often dissed as "soft" (and worse) by others.

Though color discrimination among African-Americans, born and instigated since slavery, has created a large portion of the long-standing Black middle class that is light-skinned, there is ample color diversity among the poorest and most "street authentic" among us as well. So, along with Wesley Snipes in *New Jack City,* there was the steely-eyed gangster Allen Payne. A few years ago, the actor Terrence Howard stole the show as a conniving trickster in *The Best Man* and has, since then, played a series of hardened, somewhat sinister characters. He has been the nasty light-skinned brother with light eyes from around the way.

So enter now Michael Ealy. While Terrence Howard, perhaps to stake his rightful place in the macho hip-hop cultural hierarchy, has had to play, at times, almost a caricature of heartlessness, Ealy doesn't need to drive that fast or that hard. He is also an around-the-way brother. Maybe he just got out of jail, maybe he's on parole, but he is not heartless. In both *Barbershop* films, he is the roughneck barber Ricky, who is, on the side, studying to get his G.E.D. In *Never Die Alone* he is an enforcer for a drug dealer who is the sole caretaker for a younger sister—the only family he has left. In *Their Eyes Were Watching God,* he is a rough, hardworking man who gambles, but is sensitive enough to tell the woman he loves that she is totally free to be herself, and that she "is the kind of woman who makes a man forget to grow old, forget to die." Damn.

Ealy is able to convey, with his chiseled features and blue eyes, both enough vulnerability and toughness to make him acceptable to both the male hip-hoperati and to female filmgoers, who need to see some heart. Like the better actors before him, he has the ability to communicate without words and with facial expression alone. Whereas many of our hip-hop gangsters have mainly shown how heartless the world has made them, Ealy is always more of a tortured soul who shows how he struggles to retain his center and humanity.

Never Die Alone is based on the Donald Goines novel of the same name and tells the story of the final days of King David (DMX), who returns home seeking redemption for his past misdeeds. In the process, he meets violence, and the story of his life, told in flashback through audio tapes he made, reveals the seeds of hate, violence, and death that he has sown.

One reason that Ealy's character, also named Michael, is allowed to shine is because DMX's character is such a snake, and, when Hollywood allows us, we always root for the underdog. Hip-hop has long searched for its *Godfather* in film and *Never Die Alone* is ample proof, despite its rampant misogyny (as if *The Godfather* doesn't have it, too), that we best look to our literature for dialogue, plots, and characters that are richer and more complex than what is typically offered by our standard screenplays. And we best look to actors like Ealy, who, unlike most rappers turned actors, have both the looks and emotional range to convey more than a visual style and flash.

Sometimes in April

March 19, 2005

Perhaps no film can adequately convey the horror of the Rwandan genocide of 1994, during which close to one million men, women, and children were slaughtered over the course of three months. But a new film on HBO, *Sometimes in April,* gets closer to the truth than any film so far, and, yes, that's including the acclaimed *Hotel Rwanda.*

In the mean hustle of film deals and distribution, perhaps the director of *Sometimes in April,* Raoul Peck, did not have the studio connections or the star power of Don Cheadle that allowed the independently produced *Hotel Rwanda* to tiptoe into theatrical release. While *Sometimes in April* may lack the cast and cachet, it is chock-full of the history, depth, and dimension of terror that *Hotel Rwanda* lacks. Perhaps such comparisons are unfair. There can certainly be more than one movie about this gruesome chapter in history—no doubt there will be more—just like films about the Jewish Holocaust are too numerous to count. On the other hand, with Cheadle's very deserved Oscar nomination, and with *Hotel Rwanda* still playing on some screens, comparisons are difficult to avoid.

In *Sometimes in April,* Peck shows the same passion for the history and stories of the African diaspora, told through the eyes of African people, that he showed in his 2001 film, *Lumumba.* The primary focus here is on two brothers on opposite sides of the conflict—Augustin Muganza, played impressively by Idris Elba (*The Wire*), and Honoré Muganza, played by Oris Erhuero. Their relationship serves as a lightning rod of tension throughout and allows us to understand, on an individual level, how an entire country could descend into barbaric killing, especially with the aid of mass media broadcasting hate. Honoré is a radio commentator who, perhaps unwittingly, helps to whip the Hutu majority into a killing spree against civilian Tutsis, who were ethnic minorities but long favored by the country's Belgian colonizers for being taller, lighter-skinned, and having keener features. The brothers are Hutu, but Augustin is married to a Tutsi and the couple has three children. As we watch the impact of the country's madness on this one family, we witness, in almost panoramic fashion, an entire country in the throes of self-destruction.

Adding to this panorama of horror and the quality of the storytelling is the fact that this film was shot on location inside Rwanda, as opposed to the set of *Hotel Rwanda* in South Africa. Many actual scenes of mass killings are the setting for this production. Rwanda's roads become, again, byways of quick death. The diverse faces of the country's people are featured, too, sometimes in lingering close-ups, that remind us of each human being behind the faceless death toll.

Some of the scenes are graphic, far more so than in *Hotel Rwanda.* In towns, along rural roads, and in swamps, corpses dot the landscape. And while there are a few shocking scenes of murder—in one, a mother is shot in the head at point-blank range—the rampant rape and sexual abuse of women that occurred is not depicted in a graphic manner but is described. *Sometimes in April* is not an easy story; it is a gripping one, one steeped in truth, history, and, as it promotes itself, "a million true stories," which it will not allow the world to wrap into a neat package, or forget.

Guess Who

March 25, 2005

Several seasons now of playing the "poppa don't take no mess" dad on his television show has, oddly enough, molded Bernie Mac into the perfect candidate to take on the thorny subject of interracial dating in his new movie, *Guess Who.* Shed of his annoying bug-eyed routine of the past, Mac presents the right blend of race savvy, stubbornness, belligerence, and protectiveness toward his daughter that gives *Guess Who* moments of rare authenticity for a studio comedy about race.

This isn't the funniest movie, but Mac and the rest of the cast, aided by a decent script, turn out an interracial dating movie about that tiny demographic that is the integrated MTV generation. Based on the dramas on that channel's reality television shows, young Blacks and Whites fall more easily into interracial relationships, even though we know that the predominant configuration of these relationships, and those of older couples, is between a Black man and a White woman.

In *Guess Who,* which is a takeoff on the 1963 classic *Guess Who's Coming to Dinner,* Percy Jones (Mac) is surprised when his daughter Theresa (Zoe Saldana), a photographer, brings home a White boyfriend, Simon Green (Ashton Kutcher). While it is obvious that Percy is irked by Simon's Whiteness, he is made more suspicious of him by Simon's ill-fated efforts to impress him, and by secrets that he suspects Simon is hiding. Simon, an investment banker, in turn, feels that he is walking on eggshells to prove that he is not a racist, and is intimidated by Percy's demeanor and temper. The majority of the story is a battle of wills between the father and the suitor, with Percy taking great measure to keep Simon from sleeping with his daughter while the couple is visiting. This age-old battle, combined with riffs on male-female relationships in general, gives the film its best shot at humor.

The bubbly chemistry between Kutcher and Saldana infuses the film with a sweetness and poignancy. At the same time, the story does not reveal to us what binds them to each other. And when it does deal directly with race, it usually does so just above our heads, with jokes. We know that the young couple here faces hate, but we never witness this. We know that a culture that reinforces White female standards of beauty is less comfortable with a Black woman being chosen by a White man as a partner, but no one discusses this. These are weighty matters and this film is supposed to make us laugh. In a twist toward its conclusion, the film does, very deftly and in one fell swoop, deal with bigotry versus the power of racism, and its impact on the young couple. And that moment, I think, makes this a deeper movie than it would appear, at first, to be.

Beauty Shop

March 30, 2005

Perhaps hair-care cinema has run its course.

The lukewarm comedy and well-tread themes of *Beauty Shop* give it the feel of yesterday's hairdo. And not even the likeable Queen Latifah can raise the energy to the proper level for a theatrical release. It's just okay. And a just-okay comedy pales in comparison to more cleverly written flicks, such as *Undercover Brother,* or even old Robin Harris footage.

This would have been a fresh film, say, ten years ago, when we were still yearning for Black romantic heroines and women's stories on the screen. But, for real, after the likes of *Waiting to Exhale, Soul Food* (in theaters and on TV), and more recent fare such as *Deliver Us from Eva* and the current *Diary of a Mad Black Woman,* any new film attempting to set out on the sista trail must at least rock some fresh stories or jokes.

Queen Latifah has definitely had some hits as an actress. She is certainly capable of better than this. In the fierce movie moneymaking that is going on, I hope that more of Black Hollywood can move away from the formulaic. Sure, we will continue to be lured into theaters by such comforting themes as the corner barbershop, the beauty shop, and big momma's good cooking. But if there isn't anything new to say, maybe it's time to move on.

Filmfest DC—*We Don't Die, We Multiply*
Washington, D.C.

April 13–24, 2005

Robin Harris cast such a spell during his explosion onto the comedy scene that, fifteen years after his death, there are those of us who still revere him as the funniest man ever, and as the progenitor of a new generation of comics that stand in his fading shadow.

His friend and onetime manager Topper Carew was determined that our memory of Harris would not fade, so he has produced the poignant documentary *We Don't Die, We Multiply,* a ninety-two-minute movie that explores Harris's life and legacy. This is a labor of love, foremost, and not fancy moviemaking, which brings us behind the scenes of Harris's short life and deepens our understanding of his tremendous influence.

Comedian Cedric the Entertainer, certainly one of the beneficiaries of the road paved by Harris, says it best in the film when he describes how Harris changed the nature of the stand-up routine, from a basic set-up-joke-punch-line format, to one that allowed for improvisation, including Harris's famous riffs on those in the audience. Harris's steady gig at what was the Comedy Act Theater in South-Central Los Angeles became not only a magnet for the Benz and Bentley crew from Hollywood, but was also a school for emerging comedians on the scene. It was, for these young comics, "the last great university and Robin Harris was the last professor," says comedian Louis Dix in the film. Bernie Mac adds, "If you call yourself a comedian, you need to know the essence—of what Robin Harris is."

Harris's essence, as he describes it in an interview included in the film, is that of "the average Black man." With his paunchy gait, midnight complexion, and wino eyes, he was the ultimate, unpretentious "pops," older brother, or corner sage. He talked about everyday occurrences and events and turned them into hilarious routines—about obesity, street beggars, the police, relationships, and, of course, the superbad *Bebe's Kids.*

Every Harris fan has their favorite routine, and many are included here in one of his signature performances in Chicago, which serves as a refrain throughout the movie. Raw footage from some of his few interviews is included, as well as interviews with his wife, Exetta, and other family members. From them we get to know something about Harris as a child and young man, which is really all he would ever be. He died from sleep apnea at age thirty-six.

Aside from its rich narrative about Harris, which has its excesses toward the end, one of the most valuable contributions of the movie is its evocation of Black Los Angeles in the late '80s—not only the magic of the Comedy Act Theater, but also other haunts, such as the Blueberry Hill nightclub and Aunt Kizzy's Back Porch restaurant. It also captures that particular era in Black film when directors like Robert Townsend were creating and presenting new voices for their generation. Harris brought his "average Black man" flavor to a few films, including *Do the Right Thing* and *House Party,* excerpts from which are, strangely, missing from this movie. His career, cut short just as it was starting to take off, was emblematic of that striving of a new generation to create art, movies—and comedy—on its own terms.

Black Star—Erykah Badu in *House of D*

April 15, 2005

Any film about American childhood that manages to transport us beyond the bland Disney-fication of it automatically gets some props from me. *House of D,* the directorial debut of David Duchovny (known by most from his years starring on *The X*

Files), does have its moments of oversentimentality, but it is a meaningful and often funny story about coming of age in the 1970s.

The setting is not pick-any-suburb-you-like but, rather, Greenwich Village in 1973. This is before the village became yuppie and gentrified. The twelve-year-old that we meet, Tommy (Anton Yelchin), lives in the village in a small, grungy apartment with his recently widowed mother, who obsesses over Tommy eating his brussels sprouts while smoking her cigarette at the table. Tommy attends a private school on a scholarship, and also spends his time working as a delivery boy for a butcher shop with his friend, a mentally challenged man named Pappass (Robin Williams).

Erykah Badu plays the role of Lady, who the film heavily suggests is jailed for prostitution. With her combination of slight Southern drawl and street-girl trash-talking, Lady tries to offer advice through the window to Tommy for his childhood crises. While the extent to which Tommy is helped is questionable, Lady nonetheless becomes an important link for him to a world of adult reasoning and decision-making. He learns from a woman in prison about being free, and about taking your life into your own hands.

King's Ransom

April 22, 2005

King's *Ransom* straddles that dubious netherland between a Wayans movie, a Tyler Perry stageplay, and TV sitcom. Sure, there are some laughs, but they are the kind of laughs that come from laughing at tried-and-true stereotypes: the obnoxious nouveau riche executive (Anthony Anderson), his gold-digging wife, his dumber-than-a-doornail office floozy, and some poor White trash with the vinyl siding hanging off of their house. But as it tells the story of multiple plots to kidnap our obnoxious executive, there are some clever humor touches—such as the Condoleeza Rice Halloween mask and the merciless assault on a walking hamburger. (Don't ask.) Of course, everything is *way* over the top. In fact, more and more in these movies, the top no longer exists.

OPM—*The Interpreter*

April 22, 2005

Someone must have declared 2005 as the Year of African Corruption in Cinema and didn't tell me. After *Hotel Rwanda, Sometimes in April, Sahara,* and now *The Interpreter,* we have gone from a virtual Whiteout of Africa on the screen to all the

African thug generals, politicians, and criminals that we can handle. This is an important story, about the wars, killing, and corruption that have made Africa a postcolonial wasteland. But it is weakened in part because it must be told by the daughter of a White settler family (Nicole Kidman) who, as an adult, comes to New York to work as an interpreter at the United Nations. There she overhears a plot to assasinate the corrupt leader of her homeland. I suppose, unlike Don Cheadle having the opportunity to star in *Hotel Rwanda,* no Black actress was seen capable of both playing an African woman and drawing at the box office. And, of course, Halle Berry, the Bond girl and Catwoman, would not have fit the bill at all. *The Interpreter* has moments of power and poignancy, but other moments, and the flat chemistry between Kidman and Sean Penn, leave the viewer underwhelmed and waiting for the merciful conclusion.

Death of a Dynasty

April 29, 2005

The latest hip-hop insider lifestyle flick, *Death of a Dynasty,* is a fictionalized account of the goings on at Roc-a-Fella Records, the real-life music empire of rapper Jay-Z and CEO Damon Dash, who has also, of late, morphed into a fairly prolific film producer. In recent months, Dash's credits include *State Property 2, The Woodsman* starring Kevin Bacon, and now this flick, apparently completed in 2003 and dusted off in time for this year's spring movie season.

Death of a Dynasty is all about the hustle and games played in the hip-hop world, where the dollar is king and people do all manner of ill things to get that paper. In the story, we follow David Katz (Ebon Moss-Bachrach), a cub hip-hop journalist who has just landed a dream job at *The Mic* magazine, which is modeled after *The Source* hip-hop magazine. David's first assignment, a plum one that other staffers would kill for, is to spend three weeks inside Roc-a-Fella Records, with up-close and personal access to the worlds of Dash and Jay-Z.

The script does not allow us to really feel any of the characters, and perhaps that is by design. The overall effect, however, is like watching people at a nightclub, where illusion and posturing are key, and where it takes some effort to discern what, if anything, is of substance. The vibe of *Death of a Dynasty* is that of lighthearted predator and prey. Though released for the general public, we general public may sense that there are music industry insider jokes lurking between the lines and frames. We get the sense that music-industry types will know best how much this depiction of a world without scruples or ethics is true to real life.

Black Star–Ice Cube in *XXX: State of the Union*

April 29, 2005

This sequel to the 2002 *XXX* has gone straight-up ghetto. And, in this case, that's a good thing. Rather than the old special agent, played by Vin Diesel, literally wrapping himself in the American flag, the new special agent, played by Ice Cube, is "not feeling very patriotic these days" and is more likely to burn the flag. As Cube and the other good guys, including Samuel L. Jackson, untangle a scheme by right-wing military men to overthrow a peace-seeking U.S. president, this story speaks frankly about war, the internal dangers to U.S. democracy, and the ability of folks in the hood to fight the power. Sure, the notion of a bunch of self-serving hustlers summoning the will to take on the U.S. military takes some imagination, but it beats the tired jingoistic stories of evil foreign powers and hypocritical American self-righteousness.

Black Star–Mos Def in *The Hitchhiker's Guide to the Galaxy*

April 29, 2005

The fact that the human species is so ridiculous, and treats the earth so destructively, is the subtext of this stupidly funny and original space flick, which offers surprises from the beginning to the end. You know you're in some sort of alter film world when the end of Earth as we know it is a very matter-of-fact affair, is heralded by the skyward departure of dolphins, and one hip alien, played by Mos Def, downing pints of beer in an English pub. Based on the book by Douglas Adams, who also wrote the screenplay, this movie is just as mocking of the science-fiction and space-film genres as it is of humans. And despite its easy dismissal of Earth, it is one of the most earth-loving films that I have ever seen.

29

The Changing Same

OPM—*Crash*

May 6, 2005

An auto wreck is a mighty metaphor for American race relations in this multi-layered and revealing film by Paul Haggis. Set in Los Angeles, where a myriad of folks coexist but never touch, *Crash* tells the interlocking stories of a variety of people, including police officers, a television producer, a district attorney and his wife, a store owner, a locksmith, and two carjackers. All are striving but flawed humans. No one is noble—or a noble savage.

One factor that sets *Crash* apart from other films that attempt to dissect American racism is the honesty and intimacy of the dialogue—the White gun dealer who refers to a Persian customer as "Osama," the White wife who assumes a Latino locksmith is a gang member, a Black wife who ridicules her light-skinned husband's authenticity as a Black person—and as a man.

Even if we are unaccustomed to being privy to these conversations, these moments are emotionally true—and often emotionally raw. Thandie Newton, the biracial British actress who many of us would not consider to have a strong Black identity, plays here one of the most emotionally searing parts, in recent memory, that conveys the accepted social, physical, and sexual abuse of Black women in the United States. She plays the wife of a television-show producer (Terrence Howard) who finds his position of being his own man under assault, literally, at every turn. Then there is Don Cheadle, in the role of a police investigator who balances upward mobility with the reality of his dysfunctional family background. Finally, Larenz Tate and rapper Ludacris team up as another version of L.A.'s finest—a pair of bold and seasoned carjackers.

There is plenty that is Black to see here that feels authentic, even though the film is written and directed by a White man. It certainly has more to say about race than any other recent theatrical release. Perhaps its audacity in this regard will put it outside the good graces of White film critics who believe that people do not talk or feel this way in real life. Perhaps they have become so used to race being handled as a joke, most especially if it is a Quentin Tarantino–type joke, dripping with "political incorrectness," sarcasm, irony, and brutality. Most of all, these critics don't want to be reminded of the pervasiveness and true evil of racism, or to be reminded that racism is power over people's lives every day. They want stories like Clint Eastwood's *Million Dollar Baby* that satisfy their own sense of the superiority in strength and morality of Whites. What do these "agendas" have to do with moviemaking, they ask. Are we talking cinema or politics?

Well, we are talking both, all in one breath. And so is *Crash*.

Shake Hands with the Devil

June 3, 2005

The 1994 genocide of Rwanda, which left nearly one million dead in three months, will forever haunt Lt. Gen. Romeo Daillaire, who was in charge of U.N. forces in the country during that time. As much as this documentary details Daillaire's inability to stop the carnage—which is graphic—it also details the failure of his own agency and the international community to step in while the madness might have been averted. More than *Hotel Rwanda* or *Sometimes in April*, *Shake Hands with the Devil* also documents Belgium's history of colonialism and fomenting of ethnic strife that fueled this horrific chapter in Africa's history.

The Honeymooners

June 10, 2005

The Honeymooners is a lukewarm comedy that owes much of its charm to the fact that Cedric the Entertainer can dance. Man, there's just something about seeing a chubby brother make those old-school moves like the cabbage patch, the running man, the snake—and let's not forget that ever-popular break dancing. Cedric's performances, which appear to be improvised and not scripted, are a big highlight of the movie, which is not saying much since this is not a music video.

The story, based on the 1950s television series starring Jackie Gleason, features Cedric as Ralph Kramden, a New York City bus driver, and Gabrielle Union as his wife, Alice. Their best friends, Ed and Trixie Norton (Mike Epps and Regina Hall), live upstairs in the same apartment building. Alice really wants to move into a house but her dream seems to be fading as Ralph has frittered away much cash on various business schemes over the years. For much of this story, we follow Ralph and Ed as they resort to all manner of maneuverings to make a down payment on a duplex from an elderly patron of the diner where Alice and Trixie work as waitresses.

As you sit in a darkened theater the madness and mischief will keep your attention but the script is short on originality or humor. It is also a stretch to imagine the supermodel-like Gabrielle Union actually married to the avuncular Cedric. John Leguizamo is funny just to look at but Mike Epps is not able to use his considerable comedic talents to break out of the script's predictable box.

Silverdocs Documentary Festival—*Sweet Honey in the Rock: Raise Your Voice*

Silver Spring, Maryland

June 14-19, 2005

It is impossible to experience Sweet Honey in the Rock in concert and not be transported to that place where we are all human, primal, in possession of common sense, and hauntingly beautiful. It is these moments of communion and revelation that Stanley Nelson ably captures in his documentary *Sweet Honey in the Rock: Raise Your Voice,* which airs on PBS as a part of the *American Masters* series.

If there is any shortcoming in the film, it is that it does not give us an up-close portrait of Bernice Johnson Reagon, the group's demanding and often acerbic founder. This film would have also provided a fuller portrait of the group with voices of former Sweet Honey members; twenty-two different women have passed through the group. Reagon tells her story in her 1993 book, *We Who Believe in Freedom: Sweet Honey in the Rock . . . Still on the Journey* (Anchor Books).

The group sings spirituals, civil rights anthems, traditional African songs, wordless but overpowering vocal harmonizing, and original songs that have become classics, such as "JoAnn Little," a song about a Black woman who was acquitted in 1975 of killing the White jailer who had raped her. The film captures this activism through art, including Reagon's inspirational concert talks, as much as it does the aesthetics of the group.

Rize

June 24, 2005

A dance called "krumping," a fast-paced, frenetic style of movement popular in South-Central Los Angeles, is the subject of this energetic documentary by David LaChapelle. While it includes a variety of voices from the dancers, it focuses primarily on one performer, "Tommy the Clown," and emphasizes how the dances—which are similar to some traditional African movements—create an alternative activity to gang violence and crime.

Hustle & Flow

July 22, 2005

Will somebody please save me from all these pimps?

As much as the new, much-hyped film *Hustle & Flow* is a quality, textured drama about the struggle of one down-and-out man in Memphis, it is also the latest film, video, or song, dripping with hip-hop appeal, that asks our sympathies for a lifestyle that degrades women. It also asks that we, at least temporarily, share the pimp's view of women, and his vision of what it takes to "make it." As the regretful refrain goes in the film's signature song—it's hard out here for a pimp.

Many rappers, such as 50 Cent, along with some pop stars such as Kid Rock, have promoted the pimp lifestyle with titles such as "Po Pimp," "The Great White Pimp," "Pimp of the Century," "Pimp Talk," "Chart Pimp," "Definition of a Pimp," "Pimp Your Paper," "Pimp My Girl," "Guerilla Pimpin," "Early Morning Stoned Pimp," "Big Ol Pimps," "Pimp Arrest," and, finally, "Pimp Story Street Talk, Vol. 1." Some artists even take on the moniker for themselves: Skinny Pimp, Pimp Daddy Nash, Pimp C, Evil Pimp, Pimp Black, Pimp Daddy, Geez Pimp, Star Pimp, and Pimp Playa Hustlas.

With all this focus by the hip-hop music industry on men who manage prostitutes, it is no wonder that Hollywood sees potential dollar signs with *Hustle & Flow,* and, perhaps more importantly, equates the pimp and prostitution lifestyle with urban African-American culture.

Films of this genre, starting in the 1970s with *The Mack* and *Dolemite,* always focus on and glorify the pimp. The female prostitute—along with her hard-core realities that often include AIDS, drug abuse, child prostitution, mental illness, sterility, and death—are swept under the rug in the service of keeping the narrative flowing and pimp-centered.

Popular documentaries on the subject, such as *Pimps Up, Hos Down* and *American Pimp,* keep us centered in an almost worshipful tone that focuses on the pimp's colorful street names, such as Bishop Don Magic Juan, C-Note, Gorgeous Dre, and Mr. Whitefolks. Cameras offer a sweeping view of their full-length fur coats, lime-green gator shoes, gold rings the size of paperweights, gold chains heavy enough to tow your car, and, of course, limousines and fancy cars—even if that silver Rolls Royce is actually only rented for the evening (or filming).

In *Hustle & Flow,* we are guided into the world of prostitution by the talented and mesmerizing Terrence Howard, who turns an ordinary film into an exceptional one. In contrast to the pimp image of yesteryear, Howard's DJay lives in a jainky house in the hood in Memphis. His three hookers, Lexus, Shug, and Nola, live there with him, as a sort of family with DJay as the provider, protector, and manager. DJay drives a beat-down car, his clothes look barely washed, but he does enjoy one of the benefits of pimpdom—getting his hair curled and styled with a hot iron.

But don't be fooled, the essential pimp-hooker relationship, master and servant, is still in full effect. DJay's eventual migration to music—and his attempt at rapping—puts his years of pimping on par with the legal hustle of the music industry. It's all a hustle, the film suggests to us, and the connection to hip-hop, which has renamed women as female dogs and prostitutes anyway, feels like a natural and dangerous fit. This pimp, with his sexy determination, is made more socially acceptable. And besides, he takes his ladies along for the ride to seeming success—Nola as an impromptu business manager, and Shug as a love interest and background singer. It is hardly remarkable when DJay strikes the pregnant Shug, urging her to sing her silly song hook with more soul. When, in a fit of anger, he puts Lexus and her infant son out of the house, the scene is rendered with some comedy, as director Craig Brewer shows us that the mouthy, domineering Black women is once again put in her place.

It may be hard out here for a pimp, but it should be. It's even harder out here for those of us, who work hard at all kinds of jobs that we never see on film, who are asked time and time again by big media to embrace a pimp-and-hooker lifestyle as who we are.

Black Star–Jamie Foxx in *Stealth*

July 29, 2005

Well at least Jamie Foxx's Best Actor Oscar win hasn't landed him underneath agent 007. It has landed him in this summer action flick that, at first, appears to be another rah-rah military flick in the mold of *Top Gun.* But then *Stealth* quickly settles down to offer a story about a rogue computer-operated fighter jet and, in the process, warns about blind military allegiance and blind faith in technology. There are lots of impressive explosions and firepower here but there is also a hokey love story and the obligatory typecasting of some people of color—Asians this time—as arch villains.

Four Brothers

August 12, 2005

Stories of how men come of age and grapple with manhood have always drawn director John Singleton. So his latest endeavor, *Four Brothers,* an urban action flick in the whodunit mode, feels like a natural next step after *Boyz n the Hood, Shaft, Baby Boy,* and even, on some level, *Rosewood.*

Set in working-class Detroit, Singleton tells a story of four adopted brothers, two Black and two White, who reunite in the city after their mother is gunned down in a convenience-store robbery. Set on solving the murder, and on exacting revenge, the men lead us through a series of violent encounters that provide the glue holding together a plot that feels, in spots, like it was made for TV.

The alpha male here, chosen either by Singleton or self-appointed, is Bobby, played by Mark Wahlberg, still known to many of us as the rapper Marky Mark. In this interracial family, Wahlberg plays the White thug, the city-hardened semi-criminal who must lead his brothers, literally, into battle. He is the one with the hot head and quick trigger finger. He is the "Right here, right now" man. He is the one with the brotherman quips that provide counterpoint to the assaults and murders. When his two Black brothers, Angel and Jeremiah (Tyrese Gibson and André Benjamin), wrestle in the living room of their mother's house, Bobby jokes as if he is commentating a match between two wrestlers, one named Nitro and the other named Midnight.

Though Wahlberg's acting job feels, at times, like he is trying too hard, he, oddly enough, lends the film the edge and authenticity that it needs to qualify as an urban action flick. Benjamin, the member of Outkast in his acting debut, does a credible job with what he is given. Gibson, the singer who starred in Singleton's *Baby Boy,* has a real screen presence and is really coming into his own as an actor. The youngest brother, Jack, is played by Garrett Hedlund and seems the most out of place in this gritty scenario of guns and blood.

Women are, at the very most, marginal in these Singleton flicks. The mother, Evelyn Mercer, played by Fionnula Flanagan, is a blue-eyed saintly vision, a former hippie who, despite living in a Black neighborhood surrounded by gangs and crime, had not lost her idealism, kindness, and sweetness. In a scene at the dinner table, as each man flashes back to his mother sitting at the head of the table, we see and hear her as she reminds each then-boy of his table manners, of his newfound safety, of his beauty and goodness. She is the central female figure and she is dead, just as many of the mothers and women in Singleton's past films have either wound up dead or missing in action.

After all, in Singleton's world, action and all that it entails is a very male enterprise. He begins and ends the film with a snippet of Marvin Gaye's song *Trouble Man,* for the soundtrack to the 1972 action- and violence-packed movie of the same name. Times may change. Directors, actors, and stories may change, too. But, it seems, movies stay pretty much the same.

Ralph Ellison: An American Journey

August 24, 2005

The triumphs and tragedies of a Black literary giant are movingly rendered in *Ralph Ellison: An American Journey,* which is airing as part of the *American Masters* series on PBS.

Good biographical documentaries, such as this one, cut a swath through time and history, as well as an individual's life. In this case, we journey from Ellison's childhood in segregated Oklahoma City, to his college years during the 1930s at Tuskegee Institute, and then to New York City, where he stayed for much of his life, winning the National Book Award for *Invisible Man,* his first and only novel published during his lifetime.

The connecting thread throughout is Ellison's dogged intellectualism and relentless examination of both self and society that made *Invisible Man,* published in 1952, and a subsequent collection of essays, *Shadow and Act,* published in 1964, classics of American literature. His drive, combined with the clear articulation of his own voice, allowed him to build a literary career on the basis of one book. His nonstop questioning continued, and, perhaps, continued to haunt him, until his death.

His vast impact, shortcomings, and frustrations are detailed in this ninety-minute movie written, directed, and produced by Avon Kirkland, which is filled with vintage photographs and footage, as well as interviews with scholars such as Cornel West and Ellison's friends, including writer Albert Murray. Missing is an interview with Ellison's wife, Fanny, but there are interviews with Ellison himself and the first-ever dramatizations of scenes from *Invisible Man*.

The most poignant aspect of the program is the exploration of how Ellison's examination of Black identity and American racism, which added depth to how Blacks were depicted in literature, did not better situate him in the world of Black arts during the 1960s. At a time when the influential Black Arts Movement was forging a Black aesthetic, Ellison had positioned himself in relationship to a White European and American literary lineage. Ellison also spoke disparagingly of the new arts movement, which he said put politics before "creative excellence."

While Black artists, including writers, were increasingly embracing Africa as source of culture, Ellison said that he felt no attachment to the continent. And when African-Americans were moving to proudly refer to themselves as "Black," Ellison continued to refer to himself as a "Negro." Unlike other prominent Black artists of the time, he did not criticize fellow writer William Styron for his controversial *Confessions of Nat Turner,* or march to support the civil rights movement. It almost goes without saying that, in the minds of many, Ellison was an elitist or an "Uncle Tom." The writer Amiri Baraka, interviewed here, says simply that Ellison was "a snob."

Around this same time, when Ellison was grappling with such social conflicts, he lost 350 pages of his long-awaited second novel during a devastating fire at his vacation home in Plainfield, Massachusetts. He never seemed to recover from the loss. As he continued to make a living in academia, at New York University, for the remainder of his life, he struggled unsuccessfully to finish a second novel. He died in 1994 at the age of eighty. With permission from his wife, Fanny, a portion of his vast unpublished work, the novel *Juneteenth,* was culled and published posthumously by the literary executor of his estate, John Callahan.

As this documentary makes clear, Ellison's journey did not end until long after his death.

OPM—*The Constant Gardener*

August 31, 2005

At first glance, *The Constant Gardener,* a disquieting tale of greed and murder, would seem to tell a story about Africa and African people. In reality, however, it is a tale, only the latest one, of dashing and daring Brits entering the "dark continent" on missions of intrigue and danger.

Our daring couple this time is made up of Justin Quayle, played by Ralph Fiennes, and his wife, Tessa, played by Rachel Weisz (known to most of us as the chick from *The Mummy* series—another very unfortunate chronicle of Brits in

Africa). While Justin is a stiff diplomat and yes-man, Tessa has no yes-woman in her whatsoever. When the couple travels to Northern Kenya, where Justin works as a representative for the British government, Tessa works with a health service providing care to those living in the region's squalid ghettos. Through that work, she learns that the area's poor are being used, without their knowledge, as guinea pigs to test a new drug.

As it turns out, a little bit of such knowledge can be a dangerous thing when international corporations, investments, and huge profits are on the line. One thing that *The Constant Gardener* does well is depict the good-old-boy network that often links those heading big business with those heading big government. Tessa finds herself at odds with the good old boys and in extreme danger. Eventually, so does Justin, the mild-mannered diplomat who has shown the most passion for tending his garden. The crisis forces this Clark Kent to don his tight shirt with the big S on the chest. Justin Quayle, played movingly by Fiennes, is smart and focused as he crosses continents to solve the mystery of the drugs. Through his actions, and through flashbacks to the times spent with his wife, we see and feel the love he has for her and how, in the name of love and grief, he peels away layers of good-government-job insulation and naivety.

Just as in so many Brits-in-Africa movies of the past, *The Constant Gardener,* based on the novel by John Le Carré, takes brave Brits from a place of safety and civility to an African place of unflinching misery, violence, inhumanity, and death. While delivering a stern warning about the dangers of activism, it lauds the persona of the straightlaced bureaucrat who is drawn into danger because of someone else's activism but who is willing to face that danger, or even pay the ultimate price, because of a deep sense of integrity.

Movies like these, from way back in the day, such as *David Livingstone* and the laughable *Sanders of the River* with Paul Robeson, to James Bond movies, to *The English Patient,* to today's *Lara Croft Tomb Raider* series, form their own narrative about culture and history, and all from the perspective of White Europeans or Americans. What is presented in *The Constant Gardener,* directed by Fernando Meirelles (*City of God*), is a sort of endgame where little is depicted on the continent except for mounds of garbage and people who are considered to be garbage with no will, agency—and certainly no daring—to fight European or American hegemony. If time has had any impact on this long-running cinematic narrative, we can say that now, in this endgame, there is equal opportunity corruption and equal opportunity to be a savage.

G

September 16, 2005

We first peeped this hip-hop-centered drama, starring Richard T. Jones, Blair Underwood, and Chenoa Maxwell, a few years back at the American Black Film Festrival in Miami. Since then, it seems that it has received a bit of a face-lift and a promotional push for its theatrical release. Involving a love triangle between its stars and an unwitting journalist (Andre Royo) who gets stuck in the middle, *G* cannot shake the aura of a soap opera. Good performances, particularly by Jones and Royo, keep the plot afloat but cannot infuse the story with depth beyond that of your average hip-hop radio single or performer. There is some humor, however, and lots of gangsta-wannabe shots of luxury vehicles, and this is probably Jones's best opportunity to date to look gorgeous on the big screen. It's also good to see director Christopher Scott Cherot have this new opportunity.

Proud

September 23, 2005

The story of the African-American men of the USS. *Mason,* the only crew of U.S. Black soldiers to take a warship into battle during World War II, is told for all to know in *Proud,* an uneven but heartwarming film that stars the late Ossie Davis.

What the movie has going in its favor is the story itself. Davis plays an elderly Lorenzo DuFau, who tells how in 1944 he joined in the fight against Hitler and fascism. Racial segregation was still in full effect throughout the United States and the armed forces. Black soldiers routinely faced hostility and violence when they returned home in uniform. While other Black men in the segregated navy were consigned to work as stewards or laborers, DuFau and his navy shipmates manned a destroyer escort that battled German U-boats and protected ships as they crossed often-treacherous North Atlantic waters.

Unfortunately, the film has that unnaturally lit veneer of a made-for-TV movie that strains hard for atmosphere different than that of a studio set. While we are convincingly taken to another "time" in the United States, weeks spent by the men aboard the Mason are rendered in a fashion that feels amateurish and overly claustrophobic. When the production is able to shoot on location, as this one seems to have done for a few scenes in Northern Ireland, there is a marked improvement in its sense of place and reality. The producer of the film, who should have made sure that its values and sense of atmosphere were of the highest quality, was then-sixteen-year-old Ally Hilfiger, daughter of designer Tommy Hilfiger, who apparently put up the money to make the film.

Despite these shortcomings, enough of the important story of these Black men shines through to make the movie worthwhile and to put hidden Black history into plain sight.

The Gospel

October 7, 2005

The very successful tradition of chitlin circuit gospel musicals has been reborn for a new generation with *The Gospel,* a spirited and worthwhile effort that features stars of the vibrant gospel music scene, including Donnie McClurkin, Fred Hammond, Hezekiah Walker, and Yolanda Adams. *The Gospel* is much more of a church soap opera than this year's stage play turned hit movie, *Diary of a Mad Black Woman.* While it does not have the stage pedigree of *Diary,* it still relies on tried-and-true elements of morality dramas, while making good use of lively performances and decent direction and editing. Boris Kodjoe delivers a steady, quality, and likeable performance as the prodigal son.

The Untold Story of Emmett Louis Till

October 14, 2005

Few, if any, low-budget documentaries receive as much publicity during the course of their production as Keith Beauchamp's *The Untold Story of Emmett Louis Till,* which premiered in New York City in August and is scheduled to roll out in select cities.

Produced over the course of ten years, receiving press from national news organizations and screened for small audiences as early as 2002, *The Untold Story of Emmett Louis Till* has had an unusual prelife, so much so that filmgoers might be forgiven if they assume that this film had been released long ago. Adding to the possible confusion is the fact that another documentary, *The Murder of Emmett Till,* by filmmaker Stanley Nelson, premiered nationally on PBS in January of 2003 and won an Emmy Award.

Through it all, first-time filmmaker Beauchamp and his film have been like the little engine that could. The strength of that engine has been Beauchamp's tireless investigation into the 1955 case of Till, the fourteen-year-old African-American boy who was tortured, shot, and drowned in Mississippi for allegedly whistling at a White woman. It is obvious after watching the movie that the driving force of Beauchamp's work was his investigation and the promise he made to Till's mother, Mamie Till Mobley, that he would use this production to get the infamous case reopened. His ill-advised leak of new information uncovered during his research, which drew notice from the press and federal investigators, has detracted from the eventual release of the film.

Included in the movie is new information about the case that Beauchamp uncovered, including the fact that more people were involved in the crime than the two men charged—Roy Bryant and J. W. Milam. One witness describes on-camera the swarm of cars parked outside the farm building on Milam's property on the day that Till was heard crying inside as he was beaten and tortured. The significance of this and other important discoveries, such as the fact that an arrest warrant for the White woman in question—Carolyn Bryant—was never executed, seems to get lost in the thick recounting of the drama.

This is Beauchamp's first feature-length film. (When he started it, he was twenty-four years old; now he is thirty-four.) He's done a good job of telling the riveting story about a murder that shocked the world and sparked the historic civil rights movement. Including interviews (particularly moving footage of Mamie Till Mobley), historic footage, and photographs, Beauchamp does a good job at building a compelling narrative about Mississippi's particular racism, barbarism, and sham justice system. However, the hand of a newcomer is obvious. There are some technical deficiencies, there is little that is nuanced or particularly creative, and, unlike Nelson's film, there is a lack of atmosphere and full historical context.

While these and other shortcomings might be attributed to Beauchamp's lack of experience or training, they are also signs that he worked on a shoestring budget that, according to him, included money that his parents had set aside for his eventual enrollment in law school. Despite his struggles and shortcomings, Beauchamp is ultimately triumphant in his production and purpose. What is offered is evidence of his persistence in making his film. His promise to Mobley, who died on January 6, 2003, has been fulfilled. Last year the case was reopened.

30

Get Rich or Make a Real Movie

Congo: White King, Red Rubber, Black Death

October 21, 2005

A horrible and shocking history is revealed in *Congo: White King, Red Rubber, Black Death,* which had its theatrical opening on October 21 in New York City and will be traveling to new cities in the coming weeks. The shock comes, first of all, from the fact that between 1880 and 1920 as many as ten million Congolese were murdered under the barbaric rule of King Leopold II of Belgium. Equally shocking is the fact that this macabre chapter of colonialism in Africa is so little known. As the movie's narrator says at the start, "Until Adolph Hitler arrived on the scene, the European standard for cruelty was set by a King—Leopold II, king of the Belgians. . . ."

In this low-budget but compelling documentary, director Peter Bate goes a long way to telling the history and filling the knowledge gap. Using a combination of narration, historical photographs, interviews with historians, and less-successful dramatic reenactments, Bate details how Leopold used deception, trickery, torture, and murder to rape the Congo of its resources, most especially rubber, for his personal enrichment and for the transfer of wealth to Belgium.

OPM—*Wal-Mart: The High Cost of Low Price*

November 4, 2005

This is a sobering and scary examination of global capitalism in the new millennium. A litany of business practices that increase Wal-Mart's bottom line but decrease the quality of life of its employees—wages so low that many are forced onto welfare, poor or little health-care, and vicious union-busting—are detailed in moving portraits. Add to these practices the devastating impact Wal-Mart has on small businesses, huge tax breaks the company receives, and heartbreaking conditions in its factories abroad (like three dollars for a fifteen-hour work day in China), and that smiley face usually associated with Wal-Mart begins to take on a more sinister expression.

Director Robert Greenwald is able to position the Wal-Mart debate outside the usual framework of Republican pro-business types versus Democrat pro-union or pro-worker attitudes. The owner and workers at H & H Hardware in Middlefield, Ohio, describe themselves as Republicans but they view their battle to survive with Wal-Mart as a case of unfair competition with a retailing monopoly given hefty tax breaks by local government, while they are given none. "They busted up Standard Oil," says Johnny Faenza, an employee of the hardware store. "They busted up Ma Bell—but Wal-Mart seems to be going on a rampage through the American economy and nobody seems to be paying attention. The logic of it escapes me—and I spend a lot of time thinking about it."

By totaling these costs for the low prices the company can offer, the movie asks how much Americans are willing to sacrifice for cheap goods, if slick commercials can trump reality, and how wide the gap will grow between the megarich, such as the Walton family—which owns Wal-Mart—and the rest of us.

Get Rich or Die Tryin'

November 9, 2005

The title of the new film *Get Rich or Die Tryin'* is also, of course, a powerful refrain in American society—and not just for the hip-hop generation, lest anyone get twisted about who the real gangsters are.

Enron execs, anyone? Oil execs? Blackwater mercenaries?

Of course, not all gangsters must be willing to make the ultimate sacrifice for wealth. Rather, real gangsters leave the messy business of dying to others—in sweatshops, in mines deep in the earth, in Bhopal, or in the hard choice between food, medicine, medical care, or heating a home.

It's good to keep referring back to this refrain when discussing the surprisingly moving qualities of this film, which stars rapper Curtis "50 Cent" Jackson.

This story is based loosely on the life of Jackson, who does a fairly good job of playing himself. And so, subliminally, we are also rooting for someone who is already a known commercial success, as well as a controversial artist whose sexually explicit lyrics are marketed to young audiences. In hip-hop, the drive to get rich or die tryin' is a perverted twist of the famous Malcolm X refrain: "by any means necessary." Of course, Malcolm X was talking about attaining true freedom and equality—about crushing an unjust system, not feeding it. He was not talking about the freedom to "get rich," buy new sneakers, a gold watch, and a Mercedes.

Black Star–Jeffrey Wright in *Syriana*

December 9, 2005

Syriana is a devastating tapestry of life, death, and the business of Middle East Oil. Based on the book by former CIA agent Bob Baer, it offers a complex view of this era of peak oil consumption and Persian Gulf wars. It makes complicit oil executives, the Arab ruling elite, and U.S. government operatives and assassins who all work hand in hand to ensure that business continues to run as usual—to the benefit of the United States.

The plot unfolds through a series of separate but interlocking stories: Bob Barnes (George Clooney) is a burned-out and betrayed CIA operative; Bennett Holiday (Jeffrey Wright) is a D.C.-based corporate attorney overseeing the messy merger of two oil giants; Bryan Woodman (Matt Damon) is a financial adviser whose company wants to land a ruling royal family as clients. Their stories, spliced together, are presented through key moments, conversations, and tragedies.

The interlocking of the stories adds to the film's emphasis on a machine, a machine that functions well by everyone doing their job. In the process of everyone doing their job and getting paid, questions of right and wrong, legality, morality, and principal are subordinate to the machine and mission. A prince of a Gulf royal family (Alexander Siddig), for example, who wants to improve economic conditions in his country for the average citizen, implement true democracy, and give women equal rights, is suddenly labeled an enemy of the system when he accepts a bid from the Chinese instead of the Americans for coveted natural gas drilling rights. *Syriana* has Washington, D.C., painted to scary perfection. Watch the CIA agent go home to his cookie-cutter suburban home, perhaps in Virginia, unload the screaming kids from the minivan, and then, in the next scene, order an assassination.

Director and writer Stephen Gaghan, who won an Oscar for his screenplay for *Traffic,* gives the sense of events unfolding in real time, as if we are watching a close-up documentary. Because of its sense of real time, it is not an action-packed film in the typical Hollywood sense. There are many moments of suspense and quick violence that propel the story and tension forward. It is not sentimental yet it does offer empathy for all of its main characters and for the destroyed lives of children and young men.

And yet, for all of its complexity, *Syriana* leaves much unsaid, unseen, and unexplained. Holiday comes home every day to his nice brick townhome and, typically, his father is sitting on the steps, smoking a cigarette, looking like a wino. The father never says much of anything. We know he is in a sad state; he might be homeless except for his son offering him a place to sleep every night. But we don't learn anything personal about him—or about his son for that matter.

The cumulative sense offered is that, in the machine, individual details such as family are truly secondary, and that in this cutthroat world of oil, either you are a player or you do not—or will not—exist.

Appreciation–Richard Pryor, Giant of Comedy

December 12, 2005

Richard Pryor, the cutting-edge Black comic who transformed both comedy and America's public conversations abut race, died on Saturday, December 10, of a heart attack.

His wife, Jennifer Pryor, told CNN that he died of cardiac arrest shortly before 8:00 A.M. after her efforts to resuscitate him failed and after being taken to a hospital in the Los Angeles suburb of Encino. "He was an extraordinary man, as you know," she told CNN. "He enjoyed life right up until the end. He did not suffer, he went quickly, at the end there was a smile on his face . . . he's a very, very, very amazing man and he opened doors to so many people."

Pryor, who celebrated his birthday on December 1, had been suffering from multiple sclerosis and fading from the performance scene for nearly twenty years. But before that, during the 1970s and 1980s, he, more than any other comic, brought to the comedic stage the pathos, brutality, and raw expression of his generation of African-Americans that had just staged a social revolution in the streets. His revolution was on the stage, where he regularly dropped reality bombs about America's racism, peppered his routines with the N-word (then later recanted use of the word), and made increasingly in-your-face comedy out of various street characters and events in his life, often angering Blacks and Whites.

His routines also included incidents involving the police, like the time he shot up his car when one of his wives tried to leave him, or in 1980 when he critically burned himself over much of his body while free-basing cocaine. In what many consider his finest comedy performance, in January 1979 at the Terrace Theater in Long Beach, California (recorded as *Richard Pryor: Live in Concert*), he made comedy out of a heart attack he had experienced a few years before. The excruciatingly funny routine included his heart cursing at him, making him kneel, and chiding him for "eating all that pork." At the end of the bit, when he awakes in the ambulance with all Whites staring at him, he complains that he has died and gone to the wrong (White) heaven, where he will have to "listen to Lawrence Welk" for eternity.

"Richard Pryor is a cultural giant who transformed the medium he worked in just as Miles Davis transformed music," said Reginald Hudlin, president of entertainment for BET, who met Pryor and "worked with everyone who was a disciple. Just in television alone, without *The Richard Pryor Show* you don't have *Saturday Night Live,* you don't have *In Living Color,* you don't have *Chappelle's Show.* There is no stand-up comedian today that doesn't owe him a great debt."

Pryor's signature routines frequently involved explorations of the racial-cultural divide—at a time when African-Americans were boldly asserting a new Black aesthetic that did not shy away from criticism and ridicule of "The Man." Subsequent generations of stand-up comedians and screen writers—including Martin Lawrence, Robert Townsend, Bernie Mac, Cedric the Entertainer, and D. L. Hughley—have continued to copy this and other poses of Pryor, sometimes ad nauseum, in routines that include ridiculing the supposed white-bread manner in which Whites eat, walk, dance, or even engage in sexual intimacy. The mimicry of Pryor's picking on Whites bold enough to be in his stand-up audience has become standard Black comedic fare.

Pryor's life-based routines, which expanded the usual setup and punch line of the comedy routine, were influential on all comedians, including Robin Williams and Jeff Foxworthy. Many who have written about him—including the journalist Mel Watkins in his book *On the Real Side*—have noted that Pryor's combination of wicked raw wit, pathos, and social commentary was undoubtedly kindled during his childhood in the racially polarized community of Peoria, Illinois, when he grew up in a brothel that his grandmother operated and where his mother worked as a prostitute. Despite their line of work, which first brought Pryor into contact with White men from the other side of the tracks, Pryor's family enforced strict discipline on him and wanted him to get a good education and make something out of himself.

According to Watkins, Pryor decided in 1963 to leave the chitlin circuits of the Midwest and head to the comedy stages of New York and Los Angeles, and, finally, to the big-money world of Hollywood films, where he coasted artistically during the final years of his working life in films including *Stir Crazy* and *Silver Streak.* Meatier film performances earlier in his career included a role as Billie Holiday's pianist in the 1972 film *Lady Sings the Blues* and a role as a union organizer in the important and underrated flick *Blue Collar.* He was married several times. He and his ex-wife Flynn Pryor have a son, Steven. He also has another son, Richard, as well as three daughters, Elizabeth, Rain, and Renee.

"[Richard Pryor] is the groundbreaker," comedic actor and producer Keenan Ivory Wayans is quoted as saying in *On the Real Side.* "For most of us he was the inspiration to get into comedy and also showed us that you can be Black and have a Black voice and be successful."

Filmmaker Spike Lee said in a phone interview with CNN that Pryor "was a giant, he was an innovator, he was a trailblazer, and the way he used social commentary in his humor opened up a universe to other comics to follow in his footsteps."

OPM—*King Kong*

December 14, 2005

How can you not ooh and ahh at the special effects of *King Kong*—the fierce *Tyrannosaurus rex,* the giant-sized vampire bats, the man-eating plants, and the big gorilla itself—bigger, blacker, and grander than ever?

But, unlike scores of moviegoers who have made *King Kong* number one at the box office, and unlike Peter Jackson, the talented director who also brought us *Lord of the Rings,* many of us also bring to the theater with us the fact that *King Kong* has always been a powerful and demeaning metaphor. In its many re-creations, beginning a century ago, *King Kong* has symbolized literally both the big Black beast, especially of the male variety, but, really, all of us as a collective people, and the ever-hyped beauty of the blonde White woman who alone has the bewitching power to tame that beast.

This latest production, a three-hour-plus extravaganza set during the Great Depression and rich in atmosphere, subtext, and action, if anything, reinforces this metaphor. Add to the equation the inclusion on King Kong's island of some truly crazy-looking Black "natives"—replete with bad teeth, unwashed hair, and a need to chop off heads (they look like less-disfigured versions of the orcs in *Lord of the Rings*)—and the metaphor of Black savagery is complete.

But if I might digress from this Black Studies template for the brief remainder of this review, let me offer a metaphor-freeing holiday gift to all of my Black intelligentsia, which is a perspective on the beast-and-beauty theme from a thirteen-year-old Black male who attended the movie screening with me. Like me, he watched the starving actress Ann Darrow (played by Naomi Watts) journey by boat to the mysterious Skull Island with the promise by an unscrupulous movie producer, Carl Denham (Jack

Black), that she would film on an exotic locale. On the island, we saw her kidnapped and offered by the Black natives as a sacrifice to King Kong, who quickly snatched her up and ran with her through the thick jungle.

As Kong, in these early moments of bonding, gripped her in his huge hand, shook her, roared, and scolded her, the boy laughed out loud, "She's like an action figure!" In his mind, there was no difference between Kong's relationship to Darrow and his own relationship to various action figures—those pint-sized human replications that he runs with, shakes, throws, and scolds in various games of sport and battle.

The perspective of my movie companion was further reinforced in later scenes of the movie when Darrow tried to entertain King Kong, as any good toy should, by juggling, doing back flips, and performing other stage tricks learned during her years on the vaudeville circuit.

With this new or added perspective from my companion, and no more scenes of the crazy-looking Black people, the rest of the movie was a lot more enjoyable, entertaining, and very funny.

Of course there is the necessary point of White folks transporting King Kong back to Manhattan with the idea of making money off of him as a freak show. And of course there is the necessary point of White folks then eventually attacking the big black beast when he won't cooperate. But this final attack says more about the attacker's greed and destructiveness than any shortcomings of the big monkey. After all, he would have been content to just chill, eat bamboo in the jungle, and play with his new action figure.

Gorillas just want to have fun.

Glory Road

January 13, 2006

Today's big-money world of sports media does not often remind us of the history of overt racism in the United States, including racism in the world of sports and journalism. In our inundation of information, so-called news and entertainment, I'm pleased to report that the film *Glory Road* does not take us further down the road of mindless distraction. Rather, it offers a gripping narrative that is right on time as the U.S. Congress is confirming justices to the U.S. Supreme Court who, during that same recent history, have fought integration and other gains of the civil rights movement. That inundation of information, so-called news and entertainment, is as much about competing narratives as it is about distraction.

The film is based on the story of the Texas Western basketball team and coach

Don Haskins. Both the team and coach made history in 1966, when Haskins started five Black members of the team in the NCAA championship against the storied (and all-White) team from the University of Kentucky. As this narrative reminds us, it was a game, some say the most important college game ever, that shattered racist notions about the abilities of Black basketball players to compete against Whites at the NCAA level and in the pro ranks. After the game, colleges in the South, who either had no Black players at all or restricted their playing time, ended their apartheid.

Josh Lucas delivers a solid performance in the role of Haskins, and the players, no big names except Derek Luke, are solid as well. Luke seems to be on a mini sports run. This time last year, he was remarkable as a Texas high school football player in the electrifying *Friday Night Lights.* This year, he is a cocky and risk-taking college point guard. Though there are exciting but pro forma basketball games, there are also decent portrayals of the off-court tribulations faced by the team as they traveled through hostile and racist communities and attempted to still enjoy themselves as young men in college. I learned only after my initial review of the film that it did not go far enough to really portray the long-term slander of members of the team by the White sports media, particularly by *Sports Illustrated,* and the level of racist animus directed at them and their coach by Adolph Rupp, head coach of the all-White Kentucky Wildcats.

Some of the dialogue from the Black players sounds a bit strained and unrealistic but, when in a tight spot, director James Gartner always falls back on the '60s soundtrack from Motown to lend the film more Black authenticity. And in a story so centered on race, perhaps we should have gotten a better idea of who Haskins is and what gave him a set of values different from those of so many of his colleagues. Still, despite such small annoyances, *Glory Road* is an important film.

Last Holiday

January 13, 2006

Queen Latifah's latest flick is most notable for the opportunity it gives the queen to spread her wings as an actress. Playing the part of a Louisiana sales clerk named Georgia Byrd who believes she is terminally ill, Latifah is not all comedy here and, again, she is nobody's mammy—even when the plot tries to make her into one. Byrd decides to blow her hard-earned and -saved dollars on a luxury vacation in Europe. In a somewhat formulaic narrative that alludes to Billie Holiday both in images and soundtrack, Byrd is decidedly unglamorous but is transformed by spa pampering and "international" fashions. She suddenly learns to stand up taller, speak her mind, and seek her happiness. This is all enjoyable to watch, especially after a cosmopolitan (or two). Even the predictable romance with LL Cool J is all in good fun.

On the Outs

January 20, 2006

If you are tired of Black and Latino men being depicted in film as drug dealers and junkies, a new film, *On the Outs,* serves up girls and women instead.

Written and directed by Lori Silverbush, *On the Outs* depicts slices of life from three young women living in a rough neighborhood in Jersey City, New Jersey: Suzette, the school-aged daughter of a hardworking nanny; Oz, a corner drug dealer; and Marisol, a mother who is also a crack addict.

As we meet them, all three are making bad decisions for their lives. The message of *On the Outs,* which is based on real stories gathered by Silverbush, is that being female and being on the street just don't mix.

Some of it sounds and looks a lot like your average hip-hop music video—and this feel gives a hint of the movie's major flaw—superficiality. As each woman goes deeper and deeper into her own cycle of trouble, the film becomes a pastiche of the sort of pathology that we are accustomed to consuming as occasional voyeurs. In a film, as opposed to in a music video, this steady drumbeat of immature decision, testosterone-laden violence, and lack of options begins to feel very claustrophobic. This movie about being on the outs, meaning outside of prison walls, offers its protagonists few, if any, ways out.

The Boys of Baraka

January 20, 2006

In the city of Baltimore, 76 percent of African-American males do not graduate from high school.

This shocking statistic is the subtext for *The Boys of Baraka,* a documentary that debuted last year on the film-festival scene and is opening theatrically across the country. Produced on a shoestring budget with the Independent Television Service and distributed by Thinkfilm, the two-hour production tells the stories of several "at-risk" Baltimore boys who are recruited to attend a boarding school in rural Kenya. The aim of the school, the Baraka School, is to prepare these middle-school–age males to enter and thrive at competitive high schools.

The Baltimore environment of these boys is the hood—either long stretches of mostly abandoned row houses or low-income public housing. Their families are the poor and the working poor, who are battling all manner of social ills. The mother of one boy named Devon is in and out of prison. Richard, who we learn may suffer from learning disabilities but has never been tested, visits a prison to see his father, who is serving a thirteen-year sentence for shooting Richard's mother in the leg. Classroom discipline in the public schools attended by the boys seems almost nonexistent. Most of the boys are receiving failing grades. Most of the mothers, who are not with the fathers, say they do not want their sons to grow up to be like their son's fathers.

These stories and lives of poverty are not easy to watch, even for those of us accustomed to being cinema voyeurs. The filmmakers, Heidi Ewing and Rachel Grady, are White. Except for the Baltimore recruiter, every teacher and administrator shown affiliated with the Baraka School is also White. Despite the gripping nature of the stories being told, the Black viewer might be left here in the odd position of being a voyeur of the voyeur, as if we are watching through the eyes of missionaries as they enter the "jungle." Though there is an in-depth look at the problems of the boys, this film does not delve equally into the background, funding, or problems of the school, which, in reality, faced challenges about its curriculum, depiction of White religious images, and a dearth of Black leadership. The failure to dig more deeply keeps this good movie from being great and, perhaps inadvertently, pushes it into the category of narratives that offer great White saviors and sorry Black downtrodden.

More than other recent documentaries about poor Blacks, however, *The Boys of Baraka* manages to convey both the depth of poverty's pathology and the remarkable ways that children fashion life and dreams for themselves, despite it all. It captures boys being boys, whether they are in a chaotic school cafeteria in Baltimore, or in a dormitory in Kenya, sneaking frogs and lizards into their rooms. As one boy cuddles a new spikey-haired pet, he declares, "There is something better than a cat—and it's a hedgehog!"

The Boys of Baraka puts in our faces the stark flipside to popular images of poverty chic and ghetto fabulous. There's nothing too fabulous or chic about a young life being limited or derailed because of what is, really, society's breakdown.

Black Star—Tyrese Gibson in *Annapolis*

January 27, 2006

Annapolis, starring Tyrese Gibson, functions as both a tale of triumph for the working-class underdog and an entertaining promotion for the U.S. military during a time of war. How else does a film about the U.S. Naval Academy turn into a 2006 version of *Rocky?*

Jake Huard (James Franco) has all the trappings of the soldier-hero—you know, the ones we like to root for in movies such as *Gladiator* or the current hit *Glory Road.* He's a riveter and the son of a riveter in the shipyards. His White working-class pals come replete with metal lunchboxes and after-work beers. Most pointedly, though, they are depicted as small-time bit players whose comparatively well-paying jobs—building the very ships that the academy's officers will command—are boring, mindless, and dead-end. We are to assume that the only thing these "rivets" have to look forward to is sitting on a worn couch and watching the biggest TV screen that they can afford.

The chief Black-White conflict is set up between Huard and one of his commanding officers, Midshipman Lt. Cole (Gibson), an experienced Marine who expresses disbelief in Huard's ability to become an officer. Both are talented as boxers. Conflict between the two is not depicted as centered on race and Cole is not depicted as an elitist. But it is not clear what the director and writer, David Lin and David Collard respectively, are trying to do, other than set up another *Rocky* (or *Million Dollar Baby*) scene with a racial subtext: the brutal Black boxing champ punishing the brave White underdog.

31

African-American Lives

Something New

January 29, 2006

Love stories proceed with their own gimmicks and ticks centered on the difficulty of hooking up in the modern age—cross-country romance (*Sleepless in Seattle*), single-mama drama (*Jerry Maguire*), and now two gay men (*Brokeback Mountain*).

Of the few taboo movie romances involving a Black woman and a White man in America—*The Bodyguard, Love Song,* and now *Something New*—there is the repeated motif of the haughty, de-natured Black diva rescued from her claustrophobic environment of staid, middle-class Negroes. Along comes her blond-haired beau who is salt-of-the-earth and not haughty at all. He is more down than LL Cool J! There is a reversal of the actual class conditions of most Black women and White men. And there is, perhaps, the implication that the Black woman is the one who is really racist if she—for some odd reason—prefers not to date White men.

But such movies, both feel-good and angst-driven, can't dwell on the dull business of race history, or income versus net worth. (Last year's *Guess Who* was more about the Black father and his daughter's White suitor.) And we would really have a fit if Hollywood asked us to accept a Black modern version of Pygmalion, a true around-the-way-girl, being groomed by her wealthy White suitor. Yuck!

There are two factors that allow *Something New* to break the mold of swirl as usual. First, a real actress, Sanaa Lathan, plays the lead role of Kenya, a successful Los Angeles accounting manager about to make partner at her firm, who meets a White landscape architect, Brian (Simon Baker). As our first real Black romantic heroine, from her performances in *Love and Basketball, Disappearing Acts,* and *Brown*

Sugar, Lathan is able to evoke that every-woman sympathy of the viewer that was nowhere to be found in the over-the-top performances by singers Whitney Houston and Monica Arnold in *The Bodyguard* or *Love Song* respectively. Lathan makes us like Kenya, and we want to like her, even with her particular foibles and idiosyncrasies. And besides, most of us don't want cobwebs in our hair, don't want to get our hairdo wet, don't want dogs in our house, and, while we may not want to be in that 42.4 percent of today's Black women who don't marry, we don't want to keep on dating busters, either.

This film has the added advantage of admirable and frank dialogue about race in the script by Kriss Turner, who has writer and producer credits for several television shows, including *Everybody Hates Chris, The Bernie Mac Show,* and *Whoopi.* Kenya and Brian actually have on-screen conversations where they vent about their differing ideas about how racism figures into the world both outside of their relationship and inside of it.

These conversations are not the knock-down, drag-out variety we have at Black gatherings, but they don't have to be. They give the film a refreshing sense of authenticity missing from other, more superficial, efforts. Yes, in this film also produced, written, and directed by Black women, there is something new—and it's not just a White man.

Black History Month

February 2006

African American Lives

After a couple of TV bombs, Harvard professor Henry Louis Gates has finally hit the right note with *African American Lives,* a four-part documentary series airing on PBS.

By uncovering his own genealogical history, as well as that of eight other African-Americans—Dr. Ben Carson, Whoopi Goldberg, Sara Lawrence-Lightfoot, Bishop T. D. Jakes, Mae Jemison, Quincy Jones, Oprah Winfrey, and Chris Tucker—Gates hosts a show that offers solid history lessons, as well as surprises and intrigue. What makes the series work is the research and resources put into investigating the family trees of the participants, all of whom are surprised by the findings. Using meticulous library sleuthing, as well as the latest in genetic research, the series is even able to tell participants what people in Africa are their likely ancestors.

The series is coproduced by Thirteen/WNET in New York and Kunhardt

Productions, an independent production company. With such a team in place, it is obvious that Gates did not do all the genealogical research himself. But as host and narrator, he presents findings to the participants. The result and response are better than a game-show host announcing the win of "a new car!" Oprah sheds a few tears. Jemison looks like a child on Christmas morning. Because of the often-difficult task of uncovering African-American history, each uncovered document or photo is akin to a mystery solved. There are a load of cheesy reality shows, home-improvement shows, fashion shows, and even animal shows cramming the channels these days, and, for my money and time, what is presented here beats them all for human interest and—yes—entertainment.

Gates, chairman of African-American Studies at Harvard, is not a sociologist or historian. And critics of his past TV shows have rightly stated that his specialty in Black literature and elitism did not qualify him to take on the intricacies of African history or the socioeconomic plight of today's African-American community. That argument can still be made of the current production but it succeeds anyway because, in it, Gates is primarily a presenter of facts, rather than an interpreter of them.

Many of his own musings are harmless enough, but when he begins to prattle, it often comes off like fingernails on a chalkboard. Like who cares if he is jealous of White folks who can trace their ancestry at Ellis Island? And let's get real—how did the inclusion in his family tree of White former slave owners affect his family's actual and perceived social status, their relationship to darker-skinned African-Americans, and their relationship to Whites? And, at some point, he seems to make a point of talking about racism as if it existed only in the past.

While these internecine battles that are a part of African-American "lives" are not explored, each participant's family history is woven into other social themes, as well as a timeline of the larger African-American history. Episodes one and two explore the twentieth and nineteenth centuries, along with accompanying issues of civil rights, land acquisition, and education. Episodes three and four cover the difficulties of tracing African-American lineage during slavery and before the Middle Passage.

Seldom is the past and present woven together with such edited precision. This one is worth your time.

The Beauty and Pain of *Yesterday*

Yesterday is a very moving and well-acted film about a South African woman who is caring for her young daughter when she finds out that she is HIV positive. Set in a small Zulu village, where most women fend for themselves while their husbands work in distant mines, it quietly but powerfully depicts a health crisis that is the leading cause of death on the African continent.

Yesterday is also the name of the lead character, played by Leleti Khumalo, who totally makes the film. The film likely marks the first time that Americans will see the talented Khumalo since her electrifying performances as a teenager twenty years ago on Broadway in *Sarafina!* That stage performance earned her a nomination for a Tony Award and an NAACP Image Award.

In this production, the beautiful Khumalo demonstrates her maturation as a seasoned artist. She artfully shapes Yesterday into a simple and sweet woman who finds the most joy and contentment in her little girl, named Beauty. With her kindness, gentleness, and broad smile, she is rendered nearly saintlike in a village of vicious gossips and mean-spirited biddies. Yesterday considers the more than four-hour round-trip walk to see a doctor as better for her than paying for a taxicab. Though ill and increasingly weak, she continues to take care of her daughter by gathering wood, fetching heavy jugs of water from the community well, washing clothes against rocks in the river, cooking, and cleaning.

She travels to the city where her husband (Kenneth Kambule) works as a miner. Yesterday wants her husband to know what the doctor has said. He needs to be tested. The viewer knows that, most likely, her husband has contracted the disease and has passed it on to his faithful wife. For her efforts, Yesterday is met with vicious violence from him.

Through Khumalo, and through the script by writer and director Darrell James Roodt (*Cry, the Beloved Country, Sarafina!* and *Place of Weeping*), we are made conscious of Yesterday's strength of body, quiet resolve, and her ability to negotiate the world despite her illiteracy. Though the production set and scenery is simplistic and raw (no doubt shot on a shoestring budget), there is a complex thematic swirl that includes life issues of fortitude and weakness, beauty and ugliness, faithfulness and infidelity, peace and turmoil, happiness and misery.

Roodt makes some use of the mountain desertlike landscape to show Yesterday in her environment. Her shadow on the ground works as hard as she works, or is mixed in with the silhouettes of others on a bustling sidewalk in Johannesburg. With her bare hands, she builds a hospital room for her husband from scrap and salvaged metal. As she sits in the darkened space during the day, sunlight filters through small rust holes and speckles her body and the room with light. Through images of the natural landscape, and by giving the main character and her daughter such stark monikers, Roodt lends this production the air of a timeless fable about the beauty of yesterday, about how yesterday is always our foundation for today and tomorrow.

The First Black Panthers

Battlefield victories of the Black 761st Tank Battalion of World War II, though critical to the outcome of the war, have been often overlooked by historians. Because the majority of Black soldiers were placed in segregated units and consigned to construction, engineering, and maintenance tasks, Black fighting units have not gotten their due—until now.

First To Fight: The Black Tankers of WWII, premiering on the History Channel, is the latest production to reveal and detail the accomplishments of Black soldiers who joined the U.S. military during a time of overt racism in the U.S. military, and then went on to fight on two fronts: against fascism in Europe during World War II and against racism and racial terror at home.

"Colored soldiers aren't smart enough to handle the implements of modern warfare," General George Patton had said of Black men in uniform. In 1944, however, days after the Allied landing at Normandy, when Patton found himself stuck in France and in desperate need of tanks, he ordered the 761st from their base in Texas to the front. When the unit arrived in Europe, Patton delivered a stirring speech to the Black soldiers telling them he didn't care about a soldier's color, he cared about soldiers kicking some German butt.

The battalion went on to distinguish itself in battle. Over 183 days, it helped liberate more than thirty towns under Nazi control, aided emaciated victims at a concentration camp, and played a decisive role in the historic Battle of the Bulge, which changed the direction of the war.

First to Fight is a lively and informative documentary that combines historic footage and photographs with interviews of surviving battalion members, who detail, in addition to memories of the battlefield, all the off-field drama they experienced. First, there was training in the segregated Deep South, in Fort Hood, Texas (where battalion member E. G. McConnell remembers that German prisoners of war were treated better than Black soldiers). Second, while the battalion trained and trained, probably twice as long as similar units, they were not called into battle to use their skills and prove their abilities—and the abilities of all Black men—on the field. Finally, at the point that they were sent into battle, they were derisively labeled "Eleanor Roosevelt's Niggers" because the first lady had vigorously advocated on behalf of equal rights and inclusion in battle for Black soldiers.

Members of the 761st Battalion adopted the motto "Come out Fighting" and dubbed themselves the Black Panthers. One of them, McConnell, proudly sports a panther medallion on a thick chain around his neck during his interview. Battalion members were awarded 250 purple hearts, seventy bronze stars, eleven silver stars, and a medal of honor. More than forty years after their return from the war, unit members received the Presidential Unit Citation from President Bill Clinton.

Tsotsi

February 24, 2006

In the hands of director and writer Gavin Hood, Athol Fugard's novel *Tsotsi* comes alive as a visually poetic pastiche of wealth, poverty, and violence in post-apartheid South Africa. As we follow Tsotsi, leader of a Soweto gang, in his various criminal exploits, there is the odd juxtaposition of the modern, gleaming Johannesburg—with its subways, neon, concrete, and glass—and the dusty and bleak township of Soweto, where a million of the country's Black residents, including Tsotsi, live.

We are introduced to a very hardened and merciless side of Tsotsi (which is the word for "thug" in the local vernacular; the T is silent). Actor Presley Chweneyagae commands the role with both a convincing menace and checked vulnerability. Hood keeps the tension taut, intimate, and visceral, from the opening scenes of a murder through the pivotal moments that change Tsotsi's life forever.

Those pivotal moments begin when Tsotsi decides to carjack a well-heeled woman, shoots her, and then, minutes later, realizes that the woman's infant son is riding in the backseat. At this moment, and in the coming days, Tsotsi must make decisions that allow him to reexamine his actions and his heart.

Fugard is a master at taking the pulse of South Africa and interpreting that pulse on the stage and, in this case, in fiction. While in lesser hands an action-packed story about a hardened criminal might suffice, Fugard's story adds issues of class, social mobility, South Africa's AIDS epidemic, and human decency to the mix. One of Tsotsi's gang members, Boston, challenges Tsotsi to think about human caring and the line he won't cross to get what he wants.

These issues of heart and community loom larger in this story than do issues of race and South Africa's old order of apartheid, except in a residual manner. All of the criminals and victims are Black. And in this "new" order in the country, where Blacks now hold government power but not economic power, what are legions of poor, uneducated Black people to do? Add other breakdowns in the social and family fabric, and it is clear, Hood seems to say, that there are ghettos all over the world, from Soweto, to Singapore, to San Francisco, with legions of young men who are known to the outside world simply as thugs.

In a pivotal scene in Soweto, Tsotsi asks a young widow, "How do you get money?" It seems a wonder to him that a woman can work in her home, sewing and mending clothes for a living. With the question, "How do you get money?" Fugard asks the larger question about how the modern world easily creates hardened thugs who answer that question with, "By any means necessary." They look at their own lives and scoff at any notion that there is such a thing as decency in the world.

Black Star–Cuba Gooding Jr. in *Dirty*

February 24, 2006

Watching a movie about a dirty cop is a lot like watching a monster movie.

There is something unspeakable before us, a violation of the law by the literal "law" itself. And, like the monster movie, the dirty-cop movie must, all at the same time, scare us, entertain us, and offer us new ways of considering the monster. There is, perhaps, the additional requirement that we think about the harm done to those who are supposedly protected by the police—but who are not protected at all.

With all these requirements in mind, the new film *Dirty* is an interesting effort that comes up short until its intriguing end—which comes too late to save it. By then, we have grown tired of Cuba Gooding Jr. acting way over the top, as if in some White man's interpretation of what an ignorant Black man really is. (How many times can one man put "MF" into a sentence? Can all of life be filtered through metaphors about oral sex?)

It would be a cheap shot to rate Gooding's performance as a cheesy rip-off of Denzel Washington's performance in *Training Day,* but it might not be a cheap shot to rate the construction of this character as such. Science may not have yet endorsed the practice of cloning, but, in Hollywood, the practice is in full effect.

Dave Chappelle's Block Party

March 3, 2006

Love Dave Chappelle or hate him—whether you consider him a comic genius or a nouveau jigaboo—there's no denying that he managed, in his *Chappelle's Show* on Comedy Central, to produce his own quirky vision, and have that vision wildly embraced by millions of TV viewers.

In his first movie, *Dave Chappelle's Block Party,* a portion of his TV show format—the hip-hop performance—takes center stage. The result is the best concert film to come along in a minute. If you've been on the outs with hip-hop of late, you might find yourself loving it again as you luxuriate in the beats and images of artists such as the Roots and Dead Prez. These artists are seldom, if ever, heard on commercial radio but, through the media miracle known as Dave Chappelle, suddenly loom large in a feature-length movie.

Not only does the film give deserved attention to these artists, it serves as a valuable visual document of hip-hop that lives outside the frame of a music video—Erykah Badu snatches off her wig on stage, Dead Prez still talks about "F*** the police," Mos Def airs his support for jailed political prisoners in the United States. On the milder side, there are electrifying performances by Kanye West, joined by John Legend and Common. The biggest surprise of the show is a reunion of the Fugees and a solo by Lauren Hill, looking frail and overly made-up, who is greeted by fans gone wild.

There is also the odd reality, stated most succinctly by a member of the Roots, that many of these artists, including Dave Chappelle before his TV success, often have concert audiences that are overwhelmingly White, as they are more likely to receive airplay and exposure on alternative and college stations than on mainstream Black outlets. This block party, an open-air concert staged in the heart of the Bedford Stuyvesant section of Brooklyn, uses big media, and the power associated with it, to bring Black music home to the Black community.

This arranged marriage, of sorts, is sweet to watch, even if we as viewers are painfully aware of the peculiar nature of the union. The music is still wrapped up in Dave's vision, which is peppered with foul language usually associated with a woman's sexuality and his usual barbs aimed, more pointedly in this movie, at the Black community.

This block party ultimately allows Dave Chappelle to live out his fantasy on a grand scale on the big screen. It's like he has always wanted to be one of the boys and now, with big media on his side, he's officially in the club.

He presents us proudly the official Dave Chappelle B-Boy Network.

Big Pimping at the Oscars

March 7, 2006

My review last year of *Hustle & Flow* had these closing lines: "It may be hard out here for a pimp, but it should be. It's even harder out here for those of us, who work hard at all kinds of jobs that we never see on film, who are asked time and time again by big media to embrace a pimp-and-hooker lifestyle as who we are."

I couldn't help but think back to these ideas Sunday night as I watched the Oscars, broadcast to an international audience of millions, as the song "It's Hard out Here for a Pimp" was performed by 36 Mafia and an arrangement of primarily Black dancers dressed up as prostitutes.

Surreal is the only word for the performance, except that for millions watching, there is a thin line between the surreal and reality. That's why when African-Americans travel abroad, people think it's okay to greet us with, "Yo, my nigga!" or to look askance at any attractive Black woman in a hotel lobby who is not wearing a maintenance uniform.

Oh, how the Oscars love some jainky Blackness!

Inside Man

March 24, 2006

Inside Man is a differently paced heist drama that does keep us guessing until the very end. While most cops-and-robbers stories take the perspective of either the law or the outlaw, *Inside Man* gives all sides some dap.

Detective Keith Frazier (Denzel Washington) is in the doghouse at work and needs success on this case to claw his way out. Though set in the present day, the production has a whiff of nostalgia, as if taking a style cue from the comic strip *Dick Tracy.* Like Detective Tracy, Frazier sports a brimmed hat. There are lots of men's-only environments: Madeline (Jodie Foster) passes through a men's room to reach a private barbershop where she meets with the bank president. The police and city government function as primarily a men's club where coarse language, especially as related to a women's sexuality, is used. The women in the production, with the exception of hard-edged Madeline, are ornamental, vampish characters that recall the glory days of romance serials. A cop's ex-wife comes into the police trailer in a tight dress with a small shopping bag full of tickets she'd like fixed. Frazier's girlfriend, also a cop, spends a lot of time trying to interest her man in sex and an engagement ring. When we last see her, she's on her back.

As in *25th Hour,* director Spike Lee takes New York City as his subject here, and addresses issues of race, class, and gender only occasionally within the context of the drama.

OPM–*Manderlay*

April 7, 2006

"Freedom, whether they want it or not," is the appropriate promotional tagline for *Manderlay,* an independent film that takes the peculiar institution of American slavery and makes it even more peculiar.

Written and directed by Danish filmmaker Lars von Trier, as the second piece in his trilogy about the United States, *Manderlay* is idiosyncratic and well acted by the likes of Danny Glover and Bryce Dallas Howard. But, unlike the American portrait by an outsider, *Democracy in America* by Alex de Tocqueville during the 19th century, *Manderlay* is disadvantaged by a snide dismissal of African-Americans and their history of resistance, as well as contempt for young White idealists who challenge the racist status quo. *Manderlay* could well be a public service announcement for David Duke, Ann Coulter, and Federalist Society, all rolled into one.

In *Dogville,* the first part of this trilogy released in 2003, von Trier set his sights on the oily underbelly of American life and character. That film tells the story of a young woman on the run, Grace, who seeks refuge in a small Rocky Mountain township named Dogville in Colorado. To maintain her secret, she is made into a virtual slave of the town's residents, who turn out to be a fairly sordid lot.

American enslavement as a theme is, of course, continued in *Manderlay* as Grace, escaped from her predicament, happens upon an Alabama plantation where slavery is still being practiced in the 1930s. As in *Dogville, Manderlay* is filmed as if it is on a large stage, without the trappings of location, or even the rooms of a house. The primary architectural feature is the immense and ornate front gate of the Manderlay Plantation. Over the objections of her father, who calls the situation a "local matter," Grace sets about the task of immediately freeing the plantation's slaves and punishing the Whites who have enforced this bondage seventy years after the Emancipation Proclamation.

All of Grace's ideas about creating freedom and equality are severely tested by newly freed slaves who don't immediately flee through the gates. Even though they are given good contracts, drawn up by Grace's lawyer, to be paid for their labor, the men and women—depicted for the most part as simpleminded darkies—don't rush back to work in the fields or to repair their leaky shacks. Rather, they spend their time playing cards and socializing.

Grace is further tested by her own slow evolution into a new-style overseer and big boss. She is the upholder of new community ideas that make slavery look like the good ole days of order, fullness, and plenty for all. In the hands of von

Trier, all the cynical views of Grace's father about women and about social justice are, in the end, rendered as truth. As in *Dogville,* von Trier ends on several notes that are disturbing. It takes more than artsy production and direction, however, to render convincingly the difficult idea that these Blacks at Manderlay, or any other place for that matter, don't want freedom like everyone else.

ATL—Boyz in Another Hood

April 7, 2006

ATL is a likeable though rough-hewn addition to the tradition of urban coming-of-age dramas. Starring the rapper T. I. and based on a story by Antwone Fisher (author of his own autobiographical story and screenplay), *ATL* updates the genre for those born in the late '80s or early '90s. It offers a portrait, which though sketchy, is a more realistic vision of the majority of hardworking urban Black working-class young men and families who are not caught up in the drug game or other illegal activities.

The story is set in Atlanta (the proper name for ATL) and T. I. plays the role of Rashad, who, since the death of his parents, has been in the care of his uncle. Various story lines give *ATL* and Rashad's character a sense of complexity and depth but also a sense of being somewhat disjointed. Add to this mix the music-video sensibilities of director Chris Robinson, and you wind up with a movie that, especially in the beginning, feels more like video pastiche than a film.

ATL attempts to deal with class diversity and intrarace discrimination within the Black community. Even though in *ATL* this depiction is not extremely sophisticated—the rich man, John Garnett (Keith David), is a caricature of snobbishness—it nonetheless breaks the mold of hood as usual.

Even in "new" stories from our hood, there are ways that old stories, images, and values stay the same. . . .

C.S.A.: The Confederate States of America

April 9, 2006

While reviewing films, I find myself unconsciously searching for the next gem, some production, polished or in the rough, that proves that this process of making new "Black" films is still advancing and is not stuck in the mire of *Soul Plane* foolishness or *Hustle & Flow* White imagination.

I am thankful to report that the movie *C.S.A.: The Confederate States of America* is such a gem. Written and directed by Kevin Wilmott in conjunction with Spike Lee,

C.S.A. asks us to consider what the United States would be had the South won the Civil War.

It unfolds in the form of a faux BBC documentary, which is, in turns, ticklishly funny, sobering, and surprising in the way that it meshes fiction and fact, absurdity and reality, the horrific with the hilarious. Perhaps it might be considered a meditation on the comedic mind of Lee, who thinks Black moviegoers prefer to laugh too much, rather than to think too much. *C.S.A.* allows the thinking moviegoer, Black or White, to laugh at America's chief mental illness: its obsession with race.

Organized around the obligatory talking-head narrator and history experts, the faux doc begins with the Civil War and winds its way to the present. When the North loses the Civil War, we see General Ulysses S. Grant surrender to General Robert E. Lee. Then, over the course of the following years, the North is annexed by the South and Northerners are convinced of the advantages of adopting the Southern "way of life," which means the reintroduction of slavery to the North (and the exodus to Canada of many abolitionists and other people of conscience).

In this changed world order, poor President Abraham Lincoln is considered to be an enemy of the state and, in one of the more wickedly funny sequences in the film, winds up donning blackface and following Harriet Tubman and the Underground Railroad in an attempt to flee to Canada. Years later, he is interviewed as an old man who wishes that he had "really cared for the Negro" rather than just used Black soldiers to try and win the war.

Advertising sponsors for this documentary, which is warned to be possibly unacceptable for "children and servants," include all manner of products and consumer services. Some, such as Coon Chicken and Darky Toothpaste, feature caricatures of a big-lipped, smiling sambo as a mascot. Other products, such as the high-tech wrist band that keeps a slave from running away, don't need such stereotypes to be potent symbols and accessories of White supremacy. The government public service announcement for the Office of Questionable Racial Identity takes the cake.

As the narrative winds its way through the twentieth century, more than the history of African-Americans is impacted. An American slave state is sympathetic to Adolph Hitler (and winds up creating a reservation for Jews on Long Island). The C.S.A. also has the ultimate goal of conquering and annexing all of the dark people of Central and South America, creating an entire hemisphere of plantations with White masters. Finally, in a country so sick with race, a White son of the South who runs for president must defend himself against charges that, thanks to the liaison between one of his ancestors and a Black woman, he has Black blood, or "jungle blood" running in his veins.

There are strong hints here about the ease with which such twisted fundamentalism morphs into fascism, especially with underpinnings of religion to substantiate itself. In this gem of moviemaking, Wilmott proves that truth, indeed, is often stranger than fiction.

Preaching to the Choir

April 14, 2006

With the success of Tyler Perry's *Madea's Family Reunion* and *Diary of a Mad Black Woman,* the independent film *Preaching to the Choir* might be considered in the mold of Perry's appealing church-centric soap operas that can be heavy on both morality and melodrama.

While such a comparison is legitimate, *Preaching to the Choir*—which tells the story of two brothers, one a minister and the other a rapper—also echoes other recent prodigal-son productions, including *The Gospel* and *The Fighting Temptations.* Originality is not its strong suit but it does include some good acting and musical performances.

Akeelah and the Bee

April 28, 2006

There is a freshness in the characters, dialogue, and story in *Akeelah and the Bee* that keeps it from falling into the predictable mire of movies with "good intentions" toward Black children. That mire usually includes a cheesy set, earnest but novice actors, and the sort of morality tales typical of 1970s after-school specials.

With Laurence Fishburne and Angela Bassett anchoring the cast, there is no worry here about novice actors. Keke Palmer, known to most from her TV and film work, most recently in *Madea's Family Reunion,* offers the lead role an endearing blend of early-adolescent innocence and courage.

The story is about a middle school student in South-Central Los Angeles named Akeelah (Palmer), who is a talented speller and is enlisted by her English teacher to compete in a school spelling bee. From there, we follow her quest to compete in what is arguably the most popular academic event in the United States—the annual Scripps Howard National Spelling Bee in Washington, D.C.

The Crenshaw middle school that Akeelah attends suffers from typical issues that beset many such urban centers of learning. She fears being singled out and roughed up by the school's tough girls for being a "brainiac." At home, her mother (Angela Bassett) is overwhelmed with work and a teenage son who is heading in the wrong direction. The introduction of a Black educator (Fishburne), who mentors Akeelah through her spelling competitions, enriches the story in an unpredictable way.

Black Stars—Laurence Fishburne and Ving Rhames in *Mission: Impossible III*

May 5, 2006

In this best of the *Mission: Impossible* movies, Tom Cruise goes into action-overdrive with a big assist in fierceness from Laurence Fishburne in the role of a special agent supervisor and Ving Rhames as part of the usual team, which is on the trail of a rogue arms dealer.

32

Baller, Shot Caller

Tyler Perry's Feminist Appeal

May 17, 2006

Even for Madea, Tyler Perry's gun-toting matriarch of stage and screen, one scene at the start of *Diary of a Mad Black Woman* is outrageous. Inside the walk-in closet of the mansion where her granddaughter Helen used to live, Madea furiously whirls her tall, heavy frame and shreds the new designer outfits of the other woman who has moved in with Helen's husband.

"This is for every Black woman WHO HAS EV-ER HAD A PRO-BLEM WITH A BLACK MAN!" Madea yells while ripping reams of couture garb. So goes this particular moment of Madea's gray-hair-and-red-lipstick rage. And so goes Perry, blazing his own particular path and brand of Black feminism and empowerment—first on stage, then in two hit films, and, now, even in print. His new book, *Don't Make a Black Woman Take Off Her Earrings,* debuted at number one on the *New York Times* hardcover best-seller list.

Love Perry or hate him, he has nonetheless managed to articulate a strong Black woman's voice and vision in his popular morality tales that have won audiences over to the tune of millions in profit. Some Black women dislike Perry playing a female character, but his success comes in an era when dominant hip-hop culture frames Black women as gold diggers or worse, sneers at romance, idealizes women with lighter hues and keener features, and only endows men with the toughness required for street justice. (The scene in the walk-in closet ends with the arrival of the other woman, her threat to call the police, and Madea's memorable retort: "Call the po-po ho!")

It is obvious that the rags-to-riches Perry is benefiting from the lessons learned while he toiled on the Black theater chitlin circuit (he hates that term), marketed to churches filled with Black women, honed his Christian soap operas of redemption and forgiveness, and created an audience with direct advertising on much-listened-to Black radio. But perhaps not as obvious is his ability to hammer at themes that appeal to an ignored audience of Black women hungry for portrayals of their lives, stories, and dreams that exist beyond the frame (and male-centeredness) of music videos or hood flicks. Reflected in the title of his book, he especially likes to praise, and not denigrate, the fortitude and battle savvy of the women he has known.

Exhibit 1 in this toughness is, of course, Madea, a grandmother of warmth, wit, and wildness. Perry, who transforms his six-and-half-foot frame into the character Madea with much makeup and prosthetics, says he created her as a composite of many women he knew growing up in New Orleans, most notably his mother, Maxine, and his aunt Mayola. But, citing other influences, he also dedicates his new book to "Big Mabel Murphy, Viola, Olabea, Sylvia—all those women who were on the block."

Many of Madea's fans have come to love her as a grandma-in-the-hood who isn't afraid to settle a dispute with the language and mode of the streets. In the film *Diary,* when Helen's mother (Cicely Tyson) utters the gospel lyric, "Peace Be Still," Madea responds, "Well you know what? Peace is always still around me 'cause I keeps me what they call a piece of steel." Quickly retrieving a semiautomatic weapon from her purse on the kitchen counter, she continues: "Long as you got a piece of steel, you gonna have peace."

Zeroing in on Madea's flair for the not-so-veiled threat, Perry's most recent film, *Madea's Family Reunion,* which grossed more than $63 million in theaters, was marketed heavily on Black radio and TV with a scene where two nieces ask her what a young woman should do about a boyfriend who hits her.

"Before or after his funeral?" is Madea's no-nonsense reply.

But with Perry, it's not all about toughness. Another unifying thread through his work is attention to and a genuine sympathy for the issues of love, commitment, marriage, and family that Black women focus on more than Black men. Even the fact that he made *Diary of a Mad Black Woman* his first film release exemplifies his focus on this core audience.

In *Diary,* Helen, played by the actress Kimberly Elise, makes the journey from being the wife of a successful lawyer, with a mansion and maid, to being penniless and waiting tables. But she also journeys from being with a cruel, soulless man to a relationship with a steelworker, played by Shemar Moore, who loves her and wants to marry her. He tells her: "If you're away for more than an hour, I can't stop thinking about you. I carry you in my spirit. I pray for you more than I pray for myself. And when you smile, my world is all right."

Similarly, in *Madea's Family Reunion,* a working-class single mother, Vanessa, played by Lisa Arrindell Anderson, learns to overcome her fears and embrace new love. Improbably, she gets to heal ugly wounds from her childhood and shine. In this tale, as well as others, Perry also makes pointed comments about color and class discrimination within the Black community and lets the chocolate girls be Cinderella.

Somewhere, within the Madea jokes, church-centered story lines, and frequent melodrama, Perry includes romance that, as Helen's steelworker says, feels "like a fairy tale." Sure. It is usually a syrupy sweet tale, but Black film seems to offer Black women either sweet syrup or gin and juice. (Easy to choose sweetness!)

When Perry talks about Madea's character and dialogue, he sounds as if he is channeling an ancestral spirit of a female warrior needed in these times. "In the Black community, Madea was the head of that village," he writes in *Don't Make a Black Woman Take Off Her Earrings.*

"Her name is the southern term for 'mother dear,'" he adds. "Madea used to be on every corner in every neighborhood when I was growing up and generations before . . . No matter what race you are, everybody wants to have a Madea in their family. She's not politically correct. She doesn't care about anything but what is honest and true."

Heart of the Game

June 9, 2006

Though women's sports have attracted more attention in recent decades, with the development of the WNBA, the brief flirtation in the U.S. with women's professional soccer, and better funding of women's programs at colleges and universities, it is still the stepchild of the athletic world. At least one sports aficionado I know believes that the big, unreported story of race and sports is the unequal funding received by women's programs at White, wealthier schools versus the funding that Black females receive at schools with fewer resources.

These issues of gender, race, and class in sports form a subtext of *Heart of the Game,* an energetic and probing documentary that follows a high school girls basketball team in Seattle and, in particular, the desire of one young, talented Black player, Darnellia Russell, to pursue her dream to play in the WNBA. Filmmaker Ward Serrill spent seven years following the players of Roosevelt High School, located in what is described as a middle-class to wealthy area of the city. His coverage began well before Russell came on the scene and, throughout the film, is obviously more focused on the team's unlikely coach, Bill Resler, a pudgy tax accountant who does not fit the typical mold of a hard-edged team leader.

Though narrated by Chris "Ludacris" Bridges, it is through the eyes of Serrill and Resler that the story and years unfold. Through them, we experience the sweep of emotions and time—the nail-biting drama and high-stakes emotion of each win or loss and the evolution of girls into young women. But the viewpoint is that of an observer, who, at times, is a bit distant. Part of that distance comes from the fact that, as stated in the film, Resler is not "on the court" or in the inner circle of the players from which he purposely excludes himself. The other distance factor, oddly, may be due to Serrill's dogged approach to the complex subject matter. Over the many years, it was perhaps easier to make the likeable Resler the main focus, as opposed to Russell or the other young women, who may not have been as open or forthcoming as subjects.

Even though Russell's story—including the fact that she was declared ineligible to play by the state's ruling body of high school sports—is an obvious focus of the documentary, we don't get to know her that well personally. Even though we see her in some team action, we don't hear her or anyone else talk about her signature moves or the details about what makes her a great ball player. We just know that everyone says that she is one. The viewer who comes to this story as a novice, not knowing about Russell or about this important chapter of Seattle sports history, may need more to chew on.

This is an excellent documentary but, in the end, Darnellia Russell is a highlight in the larger story of Bill Resler and the team. In a telling sequence, as we watch Resler and Russell play a little one-on-one, Resler jokes off-camera that Russell is his best shot "at being famous."

She is also the best shot, in this movie, of defining what is really the "heart" of basketball.

Silverdocs Documentary Festival—*His Big White Self* and *Beyond Freedom: The South African Journey*

Silver Spring, Maryland

June 13–18, 2006

It is not easy to "like" the documentary *His Big White Self,* which is a close-up portrait of African Nazi Party (AWB) leader Eugene Terre'Blanche, but director Nick Broomfield does his best to take an amused look at "the banality of evil."

Broomfield (who brought us *Biggie and Tupac* in 2002) tries, sometimes unsuccessfully, to maintain a delicate balance of documenting the deadly violence wrought by the party, recording the party's disintegration, and, finally, drawing a personal portrait of the portly Terre'Blanche as a husband, father, and avowed racist.

He builds on the narrative that he started in 1991 when he first followed Terre'Blanche for the documentary *The Leader, The Driver and the Driver's Wife* during the waning months of apartheid. There are moments in this documentary's ninety-four minutes when Broomfield's playful hunt for Terre'Blanche as a subject overwhelms the gravity of the subject of violent White supremacists. The fact is that, despite being imprisoned briefly, Terre'Blanche remains unrepentant for any of his acts or beliefs.

Maybe Terre'Blanche can be a joke to a visiting filmmaker or to foreign audiences, but it is not clear that, in a country where the Black majority smolders in poverty and crime is spiraling upward, Terre'Blanche and the White supremacists he represents are a joke to the people of South Africa.

Coupled with the screening of *His Big White Self* was the eye-popping *Beyond Freedom: The South African Journey,* a thoughtful, mixed-media work employing animation and other cinematic techniques that coaxes us into perhaps seeing the faces and hearing the voices of South Africa in a new way.

Waist Deep

June 23, 2006

Don't let the guns and gold teeth fool you.

Despite its formulaic gangsta trappings and just-okay script, *Waist Deep* is an intense you-and-me-against-the-world drama that is saved by Vondie Curtis-Hall's savvy direction and on-point acting by Tyrese Gibson.

The story, based in South-Central Los Angeles, is that a security guard named Otis (Gibson) is trying to walk the straight-and-narrow after serving six years in prison on theft-related charges. One day, after his cousin fails to pick up his son from school, Otis is forced to leave work abruptly to get him. After the pickup, Otis is carjacked while his son is sleeping on the backseat. In the resulting gunfight and chase on the street to retrieve his boy, Otis is drawn back into the world of crime that he is trying to steer clear of (and that will give him a "third strike" pass back to prison).

There are some silly contrivances but I give credit to Curtis-Hall for, even within the narrow confines of what Hollywood accepts as a Black or "urban" film, delivering a story that honors us, just like we honor and cheer other narratives about the search and love for children (Mel Gibson in *Ransom,* Denzel Washington in *Man on Fire*). Some credit is due to Tyrese for countering the hip-hop generation's Peter Pan syndrome and even appearing on the big screen as a father.

Little Man

July 14, 2006

Keenen Ivory Wayans's story of Calvin, a baby-sized thief who is taken in as an abandoned child, is just zany enough to overcome its boilerplate comedic format. Marlon Wayans does the facial expressions and dialogue for Calvin, while the body action is played by actual pint-sized people. Lots of cheap laughs and guy humor, from beginning to end.

Shadowboxer

July 21, 2006

The producer of the fetid film *Monster's Ball* is at it again, reveling in that seedy film space where he gleefully serves a nasty narrative of race, sex, violence, and death with as much panache as he can, and seduces us into accepting the twisted as artsy cinema.

For most of us, who don't vote on film awards, there is little to offer in Lee Daniels's new film, *Shadowboxer,* other than another stale story that glamorizes the glorious assassin. It seems now that we spend half our time in dark theaters rooting for and sympathizing with killers who dress in nice clothes and live exceptional lives with bloody money.

This time, the man with the gun is Cuba Gooding Jr., who plays the true bad boy in a vehicle far more stylish than the piteous, low-budget effort *Dirty,* which began making the rounds last year. In that film, Gooding was one half of a pair of rogue LAPD officers. In *Shadowboxer,* he is also part of a team. His name is Mikey and he and his partner, Rose (Helen Mirren), an elderly White woman, stalk their prey in sleek black clothes and while carrying long, sleek black guns.

There is, here, again, Daniels's twisted laugh at redemption. Just as a White racist can find redemption with a downtrodden Black woman, Mikey and Rose can find redemption through a child whom they allow to live. There are lots of crucifixes hanging on rooms in this film, which is set in Philadelphia and includes much old architecture and rooms filled with aging wallpaper. *Shadowboxer* represents decency's end in an old-school place.

What a way to go.

Black Star—Jamie Foxx in *Miami Vice*

July 28, 2006

Director Michael Mann is no fool.

In *Miami Vice* he gives us the requisite action, violence-that-makes-you-go-damn, sex, and neurotic characters that have become the staple of police dramas. His feature-length film is based on the iconic hit television series of the same name that helped give the 1980s its sheen of sleek decadence and superficiality.

It is an intro of quick hits and slice-and-dice editing that gives the just-okay dialogue and plot the illusion of depth and, in the best tradition of drug flicks, it is about lifestyles of the rich and criminal. Foxx gives this film some flava but this is not a Black movie. More so than in the TV series, where Don Johnson was the star, the Tubbs-Crockett team here have a bit more parity, but, still, Colin Farrell is the one involved in the film's major love triangle. Of course, Tubbs and Crockett are always in a fresh vehicle and, like the old duo, are even seen here at some point wearing fresh suits and shoes.

It's all here, minus, for me, some sense of whether it all matters. Just as the 1980s sheen and decadence is a distant memory after the savings and loan scandal, collapse of junk bonds, the devastation of crack cocaine in our neighborhoods, and two Gulf wars, the internecine battles between the super-rich who sell drugs and the super-unfunded police who fight them seem somewhat passé.

From Florida to Coahuila

August 9, 2006

The Black women, gathered together as if in worship, clap their hands and sing a familiar spiritual refrain:

"Wade in the water.
Wade in the water, children.
Wade in the water.
God's gonna trouble the water. . . ."

But the scene is not in Alabama, Philadelphia, Chicago, or Los Angeles. These women—with distinct African features—live in Mexico, in a small community founded by African-Americans more than a century ago. This startling scene, and the history behind it, is included in *From Florida to Coahuila,* a documentary directed by Rafael Rebollar Corona as part of his effort to tell the hidden story of African presence in Mexico. His documentaries were screened recently at

AfroMex: The First International Festival of Son Jarocho at the Cultural Institute of Mexico in Washington, D.C., and are also available online.

From Florida to Coahuila tells the story of the Mascogo people living in the small community of Nacimiento de los Negroes (Birth of the Negroes), near the city of Muzquiz, Coahuila, southwest of the Mexican border with the United States near San Antonio. Through interviews with community residents, oral histories, and scholars, Corona tells a fascinating story about the community that begins with colonization by Spain in 1565 of the area now known as Florida and the import to that area of enslaved Africans. Blacks who escaped bondage often formed independent communities called maroons; many also joined the Native American communities of Seminoles. After the series of wars between Spain and the Seminole nation, the Seminoles agreed to relocate to the area now known as Oklahoma and began the long trek west.

As the story has been passed down from generations, some Black members of the Seminole nation settled in Bracketville, a border town in the area of the Alamo, west of San Antonio. From there, they developed a close relationship with Mexicans and, to escape the reach of slave-catchers and violence that beset them in the Deep South, relocated to Mexico and founded Nacimiento de los Negroes in 1856. The new community thrived at its height, with agriculture and the practice of a religion that included both the spirituals they knew and interpretation of their dreams.

For a time, Nacimiento did maintain ties with Bracketville but many of those ties have diminished. Similarly, the original culture is in danger of being lost as the Mascogos marry other Mexicans or move away from the village for better opportunities. Across the border in Bracketville, however, there is a regular return of the Oklahoma Blacks for a celebration and commemoration of their heritage, which includes a cemetery in that community for those who served the U.S. Army as Seminole Indian Scouts.

Despite his obviously limited budget, Corona takes on the yeoman's task of telling this complex story with gusto, with interviews on both sides of the border, and with historical segments filled with period photographs, drawings, and maps. With so much material to cover, however, *From Florida to Caohuila* could use some streamlining in theme and content. And, as he romps through history, Corona gives some important details only sketchy treatment. It may be difficult for the viewer to absorb so much in one sitting, without reaching for the rewind button. Despite such lapses, it makes an invaluable contribution to revealing an important and fascinating chapter in a history that is, at the same time, African-American and Mexican.

Black Star—Shareeka Epps in *Half Nelson*

August 18, 2006

The angst of junior high school usually refers to the growing pains of students, not teachers. But the movie *Half Nelson,* which created a stir at this year's Sundance Film Festival, takes a fresh look at what it means to come of age in the United States during this time of turmoil, both at home and abroad.

The story, set in New York City, focuses primarily on a young White junior high school teacher named Dan Dunne (Ryan Gosling), who is bright and motivated in the classroom but seriously addicted to cocaine. The other focus is Drey (Shareeka Epps), one of his Black female students whom he also coaches on the girl's basketball team. Their simple teacher-student, coach-player relationship takes a sudden turn after a game one day when Drey catches her teacher getting high in what he thought was a deserted locker room.

From that moment, their relationship is turned on its head as Drey, who is mature far beyond her years, recognizes the precarious double life that her teacher is leading. Epps possesses that rare combination of a baby face and the knowing eyes of a mature woman. Even though the movie flirts with sexual tension between the Black teenager and White man, that tension is not explored or exploited.

Half Nelson, which takes its name from an immobilizing move in wrestling, is not a chatty film. Fleck captures intimate moments between two people, and moments that allow us to watch characters as they watch others. Then all of these snippets of conversation and life are pieced together into a whole that crosses racial, generational, and gender terrain to feel, sound, and look for real.

When the Levees Broke: A Requiem in Four Acts

August 22, 2006

When the Levees Broke: A Requiem in Four Acts is a powerful elegy for the dead of Hurricane Katrina, for the death of New Orleans, and for naivety about how the U.S. government treats its poor. Directed by Spike Lee, it is a requiem in the hands of a meditative son, on par with Mozart's *Requiem* or Earth, Wind & Fire's "Open Our Eyes."

The documentary, which premieres on HBO, is a tour de force of humanity, horror, and living history. The first two acts recount the days immediately before, during, and after Hurricane Katrina struck the U.S. Gulf Coast on August 29, 2005. While much of New Orleans was spared the brunt of the storm, which, instead, decimated coastal communities in Mississippi, ensuing heavy rains breached the city's poorly constructed levee system and 80 percent of the city was submerged beneath a toxic stew of floodwater, raw sewage, and residue from the region's petrochemical industries.

News organizations broadcasted images around the world of desperate city residents stranded on rooftops, highways, and at two emergency shelters at the city's Superdome and convention center. Though the shelters were set up to provide respite, they became islands of misery, as tens of thousands waited, and some died, without water, food, or other relief from the federal government. A police and military response to looters, and to news reports of outrageous crimes later proven to be untrue, depicted victims of this tragedy as an undeserving and dangerous criminal class.

What Lee adds to this familiar recent history is our story—close-up, firsthand accounts from those who lived to tell. "It was deplorable at that [Super] dome," says Audrey Mason, who evacuated her flooded home after hearing loud explosions come from the direction of the levee in her Gentilly neighborhood. She is one of many longtime Black New Orleans residents who believe that a section of the levee in their neighborhood was deliberately destroyed in order to prevent flooding in wealthier, White areas. "I not only heard the explosion, I felt the explosion," she says.

While Lee does not dwell long on such suspicions, he uses interviews with historians and vintage film footage to illustrate how they are rooted in history. For example, after the Great Mississippi Flood of 1927, a White Louisiana community was deliberately flooded, and during Hurricane Betsy in 1965, Black residents believe but do not have proof that their neighborhoods were also deliberately flooded.

Portions of Act I and Act II are a tragicomedy of elected leadership and "official speak." Lee reminds us, however, that the incompetence with which the federal government built levees and handled the crisis had consequences that were deadly rather than funny. He ends the second act with a finale for the dead that we rarely see in the coverage of our domestic tragedies (or from our military invasions abroad, either)—a montage of variously grotesque corpses that are bloated, mangled, or floating in floodwaters.

Lee's talent for choosing characters for this horrible story sometimes seems to mimic what he has done in his career making feature films. Just as Audrey Mason could be like the sage and no-nonsense characters played by Ruby Dee, Phyllis Montana-LeBlanc, a tart-tongued resident of New Orleans East, could be the equivalent of a sassy Rosie Perez (parents be forewarned: Cursing is definitely allowed in this requiem). Terrence Blanchard, also a native of New Orleans, provides the jazz riff here that runs through so many 40 Acres and Mule productions.

Similarly, for the combined Acts III and IV, Lee begins with a sweeping historical prelude that rivals his work on *School Daze,* his feature film that explored life at a historically Black college. While there would seem to be little left unsaid after the first half, Lee uses these two acts to follow the scattering of some of the tens of thousands of primarily Black New Orleans residents to new places around the country. Many have found a better life and vow not to return to what they feel is the scene of a crime. "If they wanted us in New Orleans, they wouldn't have tried to drown us and kill us," says Mason. "So I'm not going to go back so they can try to finish the job."

Lee also chronicles the desire of some to return to the city and rebuild their lives, though their houses have been completely destroyed or rendered uninhabitable. Graphic images make clear that, one year after Katrina, much of New Orleans still looks worse than war zones in Iraq, Afghanistan, or Beirut. "It's like someone dropped a nuclear bomb on every part of the city," says Calvin Mackie, a professor at Tulane University.

In the aftermath, there is also ongoing horror: bodies still being found in locked homes that were supposedly checked by search teams; children burying parents and parents burying children; insurance companies refusing to pay claims, even to those with flood insurance; a new tide of violence and crime from the city's dispossessed youth; a city emptied of much of its Black population; a city looking at both nature's fury and the government in bewilderment.

"They knew that this could happen," says Benny Pete, a musician from the Lower 9th Ward, of government officials. "It's almost like they let it happen."

Idlewild

August 25, 2006

The same eccentricity and whimsy that has kept Outkast on top of the music charts follows the hip-hop duo onto the big screen in *Idlewild,* a big mishmash of a film that is not short on surprise, entertainment—or confusion. Part buddy flick, part gangster flick, part romance, part whorehouse drama, and, let's not forget, part musical, *Idlewild* certainly isn't lacking in content or even in appeal, particularly for Outkast fans. But maybe this film has too much content, unfortunately of a predictable and thin quality, so that very little of it survives the mishmash.

Set in a Southern town during the 1930s, it follows the friendship between Percival (André Benjamin), the good-boy mortician's son who is a gifted pianist, and Rooster (Antwan A. Patton), a bad-boy hustler who is also a talented entertainer.

Music-video director Bryan Barber is the writer and director here and many of the musical and nonmusical scenes have music video written all over them. As a result of its jumble of stories, emotions, and textures—ranging from cold-blooded murder to animated musical notes—*Idlewild* presents itself more as ornate spectacle than a story with characters that we are really supposed to connect with and care about. The possible exception is the character of Percival, but even he is limited by what we don't know about him.

It is great to see, all in one flick, Terrence Howard, Ving Rhames, Macy Gray, Cicely Tyson, Ben Vereen, Patti LaBelle, and many emerging stars. For this gathering alone, and despite its shortcomings, the film could be one that fans will treasure as a unique contribution from two popular musicians.

Or, maybe, *Idlewild* will be forgotten as easily as the next rotation of music videos.

Crossover

September 1, 2006

Two basketball players, one who wants to go to medical school and another who wants to win a street-ball tournament, are the main characters in this well-meaning but average sports saga.

Black Star—The Rock in *Gridiron Gang*

September 15, 2006

In this very touching jock drama, Dwayne "The Rock" Johnson stars as a counselor and coach of a football team made up of young men in a juvenile detention center.

The Last King of Scotland

October 6, 2006

Idi Amin, the brutal Ugandan leader who rose to power in 1971 with assistance from the West and then murdered three hundred thousand of his own people, was, by all definitions, a monster.

So does it matter who is calling him a monster?

This is the unsettling and unsettled question for me after screening *The Last King of Scotland,* which washes over the viewer like a tsunami of political turbulence, violence, and murderous madness. Featuring a hypnotic performance by Forest Whitaker and directed by documentary filmmaker Kevin McDonald, it is based on the award-winning novel by Giles Foden, who moved from England to Uganda when he was five and lived there for some years. The novel and film are fictional accounts of a young doctor, fresh out of medical school, who goes to

Uganda to work at a mission but winds up as Amin's personal physician and one of his "closest advisors."

That's all good. I'm not trying to hate on anybody's great novel. But I prefer my history, no matter how powerfully rendered in literature or film, based on facts, not fiction. I especially need facts when the subject matter is as complicated as colonial and postcolonial Africa, the interpersonal lives and habits of African women, and the roles and attitudes of both European colonizers and the African colonized.

The story, told through the eyes of the young doctor, does, rightfully, paint a picture of him as naive and of British complicity in Amin's rise to power. But then it goes on, based on who knows what, to picture African women as easy and available sexual partners to the young doctor. One woman whom he meets on the bus, before the movie has even really started, winds up riding him like she's at a rodeo. Another fictional story line has one of Amin's shunned wives taking up with him, despite the obvious risks. If it were true, that would be one thing, but it's not. As it is, what looks deceptively like history writ large on the big screen turns out to be, partly, some White boy's wet dream.

Whitaker, who is so deserving of recognition, is already getting awards buzz for his tour de force performance. Remembering, however, the storm over "historical inaccuracy" that swirled around Denzel Washington's nomination for the film *The Hurricane,* based on the life of boxer Rubin "Hurricane" Carter, I wonder how in the world *The Last King of Scotland* can stand the same test.

Of course at the core of the Black film movement of the past twenty years has been the drive for Black people to tell our own stories. This drive is what sets apart films like *Malcolm X, Antwone Fisher,* and *Hotel Rwanda* from movies, even if they have merit, such as *Cry Freedom, Mississippi Burning, or Monster's Ball.*

This whole voice thing and vision thing is truly going in the wrong direction if an important opportunity to tell real history—even about our monsters—is instead told through someone else's fiction.

Catch a Fire

October 27, 2006

"What kind of man are you???" cries Patrick Chamusso in a South African interrogation room, where he realizes with horror that the police have harmed his family to coerce him to confess to a crime he did not commit.

Chamusso, played by actor Derek Luke in the new heart-stopping political thriller *Catch a Fire,* shouts into an opening in the wall so that he can be heard on the other side by the police, headed by the cool and calculating Nic Vos (Tim Robbins). This is a pivotal moment in the film, not just for the plot but for asking questions that are at the heart of it. What kind of man is a terrorist? What kind of man gets to label and accuse the terrorist? What is a terrorist? And what is a freedom fighter?

To answer these questions, the filmmakers tell a story based on the real life of Chamusso, who was transformed from an apolitical yes-man to a militant fighter for the liberation of South Africa's twenty-five million Blacks from the genocidal system of apartheid.

When we meet Chamusso in the story, he is with his beautiful wife, Precious, his mother, and his two young daughters. His position as a foreman at an oil refinery provides him a slightly higher standard of living than that of most Blacks in the country. His family has a small home, a car, and he even has a prized 35mm camera. What he pays in return is a studied subservience to the rigid order of White supremacy. "Yes, bossman," is his quick reply to Whites. When one of his subordinates at work is called a "cheeky kaffir" (a South African way of calling a Black person a nigger) by a White security guard, he readily agrees in order to diffuse the situation and prevent the worker's firing. At home, he scolds his mother for tuning into radio broadcasts from the banned rebels, the African National Congress (ANC). But his yes-man demeanor changes when he is falsely accused of helping to bomb the oil refinery. Arrested, beaten, and tortured—and then finally driven to his breaking point—he changes his mind about obedience to the racist status quo.

This is powerful storytelling. Director Phillip Noyce (*Rabbit-Proof Fence*) maintains an immediacy and unsparing intimacy—whether brutal or sweet—from beginning to end. The writer is Shawn Slovo, daughter of Joe Slovo, a White South African who served as head of the military wing (MK) of the African National Congress (ANC) and was a Cabinet member in Nelson Mandela's first post-apartheid government. Shawn Slovo has said in interviews that her father, who died in 1995, always told her that Chamusso's story and the story of the oil refinery bombing would be one to tell in a movie. She could have easily told an important story about her parents' pivotal role in fighting apartheid—her mother was killed by a parcel bomb sent by White extremists—but then we would have another movie like *Cry Freedom,* with a story about twenty-five million Blacks told through the eyes and experiences of one White man.

The battle of wills, and sometimes of life and death, between Chamusso and

Vos (Luke and Robbins) is riveting. After moving us in *Antwone Fisher* and *Friday Night Lights,* this is certainly Luke's biggest opportunity to show his ability to pour himself into a role. And he does it here with a lilting accent that sounds flawless (to my foreign ears). While the finished film does not give us enough time to digest and appreciate Chamusso's evolution into a revolutionary, Luke uses what is given him to carry the story and jockey for the position of his generation's Denzel. Tall, blond Tim Robbins morphs eerily into a cool torturer, a man who believes that violence and torture can yield truth, rather than easy answers from those who are physically and emotionally broken. Within the larger tale of Chamusso's life, it is the squaring off between these two men that allows the film to take a fine measure of manhood, how it is shaped—and warped.

33

Dreams and Dreams Deferred

American Blackout

November 5, 2006

The ways that Black voters in the United States were disfranchised in the 2000 and 2004 presidential elections is the subject of *American Blackout*, an unflinching and troubling documentary that is being screened around the country.

Director Ian Inaba, who was nominated in 2004 for MTV's Breakthrough Music Video Award for his video for Eminem's "Mosh," has also used American Blackout" to launch a "Video the Vote" campaign to encourage citizens to document any voting irregularities they see at their poling places on Tuesday, November 7.

Along with *Hacking Democracy*, which premiered on HBO, *American Blackout* is the latest in the new tradition of highly charged political documentaries, which began with Michael Moore's *Bowling For Columbine* and which frequently touch on the status of African-Americans within the larger American society. While the issue of suspect computer voting machines covered in *Hacking Democracy* affects Americans of all colors, Inaba makes the case with facts and passion that African-Americans have been particularly targeted for disfranchisement by Republicans because we tend to vote Democrat.

For the 2000 election irregularities, Inaba is able to piggyback on much of the material already uncovered in journalist Greg Palast's book *The Best Democracy Money Can Buy* and by the documentary *Unprecedented*, directed by Joan Sekler and Richard Perez. In 2000, Florida was the pivotal state and, well before the controversial election during November, Black voters were systematically removed from voter roles using flawed "felon purge lists." Florida is one of a few states that still has a law that prevents convicted felons from voting. Katherine Harris, Florida's secretary of state—who was also cochairman of the Bush campaign in Florida—ordered a list of felons compiled that turned out to be filled with a majority of African-Americans who had never even been arrested. Many listed felons even had conviction dates that were in the future.

For the 2004 election, *American Blackout* uncovers the specific ways that Black precincts in Ohio did not receive adequate numbers of voting machines, or even had some voting machines removed, resulting in long lines of Black voters in the rain and stretching into the wee hours of the morning. In the meantime, White Republicans in suburban districts had no such problems. Also, as did Katherine Harris in Florida, Ohio's secretary of state Ken Blackwell, a Black Republican, instituted new rules governing poling places and provisional ballots that caused many Black voters—including many young voters going to the polls for the first time—to be turned away or use a provisional ballot that would never be counted.

It also follows Georgia Democrat Cynthia McKinney in her bid to regain her seat in Congress after losing in a hotly contested and bitter race. In Georgia, registered voters are allowed to "cross over" and vote in another party's primary, and, despite this, McKinney was able to galvanize enough of her constituency to overcome both the primary and general election and head back to Congress. Her story continues this year, however, when, after the controversial altercation with a Capitol Hill police officer in Washington, DC., she again had to face a primary where fourteen thousand registered Republicans crossed over to vote against her in the primary and forced a runoff, which she lost.

By looking at both the 2000 and 2004 elections, Inaba has made a valuable contribution to the study of American elections. He has pinpointed new and high-tech ways that Black voters are stripped of this constitutional right.

OPM—*Bobby*

November 22, 2006

By resurrecting and breathing life into the day just before Robert F. Kennedy was assassinated in 1968, *Bobby* unlocks the past forty years of American life and politics and makes bold parallels to the United States today. Director Emilio Estevez explores a haunting moment from his childhood and contributes a poignant elegy (from those of us born in the 1960s) about the path from that decade's optimism to the pessimism of those that followed.

The film, just under two hours in length, is an unusual pastiche of fact and fiction that re-creates the day, June 4, 1968, leading up to the early hours of June 5 when Kennedy was shot at the Ambassador Hotel in Los Angeles. Nearly two dozen fictional characters at the hotel, played by an array of stars, remind us of some of the flavor of the times, including wide-eyed campaign workers (Shia LeBeouf), an emerging buppie (Nick Cannon), a marijuana and LSD dealer (Ashton Kutcher), aging men watching the changing times (Anthony Hopkins and Harry Belafonte), Black and Latino hotel kitchen workers (Laurence Fishburne and Freddy Rodriguez), and all kinds of White women on the verge of the Women's Movement (Demi Moore, Sharon Stone, Lindsay Lohan, and Helen Hunt).

Without fictionalizing any major events of Kennedy's life (as *The Last King of Scotland* does for Idi Amin), these various dramatic or amusing story lines are interwoven with actual news footage of the turbulent times—including Black rioters in the streets in the weeks after the assassination of Martin Luther King, Jr., which had occurred two months before. We see Kennedy as he campaigns around the country for president and heads to California for that state's primary on June 4. Most moving for me is extended footage of a stop Kennedy made in a poor rural community where he spoke of this country's ability to eliminate poverty and preserve the environment in his lifetime.

Of course the final hours of Kennedy's life are marked by his glowing speech at the Ambassador, in which he says, in part: "What I think is quite clear is that we can work together in the last analysis. And that what has been going on with the United States over the period of the last three years— the divisions, the violence, the disenchantment with our society . . . whether it's between Blacks and Whites, between the poor and the more affluent, or between age groups or over the war in Vietnam—that we can start to work together again. We are a great country, an unselfish country and a compassionate country. And I intend to make that my basis for running. . . ."

Those of us familiar with the news footage from that night, which captures the moment after the speech when Kennedy leaves the ballroom through the hotel kitchen, can guess that this is when the film most poignantly combines its factual and fictional elements.

Bobby is a tremendous feat of filmmaking that is made easier by highlighting Kennedy's eloquence, compassion, and vision. In terms of the diversity in his portrayals, Estevez leans most easily toward Latinos and the emerging Latino pride of the era, which is used in a couple of scenes to take unreturned jabs at African-Americans. Pivotal, real-life Black characters who might have been fictionalized, such as Rosie

Greer who grabbed the gun from Kennedy's killer, Sirhan B. Sirhan, are not included. Despite these noticeable rough spots, *Bobby* offers a startling portrait of perhaps the least remembered of the fallen leaders of the 1960s, and a portrait of the beginning of the end of an era.

Black Star—Denzel Washington in *Déjà Vu*

November 22, 2006

The purpose of Hollywood's star system is amply illustrated by *Déjà Vu*. As soon as we see our main man Denzel Washington coming to save the day in a fresh shirt and cool shades, it's ON. We (especially women) know, at that very moment of eye-to-screen contact, that this is a movie we are at least willing to try. The star system literally banks on the fact that we movie fans will go out and see our favorite star, rather than or in spite of the movie.

In *Déjà Vu*, Washington once again saves a somewhat dubious plot from totally bombing. As Doug Carlin, an agent for the Federal Bureau of Alcohol, Tobacco and Firearms, he comes to the scene of a horrific and deadly ferry explosion in New Orleans that he quickly determines was deliberately set. In the course of his investigation, he happens upon a secret federal project that is able to look back in time and, using the latest satellite technology, watch the past unfold in detailed three-dimensional images—just like a movie.

Understandably, he has lots of questions about this time machine and gets the young, mad scientists (including one played by Erika Alexander—yay!) to admit that their machine might also permit time travel—which would really help him solve the crime of the ferry explosion. This time-machine gimmick is at the heart of this somewhat clever whodunit, which directly touches on American fears about terrorism and our subliminal desire to make it all just go away.

But the viewer is also liable to have some questions, such as, is this real? Are they really trying to convince me that from the sleek confines of what looks like a trailer they can see and visit the past? (Oh, O.K. If Denzel says so, it must be so.)

But, I must say, what is really not O.K. about *Déjà Vu* is how our main man is always such a lone Black man whose job it is to save White people. Unlike the action movies that I remember starring Harrison Ford, Mel Gibson, and Bruce Willis, which often included them in the context of a family, a family that they were often fighting to save, Denzel rarely has a wife, girlfriend, or child whom he is trying to save who looks like him. While the dramas *John Q* and his own *Antwone*

Fisher showed him in the context of family, most of those hero movies, such as the visceral *Man on Fire*, do not.

The absence of Black surroundings also means that his love interest does not look like him. In Denzel's *Out of Time* (and in Will Smith's hit *Hitch*), Eva Mendes was chosen as an acceptable mate for a maximum crossover audience. In *Déjà Vu*, the woman Denzel falls for, Claire, is played by Paula Patton, who appears as racially ambiguous, perhaps a Creole, surrounded by White-looking family and friends.

In these big-budget action flicks, our main man star is like a chocolate chip in a sea of milk. Sure. He gives the film some flava but Black fans pay dearly when we are told, time and time again, that the flava doesn't include the rest of us.

OPM—*Three Needles*

December 1, 2006

In the world of *Three Needles,* a fable-like meditation on the AIDS pandemic premiering on Showtime, the deadly disease is not couched in terms of science, medicine, or morality. What comes subtly through the text is how money—primarily the lack of it, the want of it for survival—pushes three communities into the deadly grasp of the virus.

A coastal village in South Africa is the setting for one of the three stories told and narrated omnisciently by a nun sent there to oversee two novices at a Catholic mission. While the nun, Hilde (Olivia Dukakis), is focused on the mission of saving souls in a country with such a high death rate, one of her young novices, Clara (Chlöe Sevigny), commits herself to the survival of five orphans after their parents and grandmother have died.

More than the other two settings, in Canada and China, the South African locale has less emphasis on the African people struggling and dying from AIDS. Instead, the focus is on the good-hearted nuns and the wealthy White owner of a plantation where one-quarter of the impoverished workforce has the virus. In comparison to the close-up portraits of the indigenous people painted in other countries, this lack of emphasis is very noticeable and keeps us at a distance from the Black population, especially in light of South Africa's depicted incidence of sexual assault of virgins, mistakenly viewed by some men as a cure for AIDS. Despite this emotional distance, director-writer Thom Fitzgerald tells such an engaging tale, shot in such a way to take advantage of the haunting landscape, that it is impossible not to be drawn to it.

In China, a pregnant woman (Lucy Liu) negotiates a treacherous path as a blood smuggler when she learns that her business may be spreading the HIV virus to unsuspecting villagers eager to earn $5 for donating blood. One struggling farmer, too ill to donate blood himself, volunteers his daughter to give blood even though she is too young to be a donor. Happy to have enough money to plant a generous rice crop and buy an ox, the farmer overlooks his child's growing fatigue and the illness of many of his neighbors. His predicament is very moving and Lucy Liu is stunning as a woman in the developing world forced to make it in the best way that she can.

In the third location, Canada, a young porn actor, Denys (Shawn Ashmore), is living at home with his parents, a seriously ill father and a mother who scrapes by as a waitress. Denys's horrible secret is that he has been cheating on his blood tests, required for those in the porn industry to check for sexually transmitted diseases. When he is caught and his HIV-positive status is revealed, his life and the life of his family are irrevocably changed—and then it changes again in a very unexpected way.

All the stories in *3 Needles* are troubling and raw but they are not cheap and do not take any easy ways out. In a serious way, they depict the issue of death on a global scale—and how easily it begins with the little things that we frail humans do each day.

Ithuteng—(Never Stop Learning)

December 3, 2006

The heartbreaking stories of *Ithuteng—(Never Stop Learning),* a documentary on HBO Family, remind us that not every story of post-apartheid South Africa is a success story. By profiling several troubled young people aided by community activist Jackey Maarohanye, it chronicles the generation growing up during South Africa's difficult post-apartheid transition, which has been marked by increased crime, violence, and soaring numbers of HIV-AIDS cases.

The filmmakers, Wille Ebersol, Charlie Ebersol, and Kip Kroeger, maintain an unwavering and sympathetic eye on young folks like Victor, Lebo, and Dineo, who had been labeled "rotten apples" at their local schools and sent to a Saturday school called "Ithuteng," which means "never stop learning" in the South African vernacular. The school, based in Soweto, was originally funded by Nelson Mandela and, by January 2005, had reached more than six thousand children.

At Ithuteng, children all take academic classes, participate in rigorous physical play, peer counseling, and create their own original plays that dramatize the troubled scenarios that brought them to the school. Typically, young men like Victor had been heading into a life of full-blown crime, involved in car theft, shootings, and drugs. All the girls and young women had been raped, sometimes multiple times, and sometimes by men who were supposed to be trusted caretakers.

Documentation of these student productions is often riveting, and watching the young people as they work through tough issues of being without parents, being poor, being alone, and being traumatized physically and emotionally, can be very tough to watch. But the raw truth of what they have all endured is what gives the film its considerable strength. The other strong point is Maarohany, known as Mama Jackey, who was a young activist during South Africa's 1976 student uprisings and tries to explain to today's youth the value of growing up in this post-apartheid society that she fought for.

The shortcoming of *Ithuteng* is that it does not do enough to explain the underpinnings of today's crisis in South Africa. There is a brief mention at the start of the film about how Blacks had been denied a quality education and about the roots of Soweto as an impoverished ghetto but such a scant mention does not address the truly genocidal qualities of apartheid, or the continued inequities in a country where Blacks gained political control but not control over the economy, land, or means of production. By referring to the youth in the film as South Africa's "lost generation," it disconnects the country's poverty, pathology, and worsening statistics from their root. Viewers unfamiliar with apartheid might wonder if the youth are being so labeled because, somehow, their lives under apartheid would have been better.

The message of *Ithuteng* is self-responsibility, self-sufficiency, and self-reliance for a generation who seems to be told that they can no longer blame apartheid for its problems. With sympathy, they are told to pull themselves up by their bootstraps, even though it is obvious that apartheid has stolen their birthright, not to mention their boots.

OPM–*Apocalypto*

December 8, 2006

Apocalypto is the truth.

Mel Gibson's epic of one man's quest to survive during the waning days of the Mayan Empire is absolutely spellbinding. It is filled with action, danger, extreme violence, love, hope, and heroism—all without an uttered word of English or the superimposition of any great White savior.

When we meet Jaguar Paw, the hunter, husband, and father whom we will focus on for more than two hours, he is pursuing prey in a lush forest with his buddies, one of whom is singled out for practical jokes because his wife has not conceived a child. At this moment and throughout, *Apocalypto* concerns itself with the recurring themes of life, survival, and death. It also focuses on whether a human chooses to move through life with or without fear, with or without courage, with or without faith.

On the day after the hunting trip, Jaguar Paw's world is turned upside down when his village is attacked and he is taken captive. After first hiding his family, he is made to trek to a strange place of stone monuments that reach into the sky. With horror, he slowly realizes that he and his friends are meant to be human sacrifices that the Mayans believe will reverse their crop failures and disfavor from their god. As fate would have it, Jaguar Paw escapes the sacrifice and winds up in a run for his life, as the Mayans chase him and he tries to get back to his family.

Like Gibson's other epics, *Braveheart* and *The Passion of the Christ*, this production convincingly transports us through centuries. Research by Gibson and fellow screenwriter Farhad Safinia has brought to the screen for the first time a story that attempts to depict the sudden collapse of the mighty Mayan culture, which ruled the Americas for more than one thousand years. The re-creation of not only the hunter's village but an actual Mayan city is visually stunning, from the pyramids, to the ornate feathered costumes of the priests, to the elaborate hairdos of women, to the sights, sounds, and, we imagine, even smells of the marketplace, dungeons, and piles of rotting corpses.

Gibson hired several specialists in Mayan culture to be consultants for the film and the result is a depiction that does not feel "Hollywood," shallow, or denigrating. The Mayan warriors are tough and brutal, and one has an especially sadistic streak in his treatment of captives. But by the time we meet him, we have already been introduced to Jaguar Paw and his whole village of warm, funny, teasing, and crazy people. Not only is a language of the Yucatan Peninsula spoken, the characters look authentic to the role. Of the more than seven hundred in the cast, three came from Canada, two came from the United States, and the remainder came from Mexico and other parts of Central America.

Jaguar Paw is played by the stunning newcomer Rudy Youngblood, a Native American of the Comanchee, Cree, and Yaqui people who is a pow-wow dancer, singer, and artist. He is also a boxer and cross-country racer, (which certainly put him in a good position to do all the running he must do in this movie). He certainly is my choice for any acting award that I can vote for. The fact that Gibson establishes such an intimate and empathetic portrait of Jaguar Paw—the camera doesn't leave him for long—goes a long way to transport us back five hundred years.

Blood Diamond

December 8, 2006

The violence of *Blood Diamond*, the new movie starring Leonardo DiCaprio and Djimon Hounsou, is barbarous but cannot be accused of being over the top. The depicted civil war era in Sierra Leone during the 1990s produced at least seventy-five thousand deaths of primarily civilians, as well as shocking atrocities—most notably gang rapes of girls and amputations of limbs of children and infants. Often these acts were committed by child soldiers abducted and brainwashed by a rebel group calling itself the Revolutionary United Front (RUF), funded by diamond smuggling and backed by the corrupt government of Charles Taylor in neighboring Liberia. Almost half of the country's population of 4.5 million people, including those mutilated during the conflict, were forced to leave their homes for refugee camps.

While open warfare has ended, the RUF maintains in control of what it most wanted: Sierra Leone's rich diamond-producing rural districts. The country's diamonds, known for their fine gem quality, continue to be smuggled into Liberia for export to Europe, where they become a part of the global multibillion-dollar diamond industry. These diamonds are known as "conflict diamonds" or "blood diamonds," which give the movie its name.

In *Blood Diamond,* caught in this war era is Solomon Vandy (Hounsou), a fisherman of the Mende people who lives with his wife, Jassie, son, Dia, as well as a daughter and infant. Soon after we meet Solomon, he is fleeing from trucks, filled with RUF soldiers, barreling down a dusty road near his village. While he immediately springs into action and spirits his family to safety, he is abducted by the militia group and forced to work in a diamond work camp, where he unearths a large, rare diamond.

When Solomon is jailed after a raid on the camp, word of his discovery reaches the ear of a South African mercenary-turned-diamond-smuggler named Danny Archer (DiCaprio), who immediately starts to calculate how he can make the diamond his own. When Solomon leaves jail and finds out that his family is missing, he and Danny become locked into a deal that will get Solomon back to his family and get Danny to the prized diamond.

The uneasy alliance between the two men is handled with some care by director Ed Zwick *(Glory)* but it still degenerates, in many scenes, into a master-darkie relationship. Danny, obviously more experienced in war and killing, takes the lead to save Solomon during several battles. On back roads and in the bush of his own country, Solomon seems lost and is led by an outsider. Solomon's peaceful demeanor is rendered as somewhat childlike in some scenes and downright silly in others. When, for example, he calls out to who he thinks is his son in a passing truck filled with heavily armed RUF soldiers, he reveals his and Danny's hiding place and risks their lives. In response, Danny warns him that he will kill him if he ever does such a thing again.

In the 1980s Indiana Jones-*Romancing the Stone-Jewel of the Nile* genre, there was, usually coupled with the White hero, a White woman who routinely did stupid things that the White hero had to correct in order to save both of them in a land filled with dark people. To a lesser extent, Hounsou fills this problematic role in *Blood Diamond*, though his actions are not for comedic effect. (They don't make me laugh at least.) While Solomon is obviously passionate about saving his family, the story tells us that Danny—an obvious racist but one with some conscience—is Solomon's only ticket to survival.

DiCaprio is captivating in his role, as was Matt Dillon as the racist cop in *Crash*. These films ask us to see something good in bigots, to see that they, too, have their positive qualities. In *Blood Diamond,* this humanizing of Archer stands in stark contrast to the savage Black RUF rebels and the less-detailed portrait of Solomon. Zwick knows how to draw us into White characters, as he did on his beloved and critically acclaimed TV shows, *Thirtysomething* and *Once and Again*. He needs more work on Black characters. (He didn't write the script for *Glory*.)

Zwick deserves credit for tackling this difficult issue that is of immense importance to Africa and the whole world. And he deserves credit for not allowing Hollywood to make it into even more of an Indiana Jones type of movie. To get everyone's attention for a story about Africa, *Blood Diamond* needed a big star like DiCaprio. But, in getting the star, the movie seems locked into tired script elements that Hollywood won't yet abandon.

The Pursuit of Happyness

December 22, 2006

A film based on the true story of Chris Gardner, a struggling Black father who sought a change of career as a stockbroker, could have easily turned into another corny tale of American ambition. Instead, *The Pursuit of Happyness*, starring Will Smith, is a poignant reminder of the frailty of American families and the so-called American dream.

For its particular meditation on time, place, and Black humanity, *The Pursuit of Happyness* is destined to become one of our movie classics, alongside *Claudine*, *Cooley High*, *The Color Purple,* and *Antwone Fisher*. I can't think of another film that has so capably captured the social and economic upheaval of the 1980s, when Reaganomics and "economic restructuring" widened the gap between the very rich and poor, when legions of newly homeless filled the streets of big American cities, and the American workforce quickened its daily lockstep in order to survive.

When we meet Chris (Will Smith), he and his wife, Linda (Thandie Newton), and son, Christopher (Jaden Smith), are struggling to get by in an apartment in San Francisco. We quickly learn that the couple is behind in their rent, behind in taxes owed to the I.R.S., and that their marriage is on the brink of failure. Chris is also not having much success as a salesman of portable bone-density machines. Much of his stressful existence is spent lugging around the boxy contraption with a handle that sort of resembles a portable sewing machine.

But just as things seem to be falling apart, Chris, who is smart, instinctive. and knows how to seize an opportunity, works hard to be accepted into a stockbroker internship at Dean Witter that, unknown to him, is an unpaid position. After his wife leaves him, he faces single fatherhood with the specter of danger and homelessness looming over his head. This is the point where *The Pursuit of Happyness* gets real in a way that few hero films do, certainly in a way that I have not seen starring a Black man as a father.

The direction by Gabriele Muccino, a newcomer to American films, and the script by Steve Conrad allows many scenes to unfold as if we are watching a documentary. The narrative is drawn forward by an assembly of moments that, collectively, tell the story of one man's perhaps uniquely American travelogue—sometimes, in the course of one day, from a homeless shelter, to a corporate conference room, to a day-care center, and to sleeping on the BART train.

The Pursuit of Happyness tells, most of all, of one man's pursuit of survival. It neither praises nor condemns the financial world, on which so much of 1980s success and failure was based. It does lay bare what is, for a sizable portion of the population, the grind of American life. A phrase from the U.S. Constitution becomes a question, a quest, a joke, and a prayer.

OPM—*Children of Men*

December 25, 2006

Set in London in 2027, this intriguing, futuristic tale tells the story of a chaotic time when women have ceased to conceive children, the youngest human, at 18 years of age, has just died, and human beings are facing the possibility of extinction. Amid the chaos, a peace-activist-turned-bureaucrat (Clive Owen) works to save the life of one woman—a Black woman—who has mysteriously become pregnant.

Dreamgirls

December 25, 2006

The part of me that likes *Dreamgirls* is the part that also likes to dust off childhood albums from the '70s, tolerates the umpteenth revival of *Ain't Misbehavin',* and smiles broadly at the resurgence of the poncho. This is a lazy American part of me that is nearing circuit overload in the age of information and enjoys hearing Jennifer Hudson sing the hell out of a song—even if it is a song I dislike—or enjoys watching Eddie Murphy deliver an electric stage performance with an electric hairdo.

Dreamgirls is this year's holiday splash that is adapted from the 1981 Broadway hit of the same name. Believed to be modeled heavily on the real-life drama of the Supremes and Motown mogul Berry Gordy, it tells the story of an R&B girl group called the Dreams that includes a full-figured lead singer, Effie White (Jennifer Hudson), and backup singers Deena Jones (Beyoncé Knowles) and Lorrell Robinson (Anika Noni Rose). Not to ruin the plot of a twenty-five-year-old musical for anyone, but good ole Effie is eventually maneuvered out of her starring position in favor of Jones by the group's new manager, Curtis Taylor Jr. (Jamie Foxx). Curtis also, eventually, dumps Effie romantically and marries Deena.

In the original stage play, the White writers and producers—Tom Eyen, Henry Krieger, Michael Bennett (with financial backing from music mogul David Geffen)—utilized the Dreams saga to tell a story about the death of R&B and the ascendancy of crossover Black acts. Curtis's big ambitions to expand the reach of the Dreams, from the limited Black music audience to the bigger and more lucrative White pop audience, caused him to favor Deena's flimsier voice over the grits-and-gravy soul holler of Effie. In the original stage play, it was also obvious that the thick Effie, played by Jennifer Holiday, was being dissed and replaced by a Deena with less physical heft and more crossover appeal (Sheryl Lee Ralph).

Cut to the film version of the story—which is still backed by David Geffen, who has been holding onto the film rights for decades. The "shift" from Effie to

Deena is even more obvious, from the caramel-colored, full-figured Hudson to Knowles, who, in this film, is much thinner than her normal bootylicious self and, with her light complexion, easier for White audiences to accept. How the music industry dealt a deadly blow to Black soul divas is the one aspect of *Dreamgirls* that has some emotional truth and that keeps it from being a nostalgic trip without depth.

Other high points of the production, however, have substantially less emotional truth for me. For convenience sake, Effie is, of course, presented as neck-rolling and spiteful. Also, I don't accept as convention that women who look like the cherub-faced Hudson are not as attractive as the Beyoncés of the world. Finally, and I know this might be Black music heresy, I have always considered the hit song from the play, "And I Am Telling You I'm Not Going"— a depressing case of self-denial writ large:

And I am telling you I'm not going
You're the best man I'll ever know
There's no way I can ever go
No no no, no way
No no no, no way I'm living without you
I'm not living without you
I don't want to be free
I'm staying, I'm staying
And you, and you, you're gonna love me

(Number one: You can't make anybody love you. Number two: Why get all twisted over some skinny brother with a process? Number three: Homegirl definitely does wind up "going" after all.) For me, this song is just too much futility and pain, and not enough self-pride—words written by a White man and made famous by Jennifer Holiday—from a Black woman who has already been dumped.

No doubt, Jennifer Hudson performs the hell out of the song and, in general, steals the film, just as Effie should. Eddie Murphy is also a surprise knockout as James "Thunder" Early, a star soul singer who winds up struggling as his winds of fortune change.

Dreamgirls is the *Porgy and Bess* for its generation—a poignant tale that rings only partly true. It is a story "about" Blacks but written and produced by Whites. It is notable that is it reminiscent of a time in the early '80s—before the "new wave" of

Black film began when we weren't telling our own stories. And it is a reminder that we still do not tell them most of the time, and that we aren't the ones putting up money for green-lighting these big-budget productions. It is a reminder that Black stars are not the same as Black voices.

Dreamgirls sure does have its rush of adrenaline but it struggles to be more than the limitations that it has always had.

Epilogue
The Lists

Some Favorite Quotes

Hollywood Shuffle

Robert Townsend plays the role of a stereotypical street thing named Jimmy who puts off his enemies with the line: "I ain't be got no weapon!"

Glory

"I stand here this evening, heavenly father, to ask your blessings on all of us," says Morgan Freeman in the role of Sgt. Major John Rawlins on the night before the soldiers went into their historic and courageous battle at Fort Wagner in South Carolina. "So that if tomorrow is our great getting up morning, if tomorrow we have to face the judgment day, heavenly father we ask that you let our folks know that we went down facing the enemy, that we went down standing up amongst those who fight against our oppression. We want them to know, heavenly father, that we went down fighting for our freedom."

New Jack City

Keisha (Vanessa Williams) to a man approaching the kingpin Nino Brown on the street: "You'd better step off, grand-pop."

Nino Brown (Wesley Snipes) to G-Money (Allen Payne': "Sit your five-dollar ass down before I make change."

Nino Brown (Wesley Snipes) to Kareen Akbar (Christopher Williams): "I never liked you anyway, pretty motherf*****."

Juice

Store owner Trip (Samuel L. Jackson) to a customer: "Just 'cause you pour syrup on shit don't make it pancakes."

Deep Cover

As John considers how he has been double-crossed, he confesses that he'd "been turned out like a two-dollar ho—with no tongue and no kiss."

Passenger 57

Launching into the action-hero niche, this time Wesley Snipes plays an ex-cop, John Cutter, who is aboard a plane when terrorists take over. His memorable line to the villain: "Always bet on Black!"

Malcolm X

Prologue audio of Malcolm X (Denzel Washington) speaking to a crowd with images of the 1992 beating of Rodney King, and then a burning American flag: "Brothers and sisters, I am here to tell you that I charge the White man. I charge the White man with being the greatest murderer on earth. I charge the White man with being the greatest kidnapper on earth. There is no place in this world that that man can go and say that he created peace and harmony. Everywhere he's gone, he's created havoc. Everywhere he's gone, he's created destruction. . . .

So I charge him, I charge him with being the greatest kidnapper on this earth. I charge him with being the greatest murderer on this earth. I charge him with being the greatest robber and enslaver on this earth. I charge the White man with being the greatest swine eater on this earth, the greatest drunkard on this earth. He cannot deny the charges. You cannot deny the charges. . . . We're the living proof of those charges. . . . You and I, we've never seen any democracy . . . . All we've seen is hypocrisy. We don't see any American dream.

We've experienced only the American nightmare.

Poetic Justice

When Justice goes into a snit and gets out of the truck in the middle of some desolate California hills, Iesha is the one who talks her back into this truck and delivers one of the movie's best lines: "Girl, I KNOW you ain't gonna let no nigga make you walk all the way to Oakland."

Beloved

Baby Suggs/Grandma Baby (Beah Richards) at her sermon in the forest clearing:

> "Let the children come! Hahaha! Let your mothers hear your laugh!
> Let the grown men come! Let your wives and children see you dance!
> Women! Women! I want you to weep!
> Just weep for the living, for the dead.
> Weep!"

Diary of a Mad Black Woman

Madea's fans know her as a grandma-in-the-hood who packs heat. When Helen's mother (Cicely Tyson) utters the gospel lyric "Peace Be Still," Madea responds, "Well, you know what? Peace is always still around me 'cause I keeps me what they call a piece of steel." Quickly retrieving a semiautomatic weapon from her purse on the kitchen counter, she continues: "Long as you got a piece of steel, you gonna have peace."

MyTop Ten Films of 2000

1. *Bamboozled*
2. *Simeon*
3. *One Week*
4. *Love and Basketball*
5. *The Original Kings of Comedy*
6. *Remember the Titans*
7. *Dancing in September*
8. *The Visit*
9. *Orfeu*
10. *Boesman & Lena*

My Top Ten Films of 2001

1. *Lumumba*
2. *Life and Debt*
3. *Ali*
4. *Training Day*
5. *One Week*
6. *Baby Boy*
7. *Faat Kiné*
8. *A Huey P. Newton Story*
9. *Kingdom Come*
10. *The Caveman's Valentine*

My Top Ten Films of 2002

1. *Antwone Fisher*
2. *La Tropical*
3. *Piñero*
4. *Brown Sugar*
5. *Paid in Full*
6. *Like Mike*
7. *Undercover Brother*
8. *Karmen Geï*
9. *Ali Zaoua*
10. *Blade II*

My Top Ten Films of 2003

1. *Race: The Power of an Illusion*
2. *The Matrix Reloaded* and *The Matrix Revolutions*
3. *The Murder of Emmett Till*
4. *Amandla! A Revolution in Four-Part Harmony*
5. *Dirty Pretty Things*
6. *Unprecedented*
7. *Tears of the Sun*
8. *Bad Boys II*
9. Three-Way Tie: *Head of State, Good Fences,* and *Deacons for Defense*
10. *The Blues* series

My Top Ten Films of 2004

1. *Moolaadé*
2. *Ray*
3. *Fahrenheit 9/11*
4. *Collateral*
5. *The Battle of Algiers*
6. *Control Room*
7. *Baadasssss!*
8. *Friday Night Lights*
9. *Hotel Rwanda*
10. *Beah: A Black Woman Speaks*

My Top Ten Films of 2005

1. *Sometimes in April*
2. *Lackawanna Blues*
3. *Crash*
4. *Wal-Mart: The High Cost of Low Price*
5. *Slavery and the Making of America*
6. *Their Eyes Were Watching God*
7. *Guess Who*
8. *Diary of a Mad Black Woman*
9. *XXX: State of the Union*
10. *Congo: White King, Red Rubber, Black Death*
    Honorable Mention: *Rize* and *Sweet Honey in the Rock: Raise Your Voice*

My Top Ten Movies of 2006:

1. *When the Levees Broke: A Requiem in Four Acts*
2. *Catch a Fire*
3. *The Pursuit of Happyness*
4. *Apocalypto*
5. *Bobby*
6. *CSA: The Confederate States of America*
7. *Glory Road*
8. *Akeelah and the Bee*
9. *Yesterday*
10. *An Inconvenient Truth*
    Honorable Mention: *Waist Deep*

Movies I Loved That They Hated

1. *Meteor Man*
2. *Drop Squad*
3. *Poetic Justice*
4. *Don't Be a Menace*
5. *Set It Off*
6. *Bad Boys II*
7. *The Matrix Reloaded*
8. *The Matrix Revolutions*
9. *Head of State*
10. *XXX: State of the Union*

Movies They Loved That I Hated

1. *Eddie Murphy Raw*
2. *Clara's Heart*
3. *Ghost*
4. *Pulp Fiction*
5. *Mississippi Burning*
6. *Miss Evers Boys*
7. *Swordfish*
8. *Monster's Ball*
9. *Million Dollar Baby*
10. *The Last King of Scotland*

Favorite Black Male Characters

(in no particular order)

Laurence Fishburne as Morpheus in *The Matrix* trilogy

Wesley Snipes as *Blade*

Denzel Washington as *Malcolm X*

Denzel Washington as Trip in *Glory*

Morgan Freeman as Sgt. Major John Rawlins in *Glory*

Hill Harper as Alex Waters in *The Visit*

Eriq Ebouaney as Patrice Lumumba in *Lumumba*

Will Smith as Muhammad Ali in *Ali*

Derek Luke as *Antwone Fisher*

Jamie Foxx as Ray Charles in *Ray*

Michael Ealy as Tea Cake in *Their Eyes Were Watching God*

Robert Townsend as *Meteor Man*

Favorite Black Female Characters

(in rough chronological order)

Angela Bassett as Tina Turner in *What's Love Got to Do With it?*

Queen Latifah as Cleo in *Set It Off*

Angela Bassett as Bernadine Harris in *Waiting to Exhale*

Sanaa Lathan as Monica Wright in *Love and Basketball*

Jocelyne Beroard as Roselyne in *Simeon*
Sanaa Lathan as Syd in *Brown Sugar*
Sanaa Lathan as Alexa Woods in *AVP: Alien vs. Predator*
Jada Pinkett Smith as Niobe in *The Matrix Revolutions*
Naomie Harris as Selena in *28 Days Later*
Keisha Castle-Hughes as Paikea in *Whale Rider*
Tyler Perry as Madea in *Diary of a Mad Black Woman*
Keke Palmer as Akeelah Anderson in *Akeelah and the Bee*
Leleti Khumalo as *Yesterday*
Shareeka Epps as Drey in *Half Nelson*

Little-Known Gems

Sidewalk Stories
Rosewood
One Week
The Visit
Simeon
Unprecedented
Meteor Man
Paid in Full
La Tropical
Beah: A Black Woman Speaks

The Funniest

Hollywood Shuffle
I'm Gonna Git You Sucka
House Party
Boomerang
CB4
Meteor Man
Fear of a Black Hat
The Original Kings of Comedy
The Queens of Comedy
Pootie Tang
All About the Benjamins
Undercover Brother
Head of State
Hitch
Diary of a Mad Black Woman

The Fiercest

(in no particular order)
Antwone Fisher
When the Levees Broke: A Requiem in Four Acts
The Matrix trilogy
Malcolm X
Glory
Control Room
Ray
Race: The Power of an Illusion
Life and Debt
Ali
Bamboozled
Simeon
The Visit
Lumumba
Fahrenheit 9/11
Beloved
Blade trilogy
Mission: Impossible III
Enemy of the State
Rabbit-Proof Fence
The Corner
Apocalypto

Permissions

1989–1995 Newsday, Inc. Reprinted with permission

1) Cosby Lulled Us Into Complacency—May 17, 1992
2) In TV, It's 'A Different World' Indeed—March 24, 1993
3) Martin Lawrence—The Brother From the Corner—April 29, 1993
4) Interview: Robert Townsend and "Meteor Man"—August 9, 1993
5) Black Like Who?—October 23, 1993
6) Betcha By Golly, Wow. Black Culture Looks Back—June 19, 1994
7) Harlem's Victoria 5—August 9, 1994
8) Searched at the Cinema—July 11, 1995
9) Harry Belafonte and Sidney Poitier Pass On Their Wish—March 24, 1994
10) From Harlem to Hollywood: American Race Movies—Jan. 13, 1991
11) Showing Oscar Micheaux's Surviving Films—February 4, 1994
12) Redux "Inside Bedford-Stuyvesant"—January 21, 1992
13) A Softer Side of Tupac Shakur—July 21, 1993
14) The McDonald's Gospelfest: A Holy Singoff—June 17, 1989
15) Would You Like Funky Cold Medina?—July 8, 1989
16) Lavender Light Lesbian and Gay Gospel Choir—October 18, 1989
17) Linda Austin: A Woman on The Congo Drum—December 26, 1989
18) David Peaston Takes His Leap—November 7, 1989
19) In Concert: Sweet Honey In The Rock—January 16, 1990
20) Music Lessons—July 8, 1990
21) Carolina Slim: Getting Those Subway Blues—July 10, 1990
22) Bill Lee's Artistic Journey—February 19, 1991
23) Pop's Things: the Louis Armstrong Archive—September 6, 1991
24) Community Jazz in Brooklyn—March 10, 1992
25) Bernice Johnson Reagon's "Wade In The Water"—January 7, 1994
26) "King Chalkdust Versus The Mighty Sparrow"—August 31, 1993
27) Betty Carter: A Queen of Jazz Teaches Her Subjects—April 8, 1994
28) Bill T. Jones as Insider and Outsider—November 4, 1990
31) Dance Theater of Harlem Tries to Build Support—March 16, 1993
32) Black Theater for the Masses—February 7, 1994
33) Martin Lawrence On the Cutting Edge—April 29, 1993

34) Willie Birch: "Nairobi Series"—April 6, 1993
35) Anna Deveare Smith and Black Women Playwrights—May 27, 1994
36) "Malcolm X: The Man, The Meaning"—December 17, 1991
37) Young Black Artists Mine Their History—February 2, 1990
38) The Negro Ensemble Company: Homeless—March 27, 1991
39) Feeling Like the Venus Hottentot—August 4, 1991
40) "Urban Mythologies" and "Urban Masculinity"—December 7, 1993
41) "Art Against Apartheid"—June 17, 1990
42) Njinga The Queen King—December 3, 1993
43) Saving Harlem Renaissance Murals—August 18, 1993
44) David Hammons and His Flag: A Clashing of Symbols—February 10, 1991
45) Egypt: Black and White Perspectives—July 21, 1992
46) Nurturing The Dinizulu Legacy—August 20, 1991
47) "A Trip Between Two Cultures"—February 8, 1989
48) "Facing History: The Black Image In American Art—April 17, 1990
49) Carl Hancock Rux: "Song of Sad Young Men"—August 21, 1990
50) Leroy Campbell Paints It Black—December 14, 1993
51) Renee Cox: Posters That Challenge Racism—July 25, 1995

1995-1998 The Washington Post. Reprinted with permission

1) "Don't Be a Menace"—January 14, 1996
2) "Moesha" Breaks The Mold—February 6, 1996
3) Theresa Randle Has Hollywood's Number March 17, 1996
4) The Real Villains of 'Johnny Quest'—May 29, 1996
5) Shaquille O'Neal in Kazaam—July 17, 1996
6) Review: "Get on the Bus"—October 16, 1996
7) "Set It Off" Holds Up Well—November 6, 1996
8) Review: "The Preacher's Wife"—December 13, 1996
9) "Miss Evers' Boys" Misses the Mark—February 22, 1997
10) "Rhyme": Backstage but Not Beyond, March 7, 1997
11) Review: "B.A.P.S."—March 29, 1997
12) What About Black Romance?—May 25, 1997
13) Interview: Ice-T September 14, 1997
14) Late-Night Wannabees—October 9, 1997
15) A Little Girl's Giant Step—"Ruby Bridges"—January 17, 1998
16) Same Ole 'Porgy'—February 4, 1998
17) "Family Name"—September 15, 1998
18) "Desmond Pfeiffer" A Bad Idea Gone Wrong—October 6, 1998
19) Lisa Gay Hamilton: A Career Rejecting Traditional Roles—May 13, 1997
20) The Box: Music Television You Control?—January 21, 1996
21) Tom Joyner: Nice Guy. Great Show. Uh-Oh—May 14, 1996
22) African American Dance Goes On Another Track—March 9, 1997
23) Sinbad's 170s Soul Music Festival In Jamaica—August 24, 1996
24) Death of An Ideal: YSB Sinks Under Hip Hop's Weight—October 23, 1996
25) You Know You're Ghetto If—Dec. 27, 1996

27) Rubber Soul: The Sneaker Is Not Just A Shoe, It's A Show—August 20, 1997
28) Kickin' the Bobos: A Guide to Current Hip-Hop Slang—April 29, 1998
29) Literary 'Renaissance' Meets Reality—April 5, 1996
30) Tavis Smiley Counters Talk Radio's Conservative Citadel—June 22, 1998
31) Giving Respect: The 1996 National Black Arts Festival—July 6, 1996
32) Los Angeles' Leimert Park Village--Art and Hope—December 9, 1997
33) Sending Black Dolls to South African Children—July 25, 1996
34) In Black Culture, It's "Time for the South"—January 5, 1997
35) A Big BET: The BET Soundstage—January 17, 1997
36) Sinbad's '70s Soul Festival in Aruba—June 22, 1997
37) Going To "The Show"—April 30, 1998
38) You Remind Me Of My Jeep—December 3, 1995
39) Phyllis Hyman's Death and Life—December 28, 1995
40) The Fugee's Alien Ideas—April 14, 1996
41) Will Downing: Cool Singer Waiting to Ignite—July 26, 1996
42) Whitney Houston—October 4, 1997
43) The Philly Sound—October 26, 1997
44) After B.I.G.'s Death, Puffy Has Second Thoughts—March 28, 1997
45) Heavy D: A Whole Lot to Love—June 14, 1997
46) The Social and Spiritual Anthems of Hip Hop—September 29, 1996
47) Puff Daddy and the Family World Tour—March 23, 1998
48) Resurrection Of Soul—March 21, 1998
49) Africa: A Plunder Wonderland at the Guggenheim—August 18, 1996
50) Luba Art and The Making of History—November 10, 1996
51) Creating God in His Image—August 25, 1998
52) The Harlem Renaissance and the Black Body—April 11, 1998
53) UniverSoul Circus—July 21, 1997
54) David Driskell Creates a Black Art World—November 23, 1998